Helen Clay Frick

Helen Clay Frick

BITTERSWEET HEIRESS

MARTHA FRICK SYMINGTON SANGER

UNIVERSITY OF PITTSBURGH PRESS

Published by the University of Pittsburgh Press, Pittsburgh PA 15260

Printed on acid-free paper
10 9 8 7 6 5 4 3 2 1

Designed by Alex Castro, Castro/Arts, Baltimore
Printed in Italy

Library of Congress Cataloging-in-Publication Data

Sanger, Martha Frick Symington.
Helen Clay Frick : Bittersweet Heiress / Martha Frick Symington Sanger.
p. cm.
Includes bibliographical references and index.
ISBN-13: 978-0-8229-4341-9 (cloth : alk. paper)
ISBN-10: 0-8229-4341-7 (cloth : alk. paper)
1. Frick, Helen Clay, 1888-1984. 2. Art--Collectors and collecting--United States--Biography. 3. Philanthropists--United States--Biography. 4. Women philanthropists--United States--Biography. I. Title.
N5220.F67S26 2007
709.2--dc22
[B]
2007026397

Frontispiece:
Helen with her dog Fido, ca. 1910. Photograph by Henry Havelock Pierce.
Courtesy National Portrait Gallery, Smithsonian Institution, Washington, D.C.

Frederick A. Hetzel
former director of the University of Pittsburgh Press

Isabel Spaulding Roberts
lady of arts and letters, art historian, art patron

Arabella Symington Dane
my sister

For their wisdom, encouragement, and love.

CONTENTS

ILLUSTRATIONS

SELECTED GENEALOGY OF HENRY CLAY FRICK AND ADELAIDE HOWARD CHILDS

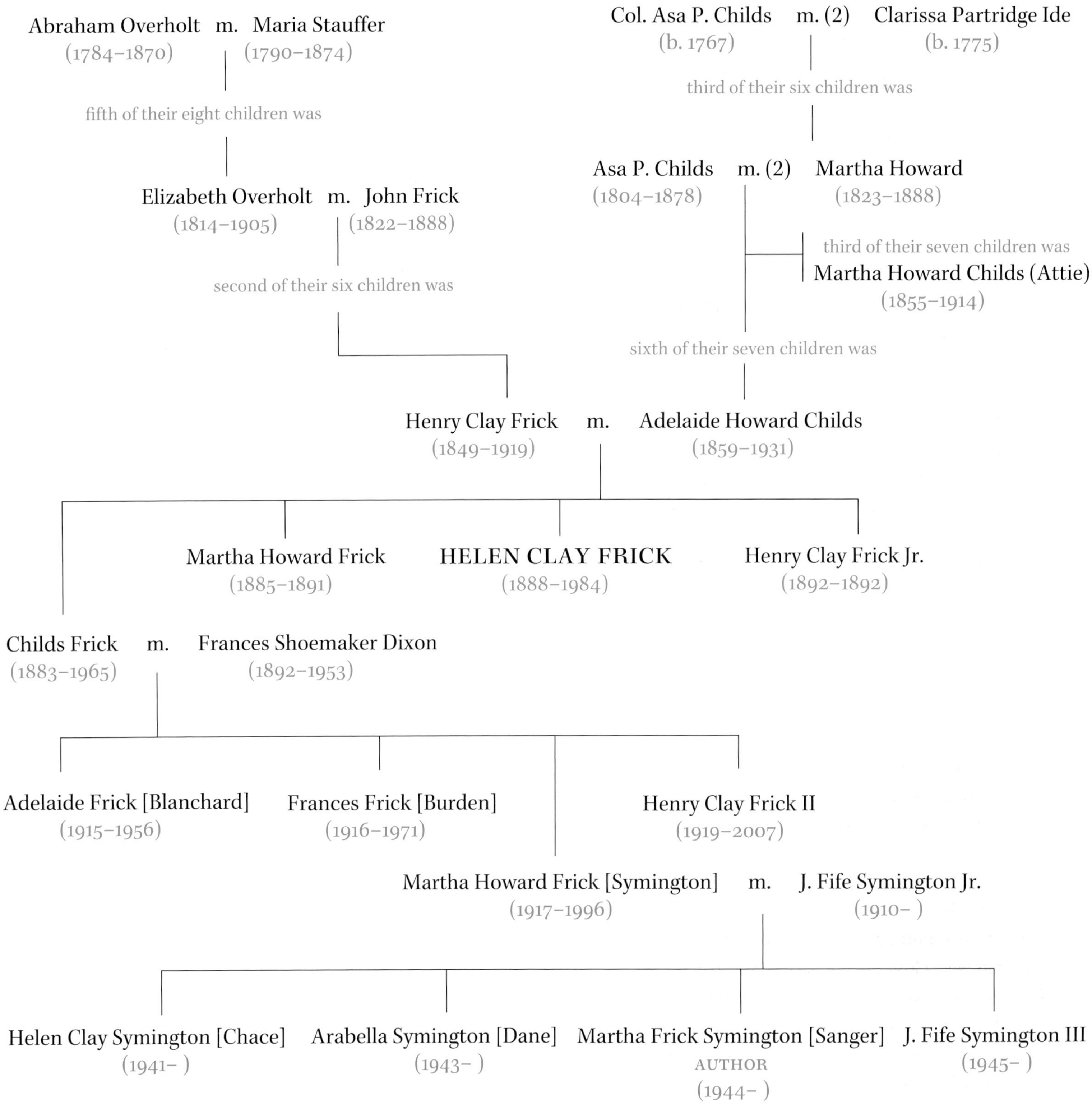

PREFACE

Sorrow fully accepted brings its own gifts.
For there is an alchemy in sorrow.
It can be transmuted into wisdom,
which if it does not bring joy, can yet bring happiness.

—Pearl S. Buck

While researching the complicated legacy of my maternal great-grandfather, Henry Clay Frick, I was surprised to find that I kept returning to his daughter, my great-aunt, Helen Clay Frick. I knew her well, as did my children, siblings, cousins, and their children. Often she visited me and my family, and more often we visited her in her various homes: Westmoreland Farm, her country place in Bedford Village, New York; Clayton, her childhood home in Pittsburgh, now established by her as a Victorian house museum; and Eagle Rock, her father's summer home on Boston's North Shore. When I was a child, she entertained me over lunch and tea in her penthouse office at the Frick Art Reference Library off Manhattan's Fifth Avenue, and on Mondays, when the Frick Collection is closed to visitors, she often opened the secret connecting door to the East Gallery and let me roam freely through her father's collection.

The summer I was fourteen brought me closer to my great-aunt, close enough to know her as both teacher and friend. She took me to Italy where we viewed the great works of art she had known and loved since girlhood and visited the famous art scholar Bernard Berenson, who was then advising her to purchase the Nicholas Lochoff frescoes now in the Henry Clay Frick Fine Arts Building at the University of Pittsburgh. From there we traveled to Switzerland where I met the family of her governess and lifelong friend, Marika Ogiz. In Paris she introduced me to the Gaston Brières, the French couple instrumental in purchasing rare books and catalogues for the Frick Art Reference Library, and in London we spent time with "her" British girls, refugees Helen had housed during World War II. Because of our close relationship and the many memories we shared, I appear, at times, as a character in this story. I have not, however, included my ten Frick first cousins as characters. Their role in our great-aunt's story is theirs to tell.

All of us were close to Helen Frick, whom my generation called Grauntie, a contraction of "Great-Auntie," yet she remained a mystery. She seemed to courageously, if not always judiciously, forge her own path; she possessed a ferocious intelligence that engaged the generosity and loyalty of her family, contemporaries, friends, and colleagues, but she often shocked us with her sometimes irrational demands, hot temper, and unpredictability. With her personal attributes—almost all of them dramatically exaggerated—my great-aunt was not always easy to admire. She was all too vulnerable to the ridicule often attached to her name and her memory: a spoiled rich girl forwarding her causes in her father's name, a woman both condemned for, and perceived as, being in love with her father.

Not until 1987, three years after Helen's death, when I began researching my Frick family, could I weigh these impressions against her personal truth. Until then I had no idea that the searing intensity of her wounds from childhood and early adulthood produced the father-adoration, impulsiveness, and impatience that seemed to drive her every action. Nor had I realized that these traumas shaped her single-minded determination, independent thinking, and often unconventional choices. In fact, like many others, I generally perceived Helen as an odd, sometimes idiosyncratic, but amusing elderly maiden lady.

During the last five years, when my research focused exclusively on my great-aunt, I finally heard her true voice—a minor chord in my previous books. As I listened for it and allowed an ever-deepening awareness to shape my understanding, her story became compelling. Born at a time of few occupations or expectations for women, Helen Frick proved to be a person quite different from the eccentric woman I thought I knew. After conducting extensive interviews; studying archival materials in more than fifty-six repositories held in art museums, archives, universities, presidential libraries, and private collections; fully examining the cultural and familial forces that shaped her; and combining this with my own insights and observations, unique to a family intimate, I came to see Helen Frick as one of America's heroines, a hidden woman of our history. Feisty, with a sureness of purpose and the guts to make her own rules, she struggled valiantly—and painfully—to achieve a philanthropy that will endure and be prized forever. Though bound to her father, she was more than the daughter of a famous and powerful industrialist and art collector. She was an intelligent, industrious, indefatigable participant in the life of twentieth-century women—a vividly independent figure in her insistent and successful fight to secure a place for herself, to have her voice heard, in the corporate, professional, museum, and business worlds of money and power.

Key episodes and experiences recorded in this biography as well as references to the Fricks' symbolic collecting pattern will be familiar to readers of my earlier work, *Henry Clay Frick: An Intimate Portrait.* Helen necessarily figured heavily in that work as a vital and influential part of her father's life, both as consoler of his sorrows and, with her highly refined aesthetic sense, assistant in his efforts to establish their New York residence as home of the Frick Collection. She thus deserves a singular focus: a larger, more comprehensive portrait of her character and her accomplishments, with all events viewed through *her* eyes, and with her own professional achievements more completely defined. Only through a biography of her own can Helen Clay Frick claim her rightful place in women's history and be fully celebrated for the critical role she played in the extension of her father's legacy, in the study of art history, social welfare, in historic and land preservation, and in museum and library building.

The British refugee girls once mused, "What an extraordinary person Miss Frick was." I concur and am honored to present her story.

Finally I just gave up and became my father.

—Sharon Olds, "Fate"

Helen Clay Frick

Sister

Sisters define their rivalry in terms of competition for the gold cup of parental love. It is never perceived as a cup which runneth over, rather a finite vessel from which the more one sister drinks, the less is left for the others.

—Elizabeth Fishel

In 1888, the year Helen Clay Frick was born, Pittsburgh, Pennsylvania, was a dark, Dickensian manufacturing town. Smoke from thousands of coke ovens, iron furnaces, steel mills, textile and glass factories, and coal-burning steamboats thickened the air. In fact, Pittsburgh was so like an inferno that Boston journalist James Parton famously referred to the city as "Hell with the lid taken off." This was a place where industrial accidents, disease, exhaustion, and despair prevailed among the laboring classes, a place where sorrow hovered over the rooftops like soot.

Helen knew little of this suffering. Born into the wealth and privilege of a steel fortune, she was the ultimate beneficiary of the success of her father, Henry Clay Frick. A glamorous, impeccably dressed man, his enormous self-made wealth was to her the very embodiment of the American dream. Her pride in his success was not based, however, on the magnitude of his fortune. Rather, for her entire life she idealized him for his triumph over seemingly insurmountable odds, for the grit and determination that enabled him to defy even death during his rise from obscurity as a poor, Mennonite farm boy to fame as a steel baron. Yet above all, Helen's greatest source of pride, indeed her whole identity, derived from the fact that she, his third child and only surviving daughter, became his closest confidant. Helen became the epitome of a father's daughter; she so worshiped her father that her self-confidence, sense of self, and competence in the world came solely from his approval. Yet her father never saw Helen as the person she was, only as what he needed her to be, his reflector.

The story of Helen Clay Frick is that of a woman holding onto an idealized image of her father, held in a childlike vise that both gripped and shaped her. Her story must, therefore, start almost forty years before her birth, with the trials of her father's childhood and life as a young adult.

Opposite: Adelaide Howard Childs Frick holding two-year-old Helen, November 1890. Courtesy the Frick Collection/Frick Art Reference Library Archives.

Henry Clay Frick, ca. 1875. Courtesy the Frick Collection/Frick Art Reference Library Archives.

A sickly boy from West Overton, Pennsylvania, Frick was an unlikely bet to reach adulthood, much less become the multimillionaire Helen worshiped. Suffering from congenital disorders, he was constantly watched over and tended by his mother, Elizabeth Overholt Frick, and his maternal grandmother, Maria Stauffer Overholt. When in 1855 six-year-old Clay, as his family called him, was separated from them for the first time, the experience nearly killed him. His father, John Frick, a farmer, had taken him to visit his paternal grandfather, Daniel Frick, in Van Buren, Ohio. On the journey, Clay contracted scarlet fever with soaring temperatures, rapid pulse, nausea, and muscle pain. The telltale red rash appeared and, as his skin began to peel, his condition progressed into rheumatic fever followed by an attack of rheumatoid arthritis. Marked by swelling of the joints and acute joint pain, the effects of this condition can take years to subside and often leaves its victims bedridden and helpless.

Since Clay was too weak to travel, he and his father remained in Van Buren for more than two months before starting the long journey back to Pennsylvania. A full year passed before he regained his former, albeit fragile, strength. But flare-ups of the disorder recurred throughout his life, particularly at moments of major transition or when separated from the nurturing women who cared for him.

Unable to walk to school, Clay helped his mother tend his four younger siblings: Anna, Aaron, Jay Edgar, and Sally. Maria, his older sister, lived with their Overholt grandparents, leaving Clay to assume the position of eldest child. When he did venture out of the house, he showed a strongly affectionate nature. In his early photographs, he looked soft and gentle, even effeminate, underscoring the comfort and safety he undoubtedly felt inside his female-centered cocoon.

This existence ended at age fourteen, when Frick began taking tentative steps into the world of business and commerce. He clerked in a dry goods store for his uncle, Christian Overholt, in West Overton. A few years later he worked a little farther from home, clerking for another uncle, Martin Overholt, in Mount Pleasant. At age eighteen, Frick, perhaps anxious to see the larger world, moved west to Allegheny City, just across the Allegheny River from Pittsburgh. He seemed to adjust well to the bustling new world he had entered, working variously in a linen-and-lace store and in another specializing in mourning clothes and black dress goods. He also broadened his mathematics training and satisfied his love of numbers by taking an accounting course. But within months he was ill again, this time with typhoid fever. He returned to West Overton and was nursed back to health by his mother, grandmother, and older sister Maria. Clay remained, as he would for the next twelve years, close to home.

Elizabeth Overholt Frick, ca. 1900. Author's collection.

Despite being frail and often ill, Henry Clay Frick was also ambitious and tough-minded. Although he would only reach only five feet, two inches in height, he was known as a giant. Frick's childhood friend Charles F. Booher recalled, "One time, when insulted by a remark made by a villager, [Frick] knocked the latter off his feet, although at that time Frick weighed not more than one-hundred and thirty pounds." Helen's memoir recalled, "Oh how proud I was of him & how little in comparison everyone else seemed."

Clay impressed almost all who came in contact with him. Upon recovering his health, he worked as a bookkeeper at Abraham Overholt's distillery in Broad Ford for an annual salary of $1,000. He amazed others with his steadfast determination to succeed at whatever he did, be it making out bills until three o'clock in the morning, measuring lumber in the freezing cold, breaking broncos, driving pigs to the slaughterhouse, playing horseshoes, or

Left: Abraham Overholt, ca. 1855. Courtesy the Frick Collection/Frick Art Reference Library Archives.

Right: Maria Stauffer Overholt, ca. 1855. Courtesy the Frick Collection/Frick Art Reference Library Archives.

balancing the distillery books to the exact cent. Booher claimed that Frick "desire[d] to get on." He was "always wanting to get into business and make money," and often said to his friends, "There is nothing to hinder me from being worth 1 million dollars and I propose to be worth that."

At the age of twenty-one, tired of his impoverished farm-boy existence, Frick entered the then-nascent industry of manufacturing coke, a purified form of coal necessary to make steel. Yet he remained utterly reliant on his mother and grandmother for nurture, guidance, and encouragement. He borrowed from their share of the inheritance left to them when Abraham Overholt died in 1870, and from banker Thomas Mellon, an Overholt family friend, to build the first of two coke works on the Broad Ford distillery property.

Henry Clay Frick, ca. 1875. Courtesy the Frick Collection/Frick Art Reference Library Archives.

During the financial panic and depression of 1873, when thousands of businesses failed, he kept his ovens working, though at a loss. He awoke before dawn to oversee his coke operations, hitched up a team of mules to canvass the countryside for coal outcroppings on properties being sold at depressed prices, then boarded the train to Pittsburgh where he sold his coke, only to return late at night to do his own bookkeeping, as well as the accounting for his grandfather's distillery. The demands of manufacturing coke turned out to be as hard—if not harder—on him than farming, and Frick's health suffered. In February 1875, just two months after his grandmother's death, a debilitated and dispirited Frick suffered a new attack of rheumatoid arthritis. Wrapped in seven pounds of wool and confined to bed for three months, he had to be washed and cared for like an infant. A full year passed before his health was restored, and even then he walked with crutches. In 1878, another attack occurred, and another long bedridden year ensued. His business, however, was beginning to show profit. He acquired new partners—his friends Edmund and Walton Ferguson, Pittsburgh brothers from a New York banking family—and changed the name of his Frick & Company to the H. C. Frick Coke Company. On December 19, 1879, healthy once more, a jubilant Frick had realized his childhood dream. The financial panic had lifted and at thirty years old he was a millionaire.

To celebrate, Frick took a whirlwind tour of Europe with his friend, banker Andrew Mellon. Then he moved to Pittsburgh in 1880, and quickly became known as the Coke King—one of the more forward-thinking, savvy businessmen of his day. Important people sought his unusually pure product, particularly Andrew Carnegie, who owned one of the largest steel manufacturing enterprises in America and needed a steady source of coke for his mills. In 1881 Carnegie approached Frick and his investors and together they negotiated a partnership: Carnegie became the majority stockholder in the H. C. Frick Coke Company, receiving a guaranteed supply of coke at a reduced rate. The Ferguson brothers were bought out and Frick became a minority shareholder but remained chairman of the company. He repaid the loans from his mother and from his grandmother's estate and, for the first time in his life, was out of debt.

While the deal was being negotiated during the summer of 1881, Frick met twenty-two-year-old Adelaide Howard Childs, the beautiful daughter of a socially prominent Pittsburgh family whose fortune had been made in textile manufacturing and as shoe merchants. Although Frick was known to be a blushing, awkward suitor, this time he turned bold and direct. He did not wait for an introduction, as etiquette required. Instead, spotting Adelaide across the room at a party he walked over and introduced himself.

Adelaide, described by the president of the Pittsburgh School of Design, Florence Speer, as "one of the talented pupils of the local artist, Agnes Caldwell Way," shared Frick's passion for art, and after a dizzying courtship the two married in December. In February 1882, after a six-week honeymoon along the East Coast, the young couple returned to Pittsburgh. When Frick married Adelaide, he was renting a three-room suite in the Monongahela House, a fashionable hotel named for the river it overlooked. He enlarged these living quarters, but when Adelaide became pregnant in June, the couple decided to find a house where they could raise a family.

Homewood (later renamed Clayton), ca. 1881. Courtesy the Frick Collection/Frick Art Reference Library Archives.

Again, as usually happened during major transitions in his life, Frick suffered an attack of inflammatory rheumatism. His grandmother Overholt was now dead, and with his mother and older sister recently moved hundreds of miles away to Wooster, Ohio, he turned to his bride for comfort and care. As Adelaide nursed her bedridden husband back to health, she rarely left his side. When she did attend a social engagement, Frick immediately complained of her "leaving him alone."

As he recovered, thirty-four-year-old Frick found just the home he and his bride desired: Homewood, a small, Italianate, pre-Civil War house on 1.43 acres in Pittsburgh's fashionable East End. Bordered by Penn Avenue to the north and South Homewood Avenue to the west—narrow dirt roads with deep ditches on each side for drainage—the house was in a rural area with freshwater springs, many varieties of wild berries, and just as important, more fresh air and sunshine than in the city. Planks aided those crossing the ditches, and in the summer the lanes were a profusion of weeds and wildflowers. To the south of the property lay a large woodland ravine, a wilderness filled with such animals as deer, fox, rabbit, quail, grouse, and pheasant.

The East End's bucolic ambience had already attracted other millionaires, including Henry John Heinz, the food-processing giant; Andrew and Richard Beatty Mellon, sons of Judge Thomas Mellon; and Philander C. Knox, attorney for Carnegie's steel concern. Living in the East End cemented Frick's status as a millionaire, provided close enough contact with Carnegie officials for quick consultations, and afforded easy commuting distance by rail to the coke region, the city, and the steel mills. Homewood was, however, far enough removed from Pittsburgh and the outlying mill towns to be safe and healthy for

Adelaide Frick on her wedding day, December 15, 1881. Private collection.

raising a family. Frick purchased the house on August 15, 1882, at the then-exorbitant cost of $25,000 and titled it to Adelaide as a delayed wedding present. He then poured another $50,000 into renovations and renamed the house Clayton.

On January 29, 1883, with Adelaide seven months pregnant, the young couple moved into their new home. They enjoyed such luxuries as indoor plumbing, telephone service,

and in 1888, the year Helen Frick was born, a new invention—electricity. Yet there was an aura of quiet modesty, if not restraint, in this new house. Indeed, Frick chose a house half the size of most Pittsburgh mansions. Nevertheless, by using D. S. Hess and Company, renowned decorators from New York, he made certain every inch of the residence was fashionably turned out and, as he would in all his subsequent architectural and design endeavors, oversaw and involved himself in all the details, including the hanging of his growing art collection.

Frick remained healthy and the children began arriving in rapid succession. First came a son, Childs, on March 12, 1883. Martha Howard, lovingly referred to as "Rosebud" because of her delicate pink skin and tiny auburn curls, followed two years later, on August 5, 1885.

Success and happiness abounded at home and at work. Henry Clay Frick was chairman of the H. C. Frick Coke Company, now operating some eleven thousand ovens in the coke region, making it the industry's largest coking operation. In 1889 he also became president of a division of Carnegie Steel—Carnegie Brothers and Company. Three years later, he became chairman of the entire united Carnegie enterprise. With more than thirty thousand employees it was one of the largest manufacturing concerns in the world. By any measurement Frick had become one of the most powerful chief executives in the world.

But the happiness would not last. During the summer of 1887, while the Fricks were visiting Paris with Childs and Martha, two-year-old Martha somehow swallowed a small black pin. Because neither parent witnessed the incident, they could not understand why the child suddenly became ill and complained of pain in her right side. They traveled to London where a doctor, without the benefit of as-yet undiscovered X-ray technology, proclaimed that Martha simply had a cold in her hip. But the pain continued, causing the Fricks' immediate return to Pittsburgh. There Dr. James McClelland, an accomplished homeopath, neighbor, and friend, treated Martha, but the little girl continued to suffer. By nature a happy child full of contagious laughter, she began, intermittently, to refuse food and to endure high fevers, sweating, digestive troubles, and hair loss. She also began to limp.

In January 1888, the family was momentarily distracted when Adelaide learned she was pregnant with a third child. Even as this pregnancy advanced, the family focus necessarily returned to Martha, whose inexplicable, excruciating illness pervaded the Frick household.

Above: Childs Frick in 1883. Private collection.

Below: Martha Howard Frick in 1885. Courtesy the Frick Collection/Frick Art Reference Library Archives.

Right: Martha (front row, fifth from left) celebrating her fourth birthday at Cresson Springs, August 5, 1889. Childs is in the front row, far right, and Nurse Grandison is holding Helen. Courtesy the Frick Collection/Frick Art Reference Library Archives.

Left: Martha, Helen, and Childs, ca. 1890. Author's collection.

Helen Clay Frick, May 16, 1889. Courtesy the Frick Collection/Frick Art Reference Library.

On September 3, 1888, Helen Childs Frick, who later changed her middle name to Clay, was born. But the event was overshadowed by a family worried and preoccupied, caught in emotional distress.

Annie Blumenschine (later Mrs. Annie Blumenschine Stephany), a teenager hired to care for the Frick children, explained the approaching crisis in her memoir. During the winter of 1889, just six months after Helen's birth and after Martha had endured two years of constant pain, "The nurse was changing Rosebud's diaper when she noticed that her right side had opened and some pus with a black pin in it came from the wound." Horrified by what they saw, yet relieved to know the cause of Martha's suffering, the Fricks immediately called Dr. McClelland. They had, at last, an answer—and reason to hope the child's worst days were over. McClelland quickly lanced and dressed the wound. But Martha did not respond to the surgery. In fact, she worsened. Unwittingly the doctor had further infected the child. Aseptic techniques such as sterile instruments had not yet been developed, nor had antibiotics.

Clayton after the 1892 renovation. Private collection.

The operation left a half-inch scar on Martha's right side and for a long time after the procedure she could not walk. Forced to ride in a carriage or be carried, she remained lame, tired easily, and complained constantly. Often Annie held her in her lap and comforted her, but her nurses thought Martha merely spoiled. She did, however, have another particularly sympathetic person around her: baby Helen. Until this moment, Childs had been Martha's constant companion and playmate, but now the new baby became her distraction, the antidote to her suffering. During her sister's worst moments Helen was brought to her bedside, in the hope that her presence would console her and restore her contagious laughter.

In 1890, Frick decided that a larger home was necessary to accommodate his family. Adelaide, however, refused to move. Thus Frick embarked on a massive reconstruction project. As work on Clayton commenced, the family moved into a rented house only a few blocks away on Lilac Street. Over the next two years, Clayton's roof was removed and various interior and exterior walls were demolished to accommodate a larger floor plan. What had once been a two-story, Italianate house would become a four-story, multi-turreted, twenty-three room Loire Valley–style château. Though still more modest than most millionaires' homes, Clayton nevertheless represented the epitome of high Victorian taste and also featured cutting-edge American technology. Aluminum, previously considered a luxury metal, had recently become a favorite in interior decoration, and was used as decorative tracery on Clayton's walls and as a glittering surface on ceilings. Plush velvet curtains and portieres, heavily appliquéd with luxurious tassels and trim or with leather strapping and sequins, complimented machine-made needlepoint lambrequins. Even a children's entrance was planned. It contained a small sink, towel racks, and an oak hallstand combining a large mirror, bench seat, and hat-and-coat rack—a sensible way to contain the mud and dirt from small children's busy feet.

By the late spring of 1891, as Clayton's expanded floor plan took shape with newly constructed exterior walls, five-year-old Martha's health was deteriorating. The doctor visited daily but insisted that she was merely cutting teeth or had a little gas in her stomach. By July, Martha had reached a critical condition, drenched in sweat and unable to retain solids or liquids, pills, or even water, the child was rapidly declining. Her bedding needed to be changed constantly, but Martha refused to let anyone touch her right side. The area around her scar was now tender and swollen.

Annie Blumenschine, later Stephany, ca. 1892. Private collection.

Almost three years old, Helen was too young to understand what was happening to Martha, but she was old enough to sense that something was very, very wrong. Her mother had been taking turns in the sickroom with her father and Annie, but by July the routine had changed. Adelaide was now worn out by lack of sleep. Ill since April with painful neuralgia of the ears, she had retreated to her bedroom. Meanwhile Martha continued to lose her strength, and her red curls, so like Helen's own, began to fall out from the high fever. To add to her discomfort, the Pittsburgh heat was excruciating. And now Helen saw an expanding raw spot on her father's hand where he allowed Martha to bite him in pain, a wound that hardened into a scar Frick took to his grave.

Recognizing the gravity of Martha's condition, and hoping a change of venue would ease her suffering, Frick decided to move his family to a resort in the Allegheny Mountains east of Pittsburgh. Andrew Carnegie made available his brother Thomas's private, Queen Anne–style cottage at the Mountain House in Cresson Springs, Cambria County—one of the finest and most impressive hotels in America. With its medicinal springs, purported to

Mountain House, front, Cresson. Courtesy the Library Company of Philadelphia, on behalf of the American Premier Underwriters, Inc.

be the purest in the world, and its clean mountain air, the family hoped that Martha would recover her strength.

Upon their arrival, those unaware of the Fricks' family crisis could only have thought there was something odd about the entourage. The man, tenderly cradling a desperately ill child, was already notorious as a heartless strikebreaker, a hard, cold, unfeeling industrialist, one of the most ruthless managers in America. In 1877, during the Pennsylvania railroad strike, he and another man had physically grabbed a striker and evicted him from his railroad-owned house. Ten years later, in 1887, Frick directly challenged Carnegie by refusing to capitulate to wildcat strikers. He resigned as chairman of the H. C. Frick Coke Company, took his family to Europe, and waited for Carnegie to capitulate and beg him to return. Frick was back on the job within months.

Henry Clay Frick's South Fork Fishing and Hunting Club stock certificate. Courtesy University of Pittsburgh Archive Center.

Then came the 1889 flood at Johnstown, a steel-manufacturing city east of Pittsburgh. Ten years earlier, Frick and his partners had purchased land near South Fork, a hamlet north of Johnstown, about fifteen miles southwest of Cresson, and there established the South Fork Fishing and Hunting Club. They dammed up a stream known as the Little Conemaugh to create a seven-hundred-acre lake. Over the Memorial Day weekend of 1889, a violent rainstorm struck the area. Suddenly the world's largest manmade earthen dam—poorly constructed and haphazardly maintained—burst. A tidal wave, estimated by some to be thirty to forty feet high, came crashing down a narrow, rock-walled gorge. It destroyed the Pennsylvania Railroad viaduct and consumed four towns in its path. By the time it reached Johnstown, the killer wave included the bodies of animals and humans; the debris of houses, trees, and trains; and every kind of rubble imaginable. When it hit Johnstown the small city was all but obliterated; more than two thousand people were killed. As news of the disaster spread, the 1889 Johnstown Flood was named the worst natural disaster in American history. Although Frick chaired the initial relief effort, and the courts declared

Eviction of workers from the Morewood Coke Works. Courtesy New York Society Library. Photo credit: Ed Watkins.

the flood an act of God, Frick was nevertheless vilified for building a faulty dam and for his role in the tragedy.

Just two years later came another ugly crisis. On April 2, 1891, more than a thousand armed workers marched on Frick's Morewood Coke Works, demanding higher wages. They tore down the fence surrounding the plant, destroyed the ovens, ripped up the railroad tracks, and smashed windows in the company store. The riot, the most severe confrontation between labor and management yet seen in America, spread throughout the coke region. Frick hired his own local deputies to protect his property; between nine and eleven strikers were reportedly shot dead and fifty wounded. Frick also began bringing in Italians and African Americans as replacement workers and commenced wholesale evictions of the strikers and their entire families. The newly elected Democratic governor, Robert Emory Pattison, having initially refused to protect Morewood, finally dispatched the National Guard. The inferno of violence and rage on both sides continued until June when the strike was successfully put down, and the striking families were evicted.

Just one month later came the incongruous sight of Henry Clay Frick at Cresson Station comforting his wife and gently holding his daughter. Four long years had passed since Martha had ingested the pin; the child was skeletal. Eight-year-old Childs knew just what was happening. He kept asking, "Is Martha going to die?" But Helen could not know. She could only hold onto Annie and watch their sad procession disembark and wind its way up the Mountain House hill in a carriage and wonder what it all meant.

Frick remained convinced he could save his daughter. When he entered Carnegie's cottage, he placed Martha, now unconscious, in her bed, and as had become the routine, little Helen was taken to Martha's room in hopes her presence would soothe the dying child. Helen, who called her sister "Tissie," pleaded after her visit to anyone who would listen, "Make my Tissie's pain go away . . . Please make my Tissie's pain go away." But nothing could restore the child to health. Cresson was almost as hot as Pittsburgh, and Martha continued to suffer intermittent chills and fever, along with the constant pain. After a few weeks at the Mountain House, she suddenly began asking for one member of the family after the other, including Helen. But when the family came to her bedside, Martha was too feeble to talk.

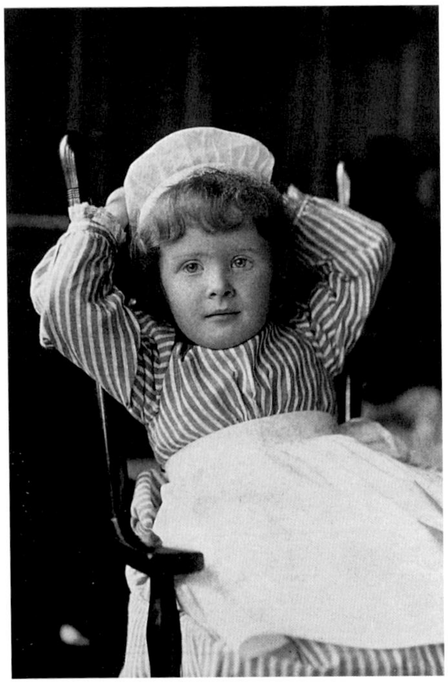

Helen dressed up as a nurse. Courtesy the Frick Collection/Frick Art Reference Library Archives.

At Andrew Carnegie's request, his own New York doctor, Jasper Garmany from Bellevue Hospital, arrived in the last week of July. After examining Martha, whose piercing screams filled the entire house while he poked and probed the area around her scar, Garmany said he could do nothing to help her. Describing what is now known as peritonitis—an inflammation of the thin membrane lining the abdominal cavity—he announced that Martha had an abdominal infection and a pus pocket had formed. Additionally he said her heart was very weak, her major organs were failing, and septicemia—infection of the bloodstream—were all contributing to the child's now-fatal condition. Garmany doubted Martha could survive an operation, but nevertheless gave the child some pills. If she would take them, he would operate in the morning and try to save her life. Frick, who was by then in tears himself, paced the halls, saying over and over, "Oh, Annie, what shall I do? What shall I do?"

That evening, Adelaide and her sister Martha Howard Childs, affectionately called Attie, comforted themselves with Helen until Annie returned from dinner and took the child, still pleading for someone to help Martha, to Martha's sickroom for what would be their final encounter. Late in the night Martha's pain became unusually severe. In the morning, when Annie returned from breakfast at the hotel, she heard Martha calling her. She ran to her bedroom, but she did not need Martha's pleading to know something terrible had happened. A very peculiar odor had greeted her as she entered the house, and intensified as she approached Martha's bed. Suspecting the worst, Annie turned down the sheets. To her horror, the child's right side had burst open. Where the old scar had once been, there oozed what already amounted to a cupful of pus.

Annie fled back to the hotel and fetched the doctors, who rushed to the cottage. They did what they could for the child, but Martha was dying. Enveloped by the putrid stench of infection and rotten flesh, the distraught family gathered to kiss her good-bye. Around noon on July 28, 1891, Martha Howard Frick died. As Annie recalled the moment, Adelaide was "hysterical with grief" in her room while Frick looked on helplessly.

Although death ended Martha's long ordeal, her passing marked the beginning of another kind of suffering, particularly for Helen. As witness to her sister's protracted agony and death, Helen became a traumatized child, a child set apart not only from other children, but also from childhood itself. Her concern about Martha in the formative years of childhood, the family's exclusive focus on Martha, the aura of the sickroom, the witnessing of her sister's suffering and death, and the sight of her distraught parents' grief created a malignant childhood reality that was to mark her for life. After Martha's death, no one in the Frick family was ever the same, most certainly not Helen.

Martha Howard Childs, known as "Attie," ca. 1895. Private collection.

A private train arrived at the Cresson platform to whisk away Helen's parents, Aunt Attie, and Annie, and carry Martha's remains back to Pittsburgh. The funeral service was held in their rented Lilac Street home and her burial took place in the recently purchased Frick family plot in Homewood Cemetery. Her grave was visible from Clayton's new, second-floor, family sitting room.

Little Helen was left behind with Childs, Martha's dog, and various servants. But her family returned to Cresson almost immediately to gather the children for a trip to New York. The adults planned to purchase the requisite mourning clothes and then to visit Fishers Island, a small island resort off the coast of Connecticut owned by Frick's former partners in the H. C. Frick Coke Company, Walton and Edmund Ferguson.

After meeting her parents' train, Helen saw that her forty-two-year-old father could hardly contain himself. He jumped from the railroad car the instant it stopped and immediately gathered his surviving daughter in his arms, "kissing you," as Annie recalled to Helen, "over and over." As Childs trailed behind asking Annie how Martha had looked and what her casket was like, Frick turned and placed Helen on her mother's lap. Adelaide fervently hugged and kissed her daughter as Frick's eyes filled with tears. But Helen, looking around for her sister, and anxious and confused by the unexpected attention, suddenly wrenched herself from her mother's embrace. As Annie described the tense moment to Helen, "you twisted around and started to look at us with a puzzled expression . . . [and] called out 'Where is my Tissie? . . . I want my Tissie.'" Annie replied patiently, "I can't get your dear sister as she has gone to Heaven." But a determined Helen was not to be put off. Her directive was: "You go to Heaven and get my Tissie for me. I want my Tissie right away." The unexpected order was too much for her parents. They began crying, and Helen, sensing she had caused their distress, turned to them: "Don't cry Mamma, don't cry Papa," she pleaded.

After a brief stop in New York, the train arrived in New London, Connecticut, where the family boarded the ferry to Fishers Island. Adelaide and Attie largely secluded themselves in their rooms and drew their blinds. Frick returned to his office in Pittsburgh during the week. So the task of consoling and entertaining Helen and her brother fell primarily to Annie. Although Childs was permitted to swim in the ocean and row on the island's freshwater ponds, Helen was not. Having lost Martha, the family did not want to take any chances with their surviving daughter.

The grief-stricken family returned to Lilac Street in September, where the mood remained despairing. The renovation of Clayton was falling behind schedule, and the first Christmas without Martha loomed. Since the family was in deep mourning, there would be no tree, no holly wreaths for the windows, no decorations of any kind. Only a few presents would be exchanged. Family friends gave the most poignant of these to Helen. As Adelaide helped her daughter unwrap a large package, out fell a life-sized wax doll with blue eyes and sparkling silver and gold wings. That night, when Adelaide and Annie looked up at the doll hanging from the chandelier in Helen's bedroom, Annie said they both turned "mute with emotion for we had the same thought—that our dear angel Martha had appeared with us in spirit."

The pall hanging over the family would not lift, even as that difficult first Christmas season came to an end. Dr. James McClelland insisted that the family stay in New York until Clayton was ready. Frick joined them in their Fifth Avenue Hotel for weekends, and Adelaide and Attie spent hours buying clothes, as well as fine china, silverware, and linens for the new house.

The women's health continued to be fragile, however, particularly Adelaide's. Her fatigue was severe, and she was newly pregnant. In addition, she had a recurring problem with her ears and, according to Annie, "some nervous condition." Dr. Garmany restricted her shopping to a few hours with rest prescribed for the balance of the day. Adding to the strain, the rooms they had taken were the same ones they had once enjoyed with Martha. Moreover, labor activists were issuing death threats and an increasingly dangerous confrontation with them loomed at the Homestead mill near Pittsburgh. Frick's weekend visits were little comfort to Adelaide. Overwhelmed by fear for her husband and family and in a deep depression, she cried herself to sleep after his departures.

By March 1892, with Clayton unfinished but habitable, the family moved back into the house. Adelaide personally supervised the unpacking along with the final details. As with any complicated reconstruction, problems lingered. More worrisome, however, was the intense, protracted mourning that continued to stalk the family. Frick, in particular, was unable to adjust to his loss. Despite his reputation as an austere businessman and a coolly calculating strikebreaker, Frick, at least during the early years, had been particularly close to his children—far more so than many of his contemporaries, who turned their progeny over to governesses and rarely interacted with them. When Childs was an infant, Frick enjoyed holding him and burping him, even if his perfectly tailored, immaculately pressed suit became soiled. Late at night, Martha would leave her bed, walk across the hall, and climb into Frick's. But Frick worried that Martha might meet with an accident because his bedroom door was at the head of the stairs. So each night before retiring he placed a chair across the top step.

With Martha gone, Frick began searching for ways to reconnect to his lost child. He had his personal checks engraved with her likeness and daily wore a pansy, her favorite flower, in his lapel. He carried her picture in his wallet and, ever longing for his dead daughter's physical presence, commissioned an important Roman sculptor, Orazio Andreoni, to

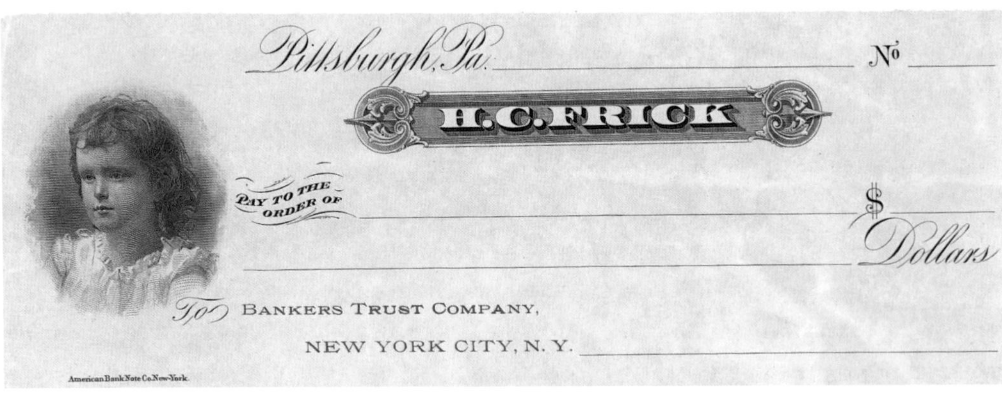

Henry Clay Frick's check with Martha's likeness. Author's collection.

Clayton breakfast room with high chair. Courtesy the Frick Collection/Frick Art Reference Library Archives.

execute a life-sized white marble bust of her. Pictures of Martha began appearing on every table in the house, including those in Helen's bedroom. But they did not satisfy Frick's longing for Martha. "When I was very little," Helen wrote, "I used to catch sight of him kissing her little high chair in the breakfast room at Clayton when he thought no one was looking." And then there was the bedtime ritual he and she enacted each evening. As Helen described it, her father "used to take out [Martha's] beautiful little curl that he kept in a box in the drawer of his bureau, & together we would kiss it. He referred to her as 'a lovely little creature.'" Then he would ask Helen to imagine the person Martha would have been, had she lived. "She was such a fascinating creature," he would sigh. When Helen retired to her bedroom, with walls painted to depict garlands of roses and morning glories and the ceiling portraying birds gliding through a sunny, summer sky, there was another reminder of Martha. Embedded within the *trompe l'oeil* of the east wall, the wall Helen faced when sitting in bed, was a single rosebud, fallen from its garland.

1892–1903

2 Daughter

Four people, four lives that boiled down to one life and that was my father's. What occupied him was what occupied us.

—Irene Selznick

As unrelenting sorrow seeped into Clayton and began to further dictate the course of Helen's childhood, another weight depressed the already overburdened family. In the spring of 1892, Carnegie's contract with the Amalgamated Association of Iron and Steel Workers entered its final months, and Frick prepared to drive the unions from Homestead, Carnegie's finest steel mill, as well as from the recently united Carnegie conglomerate. On July 6, 1892, with the labor contract expired and the workers out on strike, Frick locked the millhands out of the Homestead plant. When the furious men retaliated by storming the mill and barring both Carnegie managers and replacement workmen, Frick hired three hundred Pinkerton guards from Chicago to invade the Carnegie Steel Company grounds. Three Pinkertons and seven strikers were killed in the battle. Carnegie was pleased to win the strike and for a time publicly praised Frick, but in private he condemned his manager and partner. While as a businessman Carnegie wanted his mills to run nonunion, he also wanted the public to see him as a friend of labor. In his book, *Triumphant Democracy,* written in 1886, Carnegie had denounced the strikebreaking policy of employing replacement workers, insisting that no man should take another's job. But in May 1892, two months before the Pinkerton invasion, Carnegie had stated his fierce desire to eliminate the union, no matter the cost. He wrote Frick: "No contest will be entered into that will fail. . . . Your reputation will shorten it. . . . We all approve of anything you do, not stopping short of approval of a contest. We are with you to the end." Afraid that Carnegie might make prolabor statements to the press during the invasion, however, Frick insisted Carnegie remain in Scotland until the strike was broken.

Storming the Homestead Mill. Courtesy New York Society Library. Photo credit: Ed Watkins.

Opposite: Helen wearing her locket with Martha's likeness by Théobald Chartran. Private collection.

In the meantime, Frick and his family endured two more tragic and dramatic events. On July 8, 1892, two days after the Homestead invasion, Adelaide gave birth prematurely. All were concerned for her health and the survival of her sickly newborn, named Henry Clay Frick Jr. Simultaneously, the continuing death threats to the family intensified as a result of the labor strike. Childs, a likely target as Frick's eldest son, was sent to Fishers Island. Thin, pale, and suffering from a chronic sore throat, a shaken Childs was becoming an increasingly sensitive, retiring boy.

Helen, now almost four, was alone at Clayton with her anxious and preoccupied parents, her seriously ill infant brother, and Annie. On July 23, just two weeks after the birth of her little brother and about five days after Childs's departure, tension escalated. A Russian anarchist, Alexander Berkman, entered her father's office in downtown Pittsburgh, shot him twice in the neck, and stabbed him in the legs and chest. Dr. Bayley Buchanan, one of the first doctors in Pittsburgh to keep the newly devised black bag with sterile instruments on hand for emergencies, rushed to the scene. To better guide the surgeon to the bullets,

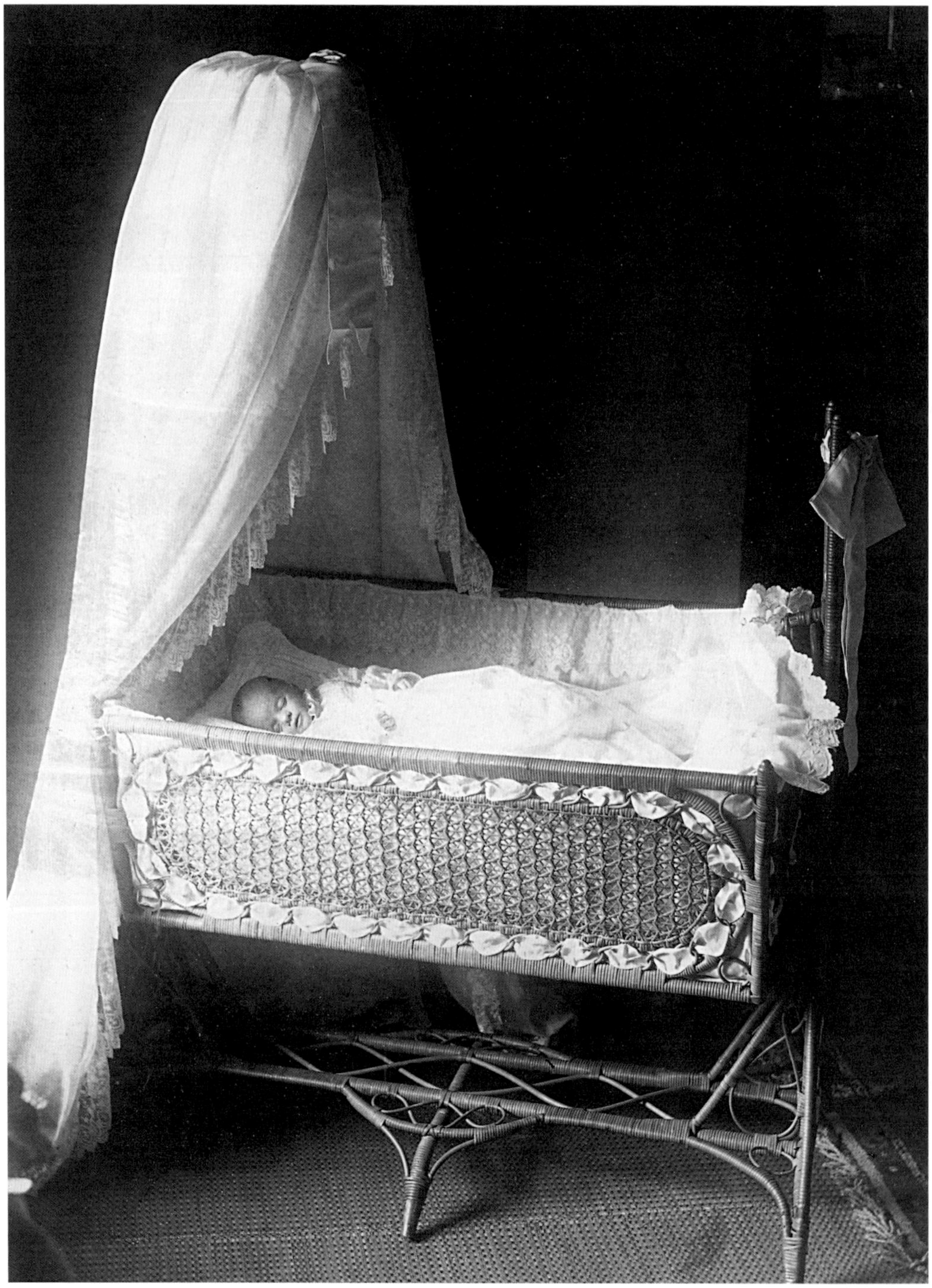

Posthumous photograph of Henry Clay Frick Jr. in his bassinet, August 3, 1892. Courtesy the Frick Collection/Frick Art Reference Library Archives.

a procedure that took four hours, Frick refused anesthesia. After the surgery, Frick suddenly bolted to his desk and completed some paperwork. Debilitated, he then returned to Clayton by horse-drawn ambulance and, swathed in bloodstained dressings, was carried by stretcher to his room. From his sickbed, Frick insisted he would run both the strike and Carnegie Steel.

Upon his arrival, Adelaide became hysterical. To calm her, the doctor moved her into her husband's room and placed her in bed beside him. Although in the next few days Adelaide's condition stabilized, the baby's health continued to decline. He refused to nurse and intermittently suffered convulsions. On August 3, he died. That morning, Frick, too weary to look at his mail, instead began organizing his infant son's funeral. Following traditional mourning and memorializing practices, a photographer was called in to take pictures of the dead child. The funeral was held the next day, downstairs in Clayton. Frick and Adelaide, both still too dangerously ill to attend, listened to the service from Frick's bedroom. They did, however, attend the burial in Homewood Cemetery, and watched as the cedar casket with a solid silver nameplate was lowered into a tiny grave beside Martha's.

Frick stayed at the bedside of his disconsolate wife throughout the night. Having had only two hours' sleep, he nevertheless returned to work on the morning of August 5—what would have been Martha's seventh birthday. Despite the more immediate emotional and physical demands on him, he was acutely aware of the significance of the date. At the time of the assassination attempt, as Frick later confessed to the *Meadow Mart,* a monthly publication in Shreve, Ohio, "the only remarkable thing . . . was that when the anarchist pointed at his head and fired, he saw his little girl, who had died the previous year, standing beside him as clearly and as real as if she had been physically present—indeed her presence was so real and corporeal that he felt like stretching out his arms to her."

Frick's immediate concern became the safety of his wife and surviving children. With Childs tucked away at Fishers Island, security at Clayton was tightened. Telephone calls were carefully screened and food was checked for poison. Neither Adelaide nor Helen was allowed outside without protection, and an intricate system was devised to alert Frick if something disastrous occurred.

But for Helen, the disaster had already occurred. She had witnessed a second sibling's death within twelve months' time, and her father, their stalwart, had very nearly been murdered. In addition, her mother had almost died in childbirth and was fast becoming a vacant presence at best. Helen no longer had Childs as a distraction, and Annie, her friend, playmate, and mother-surrogate, had a boyfriend. Although both parents would rally, the situation eerily anticipated the years ahead: Helen alone with them both safeguarding their health and fragile emotional well-being.

In September, Childs, with his health restored and the labor crisis cooling, returned from Fishers Island and entered the nearby Sterrett School. To further the boy's education, his father hired Clyde Augustus Duniway as Childs's tutor and companion. He had quite a task before him. Helen, according to Duniway, was by far the brighter of the two children, and Childs, though his health was slightly improved, remained plagued by the sore throat that

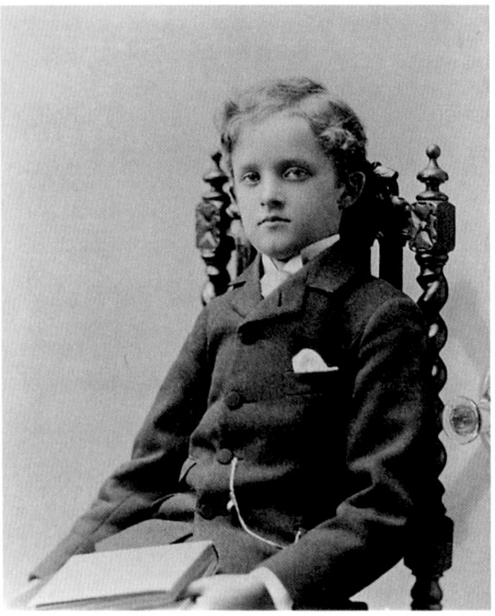

Childs when attending school in Boston. Private collection.

still needed daily medical treatment. Worse, he was not interested in his studies. Although Childs had been lucky in at least one respect, missing the most recent frightening events within the family, he returned to an acute combination of sorrow and fear.

After an uneventful 1893 springtime trip abroad with her family and Duniway, Helen returned home to yet another disruption. This time their father arranged for ten-year-old Childs to attend a day school in Cambridge, Massachusetts. Few children were sent away to school in that day, but the blow would be softened by having Childs live with Duniway, who was earning advanced degrees at Harvard University in history and political science. In return, Frick would pay all of Duniway's expenses. Frick's personal secretary, George McGrew, noted the odd nature of Frick's decision in a letter to Childs saying, "Many of the gentlemen here feel quite interested in hearing of the unusual course on which your father has started you, and they all think it a good thing." Other people expressed concern, however, about the emotional and psychological cost to Childs. Myra B. Crandall, Duniway's mentor, wrote: "Poor Childs—go away from home when so young & left to teachers who will have so little thought to his true growth and development. There are trials which come with too much money as well as from not having enough."

In the meantime, Childs's departure accelerated Adelaide's anxiety. She did not support Frick's decision to send her son away to school, and lamented that even Childs's room at Clayton had been moved to the third floor and was no longer next to hers. Having lost Martha and her infant son, not to mention having come close to losing her husband, Adelaide was now obsessed with Childs's health and safety. She begged Duniway to protect her only son from the recent outbreak of whooping cough and argued against taking him to open-air football games. This was followed by yet more pleading: "I have one more request to make of you, and it is that you will not let the little boy handle your gun. He wrote me that when he fired it off it knocked him so hard that he almost flew after it." She wrote: "I know I am a very anxious mother, but I have gone through that which has made me so."

Frick's singular concern was, apparently, with making a man out of his sweet but increasingly sorry student of a son. He wrote Childs sternly, "I hope to have good reports at all times of you. I dreamed the other night that you had written me that you stood at the head of your class. I trust such will prove to be the fact." Upon receipt of Childs's report card, however, Frick lamented on October 30, "It is about as I expected." Childs had slipped in standing and his Aunt Attie, normally sweet and comforting, pleaded, "How hard it will be to tell [your father] you have been put in a lower class because you do not care to study and keep up with the class you started in. Childs! Childs! For the sake of those who love you so dearly if for no other reason will you not try and do what is right? . . . [Do] not have Papa ashamed to mention the name of his little boy."

Childs's poor showing did indeed infuriate the steel-master. "I got the unpleasant news of your loss of class standing. This pains me very much for the reason that I am sure if you had worked as you should such result would have been avoided." He warned: "If you want to please me you must recover the lost ground quickly."

He also encouraged Duniway to create activities for the shy Childs with his schoolmates because, as Frick noted, "He is exceedingly diffident, as you know," and believed if Childs "once became well acquainted with a dozen or more of them, he would find life at school much pleasanter." Not one to let his son be nurtured—though female nurturing had saved his own life as a boy—Frick was particularly pleased to have separated Childs from his over-anxious mother. Upset at the thought of her visiting Childs, an annoyed Frick wrote Duniway, "I regret to say that Mrs. Frick has about made up her mind to visit Cambridge sometime soon, in company with Helen. I regret this very much, as I would prefer that Childs should have no interruption of this kind to his studies."

From his distance Frick quibbled, picked, and chastised, and his criticism, if well intentioned, remained unrelenting: "Using red ink is in bad taste," he scolded his son. "You should always date your letters," he commanded. "[I] was much pleased to hear from you," he wrote, "but the letter would have given me more pleasure if the spelling had been better, you do not improve in that respect as much as you should. Why I do not understand." His son's condition became fodder for more instruction: "Sorry to hear of your illness. . . . it should teach you the importance of eating plain food and of keeping regular hours."

While Frick continued to unleash a barrage of insults and disdainful personal observations at Childs, ironically, he appeared to be collapsing into the emotional vulnerabilities of midlife. The loss of his daughter and the new baby and the dissatisfactions and vicissitudes of his professional life were more and more difficult to contain. Compounding these circumstances, Adelaide was retreating more and more into depression and abdicating her role as his companion and wife.

Given his unhappiness, Frick turned to the only available female in the house able to comfort him, six-year-old Helen. She was strong-willed, bright, energetic and responsive to him. So Frick began to cultivate a father-daughter intimacy that would become the pivotal, if not the central, relationship in each of their lives. While heretofore Helen had been seated next to her mother at dinner, now her father moved her to his end of the table, where she would remain, literally, for the rest of his life. The significance of this seemingly simple act was in fact symbolic, lost neither on the industrialist's peers nor on his family. George McGrew would plant the seeds of Childs's lifelong envy and suspicion of Helen by writing the lonely, homesick boy that "Helen now occupies your place at the dinner table." With her brother in his Cambridge exile and her mother suffering from chronic headaches and colds, Helen assumed the position of the family insider. Even Andrew Carnegie noticed Helen's elevated status, referring to her in royal terms: "Lady Helen."

Helen's place was beside her father at the head of the Clayton dining room table.
Private collection.

Helen on December 9, 1892. Courtesy the Frick Collection/Frick Art Reference Library Archives.

Right: Coachman James Elmore taking Helen's doll family for a carriage ride around the neighborhood. Courtesy the Frick Collection/Frick Art Reference Library Archives.

By outward appearances Helen's life mirrored the pattern of privilege other young daughters of her social class experienced in the 1890s. At her fingertips were ivory dominos from Tiffany and playing cards from Vienna. She owned exquisite French dolls and would often place them in a carriage and ask the coachman, James Elmore, to take them for a drive around the neighborhood. She even had her own playroom on the third floor of Clayton. There she kept her beloved canaries; her favorite was named Mr. Mignon. What pleased her the most, she reported, was that the bird seemed to love only her. "Whenever a gentleman appeared, for instance my father, this gay young bird would quietly turn his back on the intruder and walk away."

Helen also entertained important visitors in her playroom. She served tea to the Andrew Carnegies and to the Mellon brothers, Andrew and Richard. These gentlemen called

Helen driving her phaeton, ca. 1895. Coachman James Elmore is seated beside Helen and governess Marika Ogiz is standing. Courtesy the Frick Collection/Frick Art Reference Library Archives.

on her father to discuss business and art, but as Helen remembered in her Clayton memoir, "they would often climb the stairs to the third floor and call upon me." Richard Mellon never left without giving her a piggyback ride, and he also gave her expensive presents, as did Andrew Carnegie. Once while traveling in Europe, Carnegie sent her a beautiful Parisian doll and a miniature sterling silver tea set.

The stable full of beautiful horses, most of them more than sixteen hands high, was another delight. She described her father's two bays and two high-stepping chestnuts as "great pets and very stunning besides." She had been given two Welsh ponies by Senator Donald Cameron, and she described them as: "full sisters, thirteen hands high, and for many years, they were my greatest joy." When she was about thirteen years old, she drove a specially built phaeton for two with a rumble seat behind. An accomplished whip, several times a week she drove the ponies, with the coachman beside her, through the neighborhood to the parks and along the boulevards. Best of all, Helen enjoyed the picnic suppers in the wagonette, a picnic carriage with seats on all sides.

Hers was an elegant, yet intimate, lifestyle. Everyone in the community knew everyone else, so much so that Helen remembered, "It was almost like a large family." She often traveled to Ohio to see her Frick relatives and also enjoyed visits from her mother's family, including Adelaide's four brothers and their families.

Her close-knit social milieu, "part and parcel of the society in which my parents moved," also involved many prominent Pittsburghers. Her parents visited Mrs. Charles Speer at Friendship Hill, where Lafayette had been entertained during his last visit to the United States. Helen described it as "a lovely old home in [La]Fayette Country on the Monongahela River. It had belonged originally to Albert Gallatin who was Secretary of the Treasury from 1801–1813."

Among Helen's playmates was Elizabeth Holmes, daughter of John Grier Holmes. They often played golf on the informal course Helen's father had staked out between Clayton and Holmhurst, the Holmes's estate. Elizabeth became, as Helen wrote, "my dearest companion, and hardly a day passed without our being together at some time." Margarita and Virginia Frew, daughters of her parents' friends, Mr. and Mrs. William Nimick Frew, were also part of Helen's circle. "[They] were real 'tom-boys' for whom I had the greatest admiration, as during our walks together, they never failed to climb to the top of the first telegraph pole we encountered, or else the highest spot on the roof at 'Clayton.'"

Helen also had high praise for the portrait painter Théobald Chartran and his wife. Chartran was commissioned to paint a posthumous portrait of Martha, as well as portraits of Helen and her father. The artist was not too busy for some levity, however. He painted a lovely picture of Helen's seven canaries, surrounded by apple blossoms, on the glass portion of the door to the enclosed porch at Clayton.

But there were some adults Helen did not like. Uncomfortable with excess formality and social pretension, Helen harbored distinct disdain for Mrs. Henry Kirk Porter, who often came to Clayton on Sunday night with her husband to enjoy the Fricks' traditional waffle and chicken dinners. Helen described Mrs. Porter as "very regal in appearance and often dressed in all white satin," reminding her of Queen Victoria. Though Mrs. Porter was "really quite handsome and wore her glistening white hair in a high pompadour and beautifully undulated," Helen admitted that her "queenly manner quite terrified me."

For the evening entertainment Helen enjoyed an orchestrion, a huge musical instrument almost twelve feet high. It arrived from Germany in 1892 complete with organ, symbols, drums, and triangle, as well as with perforated paper rolls encoded with a particular musical work. Enclosed in a large glass room off the parlor, it offered many evenings of pleasure. As Helen wrote in her Clayton memoir, "During the meal, the orchestrian [*sic*] played [my father's] favorite tunes, among which were . . . selections from *Tannhäuser, Martha, William Tell, Largo,* Gounod's *'Ave Maria.'*"

Another evening excitement for Helen was her father's weekly poker games. They were attended by such regulars as Philander C. Knox, whom Helen enjoyed as "a delightful and witty conversationalist"; David T. Watson, a brilliant trial lawyer; and the Mellon brothers. Helen remembered those evenings with pride and satisfaction: "I had the important duty of arranging the chips and took great pleasure in doing this, feeling my part was a very essential one."

Sometimes her parents gave elegant parties at home. On these formal occasions, Helen recalled "it was fun for me to peer between the banisters upstairs and see the guests as they arrived, the ladies in their lovely gowns and wraps, the gentlemen in their high hats and top coats." Other times when her parents went out, Helen watched as the special opera streetcars, "completely hung with white muslin . . . to safeguard the ladies' gowns," toured the neighborhood. "From a distance, these lighted cars all garbed in white looked ghost-like as they waited on the street corner for their passengers."

While Helen was surrounded by wealth and privilege, her parents also exposed her to philanthropy at an early age. In 1893, Frick became a founding member of Pittsburgh's Kingsley House, the first settlement house opened between Philadelphia and Chicago, located in the East End, near Clayton. Formed by the Frick family's minister, Rev. George

Montooth Kingsley House, 1902. Henry Clay Frick purchased the Montooth House and renovated it in 1901 for a settlement project called Kingsley House. Courtesy Library and Archives Division, Historical Society of Western Pennsylvania, Pittsburgh, Pennsylvania.

Hodges, at the onset of the disastrous, nationwide depression, Kingsley House was a prototype of the Protestant moral reform movement known as the Social Gospel. Its purpose was to serve the struggling immigrant workers in the nearby iron, steel, glass, and coke industries through classes in the laws and customs of America, woodworking, weaving, sewing, and home economics, among other subjects.

Adelaide Frick was an original member of both the board and the executive committee, and when Kingsley House opened on Christmas Day, 1893, with decidedly upbeat expectations, the Fricks made five-year-old Helen and ten-year-old Childs life members. By 1901, however, the enterprise was faltering. Hodges had relocated to Cambridge, Massachusetts, to further his social service. There had been a population decrease in the settlement district, a rising crime rate, and diminished family growth in the Penn Avenue area. When the directors began searching for a new site, Henry Clay Frick purchased the old Montooth mansion at Fullerton Street and Bedford Avenue, the last of the stately homes in the Hill District, as a new facility. Located in what was then the most densely populated part of the city, the Montooth mansion, central to the largest concentration of poverty in the city, represented a healthier, more viable area for community growth and settlement work. Frick spent $50,000, including the cost of a new wing, and in the fall of 1901 he turned the structure over to the Kingsley House Association debt-free. Judge Joseph Buffington wrote some thirty years later, "What this extra space meant to the neighborhood! Hundreds of boys taken from the street and its darkness, and all that goes with its forty or more clubs and classes. . . . Mothers' sewing classes, basket weaving, dressmaking, hat trimming, carpentry work, metal work, night classes for foreign-born, clinics for sickness, music, singing, community meetings." He also noted that the involvement of "earnest young men and women from many of the best homes in Pittsburgh" had in his view a "reflex of sympathy, of brotherhood and sisterhood which these young volunteer workers took back to their homes—for the homes of the rich need the Kingsley help sometimes more than the homes of the poor."

Kingsley House had just such an effect on Helen. Her childhood essays reveal both a general sensitivity to the suffering of others and a natural capacity for compassion: "If all the children had such a pretty bedroom as mine, there would not be any of them sad or unhappy," she wrote. Yet through Kingsley House she actually witnessed the tangible plight of Pittsburgh's poor and her parents' efforts on their behalf. A letter to her mother dated December 15, 1903, reveals: "This afternoon Melle and I had a very busy time at Rowes selecting clothes for the poor children." An entry in her 1904 diary dated January 9 reveals that she "arranged doll furniture for the Children of the Incurable," and on December 24 she participated in what appears to have been a long-standing Clayton Christmas tradition: "Poor children came."

For all the parties, events, and philanthropic projects involving the Frick household, underlying tensions remained. Through 1895, Adelaide continued to be miserable without her son and constantly pressured her husband for his return. In February 1896 Frick relented and Childs entered nearby Shady Side Academy. In a letter to Duniway, Frick confessed he had capitulated, saying, "We will have to give him a trial at home in order to satisfy his Mother," although, he opined, "Probably a few months' experience will convince her that it was a very unwise move to bring him home." Imprudent as Frick thought the decision, seven months later he recanted. "Very glad to be able to say that Childs is doing much better at Shady Side Academy than I expected. . . . He seems to be very industrious. Of his own accord, desired to take lessons on the mandolin. . . . He has not missed one day yet, nor been late one morning."

Indeed, Childs was much happier attending a school near home. In addition, the boy was involved with a band of twenty cadets that drilled with guns twice a week at Clayton. Thirteen-year-old Childs proudly described his guns to Duniway, "They are real and weigh 6 pounds. They are 32 cal." Helen wrote of the cadets, "On every Decoration Day, they proudly took part in the exercises that were held in the Homewood Cemetery in honor of War Dead."

Magic was another interest, as was Childs's growing collection of animals. He reported to Duniway: "The squirrel, allegator [*sic*], and pigs are well. Georgy died, but I have got another baby in his place called McKinley, because he was born on the 3d, when McKinley was elected." Adelaide caught her son's excitement and gave Childs angora rabbits for Christmas. Indeed, Childs was happier than he had ever been. He trapped animals in the woods beyond Clayton, improved his marksmanship, and practiced taxidermy on the birds he shot with "a great 12 B shotgun from Papa." A letter to Duniway boasted, "Today I shot a humming bird for our collection."

Both father and tutor hoped that Childs's developing scientific passion might spill over toward his schoolwork, but it did not. Helen, however, had enough scholastic ambition for them both. Like her father, she was hardworking and determined; she increasingly showed herself the better student and the smarter of the two, more like Frick himself and more like the son Frick had hoped for in Childs. She was also mentally tougher and more hard driving than her brother. In 1896 the famed London phrenologist, Cecil Twyford, pronounced, "[Helen] has good practical business capabilities." But Twyford also noted what he believed was Helen Frick's greatest flaw: "The head altogether is far too hot." Indeed, after Annie eloped with her beau, Lewis Stephany, Helen proved no easy charge. Generally obstreper-

Childs (center, standing) with the Clayton Cadets, ca. 1897. Courtesy the Frick Collection/Frick Art Reference Library Archives.

ous, and perhaps mimicking her father's demands and control, she could be defiant, even rude, to her governesses. She had the capacity both to outsmart and out-argue them. If her words did not persuade, she simply fought harder and often resorted to hitting. In short, Helen had the ability to make these women's lives miserable—and did.

One of them, Miss R. A. Châtelain, lasted a mere six months. After what turned out to be her final tangle with Helen Frick, she wrote her employer: "I regret having had a scene with Helen . . . for your sake, as I have always held your character & principles in the highest possible esteem. . . . [But] I was not mentally disposed that morning to accept the child's kicks & scratches very philosophically." The unfortunate woman then offered this unsolicited advice to her former employer concerning the frequency of Helen's tantrums: "Mr. Frick, you ought to consider it your duty to see that your child is surrounded by the . . . right kind of influence that will transform her into an amiable, obedient and useful member of society, and not let her through over-indulgence debase herself the way she does." Frick, however, felt he was just the right kind of influence. In this instance he sympathized with his daughter, not the governess. Helen had come down with the mumps shortly after the kicking incident. So instead of punishing his daughter, Frick penalized the woman by delaying her last paycheck.

Other times he was not so forgiving, most particularly when Helen was insubordinate. In 1896 an outraged Frick wrote his New York art dealer friend, Roland Knoedler, "Helen, since our return, has raised the question of the price I was paying her for her work, and astonished me one day by insisting that I should pay her in gold. She said she understood that was what people generally demanded, and what I was in favor of, and she did not know why she should not be paid in gold, and would accept nothing else." Frick summarily punished his eight-year-old daughter for challenging his authority and stopped buying paintings for her.

Helen's governess, Marika Ogiz, ca. 1895. Private collection.

Luckily for Helen, the right governess arrived that year and began directing the child's energies in a more constructive way. An elegant young woman from La Sarraz, Switzerland, Marika Ogiz, headed for America after a lengthy interview with Frick. Naturally, Helen, upon learning that a replacement governess had sailed, fumed. She prayed the woman's ship would sink on its Atlantic crossing. But the ship landed safely and "Melle," as the Fricks affectionately called Ogiz, found herself in charge of "a young student of precocious intelligence but of an arrogant and domineering character."

Undaunted, Melle began her duties in 1896 with a sunny personality and a delicious sense of humor that tempered Helen's emotions, encouraged her playfulness, and gently began to mold her into a finely educated, sophisticated young girl with a moral conscience and a concern for others. When Helen performed a good deed, Melle gave her a dollar, and soon her savings became significant. At Melle's urging, Helen donated the money to a tenth-century church near Ogiz's home in Switzerland so the minister could purchase a portable organ, known as a harmonium. A relieved Frick welcomed the infectious good cheer that came with this new addition to his household. Many years later Frick wrote Helen, "If it wasn't for that little Swiss woman, I don't know what would have become of you. You were so hard to manage."

Young Helen began to blossom. Although Frick was a Freemason and not a regular churchgoer, Melle taught her student hymns, and Helen now could be heard singing all day, "Jesus Loves Me," "Rock of Ages," and even the patriotic tune, "Yankee Doodle Dandy." Joined in her lessons by cousins and some children of her parents' friends, Helen studied English, French, Latin, German, U.S. history, current events, botany, mythology, and math. She learned to play the piano and took dancing and singing lessons. And she wrote essays—innocent yet revealing stories about consoling and caretaking. "The Daisy Story," for example, written in 1897, describes a family of cats—including a kitten named Rosebuddie—cared for by "a little mistress" named Daisy, who "fed them every meal."

Frick was more than pleased. "Her time is completely taken up," he wrote Duniway.

Helen (front row, second from left) with her friends. The Clayton greenhouse is in the background. Courtesy the Frick Collection/Frick Art Reference Library Archives.

And it was. For Helen was also working hard on spelling, memorization, and oration, and she was reading insatiably. On the latter discipline she received encouragement from her father: "Cultivate your mind and it will add so much to your happiness and to that of others who associate with you. Those who do not read are going back instead of progressing." As was his habit, he finished his instruction with a heart-tugging caveat: "I know you are anxious to please me and will try to do what I desire. My desire is to see you very happy and to see much of you."

Helen reading with her mother, ca. 1897. Private collection.

Unlike Childs, who showed only the most gradual improvement in his schoolwork, Helen clearly took her father's comments to heart. When she failed to live up to his expectations and caused him distress, her next grade showed significant improvement. Only in mathematics did she have difficulty. As Melle explained to her employer, "We had a good morning with our studies except for arithmetic. Helen cannot bear it and will get impatient immediately. I do not think that in this case, she is Mr. Frick's true daughter!"

In one area, however, Helen was fast becoming that true daughter. The enjoyment she began to take in her father's growing interest in art collecting was palpable. Frick had been a collector since young adulthood, and during the late 1890s, about the time Childs returned from Cambridge, he began acquiring his most important paintings to date. In her 1920s memoir, "Grandfather," Helen recalled that initially there were "pictures by Jules Breton, Cazin, Harpignie . . . Ridgway Knight, [and] Alma Tadema, [but these] gave way to those of the Barbizon School." She continued, "[The] walls of the house were rapidly being hung with Corots, Rousseaus, Millets."

Many of the new arrivals were by accomplished artists who were also family friends, such as John W. Beatty, secretary of the Art Society of Pittsburgh; A. Bryan Wall; George Hetzel of the local Scalp Level School; and their neighbor, Joseph R. Woodwell. These painters shaped the direction Frick took in these early collecting years and, thereby, influenced Helen's own developing eye. She remembered, "When my Father and I took walks together, we nearly always headed in the direction of [Woodwell's] studio and spent hours there looking over his most recent pictures and listening to the tales he told of his early years as a student in Paris." Woodwell's reaction was important to Frick. In January 1897, when a work by Narcisse Diaz de la Peña arrived, Frick wrote Knoedler eagerly, "Mr. Woodwell was over yesterday evening, and I never saw him more enthusiastic over a picture. I had made up my mind not to buy anything, but am rather glad I changed it in this case, as it seems to me that it is just what I needed in my collection."

Helen often offered a concise, profound reaction to a painting or an astute analysis of a work: "[My father] encouraged me to express my opinion about [the paintings] and it amused him to have me believe that my criticisms were of the utmost importance to him," she wrote. But his reactions were more than idle flattery. In January 1897, when

Helen was eight and a half years old, Frick advised Knoedler that he could not exchange a painting in his collection for another saying, "Helen would not consent to part with it." The following March, he returned a painting by Théobald Chartran to Knoedler because "it does not please me, nor do Mrs. Frick and my daughter seem to think it worthy of the artist." Then in December, when rejecting a new work by Charles-François Daubigny, Frick confessed to Knoedler that for fun he had told Helen "that I proposed to exchange four other pictures for it, and named them," and Helen had asserted herself. "She promptly said the Detaille could go, as she did not care much for it, but the Chevalier and the Rico could not be parted with, and although she liked the Dupre, yet she might be willing that it should go." A delighted Frick mused about his daughter's perspicacity. "So you see the difficulties I would have had to encounter, even if I had decided to propose an exchange with you." For his part, Knoedler was well aware of how precocious Helen was. When her father purchased *Portrait of a Young Artist,* then considered a work by Rembrandt, Knoedler jokingly asked Helen if she had sold it yet. Her no-nonsense reply was, "As for the Rembrant [*sic*] I have not sold it yet, so you must come here and we will have a business talk about the subject."

Helen seated on a newel post, ca. 1895. Courtesy the Frick Collection/Frick Art Reference Library Archives.

Business sense was what Frick most admired about Helen. She proudly wrote in a memoir, "Papsie was so ambitious for me—he wanted me to do things well & show good judgment. Sometimes he would go so far as to say I had 'business ability' & 'a good head on my shoulders,' & that I 'should have been a man.' At other times, he would get a little discouraged over me & say that 'Helen always thinks she knows best—she will never take advice.'" But, when Helen did disappoint, "he would relent & put out his dear hand & say, 'I love her just the same' or 'she's not perfect but she comes pretty near being it.'"

Young though she was, Helen could be as clear and direct as Frick himself. He once asked her, as they walked by the neighboring Gillespie house he had just purchased, "Now Helen, which would you prefer I should give you, this land or the pictures?" Helen's matter-of-fact reply was, "Papa, I would like the land as we can raise something on it." Then another day, after Frick sold the property and said he regretted not keeping the Gillespie place, Helen's swift reply had been, "Well, Papa you got a great deal of money for it." To Carnegie he boasted that he "had a daughter with a pretty good business head on her." Indeed Frick was well aware of his daughter's intelligence—"Helen's no slouch," he once said—and enjoyed indulging her opinions. But pleasing her father and having him brag about her came at a price. "He used to make me feel so ashamed that I was not thoughtful of him more often, when he noticed any little thing I would do, & would mention it to others."

Helen's close association with her father's early collecting efforts elevated her already lofty position within the family. She remembered: "When foreigners came to Pittsburgh, 'Clayton' was one of the homes they wished to see. My father was too busy to afford the luxury of returning home to meet these guests, and as neither he nor my mother spoke French, I was called upon to do the honors." Once Helen took the famous French actor, Monsieur Coquelin, through Clayton, and she later confessed: "But I wonder what his reaction must have been when he was obliged to listen in return to a little American girl? I am horrified every time I recall the experience!"

By now the compliant and eager-to-please Helen had usurped her brother's role as her father's favorite, the one to be molded as Frick's sounding board and heir, and the one who would have the most influence in his life. Shaping her father's destiny, not her own, and reflecting his desires would become the *leitmotif* of Helen's life. Entrapped, Helen would be caught between her powerful father's little-boy narcissism and her brother's envy.

For the moment, however, the privileges of Helen's life overshadowed any darkness. She could be seen strolling hand-in-hand with her father, albeit through the trees and shadows of the Homewood Cemetery where her sister and younger brother were buried. She had devoted parents, an apparently sweet brother, ponies, pretty clothes, expensive dolls, and even paintings of her own. She knew important artists in America and Europe, as well as the most powerful people in Pittsburgh. In 1897, she received a large new playhouse to share with her brother. As Childs described the two-story cottage to his former tutor, "It is forty feet one way, 30 the other, another story over that & then a double bowling-alley running 70 feet back." Childs had a photography lab in the rear and now kept his pet raccoon on the porch. The rest of the downstairs belonged to Helen. That was filled with child-sized wicker and oak furniture and a small gas range where she could learn to cook and bake for her young guests. The second-floor studio was intended as shared space, used for physical activities: dancing lessons, gymnasium exercises, and drills.

Clayton playhouse, ca. 1900. Private collection.

Helen played hostess in the Clayton playhouse. It was outfitted with child-size furniture. Courtesy the Frick Collection/Frick Art Reference Library Archives.

Yet the rivalry between the two children inevitably eroded the deceptively perfect facade. From 1896, when Childs entered Shady Side Academy, to 1901, when he had improved his grades sufficiently to be accepted by Princeton University for the newly established geology department, Childs teased Helen unmercifully. Though she fought back with her feet and fists, she was regularly reduced to tears. Indeed, her brother delighted in making her cry and then forcing her to look at herself in the mirror and admit she was ugly. Even Carnegie was concerned about the situation. He wrote his partner, "Wish we had Helen up here [in Scotland] away from Childs."

Teasing was an ingrained part of Frick family life, and in this one aspect, at least, Childs proved to be very much his father's son. As Helen remembered her father in a memoir, "[He] loved to tease. . . . But he rarely laughed out loud. He would chuckle though, sometimes, till the tears came. . . . He had the keenest sense of humor & the greatest knack for sizing up people, always detecting their most vulnerable point." Helen recalled how her parents "often poked fun at each other during family dinners." Adelaide did not like her age divulged so, as Helen wrote of her father, "One of his favorite methods was to bring up the subject of her age, & without telling it, let slip how old he was in a certain year, & say he was ten years older than she was." So Childs came by his teasing naturally, though taunting his sister took on a mean cast. One of his favorite pranks was to slip away from Melle and his parents in the evening and hide under Helen's bed. When his sister started to climb in, he would reach out and grab her ankles. Yet Helen seems never to have complained.

The tension between the siblings was not the only evidence of family distress. Henry Clay Frick seemed increasingly like a broken man, and the art he was collecting was a good indication of his deteriorating emotional state. In 1895, on the tenth anniversary of Martha's birth, he purchased a haunting, life-sized painting of a little girl, *L'Espièglerie (Mischievous*

Girl), by Adolphe-William Bouguereau. To keep Martha alive and present in Clayton and in Helen's mind, he placed the portrait in Helen's bedroom and hung a commemorative print by the artist above the desk in her third-floor playroom. According to the art dealer, René Gimpel, Frick bought the Bouguereau portrait of the little girl "because it resembled a daughter he had lost."

Others noticed a change as well. Carnegie, for one, was now referring to his partner as "unwell and overstrained." He observed that Frick was in an obviously "tired state" and told him "your face appears to me as it was the other night when you came to us after dinner.... [It] was worn, you were tired, over strained, long meetings, vital questions, discussions had worn you out." Carnegie had unsuccessfully urged Frick to take a vacation, but although his concerns were justified, Carnegie's solicitations concealed another agenda: Frick's removal from the firm. Criticized by Carnegie as being "too old—too infirm in health *and mind,*" Frick was under pressure to resign. In the interest of harmony, he stepped down as president of Carnegie Steel and accepted the newly created, lesser position as chairman of the board.

This demotion was the latest in a series of events that drove a wedge between Frick and Carnegie. After all, in the summer of 1887, Frick had resigned as chairman of the H. C. Frick Coke Company and had taken his family abroad, all in response to Carnegie's betrayal during the strike in the coke region. There, in Paris, Martha had swallowed the pin. When her illness became acute four years later, in the spring of 1891, Frick was occupied with the violent Morewood riots in the coke region. As an interviewer would later report in the *Meadow Mart,* "Her death was felt more keenly because he blamed himself for not

Mischievous Girl by Adolphe-William Bouguereau was the focal point of eight-year-old Helen's Clayton bedroom. Private collection.

being able to attend her more constantly during her fatal illness." Then came the death of his infant son in 1892 during the Homestead steel strike, along with what Frick regarded as Carnegie's reprehensible, two-faced behavior over unionization.

Helen wrote many years later, "The greatest sorrow of Papsie's life was the loss of his little daughter Martha. He never failed to ask me each year on August 5th if I remembered what day it was. 'Dear little soul, she would have been such & such an age today.' It made one's heart ache, just to hear the pathos in his voice when he spoke of her." Even his philanthropic efforts evidenced his grief. The recent advances in medical science that had saved Frick after the assassination attempt had not been available to Martha in her suffering. In a telling gesture Frick gave Shadyside Hospital, where Dr. McClelland practiced, a new operating room with aseptic technology. He also gave Mercy Hospital its first X-ray machine.

An essay Helen composed, entitled "Four Little Sunbeams," while typical of what the sentimental and morality-laden Victorian girl was expected to write, reveals that she had internalized the responsibility of lifting her father's heavy despair.

> Once there was [*sic*] four little Sunbeams who were talking together. I will tell you what they said. "We must try to make some people happy," they said. The first one's name was Little Rose, the second little Lily, the third For-get-me-not, and fourth Little Margaret. Well they said "let each of us go a different way, and when we shall next come back let us meet at the West where grandpapa will be waiting for us." Little Rose went to a small cottage and played with a little baby who had no toys at all, and her mamma was away washing. And so when the mamma came home she found her little darling laughing with glee. Little Lily went to see a poor old man who could not walk and brightened his little room up so that if he did not have pleasure out of doors he should have it in his home. For-get-me-not caressed a poor young girl who could not see and who was pale and thin and gave her a much rosier face than she had before. Little Margaret went to a small garden where the flowers did not bloom but now made it smell good so when its little owner came it was not the same sad little garden as before.
>
> When they reached the West their grandpapa said, "Why my dear little children you look so very happy, how is that?" Then they told him their story, and he answered . . . "Well dears, that is a lesson for you. You are much more happy when you have done some pleasure for others, than when you only think about yourself." And so now those four little sunbeams are going around the world doing good for others because it is more blessed to give than to receive.

By the late 1890s, helping others had become instilled and ingrained in Helen's evolving sense of self, so much so that she understood this to be her mission, if not her right and special honor. Another essay, "Sympathy," illustrates how deep her need had become, how through another's tragedy she sought to enhance her own self-image, and how chilling her response would be if her succor were rejected:

> "My poor Mrs. Smith, I heard that your little son was kidnapped this morning, and I have come to offer my sympathy. Oh no, you needn't thank me at all. It is my great pleasure to be able to tell you how badly I feel for you, because you will probably never see poor little Johnnie again.
>
> "I heard of a similar case that happened several years ago. The little boy in question was stolen, and five years later, his mother heard he had died because of

bad treatment. Now Mrs. Smith don't cry; it is really dreadful, but one should always expect the worst. If he doesn't come back, at least you will be able to say that I told you not to hope. Mrs. Smith, Mrs. Smith don't take on so! My but I am glad I came, because one does need sympathy in these trying times, and I'm sure you feel a good deal better now.

"Why do you start so?" A youthful voice calls out: "Mother," and Mrs. Smith rushes from the room with outstretched arms.

"It isn't Johnnie! Well I never! Well, Mrs. Smith, it's too bad in a way, that he has come back to you so soon; if he had stayed away a little longer, I could have told you so much, and you would have had other people too, no doubt, to console you. It is not often that one gets a chance of having lots of company. But good-day."

Portrait of Helen Clay Frick by Théobald Chartran as it appeared in a Pittsburgh newspaper in 1896. Courtesy the Frick Collection/Frick Art Reference Library Archives.

Try as she might to heal Frick's heart by being the perfect daughter, Helen was forced to compete with her deified sister for her father's love and approval. Yet Helen refused to live in her sister's shadow. Théobald Chartran had completed, in 1895, both the posthumous portrait of Martha and a miniature copy of it mounted in a turquoise, gold, and pearl locket for Helen to wear around her neck. He then began the portrait of Helen wearing this locket. Although there is no record of where the Fricks first intended to hang these paintings, Helen's appeared destined for a place of lesser honor. A letter Frick wrote to Knoedler suggests, however, that Helen stood up for herself and negotiated a position of equal status with her deceased sister. Soon both portraits were placed in the library, one on either side of a copy of *Christ and the Disciples at Emmaus,* painted by their friend, the French artist Pascal Adolphe Jean Dagnan-Bouveret. Frick had recently purchased the original painting, depicting the moment three days after the crucifixion when the resurrected Christ appears in a blinding visitation to his apostles. He had given it to the Carnegie Institute with a plaque reading: "In honor of Martha Howard Frick." Frick commented to Knoedler on the placement of his daughters' portraits: "Helen and her mama compromised on the library. I thought it was a pretty good business deal for Helen."

Helen and Childs in Cannes, Aix-les-Bains, ca. 1898. Courtesy the Frick Collection/Frick Art Reference Library Archives.

Helen seemed ordained to minister to her parent's emotional needs. In 1896, Cecil Twyford averred something at once convenient for her parents and devastating for Helen:

> [She] would make a splendid matron of a hospital. . . . [and] should have a nurse's training for she would become a heavenly visitor at a sick bedside, quite a patch of sunshine to light up a weariness and suffering. . . . She will always be good on an emergency—quick as lightning to arrange what requires to be done under the circumstances. . . . She must have thoroughly instilled into her mind the real pleasure of self-sacrifice—of denying herself in order to give to others, without praise or apparent appreciation. . . . [and] should never be allowed to marry.

His words anticipated the course of Helen's life: a caretaker alone both in the quicksand of sadness within her family and also in the outer world.

In 1899 another family crisis erupted when Frick failed in his attempt to buy Andrew Carnegie out, and Carnegie claimed the H. C. Frick Coke Company was inflating the price of coke to Carnegie Steel. Frick decided to end his personal and business relationship with his boss forever. When Frick tried to liquidate his holdings in Carnegie Steel, however, he met

with fierce resistance. Carnegie tried to enforce the outdated 1887 Iron Clad Agreement relating to the once Carnegie Brothers and Company, never incorporated into the Carnegie Steel Company when it was amalgamated in 1892. Under the Iron Clad, if enforceable, Frick would garner only $6 million, the book value of his 6 percent share, rather than the $16 million due him in market value.

When he learned of this, an incensed Henry Clay Frick accosted Andrew Carnegie in a near-volcanic tirade: "For years I have been convinced there isn't an honest bone in your body. Now I know that you are a god-damned thief. We will have a judge and jury of Allegheny County decide what you are to pay me." Carnegie fled Frick's office and on February 14, 1900, Frick filed suit against him. The *Pittsburgh Dispatch* noted the magnitude of this "bitter personal struggle for supremacy," saying, "The suit is the most important ever filed in this country with the steel business, and it is generally conceded that the great steel company has reached a crisis in its existence." It continued: "The entire world will watch each move with intense interest."

Frick demanded that a receiver be appointed by the court for the dissolution of Carnegie Steel and requested that the proceeds be distributed among the partners. He took a further swipe at Carnegie by announcing that the company would make a $40 million net profit that year, a heretofore privately held figure and a poor reflection on the labor-pandering Carnegie, who spoke up for the workingman yet paid him paltry wages. To further expose and embarrass his boss and partner, Frick also charged Carnegie with malice and fraud. Frick refused to meet with Carnegie or to attend settlement negotiations held in Atlantic City. Instead he greeted various partners, who served as go-betweens, either at his office in the Carnegie Building or at Clayton and, according to a March 21, 1900, press report, was "perfectly satisfied to let the matters go ahead and be made public through the medium of a court trial."

Fortune, depicted on her wheel, stained-glass window by John La Farge in the lobby of the Frick Building. Courtesy Rugby Realty, photo credit: Lawrence Henry Walsh Sr.

Only one month after the suit was filed against him, Andrew Carnegie capitulated. He saw the greater danger. As the press noted, apart from the fact that a public trial would have allowed rivals "an opportunity to gloat over coveted secrets," the affairs of Carnegie Steel would have been indefinitely tied up in litigation. Frick would have closed mills by injunctions and withdrawn a lucrative contract for steel rails for the Cape to Cairo railroad in Africa.

In a major triumph for Frick, the Carnegie Steel Company was dissolved and reorganized as the Carnegie Company, Ltd., along the lines of the syndicate Frick had formed in 1899 when trying to buy out Carnegie. Capitalized at about $320 million, with Frick retaining a 6 percent share (the same as his percentage in Carnegie Steel), the Carnegie Company was the largest steel concern then known, hailed as "encompass[ing] the mines and markets of the world."

While an astonished public stood by and watched the details of the giant firm unfold, a victorious Frick, together with his wife and Helen, traveled to Atlantic City for a month of rest. The press gleefully reported that all bitterness between Frick and Carnegie had dissolved. One report claimed, "Utmost cordiality now exists between the hitherto sturdy opponents." Yet having successfully pierced Carnegie's facade, Frick would now drive the knife deeper. He resigned as a trustee of the Carnegie Library in Pittsburgh and from the art acquisition committee of the Carnegie Institute. He also refused to lend paintings to the institute's annual exhibition. Thoroughly disgusted with Carnegie, he would never again deign to speak to his former partner.

Over the next two years, Frick played a pivotal role in merging the Carnegie Company into the $1.4 billion U.S. Steel Corporation, America's first billion-dollar company. He became both a stockholder and a director of the giant new steel trust while Carnegie relinquished his voting power by taking bonds rather than stock. Other U.S. Steel powerbrokers, J. P. Morgan and John D. Rockefeller Sr., joked about the irony: Frick was now in and Carnegie was out. They claimed they had formed U.S. Steel just to get rid of Carnegie.

Frick had fought hard to regain his stature. In 1895, during the early stages of his power struggle with Carnegie, Frick had contemplated building a new house on Gunn's Hill, overlooking the massive Carnegie steelworks along the Monongahela River, as a signal to Carnegie that he was not sidelined. But Adelaide held title to Clayton, and again refused to leave the birthplace of her children, so the project came to naught. In 1901, however, Frick began construction of a twenty-one-story, three-hundred-and-thirty-foot-high building in downtown Pittsburgh—the tallest yet in the city. It offered office space, and centralization, for the many divisions of the local U.S. Steel complex. An impressive, beaux arts style, snow-white marble edifice, it featured an entrance hall lined with Carrara marble, lit by an art nouveau stained-glass window by John La Farge entitled *Fortune,* shown on her wheel. The exquisite entrance doors were guarded by a pair of bronze lions by Alexander Phimister Proctor. The gleaming building was also fitted with a barbershop, ladies' lounge, gentleman's club reading room, and dining room paneled in Flemish Renaissance oak with a frieze depicting the heroes and heroines from Wagner's operas. It opened in March 1902, about the time the merger between the Carnegie Company and U.S. Steel was completed. Eleanor Franklin in *Frank Leslie's Weekly,* March 19, 1903, asked "Who would ever think to look for the finest office building in the world in Pittsburgh?"

The Frick Building facade during construction, September 30, 1901. Courtesy the Frick Collection/Frick Art Reference Library Archives.

With the new building, Frick had satisfied a far more significant need than merely creating a glamorous, highly praised, architecturally perfect, yet fully efficient structure to facilitate U.S. Steel operations. Frick yearned for a symbolic, yet public statement to commemorate his rise to a multimillionaire; his legal triumph over Carnegie; and his contribution to Pittsburgh's enormous industrial success. The Frick Building served this purpose. As Eleanor Franklin aptly stated, "the sun would forever rise and set on the Frick Building and immortalize its builder." In fact, this skyscraper, located east of and adjacent to the older, fourteen-story Carnegie Building, daily cast a shadow upon its smaller, now less important neighbor. Immediately upon the Frick Building's completion, Helen was given sole and secret title.

His public triumph notwithstanding, inwardly Henry Clay Frick was an embittered man, and his sharp-eyed, ever vigilant fourteen-year-old daughter was insightful. Although

she later claimed in her 1959 booklet, *My Father: Henry Clay Frick*, that her father never discussed business at the dinner table, she well understood the dispute raging between Frick and Carnegie and the devastating emotional and financial blows Carnegie had tried to inflict upon him. She read the newspapers and had witnessed with her own eyes the strain her father was under. She had listened as he recited the first part of Psalm 55, the lament of a man betrayed by a friend: "horror hath overwhelmed me. . . . Oh that I had wings like a dove! For then would I fly away and be at rest." And then she would recite the latter part of the psalm: "But thou, O God, shalt bring them down into the pit of destruction: bloody and deceitful men shalt not live out half their days; but I will trust in thee." Helen later recalled this father-daughter antiphony: when she started reciting her lines, her father "always smiled and put out his dear hand for me to squeeze." She even confided in a later memoir that she had devised a method of consoling him: "My father often got the 'fidgets' sometime during the evening, and then he and I would take a walk, arm in arm, first on one floor, then on another, steering our way around the furniture and having fun doing it. This seemed to relieve him & then he went early to bed."

The resentment Frick felt toward Andrew Carnegie passed to Helen, but she had reasons of her own to loathe the man her family once called friend. Although the creation of U.S. Steel assured her a life of ease and luxury—her father's fortune rocketed from $16 million in 1899 to $65 million in 1902—life at Clayton had forever changed. Helen was alone. Childs entered Princeton in the fall of 1901, bent on pursuing his interest in the natural sciences, and with U.S. Steel now headquartered in New York City, her parents spent increased time in their rented apartment in Sherry's Hotel. In her essay, "An Apartment at Sherry's," Helen expressed her displeasure with the New York domicile. "[An apartment] may be very attractive," she wrote, "but there is never the same feeling about it as there is about [a house] . . . for in a house you feel as though it belonged to you . . . and you use your taste more thoroughly in fixing it up." So, when her parents began spending more and more time in New York, Helen stayed behind in her favorite place, Clayton.

She was left there, however, with only the companionship of Melle, the servants, her neighborhood friends, and the constant reminders of her dead siblings. *Chagrin d'Enfant,* a painting by Emile Friant, was now in the front hall, to the left of the entrance into the reception room where the white marble bust of Martha stood. *Chagrin* depicts a suffering little girl, who in fact died shortly after the painting was completed, huddled in the lap of an older girl, just as Martha had huddled in Annie's. *Consolatrix Afflictorum,* a large painting by Dagnan-Bouveret, was placed in the dining room in front of the fireplace. *Consolatrix,* a reference to Psalm 42, shows a Madonna whose face resembles Adelaide's, a man prostrate at her feet whose profile resembles Frick's, and a Christ child who looks like the postmortem photograph of Henry Clay Frick Jr.

Although Frick was spending more time away from Clayton, he kept adding to the art collection there, and also embarked on a $100,000 renovation of the guest rooms. While the first and second floors remained in the heavy, late-Victorian style, the third-floor guest rooms suddenly featured light, air, and striped wallpaper prescribed by Edith Wharton and Ogden Codman in their book *The Decoration of Houses.* Frick also replaced the stained-glass windows on the stair landing in the family's living area. The Victorian scene entitled *Love in the Tower* gave way to one depicting four famous ladies of literature. Like *Little Red Riding Hood,* a painting by George Frederic Watts hanging in the upstairs library-sitting room, the pre-Raphaelite beauties of the new windows teach valuable lessons about the dangers of teenage girls associating with men other than one's father. Miranda from

Clayton dining room with *Consolatrix Afflictorum* by Pascal Adolphe Jean Dagnan-Bouveret, an expression of the Frick family's mourning for their deceased children. © the Collection of the Frick Art & Historical Center, Pittsburgh, Pennsylvania.

View through the dining room, past Helen's place at the table, to the front hall where *Chagrin d'Enfant* by Emile Friant is exhibited. Author's collection.

Shakespeare's *Tempest* remained loyal to her father in his time of trouble, but was only allowed to marry after her suitor passed her father's near-impossible tests. Marguerite from Goethe's *Faust* goes insane for having consorted with Faust and kills the baby she conceives with him, believing it born of the devil. Isabella from Keats's "The Pot of Basil" dies of grief because her jealous brothers murder her lover and then smash the basil pot in which she has placed his head. Finally Madeline, from Keats's "St. Agnes Eve," runs off into the storm with Porpyro, the man who watched her from a closet as she undressed, slept, and awakened.

While these images stood over Helen, her father and mother were seldom at Clayton. In their absence, Helen began to lose weight and to fear the loss of one or both of her parents. As her anxiety mounted, teenage Helen Frick assumed a new role: parent to her parents. Although Helen's letters to her parents when they were in New York could be viewed as solicitous, polite, and correct, rather than overly anxious, when seen through the eyes of a child who has witnessed the deaths of two siblings in one year and the near deaths of both parents, they assume a more noxious cast, particularly as they relate to her emotionally absent and chronically ill mother. "I hope you are not going to tire yourselves," she wrote her parents. "If you attempt to Mamma dear, Papa must correct you, and if you do, Papa dear, Mamma dear must correct you!" Another letter instructed: "Don't you be trying to do too much Mamsie dear, for you know if you do I will give you a terrific scolding when you come home! . . . Talk about wanting to hug me, I wish [I] could hug you now 'precious little baby Mamma.'"

Once, when Helen learned her mother had caught cold, real concern ensued. "I was so sorry tonight when I learned that my darling Mamma had a cold, and I hate New York more than ever now, for giving it to you!" Another directive read: "Darling little Mamma, now once more be good, and don't do too much. (I have said that not less than a 100 times.)"

Helen's growing sense of self-importance is also revealed through the protective cover of an essay entitled "Jane."

Love in the Tower, the original stained-glass windows in Clayton. Courtesy the Frick Collection/Frick Art Reference Library Archives.

Four Ladies of Literature served to educate Helen about the dangers of potential suitors. © the Collection of the Frick Art & Historical Center, Pittsburgh, Pennsylvania.

Jane was a tall, thin girl of fifteen; her appearance was very reckless as she did not care about clothes nor did she like the idea that she was rapidly growing into woman-hood.

Awkward in her movements on account of her long arms and legs . . . Jane greatly resembled a colt.

She had sharp, gray eyes that were capable of being thoughtful, funny and fierce; her mouth was accentuated, her nose long, and her thick brown hair which was her only beauty, was done up in a net (to be out of the way).

Altogether she was very ungainly, but she had a kind, warm heart, was bright and cheerful, and was looked upon as the head of her family.

Of course Helen was not as much in charge as she believed. When her father returned home from New York, without his wife, she joined in his usual rituals: walking to Martha's grave, spying on him when he kissed Martha's highchair, reciting the vengeful lines of Psalm 55 while he held her hand and she promised to avenge Carnegie's wrongs, walking Frick around the house so he could fall peacefully asleep, kissing the lock of Martha's hair and imagining what she would have been like had she lived—and now sitting on his lap and stroking his head as he resisted and then encouraged her. After her father's death in 1919, thirty-year-old Helen wrote: "I was Papsie's 'little girl' always—& he loved to have me sit on his lap & pet him & call him endearing names, & yet he would nearly always pretend that I shouldn't do it: 'Don't be foolish, don't be silly, be womanly—you never will grow up.' 'You act like a 16 yr. old girl.' 'You're too heavy',—smiling all the while with those twinkling blue eyes. . . . And he even sometimes talked baby talk to me, Papsie of all people in the world. . . . How irresistible he was."

1903 photograph of Henry Clay Frick forcing an unwelcome kiss on Helen. Childs, then a photography buff, may have taken this photograph. Author's collection.

The rituals did not stop here. Over the last few years, Helen had received numerous gifts from her father. Although Frick never permitted her to wear jewelry, except for the locket containing a copy of her sister Martha's portrait, he gave her an emerald ring on her seventeenth birthday. According to family members in whom she confided, Helen was insulted by the gift. To her, a ring whether diamond or otherwise, symbolized engagement. So infuriated was Helen by this controlling gesture she fumed about it for the balance of her life.

A 1903 photograph, probably taken by Childs, provides evidence of just how torturous the father-daughter relationship had become. In 1902, when the Frick Building opened and U.S. Steel was formed, Frick also broke ground for a family summer home—a large, neo-Georgian, limestone and brick house at Prides Crossing, overlooking the Atlantic Ocean on Boston's North Shore and named Eagle Rock for the eagles nesting there. A Republican stronghold, the North Shore was also where many of Frick's colleagues in the railroad industry summered. During the three years it was under construction—cut out of solid rock—the Fricks rented houses nearby, first Woodrock and then the Robert S. Bradley house. The photograph shows Helen near the bathhouse at Woodrock, on her way to the changing room. She is wearing a long day dress, an elaborate hat, and carrying a small shoe bag. But her father has blocked her passage down the boardwalk. In an act of stunning obscenity, he has grasped Helen with his right arm and forced her body to his. His left hand is on her face, forcing her mouth to his. Although Helen's long, thin legs are turned outward, trying to free herself, and although her face shows abject revulsion and distress over what her father is doing to her, she is not strong enough to break his hold. Helen is forced to endure her father's open-mouthed kiss.

Woodrock, ca. 1902, the house on the North Shore of Boston rented by the Frick family while Eagle Rock was under construction. Courtesy the Frick Collection/Frick Art Reference Library Archives.

Below: Helen riding sidesaddle at Woodrock, ca. 1903. Courtesy the Frick Collection/Frick Art Reference Library Archives.

The kiss probably was not the first she had endured, nor would it probably be the last. Although Helen traditionally signed letters to her mother "your loving little girl," or "your loving little kid," she signed them differently during those times when her father returned home from New York alone. In a letter to her mother dated January 5, 1900, Helen writes, "You are so sweet to write to that horrid, horrid Helen," and in 1903, revealing her confusion between her dead sister "Rosebud" Martha and her duty to soothe and care for her damaged father, she said: "keep stacks of that stuff [love] from Rose-bud Papa and your little horrid but loving girl."

Although there is no evidence Frick's advances went farther than the unwelcome inappropriate kiss, such behavior is nevertheless a violation of a daughter's sexual boundaries. Author Maureen Murdock explains a daughter's difficulty in such a situation in her book *The Hero's Daughter:* "If he violates her sexually, she has no one to turn to; she is completely abandoned."

3

1904–1912

Young Woman

The daughter then becomes . . . his bridge to his own unconscious. She becomes a walking archetype, a goddess . . . who has sacrificed her own humanity.

—Marion Woodman, *Addiction to Perfection*

By 1904, sixteen-year-old Helen was so tightly bound to her father, and he to her, she could not break free. Entries in her 1904 and 1905 composite diary reveal her dependence. Although Helen made no mention of her mother's or her brother's comings and goings, she registered all her father's departures with sorrow, and welcomed all his returns with joy.

The entries also reveal an energized young woman headstrong and mercurial yet still reliant, struggling to control her temper and a battered self-image. In January 1904, for instance, she wrote: "Was not good for 1st Sunday of 1904," and "was very naughty to Melle and did not have any lessons with her. Spent a miserable day." In February she wrote, "Was a naughty kid in morning" and two weeks later admitted, "I was a bad girl."

Helen, ca. 1904. Author's collection.

Opposite: Helen with her father in a photograph by Henry Havelock Pierce, ca. 1910. Private collection.

There were of course many good moments in Helen's sixteenth year. That same January she also started keeping records of her sightseeing trips, remarkable for their frequency and breadth. Helen was already a veteran traveler, having visited Europe with her family numerous times as a child. Extensive trips abroad were not unusual for wealthy Americans, although usually children were not included. But Frick wanted his children to be exposed to what he had been denied until he made his first million. While traveling together the family learned the history of the countries they visited, studied their art, called on Frick's artist friends, and contemplated additions to their growing collection.

In the winter of 1904 Helen's parents took her to the Breakers Hotel in Palm Beach, Florida. She expressed sorrow, as she always did, over leaving Clayton, but on arrival she threw herself into every new experience. Her daily lessons continued, and she enjoyed visits from family friends: the Horace Hardings from New York, the Roland Knoedlers, the Charles Speers from Pittsburgh, and her own friends—young Eleanor Whitney

Eagle Rock, ca. 1905. Author's collection.

from New York and Elizabeth Holmes and Henrietta Thaw from Pittsburgh. Helen swam in the ocean, visited an alligator farm, and took a sightseeing trip to Havana. What interested her most there, as it would throughout her life, was the historic setting: "was impressed with the beauty & age of the place."

At the end of March, Helen returned home with her parents, and in June she called on her ninety-five-year-old paternal grandmother, Elizabeth Overholt Frick, in Wooster, Ohio. She spent the balance of the summer riding and driving her ponies on the North Shore of Boston, watching the final construction of Eagle Rock.

But for all the carefree fun and travel and all she was learning from Melle, Helen felt a void in her life. She confided to her diary on September 1, 1904, a few days before her birthday, that she felt the need to accomplish something special: "Passed through the year into my 17th. Feel that I have not done much yet." Helen's irritability sprang from a new restlessness, an emerging impatience with the vanities of her social class. January 1905 found her in New York, sitting for yet another portrait by Théobald Chartran. To her disdain and probably her utter embarrassment, Helen was immortalized in a flirty, white, diaphanous, ankle-length lace dress, holding a parasol trimmed with pink roses and ribbon in her right hand, and in her left a matching straw hat. In an obvious reference to Eagle Rock, Helen is posed against a large cliff.

As her teenage years wore on, travel abroad increasingly became her primary interest. Each trip provided a forging, shaping, and deepening of her interest in art, architecture, and history. On July 11, 1905, despite their anxiety over Elizabeth Frick's failing health, Helen and her family left for a three-month automobile tour through France to the homelands of her Frick ancestors in Switzerland and of the Overholts in the German Palatinate on the Rhine. Wealthy families of the day generally took the grand tour to spas, the ocean, or to the mountains of Europe. But the Fricks largely went where the art was, and although Frick was still a director of U.S. Steel, as well as of railroads, banks, and insurance companies, he was retired from active business and could dictate his own schedule.

Opposite: Théobald Chartran (1849–1907), *Portrait of Helen Clay Frick* (2004.1.2), 1905. Oil on canvas, 71 ½ x 39 in. © the Collection of the Frick Art & Historical Center, Pittsburgh, Pennsylvania.

Helen wrote excitedly that this round-trip on the *Kaiser Wilhelm II,* to Cherbourg, France, was her ninth. Still, she fretted in anticipation of the ocean crossing, and her relief at having experienced an easy trip and avoided seasickness was palpable. She exclaimed:

Chartran
N.Y. 1905

Jean-Baptiste-Camille Corot (1796–1875), *Ville-d'Avray*. Acquired by Henry Clay Frick in 1898. Oil on canvas, 17 ¼ x 29 ¼ in. © the Frick Collection, New York.

"Of them all, it was the smoothest ocean crossing I have ever had. (I did not miss a meal)." Upon landing and with their chauffeur from home at the wheel, the Fricks began their long trek. Helen immediately reflected on the sudden change of pace: "It was a queer sensation to find ourselves hurrying through such beautiful country after days on the sea." But hurry they did, along the northern coast of France and then inland to view the Gothic cathedrals of Rouen and a stop to see Joseph Woodwell's colleague, the artist Ridgway Knight.

In Paris the family visited the western suburb of Ville-d'Avray, immortalized in Frick's acquisition by Jean-Baptiste-Camille Corot, deemed by Frick "the gem of my collection." The forest of Fontainebleau offered shelter when "they busted one tire," and then to their dismay they found the great château where, among other events, Napoleon had said good-bye to his soldiers was closed. But according to Helen, they gained entrance because "the guide was promised a good fee." To her delight, "we even saw more than is ordinarily shown," including Empress Josephine's apartments.

Once back in Paris, Helen visited the Luxembourg Gallery and the Louvre with her father. Since Frick was now collecting Old Masters, as well as Barbizon works by Corot and Jean-François Millet, Helen was intent on expanding her knowledge of them as well. Three paintings by Leonardo da Vinci, whose art her father would never own, were of interest: *Mona Lisa, Christ at the Holy Supper,* and *Virgin with the Scales.* She was also impressed with Millet's *Gleaners,* as well as Diego Velázquez's portrait of the red-haired Infanta Margarita, so similar in appearance to Helen's long-lost sister Martha. Not until 1911 would Frick acquire Velázquez's magnificent *Philip IV of Spain,* the single work by this artist in the Frick family collection.

Diego Velázquez (1599–1660), *Philip IV of Spain*. Acquired by Henry Clay Frick in 1911. Oil on canvas, 51 ⅛ x 39 ⅛ in. © the Frick Collection, New York.

Diego Velázquez (1599–1660), *Infanta Margarita*. Oil on canvas, 27 ½ x 23 ⅞ in. Musée du Louvre. Courtesy Art Resource. Photo credit: Alinari/Art Resource, New York.

Helen and Childs with a guide at Interlaken in 1905. Courtesy the Frick Collection/Frick Art Reference Library Archives.

The Fricks visited the Gothic cathedral at Chartres, and then, joined by Roland Knoedler, they drove through the Loire Valley, touring many grand and famous châteaux, including "the great Chenonceau," largely designed by women of the fifteenth-century French aristocracy. On touring Loches, another château, Helen entered its newly excavated, subterranean passages blocked during the French Revolution and exclaimed: "[The] deep dark caves are apt to make one's blood curdle when you think of the poor people imprisoned there." Similarly in Tours, the cathedral disturbed Helen because "so many unfortunate people were hung [*sic*] by [Tristan l'Hermite's] wicked hand." And then at Plessis-les-Tours, demolished during the Revolution and then under restoration, "We saw the room in which Louis XI died; and in my imagination, I could see that wicked king surrounded by the courtiers, and planning evil in his last hours."

The Frick party moved on to Orleans ("a little, ugly town"), Avalon, and Dijon, reaching La Sarraz, Switzerland, Melle's hometown, on August 7. Melle joined the group for the rest of their trip, and they began their perilous journey westward along Lake Geneva to Vevey and Glion on a road barely suited to an automobile. Finally the group reached the Palace Hotel in Montreux. Helen was overcome. "A height of 3,000 feet! No pen *could* describe the view from our balcony!" A few days later, they sailed down Lake Geneva and Helen noted that "the harmony of color between [the lake] and the mountains was so perfect that [from the] far end of the lake [the Geneva end], we could not distinguish what was what at the other end."

On August 16, the group headed for Interlaken where they planned to spend the night and then take a scenic drive en route to Bern and Zurich through the famous farming and cheese-making Emme Valley, homeland of Helen's paternal great-grandmother, Maria Stauffer Overholt. Helen wrote, "I have never passed more beautiful country than when we were in the gorges of the Sarine and of the Simme! There we had everything that nature produced in grandeur. . . . the typical Swiss chalets, clustered together at the foot of the giants, near the gorges, fascinated me so, that I asked Papa and Mamma if we could not have one like them on [Eagle Rock] our to-be-farm."

When they reached Interlaken, however, Adelaide became ill and incapacitated. "During the night Mamma had a very bad indigestion, and we were not able to leave [Interlaken] . . . as we had thought." Within two days, she recovered enough to take the train to Bern, accompanied by Helen and Melle, while the others drove the car through the Emme Valley. Although Helen felt this arrangement "was wise," she was not pleased. She "could see a good deal from the windows," but complained, "I was very much disappointed to miss the ride from Interlaken."

On August 21, they headed to the Falls of the Rhine at Schaffausen. "Ty," as Helen often called Childs, "took Melle and myself to a rock right under them (in a boat). It seemed very queer to be so near and the roaring, leaping water reminded me of a lot of tumbling ostrich feathers, being so light and airy." Crossing into Germany, Helen "passed little strips of the Black Forest," and went "spinning through fresh green fields, and little villages, built up with 'plastered-beamed' houses—the German fashion."

Once in "old and curious" Strasbourg with its many medieval buildings, Helen's eye turned to the Gothic cathedral with its famous rose window and its "perfect marvel" of a clock. Frick, Knoedler, and Melle departed for home, while the others, accompanied by one of Knoedler's assistants, continued east to Stuttgart and then Ulm, a largely fifteenth-century town, one of Europe's wealthiest cities, and the home of Albert Einstein. There on September 2, overlooking the Danube River, Helen celebrated her seventeenth birthday. "I was dreadfully spoiled by Mamma and Ty," she wrote. They gave her "beautiful presents" including a parasol and hatpins. Later, in Munich, Helen "ate a delicious dinner and a splendid birthday cake which Ty . . . had thoughtfully ordered for me." After a visit to the Pinakothek, she noted works by Peter Paul Rubens, not yet represented in their collection, and several by Sir Anthony Van Dyck. Frick, who eventually would own eight works by Van Dyck, bought his first, *Ottaviano Canevari,* that year.

Sir Anthony Van Dyck (1599–1641), *Ottaviano Canevari.* Acquired by Henry Clay Frick in 1905. Oil on canvas, 51 ¼ x 39 in. © the Frick Collection, New York.

Turning north they came to Nuremberg, "the most picturesque town I have ever seen," Helen wrote after viewing its moat and ancient fortifications. Albrecht Dürer's fifteenth-century timber-frame house also intrigued her, largely because of his significance in the pantheon of great artists.

Dresden, Frankfurt, and Wiesbaden followed, and then the party crossed the Rhine: "It reminded me somewhat of the Hudson," Helen noted. "It is probably a very ridiculous comparison," she admitted, only to quickly reclaim her thought, "but my observation, because it widens and narrows, in the same manner, and is surrounded by mountains." After admiring the many vineyards, the family drove south to Trier. Along the way, the chauffer noticed Queen Margareta in an auto, and as Helen described the moment, he "hurried us past her and we all looked at that good and lovely Queen of Italy." Luckily for Helen, who was an inveterate people-watcher, their hotel rooms were above the queen's, so, as Helen explained, "When we go on the balcony, we usually see her walking on her own."

As the family headed back to Paris, they drove through the Palatinate on the Rhine, homeland of her Overholt ancestors, and passed through Reims, where Joan of Arc took Charles VII to be crowned. The last leg of their journey was a dash from Reims to Paris. When Helen arrived in Paris and contemplated her extensive scenic tour—by Childs's calculation they had driven 5,800 kilometers—she wrote: "Really, it is hard for me to say whether I am glad our beautiful trip is over, or sorry. I really think it is the latter for there is nothing I love as much as sight-seeing."

Upon boarding the *Kaiser Wilhelm II* for New York in late September, Helen said goodbye to her brother, who had received an extraordinary college graduation gift: a trip with the Knoedlers to Spain and to northern Africa for a camel caravan from Algiers to Tunis through the Sahara Desert, and then an auto tour of Sicily, Monte Carlo, and France. As brother and sister parted, better friends than in early childhood, Helen said: "We felt awfully badly [*sic*] at leaving him as he doesn't expect to come home before Easter."

Added to her distress regarding the long separation was a "*very* rough passage." Relieved when the transatlantic ordeal was over, she was particularly delighted the morning of their landing, Tuesday, October 3, 1905, that her father came on board to welcome her home. "We were very glad to see him," Helen said. The reunion, however, came with sadness. Only days before, Elizabeth Frick had taken a turn for the worse. Frick had rushed to Wooster, but his mother did not recognize him and three hours later suffered a stroke. The following day she seemed much improved and free of pain, so Frick left for New York around four p.m. to greet Helen and Adelaide. But a few hours after his leaving Wooster, Elizabeth died.

Shortly after the loss of his mother, Frick made a startling decision, at least in Helen's eyes. Although the family remained legal residents of Pennsylvania and kept Clayton as the family seat, Frick wanted New York to be his permanent base. Through Roland Knoedler, he arranged to lease 640 Fifth Avenue, the former home of William Henry Vanderbilt. At one time considered the grandest private residence in New York, it was located at Fifty-first Street and Fifth Avenue, in the heart of a veritable Vanderbilt village of châteauesque-style houses.

For Frick, this was the house of his dreams, first glimpsed twenty-five years earlier, when construction had just been completed. "That is all I shall ever want," he had declared after scrutinizing the house from across the street and doing a quick calculation of interest rates and estimated cost of operation. Frick was an admirer of Vanderbilt, particularly as an art collector and railroad magnate. Among Frick's earliest acquisitions were engravings from Vanderbilt's collection, of works by George Henry Boughton, *Evangeline* and *Priscilla.*

This was not the house, however, that Helen wanted. It was not a Frick home; it was built and decorated in the Vanderbilt taste. Even though Frick spent more than $100,000 in alterations, enlarging the windows and replacing the garden facing Fifth Avenue with a high, brownstone privacy wall, and installed many of Clayton's paintings and all the furniture from the reception room, the house was nevertheless known and recognized as a Vanderbilt mansion. Resenting having to live there, and fearing that the social pretensions of the Vanderbilts might become attached to the Frick name, Helen

The Vanderbilt picture gallery at 640 Fifth Avenue. From Earl Shinn, *Mr. Vanderbilt's House and Collections*, 5 v. (Boston: G. Barrie, 1883–1884). Courtesy Special Collections of the Sheridan Libraries of The Johns Hopkins University.

later claimed that her father moved into the house chiefly because the gallery—forty-eight feet long and two stories high—"afforded such excellent hanging space."

Indeed, the reason Helen railed against 640 Fifth Avenue was her dread of being perceived as a title-seeking American heiress. She was well aware that the mansion had been used by William Henry to gain his foothold in old New York society and it, as well as the other Vanderbilt houses, bespoke that family's reputation for social climbing. From 1879 to 1914, more than $220 million had crossed the Atlantic through approximately five hundred marriages of wealthy American daughters to titled but impoverished Europeans or their sons—a staggering number by any calculation. In 1895, in an already legendary episode, Consuelo Vanderbilt was forced to marry the duke of Marlborough although she was in love with another man. An initial transfer of $2.5 million sealed her fate. Consuelo later divorced her titled husband with much accompanying international gossip and scandal.

John Singer Sargent (1856–1925), *Consuelo Vanderbilt, Duchess of Marlborough, and her Family*, 1905. Oil on canvas, 131 x 94 in. Duke of Marlborough Collection, Blenheim Palace. Courtesy Jeremy Whitaker.

Although such marriages were on the wane, many of these embittered and disillusioned heiresses were now stuck abroad or returning to the states. Helen Frick viewed this tradition with disdain and horror. Though darkened by lingering memories of family tragedy, Clayton was her home and, as she wrote, "no other place could compare with it in my opinion."

But in 1905, when Helen entered life in sophisticated New York, she lost more than Clayton's shelter and security. Her beloved home-schooling with Melle ended. Helen was enrolled in the fashionable Spence School, located just blocks from their rented residence. Although Melle remained her close friend and continued to travel abroad with the family, she was no longer Helen's primary teacher. Instructed by strangers and forced into a group of girls more socially adept than she, Helen felt, perhaps for the first time in her life, intimidated.

To the Clayton housekeeper, Miss Mary Duff, Helen wrote: "[Spence] is a most bothersome and horrible place. . . . I started there . . . not knowing a soul . . . and feeling as though I could chew everyone I saw. I did not know what to do! Every one was pushing and screaming in that tiny, *homely*, house." With equal contempt for the curriculum she continued, "I *hate* the program. Miss Spence put French on it and Latin; she told everybody that there would be no changing before two weeks time but I certainly shall complain as I am 'stuck' in with girls learning how to conjugate verbs in the former language! An awful come-down." She lagged behind in math, was forced to review algebra and was deemed not ready for geometry. Nor was she allowed to take German instead of Latin. "The villains," she complained, "are making me take Caesar—a most difficult task as nearly all the words are new. . . . Really," she railed, "this is a stupid school!"

Yet John McCarten, in a *New Yorker* profile written in 1939, described Helen as "a docile student with a tendency to swoon every now and then in an unobtrusive way. She would sink to the floor sometimes when, standing before the class, she faltered in recitation. She would collapse in a heap when her history teachers mentioned some particularly brutal detail of war or catastrophe." Helen had good reason to feel agitated and nervous. On July 20, 1905, a headline in the *New York Times* announced: "Enemy of Frick Freed." Her father's would-be assassin, Alexander Berkman, had received a commutation for good behavior. Although he had to serve another year in the Allegheny County Workhouse for carrying a concealed weapon, he would be a free man in 1906—yet was considered so dangerous that detectives would constantly shadow him.

Helen longed for Clayton. "I hope and expect to go home Friday to spend Saturday and Sunday there," she wrote to Mary Duff. "Two days are not very much but a lot of talking for more did not seem to do any good so I have stopped; but I hope to spend many days home this Winter or else my health will certainly 'break down.'" Her parents, however, decided to close Clayton and return only for Christmas. When she came down with chicken pox her first Christmas back at Clayton, the overjoyed Helen expressed delight that the illness "enabled me to stay home a little longer!" She also taught her dog "the cutest little trick": "I say: 'Fido, what would you rather do than live in New York' and Fido is supposed to die.... Then I mention a lot of other towns and as soon as I say 'Pittsburgh' he jumps up."

When back in New York, however, Helen worked hard at her studies and received high marks: honorable mentions in rhetoric and modern history, 96 percent in German, 92 percent in medieval history, and "excellent" for her architecture notebook. When she graduated in 1908 she did so with an A average.

Having moved beyond her initial impressions of the school, Helen found a kindred spirit in Miss Spence, whose background and intellectual interests were surprisingly congenial to her own. In fact, Miss Spence would guide and inspire Helen's later philanthropic goals and initiatives. She, too, was born to parents who had lost children, six of whom had perished in one week during a scarlet fever outbreak in Scotland. Clara Bebbe Spence was born in America in 1862 and grew up with an older brother, Robert, the only child to have survived the epidemic. Spence was also the female role model lacking in Helen Frick's life. Adelaide remained at the core a compliant, Victorian wife. Miss Spence, on the other hand, was a progressive schoolmistress who offered her students an upper-class version of the social consciousness then creating new opportunities for middle-class women. Miss Spence hired superlative teachers and offered a series of lectures by well-known figures. Edith Wharton gave talks there, as did Booker T. Washington, who was asked to join the students for a meal. Helen Keller spoke through her translator. George Washington Carver and Martha Berry addressed the students, as did poets, dramatists, and explorers. These experiences, along with visits to art museums, the opera, ballet, and the theater afforded Miss Spence's girls the tools, the power, and the "permission" to fulfill their chosen mission—just what Helen needed to satisfy her burning desire to do something important.

Miss Clara Bebbe Spence, 1908. Courtesy the Frick Collection/Frick Art Reference Library Archives.

While at Spence School, Helen also worked in the tenements and took courses in settlement and social work at the New York School of Philanthropy. Founded in 1898 by the Charity Organization Society, the school conducted classes in applied philanthropy, offered fieldwork in prisons, slums, almshouses, and immigration stations, and "fit men and women for social service either as professional or as volunteer workers." Its method of casework treatment called for "heroic imagination" and placed an emphasis on introducing the poor to beauty.

As an activist who promoted and advanced her theories on education in a period when women's education lagged behind that of men, Spence encouraged girls like Helen to press

Helen (front row, far left) with her Spence School classmates, possibly at her graduation in 1908. Courtesy the Frick Collection/Frick Art Reference Library Archives.

forward and to see how they could, as adults, contribute to this greater effort. Helen, retiring and socially conservative, would not, however, champion these causes in the militant, aggressive way suffragists such as her parents' friend and fellow art collector Louisine Havemeyer had. Marching with placards and taking part in hunger strikes were not for Helen, nor even for her schoolmate Electra Havemeyer, who was utterly embarrassed by her mother's conduct. For now, Helen was an enthusiastic acolyte in an era when women were powerless in the public sphere, and Spence enabled her to see for herself a place, in the distance, where she could "do" the "something" she wanted in the world.

With Miss Spence's ideas in mind, Helen soon took an independent course as a benefactress of women and children, a role that her father encouraged because it paralleled his own interests in Kingsley House. In the meantime, serving the poor and aspiring to leadership also gave Helen another kind of permission: to set limits, particularly with her father's New York social agenda. According to John McCarten, "Frick's ambition [was] to have [Helen] attend a fashionable finishing school in Manhattan and then make her debut in the most elegant manner, surrounded by Vanderbilts, Belmonts, and Astors." But in 1908, when she graduated from Spence and her father planned a debutante party at 640 Fifth Avenue in the former Vanderbilt picture gallery, Helen balked. She could not avoid being uprooted and forced to live in New York, but she could, and she would, refuse to be launched into a world and social milieu she neither respected nor desired. Harboring a natural distaste for the sophisticated party circuit and the life of idle privilege that usually followed marriage, Helen asserted herself.

One fall morning, after Frick left for his downtown office, Helen and Adelaide hopped a train to Pittsburgh. Together, mother and daughter organized a Clayton debut. The *New Yorker* profile noted the growing frequency of Helen's challenges to her father's authority: "Not infrequently the strong willed father and daughter clashed. There would be storms, then delicious reconciliation, and finally calm. Nobody could ever guess which one of them would come out on top." This time, and almost every time thereafter, Helen did. She sent her father an invitation to her reception at Clayton, planned for Wednesday afternoon, December 16, 1908, Adelaide's forty-ninth birthday, and to the dinner-dance with her friends and their escorts. Across the invitation Helen wrote: "Papa, mine, won't you come to my party?"

No match for his favorite child, Frick buckled. Since the Louis XV–style furniture from the reception room had been sent to 640 Fifth Avenue in 1905, he installed white-and-gold furniture in the Empire style then considered the height of fashion. Frick arrived the morning of the party, and Attie, living for the past seven years in the house Frick had built for her a few blocks from Clayton, penned in her diary, "It has been quite like old times to have Ada [Adelaide] & Helen at Clayton. . . . I think Ada enjoyed being with her old friends almost as much as Helen." The press reported: "As the Fricks have been in the East for the past two years, all the social contingent of [Pittsburgh], both men and women, were present to greet them and to welcome their daughter into society." Twenty-two members of the Pittsburgh orchestra played on the enclosed porch. A profusion of flowers grown in the Clayton greenhouse turned the downstairs into what one commentator called "a garden of delight." But as one report noted, "most interesting of all was the young girl herself." "[She] has a charm of manner, an earnestness, and a thoughtfulness far beyond her years; she is lovely in character. In feature she is most sweet and smiling. . . . fair with blue eyes and Titian wavy hair." Attie noted tenderly, "Helen as a young lady is certainly sweet and dainty."

Helen greeted her guests in the reception room, together with her friends: Katharine McCook from the Spence School; the Misses Whitney and Renée Gourd, also from New York; her childhood playmates Virginia Frew, Elizabeth Holmes, Mary Dilworth, Margaret Barr, and Mary Painter, as well as her cousins by marriage, Jeanette and Elsie McClintock. Helen wore a simple gown of white *point d'esprit* over white satin and trimmed with embroidered silver bands. And in her hand she carried the bouquet given to her by her father, a tiny cluster of pink rosebuds surrounded by lilies of the valley and held together by a bow of pink satin.

Frick also gave her a teardrop pearl-and-ruby necklace, and assured her that the promise he had made to her as a young girl, to grant her one wish when she became a debutante, would be honored. Helen soon made her wish known. Inspired by the pioneering efforts in land conservation of President Theodore Roosevelt, she wanted a wilderness park for the children of Pittsburgh.

The Fricks had entertained Roosevelt at Clayton on July 4, 1902, over an eight-course luncheon served by twelve waiters from the Waldorf-Astoria Hotel in New York, and accompanied by the U.S. Marine Corps Band playing marches from the lawn. A man who feared "the real and grave evils" of large business monopolies such as U.S. Steel, Roosevelt was a president to watch and befriend. Frick could only have worried over the fate of U.S. Steel when just two months before the Clayton luncheon, Roosevelt intervened in the United Mine Workers' strike to ensure that the miners received "a square deal." In 1904, still worried about U.S. Steel, Frick raised $50,000 for Roosevelt's reelection campaign. In 1907, however, Frick played a pivotal role in the purchase of $5 million of Tennessee Coal and Iron stock on the promise Roosevelt would not take antitrust action against the steel conglomerate. When Roosevelt's other progressive industrial reforms continued unabated, though, a frustrated Frick fumed, "We bought him, but he didn't stay bought."

Helen, unlike her father, was enchanted with Roosevelt. According to family lore, she argued endlessly with Frick in support of Roosevelt's social agenda and his environmental efforts. In this vein, she asked her father to donate the 150 acres of wooded ravine adjoining Clayton as a wilderness park for Pittsburgh's children. The city already had more than 900 acres of parkland, but these were all planned areas that over the years variously incorpo-

Helen (front row, far right) in the reception room at Clayton during her debutante party in 1908. Adelaide Frick is seated in the center. Courtesy the Frick Collection/Frick Art Reference Library Archives.

rated golf, tennis, ice skating, tennis, swimming, bike and equestrian trails, concert areas, and a zoo. Frick Park would be different. It was to remain an untouched forest.

Her request, while sincere, was tinged with sadness. These were the woods where father and daughter had once taken their intimate walks to Martha's grave. But after the Fricks rented the Vanderbilt house in New York and opened the summer home on Boston's North Shore, the walks ceased. These were moments Helen missed, so Frick Park was her way of preserving what was good about the past. Yet Helen was also ahead of her time in understanding the need to conserve wilderness space, particularly in an urban context. The *New York Times* declared: "The children of Pittsburg[h] who have not been so fortunate as Miss Helen Frick . . . will enjoy part of the young lady's wealth." Though the smallest of Pittsburgh's parks when established in 1908, today Frick Park, endowed by Frick with a $2 million trust fund, has expanded to become, at six hundred acres, the city's largest. Although it contains a few playgrounds and tennis courts, and the only public lawn-bowling green in Pennsylvania, as well as hiking trails and an environmental center, the land remains much as Helen Frick intended: a thriving habitat for over forty-five species of birds, as well as small animals and native wildflowers.

When 1909 dawned, twenty-year-old Helen, pleased to have the promise of Frick Park, readied herself for a winter of European travel. Helen, Adelaide, and Childs, who the previous fall had hunted elk and bear in Wyoming, and who now planned to cross New Brunswick, Canada, by canoe to hunt moose, boarded the White Star Line's steamer, the *Celtic,* for London. Later, Frick would join them in Paris, and then all would travel to Spain. Beyond the recreational aspect of the trip, the family mission was to study Spanish art, with the hope of purchasing some examples for the collection. Afterward they intended to enjoy the Riviera and thence return home via Paris and London. This journey, more than any other Helen had taken with her father, would represent a benchmark in her life—the opportunity to expand and solidify her knowledge of art, test her evolving eye, and cultivate her emerging taste. The seeds planted here would inspire multiple art initiatives throughout the course of her life.

For now, Helen was enjoying a time of peace in her family life, a moment when she and Childs could enjoy each other's company as well as their father's. Leaving Clayton for Europe so soon after her debutante party and the Clayton Christmas celebrations was, however, problematic for Helen. On January 16, 1909, the date she sailed, Helen confessed, "My feelings were of a queer mixture, for I both hated and loved to go;—hated because of leaving Papa, and loved, because of the trip in view."

Antonio Allegri Correggio (1489–1554), *The Mystic Marriage of St. Catherine of Alexandria to the Child Jesus, and Saint Sebastian*, patron saint of pins. Oil on canvas, 105 x 102 cm. Musée du Louvre. Courtesy Art Resource. Photo credit: Erich Lessing/Art Resource, New York.

Upon landing at Liverpool on January 25, Helen, Childs, and Adelaide took the train to London, and began sightseeing. Whitehall particularly fascinated Helen because she saw the "relics of the time of Nelson—the plan of Waterloo and the model of the battle of Trafalgar; Napoleon's horse's skeleton." The Record Office Museum, a place Helen called "one of the most interesting places I have *ever seen*," provided intimations of Helen's future contributions to the preservation of archival material. Among the items catching her attention was "a letter written to Geo. III, just before the Declaration of Independence of the American Colonies, and signed by J. Hancock, S. & J. Adams, Patrick Henry, Benj. Franklin & others."

Helen and Childs took in the Wallace Collection, amassed by that family over four generations and opened to the public in 1897, when Lady Wallace bequeathed it to the city of London. Helen understood that her father wanted the Frick family to pattern its collecting endeavor after the Wallace generational tradition, and studied the collection carefully: "It consists of fine old furniture, porcelains, armour, and some beautiful pictures." She proudly noted paintings by artists her father had recently acquired: Rembrandt, Frans Hals, Bartolomé Esteban Murillo, Meyndert Hobbema, Sir Joshua Reynolds, and Thomas Gainsborough.

On January 28, Helen and Childs visited the Tate Gallery. On seeing the exhibition of modern British artists, Helen was disenchanted. Presaging a lifelong distaste for contemporary painting, Helen dismissed the paintings as "Not very interesting." She wrote emphatically, "after the old masters they have no attraction for me."

On the last day in London, Helen's spirit revived when she and her mother toured the National Gallery, "this most entrancing of places!" Helen exulted. "I nearly went wild over so many pictures that I could have remained there forever. We visited first the English school"—works by Turner, George Romney, and more by Reynolds and Gainsborough. She studied the Romneys closely, as the Fricks had purchased their *Miss Mary Finch-Hatton* in 1898, *Miss Frances Mary Harford* in 1903, *Lady Hamilton as 'Nature'* in 1904, and *Henrietta, Countess of Warwick, and Her Children* in 1908. With these paintings, Frick fulfilled his passion for reuniting long-separated family portraits. In fact, these Romney women were also interconnected to Elizabeth, Countess of Warwick, subject of the Fricks' Jean-Marc Nattier portrait acquired in 1899. Reuniting portraits of married couples gave Frick particular delight; when he was in a "holiday mood," he speculated upon the fun the portrait subjects must at last be having in their reunion. In 1902, Frick had purchased Reynolds's portraits of Lord and Lady Beaumont, and in 1909 he reunited Sir Anthony Van Dyck's portrait of Margareta Snyders with that of her husband, Frans.

Bartolome Estaban Murillo (1618–1682), *Holy Family*, also called *The Virgin of Seville*. Oil on canvas, 127 x 192 cm. Musée du Louvre, Paris, France. Courtesy Art Resource. Photo credit: Erich Lessing, Art Resource, New York

Helen and her mother next visited the early Italians—Helen's absolute favorite—and then the Dutch galleries, followed by the Spanish, where Helen showed particular interest in the then fashionable Murillos and works by El Greco, whose *St. Jerome* was the pride of the Fricks' collection. So intent were they on studying these paintings, Helen said, "We stayed till the bell sounded, and even then were so slow to leave, that the guards had to hurry us away."

Then to Paris, where she visited works by Chartran and Jan van Chelminski and received a "cable from Papa about sailing. So happy!" Her next stop was the Louvre. Having visited it many times, this time she went with Childs and chose her favorites: *The Mystic Marriage of St. Catherine* by Correggio, *Infanta* by Velázquez, and another work by Murillo, *Holy Family.* They took in the medieval collection at the Cluny Museum, particularly the famed *Lady and the Unicorn* tapestries, together with furniture and porcelains, the latter being Adelaide's taste. Joseph Duveen in fact credited Adelaide as "the one who developed [Frick's] taste for collecting objets d'art. He hitherto had only put his mind to pictures."

Helen was interested in everything—paintings, tapestries, porcelains, bronzes, manuscripts, and the history behind them. On February 4, she wrote of the Musée des Archives: "It contains hundreds of letters from celebrated people, but none interested me as much as the following: Last letter written by Marie Antoinette . . . last letter written to her father by

El Greco (1541–1614), *Saint Jerome as a Cardinal*. Oil on canvas, 30.5 x 24 cm. Musée Bonnat, Bayonne, France. Courtesy Art Resource. Photo credit: Erich Lessing/Art Resource, New York.

Charlotte Corday, letters of Napoleon, Robespierre, of the many celebrated [F]rench writers. . . . those of many kings, queens, & others of the royal families." With the horrors of the French Revolution clearly on her mind, she and Childs visited St. Denis where, as she said, there were "many old royal tombs, but none more interesting than that of dear Marie Antoinette!"

Particularly fond of the pristine, gold-ground works of the Italian *trecento* and *quattrocento*, Helen, on a mission of self-education, made an extra trip to the Louvre just to study these thirteenth- and fourteenth-century pictures. The visit left her "fascinated by Cimabue, Giotto, etc." and resulted in the first of many Italian lessons. Although not works of interest to her father, the jewel-like paintings left an indelible mark on Helen.

Then on February 9, Helen, Adelaide, and Childs were privileged to visit one of the most important private collections in Paris, if not the world. It belonged to the Baroness Rothschild, widow of the famous art collector, Alphonse. Frick already owned two works from Rothschild family collections, *The River* by Jules Dupré and *Mrs. Charles Hatchett* by Thomas Gainsborough, and Alphonse had once owned the Fricks' *Cavalry Camp* by Philips Wouwerman. "Everything in the house is a gem," wrote Helen of the "marvelous collection of miniatures, tapestries, Chinese & Sèvres porcelains etc."

Frick arrived the next day and the reunited family set off for Spain. They pulled into Pau that night, at the foot of the Pyrenees in southwestern France. As interested in tapestries and porcelains as her mother, Helen noticed in the chapel of Henri IV "beautiful old Goblin & Flemish tapestries, Sèvres vases, wonderful old pieces of furniture, but most interesting of all, Jeanne d'Albret's bed, tapestry made by herself, the cradle of Henry IV (huge tortoise-shell)." A drive to Lourdes followed two days later. Helen visited the Grotte Massabielle, the cave where in 1858 Bernadette Soubirous experienced eighteen visions of the Virgin Mary, and in Bayonne, near the Spanish border, all but Adelaide, sick with a cold, visited the Musée Bonnat. Helen found the collection disappointing: "Here we saw some rather poor but interesting examples from old masters—nearly all are in poor condition." She noted, insightfully, "a small Greco just like ours [*St. Jerome*] in everything, but size and quality."

In Madrid, Helen and Childs visited the Academia de Bellas Artes where they saw many fine Goyas and "a few Velasquez," but her favorite, she noted, was *Virgin and Child* by Alonso Miguel de Tovar. That afternoon, she wrote, "We all went to the Prado! . . . Words are not strong enough to say how much I enjoyed this wonderful gallery! I nearly went crazy over so many of them that I couldn't say which ones I liked the best." Yet she chose a favorite: "Nothing could be more wonderful than *Las Meninas* by Velasquez, especially when you see it reflected in the looking-glass [mounted on the wall of the gallery facing the painting], for you actually see the room as though you were in it."

With Adelaide ill, Melle caring for her, and Frick off conducting business, Helen and Childs ventured out by themselves over the next days. On March 12, Childs's twenty-sixth birthday, they took a day trip west of Madrid to the somber but fascinating monastery-mortuary-palace of San Lorenzo de El Escorial. Built by Philip II in the sixteenth century, and considered unlike anything else in Europe, it contains the tombs of all the Spanish kings and queens from Charles V onward. Apart from the tombs, Helen was fascinated by "the wonderful library with marvelous illumined [*sic*] books, one of which is oldest on record (*Code of Laws*.)" In the basilica with its forty-five altars, she gazed at the life-size Carrara marble statue, *Christ Crucified*. "Of all the crucifixes I have seen," she wrote, "none, to my idea, can compare to the very beautiful marble one by Cellini." In the royal apartments, she noted, "My joy reached its climax when we came to those of Philip II left just as

El Greco (1541–1614), *Purification of the Temple*. Acquired by Henry Clay Frick in 1909. Oil on canvas, 16 ½ x 20 ⅝ in. © the Frick Collection, New York.

they were, chairs, inkstand and all!! Saw Charles V's spinet & closet in which Philip died, and from where he could see till the last, the high altar."

Back in Madrid, Helen accompanied her father to the studio of Señor Aureliano de Beruete. Helen often took her mother's place on such expeditions, and this time she was happier than ever to be her mother's surrogate. Father and daughter studied two El Grecos offered by Beruete, and Helen's diary notation for that day indicates that her father bought them both. Of these two, however, only *Purification of the Temple* is documented as a purchase and remains in the Fricks' collection.

Father and daughter returned to the Prado for further contemplation of Spanish art. Then on March 14 the family arrived in Seville. An ever-eager Helen grabbed Melle, who was due for a reprieve from attending Adelaide, and hurried to the massive, fifteenth-century Gothic cathedral. Both were "spellbound at its beauty & grandeur!" Ever interested in historic houses, Helen and Melle sought out Murillo's home and that of Figaro the Barber, "now nothing but a saloon." In Seville a "kind nun of Castellio" befriended her and admitted her to the fourteenth-century Alcázar, and then she dashed off to see the house where Velázquez was born. In Granada Helen described the Alhambra as "the wonderfully beautiful and fascinating palace of the Moorish kings."

On March 20, Frick and Helen visited the home of Hubert Mersmann to view his collection of tapestries. Helen wrote, "He has the most exquisite tapestries & furniture etc. of which Papa bought some of the finest." Frick's acquisitions, by Peter van den Hecke, depict scenes from the story of Don Quixote—*The Arrival of Dancers at the Wedding of Camacho* and *Sancho Panza's Departure for the Isle of Barataria.* They are the only two of the original eight to have surfaced since the French Revolution.

The tapestries were nominally a gift for Adelaide, who continued to suffer poor health. Her cold was, in fact, so bad that when Frick returned to Madrid, Helen and the others were forced to remain behind in Granada. But Helen wasted no time returning to the Alhambra, where she studied the restoration work then underway and rejoiced: "In about five years, the dear Alhambra will be all fixed over again, & other rooms will be opened to the public," she wrote in one diary entry, and in another, "How happy I am that the Alhambra is going to be repaired & arranged the way it used to be."

On March 28, Adelaide was strong enough to travel and within days the family started their two-month trip home via Barcelona, the Costa Brava, the Côte d'Azure, and thence through Paris and London. Helen despaired at "leaving my old friends" at the Prado, but Barcelona's fourteenth-century Gothic cathedral revived her—"solemn & beautiful, with exquisite stained windows, fine clustered columns." Then she and Melle toured Marseilles and continued on to Nice.

Adelaide, still suffering, spent Easter Sunday in bed and the next day, April 12, Helen and Frick left her with Melle and Childs and boarded the overnight train to Florence for a hurried three-day visit. Florence had become, and remained, Helen's favorite city. On their first day she was intent on examining "a little more carefully the interesting exteriors of both [the cathedral and baptistery] especially the bronze doors by Ghiberti & Pisano," replicated by William Henry Vanderbilt as entrance doors to 640 Fifth Avenue. Known for tearing through museums, yet nevertheless able to recall everything in detail, Frick raced through the Uffizi Gallery, to Helen's complaint, "I hated to rush through it the way we did. It was *too* wonderful to see those rare old master-pieces about which I had read and heard so much, that I felt I were in dream-land. There are so many, *many* of them."

Tapestries by Peter van den Hecke. © the Frick Collection, New York.
Above: *The Arrival of Dancers at the Wedding of Camacho*, 123 ¼ x 218 ⅝ in.
Below: *Sancho Panza's Departure for the Isle of Barataria*, 123 ⅞ x 232 ¾ in.

Nonetheless, they had only a few short days, and so they maintained an accelerated pace visiting the Loggia dei Lanzi, the medieval Palazzo Vecchio, and her favorite, Santa Maria Novella. Then to the Pitti Palace, home of the Medici family, where Helen described the gallery as "a rather heavenly gallery which gave me more pleasure than I can tell. I like it in some ways even better than the Uffizi & that is saying a very great deal." She was especially impressed by the high quality of the paintings and the intimate way the display showed how the Medici had lived with their collection, as opposed to the more sterile, strictly museum tone of the Uffizi.

Then came a dash to the Church of San Lorenzo, parish church of the Medici where their elaborate tombs are located, the Brancacci Chapel, and the Church of Santa Croce. Each stop, all of them repeat visits, reinforced Helen's love of early Italian Renaissance frescoes, contributed to her evolving connoisseurship, and marked the direction her own art collecting would take many years hence. In Santa Croce were some of Helen's favorites: Giotto di Bondone's *Life of Saint Francis* and Taddeo Gaddi's *Life of the Virgin*, particularly the *Presentation of the Virgin in the Temple*. Fra Angelico's devotional frescoes in the second-floor cells at San Marco were "gems in color," Helen remarked, "in expression, & in detail. They really should be examined with a microscope!" And then too in the Cloister and in the Chapter House she admired his immense frescoes of the crucifixion, *Saint Dominic Adoring the Crucifixion* and *Crucifixion with Saints*, masterpieces in perspective. One day Helen would purchase copies of these frescoes as teaching tools for the Henry Clay Frick Fine Arts Building at the University of Pittsburgh. But for now, when she visited the Cathedral Museum, she "admired for quite a while, the exquisite singing-lofts by Donatello [of the *Dancing Children*], but chiefly those of Luca della Robbia. . . . [of] the *Singing Children*." In about five years, Frick would copy the della Robbia as an organ screen for a third, as yet uncontemplated Frick family home, a townhouse in New York City.

The frenetic pace father and daughter set concluded with a drive to Settignano, the birthplace of Michelangelo. There they intended to call on the famous art historian Bernard Berenson, advisor to the Fricks' Boston collector-friend Isabella Stewart Gardner. Berenson would in fact become one of Helen's more important mentors when developing her art history libraries and art collections. But when Helen and her father arrived, the Berensons were out. Helen lamented their misfortune and complained again about being rushed back to Florence by her father, sorry not to have explored Settignano.

On their return to Nice the morning of April 15, father and daughter "found poor little Mamma still in bed," where she remained until April 19. In the meantime, Frick, who continued to come and go on business matters, left for Paris. Helen was eager to join him there, but had to wait until April 29 when Adelaide recovered sufficiently for them to board the night train. "Very sorry to go in a way," wrote a nostalgic Helen, "[but] very glad in many other ways." Her reward upon arrival in a rainy Paris the following morning elicited her happy remark: "Found Papa at station."

Helen was surprised, however, by her sudden disenchantment with the paintings in the Louvre. "What to me, was supremely beautiful here, has, to my surprise, greatly paled in my estimation, since we visited the Prado, & the galleries at Seville & Florence!" Yet, there was no slackening in her serious, analytical study of the artworks. "Was interested to see pictures by Velasquez, similar to ones in Prado, also old Florentine ones by same masters in Florence," she said, all the while insisting, "Still, my best favorites I shall always love dearly."

Hans Holbein the Younger (1497/98–1543), *Christina of Denmark [Duchess of Milan]*. Oil on oak, 179.1 x 82.6 cm. Presented by the National Art Collections Fund with the aid of an anonymous donation, 1909. Courtesy the National Gallery of Art, London.

For the next two weeks, Helen spent her time in fittings for a new wardrobe and daily treatments from a Parisian "nerve specialist," Dr. Gorodiche, whom Helen said "will do us all good." She scrutinized King Edward as he walked from their hotel elevator to his car: "He seems *so* nice," Helen commented. "I liked the way in which he tipped his hat to the people on the street." And she watched Childs take a "very thrilling" balloon ride at St. Cloud. These were sweet, unstructured days, as sister and brother visited St. Germain and Malmaison, the small estate near Paris purchased by Napoleon for his wife, Josephine. Both châteaux were closed, but Helen returned with Melle "excited to see so many things belonging to poor [Empress] J[osephine]—bed upon which she died, her hair etc." One of the happiest moments Helen enjoyed with her brother was the simplest, a tour "through the sweetest country & past wonderful old private places. . . . Woods most *fascinating*! Everything was so green. The shadows were so perfect & we picked the dearest wildflowers."

Their last stop was a two-night stay in London, a city Helen found "smoky as usual." On their single full day there, the entire family visited Princes Gate, the London residence of Frick's long-time friend and colleague, the seventy-two-year-old J. P. Morgan. An obsessive collector, Morgan acquired a wide range of works in bulk—entire collections formed by others—not selectively, by individual piece, as did Frick. Helen was "too entranced by everything, for he has not alone, wonderful pictures, but fine furniture, carvings; jeweled ornaments; 1000 superb miniatures of famous people, each framed by pearls & diamonds. . . . [and] Fine mural decorations by Fragonard."

Afterward, an energized Helen went to the National Gallery to reacquaint herself with what she liked to call "old friends," contemplate the evolution of her father's collection, and measure Morgan's treasures against those in the National Gallery. Helen noticed "the much discussed *Christina of Denmark [Duchess of Milan]*" by Hans Holbein, acquired by the museum through an anonymous donation, thought in part to have been made by Morgan and Frick. Christina, a young widow and possible bride for Henry VIII after his third wife, Jane Seymour, died in childbirth, refused to marry the bloodthirsty king, saying she did not have two necks—one for the king of England and one for herself. Over the next five years the Fricks acquired two paintings representative of Henry VIII's continued bloody rampage—Holbein's portrait of Sir Thomas More and his portrait of Thomas Cromwell, both beheaded by Henry VIII.

Christina influenced the evolution of the Frick collection, but the Morgan collection had a significant impact as well. In 1911, Frick bought Gainsborough's *The Hon. Frances Duncombe*, thought to have been in Morgan's residence at the time of Helen's visit. Then in 1915, two years after Morgan's death, Frick acquired the famous *Progress of Love* panels by Jean-Honoré Fragonard that Helen had referred to as "fine mural decorations." From Morgan's estate sale the Fricks' collection was greatly augmented by a large number of Italian bronzes and, among other items, Frick also acquired approximately forty impor-

tant sixteenth-century Limoges enamels, Vecchietta's bronze relief, *The Resurrection*, and over forty-six eighteenth-century Chinese porcelains. And finally in 1916 Frick bought seven decorative panels mounted on a screen, now attributed to Jacques de Lajoue. Helen's personal knowledge of, and admiration for, the quality of Morgan's collection would later influence her own acquisitions decisions for her father's collection.

On the day after the visit to Morgan's home, the Frick family sailed for home on the *Mauretania*. The ship landed in New York on May 21, after breaking the Atlantic crossing record by thirteen minutes. Helen attended her first Spence School class reunion and then left New York for Clayton—"*darling, darling* home." Old friends came to lunch and dinner, and Helen served as maid of honor at the wedding of her good friend Virginia Frew. "Great day!" Helen wrote. "Wedding came off beautifully & Ginny looked like an angel!" But she confided to her diary, "I was so scared." Walking down the aisle with the eyes of Pittsburgh's elite studying and assessing her as a potential spouse for their sons left Helen feeling exposed.

Indeed, Helen was distancing herself from the glitter and glamour of high society. When in Paris, Frick had offered her a perfectly matched string of pearls for her twenty-first birthday, just four months away. Helen, however, had another idea. Since her first summer on Boston's North Shore, she had been concerned about the plight of the underpaid, malnourished, overburdened girls working in the shoe factories of Lynn, Massachusetts, and in the textile mills of Boston, Lawrence, and Lowell. Instead of accepting the pearls, she asked for enough money to provide a place where some of these girls could

Above, left: Hans Holbein the Younger (1497/98–1543), *Sir Thomas More*. Acquired by Henry Clay Frick in 1912. Oil on oak panel, 29 ½ x 23 ¾ in. © the Frick Collection, New York.

Above, right: Hans Holbein the Younger (1497/98–1543), *Thomas Cromwell*. Acquired by Henry Clay Frick in 1915. Oil on oak panel, 30 ⅞ x 25 ⅜ in. © the Frick Collection, New York.

The stitching room in a Lynn, Massachusetts, shoe factory. Courtesy Lynn Museum and Historical Society.

rest and recover their health over the summer. Her father obliged and rented her the nearby Stillman Farm. On her return home from Paris, Helen began organizing her social welfare effort.

When she was only ten years old, Helen had written an essay called "Do All That You Can." It described "a little star [that] said, 'I can not do much to make this world bright, but as God has put me in the world I must do something, and I am going to do something good.'" The "something good" the star settled on was "help[ing] to guide the boats along the water at night.'" Now, years later, Helen wanted to help young girls who were adrift, lost in the dark confines of mill work and tenement living. Doing so revealed her affinity with the Progressive movement, as well as her ability to successfully manipulate her father and play on his conscience. The oppressed female workforce in the textile and shoe industries was, Helen knew, a direct, equivalent to the male workforce in her father's steel mills. Moreover, Frick family friends either owned the Massachusetts mills or owned stock in them, and thus were responsible for devastating the health and lives of their women employees.

Ayer Mills just after it was built in Lawrence, Massachusetts, 1909. Courtesy Collection of Immigrant City Archives and Museum, Lawrence, Massachusetts.

Frick heartily embraced his daughter's project, pleased with her choice of industry and workers to help. Though ruthless in his treatment of his male laborers, Frick never employed women in the coke fields as others did. And the textile industry was largely free of what Frick utterly detested, unions. Perhaps ironically, his own and his wife's family fortunes had been built on the backs of this laboring class, and more particularly, their ancestors' fortune had sprung from the textile and the shoe industries.

By 1909, Lowell, Lawrence, and Lynn, considered in the mid-1800s to be Utopian towns, were cesspits. Gone were the glorious views along the Merrimack as the Lowell and Lawrence mills expanded literally into one another, forming a solid mass along the river. Factory windows from Lawrence to Lowell were nailed shut and on average, 150 women were crammed into one room where they worked twelve and a half hours a day. Talking was not permitted; substandard meals were the norm; complainers and slackers were blacklisted. The fast-spinning leather belts that produced 2.5 million yards of cotton fabric per week ripped off skin and hair, and sometimes scalps. Exposed gears claimed limbs; breathing lint in the one-hundred-degree heat of the workroom with its 75 percent humidity guaranteed "brown lung" disease; and spittle on the floor spread tuberculosis. With families dependent upon a woman's supplemental wage, and mills paying an average of $8 a week, less than the average for all other industries, conditions conspired to guarantee women a life trapped in poverty.

Helen Frick, a true Republican like her father, did not look to the government, and certainly not to unions, to provide a solution. Rather, like many Americans of her day, Helen believed the business community and wealthy individuals could and should solve the problems of the poor. In the spring of 1909, she wrote letters to the South End Settlement House in Boston where the Fricks' former minister, George Hodges, was partly involved, and to various North Shore YMCAs and local churches, requesting "ten promising, needy,

The weaving room of a Lowell, Massachusetts, textile mill, ca. 1900. Courtesy American Textile History Museum.

Protestant girls [to] be selected for a free two-week stay at Stillman Farm in Beverly" that summer. In June, after purchasing books for the girls, Helen returned to Eagle Rock and welcomed the first group to her summer home.

"Promising" meant thrifty. One requirement for acceptance was that each girl come from a family that regularly put aside small amounts of money to cover expenses during months of unemployment. And she insisted on Protestant girls because their ministers

The True Blue girls in uniform. Courtesy Collection of Immigrant City Archives and Museum, Lawrence, Massachusetts.

Helen and her spaniel, Fido, at Eagle Rock, ca. 1912. Courtesy the Frick Collection/Frick Art Reference Library Archives.

often spoke the Frick language. These men had taken a leading role in teaching young women the gospel of self-improvement through hard work and individualism. They discouraged participation in strikes and walkouts and promoted the belief that labor agitators, not the mill owners, provoked labor problems.

Sixty-two girls came the first summer. Although Helen monitored every detail of management and organization, she hired a Mrs. Siefert, a family friend from Pittsburgh, to cook meals and run the home. At the house, flower gardens, a casualty of overcrowding in the mill towns, greeted the girls with a riot of color. Every room was spotless, filled with bouquets, decorated with patterned, cheerful wallpaper, windows open to catch the summer breeze, and a new New Testament inscribed with the girl's name and date of arrival on the bedside table. The half-starved girls were served lavish home-cooked meals consisting of such rarities in their diet as fresh milk from the Frick dairy herd, homegrown fruits and vegetables from the garden, and farm-raised lamb and poultry. Picnics were taken to Gloucester, and afternoons were spent swimming on the Eagle Rock beach, taking tea in the gardens, or watching a horse show or polo game at the Myopia Hunt Club. And while the girls recovered their strength, they played games, read, and gathered for evening prayers. Most welcome of all was uninterrupted sleep in beds with clean sheets.

There were rules of course: cosmetics could not be worn; hair could not be cut short; lying, gossiping, and smoking were forbidden; and male visitors were outlawed—indeed, if a man were seen on the street the girls were to lower their eyes. And the girls were required to dress in uniforms: blue bloomers with a white middy blouse. None minded. Many wrote in gratitude for their unimagined good luck. Hazel Sargent explained: "I was a very tired young girl and it was my very first vacation since I had gone to work at fourteen years of age." They adored their patron, who of course was not much older than they. Mabel Lawrence, from a Lowell mill, later said to Helen, "I'll never forget the time I first saw you. I was afraid for I thought you were above me but . . . [when] you spoke something snap [*sic*] inside my chest and I alway[s] loved you after that."

On Sunday afternoons, traditionally, Helen gathered her teenage girls in a circle on the sun porch and, with a notebook in her lap, delivered a talk based either on a stirring newspaper or magazine article, or on a passage from the Bible. Martha Cord, who worked in a Boston mill, later wrote her patron, "I recall being just spellbound as you talked. . . . in a state of very special uplift. . . . entirely speechless." But no one remained speechless for long. Helen engaged the girls in a lively discussion and later assembled them around the piano, where they sang hymns. Ida Arthur, another Lowell girl, was frankly amazed at how approachable Helen was: "You Miss Frick used to come and sit with us girls, so sweet just like a regular girl like ourselves, you always made us feel as if we were all yours." "You could do such different things with the money entrusted to you," penned a grateful Anna Morrison Ruiter, "but you chose to spend it where it was needed the most." Helen lavished an intensely personal nurturing on the girls. Poignantly, Melo Corrow Dickason recalled: "If we had little problems we could take them to you and always after our talk with you, feel that we really hadn't any problems."

Adelaide Frick in her wheelchair at Eagle Rock, ca. 1912. Courtesy the Frick Collection/Frick Art Reference Library Archives.

Even Henry Clay Frick displayed a personal interest in the girls. According to Ellen Boyd, who directed the home the following summer at its permanent location, "It was his custom to give us . . . all the apples from the farm, except the very first quality, which were reserved for the family. Sometimes there were forty barrels and once I sent away [to the girls' families] sixty-three barrels." According to Boyd, he called at the home "while we were at dinner and would ask about the progress of different individuals whose health was not quite normal." She wrote, "Mr. Frick did great things for his country but we will remember him for the many thoughtful things he did for us." So pleased was Frick with his daughter's experiment, when she asked him to expand her vacation home facility for the summer of 1910, Frick responded with the purchase of a thirty-seven-acre colonial farm in nearby Wenham, Massachusetts, as the permanent site. Named the Iron Rail for the old iron railing both fronting the property and enclosing the piazza, the vacation home was a tangible way Helen could join the young women of her day who were striving to assert themselves as social reformers, feminists, artists, and rebels.

The Iron Rail front facade. Courtesy the Frick Collection/Frick Art Reference Library Archives.

Friendship Cottage at the Iron Rail.
Private collection.

Helen began the program's second summer at the new location and immediately hired as director Ellen Boyd, the social worker with the Boston City Missionary Society, who had suggested candidates for the vacation home's previous year. Yet Helen remained very hands-on, managing the Iron Rail, making daily visits to the home, and continuing her Sunday talks, all without fanfare. Meanwhile, the girls developed such strong bonds they founded clubs in their respective towns so they could stay in contact. Helen paid the rent for these meeting places, and the girls dubbed their new quarters "True Blue Clubs," a reference to the durable, fade-resistant blue cloth manufactured in England, and assumed the motto, "For the Other Girl." The girls used their True Blue Clubs to raise money for underprivileged children, the Red Cross, old age homes, and various other charities. In addition, as a way to thank Helen Frick, every year on her birthday the girls gave a donation to Boston's Floating Hospital, a ship that cared for infants and children. The day soon became known as H.C.F. Day.

Toward the end of the Iron Rail's first full summer, twenty-two-year-old Helen began embroidering "Westmoreland" on a pillow for her father's December 1910 birthday. Westmoreland was the county of his birth and the source of his fortune; it was also the name of the all-steel private railroad car that would in the spring take Helen, Adelaide, and Childs on a one-month trip to California. Frick, touched by the pillow, wrote: "How sweet of you *Dear One* to give me such a lovely little pillow, and on it 'Westmoreland' worked with those dear little hands guided by that wonderful brain. You certainly was [*sic*] thinking of me as those letters were being formed and the evidence of your affection makes me very happy on this my 61st birthday."

At the same Helen was expanding a catalog of the family's collection she had compiled the previous Christmas as a gift to her father. It contained detailed provenances, including when and where each painting was exhibited and in what books each painting was referenced. Helen remembered how he "beamed for days because of the love & thought that had been put into this simple little gift. Later he told a friend that the fact of my having done this for him, made it worth his while having put all the money into his collection that he had spent on it!" Helen took further pride in her efforts in May 1910 when, while in Paris with her mother and admiring her father's recent acquisition, Rembrandt's *Polish Rider,* Frick exclaimed to Knoedler, "It gives me the keenest pleasure to see the interest Helen takes in art."

On her return home in April 1911, Helen opened the Iron Rail with more verve and conviction than ever, still more convinced of its need. On March 25, fire had broken out in the Triangle Shirtwaist factory, a ten-story sweatshop in Washington Park, New York, just twenty blocks from 640 Fifth Avenue. Hundreds of women, trapped behind locked doors, were incinerated alive when a pile of garments caught fire and flames consumed the building. Hundreds more jumped out of the eighth-floor windows to their deaths. The tragedy was so dreadful it prompted legislation to regulate conditions in the workplace, largely through the efforts of the Democratic Party.

Though Helen wanted to improve the lives of working girls, there were limits to her brand of conservative social reform. However real and profound her personal connection to her Iron Rail girls, she nevertheless remained an unwavering product of her time and social class. As a Republican and Henry Clay Frick's daughter, she would not, and could not, subscribe to the kind of deep economic-social reforms required to reverse the unhappy futures in store for these young women and the millions of others in their situation. Helen and her True Blue girls continued to embrace the 1830s ethic of the ministers who persuaded New England farm girls that protest was unladylike. One girl explained: "When we have trouble we go to our overseer like ladies and try to show the breeding that we have received, not like Turks, smashing and destroying everything in our way."

That fall, Childs tried to duplicate Helen's satisfying new life. In November 1911, he departed for a first-of-its-kind trip to Ethiopia and Kenya, financed by his father, to collect rare birds for the Smithsonian Institution. He already had enjoyed a five-month safari in British East Africa to hunt big game specimens for the Carnegie Institute Museum of Natural History and the American Museum of Natural History, where Henry Clay Frick was a trustee. Childs also had participated in an August 1910 shoot in British Columbia. Happily engaged in fostering the burgeoning study of natural history, he was not expected home for a year. With Adelaide still withdrawn and indecisive, and Childs gone, Helen once again became the only child at home, and the person most available to Frick. For all her hard, seasonal work with the Iron Rail project, her other job, the job that gave her little, if

The Westmoreland railway car.
Courtesy National Museum of American History, Smithsonian Institution,Washington, D.C.

any, rest, increasingly became that of a daughter attending to a father's needs. She already had assumed many of her mother's household duties, including ordering new leather covering for the chairs in the Clayton library and in the breakfast room, and hosting a dinner for poor children at Christmas. But the family then faced a new year swollen with symbolic memory: the twentieth anniversary of Alexander Berkman's assassination attempt, when Henry Clay Frick believed he saw Martha's apparition, and the death of infant Henry Clay Frick Jr.

Still grieving for his lost children even after all these years, Frick donated a second X-ray machine to Mercy Hospital in Pittsburgh and the aseptic facility to the Shadyside Hospital. On a note affirming his hope for a brighter future, Frick also decided to build a townhouse in New York, at Fifth Avenue and Seventieth Street, as the permanent resting place for his art collection, increasingly resembling a mosaic of his life. His choice of paintings was informed, always, by Martha's death and his experience of her apparition, as well as his need to surround himself with reminders of people, places, and events from his past. Riverscapes by Jan van de Cappelle, Aelbert Cuyp, Charles-François Daubigny, Jules Dupré, and Jacob van Ruisdael recall the rivers so familiar to Frick and so important to his commerce, while *Pasture in Normandy* by Constant Troyon, Rousseau's *Village of Becquigny,* and landscapes by Hobbema recall the bucolic landscapes of Frick's childhood in Westmoreland County. Rembrandt's *Polish Rider,* with its gray horse and dark hill in the background, seems reminiscent of Frick in his twenties, studying the large bluff outcropping of coal while astride his gray, high-stepping trotter. *Woman Sewing* by Millet and *Pietà with Donor* evoke Frick's relationship with and feelings for his mother. The Reynolds portraits of Elizabeth, Lady Taylor, and Selina, Lady Skipwith, and John Hoppner's portrait of Lucy Byng, who wear beautifully beribboned and plumed hats, gave Frick, who had a passion for ladies' hats, occasion to tease Helen about the large black ones she preferred. Pointing to Sir Thomas Lawrence's portrait of Julia, Lady Peel, Frick would say: "A hundred years from now, people will point out this picture and say 'This is Miss Frick.'" Helen had a ready reply. Referring to her father's El Greco's portrait of the stern, white-bearded, uncompromising Saint Jerome, with his finger firmly placed in the Bible, she quipped: "And they will point to Greco's picture of the Cardinal and say 'There's Mr. Frick.'"

Helen and her father being lowered from their ship into a tender, perhaps off Gibraltar. Courtesy the Frick Collection/Frick Art Reference Library Archives.

In this important anniversary year of 1912, perhaps to soothe her father's tortured psyche over Martha's death and apparition, Helen, as family members recall, was "hot to go to Egypt." She persuaded her father to take her there for the coming 1912 winter season, where the "evidence" he craved of a parallel universe could soothe and support his own feelings. Moreover, turn-of-the-century Egypt, under British control since 1882, also offered the most exciting of all winter activities for the wealthy.

Frick began planning a four-month overseas tour, with Egypt included. On learning of the forthcoming trip, the president of the board of trustees at the Museum of Fine Arts in Boston, Gardiner M. Lane, invited Frick to hear a talk by Egyptologist George Andrew Reisner, professor of Egyptology at Harvard, curator of the Egyptian department at the museum, and director of the Harvard University-Boston Museum of Fine Arts expedition at the Giza necropolis. Gardiner claimed that Reisner was building one of the world's finest collections of Old Kingdom treasures, "unrivaled outside of Cairo."

Frick's interest was piqued. Though unable to accompany Lane to the Reisner lecture, he accepted another of the director's invitations—to have Reisner "help you to see Egypt in a way which falls to the lot of very few travelers. . . . He can take you to all the new excavations and give you a unique chance to see the work of excavating antiquities. . . . The ruins of Egypt, the art, the present day people would all take on real life." Hopeful that treasures might be uncovered during his family's stay in Egypt, Frick gave Lane $12,500 of the $25,000 needed for Reisner's exploration fund. There were, however, conditions attached: the museum would have to raise an equal amount by January 1, 1912; and his donation must remain, as in all his philanthropy, anonymous. According to Gardiner Lane, the balance of the fund was "raised in five minutes."

With keen anticipation, on January 10, 1912, Frick and his party sailed on the *Adriatic.* Accompanying Frick and Reisner on the trip were Adelaide, Helen, Helen's friend from Baltimore, Frances Dixon, or Dixie, whom Childs was now courting, Mrs. Reisner and her daughter Mary, the art collector J. Horace Harding, who was also Frick's financial advisor, and Mrs. Harding.

When the ship docked at the Azores for a few hours on January 16, Helen and the others enjoyed a two-hour tour through gardens and narrow streets; Frick joined them the following day when the ship anchored in Madeira for a night. Unfortunately, while boarding the tender that would take them to the main part of the island, Adelaide, who had just celebrated her fifty-second birthday, slipped and broke her foot. "Papa and I rushed back & found Mama pale as a ghost," Helen recalled. Two gentlemen lifted Adelaide from the launch into a *carro* and together the party drove up a hill to their hotel, "a long & painful drive for us all for Mamma was suffering a great deal with her foot & from nervous excitement & we were so afraid she might faint, that the ride seemed never-ending."

Reisner, determined to continue the trip with his most significant underwriter, "promised [Adelaide] that I would have her carried in a carrying chair by my own men and that she would see everything that other persons would see." "So," he concluded, "the trip was carried out." The ordeal of transporting Adelaide began in the morning. As Helen recalled, "after a great deal of trouble," the group got her mother back in the tender and aboard the ship. Next the travelers docked at Gibraltar, and, after several stops along the northern Mediterranean coast—including Genoa where Helen saw Columbus's birthplace and the palace "still used by the Cattaneo family (where two portraits by Van Dyck, in our possession, came from)"—the Frick party crossed to Alexandria on January 28 and boarded the train for Cairo. On the three-and-a-half-hour trip through the Nile delta, Reisner explained the complicated irrigation system and described how the villages were built. Then they arrived in Cairo, "the mysterious town I have heard of so much," Helen sighed.

On her first morning there, Helen kept her mother company in the Savoy Hotel, but later lunched with the Hardings, Dixie, and her father at the former palace Napoleon Bonaparte had used as headquarters. It was now Shepheard's, a famous luxury hotel where many British tourists, as well the Fricks' shipmates from the *Adriatic,* were staying. Helen delighted in the number of "familiar faces." Indeed, Rudyard Kipling, amazed at the number of Americans in Egypt, commented: "You'd swear that Egypt becomes a province of the

Henry Bacon (1839–1912), *On the Way to Karnak*. Watercolor, 20 x 26 in. Commissioned in 1912. Author's collection.

U.S.A. in wintertime." Helen, feeling quite at home, later watched the first of many Egyptian sunsets, this one from a mosque in the Cairo Citadel, and experienced her "first glimpses of the pyramids, way off in the distance. How glorious it all was!"

Sightseeing brought out the very best in Helen. Young, exuberant, curious, and open to what was outside her experience, she was a carefree, happy, twenty-four-year-old. No longer the somber, responsible caretaker, she felt liberated when traveling. Her first evening in Cairo included the opera and the next day the group was off by carriage to view the pyramids and the Giza necropolis. Reisner took them on a moonlight tour of his recent excavations, including a little offering chamber in one of the *mastabas* where mourners could leave gifts for the dead. "Fine moonlight on desert and pyramids," wrote mood-sensitive Helen. "Nothing could have been more mysterious than the scene before us."

The following day, after she visited some Cairo mosques, Helen visited the studio of Henry Bacon, an artist friend of her father's, where she admired his "lovely watercolors of

Frances Dixon and Helen riding donkeys along the Nile. Courtesy the Frick Collection/Frick Art Reference Library Archives.

the desert & the Nile." Seven years later Frick bought from the E. R. Bacon estate a watercolor of Helen and Dixie riding donkeys along the Avenue of Sphinxes at Karnak.

On February 1, Reisner and the Frick party boarded the *Soudan II.* Early the following morning the steamer pulled anchor and as it "sailed along," Helen, awakened by "the lapping & rippling sound of the Nile," "watched the scenes along the bank—the passing camels & donkies [*sic*]—& on the water, the falukkas [transport boats with sails sloped toward the stern] gliding by us." Toward evening, as they passed the pyramids of Sneferu, Djoser, and the "white" pyramid of Amenemhet II, she exclaimed of the pale pinks, lavender, and gold colors, "I have never seen such coloring in my life & can't recall such a combination as the sun-set & moon 'rise' as we had this evening." The Nile, though busy with Thomas Cook and Son's tour boats and general river traffic, was calm by today's standard. So Helen could fully absorb the colors, serenity and emptiness of the landscape, and Reisner could whisk the Fricks through lines at the Nile monuments and take them to places not usually seen.

Henry Clay Frick on the *Soudan II* in a photograph taken by Helen. Courtesy the Frick Collection/Frick Art Reference Library Archives.

The Frick party landed at Beni Hassan on February 4 and began to explore the nearby rock-hewn temples, particularly those of the lion goddess Pakhet and of Amenemhet. Helen was again stunned by color, this time in the frescoes of Amenemhet's temple. Reliefs variously depicting hunting and agriculture, thousands of years old, were "in some places . . . still quite clear & the drawings really full of life & action." Saddened by the deteriorating columns, however, she explained regretfully, "Dr. Reisner says that in a hundred years or more nothing will be left of these old tombs, for they are hollowed out of the limestone rocks, and these are fast going."

The morning of February 8, the family reached Luxor, where Melle joined them. On a brief tour of the temple, Helen admired the colonnades and the statue of Rameses II but mused of his giant structures, "what a lot of conceit he must have had!" At Edfu the party saw a temple dedicated to the falcon-headed god Horus and "climbed 260 steps to [the] Pylon tower." Although Mr. Harding "had a tumble from his donkey on the way home," the group boarded the *Soudan II* safely, and as the sun set they reached Kom Ombo—"city of gold"—located at the mouth of what was once a gold mining region. More than any temple Helen had seen so far, the one in Kom Ombo dedicated to Horus and the crocodile-headed Sobek pleased her most. She studied the crocodile mummies and noted that "some reliefs are very clear & I just loved it—the setting & all!" though she lamented, "Much of it is destroyed."

The next stop was Aswan, ancient crossroads for African trade routes, and the site of the decade-old Aswan Dam, one hundred feet high, eighty-eight feet wide at the base, and one-and-a-half miles long. A delighted Helen rode a donkey to the granite quarries and studied some old and modern Arab cemeteries. She found the modern cemeteries "most curious" because "tombs have openings in the stones at each end, so that the 'spirits' can get out for an airing & lodge in the little gardens that are planted there for this purpose." She also visited the village of Bishareens where she saw a "half-clad, long-haired tribe of Bedouins," made some purchases in "the interesting bazaars," and attended a dance in the Cataract Hotel. Helen laughed, "Foreigners dance miserably, Dixie & I think." On the following day, the group traveled by train to Shellâl "to circle around the beautiful Philae Temple . . . once the 'Pearl of Egypt,' & still so, I think" on its small island. The temple was partially submerged by rising waters from the Aswan Dam. "It is already half under water," Helen despaired, "& soon there won't be anything left of it, as the inundation increases each year."

Helen and Marika Ogiz, possibly in the garden at the Winter Palace Hotel at Luxor. Courtesy the Frick Collection/Frick Art Reference Library Archives.

The Frick party began its trip back to Cairo on February 12. Helen said she was "so glad to get back" to Luxor, probably because Frick and Reisner had booked them into the luxurious Winter Palace Hotel. In the morning, the group, this time including Adelaide, split into three carriages and drove to the Valley of the Kings, the largest funeral complex in Egypt. "The poor horses," Helen complained, "found it very hard work to drag us over the sand & it was painful to see the efforts they had to make—also the flies were thick & the sand blew over us all the time." But once there she was enthralled. Tutankhamen's tomb was yet to be discovered, as was the one-hundred-room mausoleum for the sons of Rameses II. But Helen saw much that interested her: the rock-cut tombs of Set I, Rameses VI, and Amenhotep II. Of the artistry exhibited in the reliefs she said: "We were much impressed with sweetness of faces . . . & the delicacy of the features." But something even more compelling awaited her. Helen said: "Dixie & I had a great thrill in the tomb of Amenophis [*sic*]—for there was the old gentleman himself—in his coffin, where he was buried centuries ago, & all lit up by electricity."

Yet for Helen a highlight of the trip still lay ahead. On February 14, she and Dixie rode donkeys to the "wonderful" temple of Karnak, while the rest of the Frick party followed in carriages. The most important sanctuary in Egypt, the temple dedicated to the god Amen-Re required the services of thousands of people and was held so sacred only priests were permitted in the inner sanctum. Linking it to Luxor was the *dromo,* a dramatic, over one-and-a-half-mile-long entrance-causeway lined with lion-bodied and ram-headed stone sphinxes to protect the priests on their journeys to and from the temple. Mesmerized, Helen said, "I have never seen a more imposing approach than the Avenue of Sphinxes with the big gate beyond." And yet, for all its mystery and importance, Helen found Karnak "a little disappointing . . . because I had expected to find it in better preservation."

The Frick party left Luxor two days later and farther down the Nile, at Nag Hammadi, where the astonishing Biblical texts were later discovered, they called on J. P. Morgan in his

houseboat. He and his party were out, but Helen nevertheless "enjoyed seeing the beautifully planned boat." On a "splendid" mule ride to the temple of Osiris at Abydos, she applauded the "finest reliefs of all the temples."

Back in Cairo, Reisner took them to a newly opened *mastaba* tomb at Giza, uncovered just four days before. Over seven hundred *mastabas* had been excavated at Giza, with hundreds still buried. Indeed, this one, G. 2184, was discovered by chance. According to Reisner's assistant "no trace of [it] had shone" until February 13, when he was working on an adjacent tomb. In any event, the assistant recorded that he was having the "tomb care-

Above left: Excavation of the *mastaba* tomb sent by Henry Clay Frick to the Museum of Fine Arts, Boston, in 1912. Photograph © 2004 Museum of Fine Arts, Boston.

Above right: The *mastaba* chapel of Akhmeretnisut and his family, Giza tomb G 2184, with the statue of Akh-meret-Nesut, the offering slab, and the chapel frescoes. Photograph © 2004 Museum of Fine Arts, Boston.

Adelaide Frick at the Tomb of Kings, photographed by Helen. Courtesy the Frick Collection/Frick Art Reference Library Archives.

fully cleared and left with statue in place for Mr. Frick's inspection." Dating from the Old Kingdom, G. 2184 belonged to Akhmeretnisut and his parents, and even today is considered one of the finest small *mastabas* yet found. It contained a statue of the owner and was decorated with approximately fifty-nine frescoes of cattle and farming scenes, all painted without carved relief and with a dynamism atypical for this period. On exiting the *mastaba,* Frick announced: "This is the most interesting thing I have seen in Egypt." Then he delighted Reisner by asking: "How long it would take to finish our [Giza] concession and how much it would cost?" Reisner answered, "four years or so and about $100,000." "There will be no difficulty in finding that," Frick replied. He then authorized Reisner "to call on him for the expense of getting the new tomb to Boston to the extent of $3,000"—and the following December, although the purchase, packing, and shipping cost only $1,750, Frick gave the expedition an additional $12,500.

Excitement continued when, back at Reisner's house for tea, the Egyptologist opened his tomb-treasure storerooms. Helen was impressed with his collection, most of it destined for the Boston museum, and described the rooms as "filled to overflowing with priceless antiquities of all descriptions: ladies' toilet box containing fake hair & net, manicure set, & painting materials also with brass mirror on box. A plaited shirt—like ones we have seen in the reliefs—still well ironed! Quantities of bracelets, scarab & skulls, amulets & beads etc." Then father and daughter enjoyed the dinner party Reisner hosted in a large tent at the Harvard Camp, erected specially for the evening of Frick's visit.

Reisner later commissioned Mrs. C. M. Firth, wife of a British archaeologist working nearby, to execute watercolor drawings of the unique frescoes before the tomb was dismantled and shipped. His request was prescient, for a few months later, when the temple blocks with their painted scenes were en route to Boston the original frescoes, "wonderfully fresh & beautiful" according to Helen, were ruined by the water used to extinguish an onboard fire. As Reisner's assistant at the museum, Dows Dunham, reported, the "packing cases were soaked and sustained serious damage, especially to the many blocks which bore primarily painted scenes." The Firth drawings still survive, however, as do the tomb's statue and the carved exterior facade, together one of the great treasures on display in the Museum of Fine Arts in Boston.

As their Egyptian sojourn began to draw to a close, Helen sent home the items she had acquired—a Turkish lamp, a wooden face, an alabaster jar, three little figures, a small set of dishes from a tomb, and four sets of Turkish pipes. She traveled to Memphis, once capital of the Old Kingdom, and Saqqara, where the funerary monuments span Egyptian history from the earliest dynasties to the Christian era. Helen studied the two colossal statues of Rameses II, the largest one then slated for removal to the British Museum, and then continued with "a rough drive" past the Step Pyramid, the world's first, large-scale stone monument, and to the tomb of Ptah-hotep and of Ti with their "lovely rural & domestic scenes in relief." The group pressed forward to the Tomb of the Sacred Bulls, trekked through its long dark passages, and after lunch drove another fifteen miles from the extensive Saqqara burial grounds—with many pyramids and sacred animals still buried beneath their feet—to have tea on the famous Mena House terrace, at the foot of the Giza pyramid plateau. "How lovely & sandy it all was with the Giz[a] Pyramids looming up in the distance & becoming more and more distinct," wrote a nostalgic Helen. Along the way she and her party passed the funeral cortege of a sheik, a procession Helen found "melancholy & strange." On her last full day in Egypt, she toured the Cairo Museum with Reisner and bade "a sorrowful farewell to the dear Soudan."

The family sailed from Alexandria aboard the *Prince Heinrich* to Naples. Thrilled as she was to be back in her beloved Italy after an absence of three years, the last several weeks learning about Egyptian funerary practices and mummies left Helen unprepared, during a side trip to Pompeii, for the people preserved in their final, private moment of horror. In the museum there she saw "the reclining figures of men and women who were imbedded in the lava & who are now in glass cases, looking just as they did in life, but turned to stone. It was a pitiful sight, I thought."

Rome was a better experience. Visiting the city for the first time, Helen left Adelaide in Melle's competent hands while the group toured St. Peter's Cathedral. It might be "the largest in the world," Helen wrote, but "the church as a whole does not appeal to me. It is so gaudy . . . it lacks dignity." Rome itself, however, fascinated her, a repository of "all that had passed here—all the history of Europe is connected with these monuments & this is the scene of the tragedies of the world." For her, Rome was nearly overwhelming: "At every step there is some wonderfully beautiful & ancient building, tomb, or monument to admire, some historical incident or legend to recall & my head is simply spinning in ignorance." She declared: "1100 rooms. . . . what a treasure-house is the Vatican!"

March found Helen once again in Florence, revisiting her Florentine favorites. Then on the twenty-eighth, Helen and Dixie traveled to Paris where they joined Frick, again leaving Adelaide and Melle behind. Helen noted in her diary that she had some long talks with her father, and although she did not disclose the nature of their discussion, something put her in a ponderous mood. Helen felt pulled to the Luxembourg Gallery where she concentrated on works by artists represented in or reminiscent of their own collection: Emile Friant, whose *Chagrin d'Enfant* hung in Clayton's front hall; Adolphe-William Bouguereau, whose *L'Espieglèrie,* the Martha look-alike, hung in Helen's Clayton bedroom; and Bouguereau's *Madonna Consolatrix,* similar in composition to *Consolatrix Afflictorum,* Dagnan-Bouveret's portrait of mourning that dominated the Clayton dining room.

After visiting Venice and Milan, she was off to Bellagio, on the shores of Lake Como, where no garden or villa went unexplored and to Lausanne, Switzerland. There, on April 16, Helen "read in the papers of the frightful wreck of the *Titanic*" the previous morning. Of the 1,500 men, women, and children who drowned in the icy waters of the north Atlantic when the ship hit an iceberg and sank to the bottom, Helen exclaimed, "too, too, horrible!" Her reaction was more than a mere sympathetic reflex. The Fricks were meant to sail on the *Titanic,* and family speculation was that they had canceled because of Adelaide's foot. Many years later, Helen Frick told Alice Thompson, the niece of her childhood friend, Mary Painter, that she, not her mother's foot, was the reason the Frick family narrowly escaped being numbered among the dead. According to Thompson, Frick had reserved three connecting suites—B 52, 54, 56—with a promenade, and was greatly looking forward to the historic voyage. But Helen dreamed that the *Titanic* was going down—perhaps the reason for the serious talks in Paris—and "begged and begged her father not to go." According to Thompson, Helen said she "did everything but throw a temper tantrum, and her father finally gave in and canceled the reservations." The suite was reassigned to J. P. Morgan, who canceled because of business in Chartres. It was then given to the Horace Hardings, who also canceled. They took an earlier crossing to New York on the *Mauretania.* In the end, the White Star Line's managing director, J. Bruce Ismay, took the suite and perished when the ill-fated ship sank.

Helen's brush with death shook her deeply, as did the tragic drownings of many friends, such as George Widener. When Helen, Dixie, and Melle headed to Paris on April 19, leaving a dazed Adelaide and Attie behind to recover their strength in Switzerland, Helen wrote: "Left Mamma—it was awfully, awfully hard—all day we thought of the horrible sea disaster." Suffering from headaches and stomach pains, Helen spent the next week in bed. Perhaps because of the *Titanic* tragedy, when Adelaide and Attie arrived in Paris, they sailed home on the *Lusitania*, whereas Helen, Dixie, and Frick took the *Amerika* from London.

When Helen arrived safely in New York in early May, she was even more watchful and protective of her father. Once, fearing he might catch cold, she threw an overcoat to him through the car window. But Frick defied her and flung it back. Running after the car, Helen tried two more times, but Frick, like a naughty child, each time tossed it out of the window while blowing her a kiss. Frick was, however, more devoted than ever to his daughter, and as Adelaide continued to complain of her ailments, Helen stood in as never before as her father's companion.

HARPER'S WEEKLY
A JOURNAL OF CIVILIZATION
New York, February 10, 1912
MARTIAL LAW IN NEW ENGLAND

The 1912 "Bread and Roses" strike in Lawrence, Massachusetts, drew the attention of Congress to the plight of women textile workers. Courtesy Collection of Immigrant Archives and Museum, Lawrence, Massachusetts.

Returning to Eagle Rock for the summer, Helen found a changed environment, at least as far as her True Blue girls were concerned. On January 12, 1912, a few days after Helen sailed for Egypt, the most militant and massive strike in American history erupted in the Lawrence textile mills. Eighty-five thousand people in the city depended on these mills for survival. At least half the children in Lawrence worked in them, and among the adult mill workers, more than half were women. So when the mill owners cut their pay in reaction to a new law reducing working hours for women and children from fifty-six to fifty-four hours a week, the mill hands struck. They attacked the mills, slashed belts, and smashed machinery.

In response to the violence, the governor ordered in the National Guard. Two hundred mounted militia, including volunteer Harvard University students whose parents either owned the mills or held stock in them, arrived in Lawrence. With a palpable fear of socialism on the rise in America, the strikers were labeled anarchists or communists. When rioters smashed windows, threw rocks, and further tried to destroy mill equipment, mill owners retaliated by cutting off the town's food supply. Parents watched their children begin to starve.

On February 10, Margaret Sanger, a nurse and friend of the IWW union leader Bill Haywood, was enlisted to evacuate over one hundred young Lawrence residents to the homes of socialist and anarchist sympathizers in New York City, Philadelphia, and Barre, Vermont, thus easing their parents' minds. But when the second group of children was assembled, violence erupted. Women, some of them pregnant, were clubbed and trampled, and police seized the children. Driven wild by these attacks and by their own hunger, the women of Lawrence became the driving force behind the strike. They hid scissors in their dresses, slashed the clothes of policemen, stripped them of underwear, and threw the policemen into the freezing cold, polluted waters of the Merrimack River. They mugged scabs with red pepper, boiling water, gas pipes, and bowling pins.

By early March, while the Fricks were enjoying Italy and Paris, the situation had become so grave President Taft ordered a congressional hearing. So grim were the revelations that within two weeks, the mill owners, hoping to avoid further damaging publicity, capitulated and gave the demanded wage. Lawrence now symbolized the triumph of labor over capitalism, and although Helen Frick's True Blue girls probably had not participated in the strike, they were surely empowered by it.

Eagle Rock front hall. Author's collection.

In her quiet way, Helen's efforts on behalf of the mill girls had changed her, too. No longer an unhappy teenager castigating herself for bad behavior, she had learned to stand up to Frick and, within certain boundaries, often had her way with him, even in politics. According to a Frick family member, she "fought like Hell about Roosevelt," and backed the Bull Moose party platform, calling for the abolition of child labor, minimum industrial standards, equal suffrage for women, and care for the aged. Frick, on the other hand, preferred his summer golf companion, the incumbent Howard Taft, who often slipped past Secret Service guards to play poker with him at Eagle Rock. Frick raised $50,000 for Taft's run against Roosevelt and the Democratic candidate, Woodrow Wilson, but as the summer of 1912 wore on, Frick saw that with the Republican party split between Roosevelt and Taft, neither candidate could beat Wilson. Moreover, he had become disenchanted with the Taft administration's trust-busting record. It had "utterly failed to treat many of its warmest friends fairly." By August, political arguments between father and daughter cooled.

As Helen's twenty-fifth birthday approached, Frick planned the first elaborate lawn party at Eagle Rock. They would erect a large dance floor on the front lawn so all the guests, including local merchants and townspeople as well as North Shore society, could enjoy the day and evening together. But the invitation caused a furor: "Society Objects to Trades People," ran the headlines in the *Pittsburgh Post,* when the Fricks' society friends balked at what the paper referred to as a party "so ultra-democratic as to be plebian." Thus many of the hundreds of invited guests did not bother to reply. So fierce was the community reaction, the *Post* said, that Frick, "known as one who rarely takes the middle course, broke his rule yesterday. . . . [and] compromised." He first decided to cancel the party. But then, probably at Helen's urging, he made alternative arrangements. Apparently eager to make a success of the first large party he had given at Eagle Rock, not to mention the first he had given in honor of his astonishing daughter, he bowed to the demand for exclusivity and divided the guest list. The afternoon was designated for the three hundred local tradesmen while the evening was reserved for a five-hundred-guest society dinner dance. At three o'clock the famous composer and bandmaster John Philip Sousa and his musicians, brought up specially from New York on twenty-four hours' notice, began playing. With only a few of the more progressive North Shore residents attending the afternoon party, the first group had the run of Eagle Rock—the grounds, house, stable, beach, gardens, and greenhouses. Five cars and four motorboats were also placed at the guests' disposal. Since Adelaide, whose foot was still troubling her, was unable to stand for long periods, Helen took her mother's place as hostess.

At seven o'clock, after Helen changed her dress for the evening, a sixteen-piece orchestra replaced Sousa's band. To deter the uninvited, Frick hired fifty guards and stationed motorboat patrols. One newspaper noted that the police "had their hands full in straightening out the tangle" from the crush of automobiles, but once arrived, the guests first enjoyed a recital by the Fricks' $15,000-a-year salaried organist, Archer Gibson, followed by dinner on the Eagle Rock lawn, overlooking the Atlantic Ocean. The scene was described as "a veritable fairyland," with hundreds of Japanese lanterns of various sizes and shapes strung together with strands of other colorful lights. After dinner, dancing followed in the Eagle Rock music room, dining room, and hall.

Both the afternoon and evening events were huge successes, marred only by press reports rehashing the uncomfortable social facts that had resulted in the split celebration. The *Pittsburgh Gazette Times* claimed that the Fricks had been insulted by gossip that "a gathering of society notables occupying the same station—if not in wealth, at least the same relative status socially—as [Helen and her father]" balked at mingling with the townspeople. The *New York Times* called the party "an event which caused more talk than anything ever attempted on the shore." When asked to comment on the social controversy their party had caused the Fricks' response was simply: "We have nothing to say."

Helen Frick at twenty-five was a well-educated, intelligent young woman who had seen and studied more of Europe's culture—and Egypt's—than most women her age. Her all-important relationship with her father had evolved into a new phase. An oil portrait by the North Shore artist Edmund Tarbell, commissioned for Helen's twenty-first birthday in 1909, and now in the National Portrait Gallery, reveals the nature of this adult father-daughter enmeshment. The two are seated side by side, in an open-air carriage. Frick, dressed in black tie, dominates the foreground and presses Helen, in a plumed hat and white lace dress, to the background. Photographs from 1910 are equally explicit. They show Helen seated beside her father, one arm around his shoulders, the other pressed high on his inner thigh, while Frick's hand rests firmly on her knee.

Helen was proud of her father's affection. In her diary she confessed that her father often said, "Helen's my girl." And sometimes, "after perhaps giving me a little reproof he would say 'never mind—I'm so in love with her—her happiness is what I am after.'. . . Indeed Papsie would have done anything to make me happy, & he gave proof of this every day, in the dearest & most thoughtful & unusual manner. From the time I was a very little girl, I felt there was nothing he couldn't do—& I felt such strength and tender protection emanating from him—he was a stronghold to me. . . . Papsie would sometimes say to me 'Look in my eyes, my blushing fair and see thine image reflected there.'"

Edmund C. Tarbell (1862–1938), *Henry Clay Frick and Daughter Helen*, ca. 1910. This portrait was commissioned on or about Helen's twenty-first birthday. Oil on canvas, 31 x 23 ¼ in. Courtesy the National Portrait Gallery, Smithsonian Institution, Washington, D.C.

Father

It didn't matter who my father was; it matters who I remember he was.
—Anne Sexton

On May 3, 1913, Childs and Dixie officially announced their engagement, and three weeks later Helen and her parents celebrated at Clayton. The happy group then departed for a summer at Eagle Rock with Dixie's seven younger siblings. When Helen opened the Iron Rail for its third season, Dixie was there to help her. The project was thriving, and the *New York Times* praised Helen's attempt to "carry out some of her ideas in sociology." In 1912, a record eighty-two girls had joined the True Blue Clubs, and in 1913 the clubs opened their first savings account with a $50 deposit.

As summer turned to fall, Helen began to prepare for Dixie and Childs's nuptials, where she would serve as maid of honor. As the date approached—Tuesday, October 14, Dixie's twenty-first birthday—Baltimore society was understandably astir. The bride's late father, Isaac Dixon, had been a man of modest wealth but locally prominent as a founder of the Calvert School in 1897, still famous today for its home-school program. His wife, Elizabeth White, as sister to the owners of the Marlborough Blenheim Hotel, was an equally notable member of Baltimore society. But the Dixon name paled in comparison to the Fricks' notoriety.

The Saturday night before the wedding, Dixie's brother Billy and their cousin D. Stewart Ridgley hosted a coon hunt, a continuing Maryland tradition, at Hampton, just north of Baltimore. Fifty men and girls met at 8 p.m., hunted the nocturnal "masked bandits" until 2 a.m. and then enjoyed breakfast around a bonfire, accompanied by Childs's stories about his African exploits. He had just given the Smithsonian Institution more than five hundred birds felled during his recent Ethiopian expedition; and he sent more than forty species of big-game mammals to the Carnegie Museum of Natural History in Pittsburgh and to the American Museum of Natural History in New York. Many of his trophies were the first ever mounted by a museum. Dixie missed the evening's excitement, however. Suffering from a "slight indisposition," she remained at her parents' Baltimore townhouse at 823 Park Avenue and rested.

Frances Dixon, "Dixie," ca. 1913. Author's collection.

Opposite: Helen and Henry Clay Frick with two-year-old Frances Frick, 1918. Author's collection.

By noon of the wedding day, crowds lined the sidewalks near the church, hoping to get a glimpse of the Frick family and their eight hundred guests. While a crowd of several hundred pressed against the canopy in front of the church, New York detectives hired by the Fricks held them at bay, admitting only card-holding guests. When all were seated and the bridal party had gathered at the altar, maid of honor Helen Frick entered last. She wore the same style of dress as the bridesmaids, but in a different color and material, and the same black Gainsborough hat, but with a pink plume. This was at least the third time she had held this honor—she had been maid of honor to Virginia Frew and Mary McNeal, also from Pittsburgh, as well as bridesmaid to other childhood and school friends. Although pretty and feminine and comfortable in the company of Childs's bachelor friends, particularly within the setting of Eagle Rock house parties, Helen continued to loathe the superfluities of society, not to mention the formal rituals of the mating game so important to many of her contemporaries. Now Dixie, her closest friend, had succumbed. With all eyes on Helen as she completed her solitary march down the aisle, some guests must have speculated about her marital prospects, or whether there was any truth to rumors that she was a lesbian, a label often attached to unmarried women. Having just celebrated her twenty-fifth birthday, she was a ready target for such speculation, though the rumors were untrue.

Frances Dixon Frick on her wedding day, October 14, 1913. Author's collection.

As Helen finished her procession, the guests' attention turned to Dixie, walking down the aisle on the arm of her older brother Billy to the wedding march from Richard Wagner's *Lohengrin*. Small and slender, described in press reports as a "demure," "dark beauty," she carried a bouquet of white orchids.

A wedding feast followed at the Dixon house where gifts worth more than $1 million were on display. One particularly evoked the union of the two families: a *repoussé* silver pitcher, hand-embossed with the Dixon home on the Eastern Shore, Bloomfield, on one side, and Eagle Rock on the other. The young couple was not only lavished with gifts, but also money. Frick was said to have given $12 million to his son before the ceremony and a multimillion-dollar marriage settlement was rumored for Dixie. According to a *New York Times* article that ran two days after the wedding: "The many guests . . . were not taken by surprise when . . . Henry Clay Frick handed the bride a plain envelope." The *Times* claimed the envelope given Dixie contained a check for $2 million. Henry Clay Frick, furious about the false press report, gave a rare interview denying having made such a gift to his daughter-in-law, or one so vast to his son. Nonetheless, Frick gave the young bride a $32,800 pearl necklace from Tiffany & Co., an $8,000 string of pearls from Cartier & Co., as well as a Packard Brougham motorcar for Christmas that year. To Childs, perceived to be, in all likelihood, the future head of the Frick family, came only a transfer of approximately $180,000 of Frick's interest in the Susquehanna Power Company, with instructions that Childs was to visit the plant and study its reorganization to "decide what had better be done."

Childs and Dixie departed for a rugged Arizona honeymoon, and Helen prepared to move to the new residence in New York. She was far from pleased. Its slow steady rise from a basement and subbasement cavity in 1912, to its current state as a three-story building, diminished any hope she may have harbored of keeping beloved Clayton as her base. In December 1913, when Frick celebrated his sixty-fourth birthday, Helen gave him a stack of pages, one leaf dated for each day of the coming year, known as a friendship calendar. Helen previously had distributed some of the pages to family and friends, asking them to write a little saying or a wish on each leaf. On one page she pasted a photograph of Clayton's southern facade and wrote firmly beneath it: "East or West Home is Best." And tactfully, she removed the page dated August 5, the twenty-ninth anniversary of Martha's birth.

Yet Helen had little control over her personal life. Her future, particularly her romantic life, seemed bleak, ever dominated by her father. Indeed, the floor plan for the future New York residence showed how trapped she was. Helen's bedroom would be adjacent to Frick's bedroom and bath, between his and Adelaide's rooms. Down the hall and across from her father's private sitting room was a library-sitting room where Helen could continue the study she was making of the family collection and where she could update the catalogues she had made for her father in 1909 and in 1910. Elsie de Wolfe, at forty-eight America's first professional female interior decorator, would furnish the family's private quarters, including Helen's second-floor bedroom and library. According to family members, Helen did not like de Wolfe. She thought the former actress flamboyant and pushy; but Frick hired the decorator for the seven second-floor bedrooms, the four on the third floor, and the housekeeper's room. Eventually, de Wolfe was also given the ladies' powder room off the Seventieth Street entrance. In fact, Frick had such confidence in her ability he told her, "I shall not limit you as to the amount you may spend." He did of course stipulate: "I know you will not over-do it, and it will be in the best of taste."

Helen wanted her bedroom walls decorated with *trompe l'oeil* landscapes evocative of the outdoors, like the ones back in her Clayton bedroom. De Wolfe, although a proponent of *trompe l'oeil,* felt it inappropriate for a bedroom in a house as formal as the Fricks'. So even the decoration of Helen's own bedroom was not under her control. De Wolfe purchased all the interior furnishings, and Frick was often pleased with her choices, including the Louis XIV furniture, the two Ming vases made into lamps for Helen's library, two more for her bedroom, and an old stool for her dressing table covered in Beauvais tapestry.

Soon Helen's quarters began to take shape. The bedroom was lined with rose silk, trimmed by a wide gimp border in green, rose, and blue; the overcurtains and valances were of green-and-rose-shot taffeta silk. A Louis XVI marble mantel was installed in the room, now appointed with tables, chairs, and a commode of the same period, including a piece

Helen's bedroom at One East Seventieth Street after a second renovation. Author's collection.

signed "L. Peridies." Her library fabric was a green-figured moiré silk with matching fringe and a chandelier and a pair of gilt and wrought-iron torchères featured matching green silk lampshades trimmed with ribbon. Here Helen installed a small bust by her favorite sculptor, Jean-Antoine Houdon, of his daughter, Claudine, personally carried by de Wolfe from abroad. De Wolfe also provided Helen with a writing table, a desk chair signed "E. Laporte" of the same period, a Louis XVI bergère signed "Jacob," and a tulipwood inkstand, circa 1850, with Sèvres inlay plaques.

With the arrival of summer, the Fricks suddenly had to vacate 640 Fifth Avenue, their home of the last nine years. Back in March, George Vanderbilt had suffered an attack of appendicitis and died. Cornelius and Grace Vanderbilt inherited the house and now wanted immediate possession. Thus, during the turmoil of finishing One East Seventieth Street and settling the endless stream of arguments between Sir Charles Allom, decorator for the first floor, and de Wolfe—not to mention the crushing number of details regarding two new construction projects in Pittsburgh, the $6 million, twenty-story Italian Renaissance–style William Penn Hotel, and an adjacent ten-story French- and Flemish-Gothic inspired indoor shopping mall, the Union Arcade—the Fricks decided to move in June 1914 to Eagle Rock, itself undergoing a $35,000 renovation.

The summer was filled with difficulties. In July Helen's beloved Aunt Attie died of pancreatic cancer on the twenty-second anniversary of Alexander Berkman's attack and in the same week that Martha had died twenty-three years before. As the stress mounted, Frick suffered a near-fatal bout with inflammatory rheumatism. Bedridden, unable to move without assistance, and in great pain, he was more uncomfortable than he had ever been. While still recuperating, he received news of the assassination of the Archduke Francis Ferdinand, heir to the throne of Austria and Hungary, the event that triggered the onset of the Great War. The stock market suffered a drop so severe President Woodrow Wilson suspended trading and later restricted it. Sixty-five-year-old Frick, however, took a fatalistic attitude about the war. He said to S. L. Schoonmaker, his former Carnegie Steel agent and Long Island friend, "Well it is too bad we are to have a war, but it seems it had to come sometime, and it's just as well it should be over."

Frick may have been unconcerned, but Helen took action and founded a Goodwill Section of the Red Cross to help war refugees in Europe. She also busied herself with another season at the Iron Rail. By now, many of her first-year girls had married and were raising children. With the pressures of child rearing, the True Blue mothers adopted a new slogan: "When you get to the end of your rope, tie a knot in it and hang [on]."

Helen also continued to gather information on the family's art collection, asking Roland Knoedler for information on those paintings purchased over the last two years together with photographs of them to include in her ongoing catalogue of the collection—thirteen works beginning with Paolo Veronese's *Wisdom and Strength* and *The Choice Between Virtue and Vice,* acquired in 1912. She assiduously applied herself to the task—studying each painting's provenance, comparing each work to others by the same artist, and compiling the research into files.

Frick's recent purchases, like his previous ones, reflected his personal history, interests, and obsessions. He had recently attended two funerals: George Vanderbilt's, held in the next-door wing of 640 Fifth Avenue, and Attie's in Pittsburgh; James McNeill Whistler's two black-dressed portrait subjects, Rosa Corder and Robert, Comte de Montesquiou-Fezensac, invoke those moments. Whistler's *The Ocean,* however, of a smooth sea, recalls the Atlantic Ocean as seen from Frick's new third-floor bedroom at Eagle Rock on a dead calm day. The

Van Dyck portrait of Paola Adorno, Marchesa di Brignole Sala, regally dressed in a flowing, white-and-gold silk brocade dress, reflects Frick's continuing interest in portraits of women in fine clothes. The theme of children appears in two paintings. Van Dyck's *James, Seventh Earl of Derby, His Lady and Child* depicts a charming little girl standing between her parents, and the subject of Gainsborough's *Sarah, Lady Innes,* proffers a long-stemmed rose exactly like the one Martha holds in a drawing outside Frick's bedroom at Clayton.

One acquisition contained a directive meant for Helen. The satirist William Hogarth painted a portrait of Mary Edwards, the richest woman in England in her day—just as Helen might one day become in America. In the picture, Edwards's left hand rests tenderly upon the head of her black-and-white spotted spaniel, a dog remarkably like Helen's own Fido, and beside her right elbow lies an open scroll praising the value of liberty and prosperity. Edwards had married a fortune hunter and then divorced him to protect her wealth, even though their child was subsequently deemed illegitimate. Close to her father like Helen, Mary, who died at the age of thirty-six, the year after the Hogarth portrait was completed, asked to be buried with her father. Frick liked to warn Helen against marriage: "Weddings make me sad," he often complained, and yet he teased Helen about her single status. "Often in connection with the future," Helen wrote in one of her diaries, "Papsie would enjoy drawing a mental picture of the 'little old spinster,' as he would then call me. He said that . . . I would be seen going around [the Frick Building] with a little bag collecting office rent." Helen remembered: "I would always get so provoked."

William Hogarth (1697–1764), *Miss Mary Edwards.* Acquired by Henry Clay Frick in 1914. Oil on canvas, 49 ¾ x 39 ⅞ in. © the Frick Collection, New York.

Like Clayton, the new house was rife with references to Martha. The portals over the exterior doorways, except the entrance porte cochere, each depict four children, the two who lived and the two who died. Inside the house, the gilt organ screen inspired by Luca della Robbia's marble *cantoria* for the Duomo in Florence, studied so intently by Helen in 1909, depicts Psalm 150, with children singing the praises of God. Four marble columns, a pair on either side of the organ screen's central arch, support statues of children—a boy and girl to the left, a boy and girl to the right. A ram, the animal of sacrifice, is carved beneath the girl to the left and beneath the boy to the right, suggesting that the price Frick paid for his fortune was the deaths of his two children.

From portals to staircases to fences, paths, and paintings, Frick determined to live his life surrounded by referential glimmerings about death and resurrection, a perhaps perverse symbiosis that gave him comfort. Indeed, Frick's secretary, James Howard Bridge, later wrote in *Millionaires and Grubb Street,* "the portraits had become something more than mere paint and varnish." Decorator Sir Charles Allom and art dealer Joseph Duveen "invented a remarkable system of illuminating these paintings," Bridge explained. "Each one had its own spot-light concealed in the glass ceiling, so directed that the light fell only on the canvas, while the frame and surrounding wall were lost in shadow." According to Bridge, this system of lighting "gave to the portraits a weird semblance of life; and sitting alone in their midst, it was easy for me to imagine them as stepping out of the frames and joining each other in friendly talk." The lighting "enhances this illusion of vitality" and "visitors have been heard to protest that they have seen changing expressions on the faces of the men and women on the walls, as the lights were altered." Matilda Gay, wife of the artist Walter Gay, was more specific. A decade and a half later she noted in her journal: "After dinner we visited the Gallery where we had sat before an open fire before dinner. Miss Frick had arranged a curious lighting system. All the light was extinguished, with the exception of the special lights over the pictures; so that the pictures stared out of the gloom at us. This gave the effect of projections on the screen; the masterpieces therefore lost the quality of painting and looked like ghosts."

George Harvey also described the special hold the paintings had on Frick: "Often late at night, at the end of a trying day . . . he would slip noiselessly, almost furtively, into the darkened gallery, turn on the [spot] lights and sit for an hour or more, first on one divan then on another, absorbing solace and happiness through the mirrors of his heart before seeking . . . dreamless sleep."

Helen Frick never spoke on the subject of her father's peculiar lighting system or his nocturnal habits. But she certainly knew about them. Many years later, when Bridge published *Millionaires and Grubb Street,* she forced him to remove several descriptions suggesting Frick had some psychic communication with his paintings. Helen was, however, fully aware that her father sought solace in symbols of Martha. To comfort him in the most palpable way she could, she asked Knoedler to send the Chartran portrait of Martha, placed in storage during the move from 640 Fifth Avenue, to Eagle Rock. And with the first anniversary of Childs's and Dixie's wedding drawing near, and Dixie promoting herself with Frick, twenty-seven-year-old Helen engaged an artist to alter a posthumous miniature of Martha; Helen had her own likeness as a six-year-old painted into it, so she and her lost sister could look like twins.

On November 17, 1914, Helen moved into One East Seventieth Street with her parents. The residence was still unfinished. Frick, crippled from the attack of inflammatory rheumatism, fumed about the inefficiency, but nevertheless found the house "sufficient to make us comfortable." With all its emotional undercurrents, and still too grand for her quiet taste, One East Seventieth Street was, however, less offensive to Helen than had been the rented Vanderbilt house. She took particular pleasure in the happiness the move gave her father, where everything he cherished—family and art—resided splendidly and symbolically together, according to "the owner's direction."

With more paintings arriving by the end of 1914, Frick's personal themes and preoccupations became even more pronounced. Francisco de Goya's *The Forge* recalls scenes once familiar to Frick—men laboring at blazing coke ovens. J. M. W. Turner's stunning wharf scenes, *The Harbor of Dieppe* and *Cologne: The Arrival of a Packet-Boat: Evening,* recall the

Mon Wharf on the Monongahela River, Frick's place of business and the view from his hotel suite during the first years of his millionaire status.

Frick also selected a Martha look-alike: George Romney's portrait of Lady Hamilton holding a spotted dog like Martha's Brownie. Had she lived, Martha would have been the same age as Lady Hamilton when Romney painted her. For two years this was the only work of art hanging in Frick's bedroom. Then in 1916, he added another reminder of Martha, the portrait of Miss Louisa Murray by Sir Thomas Lawrence, depicting a ghostly little girl, almost floating through the air with a skirt full of Martha's favorite flower, the pansy. Back in 1914, when Frick moved into One East Seventieth Street, he had purchased another Martha-related work for his collection, a painting by Pierre-Auguste Renoir then entitled *Governess and Children,* now known as *Mother and Children.* It depicts a woman walking in a park with two little girls. The older child holds a doll dressed exactly like the governess—in a dark blue velvet jacket and a wide skirt of pale violet-gray. Coincidentally, Frick's last gift to his dying daughter was a doll that looked like her companion, Annie. Moved by the painting, Frick placed it at the entrance to the family quarters on the second floor, where it stood over Helen as she came and went, ever perpetuating her family's mourning, her task as consoler, and Frick's longing for the happy life they would have enjoyed had Martha lived.

The Rehearsal by Hilaire-Germain-Edgar Degas, depicting a bearded violin master overseeing a room full of young female ballet dancers, was instead, like Hogarth's *Miss Mary Edwards,* a warning to Helen. In his youth, Frick played the violin at dances while people literally danced to his tune. So the painting with its robot-like dancers, oppressed by

Above, left: George Romney (1734–1802), *Lady Hamilton as 'Nature'.* Acquired by Henry Clay Frick in 1904. Oil on canvas, 29 ⅞ x 24 ¾ in. © the Frick Collection, New York.

Above, right: Sir Thomas Lawrence (1769–1830), *Miss Louisa Murray.* Acquired by Henry Clay Frick in 1916. Oil on canvas, 36 ½ x 28 ⅞ in. © the Frick Collection, New York.

Pierre-Auguste Renoir (1841–1919), *Mother and Children*. Acquired by Henry Clay Frick in 1914. Oil on canvas, 67 x 42⅝ in. © the Frick Collection, New York.

their ballet masters and sold by their mothers for financial favor to wealthy men, was both Frick's slap at working women and a caution to Helen against insubordination. Frick hung it in his private sitting room, above Helen's writing desk.

The heavy mood of the Frick household as 1915 dawned—the war raging in Europe and Frick still suffering—lifted when on February 7 Dixie gave birth to the first Frick grandchild, a little girl named Adelaide. Much excitement accompanied her arrival although Dixie was slightly disappointed she had not produced a son to name after her father-in-law. The True Blue girls, now raising children of their own, also celebrated. They donated $100 of their hard-earned money to the milk fund of the Floating Hospital in the baby's honor.

To the delight of the family, by the fall Dixie was pregnant again. Perhaps as a result, on Christmas Eve, Frick showed a softer public heart than had yet been recorded when Pittsburgh's Dime Savings Bank failed, and the institution closed its doors without warning. Approximately forty thousand schoolchildren, encouraged by the city's Board of Education to make systematic deposits, lost almost $170,000 in savings. On learning of the collapse, Frick telegrammed the president of the Union Trust Company, his friend H. C. McEldowney: "Arrange at once to pay all school accounts in Pittsburgh Bank for Savings, in full so that the children shall not be deprived of their Christmas funds. Charge to my account." The newspapers were full of praise. "Mr. Frick has earned national thanks for his act of generosity," wrote one, and in Pittsburgh the press chimed, "Next to Santa Claus, Mr. Frick was the most popular man in Pittsburgh." Another account, however, credited Frick's action to Helen: "People in general looked on the 66-year-old Frick as an old curmudgeon. . . . Perhaps it was because of his daughter Helen, whom he adored, that the story of the children's loss touched Mr. Frick so deeply. Maybe it was because he knew how much she would have suffered from such a disappointment that he moved swiftly and without delay."

The Fragonard Room at the Frick Collection, 1927. Author's collection.

With baby Adelaide safely delivered, new grandfather and aunt resumed their gallery visits and discussions about potential acquisitions. Very happily the Fragonard panels, *The Progress of Love,* that Helen had so admired when she saw them in London in 1909, were now for sale as part of J. P. Morgan's estate. "Visited the Fragonards," she wrote on February 22, when she and her father went to the Metropolitan Museum to consider their purchase. Buying the panels would necessitate both a complete architectural reworking of the recently furnished drawing room by French experts and new decoration by Duveen. Weeks later the Fragonards and the porcelains acquired from Morgan's estate arrived. Frick remained "very impatient" for the room to be refitted with special French paneling, a marble mantelpiece chosen for its ivory color, new curtains, and lighting—a project that would take a full year to complete.

Although many details remained, the house and its collection were coming along well. In 1915, Frick purchased twenty-two pieces of furniture from the Morgan estate, small statues by Claude Michel Clodion, Étienne-Maurice Falconet, and Augustin Pajou, and a num-

François Boucher (1703–1770), *The Arts and Sciences: Painting and Sculpture.* Acquired by Henry Clay Frick in 1916. Oil on canvas, 85 ½ x 30 ½ in. © the Frick Collection, New York.

After François-Jacques-Joseph Saly, *Bust of a Young Girl.* Acquired by Henry Clay Frick in 1915–1916. Marble, 13 ½ in. © the Frick Collection, New York, gift of Helen Clay Frick in 1934.

ber of important symbolic paintings with personal references, by such artists as George Bellows, Titian, Rubens, Hoppner, and Francis Cotes, as well as Giovanni Bellini's masterpiece, *St. Francis in the Desert,* and *The Deposition* by Gerard David, depicting the dead Christ being taken from the cross and handed to his grieving mother. The arrival of *The Deposition* coincided with the execution or signing of Frick's will. On June 24, 1915, pleased to be both in his new home and have his affairs settled, Frick wrote Helen, who was at Eagle Rock: "The house is in complete order & is most attractive [and] only lacks you to make me perfectly happy."

Concerned by her father's recent illness and slow recovery, Helen now wanted to understand his life story. In early June 1915, she traveled to West Overton, Pennsylvania, hoping to learn more about Frick's early life. She took photographs of the Overholt Homestead, the barns, the distillery, and the houses, and even located the store in Mt. Pleasant where Frick had clerked for his Uncle Martin. Helen noted that her delighted father wrote her a letter, that he "saw the [Iron Rail] porch full of girls as I went by," and continued: "How I should like to be with you on your pilgrimage to see the scenes of my early struggles, but it will be interesting to hear all about it & we will take the trip together sometime."

Henry Clay Frick was busy, however, acquiring more art for his collection. His lifelong fascination with women's finery led to acquisitions in 1916 of Gainsborough's *The Mall in St. James's Park* and *Mrs. Peter William Baker* as well as Van Dyck's *Anne, Countess of Clanbrassil.* Frick also purchased *Old Woman with a Bible* (now called *Old Woman with a Book*) for $300,000 as a Rembrandt. When he later learned the painting was by Carel van der Pluym, he was infuriated, but he kept it in his collection. The old woman resembles his beloved grandmother Maria Stauffer Overholt, who customarily slid three fingers of her left hand through her folded reading glasses in just the same way as the portrait subject.

Tragedy from the past was never far away or forgotten. Frick bought Eugène Carrière's *Motherhood,* a portrait of an older woman who resembles Adelaide, nursing a baby. In 1916 Frick also purchased fifteen paintings by François Boucher, eight panels known as *The Arts and Sciences,* to be installed in Adelaide's boudoir. The works depict a boy and a girl enjoying, among other occupations, studying the stars, writing poetry and playing music, fowling and gardening, fishing and hunting—the many possibilities denied to the Fricks' two lost children. The panel entitled *Painting and Sculpture* depicts the small, marble bust by François-Jacques Saly, then believed to be Madame de Pompadour's daughter, who, like Martha, had died young. With 1915 being the thirtieth anniversary of Martha's birth, Adelaide suggested to Duveen, "How fascinating it would be to have the same little Bust shown in the wall picture?" So Duveen sold her a copy of Saly's sculpture, and Adelaide quickly displayed it in a prominent place, facing her when she entered her boudoir. To install the panels, however, was no easy task. The height of the boudoir ceiling had to be raised more than a foot by cutting through steel beams.

In anticipation of his second grandchild, Frick wove a new theme into his art collection. In January 1916, with Dixie now three months pregnant, Frick bought *Sir Joshua Vanneck and His Family of Roehampton House, Putney* by Arthur Devis. The work presents a prosperous, eighteenth-century international financier on the lawn of his forty-acre estate, surrounded by three generations of his family. Frick displayed the painting above the mantel in the music room at Eagle Rock, where it could be enjoyed when the three generations of Fricks assembled for the summer.

Dixie gave birth to daughter Frances in the summer of 1916 near Eagle Rock, in Beverly, Massachusetts, where Frick was renting a summer house for Dixie and Childs. The advent

Gerard David (active from 1484–1523), *The Deposition*. Acquired by Henry Clay Frick in 1915. Oil on canvas, 56 ⅛ x 44 ¼ in. © the Frick Collection, New York.

The Arthur Devis generational portrait, *Sir Joshua Vanneck and His Family of Roehampton House, Putney*, is displayed above the mantelpiece in the music room at Eagle Rock. Courtesy the Frick Collection/Frick Art Reference Library Archives.

of grandchildren, the flurry of excitement over additions to the collection, and Helen's continuing visits with her father to various galleries and dealers to study potential acquisitions had been the focus of the last two years, but now, as 1917 dawned and America prepared to enter the war against Germany, the focus changed. A much-concerned Frick gave large sums of money to various war-related charities. On March 21, 1916, the *New York Times* credited him with giving "$5,000 to Trade Schools for the Maimed French Soldiers." As time went on, Frick purchased approximately $4.5 million worth of Liberty Loans and gave an additional $300,000 to such causes as the Belgian Relief Fund, the American Ambulance Hospital in France, the families of disabled French, and the Armored Motor Squadron, and he supported an entire village of orphans. In January 1917, he shelved plans for a sculpture gallery and, always the practical businessman, wrote Thomas Hastings, "I have decided to do nothing whatever towards the erection of the proposed building until times become normal and prices reasonable. . . . how can we expect good and prompt work?"

On April 6, 1917, President Woodrow Wilson, who had long distanced himself from the fight, asked Congress to declare war. Ever a steadfast Republican, Frick nevertheless stood solidly behind Wilson and gave the president his personal vote of confidence: "While I differ from you in politics, I subscribe without reservation to all you are contending for. . . . I firmly feel you are devoted to this great work and will carry it forward fairly and honestly." In a show of patriotism, when the government took over management of privately owned railroads in December 1917, Frick was the first director of a railroad to put his private car in storage and to travel by public means. And when he sold his shares in a shipbuilding syndicate at a profit, he placed his gains in the U.S. War Work treasury, rather than chance being accused of profiteering from the conflict.

Although many Frick family friends from the North Shore volunteered in the air war, Childs had done little on behalf of the war effort. He played polo and golf when summering at Eagle Rock and although based in Bryn Mawr in the winters, he followed the polo circuit to Georgia and Florida. On April 26, 1916, he became a licensed pilot through the Wright Flying School and hoped to accrue additional hours when summering on the North Shore, but he was grounded by two months' rain. Finally, in August, he enlisted in the experimental and newly created civilian and military training camp for businessmen, students, and troops in Plattsburgh, New York, a one-month training course that was a precursor to the Reserve Officer Training Corps (ROTC), seen at the time as "an easy out for the patriotism of well-to-do educated men who would not join their state militia."

Then Childs and Dixie decided to spend a year in southern California so Childs could fly his plane and pursue his interest in vertebrate fossil mammals. On January 3, 1917, after celebrating Christmas at One East Seventieth Street, he packed up his family and moved to Redlands, California. Childs's childhood mentor, the prominent Pittsburgh naturalist and pastor Rev. William Holland, provided letters of introduction to professors and museum directors, including one to the chairman and founder of the newly created department of paleontology at the University of California, Berkeley, Professor John C. Merriam. Soon, under Merriam's guidance, Childs hired a German-trained miner, Joseph Rak, to work on the thick sections of well-exposed Late Tertiary and Quaternary continental sedimentary rock at San Timoteo Canyon, Eden Mountain, and Bautista Creek. Childs also became the proud owner of a $12,000 "flying machine," purchased as a trainer by his father, who, though upset it was secondhand, was nevertheless hopeful that Childs might soon contribute to the fight against Germany.

Helen had been intimately and financially involved in the war from its inception in 1914, when she founded a Goodwill Section of the Red Cross. In fact, she had initiated what became a four-year, hands-on campaign to relieve human suffering in war-torn France. She gathered about her a group of workers, and together they rolled bandages, taught first aid, shipped surgical dressings to the Allied soldiers in France, sent clothing and food to refugee women and children, and personally taught French to relief workers headed overseas. When America entered the war, Helen and her group expanded their activities and gave instruction in making surgical dressings and in assembling other Red Cross supplies. Far from a slapdash effort, in its four-year history this "Goodwill Section Helen Frick," as it became known, sent two soup kitchens to France and hundreds of comfort kits containing children's clothing, toilet articles, and toys. Helen Frick spent $1 million of her own money on this initiative and also helped organize and finance a Red Cross orthopedic hospital unit, known as Base Hospital No. 9 of the American Expeditionary Forces, accredited to the New York Hospital. A military medical unit created at the request of the Army and Navy, it was fully staffed with the hospital's personnel and equipment and ready for immediate deployment overseas to assist with war wounded from the field and from evacuated hospitals. She also donated a knitting machine and five hundred sets of mosquito netting to protect open wounds from flies should the unit be deployed, as was anticipated, to a hospital in France near the front, established by the British Expeditionary Forces. Fourteen of these American base hospitals would serve in the war, six of them attached to the British Expeditionary Forces.

To her delight, Frick told Helen on April 30 that to assist the French in raising money for the war effort he had "tendered through the Mayor to the French & British War Missions, the use of One East Seventieth Street with full service & automobiles & chauffeurs during their stay in New York." Anticipating the arrival of the famed French general, Marshal Joseph-Jacques-Césaire Joffre, Frick and Adelaide took rooms at the Plaza Hotel and Helen moved in with her friend Louise Freeman. There to greet Marshal Joffre and his entourage on their arrival, Helen wrote, "Papsie, Mamma, & I & Louise Freeman & [her friend] Helen Houget received." The following night Frick hosted an all-male dinner for the general, seating himself between Joffre and former president Theodore Roosevelt.

That May the war touched twenty-eight-year-old Helen in a more private way. At long last a romance had developed, between herself and Dr. Fordyce St. John. A Princeton classmate of Childs's, he had been the student president of Princeton University, as well as head of the senior council and president of the Ivy Club, and he had attended Childs and Dixie's wedding. Now an instructor at Columbia University's College of Physicians and Surgeons, an assistant visiting surgeon at Presbyterian Hospital, and on the attending staff of the First Surgical Division of the College of Physicians and Surgeons at Bellevue Hospital, he was, according to his daughter, Jane St. John Roe, extremely attractive: a "distinguished looking man, imposing in appearance, warm and charismatic." Whatever the budding relationship may have been back in 1913—the moment the courtship began is unclear—after Dixie and Childs's wedding, the romance appears to have quietly and slowly developed, and was observed by others. "Johnnie" visited Helen at least once at Eagle Rock and at One East Seventieth Street and several times the two were seen together in public, particularly on opening night of the Metropolitan Opera. Liza Fosburgh, a mutual friend of both families and Eleanor Whitney Fosburgh's daughter-in-law, said that for as much as Helen appeared to be in love with St. John, "he adored her."

Giovanni Batista Tiepolo's *Perseus Rescuing Andromeda* can be seen to the left of Helen's bedroom door. Author's collection.

As Helen considered her situation, she purchased from Knoedler a telling oil sketch by Giovanni Battista Tiepolo, a study for a ceiling fresco in the Palazzo Archinto in Milan entitled *Perseus Rescuing Andromeda,* and placed it outside her bedroom door. According to Greek myth, the Ethiopian king chained his daughter, the princess Andromeda, to a rock and offered her as a sacrifice to the sea monster who, angered by the queen's vanity, was about to destroy the kingdom. Andromeda, however, promised Perseus she would marry him if he saved her from the monster. The painting depicts the moment of her rescue. Andromeda and Perseus are flying away together on the back of Pegasus while broken chains dangle from Andromeda's arm and leg and another hangs from the rock, inches away from the sea monster's jaws.

If Helen was considering flying away, she lost her chance in April 1917, immediately after America declared war on Germany. Since 1915, St. John's Presbyterian Hospital had been organizing a base hospital unit to assist the war wounded. In 1917 the unit was officially merged into the army as Base Hospital No. 2, with a staff of twenty-five medical and surgical officers, including St. John, and sixty-five nurses. According to Childs Frick's son, Henry Clay Frick II, before St. John sailed to join the British hospital at Étretat on the northern coast of France near the Flanders front, Helen hoped to announce their engagement. But the anticipated announcement was never made. Childs, whose relationship with his sister Helen as well as with his father Henry Clay Frick had so largely been defined by mutual disappointment and dissatisfaction, even after marrying and starting a family, sabotaged the betrothal. Dixie encouraged his jealousy, perhaps fearing that if Helen married and had children, Helen's would be favored above hers. Though the *New York Times* said at the time of her engagement that Dixie was "considered one of the most beautiful young women in Baltimore Society," according to family members, Dixie was also one of the most charming and calculating, "ever running herself as family favorite." Years later Helen told her secretary, Julia

Egan, that once married to Childs, Dixie turned on her sister-in-law and dropped her as a friend, conveying the message: "I have what I want and don't need you anymore."

With Helen's engagement looming, Dixie and Childs informed St. John that his suit was useless; Frick never would permit his daughter to marry him or anyone else. Whether or not they were speaking with Frick's authorization is unknown. At the Fricks' farewell dinner for St. John, when many expected the announcement of Helen's engagement, nothing happened. On May 14, he sailed on the transport St. Louis for Étretat, and Frick sent the hospital a check for $10,000. But according to Liza Fosburgh, Helen was still hopeful. She took St. John seriously when on his departure he "promised to marry Helen after the war." Helen, furious with her brother and Dixie, symbolically rid herself of them by legally changing her name. Born Helen Childs Frick, she struck out "Childs" and substituted her father's nickname "Clay."

Whether Childs's intervention was or was not the turning point, in the end, St. John would break his promise to marry Helen. When he sailed for France in May 1917, an accomplished operating-room nurse from the Presbyterian Hospital, Jane Rignel, was on board. In July 1918, St. John became commanding officer of Mobile Hospital No. 2, funded by the British hospital at Étretat with the unused portion of $10,000 Frick had sent for the purchase of coal in 1917, and Jane Rignel was appointed his chief operating-room nurse. The two were assigned first to the Somme-Suippe line and then the Argonne. Upon Germany's surrender on November 11, 1918, St. John proposed to Jane. In January 1919 the betrothed couple sailed for home, although in the spring St. John seems to have had a change of heart and wanted to renew his relationship with Helen. In her diary Helen confided something quite startling: "Papsie wrote me a sweet letter.... said.... 'I had another proposal for your hand today which I confined to the wastebasket. You are becoming far too popular.... This is only a line to assure you that you are always in my thoughts.' " No more details are known regarding this proposal, but St. John and Jane married in August 1919.

According to anonymous sources interviewed for the *New Yorker* profile, Helen was evidently not without options, had she wanted them, and had her father given his permission: "Army officers who knew [Helen] then remember her as a vivid young woman, attractive in her uniform but very reserved. 'She was a swell person,' one of them wrote after the war, 'somewhat dominating when she was in the room, but with a great deal of force and personality, and I couldn't understand why she wasn't married and thought she certainly would be before long.' "

Over the years, Helen and the St. Johns developed a social friendship. Many, many years later, in 1954, when St. John suffered a major heart attack after his seventieth birthday celebration, Helen visited him in the hospital and promised to watch over him and his children. In fact, she provided a house for one of his daughters, Libby Marvin Fennell, and her young family, on her farm in Bedford Village, New York. And in the 1970s, when Helen was in her eighties, she attended the funerals of both Fordyce—he died at age eighty-nine—and Jane. But during his service Helen turned to her nephew, Clay Frick, by then a surgeon himself, and with a rueful smile whispered, "poor old man."

Above: Dr. Fordyce St. John on his departure, May 12, 1917, to serve in France. Courtesy the Frick Collection/Frick Art Reference Library Archives.

Below: Helen on October 30, 1917, shortly before serving with the Red Cross in France during World War I. Courtesy the Library of Congress.

On September 23, 1917, Dixie, now living in Santa Barbara, California, bore her third child—another girl. According to her brother, Billy Dixon, failing once more to deliver the longed-for son to name after her father-in-law rankled Dixie. And so to cushion the disappointment, and to further endear herself to Frick, she named her baby Martha Howard Frick after the child who, as George Harvey once said, "held first place in the shrine of his heart."

Helen had more important things on her mind than family infighting: she wanted to join the action at the front and to personally care for children in the devastated regions of France. With two New York friends, Constance Roberson and Gertrude Hill, daughter of the tobacco tycoon, George Washington Hill, she signed up with the Department of Civil Relief to establish and finance a Frick Unit under the Red Cross. On October 11, permission was granted.

Frances Frick holding her infant daughter Martha Howard Frick. Her eldest daughter Adelaide Frick is seated on the table. Author's collection.

Helen and her friends were very much needed. Thousands of refugees, women, children, and aged people, had by then fled France, passing through Belgium to Switzerland and thence to Evian, France, on the south shore of Lake Geneva, the entry point for refugees seeking relocation in Valence, Lyon, Bourg, and elsewhere in southeastern France. Margaret Curtis of Boston had initiated organized relief for these refugees by providing housing, food, and a livelihood. For Helen, fluent in French and experienced in social work, this was the perfect assignment. In fact, when she attended the New York School of Philanthropy, its director was Edward Devine, now the chief of the Bureau of Refugees for the American Red Cross in France, and Margaret Curtis was his assistant.

In her own idiosyncratic way, Helen was a participant in the broad social shift of "New Women"—well educated, for the most part unmarried, and searching for new ways to use their talents. Independent, self-motivated, patriotic, and wanting to serve, they established, often with their own money, niches within the chaos of war and its inadequate foreign services. Many women of Helen's social class were finding a way to serve. Madeleine Astor, wife of Vincent Astor, and Helen Taft, niece of the former president, sold liberty bonds. Consuelo Vanderbilt chaired the American Women's War Relief Fund. Gertrude Vanderbilt Whitney spent $250,000 to organize a Red Cross hospital at Juilly, north of Paris, and worked in one of its wards. Elizabeth Ayer established a motor corps and served food to the refugees and helped transport them from one station to another; while Annie Harriman, wife of William K. Vanderbilt, and Anne Cameron Tiffany, wife of Belmont Tiffany, did canteen work to help the troops relax. Of the expatriates, Miss Ana Dana of Boston, then married to Phillipe B'érard and living in Paris, and who had three sons in the French army, nursed at the front. Edith Wharton employed seamstresses to make clothing. She fed the homeless, offered refugees a free clinic and dispensary, delivered coal, and established a day nursery and an employment agency. The artists Mary Cassatt and Malvina Hoffman joined the cause, as did Gertrude Stein and Alice B. Toklas, who established depots to distribute supplies to hospitals. Even Elsie de Wolfe helped. She and her companion, Elizabeth Marbury, converted the house at Versailles they shared with Anne Morgan, the youngest daughter of J. P. Morgan, into a hospital, and Anne drove an ambulance.

The relief effort Helen and her friends joined had been in place since the beginning of the war. From 1914 to 1917, Herbert Hoover, then in London as head of the Commission for Relief in Belgium, organized the distribution of food to the Belgian people. Working with him was Charlotte Kellogg, who traveled to Belgium with the relief organization and established the policies Helen would soon practice. Kellogg met trains of refugees "down to the dirtiest little specimens with runny noses and lice," took their names, added the names of lost relatives to a Red Cross list, gave them coal cards, fed and clothed them, housed them, and tried to help them forget their misery, if only for a little while.

The night before she went overseas Helen had dinner with her parents. Joining them, Helen later noted, were "ten of our soldiers in training. Papsie was so interested in them. They were all from Montana & most of them farmers." According to her own diary, after dinner, when everyone started to move from the table, "Papsie told us to remain standing." He then produced a diamond, sapphire, and ruby pin and, as Helen said, "He decorated me with it."

On Friday, November 30, 1917, Helen boarded the *Rochambeau*, together with 450 passengers, two-thirds of them women. Her self-financed unit, one of the many ad hoc relief organizations created during the war, included, in addition to her friends Gertrude Hill and Constance Roberson, the woman who would be her superior in the field, a forty-three-year-old Wellesley graduate and experienced Boston social worker, Molly Dewson, and her partner, thirty-three-year-old Polly Porter. Dewson, a former superintendent of parole at the Massachusetts State Industrial School for Girls in Lancaster, a reform school, later became director general of relief for all of southern France and, still later, a trusted advisor to Franklin D. Roosevelt.

Helen and Molly Dewson in their Red Cross uniforms. Courtesy the Frick Collection/Frick Art Reference Library Archives.

Excited to be on her way, Helen nevertheless found the departure difficult. Her father, though reasonably recovered, remained noticeably weak. Knowing how hard saying goodbye would be, she asked him not to see her off. He did as she asked, but sent Knoedler to hand-deliver this letter to her:

> My dearest Helen,
> *Only* for the reason you requested it I refrained from going to see you sail.
>
> My fondest deepest love Dearest, I feel you will take the best of care of yourself and surely return to us within six months.
>
> I agreed most reluctantly to have you go, but we are much alike and I would want in your place to do just as you are doing, otherwise would be very unhappy.
>
> Your happiness is my first consideration, especially your future happiness, and to have denied you the opportunity to have this experience, would I fear always had its effect on your future.
>
> That you will accomplish something worthwhile I am sure.
>
> Our thoughts and tenderest love will always be with you and I am very proud of you
>
> Most affectionately your devoted
> Father

Helen's passage, though uneventful, was fraught with tension. Groups patrolled the decks looking for lurking submarines. On December 8, when they entered the war zone, Helen and her companions spent most of the night outside despite the cold and tried to sleep in their deck chairs. Helen managed to get only two hours of rest that night in her cabin, fully dressed in her uniform, a tailored suit for Red Cross social workers with jacket, long skirt, plain blouse, necktie, and large square hat. On Monday, December 10, when the *Rochambeau* docked at Le Havre, Helen was anxious to get to work. While awaiting their orders, the five women comprising the Frick Unit went to Paris. Dewson and Porter settled into the American Red Cross Club for Women on the Rue Cambon, and Helen, Gertrude, and Constance moved into Knoedler's flower-filled apartment. On December 12, Helen

Above, left and right: Helen on the trans-Atlantic crossing to France. Courtesy the Frick Collection/Frick Art Reference Library Archives.

wrote her mother, laughing at her sudden loss of privacy. "I have never been so promiscuous in giving my photographs & it seems as though everyone now must know where each member of the Frick family was born & everything I have ever said or done since I drew my first breath."

As she awaited her assignment, life in Paris for Helen was much as it had been before the war, though "[it] looks & is quieter than it was," she observed. "As long as we are in Paris we need no food supplies" although "candy of course is greatly desired by all." Around mid-December, the Frick Unit received its orders from the Red Cross. "Three of us are going with Miss Dewson who is a perfect wonder—she's a most experienced (one of the best) social worker from Boston & the R.C. is certainly giving us a marvelous opportunity of showing what we can do for the rapatriés." Helen may not have been going to the military front as she had hoped, but she was headed to the front of another war, to southeastern France at Evian, where the flood of refugees was entering the country. Pleased to be assigned to the rich agricultural town of Bourg-en-Bresse in the Rhône Valley, Helen bided her time in Paris helping canteen workers wrap and pack Christmas comfort bags, a total of 150,000 in all, or 3,500 a day. "And all must be finished by tomorrow night," explained Helen to her mother on December 16, Adelaide's fifty-eighth birthday, "if the men are to get them by Xmas."

Helen had two accounts in Paris, both set up for her by her father. Able to spend as much money as was needed on behalf of the Frick Unit, Helen also received special gifts from home. On Christmas morning, "there was a knock at the door, & a man from Cartier was announced. He brought four little red leather boxes, each inscribed with different initials & on opening them, we found . . . exquisite little [torch-shaped] diamond victory pins, all just alike!" Helen, touched and invigorated by her father's gesture of love and support, wrote to him, "Thank you again for the beautiful pin. I love its symbol."

Although she was "under real orders" not to give details, Helen could nevertheless give her parents a general description of her activities. In a letter of December 29, 1917, she described her arrival in Bourg-en-Bresse, in the midst of falling snow, where orphans of the *rapatriés* were being gathered in a large home in Lyon. "The stories," wrote Helen, "go on and on, and they make your heart ache." A mother of five children, including a four-day-old boy, died "of grief & terror" when Germans entered the house. A two-year-old girl, a "darling little child," had already lost her mother and her father was a prisoner in Germany. She continued, "A poor little girl of five cried so when her mother was taken from her that the Germans fired at her and hit her little brother by mistake, wounding him badly in the foot."

Helen assured her parents she was safe, "warm and comfortable in her Red Cross outfit," happy that it was "no trouble to care for." But her main task for the moment was helping the *rapatriés* get settled as quickly as possible. She later explained:

> No French people are allowed to return directly into France from occupied territory. First, they are taken to Belgium for two months, so that anything they might know of German defenses may be of no importance to the French government; from Belgium they are sent to Switzerland and then they are sent across the border to Evian. There the Minister of the Interior directs them to their destination.
>
> Our work consist[s] of helping these people after they had been placed in their homes. All who [are] able [are] urged to do farming. When we visit . . . them in our motor truck we always [take] garden implements and seeds with us, for every scrap of land must be cultivated. . . . The women who are not strong enough to work in the fields are encouraged to knit. The French government furnishes the wool and pays a franc for socks and seventy-five centimes for gloves. It is not very much money, but it helps.

Unlike Dewson and the others in her Frick unit, the one thing Helen did not have to do was learn French. She laughed at their efforts, "It's awfully funny," and said, "I'm so glad I don't have to bother on this score, it really makes things pretty easy for me." Yet knowing the language made her available for other work. "I've been fairly busy translating some French laws pertaining to the refugees . . . so that evens things up a bit."

Helen took pride and satisfaction in being able to help solve the refugees' problems. "One poor, old man landed in a little village only to find that he had been separated from his old wife. She had his sack of clothes and he had hers. Through the medium of the Red Cross, the wife was located and when we made our second visit to him, we found him at the railway station four hours before the train was due, clad in a new suit furnished by the Red Cross and eagerly awaiting the arrival of his wife. "

During the first week of January 1918, Helen wrote her parents that she had finally met her Red Cross superior, Edward Devine, from whom she had taken her course in social studies. To familiarize themselves with the many towns in their section of southern France, she, Gertrude, and Constance were apparently "studying geography until we are blue in the face." A few days later, she reported that while she was busy, very much so, she felt secure and happy in her job. "Except for the stories we hear from those who have suffered through the war and of course the difficulties the poor classes have in getting the necessities of life," she noted, "we would scarcely know there was such a thing as war. . . . When I can I will hope also to visit the village of orphans you are helping, Papa."

Her father's interest in the relief effort remained a sustaining force for Helen, and she did not hesitate to tell him one story after another about German cruelty. During the first week of January, she reported that when four prominent French women were being sent to Germany and "the townspeople wanted to pay a silent tribute to them as they were taken away . . . the Germans let a quantity of Police Dogs loose and these tore and bit the people." She admired those who dared defy the Germans: "The people are little more than prisoners in all of their actions," she explained. "Offenses send them straight to prison unless they

The arrival of "Hunkatin" as photographed by Helen. Courtesy the Frick Collection/Frick Art Reference Library Archives.

pay the penalty of six francs for every day the summons calls for, and because they don't want to help the Germans any more than they have to, even if the penalty can be afforded, these people choose the prison!"

Later that month Helen met her first convoy in Evian and accompanied 596 French refugees from northern France to Bourg. She wrote in her war diary that the train's arrival with the "quantities of old people & little children," was the "most touching scene I have ever witnessed." She took their names and histories and helped get her charges settled in any available housing—hotels, farm cottages, barracks, anything to offer them shelter in this emergency.

The last week of January an important addition to the Frick Unit arrived, a Ford wagon Helen variously called "Hunkatin" or "Honka Tin," or just "Hunkie." With gas alternately supplied by Knoedler, the military, or purchased for just under $1 per gallon, Helen could now drive to the villages and check on her "families." There was a husband and wife caring for five orphan boys while their only son was at the front. On the wooden table before them rested their evening meal, "one large dish of baked apples." Helen, touched by the sight before her, took Goodwill comfort bags from Hunkie and gave them to the boys.

On January 31, however, as Helen, Constance, and Gertrude streaked across the French countryside, they met with an accident. Constance was behind the wheel, and when she swerved to avoid some chickens in the road, Hunkie "turned completely over—wheels in air, all of us underneath . . . marvelous miracle that we all escaped."

She prepared to meet her second convoy on February 3, this one arriving south of Bourg-en-Bresse, at Valence: "[W]ith small valises full of R[ed] C[ross] 'face cards' and pencils, we started forth on our busy days [*sic*] work. . . . At 4:20 the train was announced,—a long affair of about 10 or 12 wagons, filled to their utmost capacity with the poor sorrowing victims of war. We all went through the train to welcome them back to their beloved France, while the canteen women served them hot chocolate and huge slices of war bread." After people had been classified and assigned to a town, Helen wrote, "It was time for our Unit to get busy,—we helped carry the bundles to the waiting rooms, and while two handed out R.C. coal cards, the other two took down family histories. Such sad histories," Helen lamented. After several hours, the displaced people went to hotels for meals and "we began distributing toys to the children." Trains kept coming and Helen kept on working, taking down eighty histories one day and buying more toys another. "Found a stone wall of difficulties," she wrote. "Great lack of lodgings."

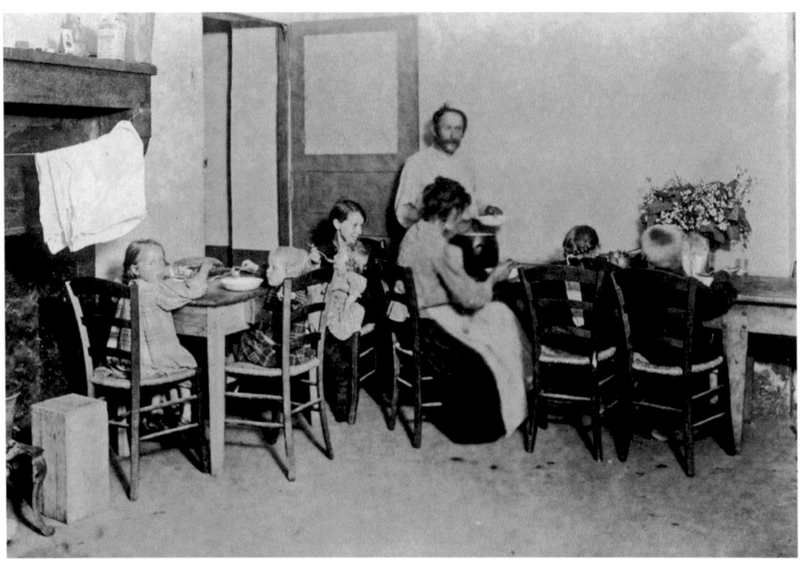

One of the refugee families at dinner, photographed by Helen. Courtesy the Frick Collection/Frick Art Reference Library Archives.

Helen wrote her parents on February 12, "Tomorrow we take the 4:50 a.m. train (don't you love the hours!) for Evian." Undaunted at the prospect of having some sixty-three villages to visit once these new refugees were settled, Helen explained, "But this is just the part of the work we love the most—& Hunkatin plays a very important part in our pleasure."

Evian now hosted two convoys daily, each train carrying six hundred refugees. Helen described the scene: "We saw one convoy arrive and just as the long train pulled in the trumpets were sounded and you've never heard a more thrilling sound in your lives! Picture these hundreds of poor souls, young and old, setting foot in their beloved France after three years. . . . Some laughed, but many cried with joy, and in one large body all marched down the wide street, following the [town's] band to the Casino [for processing], with shouts of 'Vive la France' 'Vive les Allies' rending the air."

That afternoon Helen and Miss Dewson walked through each room of the Casino and watched as the *rapatriés* were given food, clothing, baths, medical exams, and missing person forms to assist the Red Cross in locating lost family members. The following morning, Helen, Miss Dewson, Gertrude Hill, and Constance Roberson accompanied six hundred *rapatriés* to Ambérien, "four of us to take their histories and hand out coal cards, printed Red Cross letters telling of the ways in which we could help them, and blanks with indications as to how to recover lost relatives and lost baggage." The task was immense, yet by the time the train reached Ambérien and the family groups disbursed, "our lists showed with but few exceptions that everyone had had attention paid them." Helen was elated: "This is a sample of two days' work and we never have felt better in our lives!"

Refugees gathered at a French railway station, possibly Evian, photographed by Helen. Courtesy the Frick Collection/Frick Art Reference Library Archives.

Very soon Helen's unit became responsible for the comfort and care of refugees in more than seventy towns. Meanwhile, in late February, Helen had received news from her parents about Childs. Following his ten-month stay in California, working in the Badlands and flying his trainer plane, he had joined the Signal Corps, at Ellington Field in Houston, Texas, and now was commissioned as a first lieutenant in the gunnery section of the Signal Reserves Corps, Aviation Section, in Washington, D.C. Childs said to the Rev. Holland that he was "busily engaged in the study of modern machine guns," working on a cooling mechanism, or jam reducing device, for the Marlin machine gun. "I am so happy he is in something," Helen wrote, "& know he will do fine work."

Back at home the Iron Rail, now fostering its second generation of young women, contributed to the war effort, teaching more than five hundred True Blues to knit. One True Blue "mother," as the older generation was now called, made approximately five hundred dresses for French children; as a whole, the group produced fifty-five thousand garments between 1917 and 1918. Moreover, in a gesture that made their benefactress most proud, by sacrificing a day's pay the girls raised enough money to send a True Blue ambulance, known as HCF Ambulance No. 878, to France.

Helen's duties escalated. A torrent of refugees caused by the German offensive from the Oise and Somme rivers had flooded the area. Dewson said of the situation: "We thought we were busy before the offensive, but now . . . we just gape." All of them, Helen included,

Helen (last in line) and Red Cross volunteers tour the battlefield from Chemin des Dames, a roadway on the crest between the Aisne and Ailette rivers. Courtesy the Frick Collection/ the Frick Art Reference Library Archives.

worked themselves to exhaustion. In early March, while taking some children to be examined at the hospital, Helen fainted—and not for the first time. A concerned Gertrude Hill encouraged her to take a break from her Red Cross duties and rest for a few days in Knoedler's Paris apartment.

The respite was not restorative. The Germans' infamous long-range cannon, Big Bertha, was shelling the city every twelve minutes from seventy-five miles away and had caused much damage to places such as the Champs Elysées and Place Vendome. Blaring sirens constantly pierced the air, followed by more German shells and bombs. Helen later reported to her parents, "Last night . . . bombs dropped, but the 'barrage' guns kept up such an incessant firing that you couldn't distinguish which was 'Gotha' and which was anti-aircraft." She complained to her parents it "seems so never ending that it seems more like a hideous, hideous nightmare than a reality."

Frightened by the bombing, Helen became more dedicated to her cause than ever. She asked her father for permission to use his special fund to "organize and finance a convalescent home for undernourished children of rapatriés in the Ain Dept. [of the Bourg area]." As she envisioned the project, the home would be "large enough to accommodate about 20 at a time, and to keep it open for the duration of the war. . . . not too far away from the main line, and yet in the hills where the air would be cool and healthful in the summer." A few days later, upon her return to Bourg, Helen found the perfect house. It had a garden, and next door was a farm that could supply fresh milk for the children. Helen hoped to acquire it and place Melle, who lived just over the border in Switzerland, in charge. "I do want to start it well before going home. I feel it will be well worthwhile & not extravagant. . . . I refuse to go home without feeling that aside from a little personal service of my own, I haven't been able to really contribute *through you* to some really worthwhile cause, and I know it would disappoint you if I didn't when there *is* a big need to be filled."

Not a week later, on March 25, Helen received her father's permission to establish the orphanage. She selected girls aged four to fourteen, hired a nurse, an executive head, and a cook, and made all other necessary preparations. With this added activity, however, Helen's health, already stressed by her urgent and demanding work with the refugees, was

Helen (looking through binoculars) in an artillery observation post on the battlefield in the Aisne District. Courtesy the Frick Collection/the Frick Art Reference Library Archives.

seriously compromised. By the end of March she had become too ill for either Red Cross work or for running the convalescent home. Her World War I diary notation for March 25 reads: "Woke up in bed feeling faint." The March 27 entry says, "very tired," and March 28 is more ominous: "Do lots of typewriting & almost die. Feel so tired. Bed right after dinner." In her next entry she confided, "sick as a dog all day." On March 29, Gertrude took Helen back to Knoedler's apartment in Paris. Gertrude wrote her mother that her friend "hadn't been well for ten days—tired and nervous, and Thursday was very sick all day, also Friday." Eventually a doctor diagnosed fatigue and some intestinal poisoning due to the poor food in the field and said she just needed rest. But when Helen's friend, Louise Freeman, wrote Frick to follow up on the doctor's visit, she queried, "Do you know that she has had regular vomiting spells for about two years [?] They average four or five weeks apart, and of course

Helen (center) in a cantonment on the Aisne. Many of these soldiers were killed in a German offensive on May 27, 1918, eleven days after this photograph was taken. Courtesy the Frick Collection/the Frick Art Reference Library Archives.

over here with the continual work and nervous energy expended and poor food she has had them oftener." Freeman also pointed to the larger problem: "While Helen was here [in Paris], we all made her rest as much as possible, just to store up some reserve batteries, but it is the hardest job I know to make her keep quiet and relax."

Within two weeks Helen recuperated enough to return to work. Four thousand evacuees had entered the area on the first day of April, and as Helen explained to her parents on April 15, their unit needed more help. Her project had been so successful, and the need for more volunteers had become so great, the Red Cross decided to expand. May signaled the end of her six-month tour of duty, and although she advised her parents that she did not yet know her sailing date, she said, "You can be sure of this—before the middle of June, I'll be back with you & oh so happy to be home again."

While Helen was in Paris that May, awaiting her departure, the German army was advancing along a fifty-mile front toward the capital. Helen nevertheless arranged a visit to the devastated areas and to the front. On May 16 she left Paris with a French delegation and saw firsthand the physical ruin caused by German bombs and heavy artillery. Meaux, Ferte Milon, Longpont, Belleu where the Sixth Army was headquartered, Soissons—these were villages and towns now reduced to rubble. Helen walked the Chemin des Dames, a dirt road on the crest between the Aisne and Ailette river valleys, a theater of violent fighting during the 1917 French offensive and now under Allied control. Her picture was taken here as she surveyed the war-torn landscape. Later she looked into a bunker and visited soldiers in a Red Cross cantonment on the Aisne, just behind enemy lines. Her picture was taken here as well—this time with the soldiers.

Helen did not forget the grim lessons of that trip. Months later, in a scrapbook, she painstakingly juxtaposed pictures of Soissons Cathedral and other sites she had loved since childhood taken before the war and after. She also included the photographs of herself on the Chemin des Dames and in the cantonment. A caption reveals that eleven days after her visit, on May 27, the day before Helen sailed for home, most, if not all the soldiers she had met that day were killed in the German advance to the Marne River.

The Red Cross recognized Helen for having done a superb and sincere job on behalf of the millions of refugees during her six-month tour of duty, as well as in the three years before America entered the war. On May 27 a weary Helen Frick, accompanied by Gertrude Hill, boarded the *Espagne* and sailed from Bordeaux for New York. Her ship docked safely on June 5, 1918, and Helen recorded: "Papsie & Mamma [were] down at the French pier to meet me." Happy though she was to see them, Helen was alarmed. Over the winter her mother had been ill with a cold so severe a trained nurse was hired to care for her. Moreover: "My first glance at Papsie made me realize he was not well, although others said how well he looked," she complained to her diary. Frick, testing her devotion, queried: "When you got a letter from me, you always opened it first, didn't you?"

During the ensuing summer at Eagle Rock he and Helen enjoyed playing with the grandchildren and in September their bond was further cemented by Helen's thirtieth birthday present: Frick gave her title to Eagle Rock and its contents, an inheritance Helen would have received from him upon her mother's death. Although the reasons are unknown, this transfer was never completed. Nevertheless, Frick's intention to make his daughter the owner of his house said much about their relationship and how little room it left for Frick's wife. In fact, at this same time, Frick purchased for his Eagle Rock collection a portrait of Princess Sophia, then thought to be a work by John Hoppner, now attributed to William Beechey. It carried an inherent message: Sophia died unmarried at age seventy-seven.

Attributed to William Beechey (1753–1839), *Princess Sophia*. Acquired by Henry Clay Frick in 1918 as a work by John Hoppner. Oil on canvas, 36 ¼ x 23 ½ in. © the Collection of the Frick Art & Historical Center, Pittsburgh, Pennsylvania. Photo credit: Richard A. Stoner.

Meanwhile, father and daughter remained intensely involved in the effort to defeat Germany. Helen produced a short movie entitled *Home Fires* for distribution in the canteens abroad. Filmed by the well-known cinematographic photographer of birds and animals, Norman McClintock, the movie was intended to boost the morale of men in divisions from the North Shore with images of home: shots of school letting out in Manchester-by-the-Sea, a town near Eagle Rock; the Grand Army of the Republic veterans' parade in Beverly Farms honoring those who fought for the North in the Civil War; Myopia Hunt Club polo games, fox hunts, and golf tournaments; whippet racing; classes in surgical dressings, sock-knitting and canning; vignettes of tennis matches and horse shows—anything to remind the soldiers of home. After sponsoring a large benefit premiere on the lawn at Eagle Rock, Helen donated the proceeds and the film to the Red Cross for distribution.

Helen (front row, center) and members of the Red Cross Shop executive committee. Courtesy UPI/Corbis Bettman.

In addition, she continued her efforts with the Goodwill Section she had founded, this time by starting a Red Cross thrift shop in New York to raise money for convalescing soldiers. One of the first such stores established in New York, it was patterned after a $15,000-a-month enterprise for the Red Cross in Los Angeles, a model for other shops on the Pacific Coast. In private, however, Helen referred to her project as a "glorified rummage shop."

As president of this new venture, she believed she could do especially well if she could open in time for the Christmas shopping season. Determined and clever, she sent an appeal, designed like a court summons, to everyone she and her parents knew, demanding that "in the cause of humanity" all attics, basements, and closets be emptied of anything from antiques to furs, old lace, china, jewelry, paintings, tools, cigarette cases, and feathered fans, and be donated "to our great melting pot." The melting pot was a four-story brownstone at 587 Fifth Avenue, across the street from Cartier & Company. Owned by the estate of Louis T. Haggin, it was donated rent-free. Room after room displayed unique and unusual items, all fumigated as a precaution against the Spanish flu epidemic then raging in Europe and America. The "Bird Cage Tea Room" featured caged eagles and offered entertainment with music and drama. The poster room provided a slide show with pictures of the war and two large, vertical paintings by George W. Bellows, *Dawn of Peace* and *Hail to Peace,* donated by Bellows and specially commissioned by Helen through Duveen. On the second floor, a detective-protected front room called "Pandora's Box" was filled with $10,000 worth of Cartier jewelry secretly donated by Frick. Only one person at a time could enter this room, paneled by Duveen and painted in French gray to emulate the Louis XVI style. For a decorative touch, Duveen had included tapestries, a mantelpiece, and a marble bust.

Although Helen did most of the selling in the shop, she put her reclusive mother in charge of the jewelry. Helen advertised the sale of anything from "a dollar trinket to a diamond," but according to one newspaper, people were "more keen to see Mrs. Frick in person than to look at the diamonds." People were also curious about Helen. She had often been mentioned in the Pittsburgh papers and the *New York Times,* particularly in reference to her debutante party, Frick Park, the Iron Rail, and her service abroad. But Helen, who studiously avoided the press and the parade of society events, had rarely been seen in public.

George W. Bellows (1882–1925), *Dawn of Peace*. Commissioned by Helen in 1918 for the Red Cross Shop. Oil on canvas, 104 x 74 in. Courtesy Allentown Art Museum, Allentown, Pennsylvania. Gift of Estelle Reninger, 1990 (1990.15).

George W. Bellows (1882–1925), *Hail to Peace*. Commissioned by Helen in 1918 for the Red Cross Shop. Oil on canvas, 104 x 74 in. Courtesy Scott & White Hospital and Clinic, Temple, Texas.

Amidst much curiosity and fanfare, Helen's store opened just as she had hoped, during the first week of December 1918, three weeks after the Armistice. She planned to operate it for six months, until the start of the Iron Rail summer season. Right away the press understood that here was something unique in New York: an all-female-managed enterprise and one staffed entirely by "society" women.

On December 9, the *New York Sunday Herald* reported that Helen proudly gave her father a tour of the shop. Frick described the jewelry department "as 'perfect' and greatly admired a flexible bracelet of diamond and onyx and a sixteenth-century basket of crystal and gold." In addition, "he found the tea room superb, and the stock room with a system that leaves no room for improvement." Then, following an "inspection of the poster department," with never-before-seen war pictures continuously projected onto a movie screen, "Miss Frick smilingly requested her father to express his opinion. Pointing with his right forefinger he said: 'Those posters with the inscription *Give, Give, Give* should be made to read *Buy, Buy, Buy.*'"

The Red Cross Shop was a brilliant success. As profitable as the one in Los Angeles, the New York store took in $16,000 in its first three weeks. When Enrico Caruso and his bride patronized the shop, Mrs. Caruso was so impressed she unpinned her diamond and platinum brooch, put it in Helen's hands, and offered it for sale. Roland Knoedler also lent his support. His Paris office had watched over Helen during her tour in France, and after her return home, one of Knoedler's staff, Jules F. Lorin, tried to help the orphanage, failing from staffing problems and about close. Now, at the joint request of Frick and Helen, Knoedler mounted an exhibition by the artist John Elliott, known for his portraits in red chalk, pastels, and silver point, of distinguished Americans who lost their lives in the war. Frick purchased a portrait of his friend and general counsel to U.S. Steel, Colonel Raynal C. Bolling, who was the first officer of the Signal Corps, Aviation Section, to be killed in combat, and donated the work to the giant steel trust Bolling had served so well. Frick also bought a portrait of Norman Prince, a pilot friend of Childs's who had volunteered as an aviator in the service of the French army in 1915, and who was fatally wounded in an October 1916 air battle over southern Germany.

Helen (fifth lady from left) initiated Red Cross Shop bus tours of New York City for the wounded soldiers. Courtesy the Frick Collection/Frick Art Reference Library Archives.

The shop had yet another function, one that touched many veterans personally. Helen visited soldiers in the U.S. General Hospital in Colonia, New Jersey, and noticed the necklaces and bracelets the handicapped men were making as part of their occupational therapy. She gathered up the jewelry and sold it through the shop, returning all proceeds to the soldiers. In addition, she initiated educational Red Cross bus tours of New York, something she began with her True Blue girls in 1915 as a means to foster pride in America. Now she hoped that showing the city's historic monuments and buildings would give the wounded veterans "a true appreciation of the wonders of New York" and help them "cultivate," as was reported in the *Evening Mail,* "the spirit of respect for and appreciation of American ideals." Indeed, one unnamed soldier spoke to this spirit and bravely claimed, "I have not lost my leg, I merely swapped it for democracy."

Over the course of the next few months, busload after busload of veterans enjoyed these excursions. They started from Debarkation Hospital No. 5, formerly Grand Central Palace, and while a member of the Red Cross Shop spoke through a megaphone, the soldiers were shown the Bronx Zoo and Horticultural Gardens, the Soldiers' and Sailors' Monument, Grant's Tomb, the Brooklyn Bridge, the Woolworth Building, and the Battery. The Red Cross Shop paid all expenses, an average of $2,000 a week.

When the shop closed in May 1919, the *Evening Mail* reported that it had raised over $50,000, a significant financial boost to the rehabilitation of maimed and wounded men returning to the military hospitals of New York. The war had taken a devastating toll, with sixty-three out of every one hundred Allied soldiers killed. The staggering numbers—540,000 French and 430,000 German soldiers at Verdun, 60,000 British soldiers just in one day of fighting on the Somme, and 5 million civilians, remains without precedent.

Helen's desire to help ease the suffering profoundly moved Frick. During that month of May 1919, much was on his mind: a steel and coal miners' strike had idled four million workers; the Boston police were striking; the Eighteenth Amendment prohibiting the sale of alcohol had just passed, requiring the Overholt distillery to win a government contract so it could produce spirits for medicinal purposes and causing Frick to hoard his grandfather's elixir and store it by the hundreds of carloads in the Eagle Rock cellar. But Frick had also read that in New York the mayor's committee had declined to erect special viewing stands along Fifth Avenue for disabled veterans to view a parade of wounded soldiers. So Frick turned to his daughter. After he had ordered the construction of covered stands for five hundred disabled men along Fifth Avenue in One East Seventieth Street's garden, as well as a stand for nurses and war workers from the army hospital at Lexington Avenue and Forty-sixth Street, Helen wrote, "he asked me if I would make all arrangements for feeding the wounded soldiers." So she obliged, gathering up a number of her friends to serve the guests, including the soldiers' wives, mothers, girlfriends, and sisters, while her parents watched the event from the dining room.

All of this further intensified the father-daughter enmeshment. At Clayton that spring, when visiting with friends and learning that her father had arrived in Pittsburgh, Helen rushed to see him in Andrew Mellon's office. The two had hardly been separated, but she was thrilled to be back in his company. Thirty-year-old Helen remarked in her diary, "I sat on his lap & we talked a while, telling him about our visit." Later in the day, Frick seemed tired, so Helen kept him company when he took tea in bed. Later still, they had dinner at the Golf Club. "[We] went early, by way of the cemetery. Papsie picked a magnolia blossom from our garden & laid it tenderly on Martha's grave."

The pleasure they took in each other's company was palpable. Thus Helen did not mind terribly much when Dixie, pregnant with her fourth child and hopeful that this time they would finally welcome the son to bear Frick's name into the family, asked her father-in-law for a home of her own. She wanted a place where she could raise her children and Childs could pursue his scientific interests. Frick agreed, and so Helen, whose childbearing years were slipping away while she lived with her parents and to a large degree managed their houses, stood by and watched while Frick purchased the handsome estate of General Lloyd Bryce on Long Island for her sister-in-law, had it fully renovated by Sir Charles Allom and furnished with antiques, rugs, and porcelains. These included the Don Quixote tapestries, bought in Spain in 1909 with Helen at Frick's side, as well as six pieces from his important collection of sixteenth-century, French, carved walnut furniture.

On May 23, 1919, about two weeks after Frick delivered the Bryce estate deed to Dixie, and after Dixie renamed the property Clayton to honor her father-in-law, Frick surprised Helen. As they sat down to dinner one night, he presented her with a beautiful string of pearls. "My string of pearls, almost twice as long as it was before & oh, so beautiful!" Helen exclaimed. And with it came, she said, "the dearest little note. He wouldn't take the credit for it, but said it was all Mamma's idea (!)" Then Helen wrote fondly of how her father took the pearls and "clasped them around my neck in such a dear way."

In the aftermath of the Armistice and the eventual completion of her Red Cross duties, Helen had resumed her activity on the family art collection. On June 26, 1918, she noted that her father was "delighted over his purchase of 10 pictures for Eagle Rock from [the E. R.] Bacon Estate [and] said this was the best bargain he had ever made for that number of pictures." Since 1916, Frick had added fifteen paintings to the collection, including those from Bacon's estate—all of the highest quality and all consistent with his symbolic collecting pattern. When Knoedler sent Helen the information she had requested about the new pictures, she thanked him with a compliment: "The effect of the pictures up here is very attractive this year," she exclaimed, "& [it] shows what good taste you & I have!"

A few months later, on August 13, 1919, sixty-nine-year-old Frick bought what turned out to be his last painting, Johannes Vermeer's *Lady with a Letter* (now known as *Mistress and Maid*). So entranced was Frick by the picture—a scene that may have recalled his desperate correspondence with Adelaide when Martha was dying at the Mountain House—he changed his seat at the table so he could look at it during his meals. When in the fall the Fricks returned to One East Seventieth Street with their paintings, Frick showed the Vermeer to a friend, and said of his museum to be: "I can only hope that the public will get one-half the pleasure that has been offered me in enjoyment of these masterpieces in proper surroundings. I want this collection to be my monument."

Hypervigilant, Helen watched over her father obsessively. His health was her greatest concern. One July midnight when Frick left Eagle Rock for New York, she grew alarmed because he was leaving without a coat and might catch cold. So when the chauffeur, George Dupres, started to drive off, he "went down [the] drive very slowly & gave me time to run after the car & throw the coat through the window." Helen wrote that she "threw it three times & each time Papsie threw it out onto the drive. The third time he ordered George to put on speed!" Sure enough, her father left Eagle Rock as he wished, coatless.

Johannes Vermeer (1632–1675), *Mistress and Maid.* Acquired by Henry Clay Frick in 1919. Oil on canvas, 35 ½ x 31 in. © the Frick Collection, New York.

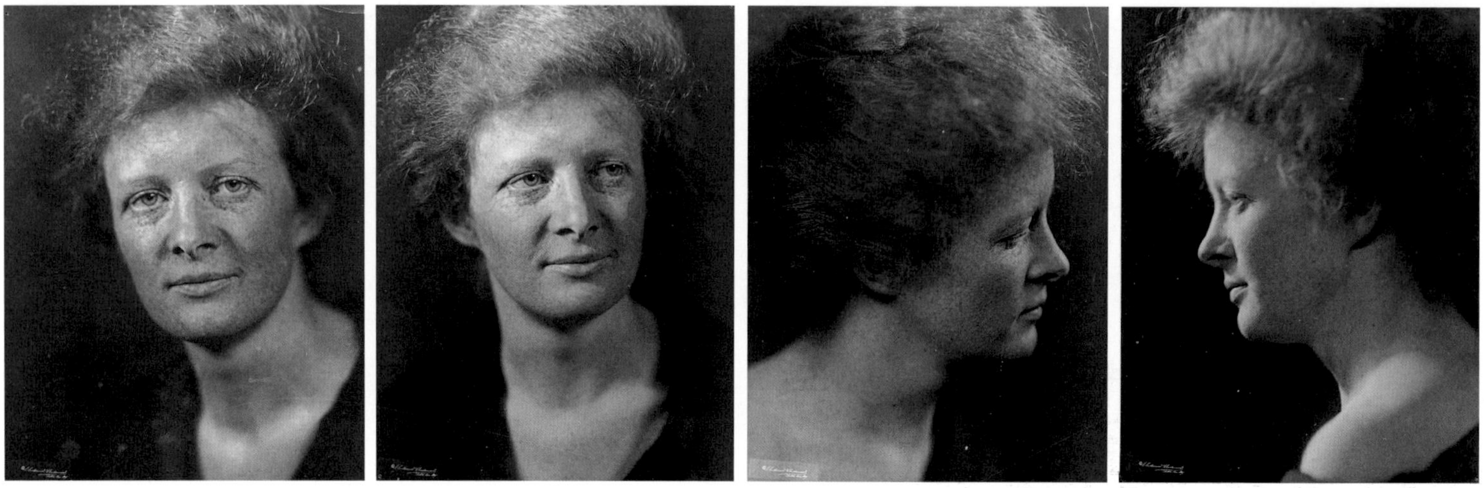

Photograph studies of thirty-year-old Helen for an intended portrait bust by Malvina Hoffman. Courtesy Research Library, The Getty Research Institute, Los Angeles.

In early October 1919, Helen's parents left Eagle Rock for winter in New York, but Helen remained behind for a few days to entertain her good friend, the American sculptor, Malvina Hoffman, who was executing Helen's portrait bust. The evening of October 18, Helen heard from her parents that earlier in the afternoon Dixie had delivered her fourth child, the long-looked-for son, Henry Clay Frick II.

When Helen returned to One East Seventieth Street on November 3, 1919, although she was anxious to see little Henry Clay Frick II, she delayed her visit. Tired and feeling unwell, she sat with her father while he had a massage and the two talked of her trip down to New York. The next morning, Frick announced that he was hosting an important luncheon the following day with a number of other prominent conservative isolationists. When Helen asked her father if he would like her to look over the menu, Frick replied that he had already "ordered the lunch," including a lobster entrée. Aghast because lobster traditionally made her father ill, Helen said she "begged him not to take that as it never agreed [with him]." Frick refused to change the menu, saying firmly: "It agrees with me perfectly now." According to her diary, Helen "still felt dubious," but went to the Garden City Hotel to visit Dixie, Childs, her two eldest nieces, and baby Clay. Two-year-old Martha was staying at One East Seventieth Street with her grandparents while her family awaited the move to their new house.

That evening, after dining with her parents, Helen complained of being tired, and announced that she "thought [she] would go to bed." As she described the scene, "Papsie was reading the papers, seated in the big chair by the table at the right of the sofa in the living hall. Mamma was playing solitaire on the other side. He asked me if I would wait for him. Mamma said, 'Oh let her go up, she's so tired.' Simultaneously with me, Papa spoke & said 'Let her answer for herself' & I said 'of course I'll wait' & went over and sat on the arm of his chair." When Frick finished reading, Helen commented: "Arm in arm, we went out of the room."

In the front hall, Frick faltered and "confessed the lobster must have disagreed with him & he felt swollen." Panicked, Helen "dashed upstairs for aromatic spirits of Ammonia, & after taking some, he said it had helped him very much." The following morning, Frick "felt better but [was] quite weak." He met with principals of the Atchison Railway and seemed "very chatty over lunch with Col. [George] Harvey." Frick in fact was so animated he managed to direct a cutting remark at Adelaide, on the controversial topic of woman suffrage, now making its way through the states' ratification process. As Helen recounted the conversation, her mother, pleased with the progress of the amendment, "said something about 'women having come into their own.'" When Helen asked her "what she meant by that," Adelaide "did not answer the question very directly." So Frick scowled, "You have not answered Helen's question about what you mean when you say 'come into their own.'" And then, laughing heartily about Dixie, busy nursing his namesake and raising his little granddaughters, he exclaimed: "Now Frances is a woman who has come into her own."

Over the next week, Frick's health did not improve, so Helen stayed close, noting in a diary the details of his condition. She overheard him confess to a friend, when walking from the living hall to the dining room for lunch, "he could not bear being an invalid—that he would rather not live if he couldn't do things." On November 10, a cold and windy day, Frick, already battling laryngitis, left the house to lunch with friends, refusing to wear an overcoat. Not as lucky as he had been before, this time his cold worsened. That night and into the next day, "he coughed a great deal." Frick's valet, Oscar Rodgers, agreed to stay up nights and watch him and Helen, increasingly concerned, summoned Dr. Garmany, Frick's long-time physician, and a Dr. Evans.

Evans believed Frick had a heart blockage, but he was hopeful, as Helen noted: "With great care Papa could get along with it probably for ten years." And with her Red Cross training, Helen was certain she could manage her father's medical care. Anyway, Helen was the only one available. Adelaide, always fragile, was more so under the strain of her husband's illness and had taken to her bed with a cold and Childs and Dixie were busy with the new house in Long Island and the new baby.

Helen remarked later that she so feared the death of her father that "a terror" would seize her when he talked about the possibility. Yet, she confessed, her panic and alarm "rather encouraged him to continue the subject." Indeed, Frick stoked her fear by his frequent talk of death and dying. At other times Frick was upbeat about his health and raised Helen's spirits by announcing that he could "live to be ninety or a hundred," although he would add quickly that he was "ready to go any time." Sometimes Frick said he had but one wish: to "go to sleep and never wake up" and then brought up the subject of his funeral plans, probably, as Helen believed, to make her mad—"to get a rise out of her." These conversations always ended at an impasse, with Helen doing her best to change the subject and Frick complaining to Adelaide: "I wish Helen would let me talk about things sensibly—but she won't hear of it." His statement was accurate. Helen explained, "I never gave him the comfort of discussing the plans he wished to make for the future, because I could not bear to visualize what life would be without him."

The reality of Frick's condition threw Helen into frenzied action. She hired nurses, made appointments with doctors, ordered his meals, studied the nurses' charts. The day Evans gave his diagnosis she presented her father with pink roses and attached a card inscribed "From Your Best Girl." Warmed by her gesture and by her continued devotion Frick replied, "You are that." The following morning, she called in a Dr. Lewis to examine her father's sore throat.

Childs visited his bedridden father and, realizing how serious his situation was, promised to bring the grandchildren for a visit. On November 14, Frick remained in bed but asked frequently when the children were coming. The two eldest, four-year-old Adelaide and three-year-old Frances, finally arrived late in the afternoon and presented him with flowers they had picked. Helen described the tender moment when young Adelaide "made a little speech all in one breath 'Grandfather we have brought these flowers for you & we're so sorry you are sick & I'll hope you'll be much better next time.'"

The library at One East Seventieth Street where, shortly before his death, Henry Clay Frick rested on the sofa beneath William Hogarth's *Miss Mary Edwards*. Author's collection.

The following day Dixie came to visit. Frick had endured a sleepless night, but according to Helen, his charming daughter-in-law made him feel marvelous. "You certainly are a remarkable person to have such a poor night & to look so well," she said as Frick smiled back at her. Dixie remained "for some time," and the two "talked about opera tickets, the children, the new house." But flattery was useless. Frick was experiencing heart failure, and his organs had started to retain fluid and swell.

With her father declining before her eyes, Helen summoned yet another physician, a Dr. Bachman, to give her father a throat treatment. Pleased and satisfied to have eased Frick's discomfort, Helen said her father "remarked on how much good it had done him." Keeping the patient quiet and amused, however, was challenging. Not used to confinement, his mood swung from congenial to cross. Little Martha came to his room often, and Helen bought what she described as "some funny Victor records" for him to hear. Indeed Frick enjoyed his tiny granddaughter and "laughed quite heartily over some of the stories [on the record player]." But even laughter had become difficult and painful. His cough was worse and he now "coughed . . . quite badly."

On November 19, Frick was able to venture downstairs and sit with his pictures, the first time since falling ill. He stretched out on the sofa in the library, as a fire blazed beneath Hogarth's portrait of Miss Mary Edwards. His friends J. P. Grier and Judge Elbert Gary of U.S. Steel came and went, but the person Frick seemed most interested in was Dixie. During her visit Frick fell in and out of sleep, asked Dixie about the grandchildren and their new governess, Annie, and mumbled, "Are you still there Frances?" Then, realizing he was drifting off he apologized and said he hoped she didn't mind his sleeping and asked her to stay with him.

Two days later, on November 21, Dr. Evans pronounced Frick well enough to take an outing, perhaps an hour's drive around Central Park. Although Frick must have been pleased, Helen was leery. "We were all nervous because he was very independent & it looked doubtful as to whether any of us would be allowed to go along—& he was too weak to go alone." So Helen, Oscar, and the nurses readied themselves, just "in case he should call on one of us." To her relief, Frick did ask Helen and Oscar to join him. Then suddenly he asked her: "Did you tell George where to go?" Helen replied that George already knew, "To the Park." "No, not to the Park," snapped Frick, "to Westbury [Roslyn]." Helen wrote, "I grew so frightened & implored him not to do such a rash thing." But Frick was adamant. "Papa told me to obey his orders or get out of the car—so I complied [but] only begged to stop [back] at the house for a moment." He relented, saying "Very well," and they returned to One East Seventieth Street for a minute or two. While her father waited, Helen called for the nurse and told her to follow them in Helen's car with her father's various medicines and to stay "out of sight."

Feeling more secure now, Helen jumped back in with her father. The ride out to Roslyn, Long Island "was full of anxiety to me . . . & it all seemed such a terrible risk. . . . We talked very little & he dozed frequently." Forty-five minutes later, when they arrived at the house, there was her car—the one with Miss Reid in it. Helen had a momentary panic, but fortunately "Papa never suspected." Indeed, he never noticed. He was too intent on watching the grandchildren playing outside and was delighted at having surprised Dixie with his visit.

"Papa walked up the steps into the front hall & sat down looking so tired & pale." Helen wanted to revive him with a drink of whiskey from a flask she carried for him, but Frick refused. Young Adelaide, however, had better success. With all the skill she would later display as a pediatrician coaxing medication down a child's throat, she pleaded sweetly, "Grandfather won't you take your medicine for me?" To Helen's amazement "he drank it all."

Then infant Henry Clay Frick II was brought downstairs and Martha, back home now, entered with her sister Frances. Frick said happily to Dixie, "At last you have your wish. You have all four together." As they roughhoused with their aunt on the floor, Frick said slyly to Helen, whom he had secretly chosen in 1915 as the chief beneficiary of his estate not left to charity, "They'd better be nice to their rich old aunt."

After lunch, Frick departed for New York. Once more Helen became agitated about Miss Reid being discovered. "On the return trip I was so scared that Papa would look back & see the car, but we got back to the house & were sitting in the front vestibule as Miss Reid arrived." Her father looked puzzled, but Helen quickly explained that the nurse, with her afternoon free, had merely been out for a drive. Frick never guessed the truth and went straight to bed.

Front entrance to Childs's and Dixie's new house, Clayton, at Roslyn, Long Island. Author's collection.

That night, Frick tossed and turned, partly because of the edema in his lungs, partly because something was evidently troubling him. Awake before dawn, he dozed first on the sofa in his sitting room and then downstairs in the library. Obviously upset now, he took breakfast in the library at nine o'clock and afterward called his friend, the railroad attorney, Victor Morawetz. Since the summer Morawetz, an expert in contract law, the U.S. monetary system, and the law of private corporations, had been advising Frick on the merits of incorporating his paintings to avoid taxation should his collection be refused as a gift to the public upon his death. Heretofore Helen was to be his primary monetary beneficiary and recipient of his paintings should they be rejected as a public gift. After seeing his four grandchildren in the new house, however, Frick apparently changed his mind and wanted Morawetz to redraft his will, making Childs, not Helen, head of the family. But Morawetz was out of town, so Frick left a message, and with the phone call his spirits seemed to improve. He announced to his nurse that he "had the upper hand with his illness." This time Frick was completely wrong.

For the next three days Frick suffered, and Helen recorded that her father was "very miserable & short of breath." Then one Sunday afternoon, he felt strong enough to walk unaided around the West Gallery. Knowing the restorative quality the paintings had for him, Helen said she toured the gallery with "Papa . . . carrying [his] blue silk comforter himself." When father and daughter reached the Limoges Room, they "drew chairs up to the window on [the] Fifth Ave. side & looked out at the Sunday strollers." Even in his weakened state, Frick had not lost his keen powers of observation. He particularly "noticed the funny walks people had & how traffic comes in bunches." On their way back through the gallery, however, he remarked wistfully: "It's strange how when you get a fine collection, it becomes ordinary to you."

A frightened Helen was incensed that Dr. Evans had not come to see her father in three days. She referred to the doctor as "indifferent" and, having already dismissed Garmany for what she considered ineptitude, ordered up an entirely new medical team. Frick was bewildered when presented with yet another new doctor, but Helen coaxed him along. This one, Lewis A. Conner, gave Frick a complete examination, advised him against eating his usual meals and instead put him on a liquid diet.

On November 25, Frick seemed better. He greeted some visitors, and although he lost a few games of Russian Bank to Grier, his sense of humor was sharp as ever. When Frick sent Oscar upstairs for his wallet, Grier said not to bother because Frick "couldn't afford to lose $34 as he was not making money these days." According to Helen, "Papsie's eyes twinkled & he said 'That's the very reason why I can afford it, because I'm not losing at the club. I'm saving money staying in.'"

Around 6:30 that evening, Helen checked on her father, in bed reading the papers. Content that he was "looking bright & well," she nevertheless felt uneasy and canceled a dinner engagement. Just as she hung up the phone, he "uttered a sharp cry of pain." The nurse ran into Frick's bedroom and Helen telephoned the doctor. By the time Dr. Conner arrived, Frick was feeling better, but "he was so fearful of a return of the pain," the doctor gave him a shot of morphine.

During the night Frick slept well for the first time in three weeks, and in the morning a Dr. Partridge, urged upon Frick by Dr. Conner, called. As Helen described the scene, Partridge "took records from his temple beats of his circulation [and] Papa was interested in the up to date method." Yet he did not entirely trust this doctor and kept asking for Garmany. Helen relented and told her father she would have him come "if it would give him any comfort." She was determined, however, to keep the serious nature of his condition from him. She instructed the nurse to keep Garmany from talking professionally to her father while Frick, suspecting just such a manipulation, insisted on seeing Garmany alone, without Helen or the nurse in his room. But when the doctor left, Frick said to Oscar, "G's a damn fool—throw all his medicines out of the window." Helen "didn't know what to think!" particularly since Frick immediately demanded the nurse tell him what his pulse rate and temperature were. The nurse, afraid that Garmany had told him something different than what she was instructed to say, pronounced that his pulse was 58 and his temperature normal. Helen was afraid to go into her father's room. "Finally Papsie sent for me & in the gentlest way asked if I had written G. to discharge him. I said yes & explained that G. had not been on the job & was not up to date & I wanted him to have the best." Frick replied, "You did quite right. G. is a fool. He told me my pulse was 42 . . . [and] also said I had 99 temp. . . . I never want to see him again. He's a bad number." Helen noted: "We felt our lucky star had been with us this time." But from now on, if she wanted to withhold information from her father, she would have to be clever. Frick was asking repeatedly to have his pulse and temperature taken, and as Helen said, "it made us so anxious for fear he might learn the truth, become thereby discouraged & lose faith in us."

When bedridden Henry Clay Frick entered his fatal decline, he turned to look at Sir Thomas Lawrence's *Miss Louisa Murray* (above) and George Romney's *Lady Hamilton* (below), portraits that recalled his lost child, Martha. Author's collection.

November 27, Thanksgiving Day, broke the tension in the sickroom. The grandchildren were coming for lunch, even though Frick's condition, now diagnosed as pleurisy, would require him to be quiet. Unbeknownst to Helen, who waited for the children downstairs "to keep them quiet for Papsie seemed so weak & tired," Frick was out of bed, fully dressed, and getting into the elevator long before the nurses had any idea what he was doing. "It broke us all up," wrote Helen, "to run such risk of catching more cold & we all flew in different directions to light the fires downstairs." Frick settled into an armchair by the library window overlooking Fifth Avenue. Young Frances came in and sat on his lap and then little Adelaide arrived, accompanied by Dixie. Frick, still concerned that he was not being told the truth about his condition, spoke to his daughter-in-law about his pulse and tested her saying "if his pulse was as he was told, a little exertion shouldn't be bad for him." He continued, "You don't suppose they are trying to deceive a man of my common sense?" Then, after telling her he had dismissed Garmany, he confided, "You know Frances you & I are the only ones in the family that have commonsense. They are all nice, but they are so fussy."

Helen and the nurses may have been fussy, but they were adept at keeping their secret. At two o'clock, when Frick went back upstairs, Helen recorded that "his pulse was 10 beats faster from the exertion & he seemed exhausted." She said he also suffered "a terrible night." Perspiring "a great deal," he sat at the front of his bed, facing the Martha look-alike,

Romney's *Lady Hamilton as 'Nature.'* Back in bed, he turned on his side to face his other Martha look-alike, Sir Thomas Lawrence's *Miss Louisa Murray.*

Afraid the end was near, Helen called Malvina Hoffman and asked her to make a drawing of her father while he rested. By now, the vicious cycle of heart failure was entrenched. Frick's weakened heart pumped harder and harder, but moved less and less blood through his circulatory system. The steel-master was at once suffocating and drowning. Nevertheless, over the next few days he fought back and continued to read his papers, tend to business matters, receive visitors, play checkers, and beat Helen at Russian Bank, quite soundly in fact. He listened intently as she read him stories and read the books she gave him, but he was uncomfortable.

On November 29, Frick asked Duveen, who owed his bankers almost $20 million, to collect works of art he had sent to Frick on approval, worth approximately $1.5 million. A van arrived under armed guard, and the rejected items were removed. Having literally cleaned house but anxious about how the collection looked, Frick, who continued to toss and turn, first looking at *Lady Hamilton* and then at *Miss Louisa Murray,* asked Helen to go and "look around & report to him how the rooms looked without the Duveen articles." Helen assured him the collection was as fine as ever.

Malvina Hoffman, Henry Clay Frick on his deathbed, November 1919, commissioned by Helen Clay Frick. Courtesy the Research Library, The Getty Research Institute, Los Angeles.

On December 1, 1919, though restless and very uncomfortable, Frick spent the day reading his papers and questioning Bridge about the November 1920 presidential election. He also seemed to know he was dying. He spoke of a "premonition of a tragic outcome of his indisposition." At ten minutes after midnight Frick called for Oscar and complained, "Oh, if I could only sleep." So Oscar gave him the sleeping tonic the nurse had ordered. Later, about five o'clock in the morning, Frick called out again, this time for a glass of water. He drank it down and fell asleep, this time forever. Henry Clay Frick died at 5:15 a.m., Tuesday, December 2, 1919.

The one thing thirty-one-year-old Helen Frick most feared had now happened. She again called Malvina Hoffman, this time to have her make deathbed studies of her father before the undertakers took his body to the funeral home. Having denied the possibility of her father's death and having refused to listen to his funeral plans, Helen was utterly devastated and forced to face them all. After a small viewing at One East Seventieth Street, the coffin was placed in the "Westmoreland," his private railroad car, and taken on the ceremonial trip back to Pittsburgh, stopping in Harrisburg, Altoona, Cresson Springs, and Johnstown, with an entourage of one hundred family and friends. A service was held at Clayton, and on December 5, Frick's remains were buried in Homewood Cemetery beside his children.

Frick's will made Helen America's wealthiest unmarried woman. Without husband, children, or a home of her own, and five years younger than her brother, who had fathered the heir to carry forward their father's legacy, she, not Childs, received the lion's share: $5 million outright; thirteen of the one hundred shares in her father's residual estate; title to

Eagle Rock and its contents on her mother's death, including the Westmoreland railroad car; $1 million for upkeep of the Frick Building valued at $12 million and owned by her since 1901; One East Seventieth Street, together with her father's entire art collection and its $15 million endowment, should the city of New York not accept it as a museum; any other bequests to charity not accepted; the entire Iron Rail property; and an extra $200,000 to "enable her to make effective certain of [her father's] wishes that are known to her."

By comparison, sixty-year-old Adelaide and thirty-six-year-old Childs were shortchanged. Adelaide retained life tenancy of One East Seventieth Street and Eagle Rock; became, like Helen, a trustee of the art collection; and received $1 million outright and $5 million in trust, an amount far below her legal right to a widow's dower of $68 million on an estate worth nearly $200 million. Childs, though also a trustee of the collection, received little in the way of a monetary bequest: $1 million outright and $2 million in trust. Dixie also received far less than anticipated. Under the will she received $2 million in trust. True, there was great value in their house, fully furnished, and Childs now assumed his father's position as director and trustee of many institutions; still as his father's only son and elder child, the arrangement was paltry and clearly humiliating and it precipitated a heightened level of animosity between brother and sister.

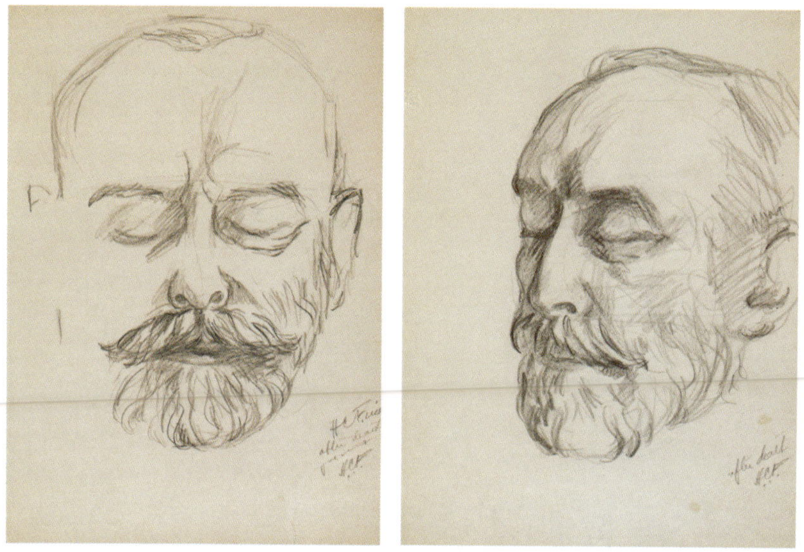

Malvina Hoffman, Henry Clay Frick after death, commissioned by Helen Clay Frick. Courtesy the Research Library, The Getty Research Institute, Los Angeles.

But this will had not always been the dead patriarch's intent. Toward the end of February 1913, just before Childs's engagement was announced, Frick had executed a will drafted by William Watson Smith, thought to have bestowed the larger portion of his fortune on his son. Two years later, although Frick continued to support Childs's scientific pursuits, finance his expeditions, and, as a trustee of the American Museum of Natural History, continued to give donations to the museum, his old antagonisms toward and disappointment in his unconventional son had again surfaced. Childs's poor showing in business matters and his lack of involvement in the war effort could not be denied. Helen seemed the more sober, capable child, particularly since her interests—in art and philanthropy—were his and furthered his own agenda. Therefore, unbeknownst to Smith, on June 24, 1915, Frick executed a second will, drawn by another of his attorneys, Lewis Cass Ledyard, in favor of Helen. Four years later, on November 22, 1919, after his visit with Dixie and the grandchildren, Frick had some misgivings about leaving so little to Childs and Dixie: hence his instructions for Morawetz to draft a new will, reinstating Childs as his principal heir.

According to family members, Frick advised Childs of this plan but died before the new instrument could be executed. The 1915 will in favor of Helen stood. Some of the press coverage must have been painful for Childs. One paper from Connellsville, Pennsylvania, near Frick's hometown of West Overton, said Frick's will "indicate[s] his appreciation of the ability and judgment of Miss Frick, his only daughter." It also credited Helen as responsible for her father's extraordinary nonsectarian generosity to the public, citing his bequests to hospitals, the Salvation Army, Harvard, Princeton, MIT, the YWCA, the News Boys' Home, the Kingsley House Association, and the Henry Clay Frick Teachers Fund: "Much of the interest of Henry Clay Frick in the institutions remembered in his will is attributed to his daughter. . . . Her wide knowledge and social work . . . is believed to have been of assistance to her father in choosing objects for his bounty."

The will was, in fact, unusual for its public generosity. According to an unidentified news article, his was "the largest single testamentary benefaction to public welfare ever made." A family friend, Hilaire S. Dean, agreed: "It so surpasses any other comparable will, in its noble humanitarian spirit, its wise generosity, and total freedom from the old standards of narrow selfish family inheritance that really. . . . this will of your father's has set a new standard."

Childs and Dixie, already envious, were now forced to accept the terms of the will. Immediately suspicious, they cornered Helen in private and accused her of killing her father. According to family members in whom Helen later confided, when Frick awoke early on the morning of December 2, he had not asked for a glass of water but for a dose of the sleeping draft, although he had already had one that night. Helen, not the nurse, answered the call, and administered what may have been the fatal second dose. There was, however, never a formal investigation.

Although Frick's will offered some guidance as to how Helen should make use of her fortune, its language should have set her free: "All amounts which I thus give to my said daughter . . . are given to her in absolute and unqualified ownership." It continued: "It would, nevertheless, be agreeable to me that she so dispose of these amounts that my general purpose in making these legacies should be accomplished; but this is merely the expression of my wish, and shall not be construed to impose upon my said daughter any duty or obligation, legal, equitable, or moral, nor in any manner to qualify or affect her absolute ownership of the amounts thus bequeathed to her."

Helen could never abandon her father, his memory, or the responsibilities of his legacy, although other heiresses of her day had done just that. When Barbara Hutton was just seven years old she inherited $25 million from her Woolworth grandfather, and Doris Duke, the only daughter of tobacco tycoon Buck Duke, was worth $100 million at birth in 1912. Both women squandered their inheritances and destroyed their reputations and health through ill-fated marriages and alcoholism. Other heiresses who struck an independent course were Electra Havemeyer, who inherited $4 million on her father's death in 1907; twenty-seven-year-old Marjorie Merriweather Post, who was still a teenager when she inherited the Postum Cereal Company (later known as the General Foods Corporation) from her father Charles William Post; and Ima Hogg, the only daughter of the late governor of Texas, James Stephen Hogg, who shared with her brothers the bounty of an oil strike bringing in an estimated gross daily income of $250,000. Twenty-one-year-old Peggy Guggenheim, who came into a $450,000 inheritance from her father in 1919, in an act of rebellion against her bourgeois origins, left New York for Paris and lived a flamboyant life among the avant-garde. But for Helen Frick, the mantle had been passed to her as neatly as if her father had stood behind her and clasped it about her neck, just as he once had clasped her pearl necklace, "in the sweetest way."

Although Helen in 1919 in some ways still exemplified the "New Woman"—single, educated, and economically independent—she was also conservative by temperament and upbringing. Now she prepared to take her seat on the board of the Frick Collection, composed of all men, save herself and her mother, men who perceived her as a threat. What Newton D. Baker, head of the New York Consumers' League, wrote about the activist Florence Kelly, was equally true about Helen Frick: she was "dangerous in the sense that she knew what she was talking about."

Westmoreland Farm in springtime. Courtesy Smithsonian Institution, Archives of American Gardens, Garden Club of America Collection, Washington, D.C.

Helen moved her father's bed to her bedroom, and then struck out beyond the walls of her family residence. She purchased the tract of land in Bedford Village, New York, and named her first home Westmoreland Farm after the county of her father's birth. While fashioning a new life for herself, she remained bound to her father, oblivious to the warning signs of what was in store: Childs lay in wait, as did the male trustees of her father's collection, who now sought to dominate her. Each had his particular bias and agenda, emboldened by envy and suspicion of this wealthy thirty-one-year-old maiden lady who had been given a voice she intended to use.

1920–1931

The Family Claim

Daughter is not a lifelong assignment.

—Shirley Abbott

During her father's lifetime, Helen Frick had in many ways remained a small child, taking her limited, first steps and then running back to the shelter of her father. Now he was gone, and her mother continued to be passive and reclusive. Adelaide Frick seldom removed her widow's weeds, and even though the women's movement was successful at winning suffrage in 1920, she never voted. Chronically ill, she looked to her daughter to care for her.

Helen, on the other hand, relished having a voice in the national agenda. A die-hard Republican like her father, she never missed casting her vote in Pittsburgh. And she assumed the responsibility of looking after her dependent mother. For Helen, a bold break from Adelaide was unimaginable. She had inherited her mother, along with everything else. At no time did she expect or ask Childs to share in that obligation.

The psychiatrist Marion Woodman says that when a father-bound daughter reaches maturity she "considers her creative ability to be the destiny her father bestowed upon her and affirms her positive relationship to him." Indeed, Helen Frick now believed herself to be the chosen guardian of her father's reputation and legacy, and thus began a decade-long effort, not to culminate until after Adelaide's death, of training herself in museum management for the moment when the New York residence would become the Frick Collection.

In the years after Frick's death Helen poured herself unreservedly into her new duties with a ferocious, obsessive passion that also blinded her to the considerable obstacles in her path. Chief among these was her brother Childs, who remained angry that his share of Henry Clay Frick's estate had been comparatively slight and was smarting over the public implications of his rejection in favor of his unmarried, younger sister. Childs's pain prevented him from seeing Helen's entrapment, or from understanding that Helen's favored position was the result of their father's abuse of power, not, as he construed it, due to her hijacking of parental affection.

Adelaide Frick continued to wear black, or "widow's weeds," after Frick's death. Here, she holds her dogs in a photograph taken by Helen at Westmoreland Farm. Courtesy the Frick Collection/Frick Art Reference Library Archives.

Opposite: Helen's library at One East Seventieth Street. The portrait of Henry Clay Frick may be the one by Sir William Orpen. Courtesy the Frick Collection/Frick Art Reference Library Archives.

The first thing Helen did in her new role was to assume use of Frick's checks, the ones engraved with Martha's likeness that he had used since 1892, for her charitable donations. As she got to work, she asked her first cousin, Karl Overholt, who ran the family office in the Frick Building, to provide her with a list of the donations her father had made to various churches in the last five years so she could match them. And then, driven perhaps by anxiety over her part in her father's death, she advised Overholt: "I would like to personally settle the bills for doctors' services rendered Papa during his illness, even if the Estate settled them," adding, "This would mean a great deal to me." With permission granted, Helen reimbursed her father's estate for the full amount of more than $11,000.

Helen traveling in Europe in 1920 to further research her father's collection, study museum management, and survey the devastation from the war. Courtesy the Frick Collection/Frick Art Reference Library Archives.

Now she turned to the Iron Rail. Since her father had largely financed her beloved institution out-of-pocket, she incorporated it as a Pennsylvania nonprofit organization with herself, her mother, her Pittsburgh friend Elizabeth Holmes, Karl Overholt, and a bookkeeper, William Naughton of the Union Trust, as directors. On April 24, 1920, Helen invited the True Blue girls to One East Seventieth Street to see the art collection and gain a further understanding of the man who had financed their vacation home and given her the wherewithal to guarantee its future. A month later, following a visit to Frick's birthplace in West Overton, Pennsylvania, Helen took other immediate measures to ensure the preservation and promotion of her father's legacy by engaging his friend George Harvey to write his biography.

Then on May 15, 1920, Helen Frick left her widowed mother behind at Eagle Rock, in the care of a companion, and sailed on the *Celtic* for a six-month tour of Europe. Only the second time she had traveled abroad without one of her parents, she boarded the ship with a maid and Karl Overholt for companionship. Her plans were both extensive and ambitious. In England, her first stop, she hoped to further research her father's art collection by visiting the houses where many of those paintings once resided. As a trustee of the Frick Collection, Helen also wanted to educate herself about museum management. Well-organized and determined, she had letters of introduction from Knoedler to various private collections and to the directors of museums and historic houses who could discuss their organizations' rules, regulations, and policies. Following that, Helen planned to trace the path of the Great War through the devastated areas of France and Belgium, a retrospective and valedictory journey back into an experience that had been so personally significant.

Helen arrived in London on May 24 and began her quest. Keith Merrill, Helen's friend from the North Shore and now the American consul in London, gave her an introduction to Sir Robert Witt, secretary of the National Gallery of Art, whose Library of Reproductions Helen was eager to see. Over the last ten years, Sir Robert and his wife had collected postcards of important paintings throughout Europe and had filed them systematically in alphabetized boxes. Until then, according to Katharine McCook Knox, Helen's school friend who later wrote *The Frick Art Reference Library: The Early Years,* "much unnecessary time was . . . lost by scholars, critics, writers, collectors, dealers . . . owing to the available material being scattered and to a great extent unorganized." The Witt collection was thus pioneering, a critically important resource to collectors and to scholars of art history, then only in its second decade as a popular branch of study. When Helen asked if she could call,

Sir Robert's wife, Mary, who was curious about the wealthy Frick heiress, replied, "How pleased we should be to see you. . . . [and] talk over the question of private collections, as my husband will be at home, & so glad to help you."

On May 30, 1920, when Helen entered the Witts' house on Portman Square, Knox later reported, "Her breath was almost taken away. All around her and far as the eye could reach in the large bright and airy rooms were shelves upon shelves filled with boxes containing photographs and reproductions of all kinds." Over 8,000 European artists from the thirteenth century to the mid-nineteenth century were represented by 150,000 reproductions, mostly postcards and photographs, with the work of another 5,000 artists and another 100,000 images soon to be entered.

Helen wasted no time asking Witt: "May I copy-cat your Library?" Witt was overjoyed at the prospect of having his life's work duplicated in America and replied: "Of course you may and shall. Not only that, but I will gladly help you to make an even better Library than this one of mine." According to Knox, "That night Miss Frick was sleepless. Kaleidoscopic visions took over. . . . the U.S.A. would have, in memory of Henry Clay Frick, a Frick Art Reference Library, founded by his daughter." At the time, there was little, if any, benefaction of art scholarship in America.

Sailing on June 15 from Dover to Calais on the brand new channel boat, *Maid of Orleans,* still accompanied by her maid and Karl Overholt, Helen traveled by train through the devastated French countryside toward Paris, more determined than ever to create in America a record of the great art produced by Western culture. Helen's friends Mary Dilworth, Margaret Barr, and Gertrude Hill joined her in Paris, and on June 19 she attended a gathering of "eminent Frenchmen to discuss their construction of devastated regions." Helen and her party traveled east, finding towns "badly shot up." She paused at the Marne "to see [the] valley which separated [the] enemy from [the] Allies," and at the Belleau Wood where 2,500 soldiers were buried. Shattered by the destruction at Reims, Helen "visited the Cathedral & the remains of the principal streets—all unspeakably sad & dreadful."

The horrible toll war had taken on French culture and the chilling lack of moral conduct and conscience by the enemy became still clearer to Helen as she traveled north to Berry-au-Bac, the Chemin des Dames, Fismes, and northwest to the ruined cathedral at Soissons and the Forest of Compiègne, where the Armistice was signed only a year and a half before. As she traveled she visited some of her former refugee "families," back home at last, before she returned to Paris.

On page after page of her diary, Helen painstakingly arranged postcards and photographs of the devastated towns she visited, showing their condition before the war and after it. Clearly she was not merely creating a souvenir snapshot album. She was accumulating evidence, documenting the consequences of a war where the survival of civilization itself had been at stake. Blind to the fact that British, French, and later American bombs also caused damage and death, Helen blamed only the Germans; they had been the aggressors. To her, in a conviction that would coalesce and strengthen on this journey and then harden over the next years and decades, the Germans were a cruel and heartless people who deserved to be distrusted, boycotted, disarmed, fined, and unilaterally rejected by the civilization it had almost destroyed. There was no telling when or if Germany might again rape Europe, its people, and its art. But if that should happen, the art history library she envisioned could at least preserve the memory of what had been. Like Witt's library, hers would have a photographic record of every work of art in Europe and the British Isles, and also in America.

St. Quentin before and after World War I. Courtesy the Frick Collection/Frick Art Reference Library Archives.

On July 10, Helen "visited Papsie's portrait"—checking in on the progress Sir William Orpen was making. She was pleased with what she saw. Not surprisingly, however, seeing her father's likeness, when he had been gone for only seven months, was a jolt. When in England, Helen had complained of being sick in bed with headaches and of being "dead tired"; now she confessed that after seeing Frick's portrait she "was very sick at [her] stomach [the] rest of [the] day."

Her spirits lifted in the morning when the conservator of paintings at the Louvre, Jules Guiffrey, showed her the Gallery of Paintings. But later, at the Château de Chantilly, the headaches returned. "Monsieur Maçon," explained Helen, "told us, vividly, about the fateful night of September 4, 1914, when Germans slept there and quartered their horses in the great art gallery. Miraculously, he had time to remove most of the paintings from the lower rows and had protected the floor with hay."

As her conviction about Germans intensified, Helen traveled to Bourg, site of her wartime service. Happy to be back in her hamlet, she penned in her album-diary "Home Again. . . . Reach our dear little Bourg at 4:45—so natural to be back! . . . I have same old room at Hotel de l'Europe." But returning to her wartime post also brought memories of the helplessness and despair of her refugees. The next day a restless Helen was visiting her "families," and "taking in lots of the adorable villages we know so well."

On July 19, Sir Robert Witt joined her in Aix-les-Bains and there the details of Helen's plan for the art history library began to take shape. She would strive for "completeness in the painters represented and in the individual works, and a classification system as swift as opening a dictionary."

Ypres before and after World War I. Courtesy the Frick Collection/Frick Art Reference Library Archives.

After a quick visit to see her former governess in La Sarraz, Switzerland, Helen readied herself to inspect the German devastation in Belgium. Her first visit was to Coucklaere, where the huge German gun, Lange Max, began firing on Dunkirk in November 1917, the month she had departed for her tour of duty in France. Helen photographed the "terrible monster" with a friend, possibly Margaret Barr, sitting on its long cannon barrel and carefully noted its 17,000-ton weight, 1,500-pound shells, and the need for the soldiers to move 200 meters away from it when firing, due to the concussion.

She continued by train to Belgium, ever noting the extent of devastation. She took time to tour Bruges, but her main goal was to see the German submarine base at the port of Zeebrugge. Her photographs of the solid concrete edifice the Germans took two years to build, as well as those of the eight-hundred-foot-long submarine beds and the eight others still under construction when the Armistice was signed, filled the pages of her album-diary. In it she also pasted her own photograph of a German mine, a weapon that had sent many innocent passengers on unarmed ocean liners to their death. On August 16, seeking relief in art, she visited the Musée des Beaux-Arts in Brussels where she was thrilled to find that one of her favorite works of art, Hubert and Jan Van Eyck's *Adoration of the Mystic Lamb,* was being exhibited for the first time since the war.

German submarine base at Zeebrugge, Belgium, photographed by Helen. Courtesy the Frick Collection/Frick Art Reference Library Archives.

The same day, Helen visited the art nouveau palace of Adolphe Stoclet. Although Stoclet primarily collected Asian art and blended it with contemporary European works, he had also developed a distinguished collection of Italian primitives. Only a handful of Americans collected these works, but Helen had loved them since childhood for the stories they told. She now anticipated building both a choice collection of her own and incorporating examples of this period into her father's collection, up until then composed of more portraits and landscapes than religious art. She was intrigued that "[Stoclet] had made an art of framing the[m]," Helen wrote, "and the lovely colors of the paintings were accentuated by the introduction of rich old velvets into the frames," a technique Helen hoped to emulate.

Tracing the path of war once again, she went to Ever where she "saw [the] great German hangar for the Zeppelin[s] which made a daily trip to London during the war. . . . on their devilish mission." Back in France, at Sedan, Helen met the director of the Société Général, who had "his own tales to tell of [German] cruelty & of the dissipation of the Crown Prince." Her anti-German feelings now quantified and qualified, she set off for a final swing that culminated at Verdun, where eight nearby towns were entirely obliterated and one million men died in savage fighting from 1916 to 1917. "Frightful destruction everywhere," Helen wrote.

Deadly mines, photographed by Helen. Courtesy the Frick Collection/Frick Art Reference Library Archives.

Back in Paris, Helen met with Walker D. Hines, a close family friend and a fellow trustee of the Frick Collection, who was so impressed with her plan for an art history library that he embraced it wholeheartedly. Hines felt Helen's proposal was entirely consistent with Henry Clay Frick's expressed intention in his will to found an educational institution "which shall encourage and develop the study of the fine arts, and which shall promote the general knowledge of kindred subjects among the public at large." He wrote to the attorney for the Frick Collection, Lewis Cass Ledyard, "As I am very much impressed with the desirability of accomplishing a similar work for the Frick Art Collection, I write to submit the matter for your consideration. . . . [a] ready reference, photographs of all pictures to be found, both in public and private Art collections, in Europe and America . . . in one place a collection of photographs of practically all [of a] painter's pictures wherever located." With this very keen and formidable ally behind her, Helen's plan was all but assured. Upon her return to New York, she immediately went to work. Reluctant to dismantle her small personal library on the second floor and equally unwilling to disturb her father's bedroom or private sitting room, she instead took over the empty billiard room and bowling alley in the subbasement with its own entrance. Always loyal to her home state, she registered the library in Pennsylvania.

Helen began her search for material by rummaging through boxes and shelves in One East Seventieth Street, looking for books, magazines, catalogues, pamphlets, periodicals, photographs, and postcards accumulated by the family over the years. She took notes, made lists, and, because the library was to be used by scholars, she consulted two of America's finest art scholarship authorities: the director of the Fogg Art Museum at Harvard University, Edward W. Forbes, and the assistant director and Harvard professor, Paul Sachs, both of whom would become her lifelong friends and mentors. They too were collectors, particularly of early Italian art, were cofounders of the first American university art collection in the Fogg Art Museum, and together they ran the Fine Arts Department at Harvard, then considered the country's best.

Adopting Witt's time frame, Helen concentrated on twelfth- through mid-nineteenth-century paintings, drawings, and sculpture. She hired a staff—a reference librarian, Hannah Johnson Howell, and a librarian, Ruth Savord—and began the arduous task of attaching each image to brownish-gray mounts with headings on the front as to artist, title, subject, collection, medium, and size. On the back was noted the date of the work, the engravings made of it, the source of the photograph, the record of reproduction, the exhibition history, collection history, a description of the work, and bibliographical notes. Then each mount was archived alphabetically by artist in an upright green box, labeled according to national school, and cross-referenced in the card file by subject, such as the Bible, mythology, or portraits, and also by objects found in the paintings, such as flowers, books, or dogs.

As Hannah Johnson Howell wrote: "Miss Frick's initial problem was to gather quickly enough material to serve the needs of art scholars. . . . Dr. Paul J. Sachs set a figure of 13,000 reproductions as a minimum working collection." Helen engaged Sir Robert Witt to purchase books, sales catalogues, and photographs in England, and on his advice she asked the librarian of the Bibliothèque d'Art et d'Archéologie of the University of Paris, Mlle. Clotilde Mismé, to similarly act on her behalf in France and Holland. All items were to be purchased in duplicate, or better triplicate, so one copy could be kept intact. Shortly after she began her work, Mismé acquired a collection of vintage art sales catalogues once owned by the Dutch antiquarian Anton Mensing and they, Helen claimed, immediately made her collection in this category "one of the greatest in the world."

As she labored to create her library, Helen worked herself to the bone. Frail by nature, and always pencil-thin, she now looked harried and worn, almost a ghost of her own shadow. On December 11, one month into her library project, she showed a number of distinguished members of the art community through the One East Seventieth Street galleries: Bernard and Mary Berenson; the head of paintings at the Metropolitan Museum of Art, Bryson Burroughs; and Paul Sachs and Edward Forbes. Mary Berenson was so startled by Helen's appearance she said to Isabella Stewart Gardner that she had visited "the Frick mausoleum inhabited by his wraith of a daughter." Burroughs, on the other hand, focused his observations on the effect of the spotlights hidden in the West Gallery skylight. "I was shocked at the aspect of the pictures in the Gallery. That abominable light! The glaring whites! One would have sworn they were not paintings at all, but reproductions." Forbes tried to calm him with the assurance that Helen Frick was capable of making intelligent decisions about the collection. "I like the spirit in which she is going at her work," he replied.

"I think she takes the matter seriously and I think she wants to fulfill her obligations in the very best possible way." Forbes did, however, agree entirely about the weird effect of the spotlights: "I told her I like [the gallery] better with the general illumination. . . . [and] Miss Frick took the criticism in good part." But Helen did not alter her father's lighting—at least not until 1929 when a letter Adelaide sent to Duveen indicates it was changed.

During the final weeks of 1920, Helen became alarmed about one of the Fragonard panels, then being relined. The conservator had started to clean it with harsh results and, fearing the trustees would not take her advice on the action she thought necessary, Helen, who felt responsible for the paintings, sought Forbes's support for halting the restoration. On December 14, she wrote him: "A great weight [is] off my shoulders . . . for I feel that now it will be possible to give the other trustees a correct diagnosis." The following April, Helen, unaccustomed to being held accountable for her decisions, found she had to explain her action and her decision to John D. Rockefeller Jr., the newly elected board chairman of the Frick Collection. "The change was so startling that the work was ordered stopped until the Trustees should get together and decide upon the wisest course to pursue." She continued: "This winter I have consulted with a number of museum directors, artists and critics, and it is interesting to note they agree that the present treatment is too radical, and that the pictures are in danger of losing a great deal of charm; while to the contrary, they run no risk for years to come in not being cleaned." Rockefeller, who according to Helen "began to usurp more and more [control] . . . especially after he had his own name confirmed as 'Chairman of the Executive Committee,'" in what became one of the few times he agreed with Helen on Frick Collection matters, concurred that it was indeed "best not to touch them."

Early in 1921 Helen expanded her library staff, hiring two typists and a cataloguer, and continued to seek the advice of scholars in the field, including Frank J. Mather Jr. of Princeton University and Bernard Berenson, who had suggested she cross-file her material in a subject index. In order to obtain original photographs of high quality, she engaged Pach Brothers, who had taken portrait studies of her father, to document over one hundred paintings; Peter Juley to record others; Stephen G. Cleveland for sixty more; and William McKillop for still another six hundred. Photography was an unusual and costly procedure, as a future director of the Frick Collection, Everett Fahy, noted. "Many of them [were] taken in the days when one could almost buy some works of art for the cost of making photographs of them."

On April 16, Helen sailed again for Europe, for a stay of four months, "reveling in beautiful pictures." In her absence the Iron Rail opened and Helen returned home in time for a Labor Day reunion with her girls on September 5. The True Blue family boasted 850 members from 600 families from all over the United States, Canada, and even Scotland.

Childs, meanwhile, was meeting with success and respect in his field of paleontology. He had assumed his father's place on the board of the American Museum of Natural History in New York, had been given a room in the museum to conduct his research on vertebrate fossil mammals, and had become honorary curator of mammals at the Carnegie Museum of Natural History. A recognized scholar, his book, *Extinct Vertebrate Faunas of the Badlands of Bautista Creek and San Timoteo Canyon, Southern California,* undertaken for his master's degree in paleontology at the University of California at Berkley, was about to be published.

Childs was also voted president of the board of the Frick Collection, even though he had never been interested in art or in his father's collection. A constitution was adopted and officers were elected, but Childs, eager to further strengthen his role, attempted to change the power structure of the institution. Lewis Cass Ledyard wrote Rockefeller that Childs "had been very set upon a constitution which would change the character of the organization contemplated by the father, who had carefully provided for a control *outside* the family. The son wanted the trustees (three family and six outsiders) increased to twelve. This of course, was to get three friends of his in—so as to break the control the father intended to vest in those he named." In addition, Childs "had a constitution drawn, and sent a draft of it, which embodied these and other changes—notably the election of *members*, other than the trustees, who should have voting power." Ledyard was firm in response. "I had to tell him I could not approve of this, as I felt it would be in violation of his father's intentions." So Ledyard drew up what he called "a simple constitution—making the existing trustees the only members—and giving them the power over any vacancies." Both Helen and her mother supported Ledyard's constitution, and to both Rockefeller and Ledyard's relief, it was adopted. Ledyard noted, "The son withdrew his opposition."

But Childs, now thirty-eight, did not take defeat lightly. Nothing would have pleased him more than stacking the board with his personal friends and seizing control of what had traditionally been his sister's domain. According to Ledyard, when Helen and Adelaide were abroad for the summer:

> [I] drew up a set of minutes for Wm. Harding to record as secretary, embodying a copy of the constitution as adopted. These were submitted to [Childs], as he had the originals of some papers that were necessary to be included (such as the waivers of the heirs of the N.Y. law preventing the bequest of more than one half the estate to charity) and we found him objecting to the . . . minutes and insisting on our changing some of the provisions of the constitution as adopted—and he then drew up a set of minutes and sent them to Wm. Harding—who, I understand, has informed him that of course he cannot certify minutes which are different from the actual proceedings of the Board.

Indeed, Ledyard expressed further concern: "As you know, I have been rather fearful that the young man would make trouble for us."

Helen made no mention of this as she traveled to Washington, D.C., Philadelphia, and Atlantic City in the fall of 1921, primarily to gather additional images for her library and to ask for donations. She contacted Anita Hart, whose recently deceased husband Charles Henry Hart owned a photograph collection of early American pictures, and asked if she had "made any plans for the disposal of this work. . . . as such an exhaustive work as this would prove of inestimable help to us in the library work to which I am devoting so much of my time and thought." Helen well knew she was treading on delicate, if not sacred ground, but mourning was a familiar condition to her, one that made her request all the more plausible. "I hope very much that you will understand the spirit in which I write this letter, for doubtless this wonderful work of your husband's must have much of the same meaning for you as my father's collection has for me," she wrote. In return, Mrs. Hart, though about to sail for London, sent her two trunks full of papers, as "a distinct pleasure" because she was "deeply interested . . . in that [the library] is to include American Art."

Predictably, when the first anniversary of her Frick Art Reference Library approached in November, and after the fledgling organization had outgrown the bowling alley and spilled over into the basement halls and corridors, Helen created a photography shop in a room off the men's hall. She turned the washroom into a darkroom, and the men's smoking room into a studio for photographing paintings. In addition, she adapted the ladies' lounge for clerical work. To ensure her library stayed current, Helen gave hundreds of museums like the Metropolitan, the Philadelphia Museum of Art, and the Museum of Fine Arts, Boston, file cards addressed to the library to be returned whenever the museum acquired a new work. Helen wrote Sir Robert Witt, whom she named godfather of the library, of her delight in its progress. He replied on November 9, 1921: "Your cable of greetings from my God child on the eve of its first birthday gave me the greatest possible pleasure and I, in return, would like to say 'Many happy returns, and God speed it.'"

On February 14, 1922, Helen orchestrated the overnight stay of Gainsborough's world-famous *Jonathan Buttall: "The Blue Boy,"* owned by Henry E. Huntington. Duveen was about to exhibit the painting for the benefit of the Fifth Avenue Hospital, and ever eager to please a client, he agreed to let Helen have it overnight. She longed to see it displayed alongside her father's stunning Gainsborough portrait of Frances Duncombe, depicted in a long, seventeenth-century silk gown of the same silver-blue color as the portrait subject in "*The Blue Boy.*"

Another wish of Helen's was also coming true—the renovation of the small farm in Bedford Village, New York, she had bought in 1920. Although she would always keep Pittsburgh as her legal residence, she needed a retreat convenient to One East Seventieth Street and her library project. Westmoreland Farm, with its white clapboard house, guesthouse (the former barn), and stable, was ideal—well away from the Manhattan bustle she loathed yet only an hour's drive to New York City. It offered a cozy setting for mother and daughter, who with Frick gone were building a closer relationship. Helen gave her mother the sunny master bedroom with a view of the meadow, and together they scoured the countryside for early American antiques. Helen told a friend she was "very well pleased with her house," but in fact she was ecstatic. Every day she recorded the happenings at Westmoreland Farm in five-year diaries, so year after year she could make comparisons: what April day the horses came down from Eagle Rock, when she saw the first trillium, the day her apple trees blossomed.

By February 1922, as her library entered its second year, the farm was becoming the intimate, informal sanctuary it would remain. Busy as Helen was, she needed such a haven. In two frantic years Helen had met her goal of thirteen thousand reproductions, and graduate students in art history from Harvard and Princeton were already using the material, as were authors, curators, and scholars, among others. The enormous task of her library weighed heavily, and the scope of it had now caught the eye of the press. The *New York Herald,* in one of several articles on the library, described the institution as "a great help not only to students of art and architecture but to all who are interested academically in professions or business with which art is linked. The historian, the novelist, the playwright, the decorator, the theatrical producer, the costumer, the furniture maker—all will have at their command . . . the most complete collection of its kind ever assembled."

Determined to expand the library's scope, Helen organized expeditions throughout America and Europe to record unphotographed works of art, with the first trip slated for Virginia. Fiske Kimball, professor of art and architecture at the University of Virginia, suggested she include the Boston architect and expert on early American paintings, Lawrence Park, on the trip. Together with Fiske, Park, and her friends Gertrude Hill and Louise Freeman Lee, Helen documented many American and British paintings. Over the next

Thomas Gainsborough (1727–1788), *Jonathan Buttall: "The Blue Boy."* Oil on canvas, 70 x 48 in. The Huntington Library, Art Collections, and Botanical Gardens, San Marino, California. Courtesy the Huntington Library/Superstock,

Thomas Gainsborough (1727–1788), *The Hon. Frances Duncombe.* Acquired by Henry Clay Frick in 1911. Oil on canvas, 92 ¼ x 61 ⅛ in. © the Frick Collection, New York.

thirty-four years, Helen and others took approximately fifty such expeditions throughout the United States and accumulated almost nine thousand photographs for the library, in addition to those taken by the photographers hired by Helen and the many taken in New York City by the library staff photographer. Helen prepared for the field trips well in advance by placing notices in local newspapers stating the date of her arrival and the intent of her mission. Soon historical societies in other locales competed with each other for her consideration. Each trip saw some two or three hundred paintings photographed, an unrelenting pace that extended over the decades.

Progress on the library collection was, however, interrupted in mid-June 1922, when a spring erupted in the bowling alley. The librarian noted that the finely laid maple floor "began to slowly rise, brick work and all." By five o'clock it had risen four inches and was still rising. The staff formed a bucket brigade and handed over boxes and books in a long line stretching up a short flight of stairs and into a service dining room. According to Ruth Savord, "by morning [the floor] had risen 14½ inches and water stood in the alcove of the bowling alley to a depth of about 3 inches." Luckily all the material was saved, but the bowling alley was unusable until the fall when the underground spring was finally clamped and diverted.

Helen was at Eagle Rock when she learned of the near disaster. "First of all," she wrote her staff, "I want to tell you that I think you all are perfect bricks the way you managed the situation and kept your heads." She continued, "I could weep with you when I think of the work undone. . . . I wish I were there at 1 East Seventieth to help and then again I am glad I am not, for I think I would be terribly discouraged to see our darling workshop so upset."

The opening of the Historical House, now known as the Henry Clay Frick Birthplace, on June 19, 1928. Courtesy the Frick Collection/Frick Art Reference Library Archives.

In reality, Helen could not possibly have been there to help. She had collapsed. A June 29, 1922, article in the *New York Times* was headlined "MISS HELEN FRICK ILL: Daughter of Late Henry Clay [Frick] Suffers a Nervous Breakdown," and insisted she was "seriously ill at her estate at Prides Crossing. . . . [from being] hard at work cooperating with her corps of assistants in New York in cataloging the works of American artists, and it was this that brought about her breakdown."

The strain of organizing the library had certainly contributed to Helen's condition, but only in part. Constant activity had exhausted her. First there was the March 1922 purchase of her father's childhood home in West Overton. The property, approximately twelve acres, included the main house, the springhouse where her father was born, and the washhouse. It is today a historic site, the only existing pre–Civil War Mennonite village in America.

Helen's nervous state was further exacerbated by the increasing publicity attending her philanthropy, making her a target for cranks and stalkers. Homes of the wealthy had become virtual tourist attractions, and many notables, such as J. P. Morgan's son Junius, were targets of assassins, as Frick had been. In 1912, a gunman broke into Morgan's Long Island house and shot him twice in the groin. Seven years later, he and twenty other prominent individuals received letter bombs, and an innocent man, mistaken for Morgan, was shot and killed in church. Now, according to a *New York Times* report on May 7, Helen's safety was threatened. A prowler named Selman Smith had been telephoning her in New York over the past year and shadowing her and Adelaide. Weeks before, in April, the deranged man entered the vestibule at One East Seventieth Street, where he was arrested and warned by police that he would be in greater trouble if he did not leave the women alone. On the afternoon of

Follower of Giotto di Bondone, Romagnole School (ca. 1266–1337). *Madonna and Child with Saints: Scenes from the Life of Christ and the Life of the Virgin.* Acquired by Adelaide and Helen Clay Frick in 1922. In 1926, Helen reimbursed her mother for $17,600—half the cost. Triptych: tempera, on panels, 28 ¾ x 38 ¾ in. © the Collection of the Frick Art & Historical Center, Pittsburgh, Pennsylvania.

May 6 he returned, rang the doorbell, and asked to see Mrs. Frick or Miss Helen Frick, claiming: "My future lies in this house." The butler recognized him and promptly called law enforcement. The stalker was whisked away to Bellevue Hospital for observation.

Shaken by this episode, and already exhausted, Helen collapsed. Although traditionally active in the summer at the Iron Rail, she could neither visit the girls nor take part in the programs. Yet the Iron Rail provided respite for a new category of guests, fifty-nine mothers of the younger True Blues. Before her collapse, Helen had been enlarging the activities available to the girls, including instruction in making dresses, hats, baskets, and trays as well as debates on topics such as whether or not women should enter industries with equal pay as men. By August, Helen was back on her feet and engaged in a ten-day trip through New England and Canada looking for paintings to photograph. That September she gave each True Blue club copies of the ten greatest pictures of the world.

Recently her mother had purchased a sizable masterpiece, *Madonna and Child with Saints: Scenes from the Life of Christ and the Life of the Virgin* by a follower of Giotto di Bondone, Romagnole School. Helen asked Edward Forbes, "Do you consider it as a good little corner-stone on which to build up something worthwhile in a more modest way, & to cultivate an appreciation for the Early Italian Pictures, something which has not yet come my way?" Helen became joint owner with her mother of this work in 1926, and in fact it became the first of many pieces Helen acquired depicting scenes of the annunciation and of the Virgin holding the Christ Child. So attached to the Giotto was Helen, she did not lend it to the Fogg's forthcoming winter exhibition. Instead she offered works from the Eagle Rock collection.

At this time, something else precious to Helen arrived. Hoffman completed the bust of Henry Clay Frick commissioned from the deathbed studies. Writing to thank her friend, Helen said, "I do want you to feel down in the bottom of *your* heart, how grateful mine is for what you have done for me in bringing almost to life the one who means more to me than all else."

Malvina Hoffman (1885–1966), *Portrait Bust of Henry Clay Frick*. Commissioned from deathbed studies by Helen Clay Frick in 1922. Marble, 28 in. © the Frick Collection, New York, gift of Helen Clay Frick, 1935.

Now Helen began to move her library material back into the restored bowling alley. Almost immediately, however, she recognized: "that unless the Library was to strangle in its sturdy and growing infancy, new quarters were necessary." So Helen cast her eye next door, toward the property at Six East Seventy-first Street, once intended as the site for her father's sculpture gallery. For the next year, while her father's estate was in the last phase of being settled, she wrangled with the Frick Collection trustees both over her proposal for a separate building to be designed by Thomas Hastings and over the terms of a joint agreement.

Progress on the library continued throughout 1923, as Helen consulted with noted scholars. The art historian, F. Mason Perkins, whom Helen had met in London in 1920, acquired more than 650 negatives of Italian paintings taken under his direction, paintings he had discovered and published. Richard Offner, who taught Italian painting at New York University, offered Helen his bibliographies on Italian art, scanned Italy for periodicals and reference books related to this field, and even sent interior shots of paintings and frescoes in churches devoid of electric light, photographs ingeniously taken by a photographer named Brogi, who created his own light source by hooking his camera lights to the batteries in his car. With a mountain of work before her, Helen quickened her pace and organized more comprehensive field trips, including the first of five successive tours of Italy. These were methodical adventures, organized so early Italian paintings and frescoes never before recorded or photographed could be found and documented. With the help of Lawrence Park, Helen also combed New England, Philadelphia, and South Carolina for unrecorded works. Finding a wealth of miniatures by such artists as Charles Willson Peale and his family, she decided to broaden the scope of her library and include miniatures as well.

Meanwhile, Helen augmented her art collection. In 1922 she had acquired a recently discovered small *Pietà* in Naples. Now attributed to a follower of Konrad Witz, it is considered a "twin" to her father's fifteenth-century French *Pietà with Donor,* acquired in 1907. To Helen's dismay, however, a controversy opened between the experts over the authenticity of her *Pietà*. Joseph Duveen argued that Frick's was the original and hers "a copy . . . by a craftsman or an inferior painter which only accentuates the beauty of the original." He even went so far as to bet his brother-in-law, the art dealer René Gimpel, that he was correct. But on June 22, 1923, Gimpel wrote in his diary that Helen "show[ed] the [pair] to

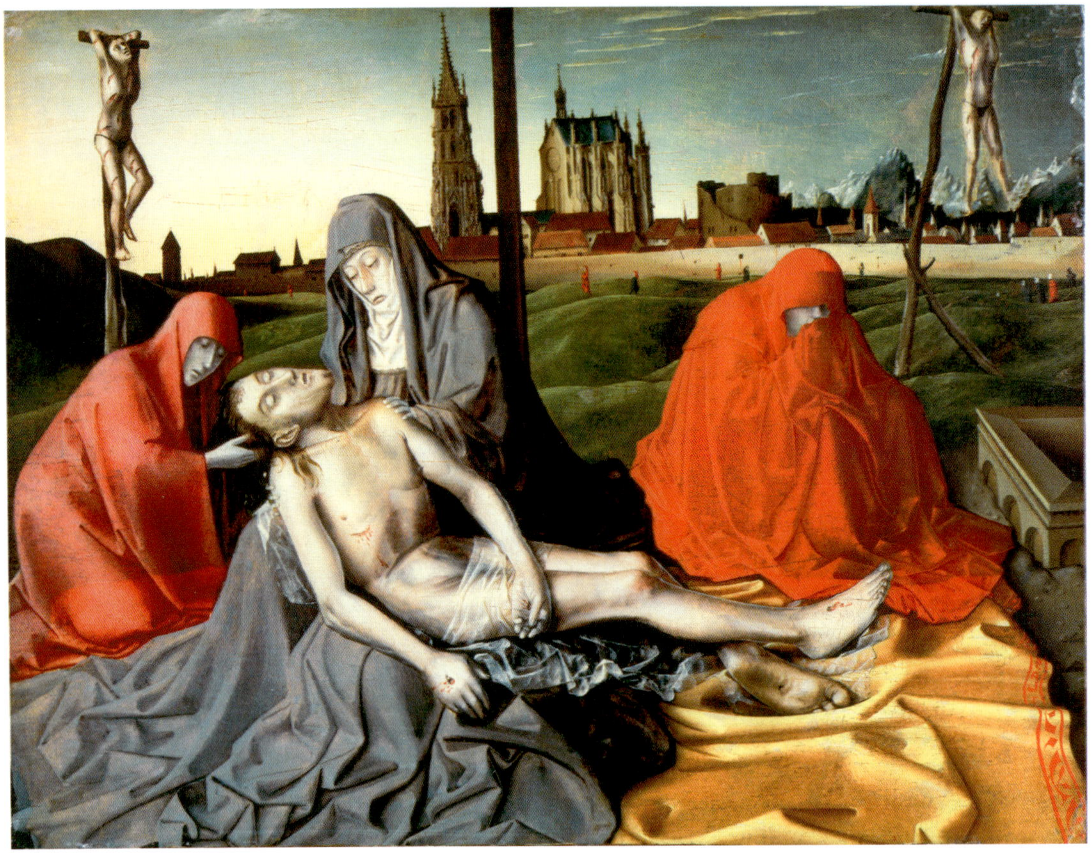

Konrad Witz (ca. 1400–1447), follower of, *Pietà*. Acquired by Helen Clay Frick for her collection in 1922. Tempera and oil on panel, 13 ½ x 17 ½ in. © the Frick Collection, New York, gift of Helen Clay Frick, 1981.

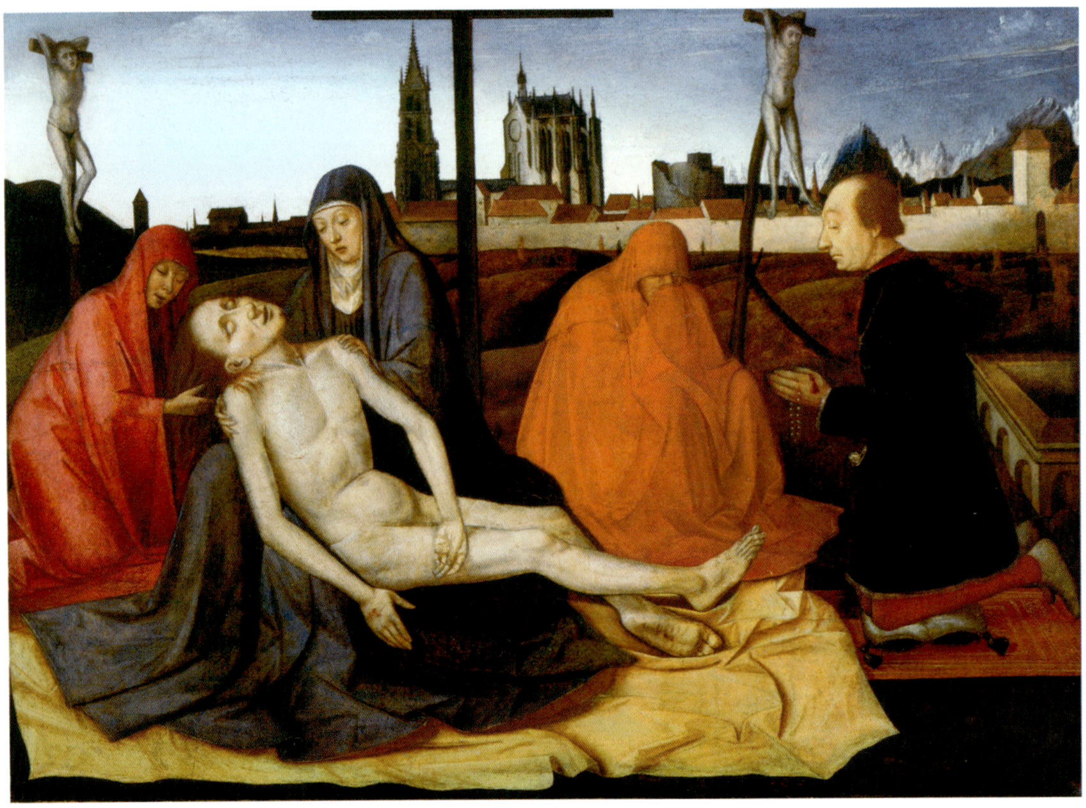

French (probably south of France), fifteenth century, *Pietà with Donor*. Acquired by Henry Clay Frick in 1907. Tempera or mixed technique on panel, 15 ⅝ x 22 in. © the Frick Collection, New York.

everyone qualified to give an opinion and has by now no less than twenty testimonials; she has told me that only one person shares Joe's [Duveen's] opinion: the curator of the Cook Collection in Richmond, who Joe said was an idiot." Helen's *Pietà* was hailed as the original, the model for her father's, and Gimpel dubbed it "the pearl of the collection." Duveen, having lost his bet with Gimpel, asked him to visit Helen and offer a $25,000 donation to her and Adelaide's favorite charity. Helen, so offended by the dealer's conduct, replied sternly, "Tell your brother-in-law that I don't take money from a lost wager. Tell him too that you've saved him $25,000, and that pride goeth before a fall."

Summer 1923 found Helen at Eagle Rock, opening the Iron Rail and welcoming her nieces and nephew for their seaside vacation while Childs and Frances took their annual trip west. Helen doted on her brother's children, now ranging from four to eight years of age. Often she took them to the Iron Rail to teach them about helping others. With service on her mind, Helen asked two people to speak at the True Blue girls' September 1923 reunion. Dr. Burton J. Lee, the youngest consulting surgeon in the American Expeditionary Force in France, decorated with the Distinguished Service Medal and the French Croix de Guerre, gave a patriotic address entitled "Glimpses of the War at the Front." The former U.S. commissioner of immigration, Frederick Wallis, discussed the Americanization process and the importance of becoming a citizen. Warren G. Harding had died on August 2, and Helen wanted these largely immigrant girls to become American citizens, so they could vote Republican, she hoped, in the next election.

Helen first used the bowling alley at One East Seventieth Street to archive the material she had amassed for her burgeoning Frick Art Reference Library. Courtesy the Frick Collection/the Frick Art Reference Library Archives.

With the advent of fall, groundbreaking for the new library was only a month away. The interior design, largely planned by Helen, was being completed. The main reading room and her private sitting room were to be in the Italian style with terra-cotta tile floors. The staff sitting room and head librarian's office, however, were to be authentic early American. Helen wanted lighting she had seen installed by Clarke & Mills of Boston, floor finishes "like the old speckled floors," office furniture in a mahogany finish, reading-room chairs in the Windsor style, and a large, fifteenth-century Italian Gothic fireplace in her sitting room. She had chosen the color for the walls and a paint that "absorbs a minimum of the light and therefore permit[s] the room to secure the best lighting" and had checked and double-checked the plans for everything else: the heating, plumbing, window shades, and the steel door in a tunnel connecting the library to One East Seventieth Street. To create the authentic early American staff sitting room and head librarian's office, she sought the services of an antique dealer, Harry D. Sleeper, to whose purchases Helen would add Americana of her own selection. Helen wrote Overholt, "I think the expense warranted, as [the rooms] will be little museums of Americana, as an adjunct to all the European things at 1 E[ast] 70 [th Street]."

Her emerging interest in Americana put her among the avant-garde. Until the 1920s, the long-held view was that "early America had no art, culture or taste worth preserv-

The original Frick Art Reference Library building designed by Thomas Hastings in 1924. Courtesy the Frick Collection/the Frick Art Reference Library Archives.

ing." In this decade, however, Electra Havemeyer Webb, Abby Aldrich Rockefeller, and Juliana Force, director of the Whitney Studio Club (precursor to the Whitney Museum of American Art), were forming their collections. Moreover, the Metropolitan Museum of Art was preparing to open its American Wing in 1924, the same year the new art reference library building would open to the public. The American Wing, financed by the renowned Americana collector, Emily Johnston de Forest, and her husband, Robert, a trustee of the Metropolitan, held the first museum-grade assemblage of period rooms.

Helen shared the design for the library with the Witts when they visited New York in October, and took them on a tour of Philadelphia, Washington, D.C., and Boston. She also introduced them to members of her family in Ligonier, showed them her father's birthplace at West Overton, and accompanied them through steel mills in Pittsburgh and art galleries in Washington. After their departure, Helen sailed with her sixty-three-year-old mother for three months in Italy and Christmas in Cannes. Never out of touch with her True Blue girls, Helen was pleased to learn through Ellen Boyd that eighty-eight barrels of Eagle Rock apples had been sent to the True Blue families. "It was quite an undertaking," Boyd wrote, "but brought untold pleasure." Boyd also distributed 960 calendars that Helen had designed and printed as Christmas gifts for the girls who, thanks to Helen, were also now under medical care for the tuberculosis running rampant in the crowded tenements and textile mills and for the stomach ailments caused by poor diet.

A refreshed Helen Frick sailed for home on February 27, 1924, and threw herself into the final months of library preparation. On May 23, the building was completed. Reference material and the much expanded Frick Art Reference Library staff of nineteen women and a lone male photographer, Ira W. Martin, moved into the new space. A few days before the opening ceremony, Sir Robert Witt sent congratulations: "I shall be thinking of how in 1920 we talked over the idea of your setting out in America on the same road that we had begun to explore some twenty-five years ago; of how slow *our* progress was at the outset and how extraordinary have been the results *you* have achieved in so short a time. . . . You have been the pioneer for your great country."

On June 9, 1924, the library women, clad in uniform pink coveralls, greeted their first readers. At its opening, the Frick Art Reference Library held more art historical reference material and photographs than any museum or library in the United States—60,000 photographs, 6,163 reference books and pamphlets, and 88,000 catalogues. "This may sound like a large number," Helen wrote as she described the project to her True Blue girls, "but in reality, it is only a beginning, as we have but a small portion of the world's output in paintings represented as yet, and the Library will have to grow and expand continually, as new pictures of standard quality are painted, and old ones that have been lost to sight, turn up again."

Helen also had a new librarian, Ethelwyn Manning, who remained a guiding force in the Frick Art Reference Library until her retirement twenty-four years later. Her dedication, like that of Ira Martin, who worked at the library until his death in 1960, typified the loyalty Helen Frick evoked in her staff.

With Miss Manning in charge and the library open and serving scholars, Helen returned to Eagle Rock for the summer of 1924, and to her girls at the Iron Rail. Times were hard in the textile industry. The wartime boom had ended, and the giant brick factories lining the Merrimack River and Lowell canals were in decay. Many Merrimack businesses moved south, and those that stayed refused to update their plants. Soon the remaining mills simply shut their doors. Thus many True Blue girls found work as domestics, waitresses, or chambermaids in mountain hotels. The shoe industry in Lynn was similarly affected. General Electric, then developing jet engines, became the city's largest employer, but of more men than women.

As mills closed, the Iron Rail opened its doors wider: "If your place of business closes for a short or a long period and you are laid off. . . . you are welcome to the full capacity of the house." That summer Helen herself was there to welcome the girls for their traditional two-week stay where they listened to a radio for the first time, enjoyed forty outings, and consumed 1,126 quarts of milk delivered by rail from the Eagle Rock dairy. And at the annual September reunion, when five hundred True Blues and their families came from sixty-one cities and towns, they enjoyed a chicken luncheon and a talk by the former Speaker of the House Frederick Gillett on the coming electoral contest between Calvin Coolidge and John W. Davis. That fall, Helen's girls enjoyed a glimpse of the Prince of Wales, the future King Edward VIII, as he came galloping through the Iron Rail property on a foxhunt with the Myopia Hunt Club. Adding to that brush with glamour, Helen sponsored a trip to New York for some of the girls. They stayed at the Hotel Astoria, and after visiting the library and One East Seventieth Street, they experienced Chinatown, walked through Central Park, attended the theater, and on the last day of their trip, drove up to Westmoreland Farm. Helen preferred an intimate and informal style of entertaining consistent with the modesty of her life at the farm: a casual picnic in the woods, spread upon blankets and served by her. In this way, she differed from many contemporary heiresses, who entertained lavishly in their showcase houses: Barbara Hutton at Winfield House in London, a private residence second in size only to Buckingham Palace, as well as at her palace on the Grand Canal in Venice, her castle in Tangier, and her Japanese-style home in Cuernavaca; or Marjorie Merriweather Post Hutton at her 129-room, Spanish-style Mar-a-Largo in Palm Beach and her elaborate compound in the Adirondacks.

In September 1924, Helen at last signed an agreement between the library and the Frick Collection trustees. The collection agreed to pay $80,000 toward construction of the

$140,000 building, and Helen, as president and director of the library, agreed to assume the balance, as well as all operating expenses, estimated at $40,000 a year. In addition, Helen agreed that in the event of her death, the library would be transferred to the Frick Collection in its entirety. She was pleased with the arrangement, but the trustees were uneasy, as they had been throughout the negotiations, particularly concerning her policy about usage of the library.

When it opened, Helen had adopted a rule to exclude Germans or people with German-sounding names from using the facility, just as she had with the One East Seventieth Street gallery. While society had moved on, Helen could not. Her policy, inflexible and extreme, would soon attach ridicule to her name, obscure the brilliance of her vision, and damage her reputation, particularly with the Frick Collection trustees. Her philanthropic work would be tainted in the public mind, scorned by many who worked with her, as well as those against her. She simply did not care. The odd circumstance that Frick was German and making Helen herself of direct German descent was mystifying. That she constantly asserted "The Fricks are Swiss, not German," particularly to family members, who well knew the Fricks came from the German sector of Switzerland and the Overholts from the German Palatinate on the Rhine, seemed irrational and self-incriminating. Without hesitation or remorse, when Hastings suggested she use a landscape architect named Max Schling to create a small garden around the Frick Art Reference Library, Helen snarled at his assistant: "I will *not* have Schling. He is a German." Helen, instead of waiting for another referral from Hastings, used her own gardener for the library project.

Preventing publication of the research by German scholars was the next point on her agenda. When she heard from Sir Robert Witt that a German, William Valentiner, the recently named director of the Detroit Institute of Arts, wanted to publish an article on her precious *Pietà*, then on loan to the Fogg Art Museum, she took action. When war broke out in 1914 Valentiner had abandoned his post as curator of the decorative arts department at the Metropolitan Museum of Art, a department he founded, to enlist in the German army. Awarded the Iron Cross for bravery during the bloody fighting at Verdun, after the Armistice he joined a radical left-wing organization in Germany, where he remained a member until his return to America in 1921. Still a German citizen, he received a cool response from his former Metropolitan Museum colleagues and from former friends, except the wife of John D. Rockefeller Jr., Abby Aldrich Rockefeller, who shared his interest in modern art. Valentiner was promoting the sale and the exhibition of German Expressionist paintings, works Helen categorically loathed. She thus demanded that Forbes put a halt to publication of Valentiner's article in *Art in America*. "The part I object to," she wrote the Fogg Museum's Edward Forbes, "is that I have no regard for Valentiner & wish to reserve the privilege of publication for some one in whom I have confidence." Forbes was apparently willing to overlook Valentiner's war record in the interest of scholarship, but he did as she asked and wrote the journal's editor, Frederic Sherman. Helen thanked Forbes for stepping in and said she wished he and Paul Sachs would write a joint article in Valentiner's stead, adding: "It would be intolerable to me to have anything of mine described by that man." She then advised Forbes that she had taken further action against Valentiner. "Only this morning," she wrote, "a request came from him to see the Collection—which of course will be refused as long as the house continues to be my mother's and my home." Helen's treatment of Valentiner backfired. Forbes wrote Helen that "[Valentiner] replied to my disappointment that he was so hurt and so angry at your letter refusing him admittance to your home that he had gone ahead and told Mr.

Sherman to publish his article in *'Art in America'*"—in spite of Helen and of never having seen the paintings together.

Through the fall of 1924, Helen remained agitated about German scholars. Sir Robert Witt had cautioned her against her German prejudice when the library opened: "If I may add a word of counsel on the future of your Library it would be that its doors are opened wide to all and sundry, with sympathy, with patience and imagination; for art and learning need space and freedom and the open door should typify the open mind within, open to new ideas, new methods and to any reform which can make good its claim to improve your system and arrangements." But Helen would not listen. In November 1924, Paul Sachs begged admittance to both Frick entities for the prominent scholar, Max Friedlander, and cautioned Helen against her bias:

> I am fully aware of your strong feeling in regard to all Germans. . . . [but] I do not know how the Frick Library can function as it properly should without turning to [Friedlander] for valuable information which he, better than any other living man, can give about North European painting. . . . I am going to go even a step further in friendship and say to you that I am fully satisfied that it is not only in the interest of the Frick Collection and the Frick Library, but in the interest of American scholarship as well (which you have so deeply at heart) that you should now and again, as in this instance, begin to make exceptions to your general rule.

Helen thanked Sachs for the help he had given the library and the collection, saying he had been "so kind," and explained that she would like to admit Friedlander "so much," but stated: "My principle, however, of not admitting Germans to the house or to the Library, is so strong, & I believe so *justifiable* that I can really make no exceptions. . . . and no advantage the Library might gain through their coming would compensate for my inability to live up to this principle."

Sachs was shocked. On the back of Helen's reply he wrote a note to Forbes: "*This is it!!* Now I have it black and white. No longer 'gossip' but is fact. Hard to believe." Fearing retaliation from Helen because the library and the gallery were important to his students, he took a milder approach in his response, writing Helen that he hoped they could remain good friends, and that he could still bring his students to the library and to the collection. Nevertheless, Sachs continued to press his point: "I venture to disagree with you in your belief that your present attitude is justifiable. To harbor hatred and to justify it by invoking a 'principle' seems to me unjustifiable, simply because 'hatreds' have nothing to do with each other."

This scenario was repeated in the fall of 1926 when Sachs asked Helen to allow his personal friend, the eminent German art historian, Hanns Swarzenski, to enter the gallery. He explained that Swarzenski was "a cultivated gentleman of charm and refinement . . . one of the best museum directors in Europe today. . . . a mediaevalist of distinction and the Director, as well, of the Staedel Institute in Frankfurt." Helen refused him entrance. An infuriated Sachs wrote Forbes: "You may not agree but I intend to keep up this pressure on my side even if in the end my relations with Miss Frick grow to be less candid."

Sachs, Witt, and others who saw Helen's fury were baffled, but in spite of her German antipathy, they could—and did—respect and admire her. With the success of the Frick Art Reference Library, Helen had become a recognized art historian as well as an astute art collector. As head of the Frick Collection's art acquisition committee, she had further enhanced her reputation by successfully urging the trustees to buy *The Annunciation* by Fra

Fra Filippo Lippi (ca. 1406–1469), *The Annunciation*. Acquired by the Frick Collection in 1924. Tempera on poplar panels: left panel, 25 ⅛ x 9 ⅞ in.; right panel, 25 ⅛ x 10 in. © the Frick Collection, New York.

Filippo Lippi. Indeed, Helen's commitment to early Italian art was deepening. In 1924 she purchased two telling works for her own collection: Apollonio di Giovanni's comment on love and loyalty entitled *Scenes from the Odyssey,* depicting Penelope waiting for the return of her husband, refusing a suitor as she daily unravels her work on a shroud, and Matteo di Giovanni's *Madonna and Child.* A reminder of Martha, Giovanni's work shows the ill-fated infant Christ with three figures: an angel; Saint Jerome, who removed a painful thorn from a lion's paw; and Saint Sebastian, the patron saint of pin-makers. Of the Giovanni, Helen merely said to Forbes she "hop[ed] he & Sachs [would] see it."

In return for their support, Helen offered an intense loyalty to her friends, particularly those who guided the library's development. In the fall of 1924, during the Friedlander debacle, Lawrence Park was diagnosed with a terminal illness. Helen wrote his friend, Henry Fuller, "It is a most heart-rending case and I want very much to do what I can to help." Grateful to Park for locating and identifying American paintings to photograph, she paid for his medical care and financed his four-volume work on Gilbert Stuart. Park wanted to

Apollonio di Giovanni (ca. 1415–1465), *Scenes from the Odyssey: Story of Penelope*, detail. Acquired by Helen Clay Frick in 1924 for her collection. Tempera on *cassone* panel, 7 ½ x 37 ⅜ in. © the Collection of the Frick Art & Historical Center, Pittsburgh, Pennsylvania.

Matteo di Giovanni (ca. 1430–1495), *Madonna and Child with Saint Jerome, Saint Sebastian and Angels*. Acquired by Helen Clay Frick in 1924 for her collection. Tempera on panel, 29 ½ x 19 ¼ in. © the Collection of the Frick Art & Historical Center, Pittsburgh, Pennsylvania. Photo credit: Richard A. Stoner.

Sir Gerard Kelly (1879–1972), *Henry Clay Frick in the West Gallery*. Commissioned by Helen Clay Frick in 1925. Oil on canvas, 48 x 40 in. © the Collection of the Frick Art & Historical Center, Pittsburgh, Pennsylvania. Photo credit: Richard A. Stoner.

dedicate the set to her, but Helen demurred. She felt too many others had played equally important roles. After his death late that year, she assembled the work at the library and brought it to publication. Although sales were slight, Helen paid Park's widow steady royalties for a number of years.

Yet those who crossed Helen felt the full force of her anger. In early 1925, Thomas Hastings found himself in trouble with her. He had been unable to make the fifteenth-century Italian fireplace in Helen's private sitting room draw properly. It needed a far larger chimney than had been constructed, so Hastings proposed a glass front or curtain to correct the draft problem. Suggesting words her secretary was to use, Helen scribbled across the back of a letter from Hastings: "Miss Fr. will *not* consider [these solutions] for one moment." She wanted Hastings to extend the chimney and add a hearth. But these alterations failed. A frustrated Hastings gave up and wrote Helen, "Alas. . . . it was expected that [the fireplace] could make friends with a flue which was never intended to go with it." When he submitted a bill for his work his infuriated client refused to pay, saying, "your work was not satisfactory, and accomplished nothing in remedying the trouble."

There were other problems with the new building: the cork floor in the main hall was already showing wear, the iron railings had rusted and were staining the stone beneath, and the paint was peeling from the walls because the plaster had not been dry when painted. The library's front door was difficult to open since Helen had reversed it to swing in not out; its molding was loose and the varnish was peeling. Her secretary complained on March 11: "It looks so very shabby and she feels that you should make it satisfactory." But Hastings refused, explaining that the interior side that Helen had now faced out was made of birch and therefore could not stand up to the harsh New York weather. And anyway, code dictated doors swing out, not in. An exasperated Helen wrote Hastings:

> It is just under a year since you so called "finished" the building of the [library]—and I regret it is necessary for me to make so many complaints regarding the way the work was done, but it is only just that you should know in order that you may rectify the mistakes. . . . that the real blame must rest on your design of the stoop which you made so narrow that any person standing there, ran the risk of being knocked down the steps each time the door was opened. For this reason the door had to be reversed. I feel that it is up to you either to supply us with a new door or else to widen the platform at your own expense. . . . These various jobs, together with others about which I have complained before make me realize how very little interest & attention were given by your firm . . . and the result has been a very disappointing one to me.

Hastings's bills remained unpaid.

At about this time, the artist Gerard Kelly became another target of Helen's anger. The portrait she had commissioned from him of her father standing in the West Gallery utterly displeased her. In June, when the artist asked if Helen would lend it to a forthcoming exhibition of his work in Pittsburgh, her response was frank and to the point:

> The opinion expressed by the two directors of the Fogg Museum on the "Gallery Interior" confirms me in the feeling to which I have adhered since the beginning. My father's figure is the poorest part of the picture—and is entirely lacking in expressing his force and personality. As you know, it is a very great disappointment to me. . . . I wish to state now, that neither my mother nor I will consider lending anything to your exhibition in Pittsburgh.

Throughout the fall of 1924, Helen's health deteriorated. She suffered from gall bladder attacks and in the weeks before Christmas became bedridden. Helen underwent an operation early in 1925; at the same time, Adelaide fell ill and was bedridden until July. Yet by the spring Helen was undertaking new projects. In May she offered to fund a fine arts department and library at the University of Pittsburgh—$100,000 over five years, as well as $5,000 to the building fund and $15,000 to the fine arts department per year. John Gabbert Bowman, appointed chancellor of the university in 1921, had been cultivating Helen as a donor, and naturally the offer appealed to him. In his memoir, he remarked that in the 1920s Pittsburgh was considered the "last great center in the country where there is not a great

Giovanni di Paolo (ca. 1403–1482), *Nativity*. Acquired by Helen Clay Frick in 1925 for her collection. Tempera on panel, 23 x 17 ½ in. © the Collection of the Frick Art & Historical Center, Pittsburgh, Pennsylvania. Photo credit: Richard A. Stoner.

university." The university was also approximately $1.6 million in debt and without hope of securing additional loans. To cut costs, Bowman had discontinued the few fine arts courses. Yet he recognized that growth, not diminishment, was critical for the future: additional land, new buildings and classrooms, books, equipment, athletic fields, and funds for faculty salaries were needed. Thanks to Andrew Mellon, who in 1921 had purchased the fourteen-acre quadrangle in Oakland from Henry Clay Frick's estate and donated the land to the university, by 1925 Bowman had room to expand. Already he had raised $9 million for the construction of a giant Gothic-style skyscraper then called the Tower of Light, later the Cathedral of Learning, "about which," a trustees' report claimed, "all the activities of the university may develop."

As Bowman was making headway in reviving a lagging institution, Helen expanded her offer: "Without making any definite promise for the future—at the end of five years, should this new department meet the requirements and prove of value to the University and Pittsburgh in general,—I may endow a permanent chair for the Department of Fine Arts." One string, however, was attached—one so tight that many years later, it would nearly strangle the university, the department, and Helen Frick. "In making this gift," the thirty-seven-year-old benefactress insisted, "I reserve privilege of having the final selection of the Department head, and I request that the advice and guidance of Mr. Edward W. Forbes, Director of the Fogg Museum of Cambridge, be obtained and followed as closely as possible." Bowman was reassuring to his young patron, and met with Helen, Forbes, and Professor Sachs on June 2. On June 11, Forbes and Sachs submitted eight names as possible department heads.

While the search proceeded, Helen departed for Italy with Gertrude Hill and Pauline Wells, a member of the library staff. Although the library owned many images of Italian art, a great many more remained undocumented and possibly unknown. When in Florence, Helen realized that the only way she could acquire photographs of every painting and fresco in Italy was to employ a full-time Italian photographer. But according to Helen, Mason Perkins, the art historian leading the expedition, firmly told her: "No Italian photographer would work by contract" and so he refused to have anything to do with the matter. Still Helen persevered. She wrote a contract, took it to a lawyer who translated it into Italian, and then met with Cavaliero Sansoni, of the firm Sansoni and Nesti, which already had been working for the library. Indeed, in addition to photographs, Sansoni provided Helen with lists of books and new publications for purchase and also bought material desired by the library. So congenial was the relationship, it continued until World War II.

On the trip the three women took copious notes and made detailed drawings of church or museum interiors with numbers indicating the location of each picture and fresco.

Stefano di Giovanni, called Sassetta (1391/1400–1450), *Annunciation*. Acquired by Helen Clay Frick in 1925 for her collection. Tempera on panels, 4 ½ x 6 in. © the Collection of the Frick Art & Historical Center, Pittsburgh, Pennsylvania. Photo credit: Richard A. Stoner.

Stefano di Giovanni, called Sassetta (1391/1400–1450), *Virgin of Humility Crowned by Two Angels*. Acquired by Adelaide Frick in 1925 and purchased by Helen Clay Frick from her mother in 1931. Tempera on panel, 14 ½ x 10 ⅜ in. © the Collection of the Frick Art & Historical Center, Pittsburgh, Pennsylvania. Photo credit: Richard A. Stoner.

Helen examined Polly's work and often made suggestions in the margins such as, "I think you have reversed #79 & 82," or indicated an artist listed out of chronological order. She clipped articles on works of art from newspapers and circled paintings or frescoes new to her, questioning Polly, "Where is this one?"

Helen wanted to find a thirteenth-century triptych known to have once been in a small church between Florence and Siena, but now considered lost. At the church she persuaded the sacristan to take her to the storeroom. Together they began rummaging around and suddenly, when Helen opened the door of a cupboard, out the triptych fell. Luckily the sacristan caught it before it hit the floor. When Helen examined it and realized it was already in very poor condition, she asked permission to send it to conservators at the Uffizi at her expense. In time the triptych was returned, fully repaired, to reclaim its original place inside the church.

Although Helen found nothing of interest for the Frick Collection in 1925, she acquired four gems for herself, all purchased in the fortieth anniversary year of Martha's birth: Giovanni di Paolo's *Nativity;* Andrea di Bartolo's *Madonna and Child;* and the *Annunciation* panels by her favorite artist, Sassetta. Her mother also bought a Sassetta this year, *Virgin of Humility Crowned by Two Angels,* a work she kept in Frick's private sitting room on the second floor of One East Seventieth Street and that was later purchased by Helen in 1931. Helen also acquired for the University of Pittsburgh two Umbrian fresco fragments, one depicting St. John the Baptist, and the other, *The Resurrected Christ.* Forbes saw them the day they arrived, and John Bowman assured Helen that Forbes considered them "splendid teaching material and valuable acquisitions for our department."

Throughout 1925, Helen's projects were growing. In a record-breaking season, over five hundred True Blues enjoyed the summer at the Iron Rail. In the fall Helen erected a screen in the Eagle Rock stables and showed the girls movies of her trip to Italy. Home movie cameras were just being introduced, and the girls were mesmerized by this innovative technology: "It was quite an unusual entertainment [with] the girls sitting in the carriages and watching the screen . . . delighted with the novelty of it all."

In their traditional manner, the girls returned their good fortune by giving impoverished children some joy and happiness during the holidays. They knitted fifty pairs of mittens to give away over Christmas, and Helen, whose annual expenses for the Iron Rail now averaged about $30,000, supplemented the girls' gift-giving to the poor with an almost equal number of dolls. Seventy-seven children from ages two to ten years came to the party in Lawrence, nearly two dozen more than anticipated. Meanwhile, far away at Westmoreland Farm, Helen and her mother entertained fifteen children from the Children's Aid Society of New York during the 1925 holiday season. "They gave us as good a time as we gave them," Helen noted.

Shortly thereafter, in January 1926, Adelaide's health again began to fail. By March she was bedridden at One East Seventieth Street with severe pain in her lower back, diagnosed as lumbago. She also was suffering from laryngitis, and in April she was placed on oxygen. Her condition did not improve for three months. One of Helen's personal secretaries, Eleanor B. Howland, explained to Ellen Boyd just how hard the situation was for Helen, who was "in New York about as much as Bedford as she comes back and forth on account of her mother. . . . still on her couch."

In March, Helen asked John D. Rockefeller Jr. to appraise two Italian primitives offered for sale by the New York collector Carl W. Hamilton: "a fine 'Crucifixion' by Piero della Francesca . . . and also a 'Madonna and Child' by Fra Filippo Lippi." "May I ask," she wrote, "that you treat this confidentially?" After much discussion the Piero was turned down as being restored to the point of ruination and the Fra Filippo Lippi rejected as not fine enough.

That same month Helen published an article in the *Garden Club of America Bulletin* entitled "Flowers in the Paintings of Old Masters." Using her own classification system, she, or perhaps members of the library staff, merely went to the card file, found "flowers," narrowed the search to artists of relevance from the fourteenth through seventeenth centuries and, after submitting the call slips, within five minutes boxes containing photograph mounts arrived, complete with the name of the artist and the painting's location.

Helen, however, remained annoyed with Thomas Hastings. In July he revisited the issue of his unpaid balance by softening her up with compliments on her library: "I was very much impressed with the quiet and general appearance of things and the seriousness of the work you are doing." When Helen refused him again, he appealed to her mother, now just recovered from her five-month illness. "Indeed," he whined to Adelaide, "I recall being somewhat hurt at the time when your daughter felt that we were remiss and negligent." On August 9, Helen issued a firm and final warning. "Your letter addressed to my mother," she wrote, "infers that you are quite satisfied with the entrance to the Frick Art Reference Library . . . in spite of the fact that [problems] have given us no end of trouble ever since the building was erected." Recognizing that Hastings had no intention of remedying the defects, she threatened that in the future, if One East Seventieth Street were expanded eastward across the Seventy-first Street driveway to connect with her library building, "as a trustee of the Frick Collection, I would seriously oppose engaging the services of your firm as architects, but would insist on obtaining the advice of those who would make it their business to give satisfaction."

Hastings declared to Adelaide: "You will probably laugh and I hope you will, when I explain that architects are never responsible, even for mistakes they make, unless these mistakes are criminal. . . . We are protected in this regard, because we could not afford to correct our errors or imperfections which are sure to happen in the best regulated families—'I mean architectural families.'" To Helen he simply replied: "Your last letter to me . . . seems so uncalled for, so unfair and so unkind, that there is nothing further for me to say." Helen remained steadfast. "Not until they have attended to everything," she told her secretary.

Helen's attention was also engaged by developments in Pittsburgh. She had settled on the candidate to head the new fine arts department, a professor from Cambridge, Massachusetts, Frederick Mortimer Clapp. Tall, elegant, with a wry sense of humor and conservative appearance, Clapp held a masters of art from Yale University, a *docteur en lettres* from the University of Paris, and was a poet, a scholar, and a world traveler. An expert in Greek and Elizabethan drama, he had written his dissertation on the sixteenth-century Florentine artist Jacopo Carucci, called Pontormo, an early exponent of Mannerism. Moreover, Clapp knew the rare book trade, spoke many languages, read Sanskrit, and his convictions about the importance of teaching art history resonated with Helen. "Art," he claimed, "reveals the story of civilization. It records the unfolding of the imagination; it keeps alive for us the hopes and fears, the activity, environment, and manner of life of each succeeding generation, whether in India or England, in China or Italy. It vividly preserves the dress, the expression, the faces of those long dead. . . . [a] light into dark places not easily reached by words."

The heiress increased her original offer to the university and agreed to donate $25,000 as startup money for the fine arts library she envisioned as a sister to the one in New York. In addition, she agreed to give Clapp a $10,000 annual salary, as well as another $10,000 a year to spend on books and photographs. She also gave the university $4,000 for an assistant professor and secretarial help. And she agreed to fund the department on a permanent basis if it met with her satisfaction after a three-year trial period, not five years as originally stated.

On October 4, 1926, Clapp formally accepted the position of full professor. To Bowman he wrote: "With your vision and Miss Frick's liberality behind us, we will be able to create and carry on at Pittsburgh a department of the history of art which in time will not fear comparison with any in the country." He then took an extended trip to Europe and, aided by Helen's contacts, within a year he assembled one thousand volumes for the university's nascent fine arts library. When Clapp and Bowman corresponded, they began referring to their patron as "The Angel" or "Donatrix." Clapp was particularly awed by Helen and diligent about keeping in her good favor. Once he explained to a friend how meticulously he had prepared for a lunch with Helen: "I shaved for a week like a seamstress making a seasonable confection."

As Clapp worked on the library for the university, Helen worked on her private collection of Italian primitives. This year she acquired a painting by the Master of San Sepolcro, then considered a Duccio, and "a little Bernardo Daddi" entitled *Madonna and Child with Saint Francis and a Bishop; Saints Peter and Paul; Crucifixion; Annunciation.* Of the latter Helen exclaimed to Edward Forbes, "The left panel of two saints bears a great resemblance to the same panel of the Fogg triptych!" For the Frick Collection she had steered the trustees toward Gentile Bellini's *The Doge* and to Jean-Baptiste-Siméon Chardin's *Lady with a Bird-Organ.* Paul Sachs had suggested the latter as a compliment to the Bouchers and Fragonards, and Helen "intend[ed] moving heaven and earth to get it into the Frick Collection." The acquisition was soon after hailed by *New York Times* art historian and art editor Royal Cortissoz as "one of the jewels in the history of painting"; it remains today a "jewel" in the history of the Frick family's autobiographic collecting pattern. After all, Chardin's scene of a room with wood paneling, large windows, and caged canaries is reminiscent of Helen's childhood and the third-floor Clayton playroom where she kept her canary family. The bird-organ recalls the harmonium she had purchased with money earned for good behavior, donated to the church in Montcherand, Switzerland.

By every measurement, then, 1926 had been a good year, capped, perhaps, by the joint commission with her mother of *The Fragonard Room* by Walter Gay, an artist who critics claimed, "has felt that a cracked wall of the past, a period table, an armchair worn out from use, seem to possess certain features similar to those of the human face, that change according to the time and the hour."

Helen also indulged her other interests. Her True Blue family, now numbering almost twelve hundred, remained a source of pride and satisfaction to her. Many had abandoned the failing textile industry for professional careers as nurses, teachers, or stenographers. All through the fall Helen continued to invite prominent speakers to the Iron Rail, whose membership was growing by about sixty a year, to address the topic of adolescent girls. And when the year drew to a close, Helen gave each True Blue a sterling silver pencil with a black ribbon and small silver clasp for Christmas. She and her mother again hosted a Christmas party for needy children at Westmoreland Farm, while her girls collected $1,081.90 and distributed it to shut-ins, orphans, widows, and the sick through the twenty missionaries of the Boston Missionary Society.

In January 1927, Adelaide became ill again and remained, as Helen said, "on her back most of the time, after another set-back," and unable to leave for Eagle Rock in May.

Bernardo Daddi (ca. 1290–ca. 1348). *Madonna and Child with Saint Francis and a Bishop; Saints Peter and Paul; Crucifixion; Annunciation.* Acquired by Helen Clay Frick in 1926 for her collection. Triptych: tempera, on panels, 17 ¼ x 16 ¾ in. © the Collection of the Frick Art & Historical Center, Pittsburgh, Pennsylvania. Photo credit: Richard A. Stoner.

Bernardo Daddi (ca. 1290–ca. 1348). *Christ on the Cross between the Virgin and Saints Mary Magdalene and John The Evangelist*; left panel: *The Agony in the Garden and Saints Peter and Paul*; right panel: *Saints Catherine of Alexandria and Margaret of Antioch, Saints James Major and Benedict,* 1334. Tempera and gold leaf on panel with engaged frame, 24 ½ x 21 ⅜ in. Courtesy Harvard University Art Museums, Fogg Art Museum, Friends of the Fogg Art Museum Fund and William M. Prichard Fund, 1918.33. Photo credit: Imaging Department, © President and Fellows of Harvard College.

Although Helen was also unwell in January, she helped Malvina Hoffman promote an exhibition for her French artist friend, Jean Julien Lemordant, at the Wildenstein Gallery. Blind as a result of traumatic wounds in the Great War, Lemordant was a close friend of Hoffman's and nothing made Helen happier than purchasing his paintings.

But this was not the only art Helen was pursuing. She persuaded the Frick Collection trustees that "should [she] purchase the French Primitive [*Virgin and Child*] at a sum not to exceed $25,000 and loan the same to the Fogg Museum of Art for their summer exhibition, as she desired . . . in the fall of 1927 the Trustees would take the picture off her hands at the purchase figure." Later that year, Helen convinced the trustees to acquire Jean-Auguste-Dominique Ingres's *Comtesse d'Haussonville*, considered by Paul Sachs to be "Ingres' masterpiece" and one of the public's favorite paintings in the collection today. Nor did she neglect her beloved Italian primitives. In July, Duveen told Adelaide that he had purchased the famed Robert Benson Collection—"a great secret. . . . [but] I naturally . . . make an exception in your case, as I am sure you will tell Miss Frick about it." Adelaide cabled an immediate response: "My daughter and I deeply interested in Benson Duccio [*Temptation of Christ on the Mountain*] and Barna [da Siena, *Christ Bearing the Cross*]." In October, Helen urged the Frick Collection trustees to purchase the Duccio at the asking price of $330,000. Originally one of nine panels in the lower row, or *predella*, of the thirty-four-piece great altar in the cathedral of Siena and known as the *Maestà*, it was then considered by the *New York Times* one of "the most valuable paintings" in the world. Although the trustees balked, Helen insisted. She already had bought Francesco di Vannuccio's acclaimed masterpiece, *Saint Catherine of Alexandria*, for her own collection, and was about to purchase Benson's Barna da Siena that Duveen was offering at $120,000. So to help Helen secure the Duccio for the Frick Collection, Paul Sachs and Sir Robert Witt suggested she offer the trustees a "bribe" of her own. She could purchase the Barna da Siena and offer it to the trustees, provided they purchase the Duccio. After much deliberation during the November 15, 1927, trustees meeting, they agreed. The Frick Collection, now owning four early Italian masterworks, was recognized as a leader in collecting paintings from this period. Thrilled with the result of her bargain, Helen wrote Paul Sachs, "The Trustees decided to purchase Duccio's 'Temptation Scene' and to accept my gift of the Barna da Siena! And so yours and Sir Robert's and my little plan of campaign has worked out most beautifully, and I am coming to you once more to thank you for your great share in its success." For Helen there was even more joy for her in the deal. The trustees agreed to allow her and Adelaide "from time to time [to] borrow [the Barna] painting and remove it to their home in the country, or lend it to exhibitions." And when Forbes saw the paintings on display he wrote her, "The glow of the beautiful color in the room where your Duccio and Barna and other primitives hang stays with me and I want to congratulate you once more on having acquired all these lovely and wonderful pictures."

French, probably Burgundian (about 1390–1400), *Virgin and Child*. Acquired by Helen Clay Frick in 1927 and purchased from her by the Frick Collection. Oil and tempera on panel, 8 ⅝ x 5 ⅝ in. © the Frick Collection, New York.

Yet the tension at the Frick Collection's board meetings was rising. In November the collection's lawyer, Lewis Cass Ledyard (still against the Duccio purchase), ran the meeting

Duccio di Buoninsegna (ca. 1255–1319), *The Temptation of Christ on the Mountain*. Acquired by the Frick Collection in 1927. Tempera on poplar panel, 17 x 18 ⅛ in. © the Frick Collection, New York.

Barna da Siena (active around 1350), *Christ Bearing the Cross, with a Dominican Friar*. Acquired by Helen Clay Frick in 1927 and given to the Frick Collection provided the trustees purchase Duccio's *The Temptation of Christ on the Mountain*. Tempera on poplar panel, 12 x 8 ½ in. © the Frick Collection, New York.

Francesco di Vannuccio (active 1361–1388), *Saint Catherine of Alexandria*. Acquired by Helen Clay Frick in 1927 for her collection. Tempera on panel, 21 ½ x 14 ⅜ in. © the Collection of the Frick Art & Historical Center, Pittsburgh, Pennsylvania. Photo credit: Richard A. Stoner.

and, according to Helen, "In spite of the fact that my mother was present for the first time in over a year—her feelings were not spared by Mr. Ledyard's garrulous tongue. He said the Collection could *not afford* to buy pictures as it would have to conserve funds for the restoration of the building when it would become a museum! [i.e., upon Adelaide's death] The only thing I can think of now is to poison this old man's tea."

Meanwhile, Sachs, having helped Helen achieve her agenda, and having received her warmest thanks for the Duccio purchase, felt secure enough to raise the delicate German question one more time. In December, he wrote to her: "Every now and again I feel obligated to revert to a subject which on first blush I know tends to irritate you," and begged admission to the collection for a Harvard University professor, Adolphe Goldschmidt. Helen's reply was predictable: "Again it is with deep regret that I am unable to grant your request . . . but my feelings and those of my Mother remain unaltered. . . . As long as we live in our present home, it must be our privilege to accept or reject applicants for admission to the Gallery, and I am only sorry that there should be friends of yours among those who must be denied." *"Here it is again!"* Sachs howled to Edward Forbes. "Frankly," he said, "It makes me *sick!*"

Yet for other aspects of Helen's work, accolades were mounting. On October 7, she received the most meaningful of all, congratulations from Sir Robert Witt on his first visit to the new Frick Art Reference Library. He scrutinized everything from the Italian-style reading room with its long refectory tables to the bouquets of fresh flowers. One particular detail caught his eye. Undoubtedly recalling her visit to Adolphe Stoclet's palace in Brussels and the innovative way he had used antique velvet to set off his paintings, Helen had hung her Giovanni di Paolo *Nativity* against such a backdrop. "It all looks so stylish, so slap-up! Who thinks of all these things?" Witt exclaimed. The answer was Helen Frick.

Helen's meticulous attention to detail was additionally evidenced in the fine arts department at the University of Pittsburgh, also opening that fall. The curriculum, approved by Helen, included a general survey of art history, Florentine art, Medieval art, French art, Dutch painting, the history of Oriental art, architecture of the Italian Renaissance, and English Church architecture, among other subjects.

Toward the end of the year Helen sailed for Italy, her third trip on behalf the library. On New Year's Eve, she wrote Ethelwyn Manning from Italy: "Is it not a strange coincidence that we are living only a stone's throw from the house where Duccio painted the *Maesta*?" How validated she would have felt to know that in 1923 Adolphe Stoclet had purchased one of the last Duccios to be owned by a private collector, *Madonna and Child*, and that in 2004, twenty years after her death, the Metropolitan Museum of Art bought this Duccio—auctioned by Christie's on behalf of Stoclet's heirs—for a record price of approximately $50 million.

But sadness did overtake her during this period, as well. Despite her frantic pace, her chronic exhaustion, her many achievements, Helen complained of being "a bad sister and a bad daughter." In letters to her mother found at Westmoreland Farm after Helen's death, she sometimes lamented: "I am unworthy. What can I do?" Moreover, in late January 1928, while Helen was still enjoying Italy, she learned that one of her dogs, a little Scottish terrier named Kelpie, missing for about a week, had been found dead in a field, hit by a car. Helen fell into despair. As was her habit when a pet died, she mourned for months and placed a minimum three-month moratorium on entertaining.

Back home in the spring, Helen attended to the cleaning and restoration of paintings in the Frick Collection. As she explained to Paul Sachs on April 2, 1928, "some of the pictures have dirty streaks on them—nearly all require a little rubbing over, & in some cases, the stretchers are making ridges on the canvas." Meanwhile, two more Walter Gay portraits of One East Seventieth Street, commissioned by Helen and her mother, had arrived, *The Boucher Room* and *The Living Hall.*

In addition, George Harvey's biography of Henry Clay Frick was almost ready for publication and Helen was readying her father's birthplace for its opening. Since purchasing the property in 1922, she had restored the homestead to its original 1830s appearance. In October 1927, the Historical Society of Western Pennsylvania in Pittsburgh agreed to create a Westmoreland-Fayette branch of their museum in the house. Helen engaged her first cousin, Luella Frick Taylor, to manage the site, then called the Historical House, and offered to pay her salary as well as the future maintenance and upkeep of the homestead. There was a stipulation, however, that would echo profoundly in her future dealings with the Frick Collection trustees: no changes to the dwelling could be made during Helen's lifetime, unless approved by her. Helen then began acquiring antiques and furniture, patterning her project after the concept for the American Wing at the Metropolitan Museum, where the Americana collection helped visitors appreciate their own country's artists and craftsmen. Particularly desirous that the birthplace help immigrants in the West Overton area learn about western Pennsylvania history, she commissioned a New York artist, June Evans Platt, for a mural in the east drawing room, to be known as the Historical Room, depicting ten events from the history of the western Pennsylvania frontier—George Washington's arrival at Frazier's cabin in the winter of 1763, scenes from the French and Indian War, and the erection of the first courthouse in Allegheny County in 1794.

Walter Gay (1856–1937), *The Boucher Room.* Commissioned by Adelaide and Helen Clay Frick in 1927–1928. Oil on canvas, 25 ¾ x 29 in. © the Collection of the Frick Art & Historical Center, Pittsburgh, Pennsylvania.

Although preserving her father's memory and her family heritage, Helen did not want the Historical House viewed as an Overholt-Frick shrine. At the opening ceremony on June 16, speakers included R. T. H. Halsey, the director of the American Wing of the Metropolitan Museum, as well as the chairman of the Pennsylvania Historical Commission and the director of the Pennsylvania State Library and Museum. Helen stood modestly to the side and took no part in the program. Instead, her first cousin, William H. Stevenson, who was president of the Historical Society of Western Pennsylvania, read her letter expressing her desire that the house "stimulate interest in the splendid early history of this locality. . . . and encourage the preservation of the few remaining relics of these days." Only one reference to her father, a small steel engraving of Frick in the hallway, was displayed.

Since purchasing the Overholt homestead in 1922, Helen had turned down many opportunities to acquire a much larger parcel—the entire eight-house, one-street village of West Overton, the seven-story Overholt distillery, and the three-hundred-acre West

Overton Farm. On June 28, after the opening of the Historical House, she nevertheless decided to protect the site and bought the distillery across the road, together with all the mill buildings and about three-and-a-half acres of land, for $7,500.

Sixty-nine-year-old Adelaide was too frail to attend the opening, but she and Helen sailed for Italy in September. This would be no tranquil respite. The art world was shaken by scandal when sculptures sold as original Renaissance works at high prices by a noted firm, Volpi and Balboni, were exposed as fakes made by a living Roman artist, Alceo Dossena. So good was Dossena's work, for a decade it had deceived both astute connoisseurs and many premier museums as well as private collectors like Helen Frick. Most stunning of all, Dossena himself revealed the deceit. Disgruntled because he had received only $35,000 against the dealers' take of over $1 million for selling his sculptures as antique masterpieces, Dossena sued.

In 1924 Helen Frick had purchased two large marble sculptures depicting *The Annunciation,* represented to her by the collector-scholar Mason Perkins as rare works by Simone Martini, an artist known only for his paintings. Perkins described *The Annunciation* group to Helen as "two statues . . . of such important artistic importance. . . . that I cannot sufficiently impress upon you the urgent necessity of silence and discretion." Though the Frick Collection trustees rejected the group, suspicious of the authenticity, Helen nonetheless moved quickly and bought them for herself. Mineral tests proved the statues genuine, and Helen believed Perkins's assurance that "this great work [was] the most *tremendous* thing that has yet come on sale in the field of Italian Sculpture." Helen placed the statues like guards on either side of the door separating the West Gallery and North Hall—the area frequented by the few scholars Helen admitted through the Seventy-first Street entrance—from the family's inner sanctum beyond. So when Dossena announced that *The Annunciation,* as well as a $100,000 marble sarcophagus sold to the Museum of Fine Arts, Boston, as a work by Mino da Fiesole, were by his hand, not a Renaissance master, Helen was among those discredited not only before her board but also the entire art world. She was, however, a good sport, and on September 13, she wrote Edward Forbes from Italy, "I suppose you have heard about Dossena of Rome?" and continued, "My mother is enjoying every minute."

The North Hall at One East Seventieth Street with *The Annunciation* figures, thought to be by Simone Martini when acquired by Helen Clay Frick in 1924 for her collection. The master copyist Alceo Dossena later revealed that they were his fakes. In 1933 Helen gave the figures to the Henry Clay Frick Fine Arts Department at the University of Pittsburgh for study purposes. Author's collection.

This mistake did not stop Helen from following through with her plans, including commissions for work by Nicholas Lochoff. For almost a decade, the art world—encouraged by Edward Forbes, Paul Sachs, and Bernard Berenson—had endorsed the work of this Russian chemist-turned-artist, who was now living in Florence. In 1911, Russia's Grand Duke Alexi Alexeivich had commissioned him to copy many of the great Italian frescoes for the Moscow Museum, today known as the Pushkin Museum of Fine Arts, for its opening in 1912. Lochoff was, however, only able to complete three old master frescoes and five oil paintings before the Great War and the 1917 Bolshevik revolution left him stranded in Italy with neither money nor commissions, but still making his stunning copies of the great but fast-crumbling Italian works. Mary Berenson gave him her blessing: "One glance around [his] studio was enough to show . . . that his copies were indeed very different from all other copies. They were almost unbelievably accurate reconstructions of the pictures." A cult had developed around the displaced Russian, and by 1926 St. Marks School in Southboro, Massachusetts, owned his copy of Giovanni Bellini's *Madonna Enthroned with Saints,* while the Fogg owned one oil painting after Titian, *The Concert,* and two fresco copies of the series *Procession of the Magi* by Benozzo Gozzoli. Helen knew of Lochoff through Forbes and Sachs and had twice before visited his studio. In 1923, four years before Duccio's *Temptation of Christ* on the Mountain became available, Helen had commissioned the Russian for a copy of Duccio's *Maestà* in the cathedral of Siena. The order was never fulfilled, however, because Lochoff felt too much "barbarous restoration was done long ago" and the original work was, thereby, too damaged to retrieve. Now, in January 1928, Helen followed up with two commissions: a reconstruction of Piero della Francesca's fresco in San Sepolcro, *The Resurrection,* for the University of Pittsburgh's fine arts department, and one of Pietro Lorenzetti's fresco of the *Madonna and Child with Saints Francis and John* in the Lower Church of St. Francis in Assisi, for her library reading room. While the debate over the aesthetic value of a good fake versus an original was raging in the art world, Helen felt that the Dossena sculptures, like the Lochoff frescoes—never represented as originals—could serve a purpose both inspirational and instructive for library scholars and fine arts students at the University of Pittsburgh. Convinced of their beauty and merit, on September 30, Helen wrote Ethelwyn Manning from Florence that she and her mother were about to visit Borgo San Sepolcro "to see the 'Piero' that Lochoff is doing for Pittsburgh," and further explained, "We spent a very interesting hour with [Lochoff] today in his [Florence] studio and saw the cartoon [sketch] he has prepared for our own fresco. I can hardly wait for it!" Professor Clapp was touched by Helen's generosity, as was Chancellor Bowman. Soon thereafter Bowman engaged the prominent architect and celebrated authority on campus planning, Charles Z. Klauder, designer of over sixty buildings for various schools, colleges, and universities in America, to begin work on a fine arts building. Klauder was also, through his father, of German descent. The chancellor undoubtedly knew of Helen's anti-German bias from Forbes and Sachs and was certainly taking a chance in hiring him, but, astonishingly, Helen did not object. Perhaps this time Helen had put her prejudice aside because Klauder was an American citizen, born and raised in Philadelphia.

By November 1928, the fine arts department was thriving. Clapp and his department were, in fact, the envy of professors as far away as California. "You are fortunate," Ernest C. Moore of the University of California, Los Angeles, wrote Clapp, "in your budget. . . . How fortunate I may tell you by saying that no department here has as much money each year as you have."

The True Blues also felt lucky. On November 30, with employment scarce, Boyd expressed her gratitude to Helen Frick for the support she had given the women for their annual Thanksgiving dinner. For one group of True Blues, who would otherwise have been alone for the holiday, Helen provided a feast. The women consumed four turkeys, dozens of pies, and other traditional goodies. And when the Christmas season neared Boyd reported that the True Blues had "wrapped 1400 packages for the girls."

Despite the festivities, Helen severed her relationship with Thomas Hastings, and on December 3, concerned about space requirements, asked Edward W. Forbes if there were any architects he might consider for a new library building in New York. Helen also gave one month's notice to her father's secretary, James Howard Bridge, who had been retained after Frick's death to show people through the galleries. Bridge, who could hardly sustain the embarrassment of being fired by a woman, sought revenge. On November 28, he advised Helen that he was sending to the printers the manuscript for a book entitled *Portraits*

Nicholas Lochoff (d. 1948), after Piero della Francesca (ca. 1415/20–1492), *The Resurrection*. Acquired by Helen Clay Frick in 1930 for the Cathedral of Learning, Room 324, University of Pittsburgh. Fresco. Museo Civic, Borgo San Sepolcro. Courtesy University of Pittsburgh. Photo credit: Ed Watkins.

and Personalities: Imaginary Conversations in the Frick Galleries—a series of fantasy conversations between the portrait subjects in the Frick Collection, including, according to McCarten's "Profiles" article, a description of Frick as "a willing but none too competent amateur in art." In doing so, Bridge appeared to have violated a March 3, 1925, agreement with the Fricks obligating him not to disclose, as Helen put it, "any other matter in connection with our family." The imaginary conversations with the portrait subjects, revealing the symbolic relationship Frick had with his paintings, cut, for Helen, to the core of her father's very private collecting impulses. A hurt and irate Helen sought to enjoin the book from publication.

At first her lawyers dissuaded her from taking such action by convincing her that suing would bring the book more publicity than if left alone. But Helen soon changed her mind and instead followed her father's example. Back in the first decade of 1900, Henry Frick had become irate when Bridge revised *The History of Carnegie Steel* to flatter Carnegie (at Carnegie's urgings). Frick insisted that Bridge suppress the book, and although it was printed, bound, and ready for release, Bridge destroyed the entire edition. Only two copies remained, copies Helen Frick threw into the fire in the living hall in 1925. Now she decided to suppress publication of *Portraits and Personalities*. Although negotiations took until April 21, 1931, Helen paid Bridge $27,500 for the remaining 1,696 copies and the book's mechanicals—photographs, lanternslides, photographic plates, and electrotype plates—and destroyed them all.

Even Helen's good friend, Roland Knoedler, felt the force of her wrath when he acted without her authority. Since Frick's death, Helen and Adelaide had controlled the publication rights to the art collection. When Gilbert Stuart's portrait of George Washington was reproduced in the November issue of *Antiquarian Magazine* with a credit to M. Knoedler & Co., not the Frick Collection, Helen immediately demanded of Knoedler's Charles R. Henschel: "I would like to know how it is that permission to publish this picture was obtained through your firm and I would like an explanation." Advised by Knoedler to duck the issue, Charles played upon her passion for privacy: "We took [the] courtesy to protect [you] from being bothered." Helen made it clear that they should not again try to overstep their bounds.

In November 1928, Helen almost fired Ellen Boyd as well. Although efficient and hardworking, she too had overstepped her authority when, before asking Helen's permission, she suggested to the True Blue girls they take a trip with her to California in February. Infuriated, Helen wrote Boyd: "[I] will support [the trip] so as not to disappoint [the] girls. However, may this be a warning to you, Mrs. Boyd, that never must you discuss plans again before consulting me." In February 1929, forty-five True Blues left with Boyd on the eight-thousand-mile, three-week journey by special train, complete with a True Blue lunchroom. The young women stopped in Washington, D.C., where they attended Herbert Hoover's inauguration, and then went on to New Orleans, San Antonio, San Diego, Los Angeles, and San Francisco, before returning East by way of the Grand Canyon, Chicago, Niagara Falls, and New York. The trip also rumbled through a flooded area in Georgia, where, as Boyd commented, "The tenements did look poor and the contrast of the comfort of New England homes with the southern houses was never more marked." On their arrival in Los Angeles, dozens of transplanted True Blue mothers, daughters, husbands, and children came out to welcome their East Coast "sisters." Describing the scene to Helen, Boyd was impressed "with the spirit and the loyalty of every one of the girls. . . . This trip has been a wonderful demonstration of fellowship and I doubt if there is anything like it in all the world." While they were on the road, another 656 True Blues sat down to lunch with Helen at the annual reunion, where Helen read a letter to the gathering from the travelers.

Yet amid all this good feeling, a major confrontation with the Frick Collection trustees was brewing. Part of the problem was the very unconventional nature of a woman sharing the boardroom with men. Gertrude Vanderbilt Whitney ran the Whitney Museum, but women rarely held such positions. Marjorie Merriweather Post, for example, was not permitted to sit on the board of her company, Postum Cereal; her place was assumed instead by her husband, Edward F. Hutton. Certainly the Frick Collection men, uncomfortable in Helen's presence, did not appreciate her knowledge about the collection or her art history expertise (in most cases greater than theirs) and for the most part they did not like her. Her authoritarian manner was deemed unfeminine, as was the power she wielded in her dual capacity as director of the library and trustee of the collection. Without question, they were palpably embarrassed by her anti-German bias. Despite Adelaide's life tenancy, they believed Helen had no right to bar German scholars from the house. Increasingly, Helen was seen as high-handed, exercising her authority in the most arbitrary manner. The trustees were frankly appalled by some of her actions. For example, when the seniors of East Huntington Township High School had wanted to dedicate their yearbook to Henry Clay Frick and had written essays around the West Overton Historical House, Helen had agreed to the project, provided their work was respectful. But when she studied the yearbook proofs her temper flared. "I cannot half express the indignation I feel on reading their sketches!" she exploded to her cousin Karl Overholt. "Positively they are not to use his name at all!" At the end of March 1928, without consulting the trustees or offering either a reason or a compromise, she closed the gallery to visitors, except Edward Forbes, who was given admittance for his students. When the trustees demanded an explanation, she complained to Forbes: "Orders were given that my mother, being ill, should not be troubled by these matters."

The trustees' long-simmering resentment finally exploded at the April 1928 board meeting. Fed up with what they deemed her nervous erraticism, her single-minded efforts to immortalize her father, and her unbalanced and irrational anti-German posture, and emboldened by the Dossena scandal, her colleagues retaliated. When Helen asked the trustees to enlarge her library building, she met with fierce opposition. Rockefeller, who had been suspicious of Childs's attempt in 1922 to seize control of the board, now switched sides, turned on Helen, and aligned himself with her brother.

As for Childs, seven years as president of the Frick Collection had not quieted his hostility and resentment. After his attempted takeover, he had completed a scientific expedition to Mexico; funded an American Museum of Natural History voyage to Santa Fe; discovered a much heralded fossil specimen of "Hemicyo," the dog-bear; and sent hundreds of boxes containing fossils from his field explorations to the American Museum of Natural History. Yet Childs remained jealous of his sister.

On April 19, 1929, Helen wrote Karl Overholt: "You will hardly believe me when I report to you the limit to which the Trustees went yesterday at the meeting, in the discussion re the Library and its future! It was easy to see from the beginning that Childs had personally talked the matter over with each one. And with the exception of Mr. Hines, they were all very much opposed to me." Angry and insulted, forty-year-old Helen described the trustees' position, confirmed by the minutes of the meeting: "They will not consider now the enlarging of the Library. . . . [Mr. Ledyard] said I had no right on counting on living [ten years], and that I might die within the year. I replied that I had no intention of doing so." She also reported, "Mr. Rockefeller, on three or four occasions, in a very religious voice, expressed his sentiments about the wonderful work, and how he admired it, but each time, stated, that in his opinion, such a wonderful work should be much more adequately housed in the Metropolitan Museum or some other N.Y. institution, where it would be more accessible to large numbers of people." Outraged, Helen responded, "that was not the object I had in financing the Library and devoting my life to the work." She countered Rockefeller "with the statement that I had been both the creator and supporter of the FARL [Frick Art Reference Library] and that it was dedicated to my father's memory and was to be a part of the Frick Collection in the future. I said that I felt certain my father would have approved of its being properly housed." Rockefeller replied: "It is unfortunate that Mr. F. is not here to speak for himself," and then he "mentioned that I should have obtained an affidavit from him." Adelaide, confined to her bed for over a month and taking seven different medications, nonetheless had managed to write the trustees embracing her daughter's cause. But the trustees dismissed Adelaide's letter. Helen reported to Overholt. "A portion was read aloud by Mr. Ledyard, but in a tone of voice that left no doubt in the minds of anyone, that her opinion deserved no great consideration." She scowled: "I could have knocked him down!" and lamented, "You now see what I had to go through with yesterday, and will not be surprised that I am anxious, out of fear, of dying within the year, of enabling Mr. Rockefeller of bestowing the Library on some other institution in N.Y., and thereby, securing another gold medal for his generosity."

Helen found her own way to retaliate. After Frick's death in 1919 she had, as an olive branch to Childs, secured his children's—her nieces' and nephew's—financial future through her will. Now she advised Overholt, a cousin more sympathetic to her than to Childs, that she wanted the terms changed "to safeguard the future of the Library." She understood that changing her will would "of course, mean that the residuary of my estate will not go to Childs's children as I had planned, but to FARL, which I am quite willing should happen, in view of Childs'[s] attitude." She continued, "my life['s] work has to be saved from people like Mr. Rockefeller and Mr. Ledyard." Setting aside her keen desire for privacy, the publicity-shy heiress further insisted, "I am anxious that great publicity should be given this matter, as only ridicule and public opinion will ever have weight with men of their mentality."

Helen further pressured the trustees. Although she purchased no paintings for her own collection this year, she and Adelaide urged the Frick Collection trustees to buy *The Wilton Diptych,* owned by the Earl of Pembroke estate and first offered to them in November 1927. A fourteenth-century English, or possibly French, altarpiece commissioned by Richard II of England for his private devotion, the diptych shows the king being presented to the Virgin and Child by his patron saint, John the Baptist, and Saints Edward the Confessor and Edmund, earlier English kings. Eleven angels in brilliant blue robes surround the Virgin, who is also in blue. Helen described it as "a supreme small Diptych" and Adelaide insisted, "It is one of the world's great masterpieces and I hope it will in time come into this Collection." Frank Mather Jr. had agreed, advising Helen that "a picture of that period of equal beauty is very unlikely to appear in the markets." Yet the arguments came to naught. As Helen later complained to her attorney William S. Moorhead, the trustees were deterred by the "high figure" cost and thereby showed "their lack of appreciation and knowledge [and] lost us this treasure." The British government raised the funds for its purchase and in 1929 gave the altarpiece to London's National Gallery of Art, where it remains one of their greatest treasures.

Meanwhile, Helen and Adelaide conspired to bolster her position with the trustees. The death of J. Horace Harding—a fellow trustee and Frick's beloved friend and advisor to

The Wilton Diptych (ca. 1395–1399). Egg on oak panel, 53 x 37 cm. Courtesy National Gallery, London, purchased with a special grant and contributions from Samuel Courtauld, Viscount Rothermere, C. T. Stoop, and the National Collection Art Fund, 1929.

whom Helen appealed "before the other Trustees [because] he always took my part, making it plain that my father and I had been very close and that I knew his wishes"—left a vacancy on the board. Adelaide preemptively proposed the vacancy be offered to Treasury Secretary Andrew W. Mellon, to prevent Childs and Rockefeller from nominating one of their friends. Adelaide and Helen knew that Mellon, a longtime friend of the Frick family, could be counted on as an ally.

Yet Helen was in a strategic predicament. If she supported Mellon, the trustees would probably refuse to elect him. So on December 10, 1929, Paul Sachs advised her "not to have any 'business' to report at the next meeting [in January 1930]—so that the Trustees would have an opportunity of realizing that unless [she] take an active interest, nothing happens." Helen complained, "I am sick at heart & weary, when I show them works of art & they do not even look at them!" Sachs warned her, "say nothing whatever about Mr. Mellon, about pictures or about anything else." On Christmas Eve, he warned her again: "Be a listener." On January 6, 1930, Andrew W. Mellon was elected a trustee of the Frick Collection. "Maybe," Helen wrote Paul Sachs, "1930 holds better luck for the Frick Collection than has the past—at least I am feeling more hopeful now!" On February 12, Mellon accepted the position and Helen, having heeded Sachs's advice, rejoiced: "I feel that you are very much responsible for this."

In the summer of 1930, the Iron Rail provided its usual respite and healthy food to hundreds of young guests, but the months were also marked by a more hands-on effort by Helen than she had been able to give since starting her library nearly a decade before. She was everywhere, assembling an exhibition of Italian objects and costumes for the girls and showing them movies of Italy, including the Palio, the colorful, brutal, bareback horse race run twice each summer around Siena's Piazza del Campo since the thirteenth century. She invited the girls to Eagle Rock, so they could see the stars through a telescope on the roof. And of course she continued to provide the traditional excursions and trips to the Eagle Rock beach, stables, and gardens.

In the fall, when sickness broke out among the young mothers and their babies, Helen stepped in again. On average, one baby in fourteen died in the United States, making it eleventh in infant mortality in the civilized world and seventeenth out of twenty nations in maternal mortality. For a time, the Sheppard-Towner Act of 1921, the first federally funded health care program in America for maternity and childcare, provided a glimmer of hope. When it came up for reauthorization in 1929, however, the bill was defeated. At Helen's urging, the girls received educational pamphlets and instruction in maternal and infant care. In fact, that season the $36,000 Helen spent on her girls—by today's standards the equivalent of $1.7 million—equaled the amount expended on the library.

In September, Helen prepared to switch her focus from the Iron Rail to the future of One East Seventieth Street as a house-museum. Nothing would happen until after her mother's death, but at that time a director would have to be appointed. Clapp was the obvious choice. He had developed a superb fine arts library at the University of Pittsburgh and ran an excellent educational program. More important, Helen liked and trusted him; he even persuaded her of the necessity to teach modern art including impressionism, neo-impressionism, cubism, futurism, and surrealism at the university. Ever since her brush with contemporary British painters at the Tate in 1909 and later after the Armory Show,

Arcangelo di Cola da Camerino (ca. 1385–1450), *Madonna and Child Enthroned; Crucifixion*. Acquired by Helen Clay Frick in 1930 for her collection. Diptych: tempera on panels, 12 x 13 ¾ in. © the Collection of the Frick Art & Historical Center, Pittsburgh, Pennsylvania.

when cubism shocked the American public in 1913, Helen had turned her back on anything created after 1850. Family members remember her spontaneous outbursts condemning most contemporary works as "trash," the representation of the destruction of cherished aesthetic values: excellence in technique, style, and composition. Clapp was able, however, to convince her to approve a course indicated by synopsis as "an attempt to give a fuller appreciation of an art that has constantly appeared to challenge the good taste and good sense of many contemporaries."

Helen considered offering Clapp the position of director of the Frick Collection now, while maintaining his position at the University of Pittsburgh. Clapp already was working very hard on an illustrated folio catalogue of the collection—an expansion of Helen's efforts during her father's life—and so was intimately familiar with its paintings, furniture, and decorative objects. On March 31, 1930, Helen invited the Clapps to dinner at One East Seventieth Street and there broached the subject of the directorship. Both were interested, though Maud had reservations about her husband's health and the importance to his career in his finishing the catalogue.

While Clapp considered the offer, Helen continued to battle the trustees for objects she wanted in her father's house-museum. She purchased for herself this year Arcangelo di Cola da Camerino's only signed masterpiece, *Madonna and Child Enthroned; Crucifixion* and persuaded the Frick Collection trustees to buy Paolo and Giovanni Veneziano's *Coronation of the Virgin*. But obtaining the Dreyfus Collection—the single most important private collection of Renaissance sculpture in the world, including bronzes, marble statues, terracottas, as well as historic coins—for the Frick Collection was foremost on her agenda. At a special meeting of the board on April 24, Helen advised the trustees that Paul Sachs recommended the purchase. Adelaide, and for once Childs, was also on her side, as was Andrew

Paolo and Giovanni Veneziano (Paolo, active 1321–1358), *The Coronation of the Virgin*. Acquired by the Frick Collection in 1930. Tempera on poplar panel, 43 ¼ x 27 in. © the Frick Collection, New York.

Mellon, who stood with Helen against the other trustees, including Rockefeller, who had the votes needed to reject the proposed acquisition.

Helen did not give up. By the end of April she had enlisted the support of Walker D. Hines, who stated: "[There] are some wonderful marbles and terra cottas . . . which could very appropriately be added to the Frick Collection as incidental to its present character and without committing the Collection to a further and general development of the matter of sculptures." Helen proposed, therefore, in a May 2, 1930, letter to Rockefeller, to buy the Dreyfus Collection for $4 million and to sell off what they did not want. Unbeknownst to Helen, however, Rockefeller had seen the collection a few years before, was already in secret negotiations with Duveen, and had already selected four pieces for himself: two marble busts and two terra-cotta busts. Months later, when Adelaide saw the collection in New York, Duveen falsely claimed that he was holding those pieces awaiting the decision of French clients. In the meantime, Rockefeller admitted to Ledyard: "Those are the four pieces in which we are interested [and] I am not a little embarrassed by the fact that I am a trustee of the Frick Collection." Ledyard advised him: "I do not think that this situation ought to cause you any embarrassment, whatever. . . . I am clearly of the opinion that there is no reason, whatsoever, why you and your wife should not . . . go on and acquire one or all of the four objects that you have in mind, and I do not think any duty rests upon you to see that the first opportunity should be given to the Frick Trustees." In the end, Frick Collection did not purchase the Dreyfus Collection. Instead, Andrew Mellon purchased it for the National Gallery in Washington, D.C.

By the spring of 1930, the Great Depression was engulfing the country. With the dire conditions in the textile and shoe towns around Boston, Boyd regularly checked in with the True Blues and monitored their needs, especially regarding health care. But lack of proper nourishment was compromising the girls' immune systems. "It is amazing how many of these mothers get along day after day on tea and bread and one meal now and then, of fish or meat without the proper vegetables," she lamented. Helen assumed more financial responsibility by paying for necessary operations and urging the girls to come to the Iron Rail to eat and rest. She boosted morale by inviting the noted Harvard astronomer Harlow Shapley to speak, continuing to buy each new girl a Bible, and encouraging them in other little ways to stay interested in life. One spring day a set of magnifying glasses arrived at the Iron Rail, and soon Boyd claimed the girls saw "many beauties in the mosses and flowers that [they] did not know existed." Fresh milk continued to arrive daily from Eagle Rock, and each girl drank on average eight-and-a-half quarts per week. The Iron Rail closed at the end of the summer except for its traditional Thanksgiving dinner, and all surplus food was distributed to the girls. For their part, the True Blue Club members chose not to hold a 1931 reunion and instead voted to put their money toward relief.

With the dawning of 1931, Adelaide was again confined to her One East Seventieth Street bedroom suffering from rheumatic pains. Helen seems to have done little through the winter and spring other than worry about Adelaide's declining health and consider the future of her father's collection should her mother die. The library staff took photography trips in March and May to Albany, where they identified many unknown works. Helen acquired a sixteenth-century French work by the studio of Corneille de Lyon, *Gabrielle de Rochechouart*, for her collection and decided not to give any additional work to Lochoff, now impoverished due to dwindling commissions, because, as she said, "a copy, no matter how fine, is always a copy."

Helen's folio catalogue of the Frick Collection was, however, moving along at a healthy pace. The first 168 pages were being printed in Pittsburgh on paper specially made of Italian linen. Meanwhile, Helen continued to woo Clapp for the director position. Toward the end of April, she treated him and Maud to a two-week New York visit and also entertained them at Westmoreland Farm amid a riot of spring blossoms.

In May, Adelaide was able to travel to Eagle Rock for the summer, but remained unwell until June, when she took a few small outings. On September 30, just as she was about to return to the city for the winter, Adelaide suffered a stroke. Childs rushed from his Long Island home to be with his mother, and Helen came by airplane, accompanied by a New York physician. At 1:00 a.m. on October 4, seventy-one-year-old Adelaide Howard Childs Frick died. Other than writing "Mother" in his diary, Childs made no remark about her passing. But Helen did. The final entry in her 1927–1931 Westmoreland Farm diary, October 4, reads: "All is over. My precious one slept away at one o'clock this morning." Then, across the envelope containing her mother's September 10 letter, the last of Adelaide's she ever received, Helen wrote: "Sacred."

Corneille de Lyon, studio of (ca. 1534–ca. 1574), *Gabrielle de Rochechouart, Dame de Lansac.* Acquired by Helen Clay Frick in 1931 for her collection. Tempera and oil on panel, 6 ⅜ x 5 ⅛ in. © the Collection of the Frick Art & Historical Center, Pittsburgh, Pennsylvania. Photo credit: Richard A. Stoner.

A short service was held at Eagle Rock the day after Adelaide's death, and then her remains were transported to Pittsburgh. On October 7, after a funeral service at Clayton, her body was buried beside her husband's in the family plot at the Homewood Cemetery. Her will was read, and to Childs's ire, Helen again inherited the larger share of the family fortune. Adelaide had executed her will four years earlier, on December 19, 1927—what would have been Frick's seventy-eighth birthday—and bequeathed all her personal effects to Helen, including her Sèvres porcelain and other valuables in her One East Seventieth Street bedroom and boudoir. Eagle Rock and its art and porcelain collections passed to Helen through her father's will together with all real estate in the surrounding area. Adelaide also left Helen what the daughter valued most: ownership of Clayton, its paintings and decorative arts collection, and the Westmoreland railroad car of enduring sentimental value.

Hoping to appease Childs in his second "disinheritance," immediately after Adelaide's burial Helen transferred to him and his heirs her half-share of the $5 million trust their father created for Adelaide's life use. In the eleven years since Frick's death, brother and sister had spoken rarely. Assured he could now maintain his and the children's future lifestyle, Childs chose, for a time, a truce. With a new era dawning, Helen, recognizing she was unpopular with the all-male board of the Frick Collection, took additional steps to ensure a better relationship with her brother and her fellow collection trustees. Helen immediately removed her personal belongings from One East Seventieth Street and vacated the premises, while twelve guards protected the house, twenty-four hours a day. Frick's New York home, no longer a private residence, was officially the Frick Collection, owned by the public and governed by the trustees appointed through Frick's will. No longer could Helen single-handedly monitor the works of art or decide who could see them.

But she did not disappear. She suggested to Childs that Clapp become director of the collection. Childs, wanting more assurance than just his sister's recommendation, asked both Paul Sachs and John Bowman for a reference. Sachs replied that Clapp was "one of America's outstanding and recognized scholars . . . a man who reacts with the utmost sensitiveness of both eye and mind to works of art of any land or epoch." Since Clapp had been working on Helen's illustrated folio catalogue of the collection, Sachs added, "He knows more than any man living about the Frick Collection." The chancellor gave Clapp a similar recommendation, as "one of the leading scholars in the world in the history of art."

At a special meeting held at the Frick Collection on November 5, 1931, just a month after Adelaide's passing, the trustees voted to close certain rooms "pending appraisal, the contents of which, under Mrs. Frick's will, pass to Miss Frick," and Helen, having long since received Bowman's permission to let Clapp take a year's absence from the university, formally proposed him as director, a position to be held in consultation with Bowman, Sachs, and Forbes. On December 9, 1931, Clapp completed his first day at the Frick Collection. But not as director. He had modestly requested that he serve in an advisory capacity and without title or publicity. Four months into the New Year Helen was able to write Edward Forbes: "The trustees meetings of the Frick Collection have improved so much since Mr. Clapp has been connected with them, that I no longer dread them as I used to and I want you & Mr. Sachs to know of the better understanding that now exists & of the cooperation on the part of the trustees with matters pertaining to the library."

Helen knew, however, that even with Clapp on her side, she was in a tough position. Fearful of her brother's erratic and arrogant behavior and his dubious motives, yet determined to remain a force in the collection, she asked her secretary "to think of either a fable or a proverb, or something like that, which tells the story of a very small insect—or possibly animal—which bothered the great big animal, [who] was so sure of himself he just thought that he was all important." No matter how "big" the male trustees were, and no matter how voiceless they rendered her, she intended to fight to uphold Frick's legacy; to wear the mantle her father had bestowed.

On Her Own

I wanted him to cherish and approve of me, not as he had when I was a child, but as the woman I was, who had her own mind, and had made her own choices.
—Adrienne Rich

As Helen prepared for a first full year without her mother, she closed Eagle Rock for an indefinite period and shifted her focus to the Iron Rail. Fifteen Boston banks had closed and unemployment and suffering continued through the fall of 1931, when a strike in Lawrence intensified the True Blues' misery. Helen changed the Iron Rail Vacation Home's charter from a Pennsylvania corporation to a Massachusetts one, and kept the program functioning. On January 11, Ellen Boyd reported, "The first load of potatoes, eggs, onions and pork goes out today to Lowell where [we] will go to each house with the gift." Over the next two weeks, during that bitter winter, Helen sent coal to forty-four families, and Boyd wrote, "[We] remembered eighty-three others with provisions." Helen also asked her Eagle Rock friend and neighbor, Frederick Prince, to hire, at her expense, one hundred unemployed men to clean up the woods around the Iron Rail.

There was also much work to do in New York. Childs had been lobbying for dramatic—and, in Helen's view, tasteless—changes to One East Seventieth Street after his mother's death: surrounding the driveway court with a colonnade and using it as an auditorium for organ recitals; relocating the main stairs; and adding a new lecture room on the second floor that would incorporate Frick's private study and connect it to the new library on its second floor. In addition, he contemplated combining the enamel room, the West Gallery, and the proposed Oval Room and East Gallery into one long gallery defined by large columns at either end. Helen opposed these ideas, particularly the one long gallery she called a "tunnel." The trustees voted down Childs's proposed changes in late January and agreed on other more refined ideas for renovation of the building from home to house-museum. The plans called for demolition of the driveway from Seventieth Street to Seventy-first Street for the incorporation of a garden court and the extension of the reconstructed Frick Collection

Opposite: Helen Clay Frick, ca. 1940. Courtesy the Frick Collection/Frick Art Reference Library Archives. Photo credit: The Misses Selby.

Construction of the new Frick Art Reference Library (left), designed by John Russell Pope, before demolition of the former library building (center), designed by Thomas Hastings. The demolition made way for the Frick Collection's east gallery (right), an eastward extension of the west gallery across the former driveway. Courtesy the Frick Collection/Frick Art Reference Library Archives.

building eastward, using part of the driveway and the library. A new library would be built to the east of the present one and adjacent to it, at no. 8 and no. 10 East Seventy-first Street, with its own entrance on Seventy-first Street. The public would have access to the house-museum's first floor only, and the collection's public rooms would be roped off in a closed system of circulation through the galleries. The trustees also embraced a plan to create a united architectural facade on Seventy-first Street incorporating the Frick Collection and the new Frick Art Reference Library building as a solid block. Helen, unsettled by the number of changes being made, wanted them to make no mistake about the independent nature of the two entities, or whose library it was. She instructed Clapp to report to the trustees: "The Library should continue its development along present lines, financed by her, as a separate organization working in the closest cooperation and harmony with the interests of The Frick Collection." As stated in the 1924 agreement, the Frick Collection would assume all construction costs.

Since the library's inception Helen had spent more than $1 million gathering material and was eager to move forward with her expansion plans. She monitored the reconstruction progress carefully, and on February 28, sketched out a floor plan for the new reading room. Moreover, with Clapp working both in New York and Pittsburgh, she decided to renovate for the Clapps the house next door to Clayton.

Helen traveled abroad over the summer, through France, Switzerland, and Holland on behalf of the library, and among her many excursions in France was a visit to the Louvre and one to Houdon's factory with Malvina Hoffman. But in all the activity of her trip,

The *boiserie* and marble mantel in Helen's library at One East Seventieth Street were reinstalled in her office at the new Frick Art Reference Library. Courtesy the Frick Collection/Frick Art Reference Library.

Helen did not neglect her projects back home. In April the Frick Collection trustees had unanimously chosen the architectural firm of John Russell Pope for the reconstruction. Helen reminded Pope to reuse as much salvage from One East Seventieth Street as possible in the library, for sentimental as well as cost-saving reasons. The paneling and bookcases from her father's study and from her bedroom were to be used in a private storage area in the library. Jacobean oak paneling from the bowling-alley-library was to be installed in the new reading rooms. Her office suite was to have one room in the French style, using the paneling and the marble mantel from her little library on the second floor of One East Seventieth Street, and her Italian-style sitting room in the current library building was to be refitted as her new one. When she received Pope's architectural plans, she returned them to Clapp with corrections and detailed suggestions, and anxiously ordered that the final plans not be submitted to the trustees until her return.

Helen's Italian sitting room at the new Frick Art Reference Library. *Nativity* by Giovanni di Paolo is above the sofa, exhibited against antique velvet. Courtesy the Frick Collection/ Frick Art Reference Library Archives.

As well as her specifications for the library, Helen insisted that in regard to the collection, her father's will be honored in every detail. Before construction began, Childs wanted the paintings and other valuable objects moved off-site, even though Frick's will firmly stated that no paintings were ever to leave his house. Helen instead demanded that a large vault be constructed beneath the old driveway. "Miss Frick said that she felt very strongly that the removal of the contents of the house to a storage warehouse was not a plan that appealed to her," wrote Clapp in a November 25, 1932, memorandum. "She said that in these times it was worth while to have such a vault and that it would be of use in the future and that her father had planned some such thing when he planned the vault now under the Frick Art Reference Library." Helen warned the trustees if they moved the contents off site, each one of them would have to assume personal liability for loss, damage, or theft. The trustees decided to construct the vault.

As tensions mounted, Helen became increasingly nervous and took out her growing anxiety on the most unlikely of people: Sir Robert Witt, beloved godfather of her library. For twelve years the two libraries had enjoyed a sharing agreement, whereby Witt could keep some of the books he purchased with Frick Art Reference Library funds for his own. Claiming now that Sir Robert had spent too much money on the purchase of library material and had withheld too many books, and furious that he had filed the photographs of American paintings she had sent him with the British, Helen abruptly closed his bank account. In despair, Witt asked Malvina Hoffman to use her "healing hand and voice" and intercede on his behalf. "This wretched what-ever-it-was took possession of her mind and changed her whole character," he wrote, hoping that "thanks to you she will reconsider her position and that she may come to see that even her wealth and position cannot justify her treating any of us as she does from time to time." Recognizing her current "state of mind and body" was much the product of her mother's death and the renovation of the New York house, he continued, "But isn't it sad that health (I mean ill-health) and wealth can lead people to behave so that they lose friends and name and everything worth having?" Helen remained unmovable. "As for my 'reputation' which you say is at stake," she wrote Hoffman, "I cannot see why! I feel perfect confidence in it & if others listen to Witt & believe his side, they are welcome to do so, as my conscience is quite clear on the subject of whatever transactions have passed between [Witt and myself]." When Sir Robert's wife Mary sent Helen a letter, hoping to visit her when next in America, Helen penned firm instructions to her secretary: "This requires no answer!" Her librarian, Ethelwyn Manning, explained to Sir Robert, "Miss Frick is now retrenching in all possible directions and she has decided that the time has come to sever all financial relations with the Witt Library."

Having failed in her role as mediator, a sorrowful Hoffman told Sir Robert, "You must . . . realize that a person who has been hurt as she has been will carry the scars until the end of her days." There are "old wounds hidden away behind frigid manners." The chill, even including Helen's refusal to accept Sir Robert's gifts of books and catalogues, would last fifteen years. Yet Sir Robert kept Helen on his Christmas card list and decided to treat her "like a sick woman, who should be humoured just because she is sick."

Throughout the spring of 1932, as the Depression increased its grip on the nation, conditions around Boston continued their downward spiral. With the coming New England thaw, Helen had suggested that small gardens could be cultivated in the field directly beside the Iron Rail, each plot about twenty-five feet square and tended by the girls. In this way the True Blues could feel self-sufficient and learn to garden and to can from the Agricultural School in Essex. Certainly potatoes and carrots would help sustain the girls over the next difficult winter and any produce not consumed by them could be sold at their clubs to increase funds.

The city of Lawrence, as Ellen Boyd wrote to Helen, was bankrupt, the conditions in Lowell were "the worst anywhere," and sixty thousand Lynn shoe workers were on the unemployment roster. Now the girls were dealt another blow: the general public began objecting to the employment of married women. Section 213 of the Federal Economy Act, enacted to eliminate wives from government payrolls, stated that only one family member could work in the federal civil service. State and local authorities followed suit, and soon other employers such as utilities, department stores, and school systems also placed restrictions on hiring wives. Even the traditionally female roles such as social worker and librarian experienced a 5 to 20 percent drop in employment. Helen was not about to let her girls suffer stigma, embarrassment, or economic defeat. She could not give them paying jobs, but she could keep them hopeful of a better future. On July 3, she telephoned from Westmoreland Farm, and took meticulous notes about each girl, particularly those from the first Iron Rail season of 1909, asking about those who were having especially hard times and about those who were ill. While she considered how to help her girls in Massachusetts, she also expanded her social welfare efforts in Pittsburgh and helped organize the Forty Plus Club of Western Pennsylvania to assist older men in finding employment. In addition, Helen supported a food distribution program at U.S. Steel and initiated a pension plan for the employees of the Frick Building. According to Pittsburgh's *Tribune Review* it was "the first such plan put into effect in a city building, [and] it was a model for others."

That fall, Helen focused her attention on the Republican campaign to reelect Hoover. But the ideals of Republicans like Helen, who were convinced that private charity and not the federal government should solve the problems of the working poor, were out of step with the times and inadequate to match the level of relief required. The New Deal was implemented with more than $14 million spent in the Boston area alone. Still the suffering continued. The Iron Rail, doing what it could to ease the distress, distributed groceries that "were worth their weight in gold to many families," as Boyd described to Helen. But these were not free handouts. Helen purchased the goods wholesale at a discount and sold them to the girls at one-third her cost, "to keep their self-respect." Boyd wrote, "So many of our families represent the refined and ambitious American families whose need cannot be known from appearances, that your generosity has saved them from most intense suffering and humiliation."

Helen's fortune, though impacted by the Depression, was relatively intact, largely because her portfolio carried no debt. So she pressed forward with new projects during 1932. In January and February, the library staff organized a series of field trips to Kentucky and planned additional trips to Cleveland, New Orleans, Nantucket, and Baltimore. To her dismay, however, no agreement had yet been reached on the relationship between the library and the Frick Collection, establishing her as the director in charge of all policy and the person financially responsible for library operations. Moreover, she was denied a place on the building committee, the organizational committee, and even the committee for the new library. Clapp noted in a memorandum, "It was only because of her *insistence,* that she was permitted to be a member of a sub-committee for the Library plans." Mrs. Walker Hines, wife of trustee Walker Hines, even questioned Rockefeller about the wisdom, if not the affront, of marginalizing Helen, but Rockefeller later justified his actions by claiming expediency. "I realized from the outset that a vast amount of work was involved and that much time, thought, and effort would be required. . . . There have been difficult problems to face and solve . . . and a number of situations that had required utmost tact in their handling because of the personalities involved."

Fearing Rockefeller and Childs might actually seize control of the library, Helen directed Clapp to tell the trustees that she insisted on remaining its director. On the same date Clapp also noted that Helen demanded to see the plans for the new library building four or five days before they were delivered to the trustees. According to Helen, when these demands were presented at the next trustees' meeting, "instantly there was a 'huddle,' [amongst the trustees] and after a short time, Mr. Hines said that my terms were unacceptable to the Trustees and that I could not be Director of FARL." Helen said, "I withdrew from the meeting" and "it took some weeks to convince the Trustees of the rights in the matter, and I threatened to move the FARL to Pittsburgh. Finally they came around. It was Rockefeller who fought the hardest, and when he finally gave in, he insisted that the name would have to be changed to the Helen Clay Frick Art Reference Library. I denied his right to make any changes whatsoever and my terms were accepted."

Since the architectural design was soon to be approved, Helen forged ahead and set a date to announce the new building to the press. To prevent leaks prior to the public announcement, she wrote a note to each staff member about the project, placed it in a sealed envelope, and marked the date it could be opened. Most of the staff waited as she had asked, but to Helen's dismay someone did divulge her closely guarded secret.

Convincing the trustees to sign an agreement duplicating the financial arrangement of 1924, however, soon proved so difficult Helen had to threaten litigation. The trustees "have always admitted that the Library was [mine]. Now that they are asked to signify their approval . . . in writing, it comes as a surprise to them!" They also continued to resist her every suggestion about the renovation of the Frick Collection, as revealed in Clapp's memo: "She is not for an artificial skylight in the enamel room and would prefer to have the windows left as they are and the room preserved as nearly as it is now possible." Helen got her way. Yet the Frick Collection trustees continued to sideline her.

John D. Rockefeller Jr. wanted the Frick Collection to distance itself completely from the library, and now blithely suggested that Helen pay for the properties on East Seventy-first Street and assume all construction costs. Thereafter, she could supervise the gathering and organizing of material for the library. Under this scheme, however, she would not be given a position of authority; from year to year the Frick Collection trustees would appoint a director—anyone but Helen—and retain ultimate control. As head of the building committee for the Frick Collection, Rockefeller held unusual sway over the other trustees. He proposed the quickest and best way to make Helen capitulate: "Miss Frick expressed herself at the last trustees' meeting in no uncertain terms as to the complete inadequacy of the present library building and of the immediate necessity for a new building. . . . [making] it quite clear she was not prepared to provide these new facilities at her own expense. . . . She will continue to be up against an intolerable situation so far as adequate space for the activity of her library is concerned. This pressure, it would seem to me, must ultimately bring her to reason." He also warned Hines about future problems the trustees would suffer if Helen were left in charge of the library. Rockefeller was, perhaps, most infuriated by Helen's ban on German scholars. In particular, her policy flouted everything the Rockefeller Foundation was trying to do at that time for Jewish refugees fleeing Hitler's Germany, among them some of the more prominent scholars in the world. Under its Special Research Aid Fund for Deposed Scholars, the Foundation was helping them find positions in American universities. So Rockefeller cautioned: "If we now yield to Miss Frick . . . are we not apt to have all sorts of difficulties with her as problems arise during the erection of the new Library building, as well as during the years of its occupancy thereafter. . . . She fears unless she has complete control some people may be permitted to visit the Library whom she would not wish to admit . . . [and this] seems to suggest that Miss Frick lacks balance and stability."

Helen would not capitulate, however. Instead she restated her position. If the Frick Collection purchased the new site and paid for construction of the new library, she would continue to pay all operating expenses and would endow the library on her death, when it would revert to the Frick Collection. She advised the trustees that she had created a $3 million trust fund at the Union Trust Company in Pittsburgh, "the income of which should be ample to maintain the Library as it is now conducted." Exasperated by the trustees' stonewalling, she informed them she would not meet with them "until they had seen [the] 'light.'" Helen promptly hired William S. Moorhead to represent her and continued to assert: "While The Frick Collection is for the use and benefit of all persons whatsoever, subject only to reasonable regulations, during my lifetime admission to the Frick Art Reference Library shall be subject to my sole discretion and its policies shall be regulated and controlled by me."

If Rockefeller was poised for a takeover, Andrew Mellon seems to have staved it off, for on May 12, 1933, Helen wrote Mellon: "A little bird tells me that the successful outcome of yesterday's meeting is entirely due to your efforts and I want you to know how very deeply I appreciate your kind and friendly interest in behalf of the Frick Art Reference Library! I will always love to feel that it was because of you, who were Papa's closest friend, that an agreement was arrived at between the Trustees and myself, permitting the Library to function as I had always hoped it might."

Yet there was a last-minute hitch when Childs insisted Helen guarantee the amount of income on the $3 million trust fund she had established for the library. Insulted, Helen nonetheless promised an annual income of $113,300. The final agreement meeting all her demands was signed on June 16, 1933, while she was storing overflow books in the bowling alley.

Helen remained furious about the attempt by Rockefeller and the other trustees to seize her library and oust her in the process, and she was also incensed by their failure to acquire works that she felt would have been important additions to her father's collection. In addition to the Dreyfus Collection and the exquisite *Wilton Diptych,* they had refused two charming Italian primitives offered by Carl Hamilton, a noted collector of that period. Helen complained to her attorney that the trustees were negligent "in the acquisition of important pictures, which, had they been purchased, would have resulted in a stronger position for the Collection today." She lamented, "Instead of owning works of intrinsic value, they now possess many securities of very little value." In fact, partially due to rising taxes, the Frick Collection did not add any paintings to its collection until 1935.

During the reconstruction of One East Seventieth Street into a public facility, Frances and Childs Frick chose statues and decorative latticework from the driveway court for their Long Island garden designed by Marian Cruger Coffin. Author's collection.

With the library matter settled in her favor, Helen turned her attention to the aesthetics of the Frick Collection's new galleries, future home of masterpieces to come. Trusting her highly cultivated eye, she challenged Clapp about details she found unsatisfactory and complimented him on others to her liking. The new East Gallery she thought was "very beautiful and dignified," but in the Oval Room, the "pilasters impress me as being somewhat heavy and the [art-nouveau] rosette insertions rather disturbing." The new lecture room on the first floor was "very satisfying, except for [the] size of [the] door, which might be made more imposing by being on a larger scale." The former butler's pantry, today known as the anteroom, she considered "quiet and gentle," but queried, "What is [the] tone of [the] wood-work?" The Reception Hall "seem[ed] in keeping with [the] present house," although she did want her father's bust by Malvina Hoffman placed in a more prominent position.

As work progressed on the second floor of the house, Helen's lawyer told the trustees "she is very anxious, if possible, not to disturb her mother's room for the present and to be allowed to keep it under lock and key." Many items bequeathed to Helen by her mother's will were stored there, and she wanted them secured while she and Childs divided the salvage material not intended for reuse in either the library or in the Frick Collection. To avoid any criticism of having profited in any way by purchasing the salvage from the house, Rockefeller insisted Helen and Childs pay for what they wanted, and at a price greater than the estimate. Brother and sister agreed to do this, and for their Long Island estate Childs and Dixie took the driveway lattice panels, together with its statues and one wrought-iron entrance gate; five semicircular panels with cherubs and freestanding columns from the porte cochere; the carved fountain and the entire pavilion feature opposite the Frick Collection on the west wall of the library; as well as the carved work at the entrance to Henry Clay Frick's office wing.

Model for the garden court fountain at One East Seventieth Street. Courtesy the Frick Collection/Frick Art Reference Library Archives.

Helen in turn, paid for the painted ceiling canvas in her mother's bedroom (this was badly damaged when it was removed), and although Dixie wanted the marble mantel in Adelaide's bedroom, Helen reminded her sister-in-law that she, Helen, had first choice and was taking it. In addition Helen claimed the wall paneling and other woodwork from Adelaide's bedroom and from the vestibule between her mother's bedroom and boudoir, as well as her safe, "as it was always a very personal one." Helen took the paneling and clock from her father's office and his upstairs bathroom marble and tiles for reinstallation in the chief librarian's bathroom. She also donated many items to the collection: three tapestries, four velvets, and one silk panel found in the third-floor cedar closet; the extra lamps from the second and third floors; waste baskets; flower vases; the dining room table fittings; pillows and chair cushions; carpeting; household furniture and equipment, including some Minton china; and the family's flag collection—national flags of France, Britain, Belgium, Italy, and the United States, along with a Red Cross flag, a New York state flag, and a "Welcome Home Heroes" flag from 1918. Believing the conversion of One East Seventieth Street to be important to the history of New York buildings, Helen decided to record the reconstruction. Alfred Cook was hired to photograph the tagged and documented items and the rooms as they were being dismantled.

St. Francis in the Desert being moved to the vault before renovations to One East Seventieth Street began. Courtesy the Frick Collection/Frick Art Reference Library Archives. Photo credit: Alfred Cook.

On June 29, Clapp gave Helen the welcome news that the renovation had passed one important hurdle. "Last night the pictures were sealed in. . . . Poor Mr. Naughton [of the Union Trust] was up until midnight. . . . Most of the furniture is down including your father's office furniture which we are taking great care of." In addition, the foundations were being dug for the new library. "Tremendous pounding today as the site is being made ready," Clapp said. "What an adventure! And what unborn eyes are winking off in the uncreated day that will scan your books and photographs, I hope in peace, generations hence. Eh?" Grateful for Helen's decision to put the folio catalogue of the Frick Collection on hold for a time while she continued to pay salaries to those who were employed to work on it, he reported, "[It] has lifted from my mind a weight that has taken the life out of me for more than a year." Clapp added, "I shall . . . put the rest of the catalogue matter in order when in Pittsburgh. I expect no snags."

Meanwhile, Helen continued to offer alternative ideas to the building committee. With her approval Clapp sent Dossena's *Annunciation* group and some of the salvage material to the University of Pittsburgh's fine arts department: "the fine ornamental iron stair banisters of the north stair, including the marble of the stair itself, the ornamental carved wooden ceiling over same, the ornamental elements in carved marble from the vestibule of this stair and the ceiling of the vestibule, which is also carved woodwork."

She also gave the Frick Collection thirty-nine pieces of French pottery and porcelain she had inherited from her mother, mostly Sèvres but including examples of Saint-Porchaire, Vincennes, and Samson. The pieces were appraised at market value and that amount was deducted from the cost of the salvage material she wanted. She released other valuable items—a small statue, *Friendship*, then believed to be by the eighteenth-century French sculptor, Étienne-Maurice Falconet, of a young woman gazing at the heart she holds in her right hand; and the Martha-related marble bust of Madame de Pompadour's ill-fated daughter, a bust shown in the Boucher panel, *Sculpture*. Helen, who had legal title to them all, gave them to the collection of her own free will, focusing on her conviction that these pieces had always been part of the house and should remain there.

Busier than ever, Helen kept the library running during the renovation of the Frick Collection and while the new library building was being constructed next door. Clapp also had appointed her head of the Frick Collection house committee, in charge of overseeing the interior decoration. For once Rockefeller was pleased. Although Clapp and Helen worked well together, tensions inevitably arose. She once explained to him: "You must know at heart that of the nine trustees, I am the last one to undermine your authority & the first one to back you in things you desire to accomplish. . . . At the same time—if you will put yourself in my position, you will realize how difficult it is very often for me, to have so many changes made when I personally have less to say than anyone else—& yet all these changes are affecting my life more than anyone else's, because they are bound up so closely with precious memories and associations."

To that end, she did all she could to maintain a status quo. On three topics, Helen brokered no discussion: the hardware from her father's bedroom would be installed in the library—the door hinges, doorknobs, and plates for light switches, as well as the large, open-face window levers reproduced as doorknobs for the library doors off the entrance hall; her former bedroom door must be used in her new private office space; and two portraits of her father were to hang in this two-room suite, one on the office door, the other, by the American portraitist John C. Johansen, in the waiting room with a Johansen portrait of Adelaide. The contractor in charge, L. W. Eisinger, explained to Helen how one of the doors would work: "When the door is closed from your office side you would see the oak door, and when open [to the waiting room] you would see your father's picture exposed in your office." This pleased Helen a great deal, but the installation of the other door, the one from her former bedroom, proved problematic. Helen wanted her father's portrait hung on it, and when the door proved difficult to install, and Eisinger suggested he make a new one and hang the portrait of her father on it, Helen's reply was firm. "*No.* I prefer the same old door which has a familiar sound to it & familiar associations!"

Helen's new office at the Frick Art Reference Library. *Bust of Claudine Houdon* by Jean-Antoine Houdon is on the mantelpiece. Above it is another portrait of Martha by Théobald Chartran. Courtesy the Frick Collection/Frick Art Reference Library Archives.

Construction was going less well in Pittsburgh. University Chancellor John Bowman by then had rejected three different proposals for the design of a fine arts building, so he decided to house the department in the Cathedral of Learning. Helen donated $5,000 toward the completion of the giant skyscraper, and promised another $20,000 in May. Apart from facilitating a permanent home for the department, the money contributed to the employment of the one thousand men working inside the building. She also gave $10,000 for the purchase of books for the fine arts library.

As for the True Blues, they had endured another fierce winter. Helen continued to help with more distributions of coal—ten tons or more for the most needy—and continued to pay for their medical care as well. Indeed, this year, when the national income had fallen by half and U.S. Steel stock had plummeted from 261 a share to 21, Helen spent nearly $44,000 (more than $2 million today) on the True Blues, about $5,000 more than she was spending on her library. Sympathetic to the plight of her girls, she offered only her impatience to members of the Iron Rail staff who grumbled about their work. When Virginia Musselman, an assistant to Boyd, complained of being unhappy, Helen took her to task:

You talk of yourself, of how you miss your music, your books, your friends. Then, of how uninteresting the Iron Rail guests are with their small problems. After all, that is not the attitude for you to take—you are there to put some happiness into the lives of those who visit the home, to try to solve their little problems as well as their big ones, not simply to sit on the rocks and contemplate and introspect! I fear it is not your field—time is precious and if you are not happy and cannot see why you are there, it is your privilege to resign.

Musselman quit.

Rendering for the garden court by John Russell Pope. Courtesy the Frick Collection/Frick Art Reference Library Archives.

As the months passed, Eleanor Howland and Ellen Boyd worried about their boss. "She is so very tired," Howland said. "The new Library has taken so much time, and so much planning." There was, in fact, trouble with the construction. After breaking ground and during excavation of the garden court, workmen struck a solid stone outcropping. It had to be chiseled away by hand, not blasted apart for fear of damaging the Frick Collection's priceless objects in the vault, and for a time, as foundation work progressed, large portions of the house rested on jacks. The fountain commissioned for the garden court also proved difficult. Eighteen ten-ton blocks of marble were quarried before Helen found one with "just the color she wanted."

Nonetheless, with the end of construction in sight, Helen wrote to Edward Forbes: "The Library appears to be a complete success, and very beautiful both inside and out." It held over two hundred thousand reproductions and photographs of European and American art, sculpture, and illuminated manuscripts; forty-five thousand books and pamphlets; and about thirteen hundred photographs were added each month. And Helen had attended to every detail—the matte finish of the oak ceiling beams in the main reading room and its soundproofed ceiling, the pattern of the floor tiles, the gray blue color of the walls with just a hint of pink, a frieze with a Renaissance motif,—everything down to moldings, railings, Venetian blinds and grilles for windows, and the design and scale of the stacks. Clapp's memorandum from November 19 directed that "the furniture throughout the Library was to be placed as planned and that nobody was to modify it without [Helen's] consent." Childs, cross about Helen's demands, complained to Clapp that the Frick Collection was assuming too many "extras" for the library. According to Clapp, Childs insisted there be "no more" because it was "planned as a public building, and any personal desires . . . should be met by Miss Frick." Helen happily paid for whatever extra costs were needed to accomplish her vision.

The Frick Collection trustees now began formulating an inscription for the dedication plaque in the entrance hall of the library, "a knotty problem . . . from the point of view of appropriateness and taste," Clapp believed. The trustees decided to give themselves credit for the library and proposed a weighty encomium: "To advance the knowledge and love of art in accordance with the wishes expressed in [Henry Clay Frick's] will [and] to provide for [the library's] growth and give full scope to its usefulness this building was erected in

The main reading room at the new Frick Art Reference Library. The fresco on the far wall is by Nicholas Lochoff, after Pietro Lorenzetti, *Madonna and Child with Saints Francis and John.* The triptych on the left is: Follower of Giotto di Bondone, Romagnole School, *Madonna and Child with Saints: Scenes from the Life of Christ and the Life of the Virgin.* Courtesy the Frick Collection/Frick Art Reference Library Archives.

1934 by the Trustees of the Frick Collection." Helen balked and insisted instead on: "This Library was founded in loving memory of Henry Clay Frick by his daughter in 1920 and was here housed in 1934 by the trustees of the Frick Collection." Clapp felt this inscription "not what might be expected in a formal entry and that criticism might be directed against her in the future." Helen replied that "she could stand such criticism and the inscription should be according to her desires." And it was.

The new Frick Art Reference Library officially opened on January 4, 1935, to a week-long celebration. The night before, members of the press and art critics had an advance peek. Then came a stream of museum directors, the Frick Collection trustees and their wives, and special friends of the Frick Art Reference Library and of Henry Clay Frick. On January 5, professors, librarians, friends of the staff, and interested members of the public had a tour. Painters, sculptors, and dealers were feted on January 7, followed by members of Helen's clubs, the Cosmopolitan Club and the Bedford Garden Club.

The library collection was housed in closed stacks throughout the thirteen-floor building while the public rooms and those used by the staff were full of fine art and personal touches by Helen, especially reminders of her father. In the main reading room, the east wall featured the frieze by Angelo Magnanti depicting Helen's dogs—a field spaniel named Bobby and an Irish terrier, named Paddy—while on the west wall was a 1924 portrait by Gerard Kelly of Henry Clay Frick in three-quarter profile. The ten Millet drawings Frick had acquired in the 1890s, kept in his Eagle Rock office as a reminder of his Mennonite origins, were exhibited in the staff reading room, paneled, along with the main reading room, using the Jacobean oak from the bowling-alley library. Helen's small library room from the second floor of One East Seventieth Street had been reinstalled as her office, decorated in the French style. The creamy yellow *boiserie,* or carved wood panels, with olive green trim matched the frame of a second version of Martha's portrait by Théobald Chartran over the marble mantel. On the east wall, the panel to the right of the fireplace was in fact a false door so "Miss Frick could rush down into her private elevator [and] go anywhere in the building." On the west side, her former bedroom door connected the office to the Italian-style sitting room where Helen placed her collection of Italian primitives and reinstalled her fifteenth-century fireplace. Most important, the two portraits of her father were hung as she wished, one on the reinstalled bedroom door, the other visible upon entering her waiting room from the hall. And there was a portrait of her mother around the corner in the waiting room at the entrance to the sitting room.

John D. Rockefeller Jr. did not attend the library opening because his wife, Abby, who was chronically depressed, was suffering a nervous breakdown. Childs was sick with bronchial pneumonia, but he came, as did Edward Forbes. The remodeled Frick Collection was due to receive the public on December 16, 1935, marking Adelaide's birthday and the fiftieth anniversary year of Martha's birth.

Just weeks after her library celebration in January 1935, however, Edward Forbes was sorry to find Helen "bothered by [the] dreadful lawsuit" brought by James Howard Bridge. Still resentful at having been fired by Helen back in 1928, and at having to sell *Portraits and Personalities* to Helen in April 1931, Bridge's bitterness had peaked in September 1931 when Helen gave him a bad reference. Bridge had approached the art director of the National Studios, H. W. Warren, seeking employment, but was rejected because Helen told Warren that the handbook Bridge had published on the Frick Collection was "full of inaccuracies and adds nothing of artistic or scholarly value in art connoisseurship." She insisted that Bridge was "not a recognized specialist in art," and although he claimed to have been curator of the Frick Collection, Helen said "he was not employed as curator . . . but merely showed visitors through the galleries." So in February 1932, the seventy-three-year-old Bridge had filed a $250,000 libel suit against Helen Frick for "slander[ing] him by calling him an 'employee' of her father's galleries when in reality he was an art expert in charge of the collection."

Some three years later, as the jury trial commenced, H. A. Rosenberg of Cosmopolitan Studios reported that Bridge had offered him a bribe for favorable testimony; since Bridge had already "gotten in the neighborhood of $75,000 . . . [for] not publishing matters pertaining to the family or collection. . . . this [case] would be easy money and if we would cooperate with him he would gladly split 50/50 on whatever he got." *Time* claimed that Helen would not appear in court but in fact, Helen hired a bodyguard and threw privacy aside to testify on her behalf. Her Westmoreland Farm diary entry on January 15, 1934, was jubilant: "Trial!"

Justice William F. Bleakley heard the case in the New York State Supreme Court in White Plains. Bridge testified he was certain Frick had hired him for life, but instead he "left my fate in the hands of his daughter." He complained about Helen's "curt note" to Warren and protested, "[She] dismissed me as she would a menial." Bridge also attacked the late Adelaide Frick, recounting: "I once had a request from a member of the English nobility to see an oil painting of the gentleman's grandmother [*Julia, Lady Peel*] by Lawrence . . . and it was my shameful duty to inform the nobleman that Mrs. Frick would not let him see the painting which was only two feet away on the other side of the door."

The *New York Times* reported that in the afternoon session, during vigorous cross-examination by Helen's attorney, the former district attorney of Westchester County, Lee Parsons Davis, Bridge was confronted with a passage from his 1931 book, *Millionaires and*

Grubb Street, contained in proofs he had given Adelaide Frick for correction: "A psychosis of unconscious arrogance of conscious wealth was common among the ultra-rich men," and "the conscious arrogance of the women of the ultra-rich denoted a moral delinquency." The proof sheet also said that the unconscious arrogance in ultra-rich men "implied a mental deficiency, and an atrophied sense of humor." Both the women and the men, it added, were in need of psychopathic treatment.

Bridge admitted under questioning that he had Frick in mind when he described the ultra-rich, and when asked on what facts he based his conclusion that Frick suffered from "the arrogance malady and needed mental treatment," Bridge "finally admitted it was all based on hearsay." Questioned about the meaning of his term "moral delinquency," Bridge replied, "I guess moral delinquency means moral delinquency. It is rather hard to define. I guess I don't know what it meant." Then, "the White Plains Supreme Court chamber was thrown into a turmoil when Bridge fainted."

He returned to the stand the following morning and withstood two more days of cross-examination. Bridge continued to complain about the arrogance of the Frick family and claimed the "'conscious arrogance' of Miss Helen Frick . . . should have required the treatment of a psychiatrist." He was then questioned as to the definition of plagiarism and asked if he had ever committed it. He quipped, "Well I suppose I have along with Shakespeare and other men." When Davis presented Bridge with an art article from the *New York Times,* transcribed by Bridge into the *Frick Collection Handbook* without citation, Bridge admitted he had "lifted" it, but had made a few "corrections."

On January 26, Helen's side presented its case. With Clapp's assistance she had compiled a three-inch-thick document listing all of Bridge's errors in the handbook and in *Portraits and Personalities*—errors in dates, spelling, provenance, genealogy, and titles of paintings, not to mention accents, punctuation, unascribed quotations and more acts of plagiarism. She attacked the poor quality of the reproductions in *Portraits and Personalities,* some images actually retouched by hand and others never before published by the Frick Collection. In the parade of witnesses, Albert N. Marquis, founder and editor-in-chief of *Who's Who in America,* testified that since 1918, when Bridge began submitting his biographical information, he had never described himself as curator of the Frick Collection—at least not until 1928, when Helen fired him. The veteran art editor for the *New York Times,* Elizabeth Luther Carey, testified that she had never heard Bridge was a curator. Thomas F. Gerrity, a salesman at Knoedler's, John Holroyd, the houseman, Frank Jewett Mather Jr., professor emeritus of art history at Princeton University, and Isabelle B. Binks, Frick Art Reference Library staff member, all swore to the truth of Helen's statements about Bridge.

Then on February 5, in the fourth week of the trial, Helen testified. According to the *New York Herald Tribune,* "Although she confessed it was the first time she had been in a lawsuit or appeared in court, Miss Frick was alert at all times and answered the questions of the attorneys in a soft quiet voice but incisive manner." During her three and a half hours of testimony Helen admitted she "never liked" James Howard Bridge. According to the *World Telegram,* she stated "in a timid, frightened voice . . . that she never said anything mean about James Howard Bridge behind his back. . . . She wept a little when the point was raised that Mr. Bridge had described her mother as an 'arrogant woman' in a book he wrote." Helen responded "in a determined whisper. . . . 'My mother was a very generous woman. . . . She loved her home. She enjoyed her friends and she was very kind to her employees and they loved her too.'" She testified that Bridge was rude and disrespectful and noted that when she outlined her plans for the 1924 library building, Bridge had exclaimed

Rendering of the Frick Collection entrance by John Russell Pope. Helen complained that the architect should have fixed the off-center portal. Courtesy the Frick Collection/Frick Art Reference Library Archives.

"very ungraciously," "[So] you're going to do this thing in a characteristic Pittsburgh millionaire way."

She also took exception to Bridge's unflattering description of Henry Clay Frick that he was "a willing but none too competent amateur in art," and asserted that Bridge's true role as Frick family employee was as "a guide not a curator." She explained: "In 1914 her father moved his office from downtown to the home, where he allowed the public to come at will to see his rare and valuable art objects. . . . It proved embarrassing to Mr. Frick to have a group of strangers barge unexpectedly into his library or sitting room when he was at work, so he limited visiting hours to Friday morning and assigned to Mr. Bridge the task of guiding them through the galleries." As for the word "curator," Helen said Childs had used it when referring to Bridge in the minutes, but that Childs did so in error: "Despite the fact he was a Princeton graduate and a scientist [he] didn't understand the full significance of the word 'curator.'"

The next day, February 6, Helen concluded her testimony after four hours on the stand. Closing arguments ensued with Bridge's lawyer, Theodore Richter, denouncing Helen's letter to Warren as "the satisfaction of a rich woman's hate. . . . [a woman who] believe[s] a man's attempt to save his good name is an assault on the Frick millions." The following day the judge instructed the jury to base its decision solely on whether or not Helen Frick had told the truth in her letter to Warren. Four hours was all the time the eleven-man jury needed to vindicate her.

Helen was elated, and her friends rejoiced with her. Now she could fully concentrate on her projects. She enriched the University of Pittsburgh's fine arts department with a $14,000 gift toward the purchase of books and for the departmental budget; provided nearly $45,000 for the Iron Rail; considered the acquisition of the famed Albertina Collection of old master prints and drawings for the Frick Collection; conducted a library trip to New Bedford, Massachusetts; and a top priority, returned to monitoring the progress of the Frick Collection interior. Immediately after conclusion of the trial, Helen toured the galleries with Clapp. One matter that troubled her greatly was the architectural imbalance of the new entrance portal on Seventieth Street leading into the new reception hall. Throughout the fall of 1934 there had been much discussion about how to remedy the problem, but no one had yet found a solution. The portal was, as it remains today, off center, with more space to the right of the door than to the left. According to Clapp, Helen "still regrets the portal is off center and thinks the architects should have done something to cure it," although she had made "the excellent suggestion" to correct the imbalance with visual weight, by adding a wrought-iron fence and a large lantern on the right side, as they remain today.

She was also determined to install a plaque in a prominent position in the garden court as a memorial to John Holroyd and Percy Monroe, two recently deceased Frick family employees who had been connected to One East Seventieth Street since 1914. Rockefeller took angry exception to the idea of a Frick family memorial in a public facility. Helen, though, would not be sidelined, making it clear at a meeting of the entire board that "as a trustee and as the daughter of the Founder, I had a double responsibility and that my father always wanted me to be interested in his greatest interest." Rockefeller was not persuaded and again reminded her that her "father was not there and that this was not to be a 'Frick Institution'!" The memorial plaque was never installed, but Helen did continue to assert her aesthetic judgments throughout the house. She already had chosen a gray-green, George I material for the walls of the new Oval Room, and in May, according to a Clapp memorandum, "she OK'd the color of the woodwork in the Oval Room, but wished it had more movement." For the new East Gallery she chose ashes-of-roses velvet, and for the new lecture hall an embroidered velvet with a Chinoiserie pattern. In the reception hall, with the wood now toned down and the telephones hidden as she suggested, she approved of the ceiling "very much, but [thought] the four adjacent areas should be made the same color, finding them dull and heavy as they are." The recently darkened color of the wood lattice in the garden court, done at Rockefeller's request, "she [did not] approve at all." But it was better than what Childs had advocated—"the lattices . . . should be of bronze" since he considered wood "rather cheap."

Predictably, Childs was not pleased with Helen's new authority in the Frick Collection. Relations between them had been correct but cold, and during Bridge's trial Childs had stood aside. Now, to avoid what he called an "amateurish and ineffectual" result, he suggested hiring a decorator for the new galleries. But according to Clapp, Helen "thought the matter of wall fabrics was something in which she, as her father's daughter, ought to have something to say. . . . each decorator had a type of treatment and style peculiar to himself and you could always tell a White-Allom room . . . or an Elsie de Wolfe room. . . .

[and] she didn't want that to happen at the Frick Collection." Helen told Childs that having fancy New York decorators "was entirely unnecessary and served no purpose and . . . she would not be a party to [having them] in any way." Finally, Helen prevailed. Together she and Clapp made the selections for brocades and marbles, and between them they achieved what Helen desired: a personal, elegant tone consistent with her father's taste, and still admired by visitors to the Frick Collection today.

In September 1935, she prevailed again. Walter Friedländer, the highly respected authority on European painting, whom Helen had previously barred from both her library and the Frick gallery, arrived in New York as visiting professor of fine arts at New York University. Although he would now have access to the Frick Collection, on Helen's orders he could not use the Frick Art Reference Library. The *New York Post* remarked on September 21 about the paradox of barring the scholar. "Being a Jew, and therefore not 'a true German' [Friedländer] was ousted by the Hitler regime. . . . But here in New York . . . the Frick Art Reference Library will not be open to him on the ground that he is a German!" Both the art world and the public were baffled and offended. But Helen alone controlled the admission policy.

French (eighteenth century [?]), *Bust of a Young Girl*, terra-cotta, 12 ½ in. Helen inherited this piece, recalling Martha, upon Adelaide Frick's death. Helen gave the bust to the Frick Collection for its opening in 1935. © the Frick Collection, New York, gift of Helen Clay Frick, 1935.

As the December opening of the Frick Collection approached, Helen prevailed once more. She offered to send twenty-one works from Eagle Rock, valued at $368,200, to the Frick for display in the new East Gallery. Initially Clapp rejected the idea. He did not know the paintings and thought the trustees should make the decision to include them, not he. Helen persisted. According to Clapp: "She said they had been selected by her father and were part of his original collection and [she] couldn't see how any objection could be raised. . . . She said [without them] they would have to choose between an empty room and a finished room." Clapp saw the point and backed down.

Helen then proposed a board meeting to confirm all the details but to her dismay her suggestion was denied. Nevertheless, she worked from nine to five every day, "without even taking off her hat," to make certain the paintings in the other rooms were hung as they had been during her father's life, and that each and every room looked homelike. As Clapp reported, "I told her the committee had voted, after I told them of her desires, to hang the West Gallery exactly as it was hung by her father. . . . [She] was pleased that it was to be hung in two rows." She was also glad that the paintings were to be illuminated, with "new reflectors that Mr. Frick liked on the larger pictures in the old [part of the] house." Helen's satisfaction with the process increased when Clapp appointed his friend Harrison Griswold Dwight as his assistant. Dwight was an assistant drafting officer in the State Department and member of the protocol division who had served as translator with the American Section of the Supreme War Council at Versailles in 1918, and in 1919 as secretary to General Tasker Bliss at the peace conference in Paris.

Helen wrote Rockefeller a cordial and complimentary letter. "The building seems to have reached a high degree of perfection & I cannot think of a single detail that I would care to have changed. I hope you feel the same way." She did, however, ask for one favor: she asked Rockefeller to remove Mr. and Mrs. Charles Schwab from the invitation list of approximately seven hundred people. When Frick was demoted in Carnegie Steel, Schwab had come to Clayton and forced Frick's resignation. Rockefeller replied, "Thank you for your charming note telling me of your complete satisfaction with the Collection building. . . . [and] it was I who suggested Mr. and Mrs. Charles M. Schwab. . . . I think no real harm would be done by withdrawing his name, as you desire, and am requesting Professor Clapp to have it stricken off the list."

Then Helen gave the collection a gift for the opening: the small terra-cotta, *Bust of a Young Girl.* Thought to be by Jean-Antoine Houdon, and purchased by Duveen for Adelaide's bedroom, the sculpted girl wears a ribbon bonnet similar to the one Martha wore as a toddler.

On the afternoon of December 11, the Frick Collection's doors opened to the preview guests—museum directors, art dealers, judges, members of the state legislature, and personal friends of the Frick family. They entered beneath a canopy at the Seventieth Street entrance into the new reception hall. Helen and Childs stood side by side in the receiving line, she in a modest black velvet hat and gown, while, as the *New York Herald* described the scene, "a marble bust by Malvina Hoffman of Mr. Frick brooded proudly."

Lazzaro Bastiani (d. 1512), *Adoration of the Magi*. Acquired by the Frick Collection in 1935. Tempera, oil on poplar panel, 20 ½ x 11 in. © the Frick Collection, New York.

The guests followed a designated path, past the new lecture hall to the new East Gallery, with Helen's Eagle Rock collection exhibited against the ashes-of-roses velvet, and to the new Oval Room, with Frick's paintings placed against the gray-green brocade. The paintings in the West Gallery included Rembrandt's self-portrait and *The Polish Rider,* along with others including the Vermeers, the Goya, and the Velázquez. From here visitors passed into the Enamel Room. The four Italian primitives added by Helen were on display here, together with the Frick Collection's most recent addition, *Adoration of the Magi,* then considered a work by Bartolomeo Vivarini, today attributed to the fifteenth-century Venetian artist, Lazzaro Bastiani. The painting came from the Morgan collection, enjoyed by Helen and her father twenty years prior. With the *Adoration of the Magi,* Helen appeared to be continuing her father's symbolic tribute to the beatified Martha, on this fiftieth anniversary year of her birth. Just as worshipers in the Bastiani painting wind their way through the landscape to revere the ill-fated infant Christ, depicted joyfully laughing while perched on the Virgin Mary's knee, the procession of guests at the Frick Collection opening wound their way into the Enamel Room, past *Adoration,* through Henry Clay Frick's monument with its symbolic references to Martha, the child who "held first place in the shrine of his heart," the child known for her contagious laughter.

The guests continued into the library, where the Italian bronzes purchased from Morgan's estate gleamed atop the bookshelves, then into the living hall, where the grouping of family furniture illustrated the private way the Fricks enjoyed their two Titians, their great Bellini of St. Francis, and their Holbeins. In the Fragonard Room everyone admired the *Progress of Love* panels, and as the visitors entered the dining room, they viewed Hoppner's portrait of Sarah and Catherine Bligh, Gainsborough's *Mall in Saint James Park,* and Romney's *Henrietta, Countess of Warwick, and Her Children.* The former butler's pantry had been refitted to display the Barbizon paintings, and the former ladies' powder room now housed a small, roped-off gallery for display of the Boucher panels, previously in Adelaide's upstairs boudoir. The Sèvres porcelain Helen had donated to the collection in 1934 was placed around the room, and both *Friendship* and the Saly bust of Madame de Pompador's tragic daughter were there too, arranged as if Adelaide still lived there. The circuit ended in the main hall, at the foot of the grand staircase where, as the *New York Herald Tribune* described, "two mysterious primitives . . . hang." These were the father-daughter "twin" *Pietàs* depicting Mary cradling her dead son.

The evening was a triumph. To Maud Clapp Helen wrote, "The opening was indeed an experience that can never be forgotten. I have been living it over ever since & the fine tribute paid to my father's memory has made me inexpressibly happy." On December 12, the *New York World Telegram* wrote: "One forgets all about Frick himself, his feud with Carnegie, the strikes, and everything else, and gives one's self up to this heart-stirring experience." Even the ailing Joseph Duveen, ever Helen's nemesis, complimented Clapp on "the very beautiful and impressive arrangement of this wonderful collection," and continued, "Its success is all the greater because the atmosphere of the old home has been so cleverly preserved in that of a public art gallery."

Clapp, too, was overjoyed. Forgetting the past strain and tension as organizing director, he remarked to Rockefeller, "I count it my great good fortune to have been chosen by fate for so interesting, and, indeed, unique [an] undertaking and that, by another stroke of fate, I have had you to help, guide and enlighten me at all times during all stages of the enterprise." Clapp received a $5,000 raise, "little enough," said Rockefeller, "in view of the heavy strain under which you have worked these past years, and the diversity and the difficulty of the burdens you have carried." Clapp set a date for a much-needed extended vacation before returning to his new post as director of the Frick Collection.

Almost immediately after the opening, members of the public began to experience the comfort and solace offered by Henry Clay Frick's sanctuary. One day Helen noticed a teenage girl sitting on a bench in the garden court, crying. She walked over to the girl, whose name was Martie Smith Perry, and asked if she would like to talk about what was upsetting her. The girl explained that her classmates teased her unmercifully for her English-Australian accent. Helen sat down beside the girl and impressed upon her the importance of perseverance. When Helen left, a guard came over and asked, "Do you know who that was?" The girl said she had no idea who the woman was, so the guard told her, "That was Miss Frick." Any time afterward when Martie Perry felt sad, she returned to the garden court and found succor in remembering Helen Frick's kindness that day.

No sooner had the Frick Collection opened to the public, however, than the power struggle with Rockefeller and Childs resumed. Rockefeller expressed his concern about "the domination of the Frick influence on the Board." Under the pretext of fellow original trustee George Baker being "ill" and Andrew Mellon being "not active much longer," Rockefeller felt the moment was ripe to seize the board by electing men under his control. Among his choices were Vanderbilt Webb of the firm Patterson Belknap Webb, the Rockefeller family lawyer and trustee of the trusts Rockefeller created for Abby and their children, and Webb's former Groton School roommate and then brother-in-law Frederick Osborn, a trustee of the Rockefeller Institute and the American Museum of Natural History. Rockefeller even considered bringing in his brother-in-law, Winthrop W. Aldrich.

Rockefeller also proposed doing away with the two committees he had chaired, the building committee and the committee on organization, since they were no longer needed, and creating instead a new three-man executive committee, chaired by him, to make all decisions. The Frick family would thus have less control than ever, as Rockefeller felt he could dominate Childs, and Helen would be excluded from the executive committee. He wrote George Baker that to circumvent the board, and especially Helen, minutes not be taken in future executive committee meetings, so there could be no obstruction, intrusion, or interference.

On January 21, 1936, Rockefeller drafted a letter to Childs setting out his plan for the executive committee and copied it to all the trustees, except Helen, for their approval. While

Rockefeller solicited Childs for support, Clapp wrote to John Henry Hammond, the attorney for the Frick Collection since the death of Lewis Cass Ledyard in 1932:

> It has become necessary for my own piece of mind that all contact between me and Mr. Frick cease. . . . I tender my resignation as Organizing Director of the Frick Collection. . . . some of the points he raises, has raised from the beginning and continually returns to are diametrically opposed to what seems to me advisable either in the interests of the public or from an aesthetic point of view. . . . He and I can never work harmoniously together. . . . It is with regret that I make this decision as I am so deeply indebted to Mr. Rockefeller, Miss Frick, & Mr. Griggs for their unfailing & generous help & support during the years in which we have worked together.

Hammond's reply was simple, "Then you can say to Mr. R. that you find you dislike Mr. F so intensely that you can neither be first to him nor to yourself."

As these powerful men maneuvered, Helen had few social or business precedents to support her position with the board. Very little had changed for women in the corporate world. While Gertrude Vanderbilt Whitney still ran her museum, Abby Rockefeller was a driving force behind the Museum of Modern Art, and powerful contemporaries such as Elizabeth Arden and Helena Rubinstein were managing cosmetic empires, all were governing their own enterprises. Mrs. Taube Coller Davis earned the very substantial annual fee of $100,000 as a consultant to department stores, but she was not making decisions. Beyond Secretary of Labor Frances Perkins and Josephine Roche, who ran a Colorado coal company before becoming assistant secretary of the treasury, there were very few women of prominence in government or business. There were no women partners at any Wall Street law firms, there were no women serving on the New York Stock Exchange or on the General Motors board, in fact, as *Fortune Magazine* wrote, "There is no woman whose business achievement would properly rank with the first or second or even the third line of male success."

In January 1936, realizing that by a simple, symbolic show of hands she was to be excluded from the executive committee and from the education committee she wanted to establish and chair, Helen was irate. Her first salvo was directed at her longtime ally, Clapp. He, not she, had been put in charge of education, and new bylaws had been written and adopted without her consultation and without her vote. She demanded to know where Clapp had been and why he had not protected her against this maneuvering.

Seated together on the sofa in her library-office, Helen confronted Clapp, who later described the interview in great detail. "Mr. Clapp," Helen said, "I have always been very frank. I have known you for about ten years, and always felt you were a friend of mine. . . . I have backed you up." Clapp responded to what he dubbed her "menacing prelude," "Yes, you certainly have." When Helen raised the matter of Rockefeller's comment that she was "a stumbling block," Clapp insisted, "I did not hear him say so," and warned Helen, "I do not like the tone you are taking . . . I resent what you are implying. . . . I owe a great deal to you, and more than to anyone else, but I will not act on the Board or with anybody else except as agent of the Board."

Helen fought back. "Why does [Rockefeller] take it for granted that he would be at variance with me? . . . You give me the impression that you would prefer my not being on any committee." And then her temper flared again. Referring to Rockefeller loyalists like Vanderbilt Webb and Frederick Osborn, she insisted, "Mr. Clapp, this has developed into a Rockefeller Foundation. I am not going to be kept out of my Father's Collection." Clapp replied, "The Board of Trustees do what they think best." When Helen reminded him that she had a responsibility as a trustee appointed by her father, Clapp backed off, saying he "was in a very awkward position." "What position do you think I am in, Mr. Clapp?" she countered. "I have always been your friend and I am coming to you." But she had come to the wrong person. The endless litany of problems, nitpicking, stream of questions, decisions, details, and the ceaseless demands and tensions of a warring family and board had worn Clapp out.

The argument continued until Helen suddenly stood up, as did Clapp, who reported: "I said 'there is only one way out of this—you know that.'" Helen did not respond, so Clapp moved toward the door and said, "*Goodnight Miss Frick.*" Again Helen did not respond. Clapp remarked, "I would not have touched [the Frick project] with a red hot iron if I had known what the conditions were here." Helen retorted in disbelief, "Do you consider that I have been disagreeable? . . . I have a mandate from my Father." Clapp threw up his hands. "I think it is ludicrous for you to ask that question. I won't answer this. . . . it is useless for us to discuss this. . . . I do not owe you anything in the world. . . . Our relationship is all over." Then Clapp admitted to what Helen had long-since sensed: the reason Rockefeller wanted her out was "based on his feeling upon acrimonious disputes of the past meetings of the Trustees, and that if this went on the whole thing would go on the rocks." Helen lamented her situation, "I am not permitted to serve on the [Executive] Committee and not permitted to express myself." Referring to her failed attempt to call a trustees' meeting before the opening she reminded him, "When I asked when there would be a Board Meeting before the opening, you said there would be no board meeting, that Mr. Baker and Mr. Morgan had been consulted, and therefore there would be no Board Meeting. You said very plainly [to me], 'Miss Frick you are not wanted.'" Desperately hurt, Helen howled, "My Father's Collection was opening." Clapp said, "The upshot of this is extremely painful and in fact there is no other way out of this." He turned and left the room.

In hindsight Clapp noted, "I see now she was in a towering passion against the Trustees none of whom had supported her and since I had not stepped into the arena she struck me instead." Nevertheless, he recalled,

> I was so upset when I got back to the office that the whole Collection was an abomination to me filled with wretched passions, stupid quarrels and the ghosts of feuds and animosities in the family and out. I thought [of Miss Frick's] essential lack of justice, of all the corpses of friends she claims to have found traitors or villains that strew her background. I vowed I would never cross the threshold of the Library again—the Library I had taken such pride and trouble in making beautiful and exceptional. She had just spewed a vile venom over everything that corroded the very stones.

On January 30, 1936, trustee George Baker wrote to Rockefeller that Junius Morgan "heartily endorses [the draft of your letter to Childs] and is decidedly of the opinion that something will have to be done along the lines [of an executive committee] that you and I discussed. . . . Childs might well be just as alive to the difficulties of the situation with the present secretary [Helen] as we all are." Rockefeller noted on the bottom of Baker's letter that the lines of discussion had been about the "possible election of officers other than

Miss and Mr. Frick to fill the offices of secretary and President." He then requested all the trustees, save Helen, sign a duplicate of the drafted letter to Childs as composed, but not mail it until February 3, 1936, as "a permanent record of the verbal approval given." Since Helen was still the secretary, and since Rockefeller's attorney, Thomas M. Debevoise, had advised Rockefeller that "the members of the Board . . . are entitled to be informed as to Executive Committee Action. . . . by signed minutes," minutes were being taken. But Rockefeller insisted, "This letter of course, cannot wisely be referred to in the minutes of the Trustees' meeting or put in the secretary's files." Rather, Rockefeller's thought was to keep it in his own files because "it indicates the basis on which I accepted the chairmanship of the Executive Committee and also because it seems to me the fact that it exists will strengthen the hands of the Director."

Now tensions really exploded. In his letter to Childs, Rockefeller said soothingly, "It is both natural and proper that any views expressed by the Trustee descendants of the Founder should be given fullest consideration. Obviously they have an intimate knowledge of the Founder's feelings, thoughts and ideas such as no other Trustee can have in the same degree." He continued, however, that there was nothing in the trust instrument to indicate "it was the Founder's wish . . . his Trustee descendants should have any different voice . . . than the other Trustees." Rockefeller advised: "Miss Frick is in complete charge of the Library. She is also a Trustee of the Collection, its Secretary, and Chairman of the Art Acquisition Committee." For his part, Childs was board president, a member of the finance committee and of the executive committee, and further "dominance [of the trustee descendants]. . . . would be fraught with danger because [it would be] susceptible to the construction that the Collection had not passed completely to the public . . . but was still largely controlled and dominated by the Founder's family."

To Clapp, Rockefeller wrote, "The situation as it exists today is intolerable and I cannot for a moment believe the Trustees will allow it to continue. . . . a satisfactory outcome will be devised and achieved, I feel confident." Indeed, on February 18, during the first executive committee meeting, the trustees adopted the very policies Rockefeller outlined to Childs, "No trustee . . . shall assume any different relation to the operation of the Collection than any other Trustee, nor be under any duty or exercise any power except as provided in the Charter, Constitution, By-Laws and Resolutions."

Shortly thereafter, on March 3, after the second executive committee meeting, Harrison Griswold Dwight, Clapp's assistant, told his superior that before the meeting: "[Childs] got it [from Rockefeller] and I'm quite sure he won't give any more trouble for a long time. . . . As for the sister, she has been on her best behavior. . . . Although she doesn't scare so easily, I envy for her the opportunity of hearing a few home truths. If she gives me the smallest opening she will hear them." At the meeting, "All went merry as a marriage bell. The *F[ils] en F[rick]* [son of Frick] having been put in his place during the past month by all present . . . agreed to everything and made one or two reasonable suggestions. . . . What he needs is the *mannière forte* [strong hand]. . . . Of course if he catches one out [making a mistake] he will make the most of it."

In mid-March 1936, Helen surprised the trustees by advising them that she wanted to remove her Eagle Rock paintings, on loan since the opening, and send them to the Fogg. Dwight complained to Clapp, "F. announced on Friday that his sister wished to withdraw the pictures she had lent the Collection. I don't know whether this is an outward and visible mark of an inward and spirited withdrawal or whether it is a preparation for [hanging the] Piero." The Piero was Piero della Francesca's *St. Simon the Apostle (?)*, purchased on March

4, 1936, with Helen as head of the Frick Collection's art acquisition committee. "I am very much impressed by [its] grandeur and monumentality," she had told Clapp after first seeing the painting. And although the price was high—$400,000—she warned, "another such opportunity may never occur again." After all, the painting was only the fourth example of the artist's work in America and certainly ranked among his finest.

Of course the withdrawal had everything to do with Helen's retaliatory anger, but she also expressed concern for the paintings. On March 16, worried about the damaging effect of the crowds, not to mention the harmful effect of the dust and drafts from the new but faulty air conditioning system, she complained to Forbes: "The condition of the pictures in the Collection worries me—Mr. Clapp is away on his much-needed & well-earned rest—in the meantime, certain blisters are growing more dangerous looking & I would so appreciate having your opinion!" But Helen only had the power to withdraw her own paintings from view, and not the Frick Collection's, so she had done what she could by rescuing hers.

No sooner did Clapp return than he began to mount a campaign to curb Helen's influence on art acquisition. Rockefeller agreed that as a condition for Clapp's accepting the directorship, Rockefeller would prevent "the usurpation of authority by individual trustees, in connection with management of the Collection, to who[m] such authority has not been specifically given by vote of the Trustees." Certain that Rockefeller had now achieved this, Clapp, who was still heading the University of Pittsburgh's fine arts department, considered resigning his post there. But on April 17, still unsure, he wrote Dwight, "You should be the director, not me. . . . I am still keeled on the reef I struck and see no light," and immediately began his fight to have full sway over acquisitions and add the works of art he, not Helen, wanted for the collection. Clapp bitterly complained to Dwight about the haphazard way the members of the art acquisition committee evaluated prospective additions. "The way in which pictures are considered does not seem to me to be conducive to well considered results. A glance by this one or that one singly or under unknown influences leads to no true consensus of opinion." And referring perhaps to Helen's restricted and unyielding aesthetic, "Besides I am sick of frozen attitudes."

Piero della Francesca (1410/20–1492), *St. Simon the Apostle (?)*. Acquired by the Frick Collection in 1936. Tempera on poplar panel, 52 ¾ x 24 ½ in. © the Frick Collection, New York.

By now Helen had read Rockefeller's February 3 letter to Childs, excluding her from the executive committee and neutralizing her voice when she raised it, and she was furious. On May 13, she sent her brother a blazing rejoinder and copied it to each trustee:

> I have come to the inescapable conclusion that [the February 3 letter] was directed at my attitude or supposed attitude towards the Collection. . . . I certainly have no desire to have any different relation to the operation of the Collection than any other trustee, but I do feel that my knowledge of my father's wishes and my intimate contact with the Collection from its inception will enable me to serve its interests if I have an active position in carrying out its purposes. Mr. Rockefeller, however, has gone to the point of seeming discourtesy in ignoring my views and my right to express them. I think he would be the first to resent such an attitude if conditions were reversed and his father had founded the Collection instead of mine.

Furthermore, as for Rockefeller's comment about her having "complete charge of the Library," Helen continued, Rockefeller "does not refer to the fact that I founded it, endowed it, and entered into a written arrangement with the Collection for its management." As far as being secretary of the collection, Helen acknowledged it was "an empty title," and she called the art acquisition committee "a committee of little importance." "If there has been dominance of any character, I feel I should say frankly it has been that assumed by Mr. Rockefeller. In his February 3 letter Rockefeller insisted the collection should be administered solely for the public benefit, not according to family traditions, individual preferences, or personal considerations." Helen found bitter argument with this statement and pointed out that despite adhering to her father's principles, "to date . . . no sincere worthwhile criticism has been made in regard to the arrangement of the Collection which my father desired; but on the contrary, insofar as I am informed, it has met with the definite and decided approval of those who have visited the Galleries." In light of this fact, Helen suggested ruefully, "I do not see that it would be harmful if I were consulted with respect to proposed substantial changes." And then responding to Rockefeller's proposal to keep no minutes of executive committee meetings, Helen wrote, "there should be some formality in regard to their meetings . . . minutes should be kept by the Secretary of the Collection if for no other reason than that the Trustees may individually inform themselves of what is going on between the meeting of the entire Board." As for Childs being on the executive committee and not herself, Helen suggested a compromise: she could take his place when he was absent. "I believe I am rightfully entitled to share equally in the activities and operation of the Collection."

The following day Helen penned a personal, more conciliatory note to Childs. She may have been disappointed in Clapp and angry that he had not defended her, yet she still wanted him to become director of the collection. "It will be the source of great regret to me should Mr. Clapp leave the Collection, as after all I am the one responsible for his having come to us in the first place. I wish to add that I have always cooperated with Mr. Clapp and intend to do so in the future." Helen wanted to meet with Childs and set some guidelines about management of the collection and acquisitions. In the meantime a still wavering Clapp confided to George Baker that he did not want the directorship, "fearing I have not the reserves of strength required to cope with a continuance of similar conditions." But by early June, Clapp changed his mind and accepted the position. He wrote a conciliatory note to Helen on June 5. "I want you to know this, remember as I always do, that it was your confidence and your appreciation of what we tried to do in Pittsburgh that in the first place brought me to the attention of the Trustees."

Helen remained steadfast, particularly about her catalogue and additions to her father's art collection. When the trustees wanted to seize the research she had compiled for the illustrated folio catalogue of the Frick Collection—the project that had sprung from the provenance research she began in her younger years, undertaken as much out of interest as to give her father pleasure and win his approval—and complete it themselves, before Helen had a chance to publish her work, Clapp merely reported, "Miss Frick told me that the catalogue being her enterprise, she will not place it in the hands of the Board of Trustees to finish." Then he complained of the burden, "Though [it] rises above me like a mountain chain full of glaciers and precipices, I refuse to be conquered by it as long as any strength is left in me." On June 19, Dwight quipped about the catalogue situation in a letter to Rockefeller: "One wonders just how much Mr. Frick had in mind when he wrote in his will, 'I am conscious that . . . I am imposing upon these gentlemen a duty which may prove very burdensome.'" No one considered for a moment the burdensome duty Frick had placed upon his daughter. Moreover, when Clapp suggested the Frick Collection acquire a painting attributed to Giorgione entitled *Salomé,* Helen responded on July 31, "[It] does not impress me too highly—I find her face rather weak and the drawing a little sloppy—This may be due to cleaning." She continued, "The drapery over her right arm is quite exquisite and the coloring is doubtless so, but . . . [I] would be reluctant to vote for the purchase . . . without having an opportunity to study the original and of having certain facts proved beyond doubt." The painting was rejected.

As if these battles weren't sufficient to absorb her energies, 1936 was an election year and Helen was determined to do what she could to reverse the results that had put Franklin D. Roosevelt into the White House. Helen promoted an organization in Pittsburgh called the Young Republicans of Allegheny County, and joined the Independent Coalition of American Women, a group of female Republican and insurgent Democrats opposed to the New Deal, headed nationally by a Democrat. She wrote to Paul Sachs, "I am deeply interested & very much concerned about our national problems, & feel that the very life of the Fogg Museum, the Frick Collection & Library is at stake & that we must all fight before it is too late!"

Helen had many allies in her cause, particularly Ellen Boyd and among the True Blues. In May, Helen had given the True Blues over two hundred cards, "Taxes and the Family Purse," to distribute; she also tried to solve the growing threat for many of losing their homes because they were unable to meet mortgage payments. Although she disapproved of Roosevelt's welfare programs, Helen suggested the girls apply to the government before asking her help to forestall foreclosures. On May 11, Miss Howland replied to Ellen Boyd's request that their boss give one of the girls, Sadie Mosley Clarke, $450 so she could keep her house. "Miss Frick would like to help the family but there are so *many* just like them!" she said. "Have they applied for Federal Housing Aid? . . . Not that Miss Frick is in sympathy with what the Government does, but so many less worthy people have received help! And the administration brags so about what they do, she would like to see yet one concrete evidence when such huge taxes are confiscated for this purpose." In the end Helen relented, but on the condition that when Sadie secured federal assistance she return the entire $450 to Helen. "On the whole," Boyd reported several months later, "I have found but three Democrats in our club and most of the girls and mothers will be [of] great help in spreading the information against the New Deal."

In her zeal Helen took her electioneering too far. In August she asked the library staff to sign cards pledging their vote to Alfred M. Landon—a violation of federal law. When

Rockefeller heard what Helen had done, he immediately contacted the Frick Collection trustees and enlisted their support in a letter of protest. Horace Havemeyer wrote Rockefeller on August 25:

> Owing to the close association in the public mind between the Frick Collection and the Frick Art Reference Library, I am quite willing to join you in a letter of protest to Miss Frick. . . . If she herself is responsible for the situation . . . she is laying herself open at least to a vote of censure from her associate trustees of the Frick Collection, and if she persists in activities of that kind it occurs to me that she might very well disqualify herself as a trustee of the Frick Collection and make herself subject to removal as a trustee.

Havemeyer continued, "In light of what has transpired, I confess that I regret that we ever put up the funds to build the Frick Art Reference Library. I confess that I feel it to be of small benefit to the Frick Collection, and, apparently, a constant source of annoyance to the trustees and administrative staff."

On August 26, Rockefeller delivered the letter of protest to Helen, signed by all the Frick Collection trustees except Childs, who ducked the issue. It stated their understanding that since the library was independent of the Frick Collection the trustees were "powerless to take any affirmative action itself" against her. Yet, "the two institutions are associated in the public mind. . . . and under the circumstances the Collection must be adversely affected if the action . . . is or has been taken." The letter warned that her attempt to influence the vote of the employees of the library was "most unwise and improper. . . . [and it was] clearly against public policy that voters should be intimidated or coerced."

Helen seems not to have replied to the letter, though clearly she continued her effort to defeat Roosevelt. When Roosevelt won by a landslide, according to Howland, "Miss Frick was just terribly upset about the outcome of the election. . . . The very first night, when the returns were coming through . . . she was sick in bed. She did work so hard and did everything in her power to help the Republican Party."

As 1936 drew to a close, there were, however, some positives. Helen had distributed more than 6,000 cans of food, 400 pairs of new shoes, 100 new dresses, and 5,400 articles of secondhand clothing in good repair to more than 1,000 households, all having suffered extreme loss from a devastating flood in Lowell and Lawrence. And she had spent approximately $42,500 on coal, medical expenses, rents, mortgage payments to forestall foreclosures, and funeral expenses for the needy.

The next summer, Helen returned to Eagle Rock for the first time since her mother's death six years before. Although pleased to see the True Blues, the house held too many memories for her, and the responsibility of running such a large establishment proved more than she wanted. She decided to raze the family wing, amounting to about one-third of the original structure, an area including her bedroom, the music room, and the indoor swimming pool. A new bedroom could be fashioned out of a former guest room. The dining room could become the new living room. And the breakfast room could be used as the dining room. Helen carefully considered the architectural plans drawn by Childs's Princeton classmate William F. Milliken, of the firm Milliken & Bevin, and as she contemplated the aesthetic impact of the demolition, she constantly visited the True Blue girls, only a few miles down the road.

A period of tranquility now developed between Helen and Childs. In a rare moment, Helen agreed to celebrate Christmas 1936 with her brother and sister-in-law on Long Island.

The Frick girls had graduated from Foxcroft, an elite boarding school in Middleburg, Virginia, and were busy with their various pursuits. Twenty-one-year-old Adelaide had completed courses at Barnard College, five months' study in Germany for college credit, and soon would arrive at the University of Pittsburgh to amass credits for medical school. Twenty-year-old Frances was pursuing social work, a field dear to her aunt's heart, and was then recovering from an emergency appendectomy. Helen was especially interested in nineteen-year-old Martha (named for "little Aunt Martha," as the children called their aunt's unfortunate sister) who was working for the Republican Party. But Dixie, hoping for a son to name after her father-in-law, had resented this daughter from birth. Clay, Dixie's much-desired son was now seventeen and preparing to graduate from St. Paul's School in Concord, Massachusetts. As for Childs and Dixie, they had just purchased a home in Bermuda named Castle Point. Their Long Island garden, designed by Marian Cruger Coffin, America's first professional landscape architect, was taking shape, as was Millstone, Childs's new research laboratory. And his book, *Horned Ruminants of North America*, was due out in March 1937.

With the start of 1937, Helen was also busy with other projects. She agreed to lend the Fogg her *Pietà* for a fall exhibition, and in return the museum agreed to remove the yellow varnish and to restore the spots where the paint had flaked. The Historical House at West Overton continued to attract the interested and curious. Of the University of Pittsburgh's fine arts department, now preparing to move from the basement of a nearby building into the Cathedral of Learning, Helen wrote Edward Forbes, "I think you will be proud of this 'offshoot' for which you [and Sachs] are both responsible." She felt confident that Walter Hovey, who had been running the department since 1932, would be a fine and trusted chairman on Clapp's resignation and that his associate, Virginia Lewis, would make a superb head librarian. The department's syllabus for 1936–1937 stated: "The Fine Arts Department is no longer an experiment. . . . It has, for use of its students, one of the most comprehensive and carefully selected libraries on art in the country." Its collection now held more than fifty thousand photographs "illustrating art in practically all lands at all times; twenty-three thousand lantern slides," and special projectors as well as "a complete sound motion picture apparatus."

Perhaps best of all, a new calm appeared to be spreading through the Frick Collection. Helen seemed determined to be less combative, making no arguments about policy or management. Rockefeller congratulated Clapp on their "smooth running machine" and speculated that "perhaps your greatest problem was your necessary contact with the descendants of the Founder; now that question has been thrashed out in its minutest details and, except on the personal side, is no longer a problem." For his part, Dwight tried to make Helen feel welcome in the collection. "I have been slyly cultivating Miss F. through the backdoor," he confided to the Clapps. "I wrote a soothing letter about all that was being done re drafts and dust; and when the Piero material arrived I inquired whether by chance it would interest the Library to have (again gratis) a set of our photographs, which would include a number of details. . . . I received a melting note. . . . I replied in no less melting tones, asking whether they preferred a glossy finish or a matte."

On the subject of acquisitions, however, Helen had not softened. A painting by the Flemish artist Jan van Eyck was being considered that year by the art acquisition committee and as Dwight explained, "I . . . wrote the Duchess," as he and the Clapps now called Helen, "quoting copiously, and sent copies of my letter to the other [trustees]." But Helen

Fra Carnevale (active by 1445, died 1484), *Presentation of the Virgin in the Temple.* Oil and tempera on panel, 57 ⅝ x 38 in. Helen rejected acquisition of this painting for the Frick Collection. Courtesy Museum of Fine Arts, Boston, Charles Potter Kling Fund.

was against the purchase. "A reply arrived, insisting that the Van Eyck is not a Van Eyck and, therefore, not worth a fraction of the price suggested." The painting was rejected.

She also made her feelings known about a work from the *Life of the Virgin* panels by the painter-priest Fra Carnevale, who had a passion for architectural form. His *Birth of the Virgin* panel was owned by the Metropolitan Museum of Art, and now the Frick Collection trustees were considering its mate, *Presentation of the Virgin in the Temple.* But Helen, defying the unanimous desire of the trustees to acquire it, did not think the painting good enough for her father's collection. Noting its "imperfect condition," and cautioning against purchasing a work by an artist whose "personality . . . is still undefined," Helen noted that the main subject, the Virgin, was not placed in a prominent position as she should have been; the work was top-heavy; and the composition lacked unity. "[It is] not a great masterpiece," she told Dwight, firmly, who later moaned to Clapp, who was in California and had not seen the painting, "How will [the trustees] reach a vote?" The rejected Fra Carnevale was purchased by the Museum of Fine Arts, Boston, and in 2005—the first time since the two panels left Italy in 1935—they were reunited as the focal point of an exhibition at the Metropolitan Museum, *Fra Carnevale and the Making of a Renaissance Master.* A description of the painting in the *New York Times* seems to vindicate Helen's strong opinions about the work. Still an enigma, the *Presentation of the Virgin in the Temple* was described as by "a second-tier somebody in mid-15th century Italy" that had "little more than a name attached to two oddball paintings of tiny figures doing inscrutable things in fantastic architectural settings." The director of the Metropolitan Museum of Art, Philippe de Montebello, admitted that the painting was "eccentric" and "perspectivally inaccurate."

In December 1936, Helen walked through the collection with Dwight, upset because she had not seen the galleries since the removal of her Eagle Rock paintings to the Fogg or known about the recent alterations in the exhibition of her father's works. She criticized the placement of Renoir's *Mother and Children* and told Dwight that "all the pictures in the East Gallery were good but that they did not go together." Dwight also reported "The Enamel Room drew praise, but a previously unnoticed flaw was discovered in the smaller Pietà, [so now] the photograph must be consulted. . . . [But] All right. It is her picture." The trustees had removed much of the furniture in the rooms, but Dwight said, "She said nothing about the 'elimination' of furniture in the Library but something about [the placement of] Lady Hamilton. . . . the Living Hall was found 'bare', the furniture [the Frick family used] too precious to be used by the hoi polloi [to sit on]. As usual I changed the subject." As for the new lighting for the Fragonard panels, they "were actually praised, but not the Boucher[s]. Too garish."

The opinions Helen offered had ripple effects. In the spring of 1937, the trustees dispatched Vanderbilt Webb, Rockefeller's personal attorney and Frick Collection trustee, to inform Helen that his brother-in-law, Frederick Osborn, also a Frick trustee, had "expressed a desire to know what the policy of the Collection was in buying works of art." Since there was no policy other than acquiring what Helen approved of, the trustees felt themselves no more than Helen Frick's rubber stamp and were galled at being placed in such a demeaning position. At Osborn's suggestion Clapp wrote "a sketch of a possible program" for the coming art acquisition committee meeting.

Helen had no objections to the first part of Clapp's sketch. He was as clear as she that the Frick Collection was "not a museum of the conventional type. It is a gentleman's house, furnished and decorated with objects of an uncommonly high level of merit, in a manner free of historical or chronological obsessions. . . . [and with] accidents of personal tastes." It continued, "So in acquiring new works of art. . . . a certain tone has already been set, from which we cannot deviate without discord. . . . The principal consideration to keep in view is quality. . . . by acquiring now and then a masterpiece." She did, however, object—most strenuously—to almost everything else. Among the guidelines and hypotheticals he proposed, Clapp suggested that the Frick Collection might acquire "a picture of uncertain attribution . . . [but] admirable in itself. . . . [or] a painting . . . [of] a conspicuously better example of a master represented in the Collection than one on the walls . . . [and] should not hesitate to buy that either, or to displace the one in the favor of the other." And he further contemplated, "We should be careful not to refuse a masterpiece because it does not harmonize with present arrangements or is too new." He also stated his objection to the pieces of Frick family furniture in the living hall—the sofa and chairs in front of the fireplace, placed as they had been during Frick's lifetime. "We have a number of pieces of very high quality [furniture], interspersed with others less notable. It would be possible here and there to key up the general tone by replacing indifferent pieces with others of greater artistic importance."

But Helen maintained her long-standing position: she wanted no paintings of uncertain attribution added to the collection and none of her father's paintings displaced by new additions. She continued to object to the acquisition of paintings aesthetically inappropriate for the collection and remained resolutely opposed to the inclusion of modern art or the removal of family furniture from the living hall. She countered that there be no written policy for art acquisition; additions should be made as they had been in the past, when a worthwhile painting became available and she approved of it. And then she went one step further. On May 19, she suggested to the trustees "that it may be wise to consider retaining the services of an agent in England or France to keep on the lookout for opportunities to buy really great works of art that may become available, before options have been secured by American dealers." The trustees did not act on her suggestion so on June 29 she wrote W. G. Constable at the Courtauld Institute of Art and asked him to be their foreign representative.

Clapp, fearing a coming tirade over any written policy, decided he and the trustees should bide their time and advised Dwight not to tangle with Helen on the subject. The reality was that both Clapp and Dwight had been doing a fine job on behalf of the collection. Attendance had increased from eight hundred people a day to one thousand—the ideal number, for as Clapp observed, "We are not made for large mobs."

During the restoration of her *Pietà* by the Fogg, Forbes subjected the painting to examination by infrared X-ray. Previous restorations and overpainting were revealed, "[the] fold in [the] drapery under [the] right thigh [is] by [a] later hand & more complicated & out of scale." So on November 4, Forbes suggested the painting "go back to [the] original, smoother [hand]." Helen was thrilled by the discovery and immediately wanted her father's "twin" to undergo the same analysis and restoration. Although all the trustees had the freedom to seek an expert opinion at any time to answer a question regarding a work of art, or to educate themselves and other board members—or even staff—Clapp felt insulted and angry that she had consulted an outside expert without speaking to him first. Rebuked, Helen made arrangements to send Eagle Rock's paintings to the Fogg for exhibition and then, after restoration by the Fogg, in 1938 the paintings went to the University of Pittsburgh.

In addition, Helen began the process of cataloguing and storing the decorative architectural elements, furniture, rugs, and lighting fixtures from Eagle Rock's family wing. She decided to sell some of the furniture and the lesser pastels and then to redistribute the balance of furniture, porcelains, and rugs throughout the house. She also commissioned a design by the important Long Island landscape architect Umberto Innocenti, who had done work for Childs, for a garden to replace the wing. Then she moved into her father's former bedroom and reupholstered some of the furniture with the identical morning-glory chintz he had used.

Helen also ordered two of her father's paintings from the Eagle Rock collection—the Chartran portrait of Martha from Frick's bedroom and the portrait of herself from his dressing room—sent back to Clayton, with specific instructions on their display. Helen had the mezzotint copy of Chartran's portrait of Martha in her Clayton bedroom replaced with the original. The mezzotint was then hung above the sofa in Frick's Clayton bedroom. Perhaps to make herself the dominant presence in his bedroom, Helen placed her own portrait beside the mezzotint.

At Clayton, Helen could exert the kind of control that by year's end was slipping away from her in New York. Yet by any reckoning, her art acquisitions that year for the collection had been significant. She had steered the trustees toward expanding her father's Boucher collection with the addition of the artist's portrait of his wife, as well as Jacques-Louis David's *The Comtesse Daru.* But Helen was not at all pleased when the trustees acquired a work by Paul Cézanne, *Chestnut Trees at Jas de Bouffan.* It was "modern art"—and also the first time the trustees succeeded in acquiring a work without her approval.

With the new year, the relationship between Helen and Childs, now forty-nine and fifty-four respectively, continued to be cold but civil. When their cousin Karl Overholt died suddenly on January 29, 1938, sister and brother traveled together to Wooster, Ohio, for the funeral and comforted Karl's ninety-year-old mother, Maria Frick Overholt, Frick's older sister.

On her return, Helen offered the Fogg still more paintings for exhibition. She wrote to Edward Forbes on February 8, "I am getting things straightened out at Prides before the work starts on the house," and wondered if he would like some of the lesser paintings for six months' loan as well. Helen tended to the restoration of her prized Sassetta, *Virgin of Humility Crowned by Two Angels,* and the painting from the school of Giotto purchased in 1922, and again loaned her *Pietà* to the Fogg.

Meanwhile, Helen watched other projects take shape. The first four Nationality Rooms in the Cathedral of Learning were being presented to the University of Pittsburgh. Helen had embraced one of these, the Russian Room, out of loyalty to her artist friend. Andrey Avinoff, a former gentleman-in-waiting and advisor to Czar Nicholas II. Now director of the Carnegie Museum, Avinoff taught courses on Oriental, Persian, and Russian art at the university and was famous for his watercolors of flora and fauna. In his honor, Helen had employed local Russian women to craft a tapestry after his painting, *Saint George and the Dragon,* for display. She specially purchased antique velvet, silk, and thread in Venice and had the women work their stitching in the medieval style. And in Wenham, Massachusetts, Helen was poised to help her True Blues open a shop to sell their handmade articles. But on February 9, when the managing director of the Made in America Club in New York, F. X. A. Eble, offered to assist Helen with promotion and publicity for the little store, he received a stiff reply on Helen's behalf, "Miss Frick regrets it is impossible to allow any publicity to be given the True Blue movement as it is a *strictly private matter,*" wrote Eleanor Howland.

Ever concerned about their welfare, Helen asked her True Blue girls to fight Roosevelt's immigration policies allowing thousands into the country (primarily Jews fleeing from Hitler's steady advance into Central Europe). She considered this a threat to "our American job holders." Enthusiastically, she sent the girls membership lists of the House and Senate and requested they write letters of protest: "We worked hard on the Senate and House lists that you sent us," wrote Boyd on April 1, "and we sent many telegrams."

Paul Cézanne (1839–1906), *Chestnut Trees at Jas de Bouffan.* Acquired by the Frick Collection in 1938. Oil on canvas, 28 x 35 ½ in. Deaccessioned in 1949. Courtesy the Minneapolis Institute of Arts.

François Boucher (1703–1770), *Madame Boucher*. Acquired by the Frick Collection in 1937. Oil on canvas, 22 ½ x 26 ⅞ in. © the Frick Collection, New York.

The Iron Rail was colored not only by Helen's political views, but also by her obsession with Germans. During its early years, in the decade before the Great War, some girls of German descent had enjoyed the benefits of the Iron Rail and had joined the True Blue Club. Now, Helen's fear of Germans intensified with the sudden influx of German refugees fleeing Hitler, and despite the fact that most of them were Jewish and running for their lives, she wanted to be reassured that no Germans were entering the vacation home or the True Blue Clubs. Boyd replied with surprising vigor, in language that left her some room to maneuver: "I received your letter yesterday about the German situation and I surely cannot blame you for wanting to know absolutely that none of your support goes to any person that is un-American. I feel most strongly on the subject and I cannot believe that any German or Italian or Frenchman or even Canadian would wish to come to the Iron Rail unless they were whole heartedly in sympathy with American principles." She reminded Helen, "We have not taken in any new German girls since you requested us not to, many years ago, but we have continued to take members of the original families." Then she explained the danger of guilt by association. "It is a hard time for all foreign born and it is sad to hear them say 'Please don't judge us by Hitler or any of the Germans across the sea.'" Indeed, Boyd quickly averred, "I do not know any Germans who are not citizens and loyal ones too."

Jacques-Louis David (1748–1825), *Comtesse Daru*. Acquired by the Frick Collection in 1937. Oil on canvas, 32 ⅛ x 25 ⅝ in. © the Frick Collection, New York.

After almost seventeen years as a trustee of the Frick Collection, Helen's suggestions were still unwelcome to the Rockefeller-controlled board. On May 12, 1938, Dwight recapped the events of the recent board meeting for Clapp who, unwell with headaches and vertigo, had again been absent. The main discussion concerned a group of girls Helen saw wandering through the collection. According to Dwight, "She thought it a pity to have no guidance, especially in these days of class feeling, when the only impression they might carry away might be that of a luxury beyond their own experience." The root of this discussion was Helen's anger that the education committee she had proposed had been bestowed upon the director instead of her, and her frustration that Clapp had faltered in matters of public education. When Helen suggested distributing art stories in the public schools, Dwight was careful not to tangle with her, telling Clapp, "These things must be quietly discussed in private with Mr. R. Also with . . . Griggs, Webb, and Osborn. . . . They are all with you on the supposition that it's idiotic to pay a man $18,000 a year to direct and then not allow him to do it." Yet he did admit, "Sooner or later something will have to be done about school children, I suppose." Dwight, unimpressed with Helen and angry with her, continued to refer to her as "the Duchess" behind her back. And now, apparently upset by the purchase of *Madame Boucher* and the *Comtesse Daru* for the Frick Collection, he snidely called her a "Francofile [*sic*] feminist." Dwight despaired over Helen's intense scrutiny of the collection, the detailed number of items she wanted fixed, and her continued insistence that her father's *Pietà* be restored and cleaned as hers had been. On June 23, he wrote irritably to Clapp, "Of course what is required according to F. is a housekeeper and one who will ask whether a pin can be picked up or left where it lies."

Childs also continued to exasperate Dwight. As an executor of Frick's will, Childs had many records of importance to the Frick Collection but he had kept them hidden away like precious jewels and refused to let Clapp or Dwight study them. Moreover, regarding an ongoing problem of the planting in the garden court Dwight said, "I don't suppose it ever occurred to [Childs] Frick that you could design an interior or lay out a garden by yourself. He couldn't, and he supposes everybody else but architects and landscape gardeners to be in the same case." He concluded astutely: "We simply have to make up our minds beforehand that as long as he lives he will screw up his face, raise objections, and call for 'expert' advice; that as long as she [Helen] lives she will follow her own traditions and methods."

Frederick Osborn was not so persuaded. He had accepted a position on the art acquisition committee for one year, but within months, due to the constant infighting, he wanted to resign. "I hope there is someone on the Board to take my place, for I very sincerely feel myself ill qualified. . . . It would be my desire that the service should not extend beyond the current year."

Meanwhile, the Frick Collection had just purchased *Diana, The Huntress,* by Helen's favorite sculptor, Houdon. The life-sized terra-cotta figure of the naked goddess gracefully poised on her left foot, her left hand holding a bow and a crescent moon set in her hair, is today considered one of the Frick Collection's great treasures. Only two other versions existed—one in marble, the other in bronze. For her own collection of Italian primitives Helen bought *Madonna and Child Enthroned with Four Seasons of the Passion; St. Francis; St. Anthony,* then thought to be a work of the Lucchese or Umbrian school, but today considered by Rainaldo di Rainuccio da Spoleto. Although meaningful additions to her father's collection continued with the purchase of Jacopo Tintoretto's *Portrait of a Venetian Procurator,* Helen made no acquisitions for other purposes for the next twenty-seven years, and then her purchases were for the University of Pittsburgh's teaching collection, not her own. As she wrote to Forbes, "everyone's purse strings have been strained."

Jean-Antoine Houdon (1741–1828), *Diana, The Huntress*. Acquired by the Frick Collection in 1939. Terra-cotta: 75 ⅛ in. © the Frick Collection, New York.

In the mill towns near Eagle Rock, eighteen thousand people were employed in cotton manufacturing when Henry Clay Frick died in 1919. In 1938 there were fewer than three thousand, and only a handful of the original textile corporations remained. In Lynn, not one of the original shoe firms from the turn of the century was still in operation. These dire conditions were reflected in the Iron Rail accounts. In 1938 the vacation home served 2,256 guests. It had been open 350 days, at a cost equivalent in today's dollars to nearly $2 million. Bearing witness to the enormous impact the facility had on people's lives, 86 percent of the original True Blue group was still alive and 93 percent had remained members. During

Rainaldo di Rainuccio da Spoleto, formerly attributed to the Lucchese or Umbrian School (ca. 1270), *Madonna and Child Enthroned with Four Scenes of the Passion; St. Francis; St. Anthony.* Acquired by Helen Clay Frick in 1938 for her collection. Triptych: tempera on panels, 49 ¾ x 41 ⅜ in. © the Collection of the the Frick Art & Historical Center, Pittsburgh, Pennsylvania.

those twenty-eight years Helen had spent nearly $47 million in today's dollars on her girls' behalf. The grandchildren of the original girls, known as Juniors, were now attending the vacation facility; with the Depression, their needs were as great as their grandmothers' so many years ago. According to Boyd, "One little girl said to another after dinner... 'I ate too much . . . and I feel awfully full, but I knew I wouldn't have another piece of chicken for a year so I filled up.'"

But if conditions were bad at home, the news from Europe alarmed everyone even more. With the German occupation of the Rhineland in 1936 and the annexation of Austria in 1938, Helen was convinced that the Germans intended to occupy the continent, just as they had in the Great War. She established a charitable, nonprofit organization called Thissell House—named for Jeffrey Thissell, who in the early seventeenth century owned much of the Eagle Rock property—to provide a foster home for British refugee children displaced by the war or by deteriorating political or social conditions. The finely paneled rooms on the second floor of the Eagle Rock stables, originally the grooms' quarters, could be converted into a dormitory, and her first cousin, Luella Frick Taylor, then at the Historical House, would be chaperone. While work began on the conversion, Helen enjoyed Christmas 1938 with Childs and his family. Her niece Martha, who had returned from Scandinavia in September 1937 with a mild case of infantile paralysis, had fully recovered, and announced her engagement on January 15, 1939, to Baltimorean J. Fife Symington Jr., who was living in nearby Port Washington, Long Island, and working for Pan-American Airways. The wedding took place sooner than expected because Pan-American asked Fife to greet the landing of its first transatlantic clipper ship at Southampton. Helen had to decline an invitation from Paul Sachs to a party in honor of Edward Forbes on March 18, because her youngest niece was getting married that day. If she did not attend, Helen said, Martha "declared she would come and 'blow up' the Fogg Museum!" Helen joined the family for the wedding service in Trinity Episcopal Church in Roslyn, Long Island, and the reception afterward at the family estate. On March 22, the young couple sailed for England. Dixie and Childs, upset because Martha was their youngest daughter but the first to marry, refused to give her an allowance. So Helen stepped in to help the young couple. She also gave them a set of silverware from the Westmoreland railroad car and rugs from Eagle Rock for their use in London.

With both the reconstruction of the Frick Collection and the construction of the new library building completed, Helen now resurrected the folio catalogue project, dormant since 1933. The trustees again tried to compel her to give it them for their use and publication. Helen steadfastly refused. In the end, even Dwight realized the futility of further attempts to commandeer the project. He told Clapp on February 9, 1939, "It doesn't seem to me that much is to be gained by jockeying her into a position where she will have to admit that she loves not the catalogue more but the trustees less."

On February 14, another effort was made to establish a policy for art acquisition. At a meeting attended by Helen, Clapp, Junius Morgan, Maitland Griggs, and Frederick Osborn, Clapp argued: "It is also in line with the founder's own policy . . . that acquisitions should include modern pictures of quality and distinction as well as Old Masters for, not only do the best modern pictures add brilliance and diversity to the general tone of the house, but they are of increasing interest to modern men and women." He continued, "Such pictures will inevitably become the old masters of the future. Corot is scarcely further away in time from the founder than Cézanne is from us" Clapp also expressed his desire to replace "less important pictures, sculpture and furniture by more important pieces," even though this violated Henry Clay Frick's will, and that he hoped to "even up the quality and size of the

Attributed to Andrea del Castagno (before 1420–1457), *The Resurrection*. Acquired by the Frick Collection in 1939. Tempera on poplar panel, 11 ¼ x 13 ¼ in. © the Frick Collection, New York.

objects displayed in [character and appeal] and make the East Gallery less of an orphan." Although use of the second-floor for gallery space had long been rejected, Clapp now recommended it as "a more intimate exhibition [space] of outstanding, if smaller, pictures. These little galleries," he continued, "might also be enriched by suitable and rare furniture."

A heated discussion ensued. Helen, enraged as before, felt Clapp's approach would destroy the fundamental character and aesthetic appeal of the work of art her father had created. Helen must have prevailed, for the only painting added to the collection in 1939 was *The Resurrection*, then considered to be by Francesco Botticini but now attributed to Andrea del Castagno. Meanwhile, anxious about the future, Helen asked the director of the National Gallery of Art in Washington, D.C., David E. Finley, to send her its acquisition policy, stipulating that acquisitions be in keeping with the quality of its core collection donated by the late Andrew W. Mellon.

On March 25, 1939, works by Fra Angelico and Antoine Le Nain were offered to the trustees. Helen did not care for either, particularly the Fra Angelico. She complained to

Forbes, "The condition is perfect & the scenes are beautifully painted & the coloring is lovely. [Nevertheless] I have seen pictures by this master that I have liked better, in spite of its many attractive features—it does not have for me, certain of Fra Angelico's characteristics that I am especially fond of." Yet she relented, "But if the rest of the Committee want it, I shall gladly vote for it." Nevertheless, much to Clapp's disappointment, neither painting was purchased.

His frustration was again mounting, and not only because of the control Helen continued to hold over acquisitions. "She has innumerable times implied," he complained, "and on several occasions said, that she has superior knowledge of her father's intentions and is the true repository of his unexpressed wishes." Moreover, Clapp confessed, the art world perceived him as Helen's puppet: "The legend that exists in New York that she is the real source of authority and decision in the Collection, the arbiter of what is bought and sole puller of strings of puppet trustees and subservient director, has not been made out of whole cloth." Referring to Helen's affection for early Italian art, Clapp thundered: "Virgins . . . are out of date—hard to look at unless supreme art in themselves." Nearing the end of his patience, and with the best days of his professional life clearly waning, Clapp wanted to make his mark on the Frick Collection and secure a place of prominence for himself in the emerging and fashionable arena of modern art.

Although the frustrated director decided that "The Committee will have to buy over her head" and imposed near-martial law in the collection—strict rules and regulations such as fingerprinting the employees and requiring a guard to accompany staff members to the bathroom—there was little risk of a real Clapp takeover. Though unwelcome and unappreciated, Helen's aesthetic sense continued to dominate. When spring turned to summer, Clapp's fury abated because most of the trustees left New York for vacation and were not interested in making decisions. Nevertheless he expressed just how far his loyalty and admiration had traveled since Helen had plucked him from Cambridge obscurity to run the University of Pittsburgh fine arts department: he wished that John D. Rockefeller Jr. would run for president in the coming 1940 election.

In April, Helen had written former president Herbert Hoover, infuriated by his support of the Wagner-Rogers Child Refugee Bill. It proposed an increase over the quota allowed for Germany for 1939 and 1940, granting entry to ten thousand German refugee children under fourteen years of age. She offered Hoover "profound regret that you have chosen to give second place to the present & future needs of American children." In early summer organizations favoring restrictive immigration defeated the bill.

Now Helen, about to return to Eagle Rock and to retrieve her freshly cleaned *Pietà* and her Sassetta from the Fogg, turned her attention to the True Blues. This summer of 1939 marked the thirtieth anniversary of the Iron Rail, and Helen constructed a brick gymnasium for the girls. Designed in the Colonial style by her Eagle Rock architects, Milliken & Bevin, it would have a stage, a basketball court, a fireplace with a hand-forged spit, locker space and double-decker beds with curtains for forty to fifty girls, six shower basins and toilets, and a kitchen large enough to serve five to six hundred.

For Helen's fifty-first birthday that September, the True Blues presented her with letters of thanks, bound by Boyd in an album with gold lettering. Gertrude Davis, a first-year girl with no family, explained the meaning of having her Thanksgiving dinner at the Iron Rail, "I'm always at the fireside there at Iron Rail, for to me it is going home."

In October, Helen purchased a small cottage on the beach at Rockport for the Iron Rail, knowing how much the girls enjoyed excursions to the seaside. Then in November the True Blues made their traditional gesture, this time knitting what Helen called "beautifully made" sweaters and socks for the Finns, now facing the invading Russian army. Helen had spent almost $64,000 (close to $3.5 million today) on her girls that year, but as Boyd wrote in her annual summary, "The expenditure of money upon these [True Blue families] is not the thing that has made the work so unique, but the friendship of the one who gave. . . . the unselfish desire to be of service and make this world better for everyone."

Helen was also working to secure her library collection as the situation in Europe quickly eroded. When Hitler began construction of the Siegfried Line, Helen knew, as did others in Great Britain, France, and America, that war would come next, and on September 1, 1939, it did. Helen, who had experienced the bombing of Paris, and now feared a bomb could hit New York City, wanted the library staff to begin microfilming the entire collection of photographic images for storage outside the city. She at least would preserve a record of Europe's artistic heritage.

While Helen pondered the future, the carefully constructed privacy around her past and present was shattered. On July 15, 1939, the *New Yorker* published the first of a two-part profile written by John McCarten entitled "Profiles: Daughter of Her Father." Since Helen never granted interviews, the information was gathered elsewhere. McCarten made fun of her anti-Roosevelt stand and referred to the Frick Collection as "the vast, unhappy building that Henry Clay Frick erected as a memorial to himself." As for the Frick Art Reference Library, McCarten gave the facility full marks, but claimed that Helen, who still refused to speak to Sir Robert Witt, was jealous of Witt's library and was competing with it. He also noted, "To Miss Frick, Germans, whether scholarly or not, are distasteful. She exercises a frenzied censorship. . . . and accepted all the wartime stories of German atrocities."

The second part of the profile appeared the following week. It noted that Helen had worked on cataloguing her father's collection since childhood and that this interest had translated into the Frick Art Reference Library. McCarten praised her library efforts and the Frick Collection, although he offered unflattering remarks about the library as being "no great shakes externally." While crediting Helen with shaping Frick Collection policy, he was wrong on two important points: "the policy of the board has always been to defer to Miss Frick's wishes," and Helen "accepts Clapp's word as law."

The article also speculated about how she was spending her $38 million inheritance and attempted to determine her current net worth. In the last paragraph, McCarten recognized that Helen was an unusual woman. "Her business judgment is acute, and her investment counselors take their consultations with her seriously," and he added, "she is, by the nature of things, probably one of the last of her kind." McCarten concluded, "It is unlikely, though, that that thought has ever crossed her mind."

1940–1950

7 War

If I should tell my history, it would seem
Like lies disdained in the reporting.

—Marina to Pericles, *Pericles, Prince of Tyre*

A severe ice storm hit Westmoreland Farm in March 1940, and Helen wrote Ellen Boyd, "I am very much upset at the present time, because of the terrible disaster in Westchester County. . . . My place and all the adjoining places have been ruined and it is heartbreaking to see these beautiful trees so crushed." Another storm was brewing, though—this one over the unresolved issue of the Frick Collection's acquisition policy. Although the trustees purchased a print by Albrecht Dürer, *Melencolia I,* they were still bent on overriding Helen's control of acquisitions and on abandoning the Old Masters in favor of modern artists. Anxious to compete with other museums in this new arena, the board warred with Helen and continued to press her for a written policy. Rockefeller explained to Frederick Osborn that he wanted to make it "clear to Miss Frick that she stands alone in her view." In an undated memorandum he wrote, "The question as to whether a contemplated work of art harmonizes with the existing collection shall not be unduly emphasized, but rather regarded as of minor importance and not to be seriously considered in reaching a decision." Thus, on April 23, Osborn could proudly report to Rockefeller that the acquisition committee had finally forced Helen into capitulation with a successful vote to purchase a colorful example of Paul Gauguin's early South Sea period, *Tahitian Landscape,* "even though we all agreed it did not fit in with anything in The Collection at present." Helen did not leave written comments on her decision to vote with the trustees, who had also elected to purchase a second Cézanne, *Antoine Dominique Sauveur Aubert, the Artist's Uncle, as a Monk.*

Helen was clearly becoming increasingly preoccupied with the war in Europe and the problem of safeguarding her library collection should America be drawn into the fight. On May 17, she told Clapp she "would like to see armored plate applied to the roof of the house

Opposite: On April 30, 1948, Helen entered the New York Supreme Court, hiding her face from photographers. Courtesy UPI/Corbis-Bettman.

Paul Gauguin (1848–1903), *Tahitian Landscape*. Oil on canvas, 26 ¾ x 36 ⅜ in.
Acquired by the Frick Collection in 1940. Deaccessioned in 1949.
Courtesy the Minneapolis Institute of Arts.

against bombing." Clapp offered words of calm and suggested a direct hit was improbable. If she wanted to protect her library materials, she could build a concrete vault "at a considerable distance from metropolitan centers" in case of an emergency.

The war was also affecting Helen's other projects. On June 12, just ten days before France surrendered to Germany, she wrote John Bowman at the University of Pittsburgh, "The world is in such an upset condition, and there are so many people starving, that I do not feel justified in spending as much on the Fine Arts as I have in the past. . . . For the present I think we had better cut out buying any photographs or books, and of course omit any salary increases." Extremely encouraged about the Republican presidential nomination of Wendell Willkie, Helen wrote Edward Forbes at the Fogg Art Museum, "This looks like the first ray of hope for our Country in a long time," and she loaned the Fogg the Louis XVI furniture from the former music room at Eagle Rock, "because . . . it seems a pity that it is not being enjoyed." Forbes replied on June 27, "I do not doubt that you are as absorbed and as heavy-hearted as we all are here at the turn the affairs have taken in Europe." And at last he vindicated Helen's longstanding refusal to grant Germans use of her library: "It is hard to believe that these terrible savage monsters are really in control of France. In the universal burst of indignation against Nazis, people will understand better than they did why you have mistrusted them so."

Paul Cézanne (1839–1906), *Antoine Dominique Sauveur Aubert, the Artist's Uncle, as a Monk.* Oil on canvas, 25 ⅝ x 21 ½ in. Acquired by the Frick Collection in 1940. Deaccessioned in 1949. Courtesy of the Metropolitan Museum of Art, the Walter H. and Leonore Annenberg Collection, gift of Walter H. and Leonore Annenberg, 1993, bequest of Walter H. Annenberg, 2002. Image © the Metropolitan Museum of Art.

After serious consideration, Helen decided there was no better place to construct a vault for emergency storage of her library collection than at Westmoreland Farm. Intending to microfilm all the photographs in its holdings, a project that could take at least a year, she concentrated first on bringing the bibliographies on art objects up to date.

She also turned her attention toward another wartime rescue measure. On July 28, Thissell House, the organization designed to provide a foster home for British refugee children, was officially designated a charitable corporation under Delaware law, so expenses could de deducted in any state, including those where Helen lived: Massachusetts, Pennsylvania, and New York. Through the New England Home for Little Wanderers, a subcommittee of the U.S. Committee for the Care of European Children, Helen offered Eagle Rock to British refugee children, as other Americans from at least twenty-one states offered their homes. She asked for one hundred children, but as was her custom, there were restrictions—only young girls, no Catholics, and since Helen did not want to take care of boys, no brothers. Her stipulations may have worried the authorities; they reduced her allotment to just twelve children.

Undaunted, and with the transformation of the Eagle Rock stables into a girls' dormitory already underway, Helen now hired a "merry and kind" British lady, a Miss Lindsay, as chaperone. In early August, to outfit the dormitory, she transferred to Thissell House all the family linen from the Westmoreland railroad car, its Gorham and Tiffany silver, and carpeting from the fourth-floor hall of Eagle Rock's demolished wing. Lastly, in anticipation of the girls' arrival later that month, Helen enrolled them in the local North Shore Country Day School.

In the end, only seven of the twelve girls arrived. On August 30, 1940, the Germans torpedoed a Dutch passenger ship with 321 children on board. No children perished, but on September 17, the Germans sank a second ship, and 77 of the 256 children on board were lost in heavy seas. So the evacuation effort was terminated, and only 3,000 children out of an anticipated 300,000 actually reached the United States.

The three Sayers sisters (from left to right), Valerie, Pixie, and Mavis. Author's collection.

The first of Helen's group to arrive were Molly Stuchbery, Sheila Inglis, Margot Horn, and Mary-Joy Shuttleworth, all twelve years old and strangers to one another. They came via Montreal, where they had been housed in a reform school. Next were three sisters, Mavis, Valerie, and Pixie Sayers, ages thirteen, twelve, and eight, respectively.

When the first four girls arrived in Boston, they sat patiently in Helen's large car and listened attentively as she began to tell them about "her little boy, Bobby," not realizing until they were almost at Eagle Rock that Bobby was her spaniel, not her child. As for Helen, because she had expected the girls to be four or five years old, not twelve or thirteen, she had decorated their rooms with bunny rabbits and had filled the closets with beautiful little dresses, placing them on neatly arranged hangers with long handles for easy reach. Helen immediately exchanged the new clothes for larger sizes, rearranged their rooms, and in an effort to make the girls feel as much at home as possible, she instructed the Thissell House staff to observe all English customs and serve only English dishes.

The girls' parents expressed relief that their daughters were out of harm's way, beyond the reach of the devastating air raids that had now started. On September 30, Molly's father, T. Alan Stuchbery, wrote Helen: "I find it difficult to put into words the feeling of gratitude and relief we feel at the kindness you and other citizens of the states are showing to our children. It was very reluctantly that my wife agreed to part with our only child but in view of the savage attacks made indiscriminately on civilian homes both by day and night Mrs. Stuchbery now is fully in agreement with me that we were fortunate in being able to avail ourselves on Molly's behalf of your wonderful offer of your hospitality extended by warm hearted people like yourself." For Phyllis Sayers, "the parting from my three babies . . . is a physical pain." And Margot's mother, Elsie Horn, in a poignant letter, conveyed the spirit of the times: "When I see the children here who spend sleepless nights and anxious days, I cannot cease to thank God that the war is not touching [Margot]."

At Eagle Rock the British girls experienced a life quite unlike anything they had ever known. Helen bought them a cocker spaniel puppy named Flush, and guinea pigs, and when the season changed from fall to winter, she provided yet another new wardrobe. The girls enjoyed ballet, skating, and skiing lessons, instruction in first aid, and making craft items for local bazaars. Often books, Bibles, and boxes of candy arrived as gifts from Helen when she was at Bedford, and bunches of flowers from the greenhouse came regularly to brighten their new home.

Over the next four years Helen nurtured her girls through bouts with mumps, measles, and chicken pox, not to mention trips to the orthodontist for teeth that needed straightening or to the oculist for eyeglasses that needed strengthening. The children attended confirmation classes and, during school vacations, went to New York for lunch at the Frick Art Reference Library and theater evenings on Broadway. Together Helen and the girls visited Boston's Isabella Stewart Gardner Museum, the Frick chemistry lab at Princeton University, and the National Gallery in Washington, D.C.

In the spring each girl was given her own garden to tend, and in the summer enjoyed swimming off Eagle Rock's beach and picnicking in the fields. Phyllis Sayers, who greatly appreciated receiving the movies Helen regularly took of the girls, still longed for her daughters. Nonetheless, she was entranced by the magical life they were having with Helen. "Never in any letter, even trying to read between the lines," she wrote, "has there been even a suggestion of anything but radiant happiness. It seems such things as 'off days' are unknown at [Eagle Rock]."

There were "off days" for Helen, a few of them being Election Day in 1940, when Roosevelt carried thirty-eight of the forty-eight states—"the terrific results make this the darkest day in American History," Helen wrote. Then a Mrs. William Beggs began writing to Helen, threatening to blow her up, together with all her belongings, unless Helen gave her $50,000. Helen contacted the FBI, and in late November, the woman was arrested and confined to a mental hospital.

Ellen Boyd provided another "off day." After thirty years, she announced her retirement, effective at the end of the year. During her time at the Iron Rail, the True Blue family had grown to 5,462 members across three generations. But Boyd, for all her contributions over the years, appeared to have used Iron Rail funds for herself. When Helen questioned certain unitemized disbursements, Boyd replied, "We have never kept a record of relief or help given, as you know, and have been proud of the fact our recipients were such close friends that we would not think of putting in writing anything that would embarrass them." Helen scrawled two words across Boyd's letter—"Such twaddle"—and asked an accounting firm to conduct an audit.

The audit took some time, after which the accountants reported, "considerable doubt exists concerning the authenticity of certain disbursements listed in [Ellen Boyd's] monthly petty cash reports." Moreover, early in her tenure, Boyd had claimed that she was a widow and that her husband had died in California. Out of sympathy, Helen had set up an Iron Rail fund in his memory for Boyd's use in True Blue emergencies, but Boyd apparently had also misused that account. According to a former member of the Iron Rail staff, Elizabeth Limmond, "after Mrs. Boyd's wedding announcement [in the 1920s] . . . many of the girls then living in California wrote back to friends in the east and stated they doubted that the wedding ever took place." The boxes of candy Boyd received at the Iron Rail from her "fiancée" were in fact purchased by Boyd and sent to herself. And the diamond ring she wore had been purchased and given to her by her mother.

Helen now designated Boyd a "forbidden person" and denied her access to the Iron Rail property. Then she challenged her former director about the many items found missing. Boyd admitted she had taken some of them, but claimed that her assistant, Thora Johnson, had taken the others. When Johnson admitted this in a letter to her former employer, Helen was not convinced. She wrote William Naughton, who monitored the finances of the Iron Rail, "Isn't this an *amazing* letter? Apparently [Johnson] has been forced by that woman to play 'stooge' & take the blame! It is very revealing." More sleuthing done by Ruth Bradley, another Iron Rail employee, revealed that Boyd had pocketed repayment of loans and money for employees she never hired.

Helen spent almost $133,000 on the continuing investigation, but moved forward, beginning with fitting up the new gym at the Iron Rail. She also decided to completely renovate Fairhaven, the house Ellen Boyd had used, "so as to eradicate the memories of the person who had lived there before." As for Boyd's decision to host competing True Blue gatherings in nearby Wenham, Helen advised the new director, Ruth Larsen, not "to be bothered by [Boyd]. . . . It's a terribly difficult situation for a new person, but I am sure it will all clear up before long."

While Helen stewed about the Boyd matter, the air was filled with other unpleasantness, most noticeably at the Frick Collection. During the past summer Clapp had complained to Dwight, "The Collection is more of a grave day by day." Clapp also registered misgivings concerning a December 1940 trustees' initiative to construct a three-story underground bombproof vault for the Frick Collection treasures and for some of the library material in the event of an emergency. Work would commence with the demolition of a house at Nine East Seventieth Street, adjacent at the rear of the Frick Collection and recently purchased by the trustees. An apprehensive Clapp wrote Dwight, "Heaven give me strength to deal with it otherwise I tremble at the time-and-strength-wasting episodes that may strew our pathway."

As the plan moved forward, the Frick Collection sought permission from the department of housing and buildings to construct its vault, a structure that could be easily converted to a bomb shelter if needed. The first of its kind in New York, it was to have iron stairs, a hydraulic elevator, electric wiring in the concrete connected to an alarm system, cork-lined walls, and an arched ceiling reinforced with concrete and steel over which six feet of clay and sand were to be placed to absorb the effects of a major hit. Designed to be self-contained, with its own heating and electrical plant, an air-conditioning unit, a well, a system of alarms and inner corridor doors, the vault necessitated drilling to a depth of one thousand feet through solid rock to render it impervious to the direct hit of a one-thousand-pound bomb. The cost of construction was estimated at a then staggering $175,000, with work to begin April 3, 1941.

Helen spent Christmas 1940 with her British girls, who were thriving. Their days had been filled with making decorations and on Christmas morning, the seven little girls gathered quietly at eight o'clock in Molly's room with a portable radio "to listen together to their Empire's Christmas greeting and their King's noble address." Among the many gifts Helen placed under the silver-trimmed tree were doll houses, sleds, skis, fountain pens, and sewing kits. Then they took a walk across the road and up the hill to Eagle Rock, to the Red Cross Room where Helen rolled bandages, and "where round a blazing fire hung long red stockings filled with more gifts and giftlets." Such golden moments were punctuated for them all by the sobering news back home. Britain's fate was much on everyone's minds. Helen sent one thousand blankets, telling John Bowman in January, "There is so much to be done to help England—and now our own defense—that it is hard to keep level-headed these days!"

With security on her mind, in March 1941 Helen strengthened the Thissell House stables with sand and steel and stored emergency equipment in the cellar. At the art reference library in New York, the staff, "busy after work knitting sweaters, socks, hats and scarves . . . [and] fold[ing] bandages and sew[ing] receiving blankets for layettes at a Red Cross Center on Madison Avenue," began microfilming the photograph collection as planned, all 275,000 mounts, with fourteen different processes employed for each side. They also began copying the 430,000-card index file by dexigraph, a photostatic process. Helen was there every day to personally supervise the work.

Although space had been provided for library material on the third story of the Frick Collection's underground vault, Helen also sought estimates for packing, removing, and storing off-site 130 tons of library material. Having abandoned the idea of a vault at Westmoreland Farm, some were to be housed near Bedford, others at Eagle Rock, and another 3,200 were to remain at the library for use by scholars. Henry Milliken, the architect for the new gym, whose firm had been advising Helen on protecting her library, sought to address her concern about the possibility of a bomb landing in New York:

> Completion of the [new] vault is tentatively set for mid-October. The Russian attack completely eliminates the chance for an emergency, such as we are planning for, arising before the vault is finished. . . . Working night and day the Library could be cleared in 2 days or 3 at the most. . . . We believe that you now have all the information necessary to set your mind completely at rest . . . at least before a declaration of war. [Should that happen], we know exactly what should go to [Eagle Rock and Bedford] and to the vault.

There had been but one disagreement in the planning—Helen's refusal to ship the library's German books to Eagle Rock. Her success at barring German scholars from her library was well known—repugnant to many, but old news. Milliken, however, in a July 22 letter, tried to suggest that the books "after all represent a pretty big investment." But Helen was resolute. In the margin of his letter she wrote, "*No German books to be included!*"

Helen was under terrific strain and fainting so often that when she entered Grand Central Station to take a train to Bedford, rather than cross through the concourse she walked around the edge, touching the wall. She also suffered an attack of shingles, and then, at the end of May, her beloved dog, Bobby, died of a seizure. By July, though Helen continued to mourn her dog, she was fully recovered from shingles and on July 4, 1941, was on hand to lead the dedication of the new Iron Rail gym. Helen and the British girls led the procession of Eagle Rock carriages from Thissell House to the new building, where Helen made a speech to a gathering of 450 True Blues.

All through the summer months Helen paid unusually close attention to the Iron Rail, this being Ruth Larsen's first summer. Here the news was most positive. The war in Europe was stimulating the U.S. economy; employment was on the rise, and as Larsen wrote Helen, "Most of our people are working and in better circumstances than they have been in a long time." In just that month the Iron Rail had served 1,410 guests and 3,072 meals. "The most marked change in the program," wrote Larsen, "has been in switching from one of entertainment to one of functional activity—one where every girl is busy in an activity of interest to her." The Iron Rail canned 200 quarts of string beans, 122 quarts of tomatoes, and 114 quarts of applesauce.

The British girls raising money for the underground children's shelters in London subways. Courtesy the Frick Collection/Frick Art Reference Library Archives.

There was good news from the Frick family as well. Helen's niece Martha Frick Symington and her husband had left London in May 1940, just when France began falling to the Germans, and the couple was now living in a cottage on Childs and Dixie's Long Island estate. In February 1941, the young couple produced their first child, Helen Clay Symington, Helen Frick's first grandniece and her namesake. Helen immediately commissioned Malvina Hoffman for a terra-cotta bas-relief and a portrait medallion of the infant, and in August the six-month-old baby—the first great-grandchild of Henry Clay Frick—visited Eagle Rock.

Meanwhile, at Thissell House, the girls were planning a dog show to benefit the five children's rooms in the London subway and railroad system that they had adopted. These shelters, code-named Thissell, Eagle, Prides, Westmoreland, and Mayflower, housed children at night to keep them off train platforms and to protect them from Nazi bombs. For their fundraiser, the girls provided homemade refreshments and awarded prizes for the dog who most resembled its owner, the most obedient dog, the dog who could perform the most tricks, the dog with the longest tail, or the shortest nose, or the curliest ears, or the loudest bark. Members of prominent North Shore families and noted individuals such as George S. Patton supported the event. The girls were able to donate almost $600 to their shelters.

Helen made a donation as well, continuing a tradition she began at the outset of the German attack on England. She sent the Women's Voluntary Services for Civil Defense in London a check for approximately £700 to be used later in the year for children's Christmas parties. In addition to its many relocation efforts, this agency also evacuated children under five years of age for placement in war nurseries run by the Junior American Red Cross.

On September 24, 1941, the library staff finally microfilmed the last photo mount, and started to check and recheck the negatives for sufficiently high-quality reproduction. On December 3, they packed the one hundred reels of film in individual tin cases, arranged them in packing cartons, and transferred them to an underground bank vault on the outskirts of New York City near Westmoreland Farm. On the very day of the Pearl Harbor attack, Helen had just ordered that the library films, weighing a total of five hundred pounds, be removed from the vault near Bedford and taken by the head of the photography department to Iowa on the Twentieth Century Limited for storage in the Des Moines National Bank and Trust safe deposit vault.

With her library material copied and stored, the Frick Collection's new bomb-proof vault completed, and evacuation plans for library books organized, Helen reconsidered the safety of her British girls. Three days after Pearl Harbor, America declared war on Italy and Germany and Helen, having rescued the girls from London, now saw them once again in a country at war. For greater protection, she decided to bring the girls to Westmoreland Farm after graduation in June and to house them in a small cottage she rented about four miles through the woods. In her usual fashion, she closely supervised its preparation. The heavy curtains from 640 Fifth Avenue were brought out of storage. "I feel we might as well reuse them! . . . They will be effective as blackouts!" she told William Naughton, and then chose the interior paint color with wallpaper to match and pondered the andirons needed for so many fireplaces. "My thought is that in the bedrooms we can use bricks instead," but for the downstairs fireplaces, "Would there be any at Eagle Rock, that are not too imposing?" Some of the big rugs from 640 Fifth Avenue "could be cut down to give a warmer look to the bedrooms," and since the farm cottage was much larger than the Thissell House apartments, she designated the chauffeur for "a lot of the heavy dusting." The girls, however, "will keep their rooms up as usual," rooms Helen decorated with prints of the paintings in the Frick Collection.

The one defensive measure Helen had yet to organize was the security of the Eagle Rock art collection. She said to Paul Sachs on December 19 that she was "satisfied in leaving all but the *Pietà* at the Fogg if they are not in the way," and would keep the *Pietà* "in the safest place I can find—if there is such a place!" Helen chose Westmoreland Farm and then suddenly changed her mind about sending the Eagle Rock collection to the Fogg. Instead she sent the paintings as far from the East Coast, and from the West Coast, as she could—to the Dallas Museum of Fine Arts, giving the museum's visitors their first exhibition of eighteenth-century British paintings.

During the Depression years, Helen had reduced her financial support of cultural institutions and had concentrated on humanitarian concerns. But with the onset of war, factory work surged 460 percent, wages rose, and over six million women filled positions vacated by men serving in the military, increasing the size of the labor force by 50 percent. With these altered circumstances Helen again shifted the focus of her financial contributions, this time to the Red Cross. She told John Bowman at the University of Pittsburgh, "I have been giving thought to all the various cultural institutions to which I have been accustomed to contribute, realizing that I must cut down drastically in my donations as you can well understand." She reduced this sort of annual giving to $10,000, with the promise to "do more after the war if things improve." She removed a large part of the wrought iron fence at Eagle Rock's entrance and the iron rail surrounding the Iron Rail property and donated it all for scrap. She further instructed Ruth Larsen to shut down the poultry plant, saying "a good deal of the chicken wire might go for scrap and help with the war effort," and to butcher the sheep and "put [the meat] up in jars." Larsen was also to use a cheaper grade of writing paper, with smaller margins, "trying so hard to save in every way," and the True Blue knitters should purchase their wool from the Red Cross, now using the Iron Rail facility to teach others how to run a canteen. Helen transferred all the property she had inherited from her parents in Wenham and Hamilton to the Iron Rail, to be used, rented, or sold. She also closed Clayton, her home in Pittsburgh, lowered the heat, wrapped and covered the furniture, cleaned, rolled, and mothproofed the rugs, and offered the city part of the property, now the site of the Frick Art Museum, for victory gardens.

The British girls, ca. 1942. Front row, seated left to right: Sheila Inglis, later Milliken; Valerie Sayers, later Goodwin; Margot Horn, later Nicol; Pixie Sayers, later Love. Standing left to right: Mavis Sayers, later Archer; Mary Joy Shuttleworth, and Molly Stuchbery, later Willcox. Courtesy the Frick Collection/Frick Art Reference Library Archives.

Helen also remained involved with the True Blue girls of working age. "Has it occurred to you," she warned, "that after the war, when the 'boys' come home, women will no longer hold many of the jobs [you] now fill, and that in the adjustment to be made, there will necessarily be difficulty for many to get other work?" She advised them, "A profession is always a great asset to have and that of nurse or practical nurse is one for which there is ever a demand. . . . The Iron Rail Vacation Home is anxious to help out if some of you feel the expense during training is beyond your ability to pay."

In the summer of 1942, with the renovated farm cottage ready, the British girls moved in and enrolled for the fall in the Horace Greeley School in nearby Chappaqua, New York. Helen temporarily closed the Historical House at West Overton and brought Luella Taylor, or "Auntie Taylor" as the girls called her, down to act as housemother. Helen continued to work hard at being a parent to them; she saw the six older ones confirmed, gave each a small New Testament like those she gave to the True Blue girls, without fail dined with them every Wednesday on her way home from New York, and every Saturday invited one

Claude-Oscar Monet (1840–1926), *Vétheuil in Winter*. Acquired by the Frick Collection in 1942. Oil on canvas, 27 x 35 ⅜ in. © the Frick Collection, New York.

of the girls to spend the night with her at the farm. On Sundays she invited the entire group for lunch; the girls could play kick the can, swim, feed sugar to the horses and cows, and walk with Helen in the woods.

She also arranged for the girls to travel to the North Woods Club in the Adirondack Mountains, where they stayed in a rustic log cabin built by Henry Clay Frick in 1897, and brought them to New York for lunch in her private dining room at the library or, on Mondays, when the Frick Collection is closed to visitors, to "wander about." Many of the more renowned paintings had been removed to the new bomb shelter and Helen had specified how Clapp was to rehang the collection, including the recent acquisition, Claude Monet's *Vétheuil in Winter*, a reminder of German-occupied France. Drawings and prints filled in gaps and the remaining paintings were rearranged to ensure their safety and make the collection seem harmonious, but the Boucher and Fragonard Rooms were stripped of their panels and closed. The two adjoining French rooms were rehung with the small early Italian Renaissance paintings, because in an emergency they could be "easily handled." Closed also were the Enamel Room facing Fifth Avenue and the East Gallery. Houdon's graceful, life-sized sculpture of Diana in the Oval Room was removed to the vault and the walls covered with drawings and etchings. Nevertheless the girls were impressed. Eventually even the Italian primitives "became very close friends of [theirs]."

The details of the collection were very much on Helen's mind. Pleased with the American painter John C. Johansen's portraits of her parents in her library waiting room, she now commissioned two of Henry Clay Frick—one for herself and the other for the collection, both with dark, brooding backgrounds suggesting the heat and fire of Pittsburgh's steel mills. After giving one of the completed works to the trustees, Helen told Childs that the condition she had attached to her gift was not being met. "Just as a matter of record for the Board of Trustees," she wrote on February 10, 1943, "I wish to put into writing what I stated on the day on which I presented The Frick Collection with the portrait of the Founder. The Trustees were so enthusiastic in accepting it that I presume[d] they agreed with the condition of the gift." Helen had said, "the portrait should always hang in a place commensurate with the dignity and character of the Founder," and that the January minutes merely recorded that the portrait would be exhibited "in an appropriate place in the Collection." The trustees had placed the portrait in the Oval Room, whereas Helen wanted it displayed over the fireplace in the library. So she asked Clapp to "have drawings made at my expense, as a preliminary study to see if the over mantel paneling [could] be changed to conform with the size of the portrait" and demanded that her February 10 letter be attached to the minutes of the January meeting.

Clapp was now utterly exhausted by Helen's demands and was suspicious of anything she proposed. He warned Rockefeller on February 26, "Of course the hanging of the picture in the place that she had chosen was involved in the resolution of the gift." While controversy continued, Rockefeller told Childs that the trustees "accepted the gift with expressions of deep satisfaction and appreciation," but he deemed Helen's "wish as to the hanging of the portrait . . . undesirable that this or any other gift to the Collection should be accepted subject to any condition which would restrict the freedom of the Board of Trustees." Rockefeller advised Helen he would not attach the letter she wrote Childs on February 10 to the minutes. Helen recalled that Rockefeller had further stated he "would not have anyone dictate where anything should go, and that he wanted the portrait to hang on the northwall [*sic*] of the library as he used to see Mr. Frick in the library when he called on him!" Helen shot back. "I reminded him that I had been accustomed to see Mr. F. in every room in

Naval exercises in the Atlantic Ocean off Eagle Rock during World War II. Private collection.

the house." In the resolution of this latest skirmish, Helen prevailed: the Johansen portrait of Henry Clay Frick can still be seen above the mantel in the library.

Not long after, though, another battle began, this time over Childs's proposal that the Frick Collection mount an exhibition of approximately seventeen paintings from the late Sir Herbert C. Cook's renowned collection of Old Masters, then coming to America from Surrey, England, for safekeeping. Helen was furious at the prospect of her father's house being used to showcase another family's collection, no matter how important. (Cook's collection included Filippo Lippi's *Adoration of the Magi*, now considered among the top five paintings in the Metropolitan Museum of Art.) Again Helen emerged the victor. A chagrined Clapp complained "Some museum not obsessed by tangled directive, possibly the Metropolitan, will probably gain great kudos by putting on the show . . . and so put thousands through their turnstiles." The Toledo Museum of Art mounted the exhibition, to critical acclaim.

A full-scale invasion of Europe was clearly imminent by the middle of 1943, and with it the potential for the massive destruction of museums, churches, monuments, and priceless works of art rose exponentially. Earlier, in the fall of 1942, four respected figures in the art world—Francis Henry Taylor, director of the Metropolitan Museum of Art; William B. Dinsmoor, president of the Archaeological Institute of America; Sumner McK. Crosby, president of the College Art Association; and David E. Finley, director of the National Gallery of Art—asked Chief Justice Harlan F. Stone to support the creation of a government commission for the protection, conservation, and salvage of European archives, works of art, and historical monuments. Stone submitted their request to President Roosevelt, who approved the idea and passed the request on to Justice Owen Roberts. By April 1943, the Roberts Commission, as it was known, was established in cooperation with Great Britain. Among its members were Helen's longtime associates Dinsmoor, Taylor, Finley, and Paul Sachs.

In mid-June 1943, Helen offered the full facilities of the Frick Art Reference Library and the services of its staff as the headquarters for making grid maps of Europe and pinpointing its treasures so invading armies and Allied bombers could avoid their destruction. Overjoyed, Sumner McK. Crosby wrote Helen "to tell you how deeply grateful we are for your interest and marvelous generosity. With the facilities of the Frick Art Reference Library behind the work of this Committee, I feel certain that we can really accomplish a great deal and ultimately render a real service."

Her offer came just in time. On July 10, 1943, the Allies invaded Sicily, a preliminary step to the invasion of Italy. German airfields, railways, and military fortifications were the primary targets, and after thirty-nine days of bombing, Sicily fell to the Allies. Although the locals had put into safe storage the most important works of art from their museums, churches, and other public or exposed buildings, the cultural destruction was enormous. In Palermo—it fell within just twelve days—many historic monuments and more than sixty churches were damaged or destroyed.

On July 15, Helen closed her library to the public and opened it to the War Department, while continuing to pay all library expenses. According to her friend from Spence School, art historian Katharine McCook Knox, under Dinsmoor's direction "more than a hundred expert scholars, art historians, collectors and artists, many of them refugees from Europe . . . compiled lists, [and] catalogues." The primary resources for their highly detailed work were the library's collection of out-of-print-books, some now returned from storage, its detailed card file and photograph mounts, and the Frick family's diaries of their many

William Burke and Jane Mull, members of the Committee on the Protection of Cultural Treasures in War Areas, American Council of Learned Societies, work in the Frick Art Reference Library with Gladys Hamlin (right), a draftswoman, during the World War II years. They are composing a grid map of Paris, pinpointing its art historical treasures. Courtesy the National Archives and Records Administration, College Park, Maryland.

European trips with their references to works of art in small villages. All of these helped scholars prepare the maps identifying the principal monuments, museums, and archives to be protected. First they placed tissue paper overlays on maps supplied by the Army Map Service. Then each map was photographed with its overlay and indexed for easy reference, along with a brief written history and description of the site to be avoided. The committee worked quickly, and when the Allies invaded southern Italy on September 3, the first 150 Frick Art Reference Library "Treasure Maps" had been indexed, photographed, and delivered to the armed services. A total of 786 maps, arranged in atlas form for each occupied country as well as for Germany, were eventually sent to the Allied strategic air force staffs, to be distributed to those who planned and directed the bombing raids, and to the high command in the infantry and artillery.

Soon the commission could also help recover stolen art. On September 19, 1943, the *New York Times* confirmed that the Germans were indeed systematically stealing art from both public and private collections in occupied Europe. The article defined the Roberts Commission's multinational task as "a test of whether or not intellectual cooperation among people of differing races, creeds and cultural traditions can succeed in preserving for mankind the fruits of 5,000 years of human experience and imagination." In this regard the role of Helen Frick and the records she had compiled at the Frick Art Reference Library were of critical importance.

As the tide of war turned in the Allies' favor, Helen, regularly updated by Dinsmoor with growing lists of art stolen or obliterated, worried that the Germans might destroy the artworks they had seized. She asked Justice Roberts, "Would it be possible for the United Nations to make a declaration now, warning the Germans that they will be forced to give up all the treasures in their own museums and private collections, should harm come to the property they have removed from invaded countries? Three days later Roberts replied, "It may well be that it would be advisable to emphasize this in a further statement."

With America's women now fully employed in war work, Helen was reconsidering the function of the Iron Rail. The festering problem of Ellen Boyd also contributed; since leaving the organization she had been encouraging the True Blues to turn against Helen. Many had boycotted the ceremonial opening of the new gym in July 1941, angry that Boyd had not been invited. They believed the former director had been wronged and they had lost confidence in Helen Frick. With the friendship and camaraderie they had enjoyed over the years eroding, Helen, disenchanted with the deteriorating situation, sought to broaden the facility's mandate. Ruth Larsen also questioned whether the Iron Rail was serving a proper purpose and whether it needed to change direction. On November 24, she wrote to Helen, "Since it is impossible to live or work any longer in the midst of the undermining and bitter spirit of the Boyd followers, I recommend that this tie be severed." Helen replied with a simple "OK." So on December 15, she told the True Blue girls that "after long and serious consideration [of] the problem of how the Iron Rail could best contribute to the needs of our Country," she was adapting its work "to the needs of the present day." She wanted the Iron Rail to "make itself available to increasing numbers of children, especially to those who at this time, are in need of physical benefit of country life and nourishing food." She terminated the leases on the True Blue clubrooms, suggested the True Blues instead form an Iron Rail alumnae association, and assured them that they could hold their reunions "now and then" at the Iron Rail.

Larsen reported, "The Lowell and Lawrence girls and mothers were very interesting in their reactions to your letter. Some were wonderful." The Boston True Blues were particularly understanding. "To some of us the need of Iron Rail's free vacations has passed." But "a few [in the other clubs were] very sulky and unwilling to give up something they considered theirs, even though they had not been to Iron Rail nor used the clubrooms in years." Helen did not care. She had moved on, and in anticipation of the Allied invasion of France she said "French Babies" were what she wanted—preschool children aged four to six years. "Our purpose would be to build them up physically and return them to France in a couple of years after conditions are such that proper care can be given them over there." Yet Helen insisted they be "old enough to ensure that they are French, with no German blood in their veins!"

In spite of the war, and with Horace Havemeyer's help in the negotiations, the acquisition committee added a number of paintings to the Frick Collection during 1943, all from the Morgan estate, in a blanket deal of $495,000: John Constable's *White Horse,* Goya's *Don Pedro, Duque de Osuna,* Jean Baptiste Greuze's *Wool Winder,* Rembrandt's *Nicolaes Ruts,* Reynolds's *General John Burgoyne,* and Jean Barbet de Lyon's bronze sculpture, *Angel.* Under a separate arrangement, encouraged by Helen, it also acquired a set of William Blake's illustrations in pencil and watercolor for *Pilgrim's Progress,* donated to the Red Cross to help its fundraising efforts. Helen also received a portrait of her mother by Andrey Avinoff's sister, Madame Elizabeth Shoumatoff, based on a photograph taken circa 1902. Yet the happy interlude enjoyed by the art acquisition committee did not last long. By January 1944, Clapp was again upset with Helen, this time for rejecting a Peter Paul Rubens, *Meleager and Atalanta.* She stated that the painting was "very crowded and not very pleasing . . . not a suitable one for the Frick Collection."

Meanwhile, Helen was working hard in the canteen at the Soldiers' and Sailors' Club and also was busy on behalf of her grandnieces Helen Clay Symington, Arabella Hambleton Symington, born in January 1943, and this author, Martha Howard Frick Symington, or "Martie." Helen was searching for a governess for the older two children and for a baby nurse.

Then in mid-July, with the skies over Britain safe again, Helen took her British girls to Bellport, Long Island, in mid-July to await their departure. On July 14, Molly Stuchbery, now sixteen, wrote her Aunt Helen, "Although this was the last time we'll see you for any length of time, I don't think you'll ever be completely away from us. If you love people you are always there." The girls boarded the ship on the twenty-fifth, and Sheila Inglis remembered, "Three of us stood in the stern of the ship as she left harbor and Aunt Helen's face just crumbled. She was devastated. It was the most terrible moment." But their relationships continued. Helen sent them home with new clothes, followed by packages of vitamin pills, apricots, surprise gifts like Mother Goose figures, tea, books, seeds, soap flakes, and other items either in short supply in Great Britain, or delicacies that had long since disappeared. She wrote them letters, and sent birthday presents, and later, paid for their college educations and for the schooling of their children. And when traveling abroad Helen always visited the girls and bought them a good piece of furniture "so each had something nice."

After the girls departed, Helen went to Nantucket for a ten-day rest with her friend Louise Freeman Lee and asked her secretary "not to mention business of any kind to her, nor to send her any business mail." Then, in September, a devastating hurricane hit Westmoreland Farm, uprooting its trees, leaving Helen, as she wailed to Edward Forbes, "sick at heart!"

With one loss compounding another, Helen remained steadfast about the library's war effort. She invited William B. Dinsmoor to continue working in the library "as long as your committee finds it necessary to consult our files of photographs. . . . in the work that is being done to preserve and restore the works of art that have suffered through the war." Professor Rensselaer W. Lee of Smith College and the Institute for Advanced Study in Princeton noted: "[The] damage to historical monuments in France has been very small indeed and . . . the accuracy of the bombers was largely due to the special maps which were prepared here in New York." In fact, of the twenty-five famous cathedrals, châteaux, and other historic buildings listed by the French government, all but one was either intact or only slightly damaged.

By April 1945, the Allies were finally across the Rhine and on their way to victory. Then on April 12, Franklin D. Roosevelt died. Helen, unlike other directors of institutions in New York and across the nation, did not despair. She refused to lower the flag at the Frick Art Reference Library to half-mast. In fact she flew no flags at all. Frank Mather Jr. happened to be in the library at the time, and wrote to Helen:

> I was surprised and shocked to see three bare flagpoles over the entrance . . . at a moment when every other flag staff in the city carried its flag at half mast for the President. For any American institution that has a flagpole to omit the formal act of respect, due the presidential office, indicates on the part of the person responsible for such discourtesy, a deplorable lack of good judgment, good taste, and American loyalty. . . . The three bare flagpoles over the portal of the F.A.R.L. would be a very gratifying exhibit for Goebbels [the official propagandist of Nazi Germany] and Hitler."

Helen replied sternly:

> The flags have been omitted at my direction. I cannot compromise even if it should bring criticism upon me. I want to be sincere at all times—in fact I cannot be otherwise. Perhaps I have greater respect for the office of The President of the U.S. than have those who voted for Franklin Delano Roosevelt, whom I consider responsible for bringing class hatred to our country, & many other objectionable features that never existed before. As long as I live, the FARL will be an expression of its Director & will stand for the best interests of the Country, in spite of what others may think or say.

The stunned Mather stood up to her, "You are so desperately muddled that I fear your case is beyond psychological surgery. Please think that over." As for her alleged sincerity, he found it "monstrously sophistical and false, entirely unworthy of your character and intelligence," and complained, "[I] hate to think of you suffering from such wrong headedness and wrong heartedness."

Helen's opinions were often the subject of criticism, but the great news of May 7—Germany's capitulation to the Allied powers—was a validation and vindication of her anti-German policies. She wrote in her diary, "This morning heard that unconditional surrender of German Army took place last evening—beautiful day, worked in garden, cat birds here, wood thrushes here." The cruelty of the Nazi regime was now exposed more graphically than ever as the first images of the human suffering in the death camps made their way around the world. Moreover, with the liberation of the concentration camps came the discovery of thousands of paintings and other art treasures stolen from public and private collections in occupied Europe, hidden in salt mines. Thanks to the Roberts Commission and in part to the Frick Art Reference Library, the majority of Europe's treasures would be restored to their rightful homes. In addition, two hundred of the finest works of German art came to the National Gallery in Washington, D.C., for conservation, and then toured America before returning to Germany. The Frick library, though reopened to scholars on January 4, 1944, nevertheless remained headquarters for the commission, reduced in size and operating out of a special section. Its work continued while intelligence organizations built up their files, and while the commission continued to aid in the restitution of stolen works. Helen congratulated her head librarian, Ethelwyn Manning: "Under your generalship [crossed out to read 'guidance'] the FARL has grown from a puny infant into an important adult whose place in the world of art is undisputed."

As the war drew to a close, the changes it had wrought were apparent in all the places Helen held dear. The Iron Rail had remade itself during the war years, but soon began to falter. Returning veterans reclaimed their former jobs, leaving many of the girls unemployed, and, to make matters worse, the last three surviving mills in Lowell closed. Many True Blues, having taken Helen's advice, had gone into nursing and teaching. The Iron Rail helped them with tuition but now its greater purpose had become, as Helen had predicted, caring for orphans. The Iron Rail also opened its doors to other agencies, including Everett House, whose children, according to Ruth Larsen, "never get to go anywhere."

In New York, the library books were returned and the paintings stored in the Frick Collection's bombproof vault were redistributed throughout the house. And there was a vacancy on the board of trustees left by David Bruce, who resigned because he was seeking a divorce from Andrew W. Mellon's daughter, Ailsa. Helen pushed for the nomination of a Frick family loyalist as trustee, her friend and Bedford neighbor Edwin deT. Bechtel.

Yet whatever hopes Helen had for preserving the unique character of the Frick Collection as the display of one man's taste were once again about to be severely challenged. John D. Rockefeller Jr., now seventy-one and in increasingly poor health, remained bent on acquiring modern art for the Frick Collection—even though he did not like it and objected to his wife's interest in it, and despite Helen's protests. In addition, on March 1, 1945, Rockefeller became energized by the possibility of having his own art collection permanently exhibited in the Frick Collection. Stephen C. Clark, the chairman of the Museum of Modern Art, sparked this excitement by asking Abby Rockefeller if the Frick Collection could accept a bequest of his artworks. Rockefeller confessed that Clark's inquiry then "turned my mind to the possibility of that institution as the recipient of one or more of our paintings or porcelains." Rockefeller pushed forward and decided the matter should be taken up in the executive committee "where we could get Mr. [Childs] Frick's reaction and as a result of which he would have a chance to discuss the matter with Miss Frick before it was taken up in the trustees' meeting."

Childs apprised Helen of the situation on March 21, and as Helen said, "I . . . hit the skies!" She wrote William Moorhead, "I am very much concerned over something Childs mentioned to me yesterday and I feel certain you will see, as I do, the implications." She explained: "the name of JDR would be all over the place and The Frick Collection would cease to be a 'Frick Institution.'" Helen called on precedent. When Maitland Griggs once offered pieces from his collection, she advised him that the collection did not accept gifts, under the reasoning she explained to Moorhead: "The Frick Collection just *breathes* my father's and mother's taste and I see no reason why it should not remain that way." Helen pleaded with Moorhead to "study the Will and [the] Charter and interpret them in such a way that there can be no misunderstanding." She knew her brother was against her. "Childs will not fight [against Rockefeller] and I am probably the only Trustee who cares what happens, but I see the great danger that lies ahead." Moorhead prepared an opinion for Helen to hand the trustees, warning them they had no legal right to accept gifts for the collection because Frick had made no provision for such action under his will. Article 4, section 2, stated that the Frick Collection "shall encourage and develop the study of the fine arts and . . . promote the general knowledge of kindred subjects among the public at large," but did not include a provision for acceptance of gifts. Article 4, section 4, stated that the income surplus of the $15 million endowment fund—after care, maintenance, and protection of the building and the collection, and necessary alterations and improvements was "to be expended from time to time . . . in the purchase of other suitable works of art," but again did not mention gifts to the collection.

But on June 12, Vanderbilt Webb wrote the Frick Collection's legal counsel, John Henry Hammond, to confirm what had been said to Helen in the trustees' meeting. "Mr. Moorhead's conclusions are unjustified by the facts and the law, and are contrary to the terms of the Will of Mr. Frick and the Act of Incorporation." Hammond formally challenged Moorhead's opinion and stated that in fact gifts had already been made to the Frick Collection—by Helen. Although he made no mention of the Johansen portrait of Frick, according to a 1947 memorandum, he claimed Helen's previous gifts included the Sèvres porcelain, the furniture from the servants' rooms, the carpet and furniture in the Boucher Room, the bust of Madame de Pompadour's daughter, Falconet's *Friendship,* the bust of a little girl in a beribboned bonnet she had purchased in 1914, the 1922 Malvina Hoffman bust of Henry Clay Frick, the French Burgundian *Virgin and Child,* and the Barna da Siena *Christ Bearing the Cross.* He also claimed a color print of Whistler's *Rosa Corder* was a gift, as well as a letter from Whistler to Richard A. Canfield, from whom Frick had purchased four Whistler portraits in 1914. Since the Frick Art Reference Library would pass to the collection on Helen's death, he deemed it a gift from Helen, as well. Childs too was named as having given the collection a gift, Andrey Avinoff's drawings based on George Golokhvasoff's epic poem, "The Fall of Atlantis." In any event, argued Hammond, "a man's will should be interpreted by the practical construction thereof made by the trustees thereunder."

An irate Helen complained to Moorhead, "This list is what I thought it would be! It represents various articles for which I had no special use when I removed my personal belongings and others I had inherited from my mother's estate from the house at 1 East 70th Street. . . . It is quibbling," she continued, "to list furniture in servants' rooms that I did not remove. It belonged to the Collection just as much as it did to me! I could have had it carted away—but the Frick Collection employees needed chairs to sit on! . . . I was very careful," she noted, "not to take anything that could be questioned as Frick Collection property, so now they are making up a list in the hope of strengthening their case against me!"

Helen responded that she had indeed been offered the Canfield letter, but "felt it belonged in [the] Collection as it had specifically to do with the 'Rosa Corder' Portrait." *Virgin and Child,* she explained, was purchased in May 1927 by agreement with the Frick Collection and sold to the collection, under the agreement, for the purchase price. *Christ Bearing the Cross* by Barna da Siena also came into the collection "by agreement," in part consideration for the purchase of Duccio's *Temptation of Christ on the Mountain.* She had released the porcelains to the Frick Collection at market value as partial payment for the salvage material she took for her art library. It too was "an agreed exchange." As for the Frick Art Reference Library itself, there was no way it could be perceived as a gift. A joint venture, it was governed by a signed, legal agreement between herself, the Frick Collection, and the library.

On July 9, Henry Clay Frick's former attorney, William Watson Smith, who was also one of Helen's lawyers, concurred that the items Hammond listed were not gifts and further stated that the Frick Collection was Frick's "strictly personal creation." "There is no question," he emphasized, "that a testator can create a memorial in the form of an art collection for the benefit of the public . . . personal to himself." He believed that the language of Frick's will limited the trustees' power to carrying out the "spirit and purpose of the gifts" made by the will, and according to that logic, works of art could enter the collection only if purchased through Frick's endowment or given by a family member. "Surely," Smith said, "What [Mr. Frick] did by his Will was to establish 'The Frick Collection.' He neither established, nor intended to establish, 'the Frick, Smith, Brown, Jones, Robinson, Jackson, Taylor Collection,' yet some such conglomeration would result. . . . regardless of whether or not such gifts by others were identified by plaques or otherwise." He continued: "If [Frick] had intended that pictures and objects of art might be contributed by others, he would naturally have said so when he dealt with additions to the collection. The omission of any such provision could not have been an oversight."

According to Helen, Childs then asked Clapp "to prepare a list of artists that might be considered important, & whose pictures should be acquired in case the opportunity should come our way." In mid-October, Clapp presented the trustees with his analysis of the Frick Collection. On one hand the director complimented "the high points of the Collection" and advised that "a policy of buying to fill 'gaps' might ruin the character of the Collection by lowering its quality," but on the other hand he suggested the collection "to raise its quality" and "prevent [it] from becoming fatally static," should add works by well over one hundred artists not yet represented, and listed names from every country and every school from the Byzantine period to contemporary art.

Helen wrote Edward Forbes on October 19, "Mr. Clapp's uncomplimentary remarks about The Frick Collection as a whole have irritated me beyond measure, as they cast a reflection on the taste & judgment of the Founder & I think they are uncalled for. The Frick Collection is too small to include masterpieces by all the great artists—but most critics & connoisseurs seem to agree that most of the works of art contained in [the Frick] are of high quality." She also raised the issue of the foreword Clapp was to write for the folio catalogue. "I want to frankly say that I will feel very much averse to having him write the foreword in the Catalogue. . . . If the foreword should distort the facts & minimize the importance of the collection, I would consider that the 'Memorial' would be irretrievably hurt!"

Forbes agreed to remove Clapp from writing the foreword but added that his report was not so bad as Helen thought. He said "the distinction of the collection is self-evident, and I suppose that [Clapp] did not feel it necessary to dwell on the obvious." Rather, Forbes said, the question was one of policy, that the trustees "will have to decide, as to whether they will purchase largely modern works so as to try to keep up with the times, or whether they will try to fill the gaps in the ranks of the great masters between the 13th and 18th centuries, or whether they will concentrate on the 18th and 19th centuries." He continued, "My personal preference . . . is to fill up the gaps in the earlier fields if opportunity offers."

Helen was not consoled. She sent Clapp's report to Moorhead with a comment in the margin, "TRIPE," and advised her lawyer, "Should this paper be shown to art critics here & abroad there would ensue a very lively discussion." Moorhead agreed with her. "If paintings by all of the artists mentioned were acquired, it would seem to me the Collection would become one of the largest collections in the country." He also thought "it would be wise to adopt a general policy against receiving gifts, otherwise the Trustees might have some very difficult questions to decide on [and] there would be differences of opinion and the decisions . . . might subject them to criticism in accepting a gift from one donor and declining that of another. Without such a policy," he warned, "it might be embarrassing to refuse a gift from a Trustee, for instance."

Although Moorhead and Helen were working against the gifts Rockefeller intended to make, neither anticipated the scale of his plans. The Arthur Curtis James house, east of the collection, was for sale, and unbeknownst to Helen, Rockefeller was having architectural plans drawn for a two-story addition to the Frick Collection on the James site, an addition he called the "Rockefeller Memorial Room."

On October 23, Helen submitted a memorandum from Moorhead to the trustees warning them against adopting Clapp's "Special Report on The Frick Collection" because, among other reasons, implementing such a plan would require a building three times its present size. As Helen complained to Malvina Hoffman, Clapp "hints that we should invest in Impressionists and Post-Impressionists now as they will become the antiques of the future."

Yet when the board met, Frederick Osborn, Vanderbilt Webb, and new trustee Charles Dickey aligned with Childs and Rockefeller against Helen on the issue of accepting gifts. Two trustees, Horace Havemeyer, the only original, nonfamily trustee remaining on the board, and Junius Morgan, a trustee since 1932, cautiously suggested John Henry Hammond approach the attorney general because "it is too intimate and serious a question to decide among Trustees." But "Counsel was very sure of himself," Helen explained. "Childs was entirely on Rockefeller's side," and Vanderbilt Webb, whom she had once called "J.D.R.'s 'henchman,'" assured her, "There's no distinction between buying and accepting gifts." To evade Helen, Hammond and Childs suggested Hammond's report on other cases involving gifts be taken up at the next three-man executive committee meeting. Helen said "*No.* There will be no discussion of this matter unless the *Board* was present." Reminding the men that she too was a trustee, Helen complained she was "not represented" and that she would go to a higher court if necessary, to get proper interpretation. She told Moorhead, "Rockefeller was very disagreeable and terribly put out not to have [the] matter voted on today [and] his expression was furious."

In 1945, the sole painting acquired by the Frick Collection was Jean-Baptiste-Siméon Chardin's *Still Life with Plums.* This was the fourth work by Chardin Helen had been instrumental in buying (in 1935 she purchased *Attributes of the Painter* and *Attributes of the Architect* for the Princeton Art Gallery), and the second one she had urged on the Frick Collection. Helen noted with irony that "the Board has never in the past shown any great interest to acquire works of art, even when the *superlative* things were available!" She queried, "So why the eagerness now to accept gifts? I fear the interest lies in providing a handsome background for such collectors as R. himself! Otherwise there is too great [an] inconsistency."

Frustrated and worried, Helen directed her attorney to go to court rather than negotiate the matter. "I would not wish to have this matter settled out of court," she advised

Jean-Baptiste-Siméon Chardin (1699–1779), *Still Life with Plums*. Acquired by the Frick Collection in 1945. Oil on canvas, 17 ¾ x 19 ¾ in. © the Frick Collection, New York.

Jean-Baptiste-Siméon Chardin (1699–1779), *Attributes of the Painter*. Oil on canvas, 19 ¾ x 33 ⅞ in. Courtesy Princeton University Art Museum, gift of Miss Helen Clay Frick, 1935. Photo credit: Bruce M. White.

Jean-Baptiste-Siméon Chardin (1699–1779), *Attributes of the Architect*. Oil on canvas, 19 ¾ x 33 ⅞ in. Courtesy Princeton University Art Museum, gift of Miss Helen Clay Frick, 1935. Photo credit: Bruce M. White.

Moorhead, "as I feel that this is a long looked-forward to opportunity to have the whole Trustee matter cleared up once & for all." Saying she was "sorry that Childs is not with us," Helen, nevertheless, felt, "It may be easier to handle the case without him." She also asked Moorhead "to remove Childs' name as one of the executors of my estate." In his place, Helen appointed her twenty-six-year-old nephew Henry Clay Frick II, newly married and just graduated from medical school, and her twenty-eight-year-old niece Martha. By 1946, Helen was certain "some of the trustees are a bit scared over the thought of litigation," while she remained fully convinced of the rightfulness of her suit. When Childs asked her if she would unilaterally accept the court decision, she replied, "I would not do so if it were contrary."

Helen with her namesake grandniece Helen Clay Symington, later Chace, on the Atlantic Beach at Eagle Rock. Author's collection.

As attorneys for both sides prepared for court, Helen stayed her course, beginning, more happily, with the Iron Rail, where she remained as committed as she had been in the past. The farm was thriving—400 baby chicks were born in January—and Larsen reported, "Every mail contains requests from special agencies for camp placements. . . . The days and evenings [will be] crowded to the limit."

In mid-March, three-year-old Arabella Symington came for a one-week stay with "Grauntie," as Helen was known by her growing band of grandnieces and grandnephews. A dog had bitten the child in the leg and her mother, burdened by her fourth child, seven-month-old J. Fife Symington III, feared Arabella might have contracted rabies. So she was sent to Helen while she underwent the long, painful treatment. Then, when her five-year-old sister, Helen Clay, came down with scarlet fever, Arabella stayed on. "Of course they have just moved to Baltimore," Eleanor Howland explained to Larsen, "and were not settled at all! . . . Miss Frick is delighted to have Arabella with her." Worried about the strain of a sick child and a newborn on Helen's niece Martha, Helen decided to open Eagle Rock for the summer, "for Mrs. Symington and her four babies," and on July 14 Helen wrote Edward Forbes, "I have undertaken a big job in opening this house & in trying to run it at this time when housekeeping is less easy than it used to be." Nevertheless, opening Eagle Rock provided much satisfaction. Larsen reported to Howland, "[Miss Frick] is certainly enjoying the [Symington] children." She did, however, decide to close Thissell House. Having hoped to keep it running in case she was sent some French war orphans, on July 10 Helen dissolved the corporation. She also agreed with the decision of her head librarian, Miss Manning, to assume no new work at the library "because we are all swamped with material that has accumulated since the beginning of the war," and that "the foreign material should be catalogued as soon as possible as we have many requests for it."

Over the summer of 1946 and into the fall, the debate over the legal right of the Frick Collection trustees to accept Rockefeller's artworks escalated. Rockefeller, eager to move ahead, wanted to call a special meeting to initiate legal action, "otherwise six months time will be lost in getting forward with the legal proceedings." Claiming he had "no personal interest," and frustrated by what he referred to as "the undesirability of this continued inaction," Rockefeller moved for the immediate adoption of a resolution to seek a declara-

Thomas Gainsborough (1727–1788), *Grace Dalrymple Elliott.* Acquired by the Frick Collection in 1946. Oil on canvas, 30 ⅛ x 25 in. © the Frick Collection, New York.

Thomas Gainsborough (1727–1788), *Richard Paul Jodrell.* Acquired by the Frick Collection in 1946. Oil on canvas, 30 ¼ x 25 ⅛ in. © the Frick Collection, New York.

tion of judgment. Although Helen, too, was anxious for a court resolution, she opposed any vote on the matter on procedural grounds: Horace Havemeyer, Frederick Osborn, and Richard K. Mellon, who had taken David Bruce's place on the board, were not present. She further insisted that if the resolution prepared by Hammond and Rockefeller for the meeting was changed in any way, it would have to be circulated to all the trustees and she must be given time to consider it. In a surprising turnaround Childs then said to Hammond, "Put my name in with that of my sister and the Attorney General, as defendants. This is a more graceful way of doing it to have the family together." Skeptical rather than grateful, Helen viewed Childs's offer as an empty gesture. She "rather heatedly inquired if [Childs's] 'boss' [Rockefeller] had dictated this!" "What will happen after the declaratory judgment," she had asked Childs, "in case I should find it necessary to carry the case to a higher court? Will you still be with me?" "I can pull out quietly," he had replied.

No vote was taken, and Helen exclaimed to Moorhead, "Rockefeller was *furious* that the resolution was not acted upon, and showed his displeasure very plainly." A few days later Childs officially withdrew his offer to join his sister as a defendant.

Helen, unaware until now of the availability of the James house for purchase, and knowing nothing about Rockefeller's plans for his Memorial Room, guessed his agenda. "I can see the prospect they are entertaining, that of converting it into a new gallery for *gifts received!* More than ever the Founder's bequest would be used *to show off* the collections of other persons!" Frightened and distrustful, she reminded Moorhead, "Don't forget the Executive Committee enjoy [*sic*] keeping me in the dark as long as possible about everything!"

Helen was, however, determined not to allow the pending litigation to stall her efforts as chair of the acquisition committee. In May, the Frick Collection acquired *Richard Paul Jodrell* and *Grace Dalrymple Elliott*, increasing its Gainsborough holdings to seven. Yet the trustees were in fact pushing her further and further out of the loop. Clapp refused to answer her calls, and Dwight informed Helen that according to a May 14, 1936, resolution, no trustee could approach the director with an inquiry or a recommendation. Helen challenged Dwight, while Clapp insisted to Vanderbilt Webb, "such a right is, of course, inherent in the Trustees."

Meanwhile, Harrison Griswold Dwight resigned to pursue literary aspirations, and in 1947, Franklin Matthews Biebel, a native Pittsburgher, took his place as assistant director. Clapp remained director, however, and John Henry Hammond the legal counsel. Helen's lawyers launched a counterattack against these two adversaries concerning her legal right to talk to Clapp. On January 30, Moorhead recommended to Hammond that Clapp be "officially advised he has been operating under a misapprehension with regard to the rights of individual trustees." The 1936 minutes stated that "any trustee could make recommendations directly to the Director. . . . in the performance of his or her function." Clapp responded with a letter, but Helen said she was "very much dissatisfied. . . . I gave the whole correspondence to Prof. Sachs to read," she told Moorhead. "[Sachs] regretted the whole business & I told him that sooner or later I would be demanding Clapp's resignation."

In March, Helen enjoyed the company of Sheila Inglis who was now attending college in New York, taking her to Virginia for her spring break, and then prepared for a week's visit at Westmoreland Farm from four-year-old Arabella and three-year-old Martie in April. "Miss Frick . . . is making all sorts of preparations for their arrival," Howland wrote Larsen. The arrangements included placing carefully wrapped children's books on their pillows, arranging flowers from the garden on the dressing table, putting bottles of lavender bath salts beside the bathtub, and purchasing extra boxes of sugar lumps to feed the horse, Roman

Helen's grandniece Arabella Symington, later Dane, at Westmoreland Farm with the horse called Roman Nose, photographed by Helen. Courtesy the Frick Collection/Frick Art Reference Library Archives.

The author, Martha Symington, later Sanger (left), and her sister, Arabella Symington, later Dane, with their toy nursing kits, photographed by Helen at Westmoreland Farm. Author's collection.

Nose, and the cows, Buttercup and Honeybun. When the little girls arrived, Helen strolled down the pebbled driveway with them to the barn and they watched the farmer, Flemming, churn butter, fed sugar to the animals, smelled the spring blossoms, listened to the waterfall as they picked daffodils, and planted seeds in the flower and vegetable garden. When the sun was strong enough, Helen and the girls lunched on the terrace beneath a pair of tall pines. There, the grandnieces fed a pair of nesting mockingbirds, who flew down, unafraid, to collect tidbits. Helen's custom with her houseguests, whether a child or an adult, was to give them a parting gift, sometimes flowers, sometimes some fresh butter, but more often, homemade cookies or bread. Children generally received a toy. This time the Symington grandnieces went home with matching nurses' kits.

Clapp, during this period, was considering the acquisition of a number of paintings offered by the Duveen and Wildenstein galleries. Helen told Frederick Osborn, "I am familiar with some of the paintings you have seen and I will be glad to look at the others at the dealers' galleries and to discuss their merits with art critics of my acquaintance," but she warned, "I will have nothing to do with Mr. Clapp, as you can readily understand." On March 22, Helen rejected all but one of Clapp's choices and sent her carefully documented reasons to Osborn. She had asked Paul Sachs for his opinion, as she always did when contemplating a purchase, and when Clapp learned that she had once again gone behind his back, he became enraged. To Sachs he wrote, "Your opinion I should naturally value highly, but I don't take with much grace, after fifteen years, the lack of confidence in certain quarters, that running behind my back implies."

After two years of wrangling over what was now the open issue of Rockefeller's intended bequest, the request for a declaratory judgment still had not been submitted to the courts. To force the issue, on April 23, 1947, Rockefeller resigned as a trustee and made a specific offer to the Frick Collection, in writing, of six paintings and two portrait busts he wanted to donate to the collection through his will—all sanctioned by Clapp, Osborn, Morgan, and Havemeyer. At the same time, to avoid the appearance of a conflict of interest and to clear the way for monetary gifts to be given the collection, he returned the $50,000 honorarium given him under Frick's will for serving as an original trustee. This action, Rockefeller said, would give a "tangible basis for a consideration of the questions submitted" and would give the court "something to shoot at." The bequest would "add to the interest of the Museum and further the testator's purposes." His personal attorney, Thomas Debevoise, added, "to take the narrow view that the testator intended to bar gifts of great works of art would deal a severe blow to the Collection. Those offered by Mr. Rockefeller are practically priceless. If the gift is rejected they will be lost to the Collection and, for all we know, to the people of New York."

The following day John Hammond, worried that Rockefeller was stepping down, wrote Vanderbilt Webb, "The success of the Collection is so largely due to the devotion and vision which he [Rockefeller] has shown as a trustee." And Osborn, anxious to win Helen over to Rockefeller's side, proposed that she come with him and Junius Morgan to have another look at the Rockefeller paintings. On April 29, Helen replied curtly, "My understanding is that [the] function of [the] Acquisitions Committee is to pass on proposed purchases. The pictures to which you refer do not come within that category. Therefore I do not care to see them." Helen was, in fact, familiar with the works, and sent Rockefeller detailed critiques of each. Well-acquainted with Piero della Francesca's *The Crucifixion*, the painting she had once considered for the Frick Collection, Helen said it was then "still a great work of art," but Rockefeller himself had turned it down for the Frick Collection. She reminded him,

"Before Duveen sold it to your father, it was completely repainted." Now it was so fully, and so badly, restored, little evidence of Piero's hand remained—famed art historian Kenneth Clark had long since dubbed it a workshop piece, not an original.

Yet Rockefeller invited Clapp to study his Chinese porcelain collection and to make a list of what he should sell and what Clapp "would feel like recommending for acquisition by the Frick Collection." Clapp was "deeply impressed" by the porcelains and said, "I feel sure that there does not exist anywhere in private hands a collection of Ming and Ching porcelains . . . [that] can be compared with yours." Since Clapp wanted them all, Rockefeller began devising a second bequest. Still corresponding with Dwight, though both had retired from their duties at the Frick, Rockefeller wrote, "The male members of the acquisitions committee and the director . . . have expressed their approval of them and their desire to accept them."

On May 6, two days before the board meeting, Childs asked his sister if, since she was out of step with the board, and in light of Rockefeller's April 23 resignation letter, "she [was] going to resign" as well. Helen's icy reply was "No." With Clapp continuing to snub her, she chose not to attend the meeting. Instead she sent a letter to the trustees cautioning them against taking any action on Rockefeller's recent letter and bequest. "Were the trustees to do so," the letter read, "it seems to me that they would be acting in defiance of their own prior resolutions by attempting to exercise a power, the existence of which is still to be decided by the Courts. . . . The board should not undertake to prejudge its power in this regard, and that before it gives Mr. Rockefeller any assurances, conditional or otherwise, as to the acceptance of any of his propositions, it should first proceed to have its power determined by the Courts."

Above: Conservation study photograph of *The Crucifixion* by Piero della Francesca showing additions made by Sir Joseph Duveen. Courtesy Research Library, The Getty Research Institute, Los Angeles.

Below: Conservation study photograph of *The Crucifixion* after restoration by William Suhr. Courtesy Research Library, The Getty Research Institute, Los Angeles.

The trustees voted to secure a judgment from the Supreme Court of the State of New York. As Rockefeller reported to Dwight, "the application to the court is going forward slowly but I am told as much as a year may pass before it is finally disposed of. This is regrettable but unavoidable."

Helen was jubilant. "I want to say to you how delighted I am that the first step has been in our favor & that the trustees & the director have had to back down from their high horses!" she wrote Moorhead. "The big thing is that [Clapp] had to climb down off his high perch & the trustees as well." She continued, "They still insist that the trustees are to be treated alike in that no one person can have more to say about the collection than another." Yet, "if the three men on the Executive Committee make all the decisions the other six are merely figure-heads & JDR always *does* run it!" Then she complained, "Another point—I am the only trustee who has never been given a chance to serve on the Ex[ecutive] Committee & I probably will always be discriminated against by the men."

On May 31, 1947, Helen took precautionary measures and established the Helen Clay Frick Foundation. She placed all her trust funds and paintings in it, including a $33 million trust for the Frick Art Reference Library. The foundation would continue to pay the library's operating expenses during her lifetime, per her original agreement with the Frick Collection, but upon her death, neither the library nor the Frick Collection would be given an endowment nor would they be named as beneficiaries under her will. If either entity needed funding, it would have to submit a grant proposal to "her" trustees. Then, she hoped, the Frick Collection trustees would realize the significance of her creation and the extent of her prior generosity. If they were forced to close the library for lack of funds, so be it. The shame of its death would rest on their shoulders, not hers.

In this frame of mind Helen began to work on her court testimony, premised on the argument that her father never intended for gifts to be donated to the collection, unless by family members, and that as his daughter, she had special knowledge of this fact. To evidence the all-Frick, homelike atmosphere of the collection, the harmony of every room, and what she cherished as the handiwork of a great connoisseur, Helen gathered together a series of photographs taken of the collection in 1927, still appearing just as it had on the day of her father's death, and showing a framed picture of Frick in each room. She assembled her father's letters with his comments about the art he purchased from 1885 to 1918; located a copy of an early will dated February 27, 1913, and his last will dated May 17, 1915; and she asked scholar Richard Offner, whom she had consulted regarding Rockefeller's intended gifts, to substantiate his "opinion as to the artistic quality" of those works. William Moorhead then drew up a list of "closed" collections such as the Freer Gallery of Art in Washington, D.C., the Isabella Stewart Gardner Museum in Boston, the Jacquemart-André Museum in Paris, and the Wallace Collection in London. No paintings in these collections bore the additional recording of a donor's name, nor had they provided anyone with a tax deduction.

Preoccupied with the case, Helen was forced to withdraw a manuscript that she had been working on for a book on her favorite sculptor, Jean-Antoine Houdon. The Harvard University Press had accepted it, but had asked her to "go over all the letters [she] had translated and, really, the entire book." As Helen later recalled, "At that time my eyes were very tired and I was trying to save the Frick Collection from accepting the John D. Rockefeller gifts and I therefore took back the manuscript," something Helen said she regretted "many times because perhaps no one now will want to publish it." In the fall of 1947, however, she did publish an article on Houdon's wife in the *Art Bulletin.* The article included many previously unpublished letters from the Houdon archives, acquired by Helen from his descendents.

When the court finally ruled, to Helen's utter disbelief, the declaratory judgment went against her. The Frick Collection trustees could accept gifts of money or art from the public. Nothing in Frick's will proved otherwise. A rejoicing Rockefeller wrote Clapp, "While [the court] decision is most gratifying I assume Miss Frick will appeal it, and that it may be some time before the highest court rules on the question. In any event the Collection is that much nearer its goal." He also extended this olive branch to Helen: "You will agree, I am sure, that your father would not have asked me . . . to serve as a trustee if he had not felt that I would use my best judgment at all times in seeking to carry out what I believed to be his wishes in founding the Collection. . . . I shall always regard it as a privilege to have been able to be of service to your father in carrying out the high purposes which led him to establish The Frick Collection."

Helen delivered a scathing response.

> Whether your letter of July 17th was dictated out of a sense of contrition for the unfriendly and dictatorial attitude towards me which I am convinced was your conception of the method of exercising what you term your "best judgment" as a trustee of my father's collection or whether your letter was written for some other reason, I have no certain way of knowing. I should prefer to disregard your letter by not answering it. But that, I fear, would be misconstrued, particularly as it might seem to denote that I agreed with your estimate of your acts as trustee. . . .
>
> The high purposes of my father in establishing the Frick Collection are surely as familiar and sacred to me as to anyone. My father relied on my knowledge of his purposes and intentions and he had confidence in my loyalty and devotion to the purposes and intentions he so earnestly had in mind. They did not include the attempted amendment or thwarting of his plans for the continued maintenance of his collection. If he were alive, I believe that he would be shocked and indignant to realize what has happened; and I, as his daughter, can neither forgive nor condone.

Rockefeller shared this letter with his lawyer, Thomas Debevoise, who commented, "'Obsession' is a polite and charitable word to describe Miss Frick's feeling about the Museum. I never heard of a more disagreeable response to a gracious gesture. No court I am sure will ever be tempted to believe that the Trustees Mr. Frick chose were men he thought would follow the dictates of his daughter." Vanderbilt Webb echoed, "Her letter was the last thing needed to convince me that the lady can not really be regarded as normal."

Helen, in need of a rest, traveled to Europe in the fall of 1947. There, people noticed that she seemed quieter and less intense. When in London she visited with her British girls and mended her breach with Sir Robert Witt, sympathetic in finding him badly crippled by his arthritis. He and his wife Mary had spent many harrowing nights during the London bombings fighting fires. Witt and Helen reminisced about the time "many years ago now we sat under an apple tree . . . and made plans together and dreamed dreams, which have come true. . . . and how glad I am . . . to rejoice with you at all you have achieved."

Upon her return, Helen took up the fight against the trustees with renewed vigor. On January 30, 1948, the art world was stunned by the headline of an article in the *New York Times:*

> Rockefeller Gift of Art Is Refused [by Helen Frick]
> Trustees of Frick Collection File Suit
> Against Daughter of Steel Maker Over Ban

From this point on, the case took on electric momentum as museums across the country debated whether or not a connoisseur's one-person collection or an open collection better served the public. Friends of Clapp, particularly those at the Museum of Modern Art, cheered him and the trustees, while scholars and museum directors from around the world supported Helen. "Miss Frick seems to be taking this trial business in a very gay mood," Eleanor Howland told Miss Manning, "and the newspaper articles didn't bother her a whit. She is so anxious to get it over with." Clapp was equally anxious, and in mid-March wrote Rockefeller, "Acquisition of pictures has become even more involved and long-drawn out than in the past" and, referring to Helen, "for the same reason. We have bought nothing. The matter of gifts has turned into an inquiry into our records. . . . Why I cannot understand."

On April 4, Abby Rockefeller, who initiated the idea of a gift to the Frick Collection when she reported her conversation with Stephen Clark on that subject, died unexpectedly of a heart attack. News reports claimed that John D. Rockefeller Jr. dissolved into acute mourning. Now, more than ever, he intensified his efforts regarding a bequest to the Frick Collection.

The trial in the New York State Supreme Court was set for April 30, and the Frick Collection, given the media attention now beginning, began a public relations initiative to downplay the strain and deflect criticism. The trustees described the suit to the press as "friendly action," but tried to prevent Helen's testimony. The first and only day in court, Helen arrived holding a large, black, silk scarf across her face to thwart the waiting bank of photographers. Clapp testified on behalf of the trustees. He valued Rockefeller's artworks at $1.7 million and said that since Frick's death the collection had spent $2.9 million on thirty-three additions. He testified that there was no language in the will to prevent gifts from the public, and that by omitting such language Frick obviously intended gifts to be made. According to the *Pittsburgh Post-Gazette,* the trustees felt "the art collection [was] too broad in nature to be confined to one individual's collection." Clapp was forced to admit, however, that to date this was a family enterprise; all acquisitions had been purchased through Frick's endowment (now exceeding $22 million, an increase of $7 million since Frick's death in 1919 and growing at an annual rate of $500,000) or had been gifted by members of the Frick family.

Then, a "slight, graying" sixty-year-old Helen Frick took the stand. Dressed in a "conservative brown suit and a small hat with a half veil," she testified under questioning by her lawyer John H. Harlan about the personal nature of the collection, the family effort that had created it, and her father's intention to have it remain his alone. It was "his monument," she said, noting that Frick referred to it as "my collection" or "our collection," and to the paintings as "my paintings." She stated, "that acceptance of outside gifts would have the effect of diluting the family character of the collection." To further support her claim that the collection should not be aided in any way by the public, Helen said her father always disagreed with how Andrew Carnegie built libraries in his name but left the book-buying to others.

Justice Benjamin Schreiber offered no ruling at the conclusion of the testimony. Helen, "relieved to have this ordeal over with," left the courthouse and rushed into a waiting car. "Bedford as fast as possible and bed!" According to Howland, "Miss Frick seemed pleased with the outcome of the court case on Friday, but she won't know the final decision for another month. . . . She felt things went as they should."

The *New York Times* stunned Helen on July 13 by announcing her defeat: "Court Opens Way to Frick Art Gifts—Daughter Loses Fight." Schreiber ruled that the language of Frick's will, the language of Frick's prior wills, and the evidence submitted "affords no ground for imputing to the testator the restrictive intention which the defendant [Miss Frick] professes to find there." Clapp told Rockefeller he was overjoyed that "this morning's paper carried the big news for which we have waited impatiently. Right-thinking has prevailed. The suit is won."

Helen's diary confessed, "In a rage for the next two days over the unfairness [of] this world! Terrible congestion at back of my neck & rheumatic pains in all my joints." By July 15 she was no better. "So depressing. There is nothing I can think of but this!!" Helen's options were many. She could approach the Court of Appeals, and if she failed there she could go before the Appellate Division; she could also try to find grounds for reargument of the case. The U.S. Supreme Court was a last recourse—one Helen could very well petition should all appeals fail.

As the year drew to a close, although the appeal was much on Helen's mind, she did not let it take her attention from her philanthropic projects. During 1948 she had spent more money than ever on the Iron Rail, almost $55,000. She had severed her formal ties with the True Blues in favor of orphans, but many girls were still loyal to her and continued their tradition of contributing to the Floating Hospital on her birthday. To end the year Helen celebrated the Christmas season with a tea party and a vesper service at the Iron Rail for the faithful True Blue alumnae and their families.

The new year, 1949, marked the one hundredth anniversary of Henry Clay Frick's birth. In late 1946 the collection had acquired Georges de La Tour's depiction of St. Anne, a near look-alike to Melle, educating the Virgin, and now, in January of this anniversary year, it added Jacob van Ruisdael's *Landscape with a Footbridge,* depicting a scene reminiscent of the West Overton countryside of her father's birth. Among the works Helen rejected as not worthy of the collection were the Knoedler Gallery's Giorgione panels, *Abundance,* two Piero panels, *St. Augustine* and *St. Monica,* and Titian's *The Death of Actaeon,* now at the National Gallery, London.

On January 24, Helen learned that the Court of Appeals had unanimously and without opinion affirmed the lower court ruling granting the Frick Collection trustees the right to accept Rockefeller's bequest and other gifts from the public. Labeling the ruling "rank injustice," she subsequently came down with a very bad cold and Eleanor Howland commented, "She is fighting mad about it, and says she will carry it to the higher courts. I know how she feels, but I do wish she would save her energy, as it all looks so sort of hopeless. And then it is so expensive paying out so much money to lawyers."

Titian, Tiziano Vecellio (1477/90–1576), *The Death of Actaeon.* Oil on canvas, 178.4 x 198.1 cm. Helen rejected this painting for the Frick Collection in favor of Cimabue's *Flagellation of Christ.* Courtesy the National Gallery, London, purchased with a special grant and contributions from the National Art Collections Fund, the Pilgrim Trust and through public appeal.

Helen absolutely refused to admit defeat. She drafted a letter to the court on February 8, addressed it to "Your Honors," and sent it to Moorhead for his review. Her letter expressed indignation over the ruling and referred to Rockefeller as a brood parasite, a cowbird "called 'Cuckoo' in Europe, who lays eggs in tiny nests belonging to other birds, eventually driving them out." In addition, her letter read, the Frick Collection did not need help from outsiders. It was financially sound. The $15 million endowment established by her father in 1919 had increased by a net gain of 50 percent after operating expenses and the purchase of paintings. Whether or not the letter was sent remains unknown.

As winter gave way to spring, Helen attended to other matters, including an important change for the Historical House at her father's birthplace. Originally established as a branch of the Historical Society of Western Pennsylvania, it now was more like a foundling. The society was no longer interested in it and Helen, despairing for its survival, terminated her lease with the society, set up her own nonprofit corporation, and dedicated the site as the Henry Clay Frick Birthplace. In April she expanded the Iron Rail complex by purchasing a wooded forty-two-acre property on nearby Chebacco Lake with majestic pine trees, rocks, and two thousand feet of waterfront. Located four miles from the Iron Rail, Crow's Point, as the spot was called, provided a work program for foreign college girls, who cleaned up the camp buildings and gave the True Blue girls and Iron Rail children a place to row, swim, learn about wildflowers, and study the stars. Helen also entertained the two eldest Symington grandnieces, Helen Clay and Arabella, at Westmoreland Farm.

On May 26, Helen wrote: "Terrific blow in afternoon when I heard the Court of Appeals won't hear case! Miscarriage of justice is *dreadful!*" But, she added, "I will fight on!" Ten days later, on June 4, she sent Moorhead a draft of the letter she proposed to send to the *Herald Tribune*, but first asked his secretary to forewarn him that any "similarity . . . to the matter uppermost in her mind is purely coincidental. . . . Libel, [Miss Frick] knows."

> As a bird lover, I have been greatly troubled this spring by an infestation of cowbirds. It is a well-known fact that these noisy and unmusical birds have very lazy habits. Unlike our welcome and industrious songbirds, these ungainly creatures do not build nests of their own but indulge in the questionable habit of laying eggs in the nests of other birds. Most often, they select the exquisite little nests of the warblers and vireos and the cowbirds are the first to hatch out in the spring and the rightful owners are dispossessed.
>
> Unfortunately the law protects these marauders. Is there any way of overcoming this injustice and give protection to the nests of those who through their industry have built their own?

She wrote Judge John T. Loughran on June 22 to express, as she said, "the utter unhappiness I have felt since learning that your Court refused to hear my appeal in the Case of The Frick Collection." She explained, "For the past thirty years, my chief objective in life has been to carry out my father's wishes and to be worthy of the trust he reposed in me, and there is no need of my saying that we were as close to each other as it is possible for a father and daughter to be. . . . As things now stand, I feel that a great American citizen—my father—has been grievously wronged. . . . [and] my own personal confidence in the justice of our American courts has received a terrific blow and no longer can I rely on the protection that I always felt before, [that] was given to those who strive to do right." To William Moorhead she confessed, "Not another soul knows about this. Perhaps I may never receive an answer but at least I have gotten this much off my chest!" Then, in June, the collection's counsel, John Hammond, passed away. On July 1, Helen sent a chilly note to Childs. "Now that Hammond is dead and a new counsel for the Collection must be appointed, I hope the man who is chosen will be one whose aim will be to serve the interests of the Collection and not those of any particular individual."

Helen may have lost the larger war in court, but throughout the 1949 centennial year she was nevertheless winning a series of smaller skirmishes. She continued to argue against the two Cézannes and the Gauguin, bought over her objections. Childs wanted them to remain at least until the Rockefeller case was settled, but in May 1949 the "discordant notes" were to leave the collection forever. According to a confidential May 26 memorandum of a phone conversation between the assistant director of the Minneapolis Museum of Art, Harold D. M. Grier, and the assistant director of the Frick Collection, Franklin M. Biebel, the Frick trustees wanted to dispose of the paintings. Although Biebel claimed, "The decision was a matter of opinion on the part of the Trustees and cannot as yet be considered as a statement of [Frick Collection] policy," and further stated, "the decision to part with these pictures is purely a matter of personal opinions and ideas of the trustees," the truth was slightly more complicated.

The Frick Collection's decision to remove the more modern paintings reflected the contemporary political climate. The late 1940s marked the beginning of the McCarthy era, the period of ruthless attempts to root out suspected Communists from the government and military, as well as from the worlds of art, letters, and entertainment. In October 1946, the State Department exhibition "Advancing American Art" opened at the Metropolitan Museum of Art. The 117 Abstract and Expressionist paintings, all specially purchased by the State Department for the exhibition, included examples of antiwar themes and the Social Realists. There was an unprecedented public outcry in response. Not only had public money been used to buy the paintings, but many of the works were by artists whose names appeared on the attorney general's list of Communists and Communist sympathizers. So heated were the Congressional debates, according to Ross C. Anderson, director of the Montgomery Museum of Fine Arts, whose museum eventually bought many of the paintings, the State Department was accused of being "a haven for Communist sympathizers who were believed to have entered the information services during World War II as an alternative to the armed forces." After the exhibition at the Met, the paintings, divided into two groups, were sent on a five-year diplomatic tour of South America and Europe, with the State Department's hope that the exhibition would further international diplomacy. But on April 4, 1947, the *Journal-American* headline read "[Secretary of State George C.] Marshall Halts World Tour of Red-Linked U.S. Art." On June 11, 1947, Marshall recalled the exhibition from Prague and Haiti, sold the 117 paintings as war surplus to publicly supported universities, and announced that no artists with Communist associations would again be exhibited at the government's expense.

Then, on March 25, 1949, Congressman George Anthony Dondero delivered modern art a *coup de grâce.* In an address to Congress, "Communists Maneuver to Control Art in the United States," he attacked the Artists Equity Association, established in April 1947, claiming its board was "controlled and manned overwhelmingly by Communists and fellow travelers" and its membership included the artist Ben Shahn (who worked with the Mexican Communist Diego Rivera on the later destroyed Rockefeller Center mural) and Max Weber, "an intimate of Picasso, the Communist artist in Paris." Quoting Rivera's statement that "the role of the artist is that of the soldier of the revolution," the Congressman warned, "We are dealing with a subtle enemy. Let every loyal citizen be on guard against this insidious menace to our way of life."

Thanks to this overheated backlash against modern art, in May 1949, the Gauguin and Cézanne's *Chestnut Trees at Jas de Bouffan* left the Frick Collection for Minneapolis. The portrait of Cézanne's uncle Dominique as a monk was returned to Wildenstein for the purchase price and is now at the Metropolitan Museum of Art, gifted by Walter and Leonore Annenberg. The departure of these works signaled that the Frick Collection would no longer purchase modern art, European or American. Naturally, the Frick Collection staff did not share Helen's happiness at the exit of the Cézannes and the Gauguin. In his memorandum Harry Grier remarked, "Mr. Biebel stated confidentially that the staff was very unhappy regarding the decision and that they felt that the decision to dispose of those pictures had nothing at all to do with the intrinsic value of the pictures. In other words those pictures are just as good as when they were purchased."

With the Frick Collection in turmoil, Helen pursued her appeal through the Appellate Division, but Rockefeller upped the stakes. He advised Frederick Osborn, Vanderbilt Webb, and Frederick Mortimer Clapp that he now wanted to give the collection his Ucello portrait of Michael Olivieri, together with his entire Ming and Kangxi porcelain collection, five animal rugs, thirteen Polonaise rugs (five in storage because they were too large for his Park Avenue apartment), and two Isfahan rugs from the apartment's entrance hall and drawing room. Such a large bequest might create a space problem, but Rockefeller had already thought about possible solutions. He told Clapp, "When we were speaking of my Chinese porcelains, at lunch the other day and their possible ultimate acquisition by The Frick Collection, the question came up as to whether they might be put in the old James house, purchased by the Collection in 1946," using the Rockefeller Memorial Room plans, "or whether a new room on that site properly connected with the Collection should be constructed." Now he proposed another alternative, using the former Frick family bedrooms on the second floor (the staff offices). They "could easily be arranged for the display of these porcelains."

Childs expressed appreciation to Rockefeller for his "generosity and for the tribute which you have paid to the Founder of the Collection." Yet Rockefeller remained anxious, particularly about the fate of his second bequest. The trustees were not acting, so his lawyer, Thomas Debevoise, suggested he give those items to the Metropolitan Museum of Art if the Frick Collection "cannot accept or decline to accept."

Helen attended the trustees' meeting on October 13 and confided to her diary, "most difficult." She tried to "tame . . . [her] temper," and the following day she felt the full effect. To her diary she complained of being "dead tired. Spent morning in bed." She revived somewhat when on October 31 she "listened to [Norman] Spicer [Chaplin of the Episcopal Diocese of New York] play the organ at 1 East 70" in preparation for the December concert planned for her father's centennial celebration. Still anxious and waiting to hear from the court, she passed the time by working once again on her Houdon manuscript, checking her translations, still hoping to publish it. Despite her sour mood, compounded by a "nasty spill" (on pavement, hurting her knees and making her feel "quite sick" for a number of weeks)—Helen's plans for her father's centennial went forward. In preparation were an exhibition of the Eagle Rock collection, now back from the Dallas Museum of Art, to be held at the University of Pittsburgh; the organ concert at the Frick Collection; and the presentation of the first three volumes of the illustrated Frick Collection folio catalogue at the Frick Collection and at the library. And to ensure that the "bare and institutional" house museum would have the "homelike feeling" once enjoyed by her father, Helen had persuaded Clapp to hang three small Corots and Rousseau's *Village of Becquigny* in the southwest hall, as they had been during Henry Clay Frick's lifetime, and to reinstall the furniture in the library and living hall.

On December 18, Helen wrote in her diary: "The Great Centennial Celebration. This big day! Everything beautiful in readiness! A very deep feeling of happiness over this lovely celebration. Catalogue beautiful!" At the Frick Art Reference Library, twenty people, including Helen's niece Martha and her namesake grandniece, eight-year-old Helen Clay Symington, dined with her and afterward all walked through the connecting door into the Frick Collection's East Gallery for the organ concert. The guests wandered throughout the house accompanied by strains of Henry Clay Frick's favorite music, all selected by Helen.

Then came the unveiling of the first three volumes of the folio catalogue (twelve were anticipated), the first ever to fully document a public collection in the United States. Limited to 175 copies, these initial volumes describe and illustrate all works of art the Frick family and the Frick Collection trustees had collected up to 1931, the year of Adelaide Frick's death. In 1942 Helen had relieved Clapp, who had served as its original editor and director of research, and had delegated supervision to the Fogg Art Museum. She decided to manufacture the catalogue in Pittsburgh, and back in the 1920s had chosen the well-regarded printer and book designer, Porter Garnett. He had purchased the type abroad, a special modification of Jan van Krimper's Lutettia, and intended to hand-set the text on Kelmscott paper, handmade of Italian linen at England's Little Chart Mill. Helen purchased the paper in the late 1920s and had insured it against damage during the Nazi blitz of London. She engaged top scholars to write essays, among them Sir Charles Holmes for the American and British paintings; M. Paul Alfassa, Frank J. Mather Jr., and Agnes Mongan for the French works; Margaret E. Gilman for the Italian paintings; and Paul Sachs for the Oriental porcelains.

Inevitably, Helen's anger over the Rockefeller bequest made its way into the catalogue. In spite of the fact that it would have the most minor of circulations, Helen saw in it both the opportunity to make a compelling legal argument, heightened by the powerful occasion of the centenary, and the opportunity to write the epitaph to a house and a vision whose moment appeared to be passing. If all legal options failed, the catalogue would record the collection as it was and might never be again. On July 5, 1949, she told Sir Osbert Sitwell, who was writing the introduction in place of Clapp, "Your beautiful tributes to my father and to his taste, warm my heart at a very critical time for, as you may have heard, the highest court in the State of New York has even refused to hear my appeal." She stressed the gravity of task before Sitwell: "You are making the world of art understand for all time the place The Frick Collection occupies, and why. In this way, your Introduction must carry more legal weight than the best of legal documents, and you have given me hope for the final successful outcome in spite of my defeats up to the present time." Certainly Sitwell's introduction gave her what she wanted. His last few sentences read:

> That which sets [the Frick Collection] apart from most other collections, is that it remains a home, not a gallery. It is, on the contrary, the cultural nucleus of one family in America at a given time, preserving for us the character of him who made it, and not the dusty lumber room of a royal palace, or the dry-as-dust arrangement in the taste of a museum, where all is safe and sterilized, all finished and done with. No, the Frick mansion still exhales an air, still throbs with energy of the man who created it. Though alterations have been effected in the house since he lived there, the artistic personality of Henry Clay Frick happily still pervades it, and his would prove, indeed, were anyone rash enough to attempt it, a difficult memory and presence to destroy.

In her own essay, "Henry Clay Frick and His Collection," Helen tried once more to set the record straight about the Rockefeller bequest.

> There never was any question regarding the possibility of "gifts from others" being acceptable, and such a thought was never entertained by the founder. . . . Had his purpose been different, he simply would have given his art collection to one of the many public museums already in existence. The value of an endowed collection representing the taste of the founder and located in his private dwelling is uncontestable from an artistic point of view. It is comparable to an exquisite jewel within a setting specially designed to show off its beauty.

On December 19, Henry Clay Frick's actual birthday, Helen held a second unveiling of the catalogue at the Frick Art Reference Library. The noted historian of early America and the Peale family, Charles Coleman Sellers, who had worked on drafts of the catalogue, wrote, "I can think of no finer memorial to a great figure such as your father than this living and growing search for truth and beauty. It is so much more noble and enduring than any physical monument could be."

Frederick Osborn, eager to have Rockefeller's bequests accepted by the Frick Collection, suggested in a memorandum to the trustees on January 10, 1950, that since the purchase of the James house next door had been accomplished, "additions to The Collection could then be housed in the adjoining halls or buildings without conflict with the original Collection. . . . [and that there] would be opportunities for special types of exhibits, and the whole program would assure that the Collection would not become static but would encourage an expanding public interest." Exhibiting further gifts in the James house would in fact prevent "injury . . . to the wholeness of Mr. Frick's Collection." Two days later, in a trustees' meeting, the memorandum was approved over "the dissent of a minority of one." Osborn told Rockefeller, "Miss Frick is pretty upset, but I do not know what she is going to do about it."

Helen quickly warned Osborn: "I wish to state that I am not yet through fighting to carry out my father's Will." She retreated to Westmoreland Farm to wait for the Appellate Division's ruling. Her diary reads, "Trustees meeting—awful as usual. Home. Dressed my old dolls." Several months later, Helen told the trustees, who were hoping to purchase the George Widener house next door, that if they carried through with their plan and created "a museum housing the art collection of others, in buildings to be purchased, altered or built by diverting [money] from the endowment fund income to a purpose not specified or designated by the testator. . . . [and thus] imperil the proper maintenance of the Founder's Collection, and ultimately destroy it as a unique service to the public. . . . the trustees may find that they have failed in a public trust by undermining and destroying the unique artistic property belonging to the public, and of which they are the responsible guardians."

Then on January 16, 1951, Helen received the news that the Appellate Division had affirmed Justice Schreiber's ruling. While she waited to hear if she could reargue the case, as she had promised to do, she resorted to one of her favorite pastimes, spending time with her nieces. Adelaide Frick had recently married Peter Parrott Blanchard Jr. and was now a practicing pediatrician. So Helen took the newlyweds to the North Shore "to see if there is some furniture in the house at Prides Crossing that they can use in the new house they are building over in New Jersey." But all too soon, on February 23, came the discouraging news that Helen's motion for reargument was denied. The way was now entirely clear for all

Rockefeller's numerous items to enter the Frick Collection on his death and to be installed in the Rockefeller Memorial Room. Vanderbilt Webb wrote to Osborn, "We shall have to be extremely careful in taking any action, in view of the language in Mr. Frick's will, so as not to be vulnerable in the event of any further lawsuit which Miss Frick will undoubtedly bring to enjoin any further steps which we may decide to take along the lines indicated in your memorandum."

Helen now fastened on the stratagem of a radio campaign to solicit letters from the public protesting gifts to the Frick Collection—a tactical move against the trustees to be sure, but also a preemptive strike against members of the public who might suddenly want to donate artworks. She proposed to tell the story of a leopard in the Oklahoma Zoo, confined in a deep pit, who in seeking its freedom, leapt over an eighteen-foot wall and was killed. "My listeners," she wrote, "I feel very much like that leopard in my desperation of finding a solution to this dreadful decree of the courts. My father trusted me, and I am here to carry out his wishes which I know far better than anyone else now living."

Before delivering the address, however, she sought the advice of National Gallery director David Finley. He wrote a diplomatic reply on March 8. "This very good piece of ammunition should be held back for now," he counseled. "I am not one of those to tell you that you have lost the fight and must give in gracefully. It is not in your nature, nor would that be consistent with the trust you feel has been placed upon you. . . . You have suffered a terrific set-back in the legal arena. But," he said, "this never was a legal question. . . . It is a moral question." Finley pointed out that Osborn's plan for a separate gallery adjacent to the Frick Collection to house Rockefeller's gifts "recognizes in a left-handed way the justice of your argument that the Collection should be preserved as an entity, and furthermore leads [the trustees] to the absurd and vulnerable position of establishing *another* gallery with the Collection funds. . . . [affording an] opportunity for [more] legal attacks." In the meantime, "I believe you ought quietly to seek every ounce of prestige, influence and respect to which you are entitled." Although Finley recognized "this would be difficult for a woman to do," he nevertheless suggested it was "not impossible" for Helen to "gradually take the leadership of the Board." In his opinion, the collection had lacked "thoughtful and sensible leadership." He took a dim view of the board, whose members he described as "not primarily interested in the arts, nor in the Collection," and he said, "the Director ought to be attacked." But he cautioned Helen, "Let it be a recognized art scholar who speaks in board meetings against a man [Rockefeller] who does not have any standing other than what his money can buy in the art world. . . . And last of all, public opinion must be built up to sustain your point of view about the Collection in opposition to that of Rockefeller. . . . They must be made to see that the Collection would be hurt."

Helen abandoned the idea of a radio address, and although nothing would have pleased her more than assuming control of the board right then and there, she recognized its absolute impossibility. On March 15 of the previous year, she had written to Theodore Rousseau, whose son-in-law, Giovanni Bagarotti, a violinist and former secretary to the mayor of New York City, wanted to play at a forthcoming recital at the Frick Collection. "I feel that your son-in-law's chances are better if I do not have anything to do with [your query]." She explained the details of her protracted fight through the court system, and her defeat, but she said fiercely, "I am going to find other means of fighting and finally win!" When the New York dealer Germain Seligman offered the Frick Collection a work by Honoré Daumier, who died in 1879, twenty years after Helen's 1850 cutoff date, *L'Amateur d'Estampes, Le Malade Imaginaire,* her secretary replied icily, "Miss Frick regrets she does not feel that the paintings of the Modern School would be of interest to the Frick Collection."

Rockefeller suffered a setback when, on May 12, Frederick Osborn advised him that although the trustees accepted his first bequest of paintings and sculpture, as well as the portrait of Michael Olivieri, as far as the porcelains and rugs were concerned "a number of the Trustees feel that the present facilities of The Collection are insufficient . . . and [they] would like more time to consider the matters of policy involved." He thought they should "carry the thing along for the next two or three months," so they might "get a more wholly favorable result." Horace Harding's son, Charles, a recent addition to the board of trustees, reported, "There is to say the least grave doubt in the minds of some of the trustees about the wisdom of expansion." The hesitation of some trustees notwithstanding, Vanderbilt Webb was proceeding on what Helen called a "piecemeal or step-by-step basis" with the Osborn plan, as it was now known. Helen threatened, "I am sure that every responsible trustee will wish to weigh the consequences of your plans and objectives, and I shall await with interest the response giving your position in regard to the questions raised."

Rockefeller's reply amounted to more than an apology: "In my attempt to help the Frick Collection clarify its legal status as regards the acceptance by gift of works of art which the trustees regard as desirable acquisitions, I have only embroiled them in endless controversy, I fear. I am sorry." It was also something of a capitulation. Much to Helen's delight, the director of the Metropolitan Museum, Henry Francis Taylor, informed Rockefeller that the museum was "planning certain additions to their building . . . [with] adequate space" for his porcelains. "That they should go to the Metropolitan has always been my thought and intention," Rockefeller now told Vanderbilt Webb. Rockefeller's original bequest, however, remained in place.

While Helen worried about protecting her father's collection from Rockefeller, she became concerned once again for the physical safety of the paintings. On June 25, 1950, North Korea, with Russia and China assisting, invaded South Korea, and Helen insisted to Webb, "Time should be taken by the forelock" in ensuring that no harm could come to the artworks. At the same time, earaches were troubling Helen to the point of deafness and she was receiving what Howland called "pretty drastic treatment in New York." Possibly for this reason, permission was granted for Helen to submit a plan for the removal of certain valuables to the vault, just as she had done during World War II. Clapp allowed that circumstances "requiring such a program [had] not yet arrived," but having recently turned seventy-one, he was not prepared to continue sparring with Helen. Drawing more battle lines, Helen instituted a new policy for the Frick Art Reference Library that included a ban on hiring employees unless "American, and Americans of American extraction."

Happily for Helen, the Republicans did well in the midterm elections, leaving her, as Eleanor Howland described, "on top of the world." That same November, Knoedler offered the Frick Collection *The Flagellation of Christ* by Cimabue, "a superb example of this master's work." Helen wanted it badly and wrote Charles Harding, "This is really most unusual and very beautiful and would be a very rare addition to the Frick Collection." She still exercised strict control over what was suggested for her father's collection, having turned down a Bartolo di Fredi and Manet's portrait of his mother and his wife, feeling instead that the "Cimabue would be the greatest acquisition." The Frick bought the Cimabue, later referred to as of the Tuscan School, but in 2006 reaffirmed as Cimabue and celebrated in a Frick

Édouard Manet (1832–1883), *Les Hirondelles (Swallows), The Painter's Mother and His Wife in Berck-sur-Mer, Summer* 1873. Oil on canvas, 65 x 81 cm. Helen also rejected this painting for the Frick Collection in favor of Cimabue's *The Flagellation of Christ.* E. G. Buehrle Foundation, Zurich, Switzerland. Courtesy Art Resource. Photo credit: Erich Lessing. /Art Resource, New York.

Collection exhibition where it was paired with the recently discovered Cimabue panels *Virgin and Child Enthroned with Angels,* now in the National Gallery of Art, London. The *New York Times* dubbed the show, "New Reunion for Long-Lost Siblings."

Two other paintings were added to the Frick Collection in 1950: panels from the workshop of Piero della Francesca—*An Augustinian Monk* and *An Augustinian Nun*—compliments to the growing collection of Italian primitives. Then, at last, after eighteen years of service, Frederick Mortimer Clapp tendered his resignation as director of the Frick Collection, effective January 11, 1951. Rockefeller's longtime legal advisor on the board for twelve years, Vanderbilt Webb, also announced his resignation. Neither left happily. Clapp told Rockefeller. "I cannot now truthfully say I am sorry to be taking my hand off the tiller realizing, as I do, that as far as I am concerned the sultry atmosphere can never change or my activity be really liberated. Besides," he said, "it is time for me to withdraw even if I do so with a sense of failure to achieve many things that I saw quite clearly should be done. Among them the problem of acquisitions remains the knottiest and I see no hope of its being effectively solved."

For his part, Rockefeller regretted that the Frick Collection had not accepted his porcelains and rugs. He said to Vanderbilt Webb, "While I feel with Dr. Clapp, and always have felt, that this collection of porcelains, unique in the world, would have been a very valuable addition to The Frick Collection, it seems to me that I have done everything that I wisely could do—and perhaps even gone too far—to make that belief possible of realization." From this debacle, perhaps only Webb had a small victory to celebrate. Regarding the decision to leave the porcelains to the Metropolitan Museum, Webb, who was also a trustee of the Metropolitan, told Rockefeller, "It seems to me that the final conclusion which you

Cimabue, Cenni di Pepi (active ca. 1272–1302), *The Flagellation of Christ*. Acquired by the Frick Collection in 1950. Tempera on poplar panel, 9 ¾ x 7 ⅞ in. © the Frick Collection, New York.

have reached . . . is entirely wise. . . . Now that I am no longer the victim of divided loyalties, I cannot help expressing my delight."

After eighteen years, the relationship between Clapp and Helen, begun with strong friendship and an appreciation of each other, had ended in bitterness and estrangement. They held mutually exclusive visions of the future of the Frick Collection. Maud Clapp, who once sang Helen's praises, now wrote a final letter.

> All you aspire to is done by reason of the money of which you never could have had even the degree of intelligence necessary to earn a penny of it. From that pedistal [*sic*] your one ambition has been to surround yourself by lackeys low enough in mental energy & lack of moral courage to play your game for you. . . . As long as [my husband] carried out *your* wishes, built a library for *you,* initiated perhaps the most perfect Catalogue for your father's collection, outstanding in the spirit of experts, & accepted the Directorship of the collection that took him away from your direct dictation and made him the servant of the Board of Trustees of which your influence by your fathers [*sic*] wishes was only ⅛ of the Board—From that time on nothing but conflict. . . . He has given [eighteen] years of his intelligent and outstanding talents to running and glorifying your father's memory. . . . But that was apparently not what you wanted. Your limited vision would have turned the F.C. into a funeral monument. What cannot expand dies.

On January 11, 1951, Helen attended the Frick Collection trustees' meeting and remarked in her Westmoreland Farm diary, "Trustees meeting—Very Weary!" But she had endured. Rockefeller was gone, as were Clapp and Webb. And no modern art remained in the collection. In the battle of wills marking the first quarter-century or so of the Frick Collection's story, Helen still stood.

8 The Mantle

1951–1964

Is it age or was it always my nature, to take a bad time, block out the good times, until any success became an accident and failure became the only truth?

—Lillian Hellman

In the aftermath of her court defeat, Helen's engagement calendars, written in her own hand, indicate that she increasingly sought the company of those she loved, entertaining at her farm, Eagle Rock, and Clayton. While she gathered friends and family about her, she was fortunate to have a new ally in charge at the Frick Collection: Franklin Matthews Biebel, forty-three, who became the collection's assistant director when Harrison Griswold Dwight resigned in 1946, and assumed the position of director upon the departure of Clapp. Childs was still president of the board, but with fewer Rockefeller loyalists about, he had lost his power base and Helen could at last make her voice heard. Her first request had to do with the escalating level of Cold War insecurities and concern for the collection. Though the trustees did not remove paintings as Helen requested, they did prepare an evacuation plan and ordered the Frick Collection guards to carry revolvers.

With her position more secure, Helen took firmer control of the acquisition committee. On May 21, 1951, she proposed a resolution: "It is the policy of the Frick Collection to consider for acquisition only great works of art of the highest quality of preservation, and then only if they obviously 'belong' in The Frick Collection by harmonizing with the tastes and intentions of the Founder as expressed by his own selection of works of art." All potential acquisitions were first to be shown to the director and to Helen, and then, if they both agreed to proceed with the purchase, the work would be presented to the trustees for their approval. Subsequently she rejected a Titian, a fresco by Francesco de Giorgio, and a $300,000 altarpiece by Sassetta.

Helen then turned her attention to other matters. She continued to monitor the Iron Rail and was particularly interested in broadening the horizons of the children. That March, Ruth Larsen had taken the girls to West Beach, Massachusetts, all sporting straw hats sent

Opposite: Helen Clay Frick, ca. 1950. Courtesy the Frick Collection/Frick Art Reference Library Archives.

by Helen for protection against the sun. There they watched birds migrating north and attended a New England folk festival. Nevertheless, self-motivation and creativity at the Iron Rail began to dwindle when television became the new entertainment. "We have taken quite a strong stand against television as it now is," Larsen wrote Helen, "because all of our children have them at home and they have done the children no good, whatsoever. Their eyes are strained. They are worn out . . . from the late hours, watching it, the programs are not fit for adults, much less children, and all original and creative activity is smothered."

Also troubling to Helen was a book some of the girls were reading, *Partners: The United Nations and Youth.* Partnering through cooperation with a diverse group had always been fostered at the Iron Rail through its various activities, but Helen was vehemently opposed to the UN. Only recently, in another bitter struggle against Rockefeller, she had succeeded in keeping the United Nations out of Westchester County. "My personal opinion of the U.N. is anything but flattering and it seems likely that the war we are fighting in Korea would be over today if MacArthur [commander of the UN forces in Korea] had not been held up last summer at a very crucial moment, waiting for the U.N. to make up its mind!" Her feelings were such that she demanded the Iron Rail staff ban the book. "We have found that [it] is by Eleanor Roosevelt and that is an anathema to me, as you know . . . [as] I have no faith in the U.N. . . . [and] my wishes in this matter should be adhered to."

In the summer of 1951, before Helen traveled to England, she executed a new will directing her foundation trustees to "perpetuate [Clayton] and [its] contents as a landmark of the Victorian era." Upon her arrival in London she bought a red cocker spaniel puppy she named Warey and then scoured public and private collections in Scotland and Ireland for paintings to photograph for the Frick Art Reference Library. The summer's field trip yielded many works of art not previously documented for the library. It also fueled a new initiative. The homes in which she found these paintings intensified her interest in the preservation of her childhood home, Clayton, as an all-Frick house-museum. Pittsburgh was undergoing rapid urban redevelopment—smoke and flood control, a new airport, and a new parkway connecting the city to the Pennsylvania Turnpike. Many of the East End millionaires' houses that Helen had known in childhood were falling to the wrecker's ball. Taking no risk with Clayton, she swung into action. Having just become a life member of the National Trust for Historic Places, she offered the Clayton house and grounds, together with an endowment, to the trust at her death.

Moreover, use of the trust fit nicely into Helen's anti-Communist agenda. Formed by an act of Congress in October 1949, it promoted its cause of preserving America's historical and architectural history by citing the dangers of Communism. That May of 1951 the chairman of the National Trust, David E. Finley, still also director of the National Gallery, was pleased to consider the Clayton property. "[I am] deeply impressed with the importance of preserving Clayton," he wrote, "as a representative house of the [late nineteenth-century] period and one of the country's great industrialists, philanthropists, and the donor of the Frick Collection."

On January 9, 1952, the Frick Collection adopted Helen's proposed acquisition policy, and in March she learned the good news that the National Trust had accepted Clayton. Helen rushed to Fairfax, Virginia, where she visited Woodlawn Plantation, the early-nineteenth-century home of Major Lawrence Lewis and Eleanor (Nelly) Parke Custis—respectively nephew and step-granddaughter of George Washington. The previous year, the National Trust had accepted Woodlawn as their flagship property, and Helen wanted to study its restoration program. Anxious there be no confusion about how Clayton was to be handled once it passed into the trust, she told the Helen Clay Frick Foundation trustees of "a scrapbook in my possession at Bedford containing [seventy-five] photographs of Clayton by Lewis Stephany [from the late 1890s], [to] serve as guide to those whose responsibility it will be to hang the paintings or to place the furniture. Everything should be as nearly [as] possible like it was in the days the family lived there." To the Clayton project's great advantage, when Frick died in 1919, Helen had retained the massive Frick family archive totaling more than a thousand linear feet and dating from the 1800s. This vast collection—the complete social, business, philanthropic, and art collecting history of the Frick family—was preserved, together with nearly all the original furniture, paintings, and decorative objects. The authenticity of her father's home as a late-Victorian house-museum would be nearly unprecedented in the United States.

Helen began to prepare Clayton. She had the walls in the upstairs and downstairs halls re-stenciled, and for the walls of the reception room, where she planned to place the Eagle Rock paintings and the Garland Collection (miniature porcelains her father had purchased from the Morgan estate sale) she ordered a pink, French silk damask, similar to the one her father had used. "As far as possible, the paintings that were removed from Clayton to Prides [Eagle Rock] will be returned. I have indicated on slips glued to the back of canvases which pictures I intend to leave to the Helen Clay Frick Foundation and these will be hung at Clayton. There are some paintings that were never [at Clayton], but these will add to the beauty and interest and value of the Collection, and they need not all be hung at one time."

Curtains were restored throughout the house, and in both the breakfast room and dining room the chairs were reupholstered in hand-tooled leather. Helen also engaged Howard F. Haverstock of the Clark Music Company in Syracuse, New York, to repair the large orchestrion and shipped it to him in fourteen crates. To document her parents' lives she began to compose detailed scrapbooks with photographs, anecdotes, hand-drawn sketches of floor plans of various Frick houses, and other memorabilia. She stacked H. C. Frick Coke Company ledgers in her father's bedroom closet and wrapped little mementos from her father's life in tissue paper—his opera tickets, Martha's bonnets, pencils from the Carnegie Steel Company, her father's letterhead stationery—all tucked away in his bureau drawer. In a memoir of Clayton, written for future use by the National Trust, Helen lamented that she had found it hard "to choose from among my thousand memories of 'Clayton.' . . . Many of them are so personal, and yet they may serve to revive the past in the dear old home that is to be preserved and future generations may better understand the kind of life that was lived within its walls."

With the arrival of summer 1952, Helen traveled abroad again in search of paintings to photograph for her library, this time to France and Switzerland. But Clayton remained foremost on her mind. In August, while Helen was still overseas, Fred L. Rath, the director of the National Trust, noted in a memorandum that she had signed a stopgap codicil to her newly executed will, leaving Clayton to the National Trust—a legal maneuver should anything happen to her before return. She wrote: "I wish to make it clear and definite that 'Clayton' was the residence of Mr. Henry Clay Frick and his family, and as such it can never accept gifts or loans from anyone who is not closely related by blood to the family." She also outlawed any structural alterations to Clayton, and later, when her thoughts further crystallized, she stipulated in a revised will that objects given or loaned by Frick family members of direct descent must be in keeping with the house. If objects for interpretive display were accepted, provisions for their exhibition had to made outside the main house.

While abroad, Helen also followed the 1952 presidential race between the Republicans, Dwight D. Eisenhower and Richard M. Nixon, and their Democratic opponents, Governor Adlai E. Stevenson and Senator John J. Sparkman. The Democrats claimed that an $18,000 fund, raised by Nixon's California supporters, was actually a slush fund for his personal use. On September 23, Nixon gave a radio and television address detailing his finances, later known as his "Checkers Speech." "Pat does not have a mink coat. But she does have a respectable Republican cloth coat," he said. Then he did admit to having accepted one gift, on behalf of his daughters. Flashing a wide grin he referred to their black-and-white cocker spaniel puppy named Checkers, and said he intended to keep it. Republicans immediately raised Nixon to hero status and when he and Eisenhower next met, Eisenhower put his arm around Nixon and said, "You're my boy."

Overnight, Nixon became Helen Frick's man. Her favorite breed of dog just happened to be the spaniel. And she identified with Pat Nixon, who spurned fashionable fur coats for "respectable Republican cloth." Moreover, Nixon's record against Communism was unimpeachable. Helen, fully smitten, responded with financial support. The vice president of the Pittsburgh & West Virginia Railway, R. W. Bramwell, a Nixon supporter, later wrote the candidate:

> When you made [your] television appearance, explaining the Eighteen Thousand Dollar item, Miss Helen Frick, who was sojourning in Zurich, Switzerland, learned of the situation, and cabled her Pittsburgh Office to . . . determine whether or not you needed additional financing for Radio and Television appearances, and if so to send you a check. . . . Her check was accepted for Three Thousand Dollars and placed in the general fund for Radio and Television appearances, this contribution being in addition to the Twenty-One Thousand Dollars for the Eisenhower-Nixon Campaign which she had already contributed.

As the year drew to a close, Helen was secure and at peace. Clayton was safe; Nixon was her hero, and she had outlasted her critics at the Frick Collection. She had also completed the fourth volume of the illustrated folio catalogue, and saw the acceptance of her policy on acquisitions, albeit with minor alterations: "Resolved: That it is the policy of the Frick Collection to consider for acquisition only works of the highest quality and in excellent state of preservation, and then only if they 'belong' to the Frick Collection by harmonizing with existing exhibits." The resolution precluded—forever—the purchase of modern art. Also in 1952, the collection bought a portrait of the nineteenth-century musician-composer-conductor Antonio Bartolomeo Bruni, a work then thought to be by Jacques-Louis David, but later assigned to Madame Césarine-Henriette-Flore Davin-Mirvault—the only work of art by a female artist in the Frick Collection today.

On January 26, 1953, Helen learned something unexpected and satisfying: "It concerns me more personally than anyone else in the entire world! . . . JDR has *withdrawn* his gift from the Frick Collection!" she wrote her William Knox, who had become her attorney after the passing of William Moorhead. She was at a loss to understand his change of heart. "What induced him to do this, I do not know—but I understand he is planning to make substantial gifts to the Metropolitan Museum & this is certainly the place for them." The following year, however, Rockefeller changed his mind again, informing the trustees that he had decided to go forward with his first bequest but to give his family the right of first refusal over the paintings willed to the Frick. His decision meant that only the leftovers, rejections of the Rockefeller family, would join the collection. The trustees were, however,

Hans Memling (ca. 1440–1494), *Virgin and Child with Saints and Donors*. Triptych: Oil on oak, 71 x 70.3 cm. Helen hoped to acquire this triptych for the Frick Collection but lost it to the National Gallery in London. Courtesy the National Gallery, London, acquired under the terms of the Finance Act from the Duke of Devonshire's Collection, 1957.

oblivious to the insult. Childs wrote Rockefeller, "I may only say that I can thoroughly appreciate your desire for these exquisite treasures to become family heirlooms."

Meanwhile, Helen began stripping Eagle Rock of its treasures. In a gift-giving mood, she set aside a number of the lesser paintings, such as Francis Cotes's portrait of Sir Griffith Boynton, as Christmas presents for her nieces and nephew. Then in June, when the Frick Collection was negotiating for a Hans Memling triptych owned by the Duke of Devonshire, *Virgin and Child with Saints and Donors,* also known as the Donne Triptych, she gave the collection a tapestry fire screen from the former music room at Eagle Rock. It was part of a set of French Regency furniture formerly owned by the ninth duke of Devonshire, purchased by her father for the New York house in 1914. Frick had admired the Memling triptych in September 1915 and had inquired if it was for sale. Now the painting might at last be available, unless the British Inland Revenue barred it for export. Helen donated the fire screen both to keep her hopes up for the Memling her father had admired and to reunite the Devonshire set of furniture her father had purchased.

The balance of the Eagle Rock paintings were packed off to Clayton as intended bequests to the National Trust, with the provision that she could retain a life interest. Turning her attention to Clayton, Helen had the hand-painted ceilings in her bedroom and bathroom removed, restored, and reinstalled. She hired Innocenti & Webel, the landscaping firm that in the 1930s had designed the small garden at Eagle Rock, to identify the trees on the Clayton property and to make a tree plan, and asked Fred Rath to study the Frick family cars dating from the turn of the twentieth century, and the carriages dating from 1881 to 1900, for installation in a new brick carriage house planned near the site of the former stables. He was also to determine how best to transport the Westmoreland railroad car to Clayton for exhibition. Helen's office manager, Walter Cooley, who had succeeded Karl Overholt, pronounced that shipment by tractor-trailer would cost $12,000, and since the roads were "not wide enough [for the car] to turn," they would "have to cut it in two."

On June 21, Helen sailed from Quebec on the *Franconia* with Martha Symington and her four children. They landed at Greneock, Scotland, on July 1, and soon settled into Auchinbowie House, owned by Colonel and the Right Honourable Mrs. Alexander Monroe, on the outskirts of Stirling. Helen wanted to find still more paintings to photograph for the Frick Art Reference Library and intended to visit and study the Scottish National Trust properties for ideas about Clayton. As was her habit, she compiled a meticulous album-diary that included descriptions of each place she visited; the history of every abbey, cathedral, castle, or ruin she saw; pictures of all the sites and of the Symingtons; and a record of the paintings she saw in private homes, National Trust houses, and museum collections.

Shortly after Martha's husband Fife joined the family on July 23, they received word that Dixie, Helen's sister-in-law and once best friend, had required emergency surgery for pancreatic cancer. For many years Dixie had suffered from depression and alcoholism, often spending weeks, even months, in a sanatorium. The cancer had been diagnosed in May, and now it was so advanced she did not have long to live. Martha flew home immediately. Helen and Fife remained behind with the children and a governess.

Dixie died on August 5, 1953, the sixty-eighth anniversary of Martha Frick's birth. Fife and his twelve-year-old daughter Helen Clay flew home for the funeral, but Helen, then in London visiting her British girls, did not. Nor did she mention her sister-in-law's death in the copious diary she was keeping. From July 29, when Dixie began to fail, until August 15, well after the funeral, Helen did not even date her diary entries. Although she did not record her sister-in-law's passing, the loss did seem to affect her. On August 15, when she was having tea with Valerie Sayers and her family, she "tumbled down [the] stairs." Sailing home on August 22, she was "having a great deal of trouble with one of her front teeth" and badly cut lip.

Despite these setbacks, Helen was invigorated by her trip and overflowing with ideas for Clayton. But on October 12 her plan began to unravel. Ned Burns, who had drawn the National Trust's master plan for Clayton, died suddenly of hepatitis. Helen had come to adore him and had been looking forward to many years of working together. She wrote Fred Rath that she was "overcome by [the] bad news. . . . His wonderful work at Clayton is a monument to his ability." She set up an education fund for Burns's children, put his son, John, through dentistry school, and gave a $1,000 donation to the National Trust in Burns's memory. Helen then announced that she was endowing Clayton with $1.25 million.

The turning of the year often brought change, and in February 1954, Helen made a major adjustment in her life. Suddenly and without warning, she transferred the entire Iron Rail facility, the land and the buildings, to the Girls Clubs of America. Although she continued to underwrite the program, make provisions for True Blue vacations at Crow's Point on Chebacco Lake, pay for the girls' education, attend their annual reunions in Boston, and visit those confined to nursing homes, she divested herself of management responsibilities. The reason for Helen's decision after forty-five years dedicated to the project remains unknown. She may have wished to concentrate more fully on Clayton. Whatever prompted her change of heart, the recipient organization was ecstatic over its windfall. Jane Bedford Gooch, president of Girls Clubs of America, later described how it happened. Apparently on the evening of February 11, former president Herbert Hoover and Frank E. Mason, among others, attended a small dinner party at the Frick Art Reference Library hosted by Helen. In the course of conversation, according to Gooch, Helen "mentioned that she owned a large piece of property in Massachusetts [three hundred acres in Wenham, Hamilton, and Essex] which she would like to give to some worthy organization." Hoover, then chairman of the board of Boys Clubs of America, suggested she give it to the Girls Clubs as their national camp, to serve as a model for Girls Clubs all over the country. Helen leapt at the idea, and by April had arranged the transfer.

Naturally Ruth Larsen was stunned. She and the rest of the staff were suddenly without jobs, and Larsen would have to vacate Fairhaven, her residence for over a decade, by June. Helen tried to explain the reason for such a precipitous step saying "the thought had never occurred to me even a month ago, so that I too am a bit bewildered by the rapidity with which the transfer has been made." She gave Larsen a pension and on April 10 apologized for terminating her use of Fairhaven, albeit not too sympathetically. "I know this is not easy, but having had the experience in emptying 'Eagle Rock' in two weeks' time, I know I am not asking the impossible."

Clayton now became Helen Frick's priority. The National Trust found a Belgian couple, Emile Denys, and his wife, to act as caretakers. A two-story brick carriage house was already under construction, and five vans were being readied to transport the Frick family's vehicles—antique cars, a dozen or more carriages, two sleighs, and trunks full of harnesses. Helen contacted experts in refinishing and reupholstering and gave eight enlarged snapshots "taken many years ago of different horses and carriages" to Walter Cooley in Helen's Frick Building office "to be framed and used in the new Carriage Museum to be opened in April 1956."

What "shocked [and] distressed" Helen, however, was the "appearance in the Pittsburgh papers of a 'leak' about [her] Clayton plans." Fred Rath assured her that the National Trust was not responsible for the article. But on June 5, a second article appeared, this one in the *Pittsburgh Post-Gazette,* based on an interview with the railway executive and former Allegheny County Republican finance chairman, seventy-one-year-old Charles J. Graham. In 1941, Helen had given him lifetime use of the Westmoreland railroad car so he might better conduct his fundraising and railroad duties. Now, in her estimation, he had repaid her generosity with misstatements and a flagrant and unwarranted invasion of her privacy. Apart from referring to Clayton as Claymont, and saying Helen was a child when the Westmoreland carried "the Frick family . . . to all parts of the country," when in fact Helen was twenty-two years old when the car was delivered in 1910, Graham divulged many intimate details about Helen and her gifts to Nixon and the Republican Party.

On June 5, Helen corrected the finance chairman's factual errors in a *Pittsburgh Sun Telegraph* interview and explained that Clayton was to be "opened to the public as an educational and historical exhibit, of interest to students of history, architecture, decoration, and art, and also as an example of a 'mode of life' as it existed in the Twentieth Century." Two days later she chastised Graham: "Your discussion of me in any way whatsoever, with a newspaper reporter, showed extremely bad taste and is most upsetting to me." Although she had hoped to place the Westmoreland on exhibition at Clayton, she was so insulted by Graham she ordered the Westmoreland car destroyed. "In view of your disclosure of my plans for 'Clayton,' I prefer that at the end of your personal use of the 'Westmoreland,' that the car be completely dismantled and destroyed inside and out, as was first agreed upon. You have done me more harm than you can realize," she wrote Graham. Helen Duprey Bullock of the National Trust tried to calm the situation and on June 9 wrote Walter Cooley, "With all the building activity going on, and the bringing in of paintings and other

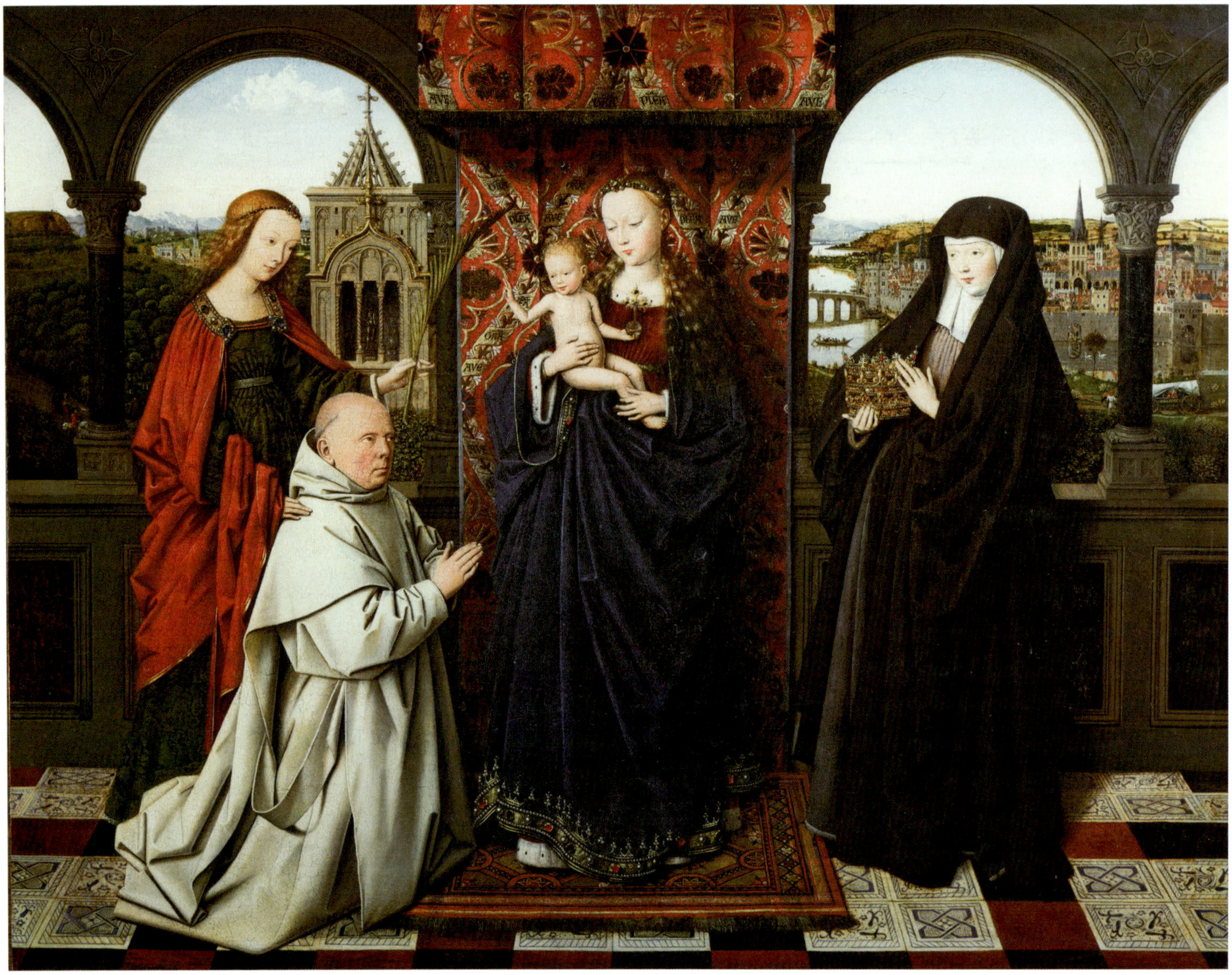

Jan van Eyck (active 1422–1441) and workshop, *Virgin and Child with Saints and Donor*. Acquired by the Frick Collection in 1954. Oil on panel, 18 ⅝ x 24 ⅛ in.
© the Frick Collection, New York.

objects to Clayton, it is inevitable that an alert press would notice something." But Helen was not consoled. She never again spoke to Graham and destroyed the historic car—a significant loss to Clayton—telling her cousin James Stevenson she had done so because the Westmoreland was no longer decorated in her father's taste.

Despite the furor during this time, Helen completed the fifth volume of the illustrated folio catalogue and received thanks from the Frick Collection trustees. Pleased with their response, she gave the collection the guest book for One East Seventieth Street (1917–1931), together with letters, bill books, and vouchers from the same period and considered the possibility of allowing the Frick Collection to publish a smaller version of the oversized folio catalogue. In addition, she discovered that Jan van Eyck's *Virgin and Child with Saints and Donor* was available for purchase. Since the situation with the Memling triptych had not yet been resolved, Helen suggested the trustees first buy the Memling and then negotiate downward from Knoedler's $1 million asking price for the Van Eyck. The situation clarified substantially when the British government decided to exercise its right under the terms of the Finance Act and then finally purchased the Memling in 1957 for the National Gallery. So on June 2, 1954, the Frick Collection purchased the van Eyck for $750,000. Helen had advised the trustees on June 10, 1953, that the work "may not be *all* Van Eyck," and was correct in her analysis. Today the painting is considered drawn by van Eyck, but completed by another hand, possibly Petrus Christus. Nevertheless, the *New York Herald Tribune* hailed it as the "most important ever acquired by the Collection" and "perhaps the most important single painting to be purchased by a New York Museum in years."

The trustees now decided, without consulting Helen, to publish the smaller version of the folio catalogue for their use, although the Frick Collection had no right to do so and played no role, financial or otherwise, in preparing the original work. Helen wrote Childs a curt note. "The other day I was stunned at the meeting when you suggested that the Catalogue Matter should be taken up by the Executive Committee and not before the Board!" She reminded him, "In view of the fact that I have paid $522,000 to date for the big Catalogue, if I do not have a great deal to say about the small Catalogue that is to be taken from the folio catalogue it will certainly be extraordinary." She warned, "I merely bring this to your attention so that in the future you will agree with me that I should be consulted on every detail that has anything to do with the Catalogue." Childs and the trustees capitulated.

The following year, 1955, she had to fend off another attempt to reproduce her work. The National Gallery in Washington, D.C., asked the Frick Collection for a duplicate microfilm of the Frick Art Reference Library photo mounts for use in its library. Fulfilling this request would severely undercut the value of what the Frick Art Reference Library offered researchers and thereby eclipse its reason for being. "It is my desire that the library shall continue to be unique," Helen wrote the trustees. "It is the only institution in the world that has compiled all this information and collected all these photographs. It represents a lifetime of effort on my part and a fortune spent on it." She stated that when the library became part of the Frick Collection on her death, "It is my hope and expectation that you will honor my wishes that any such requests be refused so that the unique character of the Library will always be preserved."

After thirty-four years of making important contributions to the Frick Collection, and after a reasonably peaceful period on the board, Helen still felt keenly disrespected by the trustees. Then, of course, there was the continuing animosity with Childs. The episode that would sever the already frayed relationship between them took place at a family Christmas gathering at Childs's Long Island house in 1954, just sixteen months after Dixie's death. Childs, exasperated and embarrassed by Helen's continued intense anti-German bias, launched a practical joke at Christmas lunch, in front of a group consisting of their first cousin Luella Taylor, Helen's good friend Katharine McCook Knox, her British girl Mavis Sayers Archer, who had become a pediatrician, and her fifteen grandnieces and grandnephews. With Childs's cooperation, two of his sons-in-law, Fife Symington and Townsend Burden, both Republican fundraisers and faithful McCarthyites, ordered calling cards engraved with the name of the art thief and executed war criminal Wilhelm Frick and rented a pair of authentic SS uniforms. When Helen and the group of family and friends gathered for cocktails in the elegant and beautifully appointed pine-paneled North Room, Childs's butler presented Helen with a small silver tray holding the calling card engraved with Wilhelm Frick's name. As a stunned Helen looked at it, the two "Nazis" goose-stepped into the room and grabbed her. They pushed her around the room and forced kisses on her. Helen nearly fainted, but when the men began to laugh heartily she realized the attack was a hoax and recognized the "Nazis" as her nephews-in-law. She recovered her balance as best she could and tried to get through the Christmas lunch. But when Childs stood to give his holiday toast, he proceeded to empty a bottle of champagne over Helen's head. Helen later pasted the photograph her niece Martha Symington took of the "Nazi" attack in her 1954 album and wrote "Prisoner of the Nazis" beneath it, but her good humor over the incident was only superficial. She did not return to her brother's house until 1965, when he was dying.

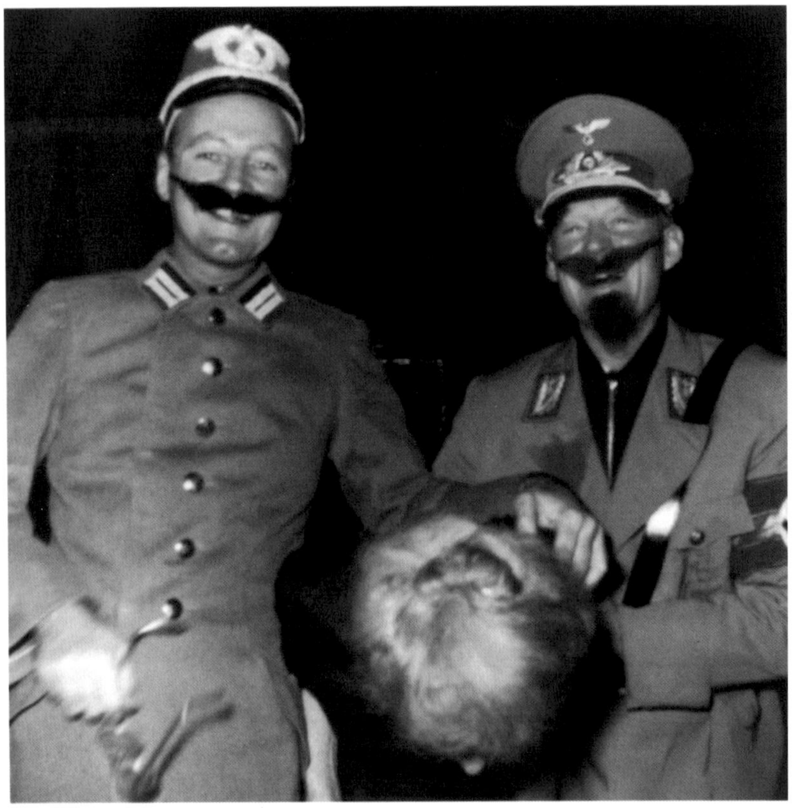

Helen's nephews-in-law Townsend Burden (left) and J. Fife Symington Jr. (right) dressed in SS uniforms, with Helen (center) as a self-described "Prisoner of the Nazis." Courtesy the Frick Collection/Frick Art Reference Library Archives.

On December 19, 1955, the Frick family gathered once more, this time at the Frick Collection, to celebrate the twentieth anniversary of its opening to the public. Although Helen was still upset about the Nazi episode and her relationship with Childs remained tense, she included him in the family luncheon she held on the penthouse floor of the library. Afterward the family took the elevator to the main floor and lined up to enter the Frick Collection through the connecting door into the East Gallery. There, displayed on an easel, was a painting never exhibited in the Frick Collection and usually confined to the vault as a lesser work—Sir Thomas Lawrence's eerie portrait of Miss Louisa Murray, the Martha lookalike Henry Clay Frick had kept in his bedroom. Childs, not to be outdone by Helen's reference to Martha and the seventieth anniversary of her birth, delivered a silent retaliation. Taking his teenage granddaughter, Frances Dixon Burden, whom the family called Dixie, by the arm, he went to the head of the line and led the procession into the East Gallery.

During the party, Helen gathered her grandnieces and grandnephews around the celebrated van Eyck in the Enamel Room, opened a tiny secret door in the paneling, and produced a large magnifying glass. Each child in turn stood on the small wooden steps she had provided and admired the extraordinary details in the painting barely visible to the naked eye. Having also engaged a photographer for the event, she carefully posed the children beside certain paintings to create symbolical links between them and their great-grandfather. In the West Gallery, for instance, she posed four of them in front of Rembrandt's self-portrait, so closely resembling their great-great-great-grandfather, Abraham Overholt. In the dining room she placed little Henry Clay Frick III in her father's seat at the head of the table, facing John Hoppner's portrait of the Bligh sisters, so similar to Adelaide Frick and her sister, Attie. Opposite little Clay was his sister, young Adelaide, seated in the place once occupied by her namesake great-grandmother, Adelaide Frick. Although Helen never permitted herself to be photographed, she now posed with the children beneath Turner's *Fishing Boats Entering Calais Harbor.* The painting recalled the many ocean crossings Helen had made with her father as well as her recent trip to France with her fourteen-year-old grandniece, Helen Clay Symington, and also anticipated the trips she intended to take when each of her other grandnieces or grandnephews reached age fourteen. No doubt hoping all the children would become instruments in perpetuating Henry Clay Frick's legacy, she posed them beneath one of his favorite paintings, Giovanni Bellini's portrait of St. Francis, who prayed, "Oh Lord, make me an instrument of your peace." Even Renoir's *Mother and Children,* recalling the doll Frick gave Martha in 1891 just days before her death, played a role in Helen Frick's choreographed silent drama. Helen arranged Mrs. Henry Clay Frick II, formerly Jane Coates, and her two little strawberry-haired daughters in the same positions as the portrait subjects. A decade later, when one of the girls became ill, Helen duplicated the arrangement for another photograph.

With family on her mind, on January 28, 1956, sixty-seven-year-old Helen revised her estate planning. She made an inventory of Westmoreland Farm, noting each and every item in the house, where it had come from, and to whom it was to be given in the event of

Below, left: Frick family members at a reunion, seated beneath J. M. W. Turner's *Fishing Boats Entering Calais Harbor*. On the floor in front from left to right are Jane, Elise, and Adelaide Frick. Behind them from left to right are Peter Blanchard, Helen Clay Symington, later Chace, Helen Clay Frick, the author, and Arabella Symington, later Dane.

Below, right: In this later rendition, Helen again posed her grandnieces, Elise and Adelaide Frick, then ill (right, holding rose), with their mother in the same positions as the portrait subjects in Pierre-Auguste Renoir's *Mother and Children.*

her death. Later that year, Helen presented the sixth volume of the illustrated folio catalogue to the Frick Collection, and on November 21, she made a further gift, two palace jars of the Yongzheng period, presented to her father by his good friend Horace Harding, whose son, Charles, had become a trustee of the Frick Collection in 1949.

While strengthening her connections with the Frick Collection, in mid-1957, Helen broke with the Fogg Museum. Paul Sachs's assistant Rudolfe Riefstrahl had expressed concern to John Coolidge, now the museum's director, about the Louis XVI furniture Helen had loaned them in 1940. "They are . . . getting to look rather crumbly and will shortly go with nothing unless they are cheered up. Also should Miss Frick or one of her carpetbaggers see them I should hesitate to envision the consequences!" Coolidge then wrote to Helen, "I fear that I have some distressing news . . . when moving the furniture . . . some of the painted and gilded gesso [wa]s flaking off." Torn between placing the pieces in storage to await restoration or leaving them in the gallery for teaching purposes, he asked for Helen's advice. But Helen was livid and not prepared merely to give advice. "I am both shocked and grieved to receive your letter, and to learn the astonishing news that you have taken such poor care of the very valuable and beautiful eighteenth-century tapestry furniture that I lent to the Fogg Museum. To repair will, as you say, involve great cost and the value will never be the same again." Her solution was characteristically draconian: "Because my faith in your directorship has been so severely shaken, I will have to ask for the immediate return of everything belonging to me at the Fogg."

The Fogg was flabbergasted. Since Henry Clay Frick's death in 1919, Helen had been extremely generous with her artworks, both those inherited from her father and those in her personal collection. The Fogg, in turn, had served as her primary mentor in the development of the Frick Art Reference Library, the Frick Collection, and the fine arts department at the University of Pittsburgh. But the deterioration of the objects was, of course, not all that prompted her sudden decision: Riefstrahl was German. "Her letter is an outrageous and typical communication," confessed Sachs to John Coolidge. "When next we meet I'll tell you of some of my own experiences with her over the years, up to the day, at long last, when I could no longer cope with the one time 'poor little rich girl,' turned into a 'thwarted female.' We used to be on 'Helen' basis. Now our relationship is correct but formal." He counseled, "Don't let her get under your skin. You are in good company—a long list. Among many others you will find Tim Clapp and all scholars of German extraction."

Riefstrahl hoped to keep the furniture at the Fogg and told Coolidge on July 12, 1957, that Agnes Mongan, the museum's widely regarded curator, "thinks that Miss Frick should be told that things are liable to get infinitely worse with her furniture when it leaves our atmosphere of controlled humidity . . . via a jouncy, perhaps steamy, perhaps bone-dry truck ride." He continued, "Miss Mongan says that had preventative measures been taken *prior* to the arrival of the furniture in 1940, the present damage probably would not have occurred." Nonetheless a steadfast and determined Helen wanted her artworks and furniture returned. "I am deeply distressed," Coolidge wrote her, "to 'have shocked and grieved you.' Your loans were a noticeable factor in making our work effective. . . . I have told Mr. Riefstrahl to prepare to return all the works of art. . . . We are so sorry to see them go."

Helen's artistic and philanthropic interests were, however, taking her elsewhere. In November 1957 the University of Pittsburgh had revisited its plan to house the fine arts department in a separate building, together with an art museum. Walter Reed Hovey, the department chair, wrote the new chancellor, Edward Harry Litchfield, that an art museum was an important part of university planning and would enable students to enjoy "art as a . . . direct road to knowledge." He said, "creditable museums are needed on every campus. . . . The institutions with no museums at all are as a class the backward colleges." But he also cautioned that a university art museum should not compete with existing museums but rather serve as "a place of study, of research for the student. . . . The objects need not be famous, and great works . . . are costly," but original works could be included, as well as reproductions, photographs, and color prints. Helen had once envisioned an institute of nineteenth-century studies at Clayton under the direction of the fine arts department, but as Hovey explained, "the residence has now been turned over to the National Trust." So, he suggested, perhaps the university could approach Helen for a building.

On November 12, 1957, the head of university planning and development A. C. Van Dusen warned Chancellor Litchfield—previously a political scientist who had helped restore civilian government in the American areas of Germany after the war—of Helen's idiosyncrasies. "Miss Frick apparently has a very strong dislike for (a) Germans (b) Modern Art (c) Democrats (d) Carnegie. This means that she probably would not like to have the suggestion that . . . [a] Modern Art Collection be sought for her museum gallery. She apparently has expressed displeasure at the prospects of the [triannual] International Show [of contemporary art] at the Carnegie Museum." Thanks to Carnegie, and the Pittsburgh International show, Pittsburgh had in fact become a center for the modern art Helen loathed. According to John Walker, director of the National Gallery of Art, with the exception of New York City's Museum of Modern Art, anyone interested in "what was happening in [modern] European painting . . . had to travel to Pittsburgh." But Helen Frick questioned "the worth" of the Pittsburgh International in a letter to the *Post-Gazette*, claiming it was "neither beautiful nor educational." Knowing this, Van Dusen and Litchfield nevertheless decided to approach Helen, albeit cautiously, "try[ing] to avoid any estimates of cost at this time," for a 35,700-square-foot building.

While the university contemplated the situation, still another project had beckoned to Helen. In December 1957, the *New York Herald Tribune* reported that the sixty-nine-year-old heiress had created a wildlife sanctuary abutting her Westmoreland Farm, "wherein wild bird and animal life as well as native flowers, shrubs, plants and trees will be cherished, protected, and preserved." With the turn of the year, on January 1, 1958, the *New York Times* announced that these ninety-four acres, purchased from the Glen Ridge Corporation by the Helen Clay Frick Foundation, were open to the public as the Westmoreland Sanctuary. This was a gift comparable to Frick Park, founded as the debutante gift Helen had requested of her father; both sites expressed her love of nature and her interest in environmental protection. While large tracts of land around her Bedford Village home were being subdivided and developed, Westmoreland Sanctuary became one of several privately funded preserves in the area designed to offset encroachment by new roads and housing developments. The neighboring Arthur W. Butler Memorial Sanctuary, the 161-acre Mianus River Gorge Preserve, the Eugene and Agnes Meyer Nature Preserve, and the Audubon Center are all part of closely connected, first-of-their-kind properties in New York, all pioneered by women. Helen announced that under the terms of her will "substantial additional acreage" would be added from her adjoining four-hundred-acre Bedford Village farm.

Helen, although suffering from a cancerous ulcer on the little toe of her left foot, now prepared for a one-month trip to Italy with her fourteen-year-old grandniece Martie. Helen

Robert Campin (active by 1405, d. 1444) and assistant, *The Annunciation Triptych* (Merode Altarpiece). Oil on wood, central panel 25 ¼ x 24 ⅞ in. Helen hoped to acquire this triptych for the Frick Collection. Instead it was sold to the Metropolitan Museum of Art for its Cloisters Collection. Courtesy the Metropolitan Museum of Art, the Cloisters Collection, 1958 (56.70) Image © the Metropolitan Museum of Art.

was seeking to educate the teenager and to find worthy additions to the Frick Collection. A string of recent failures had left her angry and frustrated. "It looks as though we might never be able to add a superlative painting to those we now have. . . . The trustees were offered the Merode Altarpiece two years ago and we made a very generous offer but were unable to get an answer from the agent." Then, "last summer, when I was in Brussels, I tried every which way to see the owner or track down the painting and it was so disappointing on my return home to find it had been bought by the Metropolitan a whole year before."

On March 28, when Helen was preparing her itinerary, she thanked Bernard Berenson "for [his] kind letter and assurance that Martie and I may call upon you when we are in Florence. . . . There are so many things I would like to discuss with you and I need your advice very much on behalf of the Frick Collection." The only painting Berenson found that was suitable for the Frick Collection was Leonardo da Vinci's portrait of Ginevra dei Benci, owned by Prince Frans Josef of Liechtenstein at Vaduz. In the end, though, the Leonardo did not come up for sale, at least not until 1967 when John Walker purchased it for the National Gallery. Berenson recommended something else for Helen, however, perhaps for the University of Pittsburgh. The Russian copyist Nicholas Lochoff, whose work Helen had previously purchased, had died in 1948. At the time, Edward Forbes had written to Berenson, "I wonder what is to become of the pictures which he left. They really ought to be kept together in one museum." A decade later, twenty-three Lochoff fresco reconstructions were available for purchase through the artist's son, Boris, and the perfect client had surfaced in Helen Frick. As Forbes had noted to Berenson, the most likely buyer would be a private individual, because "museums would rather spend their money on originals than even these fine facsimiles." Helen asked Berenson "if the Lochoff collection was still available and what he thought of the possibility of acquiring it for Pittsburgh." As she later recalled, "He was very encouraging."

Helen's itinerary allowed her to study the originals Lochoff had copied, and soon she decided she must purchase the facsimiles. They were very good, and in addition to the photo mounts already in the library, they provided yet another record of the fast-deteriorating original works. And, she reasoned, the frescoes probably would not cost her very much since they had been in Lochoff's estate for a decade. On July 3, during a private talk with Berenson about the Lochoffs, Helen agreed to make the purchase. Not unlike the moment years before, when she entered Sir Robert Witt's library "and kaleidoscopic visions took over" giving her the idea to establish the Frick Art Reference Library, Helen was seized by yet another vision: "Should I erect a building on the Clayton property. . . . and should it be a copy of a famous building in Italy, such as the Arena Chapel in Padua?"—the tiny, fourteenth-century holy place erected by Enrico Scrovegni, who hoped the chapel, filled with Giotto's fresco scenes from the life of the Virgin Mary and Christ, would save the soul of his money-lending father, whom Dante condemned to hell in his *Divine Comedy*. If she did, it could be dedicated to *her* father, and its walls decorated with the Lochoff frescoes.

While Helen contemplated this newest monument to her father's memory, she and her grandniece traveled to Switzerland, visited Melle's family, and then went on to London. They saw the British girls, now married with families of their own, and took in the Wilton Diptych at the National Gallery. They went on to Paris but canceled their visit to the Louvre because of the "bus-loads after bus-loads of Germans waiting to get in." They sailed home on the *Mauretania* on July 18, and on July 30, Helen's attorney and her bankers consummated the purchase of the Lochoff frescoes. The Helen Clay Frick Foundation paid $40,000 for the twenty-three frescoes, $20,000 less than the asking price two years before.

Helen's intention was to give the Lochoffs to Clayton, not to the University of Pittsburgh. The university had not yet decided how to house the fine arts department—in a wing off a new library building or in an independent structure of its own—and Chancellor Litchfield, who had been warned by Walter Hovey, the department chair, was more than ever concerned about being involved with Helen. On November 12, Hovey wrote, "As you know Miss Frick has definite likes and dislikes. She is violently opposed to modern trends in art and even said that if the new University Library building . . . were modern in design she would not be interested in adding a wing." Litchfield wrote the vice-chancellor of academic disciplines, Charles H. Peake, on December 11 to expand on his concerns.

> Our problem is to keep [the architect, Theodore] Bowman, Frick, Hovey, and [trustee and treasurer Adolph W.] Schmidt all more or less satisfied and they by no means agree with one another. Bowman [the former chancellor's nephew], thinks Hovey is incompetent and I gather the feeling is mutual. Furthermore, Bowman is insistent that this building be of a particular design which Miss Frick can't afford and he wants it in a location which the Mellons won't agree to and which the Board has promised that it won't be. . . . I would much rather see her [Helen] put her money into endowment for the department than into [an] additional building.

Helen "gradually" abandoned her idea of re-creating the Arena Chapel at Clayton and instead concluded the Lochoff frescoes "should be given to the Henry Clay Frick Fine Arts Dept. in the University of Pittsburgh." As she recalled in a later interview, she came to the realization that "an appropriate building would have to be erected for them [there], and, that in this way I would honor my father's memory in Pittsburgh and contribute pleasure to . . . my hometown, and . . . increase the opportunity for the students of the Fine Arts Dept. of the University." Helen was now persuaded that a fine arts building in the Italian Renais-

Above, left: Fra Angelico (1387–1455), *Crucifix with Saint Dominic*. Fresco. Cloister of San Marco, Florence. Courtesy Art Resource. Photo credit: Scala/Art Resource, New York.

Above, right: Nicholas Lochoff (d. 1948), After Fra Angelico's fresco, *Crucifix with Saint Dominic*, in the Cloister of San Marco, Florence. Courtesy University of Pittsburgh. Photo credit: Richard A. Stoner.

sance style, designed around a Nicholas Lochoff cloister, "seemed . . . the only suitable place for the frescoes."

Peake felt that the separate building would "contribute significantly to the intellectual and aesthetic atmosphere of the campus, and would assist materially the Department of Fine Arts to play its important role in the educational program of the University." But on March 31, 1959, he complained to Litchfield, "1.2 million is *all* we can get from Miss Frick," and warned, "You have already spent the 1.2 M. Hence we will have to scale [the] size [of the proposed library building] down." He was, nevertheless, upbeat about the prospect of having a building with a museum. "While photographs are a proper means for the study of most of the problems which face the student there is no substitute for the close association with original works of art. Since the greatest examples are unattainable, a collection of copies such as the Lochoff Collection when effectively displayed would be of great significance. . . . There is a reason to believe that important objects might be acquired were a suitable setting available and such a development would greatly enhance the importance of the University to the community."

The frescoes arrived in Pittsburgh early that summer. On October 6, 1959, in another gesture to her father's memory, Helen donated to the university the Aeolian pipe organ custom made for Eagle Rock in 1906. She told the university, "In the old days I felt [the organ] had the loveliest tone of any . . . I had ever heard," and agreed to "bear the entire cost of taking it down, shipping it, and installing it in condition for use."

An exhibition of the Lochoffs in the Commons Room of the Cathedral of Learning opened on November 4. Twelve frescoes were selected for display, and plans for the new fine arts building were announced: a fifty-thousand-square-foot Renaissance-style building, with a cloister for the frescoes; office, classroom, and studio space; exhibition rooms and a gallery for a small permanent collection "displaying the history of the arts"; and a wing for the library and reading room. Citing her desire for privacy, the name of the building was not divulged, and Helen asked the university not to name her as the donor. Caught up in the pleasure of the moment, Helen also gave $10,000 to the Frick Hospital near the Henry Clay Frick Birthplace for its new wing.

During the past two years, two works of art had been added to the Frick Collection, a print of *Portrait of Snyders (Franciscus Snyders)* by Sir Anthony Van Dyck and Pieter Neeffs in 1958, and Ingres's study drawing for *Comtesse d'Haussonville* in 1959. But with the one-hundredth birthday of her mother approaching on December 16, Helen felt the time had come to specifically recognize her mother. The public had long been curious about Adelaide—who she was and what she looked like. So Helen gave the Frick Collection a second watercolor of her mother by Elizabeth Shoumatoff, also based on the photograph taken circa 1902.

Elizabeth Shoumatoff (1888–1980), *Adelaide Howard Childs Frick.* Watercolor on cardboard, 14 ⅜ x 14 ⅜ in. © the Frick Collection, New York, gift of Helen Clay Frick, 1959.

The Frick Collection remained foremost in Helen's mind as the 1960s dawned. A Claude Lorrain painting, *The Sermon on the Mount,* became available, and Helen was "very much impressed with its beauty and the originality of its composition. It is a masterpiece with a remarkable history." The Sermon on the Mount had, too, been her father's favorite biblical passage. Although hospitalized in the Harkness Pavilion at the Presbyterian Hospital for removal of the ulcerated little toe, and ironically under the care of her former beau Fordyce St. John, she worked assiduously on the provenance of the painting.

Then, on May 11, 1960, John D. Rockefeller Jr.'s death in Tucson, Arizona, made his bequest to the Frick Collection official. Childs, Helen, and Frederick Osborn were the only trustees who had been on the board in 1947 when Rockefeller offered his original bequest, so Helen hoped that the new class of trustees would side with her and reject the intrusion of Rockefeller's works. Fostering this hope was the presence on the art acquisition committee of her nephew Clay Frick and of Charles Harding, the son of the Frick family's great friend Horace Harding. In addition, she had circulated to the trustees a 1958 letter from the widely revered Berenson, who had written about the danger of accepting gifts when she was discussing the purchase of the Lochoff frescoes with him. Berenson warned that people "may try to dump their acquisitions on your collection. This must be avoided, for it would utterly destroy the harmonious relation of each work of art to the other so carefully thought out by [Frick]." While awaiting the decision of the trustees, she presented the Lorrain to the board on May 12 at a purchase price of $210,000. "Should the Trustees vote to purchase this picture it will be a red letter day for the Frick Collection."

Since 1960 was an election year, Helen was also busily championing Vice President Richard Nixon in his run for the White House. First, however, he had to beat back the opposition of Nelson Rockefeller, governor of New York and son of her old nemesis, to win the Republican nomination. For Helen the race was personal. She funded the "Nixon for President" headquarters in the Frick Building, hosted a tea for three thousand supporters in the Pittsburgh Hilton, and declared Nixon "would go down in history as our greatest president." But according to one news article, she refused "to comment directly on reports the Frick family and the Rockefellers were at odds [over the Frick Collection bequest], and that this was a source for her Nixon support." Also involved in an election this year was William Singer Moorhead, son of the lawyer who had guided her through the early rounds of the legal battle with Rockefeller and the trustees. Moorhead had run for and won a congressional seat from Pennsylvania in 1958 and was now seeking reelection. Initially, loyalty had compelled her to support young Moorhead, of whom she was fond despite his being a Democrat. This time, however, his voting record caused her to throw her loyalty to his Republican opponent, and over the years she grew increasingly distant from the young couple she had once loved and enjoyed.

The ruthlessness of Helen's convictions often meant the sacrifice of a friend or her reputation. Now Helen appeared to be headed down the same road with the University of Pittsburgh administration. Architects Otto R. Eggers and Daniel P. Higgins were assigned to work on the Fine Arts Building plans but did not seem to understand what Helen desired. "The court is really lovely," she wrote Edward Litchfield on August 15, "but I do not think the exterior of [the] building is very like the Italian Renaissance style that we wanted. Also the cost has risen so much that certain changes may be necessary."

Litchfield, however, was not a person who considered costs. In his quest to raise the university's profile from that of a provincial institution to one with a national standing, he was spending so much money so fast on so many projects he had the university headed toward certain bankruptcy. And no one, not even the trustees, knew. He provided them with no interim financial reports, and those he did submit were full of inaccuracies. As the first budget director under Litchfield, Edison Montgomery, later confessed, Litchfield deliberately falsified the income side of his proposed annual budget report. "Each year I would present the budget to Litchfield to present to the board. I'd give it to him in a draft form showing him a massive deficit, and he would say, 'Well let's up this item here in gift income,' and he would raise it by a million dollars."

Helen had no way of knowing this, but she did not like Litchfield and took immediate exception to how he wanted to staff the fine arts department. Sixty-five-year-old Walter Reed Hovey had run the department since the 1930s when Clapp became involved with the Frick Collection, but Litchfield wanted him to resign in July. Helen wanted Hovey to continue teaching and to be awarded a doctorate. Her lawyer warned, "If [Hovey] was forced to step down even before construction began on the fine arts building, she would not hold the same views about some of the art objects she had intended to donate."

The threat worked. To keep the project moving forward, Litchfield agreed to let Hovey stay and permitted Helen to give him the title she had created: Henry Clay Frick Professor of Fine Arts. But the consensus among Hovey's peers on campus was that Litchfield had wrongly capitulated. Litchfield then appointed Frank Whittmore Wadsworth as dean of humanities. The fine arts department was one of eleven under his supervision, so Wadsworth wrote Helen often, apprising her of every development concerning the new building and the fine arts department. Yet their visions were highly divergent. Helen's ideas about course content represented more than her resistance to contemporary art; she was as determined as she had ever been to keep out Germans. In addition from her usual mistrust, Helen resented how many of the scholars who fled Germany during

World War II to teach in American universities were now changing the discipline of art history in America. Traditionalists like Helen valued connoisseurship—the individual's "personal" response to the aesthetic or intrinsic beauty of a work, based on a deep understanding of the artist's particular style and technique. But the "New Art History" advocated by some European scholars emphasized an interdisciplinary method combining philosophy, anthropology, psychology, and politics. Long-held boundaries and standards were collapsing in art history, and iconic works were being reexamined according to new criteria. The *New York Times* critic Michael Brenson wrote in 1989 that traditional art history was "a force that gave a privileged elite the authority to decide what is good and bad, what is in and out, who belongs and who doesn't, what is mainstream and what is provincial."

Meanwhile, the university wanted to release an advance story to the local newspapers announcing the groundbreaking for the new building. But publicity-shy Helen had again balked. After some gentle urging, she agreed to give an interview to Mary O'Hara, whom Peake described as "about the only newspaper person who has ever been able to obtain Miss Frick's confidence." After further conversations, Helen finally agreed to permit the use of her name as donor of the building, but reiterated, "*no statement on the cost of the building [is to] be made.*"

On June 16, Helen left for Ireland, Scotland, and London with her grandnephew, fifteen-year-old Fifie Symington, and her fourteen-year-old grandniece, Jane Frick. Together they explored castles, ruins, and homes with important collections, and enjoyed picnics by streams so Fifie could fish. When Helen returned home, she anxiously began to follow the fall presidential campaign as it entered its last weeks, and in November came the huge disappointment of Richard Nixon's defeat by John Kennedy.

Since Nixon intended not to run again, Helen lent financial support to the next Republican hopeful, Barry Goldwater. His desire to limit the powers of the federal government and to take a strong stand against Communists was appealing. But she was cautious and considerate of Nixon. "Although we Republicans have not yet recovered from our very great disappointment regarding the election, I feel certain that you are going to be much more carefree during the coming four years than that man now in the White House," she wrote him in a postelection consolation note, "and I hope that until you are called to succeed him, that you will enjoy each day as it comes along."

Helen felt that New York's governor, the liberal Republican Nelson Rockefeller, had handed the election to Kennedy. Her extreme disdain for the Rockefeller family was compounded by the imminent decision of the Frick Collection trustees about John D. Rockefeller Jr.'s bequest. The family had exercised its right of first refusal and only three out of seven items in the bequest remained: two were the marble busts Rockefeller had bought from the Dreyfus Collection—Andrea del Verrocchio's *Bust of a Young Woman* and Francesco Laurana's bust called *Beatrice of Aragon.* The last piece was Piero della Francesca's *Crucifixion,* the controversial painting Helen had advised the trustees against in 1947 as a ruined work. Moreover, the Verrochio bust was badly damaged. According to the collection's curatorial records, "The head [had been] broken off and replaced. The tip of the nose [had been] broken and repaired and [the] damage extend[ed along] the whole of the left part of the right nostril." There was damage on "the jaw to the left of the chin, pitting in the left upper eyelid and on [the] right temple has been repaired." Even the hair had been "extensively made up." And as for the Laurana, though in better condition than the Verrochio, it was a far lesser work than the one Frick had purchased in 1916.

Piero's *Crucifixion* really was a ruined painting. Duveen was famous for repainting everything he sold, irreparably altering the original works so they would be "both bright and pretty" for his clients. He had given the *Crucifixion* exactly this treatment when in the early 1920s he sold it to the young collector Carl Hamilton and had it restored before the transfer. In May 1929, Hamilton was forced to sell his collection. Shortly thereafter, when Duveen was in the gallery prior to the *Crucifixion* being sold at auction, he bad-mouthed the painting so loudly that others heard his claim that it was not even by Piero della Francesca. Duveen, however, became the successful bidder for the painting at $375,000—well below the estimate. He promptly resold it to Abby Rockefeller for the same amount, and Hamilton filed a $1 million suit against Duveen for harming the price with his remarks and for rigging the sale. The suit dragged on until 1939 and was settled out of court. In 1951, long after Duveen's death, Rockefeller asked the Frick Collection's conservator, Billy Suhr, with his "skillful and artistic work," to freshen up the painting. Suhr, a consummate and thoroughgoing professional, was in fact restoring all the paintings in the Rockefeller bequest under Clapp's supervision, and reported to Rockefeller that Duveen had so altered the *Crucifixion* it was hardly recognizable. Helen simply referred to the painting as "that rag."

Childs had spent the past year bringing up the subject of the bequest, "teasing and tormenting" Helen about it, and she subsequently began suffering migraine headaches. At the January 1961 board meeting, Frederick Osborn made a motion to accept the three Rockefeller pieces, and even though none of the trustees had bothered to look at the works, Childs called for a standing vote. According to a family member, each trustee, one by one, stood up and "had to declare out loud, one at a time, their vote." Helen's nephew, Clay Frick, caught between loyalty to his father, Childs, and to his Aunt Helen, abstained. Charles Harding, the third member of the art acquisition committee with Helen and Clay, voted no. The five other trustees, including Childs, stood against Helen. After more than forty years of conflict with Rockefeller, angry exchanges, hurtful words, and damaging charges, and all the years of effort to prevent this moment, the Rockefeller bequest officially entered the Frick Collection.

Scalded, enraged, and defeated, Helen, now seventy-two, jumped from her seat and spat, "I am leaving this organization forever." After accusing her nephew of having "shown yourself to be incompetent," she turned on her heel and fled the trustees' room. With her anger mounting at every stride, she raced down the grand staircase, marched through the living hall, garden court, and Oval Room into the East Gallery and barked to the guard as she flew through the connecting door into the library, "Lock it and make sure it stays locked."

Bill Rea, Helen's cousin, and his wife, Ingrid, whom she had invited for lunch that day, were at the table when Helen entered. Bill recalled, "Cousin Helen was in terrible shape." She was not through fighting. When the press stormed into the dining room, apparently tipped off by Childs, Helen "did not get up." Instead, she reinvoked the image she had used at every opportunity. "The Rockefellers are like cowbirds," she charged, describing the parasite breed that drives defenseless songbirds from their habitat. "They leave their droppings in other people's nests."

On January 16, Helen followed through with her threat and resigned from the board of the Frick Collection after serving it for forty-one years. Rather than submit her resignation directly to the trustees, she took the unusual step of first doing so in an open letter to the *New York Herald Tribune* so "that my reason for doing so might be understood." She explained: "I could not see inferior works of art in damaged condition enter the Frick

Collection which has always stood for the highest quality and authenticity. Furthermore, having known my father's wishes at first hand (whereas most of the Trustees had never met him), I could not accede to the resolution passed by the majority, accepting *sight unseen* the bequest of John D. Rockefeller Jr." And she continued, "I have served as Chairman of the Art Acquisitions Committee since its inception, and have consulted the most eminent scholars both in this country and abroad, and they are in accord with the questionable authenticity and damaged condition of two of these works."

The *Herald Tribune* published the letter on January 18, and tried to elicit comment from Childs about his sister's resignation, but he and the other trustees refused an interview. Childs claimed "he could make no statement because he had received no formal letter of resignation from his sister." In the meantime, one of the trustees who had voted against Helen, Thomas H. Higginson, a friend of Childs's who had joined the board in 1957, tried to lure Helen back with a long, flattering letter. "Your knowledge of the Collection in particular and of painting, sculpture and fine arts in general is something which is of great value to the Collection and your associates on the board. We need you to help us carry on the trust which your father and the law has imposed on all of us, and I sincerely hope that you will continue to do so." He pleaded, "I know that it would be a severe disappointment to your father, as well as a personal loss to me and all the members of the Board and the staff of the Collection, if you were to take a contrary course."

His words were about four decades too late. Helen had had enough of her brother's behavior and what she considered his and the trustees' abject stupidity. But to remind them that their action had cost the board more than her resignation, according to the minutes of the January 1961 annual meeting, "Miss Frick stated that in view of the fact that the Frick Collection would eventually have the responsibility of operating the Frick Art Reference Library in accordance with the existing agreement, she wished to present a report on the present expenses of operating [the library] and an estimate of the cost of operation for the next ten years." The deficit was estimated at about $1.6 million. She did not, however, tell them of the change she had made to her will in 1947, eliminating an endowment for both the Frick Art Reference Library and the Frick Collection from her will, thus leaving to the trustees the entire financial burden of running the library.

Hundreds of scholars and friends in the United States and abroad rallied to her side. A writer for the *New York Herald Tribune*, Mrs. E. A. Walz, wrote, "If Miss Helen C. Frick has resigned from the Board of Trustees of the Frick Collection because the offered works are 'inferior'—then, I applaud her!" Richard Offner, who had testified to the terrible condition of the *Crucifixion* in Helen's 1948 court fight, felt the painting was "far below [the] average of [the] Collection," and said "I applaud your courageous position." Acceptance of the marble busts particularly offended Yale University professor Charles Seymour Jr. "Neither bust would seem in any case to fit the needs or the standards of the Frick Collection." He reasoned, "They might on the other hand be of value to a larger and more heterogeneous type of collection where completeness and variety of *types* are of importance rather than absolute quality of the individual piece." And Kenneth Clark congratulated her from London's National Gallery "on the magnificent way in which you have upheld your father's tradition of only purchasing pictures of the highest quality" and not permitting the inclusion of lesser quality works. He continued, "It takes only one or two damaged or repainted pictures to make a bad smell in a Gallery; it seems to permeate the whole place!"

On January 20, 1961, after a lifetime of devotion to her father's collection, seventy-two-year-old Helen officially tendered her resignation in a signed letter to her brother and the trustees. "The desire to preserve the Frick Collection intact with its high standard of perfection seems to be entirely lacking." Even so, Helen continued to work behind the scenes on the only thing that still mattered to her: ensuring that the Rockefeller cast-offs were never exhibited in the Frick Collection. She struck a deal with the only real weapon left in her arsenal, her "twin" *Pietà*, always coveted by the Frick Collection. Helen offered the trustees a quid pro quo: she would give her *Pietà* to the collection on permanent loan provided the trustees never placed the Rockefeller works on exhibition. After much deliberation, the trustees accepted. The three pieces were locked away in the Frick Collection vault, and were later sent to the Princeton University Art Gallery for exhibition.

For Helen, a door had closed and with it a large piece of her life. Involvement with the development of her father's collection was over, and now she moved on. Politics had always been important to her, and in the spring of 1961 she turned her attention to it again when she sent her cousin Harvey Childs, finance chairman of the Republican party in Westmoreland County, Pennsylvania, a $1,000 check. "I hope sufficient interest will be awakened & good candidates found," she urged, "so that by the next primary there will be an unpleasant surprise for the Democrats & a still more unpleasant one for them in November!" On April 13, she began making annual $1,000 donations to the Committee of One Million Against the Admission of Communist China to the United Nations, founded in 1953 and at the time considered the most powerful and successful anti-Communist organization in the United States.

Helen also remained determined to move the Henry Clay Frick Fine Arts Building project along. The architects had not yet completed a plan, and the university had not yet located a building site. In February, Helen made a $450,000 contribution toward scholarships for fine arts students but, anxious and upset about the building's progress, on June 5, she advised Chancellor Litchfield that she was losing interest in the project.

Litchfield could not afford to lose Helen, and Helen was still unaware of the university's mounting debt. When Eggers and Higgins resigned as architects on July 11, frustrated that Helen had still not approved a design, the university, without her consent, paid them $10,000 out of the fund she had created. Another Pittsburgh architect, B. Kenneth Johnstone, winner of an American Academy of Rome prize and dean of the College of Fine Arts and head of the architecture department at Carnegie Tech, took over. He reduced the building to fifty-seven thousand square feet, flattened its facade, retained the cloister and rotunda, and presented Helen with a plan both acceptable and affordable. But by August, Helen confronted Litchfield again, this time over the lack of a suitable site. She gave him until December 1 to find a location. If he failed, Helen said, "I would like to feel free to go ahead with my own plans."

Early in 1962, Helen's maternal cousin, Bill Rea, also a trustee of the university, was able to secure a site for the fine arts building. He obtained permission from the city to erect it on city-owned parkland at Schenley Plaza, on the southern perimeter of the university campus, across the street from the Carnegie Library and, more important to Helen, around the corner from the Carnegie Museum of Art. Thrilled with the building location, Helen offered the university the twenty-by-thirty-foot rug from Eagle Rock's former music room, together with lamps and porcelains for use in the period rooms. She promised to provide all the antique furniture for the building and also suggested that she would buy some paintings for the gallery. Working with Johnstone on the building, Helen reserved the first floor as a museum and placed the classrooms and studio space underground.

As was her habit, Helen considered every detail. She dedicated the rotunda with the organ from Eagle Rock to her mother, decided that it would have a mahogany wainscot with plaster arches filled in with gray fabric, and chose decorations that Adelaide had loved—two sixteenth-century French tapestries. The Print Room was to have the Jacobean paneling from her father's Eagle Rock office; the French Room would boast *boiserie,* several-hundred-year-old paneling from a house in Paris as backdrop for the furniture she had donated. For the two-story library, she added the innovative touch of roller shelves for handling the large volumes and designed a balcony with plain wrought-iron railing. She personally selected the $100,000 natural cherry paneling to frame the books, chose the design of the custom-made tables and chairs, the pecan wood floors, and the cherry wood plaque bearing the carved gold leaf dedication to her father: "Pioneer in Coke, Manufacturer of Steel, Benefactor and Art Collector, This Building is Dedicated in Loving Memory by his Daughter." To meet with her standard—the grain in the cherry plaque had to match the letters in her father's name—the plaque was redone three times. In addition, two bas-reliefs were designed, one by Malvina Hoffman of Henry Clay Frick above the entrance doors, and one of an Indian elephant bearing a scroll over the door between the cloister and the rotunda. The Indian elephant, according to Pliny's *Natural History,* even though it has a short tail, is one who "does not fear gnats." Instead it entices them into the folds of its skin and crushes them in the crevices.

When the groundbreaking ceremony was set for September 17, 1962, Helen met with the university's public relations department about the role she was to play. The vice-chancellor for development, E. B. Cale, wrote Litchfield, "Miss Frick indicated that it was not necessary for her to be present. She intimated that she would like to miss the groundbreaking. And as a matter of fact, miss the dedication." Rather than draw attention to herself, Helen wanted the ceremony to focus on the university's 175th anniversary. Cale asked Litchfield, "Do we insist that she be present?" Litchfield replied in firm red pencil, "Let her do as she pleases."

A week before the groundbreaking, on September 11, Litchfield sent a hand-carried telegram to Helen. "This handsome memorial to your father's interest in the fine arts and the beauty it will house and inspire will mean much both to countless generations of students and to the community as a whole." At the ceremony, full credit was given to Helen for her patronage. Overjoyed, she wrote Charles Peake on September 27, "I am so delighted that everything went so well, and now I am starting to count the months till the building is finished and can be enjoyed." Just months, later, in fact, on January 22, 1963, Helen accepted the final architectural revision for the fine arts building and gave the order to Litchfield: "Proceed." "It is beautiful!" seventy-four-year-old Helen exclaimed of the new building and in April, when visiting Clayton, she proudly showed the architectural plans to her beloved British girl, Mavis Sayers Archer.

Despite the glow cast by the new building plans and the honor Helen received in October 1963 of becoming a Distinguished Daughter of Pennsylvania as cited by the Pennsylvania legislature, a new cloud was forming as Helen's relationship with Litchfield again deteriorated. He wanted Helen's loyalists in the department, Walter Hovey and Hovey's colleague Virginia Lewis, both in their late sixties, to retire. But Helen panicked at the thought of losing them so early in the construction phase. Her attorney, William F. Knox, threatened Peake, "[Miss Frick] is making no commitment at this time for the creation of an endowment fund for maintaining in perpetuity the Henry Clay Frick Professorship of Fine Arts." In March, Helen warned Dean Wadsworth, who also sought to have Hovey replaced as chairman, "I . . . want [Hovey] to have a great deal to say about the new building and its installation when the time comes to 'dress it up.'" Yet over Helen's objections, the search was on for a new department chair. On April 4, Wadsworth informed her he was considering Karl Birkmeyer, a prominent Northern Renaissance historian of German origin who was naturalized in 1955. Helen replied angrily, "I do not look with favor upon German scholars for this Department—in fact I sincerely request that you dismiss the thought of engaging one, no matter how qualified he may be. There must be American scholars as well-qualified as Professor Birkmeyer," she continued, "or else some that come from those countries that were our Allies during two world wars." Then she warned, "This is a very personal request—I could never feel content with a German Director, and this building is a large undertaking for me, and one that involves great expense, so I feel justified in asking you to meet my request."

On May 2, Wadsworth stood his ground.

> Let me first try to answer the question raised in your letter. . . . Although I do not agree with your position about German scholars I fully realize how important the matter is to you and I should not personally wish to do anything to cause you uneasiness. At the same time, I should be less than honest were I not to state that I too feel strongly about a great university's obligation to society. I believe these obligations include the duty to recognize and honor scholarly excellence irregardless [*sic*] of peoples' origins. As one who served as a pilot in the last war and lost many dear friends, I take great pride in my country's willingness to forgive and to extend citizenship to people who love and respect her even though their own countries may once have been her enemies.

The Birkmeyer question, however, was now "academic," he continued, because Birkmeyer was in fact "not interested in administration." Wadsworth assured Helen, "The other persons who have been recommended to us are all Americans and we need not, either of us, worry further on that score." Referring to a professor at Bryn Mawr College, William C. Loerke, Wadsworth reported that there was an American who "made a very favorable impression."

Immediately suspicious, Helen inquired about Loerke's nationality. Wadsworth was so offended he relayed the conversation he had with Helen's secretary, Walter Cooley, to Vice-Chancellor Charles Peake on June 5. He confided, "I think her attitude raises serious questions," and stated, "I do not think that Miss Frick should be allowed to think that she can in any way dictate the choice of personnel. . . . The Department has a bad reputation around the country and if Miss Frick's Germanic phobia is encouraged it will have a worse one." Wadsworth felt clear boundaries had to be established between university autonomy and those areas where the university "can afford to allow her and/or Walter Hovey to dictate."

Wadsworth assured Helen that Loerke "is an American, about as American as a man can be. He was born in Toledo, Ohio, served as a naval officer during the war, did his undergraduate work at Oberlin, one of the country's top colleges, and [did] his graduate work . . . at Princeton." He further explained, "He is a first-class person in every respect, highly thought of by his students and by his colleagues across the country. . . . and he is by all reports an impeccable scholar. In his early forties, he is one of the most promising younger people in the field of art history." Wadsworth had one reservation, however, and confessed to Litchfield: "Loerke is a very masculine, aggressive person who not only quivers with energy but is unusually direct. . . . [and these qualities] might be a handicap in this particular situation. . . . in view of our relationship with Miss Frick."

Wadsworth sent his entire correspondence with Helen to Litchfield and using red pencil he "marked those sections having to do with her prejudice against German scholars." Although Loerke was not German, and Helen had no reason to dislike him, Wadsworth was nevertheless concerned about a potential personality clash between the two. He warned Loerke not to discuss departmental matters with Helen, and Loerke seemed to understand for on June 6, when he formally accepted chairmanship of the fine arts department, he advised Wadsworth, "My belief is that donors are donors to the whole University and that this is true also when it is clear that only one department could conceivably benefit. I shall therefore never broach any matter of departmental or University concern, without your prior knowledge and approval, to Miss Frick." Litchfield was confident that the situation could be mollified through Loerke's forthcoming statement to the press about his appointment. It would note "the fine library we already have in this field," "what an addition the new Frick Building is going to be," "how the Lochoff Collection contributes to our total teaching program," and "how much Miss Frick has done through the years in the Library, in supporting funds, in the professorship that Hovey holds, in the Lochoff Collection and in the building itself."

With his offer accepted, and a statement intended to flatter Helen prepared, on June 19, 1963, Wadsworth advised Helen that Loerke would be the new chair. Helen seemed pleased to finally have a chairman in place, but a few days later, when she learned that Birkmeyer was to be a visiting professor in the fall, she contacted Wadsworth. "I would have thought that in consideration of what I wrote you regarding my feeling about Germans, you would not have engaged one as a Professor for the Henry Clay Frick Fine Arts Department! I could not have expressed myself more clearly, and I am surprised that you did not respect my wishes." She warned, "Please remember that, as the sole donor of the new building, I expect that amount of courtesy." Wadsworth simply replied that they needed Birkmeyer, time was short, and he was "most anxious to respect [her] wishes as fully as my own obligations to the University will allow."

Helen wrote Litchfield on July 6, "I am glad that although Dean Wadsworth first tried to engage a German [director], he was unable to do so and was able to make a wiser choice. That he engaged Dr. Birkmeyer as [visiting] Professor and that he will become a Mellon Professor [not a Henry Clay Frick professor], lessens the disappointment that I have felt that a German should fill a position on the staff." Then Helen moved in: "I do not wish to be autocratic, and have not been so in the many years that [the fine arts department] has functioned. . . . But neither my father nor I were able to feel that we could place faith in Germans, and the future is still uncertain." Helen hoped that "Dr. Birkmeyer is an exception, and that his appointment will not be regretted."

Litchfield advised Wadsworth that stringing Helen along was "a gamble worth taking"; maybe if he did what Helen wanted some of the time he could keep her somewhat under control and maybe land an even larger bequest. He was playing a dangerous game, and not only regarding Helen Frick. According to Robert C. Alberts, "1963 was the crucial year in the history of the university and in the career of Edward Litchfield." The "mounting deficits and alarming revelations of the circumstances under which they were operating" indicated that the university "was close to being out of control." Five campus buildings were already mortgaged as collateral—the Cathedral of Learning, Clapp Hall, the Stephen Foster Memorial, the nurses' residence, and Falk Clinic. In the five years since 1959, when

Helen Frick agreed to erect and endow the Henry Clay Frick Fine Arts Building, Litchfield had run up operating deficits totaling more than $11 million. Yet he remained hopeful he could manage his volatile donor.

In September 1963, Helen invited Nixon and his family to Westmoreland Farm for lunch. On their departure, Helen presented them with homegrown apples and "other fresh farm products." In return Nixon thanked her for "one of the most pleasant afternoons it has ever been our privilege to enjoy." In addition, he sent her a biography of Kennedy by Victor Laskey. "In view of what you told me about your opinion of JFK, I think you might find it most interesting." Helen replied, "I have started to read it. But I must again say, that my dislike of that man & everything about him is so intense, that I may not be able to read the book through, no matter how informative it is!" Their friendly correspondence continued through the fall, and promises were made for "a mutually convenient date" to visit the Frick Collection.

Then, on November 22, 1963, John F. Kennedy was assassinated in Dallas, and Lyndon B. Johnson was sworn in as president of the United States. Nixon decided to run for president, and Helen rushed to back him "in every way," as she wrote in a January 29, 1964, letter, cautioning, "This time *you must win* and it is going to be necessary for you to overcome a lot of prejudice that was undoubtedly inspired by the Communists who like you as little as you like them." She also invited him to speak at the Bedford Golf and Tennis Club in early March. Nixon drew a large bracket around Helen's comment about communists, and asked Miss Woods to "work out dates by phone."

On October 5, 1963, the cornerstone was laid for the Henry Clay Frick Fine Arts Building, and two days later Helen traveled to Baltimore for the wedding of her nineteen-year-old grandniece Martie Symington. A month later Helen returned to the business of her new building. She gave the university more Eagle Rock treasures for the new art gallery—twelve barrels packed with her father's Chinese porcelains from the Morgan collection, the French-style drawing room suite covered in Aubusson tapestry, and her father's Italian Renaissance bronzes from the Morgan collection.

Charles Peake was now looking ahead, planning the opening ceremony "a year hence" and the possibility of "asking Miss Frick for a temporary exhibit of some of the great works of art in the Frick Gallery in New York as a special feature of the dedication ceremony and the period following it." Litchfield replied, "It's a good idea but she is no longer connected in the Frick Gallery." And anyway, Frick's will stipulated that all the paintings must remain in the building.

At this time, the director of the Frick Collection, fifty-six-year-old Franklin Biebel, was in the early stages of Alzheimer's disease. During his tenure, he often wandered out of the Frick Collection and disappeared, to be found later, in a daze, some fifteen blocks away. Fifty-year-old Harry Grier had first assumed Dwight's position, and now Biebel's post. Grier quickly became one of the most beloved directors in the history of the collection. A self-effacing man who grew up on a farm in Oxford, Pennsylvania, he had been a major in the Army Counter-Intelligence Corps in Europe during the war and afterward was acting chief of the Museum and Fine Arts and Archives section of the United States military office in Berlin.

Determined to halt the policy of "run[ning the collection] very sternly," where "nobody did anything but read the circulating mail folders and say 'No' to every request," he wanted to promote a warm, friendly, happy atmosphere. One way he orchestrated this was by preserving the character of the collection as a private residence. Grier wound the clocks, put back lamps, and every Monday he and Billy Suhr arranged glorious, fresh-cut flowers and placed them throughout the galleries. Grier respected Helen for her knowledge and ability, and instead of being threatened by her, he drew her out. Often the new director took Helen to lunch, and the two of them spent a happy time discussing the collection and the changing times in society and the art world. Soon she began coming to the collection on Mondays, when it is closed to visitors, "to look around and see how things were."

While Helen was enjoying a revitalized connection to her father's collection, the university department she had dedicated to him was in chaos. Virginia Lewis had been placed in charge of the library until a professional librarian could be hired, and she and Hovey continued to consult Helen and offer their opinions to Loerke, opinions that neither Loerke nor the Litchfield administration welcomed. In February 1964, Virginia Lewis announced that over the last ten to fifteen years, 353 books had disappeared from the fine arts library. To enact stricter control, she issued stack permits to faculty members and graduate students and even turned away one professor because he did not have a card. On February 7, Loerke, still at Bryn Mawr College, sent a harsh letter to Lewis. "No policy decision in respect to the library is ever to be made or promulgated without my approval," he wrote, and called her behavior "so brazen an arrogation of authority beyond your competence that I must spell out in detail what should have been clear to you long ago. . . . I will never permit any librarian to assume the kind of authority you have tried to assert." He then countermanded her action. "I have . . . instructed [them] they are not to submit to the insulting nonsense of signing in and out of the stacks. Furthermore, I will not permit any rules to be set which imply that the faculty and graduate students are thieves." He made an itemized list of directives with each command preceded by the words "You Will," and concluded: "A library is supposed to be an efficient pleasant center for serious study; it is not to be turned into a malevolent, penal institution to which pettifogging martinets maintain a constant state of irritation."

Lewis showed the letter to Helen, who advised Loerke that first of all he should address Virginia Lewis as "Miss" and that his directive was "very insulting . . . as it was addressed on stationery with the letterhead of my father Henry Clay Frick—and on stationery of the Fine Arts Department which was created by me. I take great exception to its tone." She reminded him, "Miss Lewis has served a great many years in this department, and at my suggestion with the approval of Chancellor Litchfield, she was made librarian of the department." She continued: "As the founder of the Fine Arts Department and as the donor of the new building, I would feel very regretful should you be continued as the Director. In fact, I would change many of my plans and will do so unless you write a letter of apology to Miss Lewis."

Loerke replied that he had already apologized to Miss Lewis "for the tone of my letter to her, to which you quite rightly took exception." He flattered Helen about the library, "which astonishes all visiting art historians and rouses the envy of most of them," and about the new building, referencing universities such as Harvard, Yale, Princeton, Ohio State, and Wisconsin as "either moving into a new art building, or are now embarking upon their construction. Without the new building in honor of your father, the department could scarcely aspire to that position among the nation's art departments for which we can now confidently labor."

But Helen wrote Richard K. Mellon, a trustee of the university, "that a man capable of such boorishness is not the type of man fit to be the Director of the Henry Clay Frick Fine

Arts Building," and if he were not replaced at the end of the semester, she said, "I would be reluctant to carry out my cherished plans for [the new building]." As for Dean Wadsworth, he "has made an unfavorable impression on me. . . . He is much too immature." She concluded, "All I want is to have the Henry Clay Frick Fine Arts Department worthy of the name."

Mellon organized a meeting attended by Chancellor Litchfield, Helen's cousin and university trustee Bill Rea, and Henry Hillman. The men were in full agreement that Loerke had crossed the line, as Litchfield stated: "Professor Loerke should never have written the letter to Miss Lewis. He knows it. He regrets it. He did it in anger and like many young men, has not yet learned to get his anger off his chest and then rewrite his letters in a more temperate form. He is a first rate-man and this indiscretion reflects no real blemish in his character." Rather than fire him, however, Litchfield decided to overlook the incident. "He is a hot-tempered artist and if he weren't he probably would not be a very good artist. . . . [and Miss Lewis] had no business making the decisions in the first place. . . . This is typical of her defiance. . . . The whole matter from where you and I sit . . . is only an example of a larger problem. . . . Decisions are made between Hovey and Miss Frick, which the rest of the University has little opportunity to participate in." As the chancellor continued, he acknowledged as carefully as he could the delicacy of their problem. "Miss Frick is a delightful lady with great competence in her field and with a dedication to Pittsburgh and the University . . . absolutely essential to maintain. . . . Whatever is done in the future must be guided by the necessity of preserving her interest here. I take this as a position of cardinal importance." Yet Litchfield said they had to recognize that Helen had "'unorthodox' views about the academic world," and her strong opposition "to the appointment of anyone . . . who is of Germanic extraction even of several generations removed. . . . These are just things one can't do in the academic world despite the views of a wonderfully well-intentioned and generous donor." Litchfield conceded the situation was "both delicate and complex," but understood from "Pittsburgh's and the University's point of view, it is terribly important."

Bill Rea echoed these sentiments. "The pressure is getting intense. I think I have been able to stave off a couple new undesirable moves on [Helen's] part, at least for a while. I am quite aware as to the delicate nature of this Art Department problem and have been as tactful as possible in trying to meet her many thrusts which I am sure other members of the Board are also receiving." Nevertheless, that April, Rea was in the awkward position of having to inform Helen that since Professor Loerke had been granted tenure "it would be absolutely impossible for the University to force him out without completely wrecking the whole educational reputation of the University and particularly that of the Art Department." He hoped that with the enthusiasm for the "truly magnificent structure just as you had conceived it would be. . . . [and because all were] very interested and enthusiastic in working with you on finishing it . . . that cooperation with you can be reestablished and that you can be kept fully advised on every development. . . . I can assure you that this whole thing is not being taken lightly by anyone."

But Helen wasn't about to change her opinion. "I am deeply sorry that those of you who have discussed the matter with Dr. Litchfield have come to the conclusion that Prof. Loerke must be retained," she replied. "Personally, I will still do everything in my power to have him removed." Then came her ultimatum. "If Prof. Loerke is not removed from the Department of Fine Arts, I will not allow any furniture I have collected to be placed in the building and there will be other plans that I have in mind that will be altered. I say this regretfully but mean every word."

In August, after a visit to the Iron Rail to see how it was progressing under the Girls Clubs of America, Helen solicited John Walker for support in removing Loerke before he came to the university in the fall. The former Pittsburgher and director of the National Gallery often advised Helen, and the two were close friends. Walker wrote that he was "distressed beyond description" by the Loerke incident and felt "it is both wise and fair to give consideration to the wishes of those benefactors who have made our museums and universities the superb institutions they are." Still, Walker hoped Helen would "give him a chance to show what ability he has." Helen answered: "You suggest that I 'forgive him,' but that would be an impossibility for he will never measure up to what I so deeply want. This age that we are living in is a very strange one and the future of our country depends on those who are now in their teens and twenties and they need to be inspired and directed by fine men of character." Helen began looking for Loerke's immediate replacement. On August 25, she asked Professor Ernest De Wald at Princeton University to suggest someone and described the incoming department chairman as a man "of uncontrollable temper and great conceit . . . [and] unfit to fill this position. . . . [and] I am not going to give in."

Arabella Hambleton Symington, wearing her maternal great-grandmother, Adelaide Frick's, wedding dress (pictured on page 7), with her husband, Edward Nathan Dane, September 12, 1964. Author's collection. Photo credit: Winants Brothers.

Wadsworth and Litchfield continued to play for time. On one hand they felt "a campaign to overwhelm Miss Frick with Public Honors," could be implemented, "to put Miss Frick in such a public posture that she could not easily refuse to go along with her original plans. This might be done by much publicity emphasizing . . . and extolling her generosity to the *educational* world. An attempt could be made to reach national publications such as *Time*. The Chancellor and other important people could publicly thank her for the splendid teaching building. . . . [and] this might even be dressed up to the point of offering her an honorary degree which, if she accepted it, might then make it difficult for her to turn and bite the hand that had fed her." On the other hand, "Strategically, there is much to be said for . . . a waiting game," such as delayed occupancy of the building. "Miss Frick is no longer young and the passage of time is very much in our favor."

Never susceptible to flattery, and having already told Peake, "I will not have that man in my building," on October 5 Helen stated, "You will be wise if you make no further appointments to the Henry Clay Frick Fine Arts Building until I have been fully satisfied that Professor Loerke has been transferred elsewhere." Once again she ominously promised: "The lack of courtesy and consideration shown me . . . serves no good purpose and may result in my with-holding the building from the University." Yet, not two weeks later, the university further inflamed the situation by adding modern art as a core course.

While much of Helen's attention was focused on the university, other events also occupied her. She attended the August 30, 1964, wedding of her grandniece Helen Clay Symington in Baltimore, and not two weeks later returned for Arabella's wedding on September 12. "It seems very strange that my three very precious little grandnieces should grow up & and become [married] all of a sudden," she wrote. "It makes me feel very old indeed—but I hope it does not mean that the intervals between our 'get-togethers' will be any longer than in the past—& I hope we can stay just as close together, or matter to each other, as ever."

She also continued to encourage Nixon's presidential hopes. On August 13, she thanked him for sending her the transcript of a speech he gave in San Francisco and one from the *Reader's Digest*. She was disheartened at year's end, however, when the Republican presidential candidate, this time Barry Goldwater, was crushed in a landslide by Lyndon B. Johnson. At the same time, her dog, "darling little Skipper was freed from his sad life."

Now Helen was about to enter what became her most harrowing period, a time that forever ruined her good reputation and gave evidence to her critics that she was lost, tormented, and a bigot. Her Overholt cousin, James B. Stevenson, publisher of the *Titusville Herald,* had given Helen a 1964 book by the Commonwealth of Pennsylvania's state historian, Sylvester K. Stevens, entitled *Pennsylvania: Birthplace of a Nation,* slated to become "the basis for textbooks for high schools and colleges." Helen went to the index, looked up her father's name, read what Stevens had written about him, and was shocked. The historian referred to Henry Clay Frick as "stern," "brusque," "autocratic," and charged him with "low pay," the "longest hours," and using "no modern safety appliances." The abuse of the company towns and stores in the coke region was entirely blamed on Frick, and Stevens claimed that the industrialist's wealth was "amassed not in exact accord with Christian principles and practices." He gave credit to many Pittsburghers such as the Mellons and the Heinzes for their local philanthropy, but did not mention Frick's contributions—Frick Park, the park in Homestead, the Kingsley House Association, the Henry Clay Frick Teachers' Fund, the X-ray machines and endowment for Mercy Hospital, funding for the Allegheny Observatory, the newsboys' homes, and various cultural organizations such as the Pittsburgh symphony.

Tucked in the back of Helen's 1964 diary is the draft of a letter she wrote Stevens.

> Your book was given to me as a Christmas present. Naturally my first interest was to see what you had written about my father. I then realized that you had done a very poor research job about him as you had accepted unfounded & incorrect reports about him without trying to learn the truth. Had you gone further into your research you would have learned [it]. It is unfortunate that you should try to tarnish the reputation of one of the greatest Pennsylvania citizens of this past century who did so much in the development of the country & gave so much to charity. . . . [and] I am certain many others will feel the same when it is realized how biased you are.

On December 30, she wrote Republican Governor Scranton. "As you have endorsed this book, I feel it is only right that you should know that his insulting charges against my father's actions & character are wholly unjust and that as a historian Dr. Stevens must be very biased and unreliable." To both men she sent copies of George Harvey's *Henry Clay Frick: The Man.*

Naturally, Stevens was greatly unnerved and upset by Helen's diatribe. Trying to calm the situation, he wrote her on January 7, 1965: "I have tried to make it clear that the situation was not due to one man but to the temper of those times when few leaders of business believed at all in the right of labor to form unions and still less strikes. . . . The fact that your father did not believe in trade unions is not something, if viewed in the light of those times, which in any way condemns him." The following day Governor Scranton replied smoothly, "I got a copy of the book and checked the references to which you refer, and I shall talk with Dr. Stevens about them. . . . Like all great men who do things [Frick] was both admired and severely criticized, but as you look back, you recognize, as I do, that if we had many more Henry Clay Fricks in this world, Pennsylvania would be economically on top of the heap." In closing, the governor attempted to console her by remembering "what he did and what this meant to the development of our Commonwealth as well as the Nation, and no matter what anyone says, that lives with you and with those of us who carry on in another generation."

Helen was not persuaded and immediately asked her lawyer William F. Knox to sue Stevens. "In my opinion," Knox replied diplomatically, "no basis exists under Pennsylvania law for the institution by you of a civil suit against Dr. Stevens for damages and an injunction. No civil remedy is available for libeling a person who is dead." He did, however, mention a statute in the Pennsylvania criminal code that permitted a legal challenge of statements "'tending to blacken the memory' of the dead in a way that lowers living descendants 'in the esteem of the community'," a statute that carried a fine of $500 and one year in prison. But Knox dismissed the statute as useless since it had "never been instituted. The fact that the events involved happened over seventy years ago lead me to the opinion that great difficulty would be encountered in securing an indictment and a conviction."

By informing her of the statute, however, Knox had given Helen all the encouragement she needed. She switched lawyers. Under her instructions, David B. Buerger warned Stevens on January 8, "If you wish to avoid litigation it will be necessary to arrange for a full and prompt retraction." Stevens refused to back down. "I might add that I have discussed this situation with the Chairman of the Pennsylvania Historical and Museum Commission, James B. Stevenson, President of the Pennsylvania Newspaper Publishers Association, and a relative of Miss Frick," the historian replied to Buerger. "He agrees with me there is no occasion for such a position as is implied in your letter."

On January 19, 1965, Helen Frick filed a suit in equity against Stevens in the Court of Common Pleas of Cumberland County, Pennsylvania, where he lived. She claimed that the passages blackening her father's name had damaged her own reputation and public esteem, and that she was adversely affected by the book because she "has devoted her life to the promotion of projects of public welfare of the type encouraged and instituted by her father. ... [and] has sought to honor the memory of her father." In addition, Helen filed an injunction against Random House, Stevens's publisher, prohibiting the sale and distribution of the book. Random House immediately agreed to "delete what was offensive," and to "publish an errata [slip] retracting the statement on Christian principles and any other statements Judge Weidner finds libelous." So Helen did not sue Random House for monetary damages. She just wanted the book withdrawn. Having failed to achieve a ban on gifts to the Frick Collection, there were few remaining chances to redeem herself in her father's eyes. The Stevens suit gave her just such an opportunity to tell her story and to vindicate her father and herself.

1965–1980

9 Last Stand

I will die as I have lived, misunderstood by those I love best and serve most.

—Abigail Scott Duniway

Although Helen Frick's lawsuit against Sylvester Stevens in 1965 began a difficult time, it also provided her the opportunity to repair some old relationships. Since Helen was responsible for forming both the university art gallery and the teaching collection at University of Pittsburgh, she took the extraordinary step of seeking Clapp's opinion. His wife, Maud, had died in 1960, and shortly afterward Clapp had asked Helen if he could pay her a visit. "I want to erase from the record any miserable blur that may mar it mindful as I am of the days that have gone downstream into *their* silence—days when we worked in close harmony on projects that have not lost and will not lose their beauty and reality." In a remarkable act, the characteristically unforgiving Helen had replied, "It is a lot of water over the dam & bygones are bygones." Now, with the death that February of her mentor Paul Sachs, who had first brought Helen and Clapp together at the University of Pittsburgh, she was particularly pleased by the reconciliation. Clapp, too, had a vested interest in both the development of the university collection and in the outcome of Helen's problems there, and he understood her frustration in dealing with the present administration, "not of the caliber of Dr. Bowman, who so singularly stood behind our efforts to create something that would be outstanding." With Clapp's guidance, Helen purchased two eighteenth-century paintings of gardens at Versailles, writing to Walter Reed Hovey, "I want to tell you something exciting—but don't tell anyone but Miss Lewis. I have bought two lovely and exciting French pictures. . . . and the wonderful part is that they are by the artist I most wanted, Hubert Robert!" *Grotto Baths of Apollo* depicts the artist's design for a romantic garden still open to the public. *Memorial Garden of Lenoir's Museum of French Monuments* shows the tombs of famous men such as Descartes, Molière, and La Fontaine in an avenue of trees. Both paintings illustrate the design principle Helen most wanted fine arts students to fol-

Opposite: Elizabeth Shoumatoff (1888–1980), *Portrait of Helen Clay Frick*, 1973. Watercolor. Gift of the artist to Helen. © the Collection of the Frick Art & Historical Center, Pittsburgh, Pennsylvania. Photo credit: Richard A. Stoner.

Hubert Robert (1733–1808), *Grotto Baths of Apollo*. Oil on canvas, 24 ⅞ x 31 ⅜ in. Acquired in 1965 by Helen Clay Frick for the University of Pittsburgh Collection. © the Collection of the Frick Art & Historical Center, Pittsburgh, Pennsylvania. Photo credit: Richard A. Stoner.

Hubert Robert (1733–1808), *Memorial Garden of Lenoir's Museum of French Monuments*. Acquired in 1965 by Helen Clay Frick for the University of Pittsburgh Collection. Oil on canvas, 24 ⅞ x 31 ⅜. © the Collection of the Frick Art & Historical Center, Pittsburgh, Pennsylvania. Photo credit: Richard A. Stoner.

low with their compositions: the harmonious relationship between architecture, sculpture, and landscape.

Clapp then began to search for other Old Master paintings she could purchase. Six religious works were bought, one formerly in the Flines Convent, *Virgin and Child with Rosary* by the Netherlandish artist Jean Bellegambe, and five from the Italian Renaissance: *St. Agnes* and *St. Anthony,* two panels by Lippo Memmi; *The Calling of Sts. Peter and Andrew* by Luca Giordano; *Madonna and Child with St. Catherine* by Biagio di Goro Ghezzi; a fourteenth-century Sienese work, *Madonna and Child with St. Catherine and St. John;* and *Susannah and the Elders* from the School of Tintoretto. To further expand the French collection, Helen exchanged her Lazzaro Bastiani, *Madonna and Child with St. Dorothy and St. John the Baptist,* for a third Hubert Robert, *Adoration of the Magi.* She thus created a bridge between her collection and her father's through subject matter, linking Hubert Robert's *Adoration of the Magi* to the Bastiani *Adoration of the Magi* that she had encouraged the Frick Collection to purchase in 1935. Helen also bought Jean-Louis Demarne's *The Seine at Saint Cloud,* recalling her father's Monet, *Bords de la Seine à Lavacort* at Clayton, and the Frick Collection's Monet, *Vétheuil in Winter.*

Jean-Louis Demarne (1744–1829). *The Seine at Saint Cloud.* Acquired by Helen Clay Frick in 1965 for the University of Pittsburgh Collection. Oil on canvas, 21¼ x 17½ in. © the Collection of the Frick Art & Historical Center, Pittsburgh, Pennsylvania.

In the controversy over the art department, the university, anxious to maintain Helen's funding, tried to calm her and work out a compromise. To do this, the administration made the astonishing offer to split the department. William Loerke would teach and have his office in the Cathedral of Learning, whereas Hovey, who was granted the honor of arranging the first exhibition, and Virginia Lewis would have their offices in the new fine arts building. In another peacekeeping maneuver, the university agreed to let Helen hold her own opening ceremony on May 28, 1965, and the university would hold another in the fall, at the start of the semester. "This as you well know," Litchfield confessed to Bill Rea, "is a most unusual procedure. However. . . . it is another move on our part to try to keep things moving forward when there is no major sacrifice of principle involved."

Although tensions temporarily eased, within the small world of academia the department's unhappy state was already well known. The university was having difficulty in hiring faculty for the fine arts department. Aaron Sheon, an expert in late nineteenth-century French art then being recruited by Loerke, wondered on February 22, 1965, "One important apprehension keeps coming up frequently: Miss Frick. This is a delicate situation that you have to contend with, I understand, but I wonder if once I came to Pittsburgh I would have some difficulty staying there because of her." On March 27, Joseph C. Sloane, the director of the Ackland Art Museum in North Carolina, refused the position of building

The Henry Clay Frick Fine Arts Building with the Cathedral of Learning looming in the background, February 9, 1967. Courtesy *Pittsburgh Post-Gazette*, 2005, all rights reserved. Reprinted with permission.

director: "I fear that if I were to please [Miss Frick], I would run the real risk of losing the support of the University, and *vice versa*. The thought that I might end by becoming *persona non grata* to everyone was too vivid to be ignored." He continued, "It is, in my opinion, little short of tragic that. . . . personalities, past events, and a lack of a clear understanding of the nature of academic institutions on the part of Miss Frick account for much of the difficulty, and now it seems almost too late to arrive at a mutually satisfactory accommodation." Meanwhile, Frank Wadsworth complained to Charles Peake, "Hovey and Lewis are going ahead in spite of everything. . . . You will be interested in learning (1) that Miss Frick has sent her emissaries to various art historians to ask questions about Bill Loerke in what is a most unprofessional manner and (2) she yesterday quite suddenly told [Professor John F.] Haskins [internationally recognized for his research on ancient art of Central and Eastern Asia] that he could no longer rent the [Clapps' former] house after he has been led to believe since January that she would sign a lease for next year." Peake complained, "I don't know how much longer I can continue to try to work things out in this affair. The whole thing is time consuming, exhaustive of energy, patience and hopes."

During the first week of May, in anticipation of her opening ceremony a few weeks later, Helen ordered Virginia Lewis to remove the books from the fine arts library in the Cathedral of Learning and reinstall them in the new building. Helen had architecturally designed and planned specific locations for the folio-sized ones and wanted them placed according to her wishes. No matter that the students would be deprived of books in the last four weeks of the semester. She wanted the library to look finished for her opening.

The university found this untenable. To establish clear policies going forward, the administration drafted a joint agreement with Helen for management of the new building and the fine arts department. Called the Memorandum of Understanding, it recognized her "special competence in the field of fine arts far beyond that of most donors to universities," and stated that it was "very much in the interest of the University and the community that on certain matters relating to the management of the Building, she would be consulted or her approval attained." Helen would annually provide funds for the salaries of the museum staff, such as the two guards and the groundskeeper, as well as for the Frick Professor of Fine Arts and Virginia Lewis, whom Helen wanted as assistant director of the building. In addition, Helen would be responsible for buying pictures for the teaching collection and fine arts books and would control all exhibits, catalogue publications, and expenses for an international advisory board. Finally, she would provide through her foundation or her estate a $3.5 million endowment for the operation and maintenance of the building and the library. The university, in turn, would provide two guards, secure the library and art collection, monitor the fire alarm panel, move the slide collection from the Cathedral of Learning to the new building and—most important to Helen—neither exhibit nor teach modern art. For this she would contribute an additional $65,000 a year for books, slides, photography, equipment, and fellowships.

Dean Wadsworth argued strenuously against the agreement and was adamant on the subject of "the financial consideration between the University and Miss Frick." Wanting to wrest financial control of the department from her, he lobbied for Helen's removal as the donor. "It is important that the basic allocation upon which the department depends to operate not be in Miss Frick's hands. . . . [and] that Miss Frick does not feel that her financial support gives her an improper influence over the department itself." In addition he proposed that the Memorandum of Understanding should allow the museum "to sponsor exhibitions or lectures concerning phases of art that Miss Frick would never be willing to support, even if this meant going out and finding other sources for funds."

In the middle of these negotiations, Childs fell seriously ill with heart problems, perhaps from being stung by a swarm of bees. Fearing her brother's death was near and hoping to reconcile their differences Helen went to see him at his Long Island home. Ten years had passed since the "Nazi" Christmas episode, and since Helen was no longer on the Frick Collection board, the two had rarely seen each other. Although she had called ahead for an appointment, on her arrival the butler said she must wait downstairs in the hall. Helen did as asked but after an hour, when she still had not been shown upstairs to Childs's bedroom, Helen left. She noted in her diary, "He was sleeping," but upon later learning through family members that Childs was in fact awake, told her secretary, Julia Egan, "Childs wouldn't receive me." This time, however, there was no sparring. Time had run out. The night of May 8, Childs Frick passed away. Still hurt and angry, Helen did not attend his funeral on Long Island. Instead, on May 13, she gathered relatives in Pittsburgh for a memorial service at Clayton. When in 1969 the Long Island house was sold to Nassau County, Childs's remains as well as Dixie's (then buried in the rose garden on the Long Island estate) were interred in the Frick plot at the Homewood Cemetery, but placed well beyond the graves of Henry Clay Frick, Adelaide, Martha, and little Henry Clay Frick Jr.

By the terms of his will, Childs gave the Frick Collection the carved walnut sixteenth-century French furniture given to him by his father and the *Don Quixote* tapestries Frick had bought in 1909 on the family's trip to Spain. But the $2.5 million Helen had inherited from their mother and immediately had transferred to Childs as a peace offering—with the verbal understanding that the money would pass to Childs's children—was instead designated as an endowment for his paleontology collection, eventually housed in a new seven-story Frick Building wing at the American Natural History Museum in New York.

Meanwhile, Helen's negotiations with the university stalled over the wording Peake wanted in the Memorandum of Understanding: "nothing could alter in any way the jurisdiction of the Pitt Trustees and the authority and responsibility of the Administration to carry out established academic policies and practices." So she removed her long-time lawyer William Knox from the case and turned to David B. Buerger, the Pittsburgh litigator already representing her on the suit against Sylvester K. Stevens.

Buerger tried to move the issues into new territory by luring Peake into a secret side agreement, placing a restriction that would confine Loerke to teaching in the Cathedral of Learning. The university would agree to cancellation of Helen's commitments if Loerke taught in the fine arts building, and further, "no publicity will be given to this understanding by [Peake] or Miss Frick." Peake went wild. Such an agreement was an outright violation of the administration's ethical and professional codes, not to mention those of the greater academic world. "Morally offended," Peake replied to Buerger, "I reject categorically and absolutely your proposed secret agreement. I will not dishonor myself in my profession, nor will I jeopardize the integrity of the University in the academic community by being a party to such an unethical agreement."

On May 28, Helen Frick held her own private ceremony for the opening of the Frick Fine Arts Building, although she had not yet signed the Memorandum of Understanding. She noted in her diary, "The great day has come. . . . Family drift in and out." The employees of the Frick Art Reference Library arrived by charter bus from New York, were each given a white carnation upon their arrival to identify them as Helen's guests, and lunched at Clayton, many of them visiting the birthplace of their boss for the first time. Later that evening, Helen's close friend, the Episcopal bishop of Pittsburgh, Austin Pardue, blessed the building. It was surrounded by a seven-foot wire fence pointedly likened in the press as evocative of the wooden one her father had erected around the Homestead plant to bar workers during the 1892 strike. Helen, dressed in her traditional black evening gown and a three-quarter-length velvet jacket lined with mauve, greeted her five hundred invited guests. Notably absent were all the members of the university administration, Chancellor Litchfield included.

Clapp paid a visit four days later, and shortly after, on June 19, Helen finally signed the Memorandum of Understanding. Her friend, John Walker hailed Peake: "It seems to me you are making progress in a complicated situation, and I congratulate you." But the faculty and staff of the fine arts department were less generous. They referred to the agreement as a "Memorandum of Submission," criticizing Charles Peake for "selling the University short without consulting the faculty" and for pacifying Helen Frick "on the grounds . . . she would leave a vast sum of money to the University for art." Potential faculty around the country continued to refuse job offers and now included the memorandum as further justification.

In May, Litchfield attended a three-day financial meeting when the trustees finally confronted him on his spending habits. He suffered a heart attack and collapsed on the spot. Although Litchfield survived, Stanton Chapman Crawford took over as acting chancellor and had the unpleasant task of asking the state legislature for an emergency injection of $5 million just to cover the year's operating deficits. The trustees fully and finally realized the extent of Litchfield's "overzealous bookkeeping" and on July 20 forced his retirement.

Immediately, Helen took steps to prevent Charles Peake from succeeding Litchfield. If he were made chancellor, she notified the university trustees, she would simply cancel the Memorandum of Understanding. On August 23, Peake's name was removed from the list of candidates. To be sure there was no misinterpretation of her intent, when the university held its dedication ceremony for the Henry Clay Frick Fine Arts Building in the fall, Helen pointedly sent her lawyer, David Buerger, as her representative.

During this time Helen was also pressing ahead with the suit against Sylvester K. Stevens. Her cousin James B. Stevenson, who had given her Stevens's book and inadvertently precipitated the crisis, had warned Helen in March, "The newspapers, especially in Pittsburgh and New York, will have a field day at your expense." And indeed, when word of the mid-July hearing hit the national press, the *Chicago Daily News* cited First and Fourteenth Amendment issues and Civil Rights Act infringement: "The urgent purpose of history is not to protect the reputation of the deceased but to illuminate the present and future for the living. . . . Dictatorships have for their own reasons seen fit to hamstring their contemporary historians, with results both tragic and ludicrous."

Helen did not care. She defied the press, historians, friends, family, not to mention the First Amendment, and prepared to testify against Stevens. According to a *Wall Street Journal* reporter, Roger B. May, the Stevens case was "not unusual." In "Stop the Presses!" May claimed, "non-fiction has stolen the fiction market," and "as more writers and publishers turn their efforts toward serious nonfiction works—which often probe into sensitive and controversial areas—more and more persons are suing to block publication of works." Alistair Cooke of the *Manchester Guardian* echoed, "The courts are bulging with suits brought by celebrated people, or their heirs, to restrain the publication of biographies and memoirs more or less unflattering." Eric Maria Remarque's widow Paulette Goddard tried to prevent publication of a biography of her husband; Mary Hedy Lamarr Welsh attempted to enjoin books about her husband Ernest Hemingway; and baseball pitcher Warren Spahn went to court to keep books about him out of circulation. Two publishers were just then in court over biographies of Howard Hughes. And Jacqueline Kennedy was using out-of-court measures to prevent publication of certain passages of William Manchester's authorized biography of her late husband, *Death of a President,* by asking sources not to cooperate and by personally appealing to the publisher, Random House. She was also thwarting newspaper columnist Jim Bishop's unauthorized attempt to write a book about Kennedy's assassination. The former director of the American Book Publishers Council, Dan Lacy, was "concerned about the increase in the number of suits," and confirmed, "There's not enough to say there's a trend, but it is a disturbing phenomenon."

If there was a trend, it was one that Helen Frick could embrace, and she had no intention of being left behind. In July 1965, the case went to trial before Judge Clinton R. Weidner in Cumberland County. Helen was "an interested attendant at court sessions all . . . week," but to avoid photographers during the lunch break she reserved a private dining room in a hotel near the courthouse. When Stevens was called to testify, Helen complained to the judge that she was hard of hearing and needed to sit closer to the witness stand. The judge let her move to the jury box, so she "could hear better," and Helen seated herself in the chair most prominently in front of the witness stand.

In a July 26 interview with the *Pittsburgh Post-Gazette,* in the midst of the hearing, Buerger claimed that Stevens had "so far admitted that three of his comments about Henry Clay Frick were erroneous and had directed his publishers to correct them." Buerger assured Helen, "People will get a strong feeling that Stevens has been caught in falsehoods." Weidner had in fact ruled that Stevens must "produce detailed original source materials, such as contemporary newspaper reports and government documents, to support their interpretation." He was not permitted to call expert witnesses such as other historians. An astonished *New York Times* admonished that the judge's decision held "sweeping constitutional and practical implications for historians and book publishers." But Weidner intended to conduct his own research on Henry Clay Frick and weigh his findings against the testimony and the book. "[I] am just as capable as an Historian to read the original source material, and determine what it says," he had claimed. For his part Stevens said the whole affair had "denigrated into the questioning of historical facts in a general history

[and] means that any history might be dragged into court by any descendant of anyone mentioned in a book who is able to dig up the legal fees to start action." Regardless of his eventual decision in the case, with hearings on legal and constitutional issues to follow, an appeal from either party seemed certain. Some even believed the case could reach the U.S. Supreme Court.

Helen, ca. 1965. Courtesy the Frick Collection/ Frick Art Reference Library Archives.

Whatever pleasure Helen might have felt when the early rounds of the Stevens trial went her way faded after a thorough inspection of the Henry Clay Frick Fine Arts Building. Vice-Chancellor Charles Peake had moved a professor from the classics department into the fine arts office she had furnished for the Mellon Professor of Fine Arts. Worse, the office reserved for the Henry Clay Frick Fine Arts Professor was, as she complained to trustee Edward Weidline on August 31, "crammed full of the most hideous modern furniture you have ever seen!" She considered this "a flagrant disregard on the part of Dr. Peake of the Agreement that was signed by the University and myself! . . . I have ordered the [Henry Clay Frick Professor's office] . . . redecorated." She noted, "classes other than Fine Arts will be taught in the new building!" in order "to save Loerke's face." The acting chancellor, Stanton C. Crawford, tried to defuse the situation by instructing the budget director Robert Dunkelman "not [to] give a negative report to any request concerning that building without letting me know about it. I may not be able to solve the problem in every case, but I should like to feel that I am in a position to head off any troubles before the fact."

Soon Helen had another fight on her hands when New York governor Nelson Rockefeller announced that a six-lane superhighway was needed to accommodate north-south traffic between the Hudson River Valley and Manhattan. Two of the routes proposed for Interstate 87 ran through the Bedford area, one slated to pass along Chestnut Ridge and split Helen's Westmoreland Sanctuary from the Arthur W. Butler Memorial Sanctuary, though the two reserves were designed as one large tract. Concerned citizens, including Helen, formed an organization called the Road Review League and brought suit against the federal government. When it lost the case in February 1967, an angry, disappointed Helen made her namesake grandniece, who had moved to Mt. Kisco, "promise that [she] would never drive on it."

Also on Helen's mind was that the Frick Collection had accepted a bequest from Childs in memory of Dixie—220 pieces of blue-and-white Ming and Kangxi porcelain manufactured in Jingdezhen, China. Immediately after her father-in-law's death, Dixie had purchased most of these fifteenth- to nineteenth-century pieces from Duveen. Although a prized collection, it was offensive to Helen because it had been Dixie's. Having resigned from the Frick board, her hands were tied. Nevertheless, she found a way to voice her opposition. At Christmas, with a rueful smile, Helen gave the Frick Collection staff boxes of bittersweet chocolates, each piece carefully wrapped in blue and white paper with an Oriental motif.

The new year, 1966, began hopefully as the University of Pittsburgh considered a policy of appeasement. One suggestion was that Helen Pool Rush, dean of women, host a ladies-only tea for Helen Frick in the Heinz Room on the twelfth floor of the Cathedral of Learning. As Acting Chancellor Crawford said to Wadsworth, "Certain misunderstandings have been built up involving men, and it would be better to omit them at this stage." The trustees even revived the idea of awarding Helen an honorary doctorate of fine arts at the June 1966 commencement, or maybe at a private dinner in the fine arts building, or, if she thought that too ostentatious, at a ceremony in Crawford's office. But before any of these plans were fully discussed, Crawford, on January 26, suffered a fatal heart attack, putting everything on hold.

The university was in a real bind. Despite the elimination of Peake's name from the short list of candidates the previous year, he really was the obvious and best choice for chancellor. But Helen despised him, and, with the university's debt at a staggering $25 million, the administration simply could not risk losing Helen Frick's funding. Peake, however, was absolutely through with Helen. She refused to speak to him, and in February 1966 he complained to John Walker about "how very serious and how very difficult the situation is. I have to work constantly to keep things from blowing up. I wish so much that Miss Frick could get some insight into the nature of the academic world and understand how powerful are the sanctions of the Faculty." Indeed, Peake had tried hard to ease their differences in the Memorandum of Understanding. On March 7, he wrote to the newly appointed acting chancellor, David Harold Kurtzman, "The Department of Fine Arts is reaching a crisis in which we can no longer sustain the position of patient forbearance, of yielding to the continuing personal demands of Miss Frick . . . [and] of suffering the restraints and indignities to the University's rightful prerogatives of operation." He continued, "We have tried to avoid a direct confrontation, but it is now clear that the University is paying too great a price in the vague hope of some future bequest." He proposed a remedy: "I believe that the time has come when the University must take a firm stand against Miss Frick's prejudices and personal interferences with the proper operations of the University." Worried about "the potential repercussions of such a stand," he suggested "that a confidential meeting be held to discuss the whole situation and to agree on a plan of action."

Kurtzman tried, as had others before him, to alleviate tensions with peaceful overtures but Helen did not respond. "Unfortunately, there have been too many of these [problems] and I never envisioned such a thing when I planned to give the building to the University," she wrote on March 24. "Ever since the Fine Arts Department was founded in 1928, peace has reigned, and also with Mr. Hovey in charge since 1932. As soon as Dr. Peake arrived, everything blew up! The future does not look very happy if this attitude continues, and I did have such high hopes for this new undertaking."

In the meantime, because small art objects had been stolen from the building, Helen had hired uniformed armed guards and even had them posted during student lectures in the rotunda. Wadsworth simply could not believe his eyes. "I was both outraged and embarrassed by the very obvious presence of armed guards," he complained to Peake on March 29. They were an inappropriate, "menacing presence." Loerke complained to Kurtzman, "Miss Lewis and the guards have created a prison-like atmosphere [and] have treated both faculty and students as distinctly second-class citizens. . . . When my wife and I were in the building in the evening, Miller (a security guard) threatened that anyone entering the building after closing hours is taking a chance because he would draw his gun and shoot." According to Loerke, "Guards have even interrupted classes, walked into them and criticized student work, have stood in the hall and bellowed the name of a student to come out for some trivial reason."

The university's fine arts professors were resigning. Professor Charles Minott tendered his resignation on April 7, describing the department as a "progressively worsening situation," followed on May 11 by Assistant Professor Leonard Slatkes. "I, as well as the rest of the faculty, was appalled, not only by the contents [of the Memorandum of Understanding] but by the fact a policy statement clearly relating to the present, as well as future conditions governing the art department had not only been drafted without consulting the department, but that the document had been kept secret from the faculty." Shortly after, Professor John Haskins and instructor Virgil D. Cantini threatened to quit.

A discouraged Dean Wadsworth told Kurtzman, "The Fine Arts Department has now become known in this country and abroad as an unhealthy place to be." But the university clung stubbornly to the lure of Helen's money. Once again the administration entered into discussions with their wealthy benefactress, hoping to forge a new workable agreement. In preliminary discussions, the university said it would change the name of the building to the Henry Clay Frick Art Center and make it an independent entity with a board composed of several trustees from the Helen Clay Frick Foundation and one from the university. Walter Hovey would be the director and Virginia Lewis his assistant. The Helen Clay Frick Foundation would assume all costs.

There was precedent for such an independent organization on a university campus, perhaps the most prominent example being the John F. Kennedy School of Government at Harvard. The Kennedy family had heavily endowed the endeavor and with its independent board, according to the *Pittsburgh Press* reporter Ralph Brem, had won even "more controls than Pitt ever dreamed of handing over [to Helen Frick]. . . . Pitt was 'not alone' . . . when it comes to taking gifts with purse strings attached."

Although his plans were not announced until December 1966, Paul Mellon had embarked on a similar project but with an even more restrictive covenant to build and endow the Yale Center for British Art for his alma mater. The center, to be run independently of the university and established solely as a teaching instrument, would focus on his collection exclusively; it could not be used for interdisciplinary research. The public could visit the museum, but the building would be reserved for graduate students and others absorbed in serious study. Excited that her building would follow Mellon's model, Helen told John Walker, who was assisting Paul Mellon, "The University [of Pittsburgh] will have no jurisdiction whatever but the building will still belong to it and be related to it." Walker replied three days later. "You can count on my help to the utmost of my ability."

The University of Pittsburgh, however, changed its mind. On October 28, Buerger notified Helen, "All these discussions have been negated by the University draft which takes seven pages to say that Dean Wadsworth can do anything he wants with your money and that any disagreement will be finally settled by the Chancellor of the University." Buerger responded by telling the university attorney that "his draft was completely unacceptable" and that in his opinion the university was in flagrant breach of just about every provision of the Memorandum of Understanding anyway. Among other infractions, it had never provided Helen with a year-end financial statement, had not expended its required $65,000 for the operation of the library and building, had terminated Walter Hovey as a teacher without Helen's knowledge, had not moved the slide collection to the new building, and had never enforced the protection of books. Moreover, the university had "on at least one occasion . . . authorized the exhibition of modernistic 'art'. . . . [and] the university [claimed] it had 'no power' to agree to exclude modern art." By this logic, Buerger concluded, "Obviously, if the University has 'no power' to give you any 'control' under a new agreement, it had no power to grant you the rights it promised in the [Memorandum of Understanding]." Therefore he suggested his client do the following:

1. Decline to make any present payments whatever.
2. Remove the works of art which do not belong to the University to a place with more adequate security.
3. Insist that the University live up to its agreement, make good the breaches it has already made, and give you adequate assurance that it will keep its word in the future.

"I think the enclosed statement [from Pitt]," Helen wrote John Walker on November 2, "will shock you & I am certainly not going to accept their 'dictum.' But I am trying to control myself until after Nov. 22nd on which date we will hear the decision by Judge Weidner ré the book written by Sylvester K. Stevens containing the libel against my father. I am very hopeful of this outcome & will be in a stronger position to oppose the University if I win. . . . Of course if the University should persist successfully, I would remove everything now on loan at the Building & not another cent would I ever give towards its support."

As for the Stevens case, debate intensified in the public media. In February 1966, Stevens, overwhelmed by the financial burden incurred by Helen's suit, was hospitalized with hypertension. By March he had stabilized, and a band of prominent historians from across America had come to his financial rescue. The serious constitutional issues raised by the suit had prompted Julien Boyd, editor of the Thomas Jefferson papers at Princeton, to form a Joint Committee for the Defense of the Rights of Historians under the First Amendment—a consortium of eminent historians from the American Historical Association, the Organization of American Historians, the Society of American Historians, and *American Heritage* magazine. Helen's "ridiculous and tragic position" convinced them that her suit "presents a serious danger to the constitutional rights of all historians and authors." Her "assault . . . if successful, would inhibit [the ability of scholars] . . . to speak freely about the past based upon [their] research, and . . . would permit the descendants of long-dead historical figures to have serious books removed from circulation simply because something critical was said about their ancestors. Success in her suit would lead to direct censorship." The committee claimed that the Stevens case was in fact "the first case we know of in which a serious work has been challenged in the Courts, in which the Court has been asked to ban a book, and in which the Court has proceeded to hear the suit on the merits." Fearing Helen's possible victory or her appeal to the Pennsylvania Supreme Court or U.S. Supreme Court if she lost, Stevens's lawyer, George F. Douglas, noted she had "unlimited funds." The joint committee worried that her "victory . . . would encourage others to take similar action and soon we would be spending all our time defending lawsuits instead of studying and writing. . . . a crippling blow to scholarly study . . . and [the] unfettered flow and exchange of ideas. . . . An attack on one book is an attack on all learning."

In August 1966, Stevens appealed to the U.S. District Court in New York and asked it to dismiss the Pennsylvania case as unconstitutional interference with the right of free speech. Although the attempt generated publicity and garnered support for Stevens, the appeal failed. The federal court refused to intervene in state action. Yet this federal decision and the state ruling, still forthcoming in Pennsylvania, were subject to appeal and no one doubted that either Stevens or Helen would take advantage of this remedy.

On September 17, David Buerger defended his client to the student editor of the *Pitt News:* "Miss Frick is not conducting a crusade against academic freedom. She has sued to enjoin further publication of statements which are false . . . and defamatory. . . . The United States Supreme Court has repeatedly held that malicious libel, like pornography, is entitled to no constitutional protection whatever. . . . Miss Frick does not object to the book simply because anything critical was said about her father, but because the statements were false."

Francesco Melzi (1493–ca. 1570), *Madonna and Child in a Jasmine Bower*. Acquired by Helen Clay Frick in 1966 for the University of Pittsburgh Collection. Oil on panel, 34 ⅜ x 26 in.© the Collection of the Frick Art & Historical Center, Pittsburgh, Pennsylvania.

In the midst of such contention came news that lifted Helen's spirits. Her diary entry for November 8, election day, read, "Wonderful Republican victory!" She could take satisfaction in having played, along with a few other wealthy Republicans, a significant role in the outcome. Helen had asked for and received a list of candidates. who needed financial aid, and sent Nixon $15,000 in "early money" checks of $1,000 each for those candidates. Although June headlines in a *New York Times* article read "G.O.P. Candidates Aided by Heiress," the *New York Daily News* reported, "Nixon is Mum on Angel Role." Of the twenty Republicans on the list Nixon suggested that Helen support, sixteen won.

The Frick Collection also had reason to celebrate that fall—the final volume of the illustrated folio catalogue was finished. It again represented the first time the holdings of an American museum had been fully catalogued. Helen was also excited about her acquisitions for the University of Pittsburgh's teaching collection: a fifteenth-century Italian painting, *Madonna and Child in a Jasmine Bower* by a pupil of Leonard da Vinci's, Francesco Melzi; and three French paintings, two by artists her father had collected, *Young Boy in a White Collar* by Jean-Honoré Fragonard (now considered by either Henri-Pierre Danloux or Jeanne-Philiberte Lidoux) and Jean-Baptiste Pater's *Le Repose dans le Parc.* The third, *The Arts in Supplication,* by Carle Van Loo, is most interesting for what it revealed about the collapsing negotiations with the university. Commissioned by the Marquis de Marigny, director general of buildings, gardens, and arts for the French government in the eighteenth century and brother of Madame de Pompadour, who was then dying, the work depicts painting, sculpture, architecture, and music pleading desperately with the goddess of death, Atropos, not to cut the thread perilously resting between the sharp blades of her scissors.

But by January 1967, matters at the university had again deteriorated. Helen's cousin Bill Rea, the recently elected chairman of Pitt's board of trustees, visited her at Clayton to see if they could reach an agreement on use of the fine arts building. Also on his agenda were her delinquent 1965 and 1966 payments for maintenance and staff salaries, sums

Carle van Loo (1705–1765), *The Arts in Supplication.* Oil on canvas, 30 ¼ x 26 ⅛ in. Acquired by Helen Clay Frick in 1966 for the University of Pittsburgh Collection. © the Collection of the Frick Art & Historical Center, Pittsburgh, Pennsylvania. Photo credit: Richard A. Stoner.

amounting to $135,000. Helen stood her ground and, according to Rea, she "excommunicated" him. Since both parties had breached the Memorandum of Understanding and the trustees felt there was no future in dealing with their donor, they seized the building from her. Loerke moved into it, took complete control of the fine arts program, and terminated the employment of Hovey and Lewis effective in April. "It really was a phenomenal thing," Rea later recalled. But as chairman of the board he took full responsibility for breaking with his cousin. He turned to the state legislature for additional funding.

As the historian Robert C. Alberts noted, this "rare, perhaps unique, act of a university—especially one known to be in financial trouble—[of] telling off one of its big donors was national news." On February 8, a full week of press coverage began; some articles hailed academic freedom and others described Helen as the victim of duplicitous university administrators. Headlines in the *Pittsburgh Press* blared, "Pitt Gives Up Frick Millions in Art Fight: Friction Blamed on Restrictions, Hovey Is Out, Dr. Loerke Is In," and claimed that Pitt's "quest for academic freedom in the teaching of contemporary art" had caused the rupture. "We were given to understand that we must . . . eliminate outright contemporary art," Loerke told the *New York Times*. "It was either this or lose the department," added Acting Chancellor Kurtzman, who received one letter suggesting, "that you tell Helen Frick to 'go fly a kite.' She needs a sound kick in the anatomy. . . . Besides you and I know that her taste in art is unbelievably bad and snobbish. In short she is an [*sic*] humbug!" The next day, a *Pitt News* headline cheered, "A Brave and Wise Stand."

Although the press uniformly backed academic freedom, it offered Helen some sympathy. In its February 10 editorial, "The Frick Museum/School," the *Pittsburgh Press* reflected, "Whatever the facts, it is an affront of sorts to Miss Frick, who has been a friend and patron of the university for many years; it is an embarrassment to the university and it doesn't help the cause of art appreciation." Noting, "our art resources are not so rich that we can afford to treat in a cavalier manner any new beneficiaries," the editors recognized that there were no winners for "this will be regretted by Pittsburgh art lovers, present and future."

Helen who by now had spent $4 to $5 million just on the building, told the *Pittsburgh Press* she was "sorry that there has been such a misunderstanding and that my collection was not appreciated." The building was never intended to be "a working department of art. . . . for the mechanics of teaching art," more properly housed as it was in the Cathedral of Learning. Neither had Helen wanted her "historical museum of art. . . . changed with the addition of contemporary art. . . . There were many other galleries for exposure of contemporary art in the City but nothing exactly like the Frick building." Through Hovey she sarcastically promised that she would "not give any more money [to the fine arts department] because 'it might interfere with Pitt's academic freedom,'" and that "Miss Frick will not permit the phrase 'academic freedom' to be used as an example for vandalism in the Fine Arts Building."

Helen even discussed the situation with Nixon. On February 9, she gave the Nixons a tour of the Frick Collection and entertained them over dinner at the Frick Art Reference Library. Afterward she asked her secretary, Julia Egan, to send photographs of the Henry Clay Frick Fine Arts Building to Nixon's secretary, Rose Mary Woods. "Miss Frick thought you might hand them to Mr. Nixon to look at when he is not too busy (if ever such a moment could happen!). This is the building from which Miss Frick has been ejected."

Other friends rallied around. "I can't tell you how distressed I am," wrote John Walker on February 14, "to learn of the action of the University. . . . Pittsburgh has lost a great opportunity. . . . How could people be so foolish?" Clapp wrote Helen on February 16, "It seems to me incredible that such people would not understand, not only the great things you have done for the University, but the things you want to do. . . . It was a real shock to me that they were going to force you to accept their interpretation of its use." Helen thanked Clapp for his "nice letter" saying, "I know how it must sadden you to feel that your wonderful library should be in the hands of the Philistines! It is sad, also, that the paintings and other works of art that I have collected should not be appreciated by the Pitt faculty and trustees, but Pittsburgh at large is on my side and is waging a hot battle. It is doubtful that I may win [the building back], but I have other plans."

The heiress, now seventy-nine, was indeed building a new museum, this one on the Clayton grounds where she had once considered re-creating Padua's Arena Chapel. Under their settlement, the university kept the Eagle Rock organ, the Dossena *Annunciation* group, the Lochoff frescoes, the library books, and the office furniture. Helen was allowed to dismantle the unfinished Jacobean Room and the partially completed French Room and to remove the items she had intended for the fine arts gallery: thirteen recently acquired paintings, twenty-two Eagle Rock Chinese porcelains, thirty-three Eagle Rock Italian Renaissance bronzes, and her seven-piece suite of antique French furniture. They were, as Theodore Bowman, who was in charge of removing Helen's property, said to Kurtzman, "from the home of her father and mother and are full of personal associations." These items, combined with her father's Eagle Rock art collection, her own select group of Italian primitives, and the Flemish, French, and Italian paintings she intended to purchase for this new museum, would form an interesting small collection of Old Masters limited to her favorite periods in art. David Finley, still head of the National Trust, wrote her enthusiastically of her plan to offer an art museum at Clayton.

Reign of Qianlong (1736–1795), Bottle-shaped vase, *famille rose*, enamel colors. Height: 20 in. Circumference: 46 ½ in. © the Collection of the Frick Art & Historical Center, Pittsburgh, Pennsylvania.

New plans and projects had always elevated Helen's spirits, and the final arguments in the Stevens case on January 11, 1967, had left her happier than ever. Again seated in the jury box, Helen had listened intently as Buerger argued that Stevens was "a 'fast buck' operator, interested only in the money the 'book might make, at the expense of the still-mourning Miss Frick,'" and threatened that he would "press the issue to the highest court of the United States in the event of negation of her suit" because "First Amendment protection did not apply in cases of 'fictitious' biography." In a letter to his lawyers, Stevens condemned the judge for making "himself an arbiter on the soundness of historical writing."

But on May 24, 1967, the ruling handed down stunned Helen badly. In his decision, Judge Weidner resoundingly declared that his own research proved that Stevens's facts, except those he and Random House had agreed to amend, were accurate. In dismissing the suit as constitutionally invalid, he took the ruling as an opportunity to deride and scold Helen Frick. He found Stevens's book "milder" than most commentaries on Henry Clay Frick and even suggested Frick himself would have been "proud" of later historians' harsh representation of him. And anyway, "If everyone read a book as [Helen Frick] read this one, by looking in the index for an ancestor's name and, on cursory examination, started action to enjoin or correct the book, our bookshelves would be either empty or contain books written only by relatives of the subject." Weidner ruled: "By analogy, Miss Frick might as well try to enjoin publication of the Holy Bible because, being a descendant of Eve, she doesn't believe Eve gave Adam the forbidden fruit in the Garden of Eden, and that her senses are offended by such a statement about an ancestor of hers."

Stevens called the opinion "really something of a masterpiece." Though pleased to have won, he was nevertheless worried about an appeal. He wrote the head of the Joint Committee for the Defense of the Rights of Historians, Julien Boyd, "Miss Frick is bound to appeal in view of her personal spirit of revenge or whatever you might call it." The judge had indeed identified ninety findings of fact that went Helen's way, and Buerger intended to appeal to the Pennsylvania Supreme Court on the basis of about twenty-five of them—and he intended to file an opinion on 103 exceptions to what he considered Weidner's unsound ruling. Helen's legal team now included David F. Maxwell, former president of the American Bar Association, who was persuaded to join Buerger when Helen pleaded, "I am hopeful that we will win as this is the most important thing in my life." Stevens, on the other hand, remained concerned. "As it stands, just about any crackpot with a little money can start taking potshots at just about anything any historian might write."

In the shadow of the uncertain outcomes of continuing litigation, Helen and Stevens reached an out-of-court settlement. Helen withdrew her suit "with prejudice," meaning without option to reopen the case, on the condition that Stevens consent to correct certain erroneous statements and facts and to insert new language where it negatively reflected on her father. Both agreed there would be no publicity in the matter, although Helen's lawyers warned, "You know we can't control Miss Frick." On August 8, the day after the settlement, Helen issued a press release, copied to family and friends and to Richard Nixon, claiming victory and vindication in the Stevens matter. "I am delighted to announce that Dr. Sylvester K. Stevens has finally retracted the false statements made by him in his book about my father," read her statement. "While some other inaccuracies remain in the book," Helen said, "the really important falsehoods have been eliminated and I am very happy."

Nixon was "delighted" for Helen and sympathized "this has been a very unpleasant incident for you but you certainly have won the admiration of people across the country for the courage and tenacity you displayed in pursuing your cause." But when Stevens saw the press release—it appeared in the *New York Times* and various Pennsylvania papers—he was incensed. Her action was, he said to the press, "positively vicious and obviously face-saving. This whole thing . . . is designed to make it look as though I am retracting something and Miss Frick is graciously consenting to withdraw. . . . This is bad faith in any way you look at it." He had made revisions on only "very minor points," had corrected a few erroneous quotes and some language that might "give rise to misinterpretation." He charged Helen with "deception" in her withdrawal of the case because, as he discovered, when her attorneys withdrew the suit they had already written the "undisclosed" press release and were therefore in breach of their signed agreement. Stevens asked the Pennsylvania court to revoke the dismissal of her suit, appealed for a reopening of the case, and asked the justices "to file an opinion on the 103 exceptions so the public will see that everything [I wrote] . . . was true." To his attorney George Douglas, he complained that Helen's statements had placed him "in the minds of many of my fellow historians in the position of having deserted their cause and thus becoming the Benedict Arnold of the profession. . . . Miss Frick [has] won a major victory in terms of defaming my reputation as a historian and scholar . . . a major objective of hers from the start." Stevens's legal team also asked the U.S. Supreme Court to hear the case as a violation of the constitution. The Court refused to intervene.

On August 16, Helen sent out a second press release declaring victory over Stevens's appeal. "I realize that my success in vindicating my father will offend two classes of people: historians who write without proper research, and publishers who want to discourage all actions for libel. But," she continued, "it will encourage honorable and decent people to enter public life without the fear of having their reputations lessened by false statements about them." Indeed, in September, when Judge Weidner's ruling was upheld, Helen delivered a last counterpunch. She declared that she had "finally [been] able to clear her father's name."

The summer had been a difficult one for Helen, and not just because of the Stevens case. Her first cousin Luella Taylor was killed in a car crash on July 28, and soon after, her cocker spaniel Warey, who had been ill for quite some time, followed. "I must go abroad," she wrote in her diary. On August 30, Helen sailed for Europe.

When she returned in the fall, little had changed. Helen was disgusted to learn that the university was mounting an exhibition of modern art in the Henry Clay Frick Fine Arts Building. She was further shaken by an essay in the October issue of *American Heritage*, "Filial Piety and the First Amendment," by Oliver Jensen. Although she considered taking libel action against Jensen and *American Heritage*, she did neither. Instead, when she learned that the National Trust had given Sylvester K. Stevens an award, she dumped her anger on the Trust and cancelled her planned bequest of Clayton. In a scathing letter to the new director, Gordon Gray, who had succeeded David Finley, David Buerger wrote: "Your organization has chosen to glorify and ally itself with one Sylvester K. Stevens. . . . It would be mockery to have Mr. Frick's residence pass into the control of an organization affiliated with such a person. . . . I beg to inform you, therefore, that Miss Frick will make other plans for her residence and museum." Stevens reacted in a letter to Gray: "The Trust may be better off if it doesn't get this property. . . . It probably would have to be kept exactly as it was 'when Papa died.'"

The Stevens suit was over, but Helen continued to cast doubt on his credibility as a historian and to cloud what had otherwise been his clear victory. Her cousin Bill Rea later claimed that Helen destroyed Stevens by causing him to go into bankruptcy. "She could be absolutely ruthless," he recalled, "like a bulldog." Helen looked to her supporters to keep the pressure on and obscure the trial's outcome. Howard B. King, president of the Westmoreland-Fayette Historical Society, the governing body of the Henry Clay Frick Birthplace, distributed a letter to the society's members about the "unprecedented law suit" between "our Society's Sponsor, Miss Frick, and Sylvester K. Stevens." According to King, "the judge finally confessed his anti-capitalist prejudice" and Stevens his "amazing lack of historical research." With the many retractions Stevens was forced to make, Miss Frick had won her fight "for truth in history." "I compliment you," the harassed Stevens wrote King, "upon having added to . . . misinformation. . . . I think I know who wrote the report you sent out but I think you owe me a personal apology for having distributed it. It is vicious and full of untruths." When Stevens became the first recipient of the Freedom of the Press award given by the Professional Journalistic Society, David

Buerger wrote the *Pittsburgh Post-Gazette*, "It is hard to understand why a 'professional journalistic society' should honor a man because he unsuccessfully claimed a right to repeat statements which he admitted on the witness stand were false and which he finally retracted. If that be 'freedom of the press,' I'll take spinach."

In the early months of 1968 Helen Frick turned her attention to Richard Nixon's bid for the White House. After the rout of Barry Goldwater in the 1964 election, Nelson Rockefeller was mounting a challenge serious enough to threaten the former vice president's nomination. In a bristling January 10 letter to James Fulton, a Republican U.S. congressman from Pittsburgh, Helen wrote: "I think something should be done about the propaganda to the effect that Rockefeller would be more able to beat Johnson than Nixon! This is a great lie—but then Nelson Rockefeller will use his money to win if he can. This is so ridiculous—but it will get votes for Rockefeller!" She became Nixon's staunchest advocate and ad hoc publicist. The following day, her secretary, Julia Eagan, advised Nixon's secretary, Rose Mary Woods, "Miss Frick has reproduced two photographs of Mr. Nixon and Mr. Rockefeller which appeared in connection with an article in *U.S News and World Report* of January 1, 1968. Miss Frick felt that these two photographs were a very interesting contrast, and that anyone seeing these two faces side by side would be sure to vote for Mr. Nixon! Miss Frick would like to have Mr. Nixon's permission to have the photographs reproduced for a limited distribution to her friends."

While the race between Nixon and Rockefeller continued, Helen learned of the March 9 death of Edward Litchfield, killed with his wife, mother, and two youngest children when his private, twin-engine airplane crashed into Lake Michigan en route to Chicago. The plane had taken off despite marginal weather, the pilot was tired and unfamiliar with the Chicago area, and there were mechanical problems with the aircraft. Litchfield's body, the only one found in a life preserver, was located floating in the water five miles off Meigs Field. The pilot's body was recovered within days, but the bodies of the former chancellor's wife, mother, and ten-year-old son were not found until May. The body of Litchfield's five-year-old son was never found.

Helen, stunned by Litchfield's tragedy, was cheered by Nixon's victory in the New Hampshire primary on March 12. "I hope that yesterday's results in New Hampshire will influence some of these stupid people who say they are for Rockefeller," she wrote the candidate the next day. To her delight and "great rejoicing," Nixon continued to defeat Nelson Rockefeller in the primaries, and in August he became the Republican nominee for president.

During this period Helen was also busy with her new museum, reviewing plans by the Pittsburgh architectural firm Pratt, Schafer, and Slowick for a one-story, eighteen-thousand-square-foot building in the style of the Florentine master, Brunelleschi. The design called for an Alabama limestone facade like that of the Frick Collection, and an interior of red and pink marble, still with its fossil forms, quarried in Northern Italy near Lake Garda and in the Sierra de Sintra region of Portugal. An entrance rotunda would display the *mille-fleurs* tapestries she had removed from the Henry Clay Frick Fine Arts Building. The French and Jacobean period rooms once intended for the university would be installed, and an Italian gallery would be created for her private collection of primitives, among them her recently purchased painting by Francesco Ubertini, *Madonna and Child with Saint Elizabeth and*

Saint John. Other works would hang in the French and Flemish gallery, including another recent purchase, a work by Maurice-Quentin de La Tour, *Charles-Marie de la Condamine.* Also planned were a gallery for the decorative arts and a concert and lecture hall in rose-bud-pink velvet and damask. Helen's vision for the museum, reflecting as it did her taste in art, was unusual for Pittsburgh. According to John Walker, "the Early Italian Rooms in the National Gallery of Art and the Metropolitan Museum are the least visited of all." Furthermore, Helen was purchasing Old Masters at a time "when few Pittsburghers were either collecting on that scale or collecting works from those periods."

Francesco Ubertini, called Il Bacchiacca (ca. 1494–1557), *Madonna and Child with Saint Elizabeth and Saint John.* Acquired by Helen Clay Frick in 1969 for the Frick Art Museum. Oil on panel, 47 ¾ x 35 ⅝ in. © the Collection of the Frick Art & Historical Center, Pittsburgh, Pennsylvania. Photo credit: Richard A. Stoner.

Absorbed in her plans for the new museum, Helen nevertheless found time to support Nixon's presidential campaign by attending a rally at the Pittsburgh Arena and having the pleasure of visiting with him in his apartment afterward. "An exciting evening," she noted in her diary. Two days later, however, she entered the Western Pennsylvania Hospital for removal of a skin cancer on her eyelid.

Helen had just celebrated her eightieth birthday in September, and in the months that followed she received two especially satisfying gifts. One was a small volume of the Frick Collection paintings based on her folio catalogue and dedicated to her. The collection thanked Helen for "preserving the records of Henry Clay Frick, . . . enhanc[ing] appreciation of him as a connoisseur and collector . . . provid[ing] valuable documentation on the history of the Collection . . . [and] contribut[ing] greatly to scholarship in art history by founding and maintaining the Frick Art Reference Library." The other was the triumph on November 5 of Nixon over Hubert Humphrey. On January 21, 1969, she attended a 10:00 a.m. White House reception but stayed for only about half an hour: "Crowds. Didn't see Pres. or Mrs. Nixon but heard they arrived at 11! Raining very hard. Spent 45 min. looking for [her chauffeur] Ralph." Helen returned to Pittsburgh where she remained until February 3.

She did not slow down, however. At the Frick Art Reference Library, Helen could, and would, give directions right and left while walking to her office and attending to multiple small details. She continued to hold her annual picnic for the library staff at Westmoreland Farm, entertained friends and family there or in Pittsburgh, and added another eighty-five acres to the Westmoreland Sanctuary during 1969. After much deliberation, however, she decided to raze Eagle Rock. The house was too big and expensive to run, and many of her North Shore friends had died. Moreover, her focus was now on Pittsburgh. But in tearing down the neo-Georgian colossus, Helen was careful to preserve many of its architectural elements, both inside and out. The *Beverly Times* reported that the process was being done "with the care given to the cutting of a precious diamond," literally piece by piece, with much of the marble, the mantels, brickwork, and priceless paneling shipped to Clayton for use in the Frick Art Museum, and the wrought-iron and brick entrance gates reassembled for the new museum's parking lot. Many architectural items were also distributed among family members, and the land was given to Arabella Symington Dane, Helen's grandniece, who built her own house slightly behind the original foundations, incorporating in her design many of Eagle Rock's features.

The dining room table Helen offered to Richard Nixon for his use in the family quarters of the White House. Author's collection.

In June, Helen was invited to a White House reception for the president of Colombia. Wearing a long black gown, she was greeted by a military aide as she emerged from her limousine. Helen was escorted through the receiving line and later ushered upstairs to join a select gathering in the Nixons' private quarters. It was an exhilarating event marred only by one intensely irritating incident. According to her friend Liza Fosburgh, "A man came up and said 'Hello, how are you,' and she replied politely, 'I'm fine, thank you.' Wondering who the man was, she asked the aide to identify him. 'David Rockefeller,' he replied." An incensed Helen called Fosburgh the next morning. "He had the nerve to speak to me! Imagine!" she scoffed. "I spent the evening staying away from him."

Other old grudges still lived as well. Helen offered Nixon the table and chairs from the Eagle Rock breakfast room for his use in the family's private dining room, but not without her traditional tight string attached. She submitted a detailed list to the president of the United States advising him who could, and who could not, sit at her father's table—a list pointedly excluding Germans and Communists. Quite naturally, Nixon demurred. Helen thus informed her grandniece Arabella that she was giving the table to her. When Arabella replied that she wasn't sure she could use it, Helen snapped, "I didn't ask if you wanted it. I am telling you it's coming."

Although Nixon declined Helen's table, he remained a close friend. As a favor, Nixon agreed to consider her nephew-in-law J. Fife Symington Jr. for an ambassadorial post. Although he had failed in three consecutive congressional bids—1958, 1960, and 1962—Fife had been the Republican finance chairman for Maryland, cochair of the Nixon-Agnew finance committee of Maryland, and vice-chairman of the Nixon-Agnew national finance committee for the mid-Atlantic and southeastern states. In 1968, with his wife's financial assistance, he had donated $50,000 to Nixon's campaign. He "desired a European post," writing, "I have had a life long ambition to be ambassador to the Court of St. James or to Spain." In October, Fife received his ambassadorship—but to Trinidad and Tobago.

By fall, Helen's new museum at Clayton was taking shape. She purchased two sixteenth-century Flemish tapestries and two paintings for exhibition: a Flemish work by Peter Paul Rubens, *Charlotte-Marguerite de Montmorency, Princess of Condé;* and one Italian, a fifteenth-century *Madonna and Child with Scroll* by the Master of the Bambino Vispo. To broaden the architectural field in her museum, she bought an 1839 edition of *Picturesque Architecture in Paris, Ghent, Antwerp, and Rouen*, a book of twenty-nine lithographs by Thomas Shotter Boys, the print-seller to the British royal family.

Peter Paul Rubens (1577–1640), *Portrait of Charlotte-Marguerite de Montmorency, Princess of Condé*. Acquired by Helen Clay Frick in 1969 for the Frick Art Museum. Oil on canvas, 43 x 34 in. © the Collection of the Frick Art & Historical Center, Pittsburgh, Pennsylvania. Photo credit: Richard A. Stoner.

Helen took satisfaction in Clayton, as well as in other events at the end of 1969. William Loerke resigned as chairman of the fine arts department after six years and became professor of Byzantine Art at Dumbarton Oaks. And in December, the Frick Collection celebrated the fiftieth anniversary of its founding. Harry Grier hosted a series of events over several months, the first being "a small reception on December 19, Mr. Frick's 120th birthday, to thank the founder and the founder's family."

As the decade turned, Helen was concerned for the safety and security of the Henry Clay Frick Fine Arts Building, especially its library and the Lochoff frescoes. In January 1969, the university had experienced an uprising when approximately thirty members of the Black Action Society had seized the computer room on the eighth floor of the Cathedral of Learning and demanded changes in the university's policies regarding black students and culture. This situation was resolved through negotiation, but with an active ROTC unit on campus, Pitt seemed at risk for further unrest—even, ironically enough, because of the fine arts building itself. On March 4, 1970, at Helen's urging, her attorney warned the new chancellor, Wesley W. Posvar, against future exhibitions of modern art, stating that the purpose behind the Henry Clay Frick Fine Arts Building and the Lochoff frescoes "was not merely to honor a great American, but was more importantly to provide an inspiration to modern day students to follow his principles rather than be attracted to those of our current hippies and anarchists." The new head of the fine arts department, Donald E. Gordon, author of three studies on the twentieth-century German Expressionist E. L. Kirchner, was outraged. He issued a challenge of his own.

> One of the discussed targets of dissident protest in the Oakland area is the Frick Fine Arts Building. The reason given is its relative luxury and ostentation, considered anachronisms in an urban university. . . . I realize now that there is apparently a more specific focus to this particular protest [by Miss Frick]: the Lochoff frescoes. . . . Art and architecture students . . . appear unnaturally incensed at the stress on imitations, rather than genuineness, in art as in life. . . . If she were to believe, as I do, that the Lochoff frescoes would be safer in her new museum remote from the current crisis, then their early removal would certainly be in the best interest of all concerned.

The frescoes, however, stayed in place, and the students did not attack the building.

Helen quietly turned back to the task of accumulating more paintings for the Frick Art Museum. She acquired a serene triptych attributed to Hans Vereycke, a Belgian artist known as the Master of the Female Half-Figure, *Madonna and Child with Angel, St. Catherine, St. Barbara,* and a French work, *La Femme Qui Joué de la Guitare,* then attributed to Louis Leopold Boilly and now to Michel Garnier.

Although sixteen years had passed since Helen transferred the Iron Rail to the Girls Clubs of America, Helen had not abandoned her True Blue Girls. On August 23, 1970, she attended their Boston reunion, and she continued to help some of the women financially. Helen had long stopped funding the Iron Rail itself because increasingly the property was

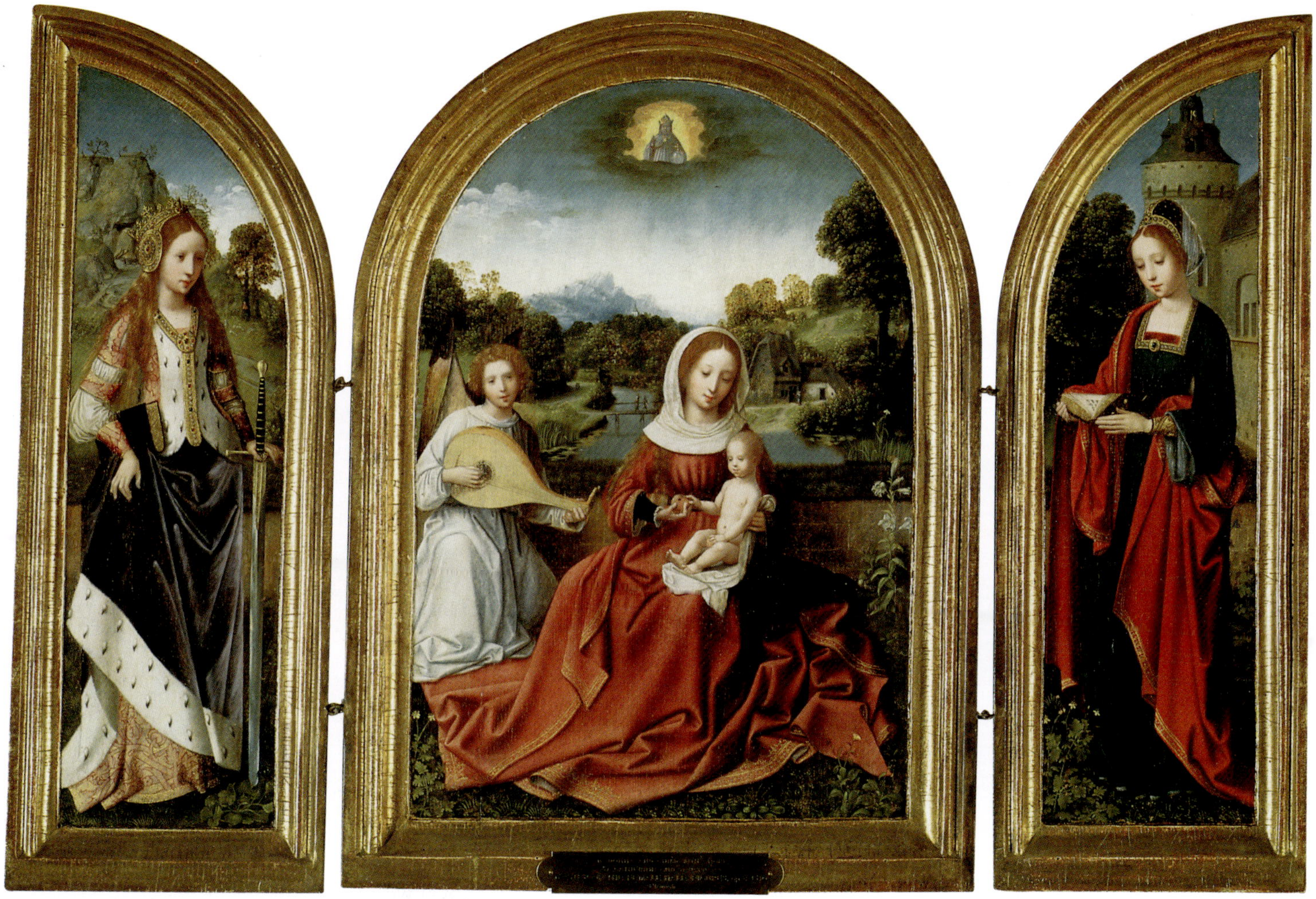

Hans Vereycke, Master of the Female Half-Figure (early sixteenth century), *Madonna and Child with Angel; St. Catherine; St. Barbara*. Acquired by Helen Clay Frick in 1970 for the Frick Art Museum. Triptych: oil on panels, 18 ½ x 22 ½ in. © the Collection of the Frick Art & Historical Center, Pittsburgh, Pennsylvania. Photo credit: Richard A. Stoner.

being used for staff retreats, not for girls in need. Gardening had ceased. Animals were nowhere to be found. And instead of hosting orphans or girls suffering from drug problems, the Iron Rail now invited only the "best" of the Brownie troops. So Helen withdrew her financial support and the Girls Clubs, unable to afford the program, sold the property to the town of Wenham. Much of the land was later developed, but the three-hundred-year-old precolonial Iron Rail house was saved. In 1976, a North Shore resident moved it to a lot in Hamilton, Massachusetts. The dwelling became an individual's home and still stands at that location. Although this private welfare project had ended after sixty years of service to impoverished working girls, Helen took satisfaction in knowing she had touched many lives. In 1981, when preparing her obituary for the *New York Times,* Helen insisted that of all the things in her life, her "greatest interest" was the Iron Rail.

Yet Helen was best known to others for her contributions in the institutional art world. Now, her newest initiative was celebrated with the October 10 opening of the Frick Art Museum at Clayton. Clapp did not live to enjoy the event; he had died at age ninety in 1969. Nevertheless, Helen had another important scholar at her side, a professor at the Institute for Advanced Study in Princeton, New Jersey, Millard Meiss. "Opening of FAM. Many out of town guests," Helen recorded in her diary. "It was an exciting evening & a very successful occasion," she wrote the FARL staff. "There were not as many people as I had hoped on account of some [steeplechase] races [at the Rolling Rock Club in Ligonier, Pennsylvania] but over a hundred came & they made up for the lack of numbers by their enthusiasm. The museum looked lovelier than I had hoped."

Helen had monitored every detail from construction to installation. According to Walter Hovey, she wanted the Frick Art Museum to have "the same delightfully warm and intimate atmosphere . . . [as] the Frick Collection in New York." After the opening, Helen began recording in her diary the number of visitors per day; in the month of November the total was 6,102. She accompanied one special guest when he toured the galleries—Donald Miller, art and architecture critic for the *Pittsburgh Post-Gazette.* When the two discussed Houdon's *Diana, the Huntress* in the Gulbenkian Museum in Lisbon, Miller was amazed by her recall. "She remembered every detail . . . even the vegetative support about its feet. I didn't. She was correct. I checked against a slide I had taken. The grasp of her mind! She would seize a subject and hold it like a trap. I had never met anyone with such concentration, such strength in a frail body. *Now I know what her father was like,* I thought." Another incident touched him for what it revealed about a side of Helen few outsiders saw. When they entered the Jacobean Room with the portrait of Princess Sophia on the east wall, Helen "walked to a draped grand piano that contained a framed photograph of her father. . . . She touched it with exquisite tenderness, oblivious to everything but memory. The unconscious gesture completely revealed her love. It was so touching; it could not have been misinterpreted."

With her new museum launched, Helen turned her attention to nephew-in-law Fife Symington. In March 1970, Fife, never happy in Trinidad, decided to lobby for the post he coveted in western Europe, and his lawyer, J. Nicholas Shriver, began working on the reappointment. In July, Fife wrote to Peter Flanigan, Nixon's assistant in selecting noncareer diplomatic career posts, that he was "encouraged that you 'at the top' are keeping me in

Helen installed the paneling from her father's Eagle Rock office to create the Jacobean Room in the Frick Art Museum. The portrait of George III's unmarried daughter, Princess Sophia, is above the sofa, facing the photograph of Henry Clay Frick on the piano. Courtesy the Frick Collection/Frick Art Reference Library Archives. Photo credit: Harold Corsini.

mind for another assignment." Symington flew to Los Angeles on September 19, to meet with Herbert Kalmbach, Nixon's personal lawyer, and to further express his dissatisfaction with Trinidad and his desire to be relocated.

Kalmbach was raising money for the Committee to Re-elect the President, known as CREEP. Among the many illegal fund-raising activities surrounding CREEP was a secret project Kalmbach had organized during the last campaign, located in a back room in the basement of a rented townhouse, and run by the White House. The Townhouse Project was devised to circumvent the $3,000 limit per candidate established in April 1970. It funneled "dirty money" to Republican candidates in the November 1970 campaign, violating the Federal Corrupt Practices Act for attempting to influence an election. Over $3.9 million was raised through the project, and Nixon himself often personally distributed the money. Because the candidates did not report the contributions, the White House gained leverage over those elected.

To raise money for Nixon's coming reelection campaign, Kalmbach was also selling ambassadorships to wealthy Republicans, a felony later cited in the Articles of Impeachment against Nixon as an abuse of power: promising employment in return for political support. Fife Symington came prepared for his Los Angeles meeting. He offered Kalmbach $100,000 on the promise of a new ambassadorial post. According to Kalmbach's worksheet, Fife wanted "Spain, Portugal, Italy, Belgium, Holland, Switzerland, Norway, Germany, Ireland,

Sweden. His wife Martha F. Symington . . . is a niece of Miss Helen Clay Frick & would be the one making any contributions to the program. Fife says that he will find out if Miss Frick can see me in NY." Kalmbach noted on his worksheet, "I want 50 [thousand dollars] this year and 50 in '72 in addition to the 16 [thousand dollars] he's already given. . . . Also, I think I am going to hit Miss Frick for 50 (with credit to be given her for what she has already given)" to give to Jack Gleason, who ran the Townhouse funds distribution. Kalmbach arranged a luncheon for Fife at the White House with President Nixon; H. R. Haldeman, Nixon's chief of staff; and the national security advisor, Henry A. Kissinger. Fife quipped to Kalmbach, "It certainly was the most expensive lunch either of us attended, I hope, but I know it was the most productive session I have ever had." On October 5, Martha Symington sent $50,000 to Jack Gleason.

Unbeknownst to the Symingtons or to Helen, the State Department was not keen on moving Fife Symington to Europe. He tended to overreact in emergencies. In April 1970, a racially motivated mutiny and riot threatened the stability of the newly independent state of Trinidad, freed from British rule in 1962. Bus workers struck over racial and economic imbalances. Black Power rioters and mutinous soldiers seized control of military barracks, and, together with armed militant trade-union workers, started to march on the capital, Port of Spain. Prime Minister Eric Williams ordered the police to shoot the rioters, declared a state of emergency, and issued a dusk-to-dawn curfew, the first since World War II. Williams ordered two Venezuelan ships that had come to the government's rescue to leave, negotiated a ceasefire, and initiated peace talks, yet he asked Fife to take the further precaution of calling in the U.S. Navy. Fife obliged, much to the concern of the State Department. Peter Flanigan wrote to Haldeman on June 17, "Regarding the 'commitment to move Fyfe [*sic*] Symington,' I did not know that one had been entered into. Symington's performance has been marginal at best, and I would strongly recommend that his desire to move up—preferably to Europe—not be fulfilled."

In the midst of these unflattering reports about Helen's nephew-in-law, the Nixons invited Helen to the June 12 wedding of their daughter, Tricia, to Edward Cox. Helen, never one for large gatherings, sent her regrets. On the day after the wedding, the *Washington Post,* followed by the *New York Times,* began publishing a series of articles based on the top-secret Pentagon Papers containing revelations about America's military involvement in Vietnam since World War II. Nixon immediately formed an intelligence unit inside the White House known as "the plumbers" to prevent further leaks to the press. Helen unwittingly chose this tense political moment to ask Nixon for a favor. On June 16, 1971, she wrote him without the knowledge of the Symingtons, and asked that her nephew-in-law be reassigned: "I am not accustomed to ask favors so this letter is difficult to write! It concerns J. Fife Symington, Jr., my nephew-in-law, who was appointed by you in 1969 as Ambassador to Trinidad and Tobago. From what I hear, he and his wife have done a very good job and my niece, especially, loves it there but Fife's health does not tolerate the hot climate. Should a diplomatic vacancy occur in one of the small countries of western Europe, I feel certain they would love to be assigned there, and it would be deeply appreciated." Nixon replied in a cordial, upbeat letter. "Knowing what a splendid job he is doing in Port of Spain, I was naturally distressed to learn of the discomfort he is suffering because of the climate there, and I do want to assure you that should the opportunity present itself, finding a more suitable post for Fife would be given the careful consideration it clearly deserves."

Meanwhile, Haldeman's assistant, Gordon C. Strachan, and Herb Kalmbach struggled to devise a solution that would keep the Frick money flowing and Fife happy. On August

10, Strachan suggested to Haldeman that Fife "be encouraged to resign and return to the United States to work for the President's re-election with firm assurance that [he] would receive a 'top European post' after January 20, 1973." Haldeman penciled a firm "NO" across the letter. Kalmbach and Haldeman agreed in late September that Symington's $100,000 contribution "should be returned since the European commitment could not be met."

Kalmbach relayed the bad news to Fife on October 9, and, as Strachan later recorded, "Symington exploded. Kalmbach says he has 'never seen anyone in such a lather.' Symington said this is a 'breach of an agreement . . . I expect men of honor to live up to it. . . . This administration has a basic lack of integrity.'" Then Symington reminded Kalmbach "his first cousin was Senator [Stuart] Symington and that Helen Frick would hear of this incident if the agreement was not honored. Symington demands that he either be physically relocated or have received orders by December . . . to be in Spain, Portugal, Italy, Belgium, Holland, Ireland, Germany, Switzerland, Norway or Sweden. . . . [He] would come in with another 25 [thousand] if one of the first six countries . . . were assured him by December 31, 1971."

The next day, Fife Symington tendered his resignation to President Nixon, after only one year and eight months as ambassador to Trinidad and Tobago. He told Haldeman on November 13, "I feel sure that Peter [Flanigan] will work things out in accordance with Herb's commitment to me." Then Fife met with the president's deputy campaign director, Jeb Stuart Magruder, but no offer was forthcoming. In an October 11, 1971, letter to Haldeman, Strachan had reported that Symington accused Flanigan of being dishonest for telling Fife he was "a terrific ambassador" while telling Kalmbach that he was "incompetent." Immediately fearful, Kalmbach wanted "to discuss the matter with the attorney general to prevent Symington's undermining the administration's record of integrity."

Two days before Nixon's February 18 departure for China and his historic meeting with the Chinese premier, Zhou Enlai, Nixon's secretary, Rose Mary Woods, contacted Helen. Woods was concerned about Helen's expressed disapproval of Nixon's trip and of her aversion to the United States establishing trade with the Communist nation. As evidence of the high value Nixon placed on Helen's good opinion, his secretary wrote her, "Before we leave for the trip to China tomorrow, I want to repeat what I have told you on the telephone! Please never hesitate to write or call me on any subject—whether you agree or disagree with policies or actions. You are a dear friend and the President is always glad to have your views." Helen remained a loyal supporter and gave $10,000 to CREEP.

She also continued to hope that her loyalty and generosity would result in a new post for Fife. For his part, Symington was also busy trying to secure it. After having refused to take back the $50,000 he had given Kalmbach, Symington donated the second $50,000 installment on April 4, 1972, as agreed to in 1970. But Gordon Strachan wrote Haldeman the next day, "Concerning Fife Symington, Flanigan remains vehemently opposed on the basis of competence. . . . Flanigan believes it would be 'stupid' to submit Fife Symington . . . [for appointment approval to Congress on] . . . cases that he so firmly opposes." Nevertheless, Fife Symington was now being considered for a post in Portugal or Yugoslavia.

While Helen waited for news about him, she continued to purchase paintings from her favorite schools for the Frick Art Museum. She bought two French works in 1971—Antoine Le Nain's *Le Bénédicité*, reminiscent of the scenes she saw when in France helping her refugee families, and Jean-François de Troy's *Portrait of a Gentleman*. The next year, Helen's acquisitions included several by artists her father had collected: Arthur Devis's *The Gardnor Family* (now considered a work by Edward Haytley), recalling her father's *Sir Joshua Vanneck and His Family*, also by Devis; *Pastorale: Peasant Boy Fishing* by François

Boucher; a portrait study of a head by Jean-Honoré Fragonard, thought to be of his cook, and now considered a work by Alexis Grimou; and Nicholas B. Lépicié's *Mother Feeding Her Child.* In 1973 Helen gave to the Frick Art Museum a Fragonard study for *The Pursuit* panel at the Frick Collection. For the Frick Art Museum she also purchased Nicholas Lancret's *Young Lovers in a Landscape* recalling the romantic Fragonard panels and *The Music Lesson* by the Dutch artist Jan Steen, echoing her father's Vermeer, *Girl Interrupted at Her Music.* For the decorative arts gallery she purchased a collection of eighteenth-century parcel-gilt Russian silver, an unusual choice for an American museum at the time. The pieces once belonged to Jean C. Herbette, the French ambassador to the Soviet Union in the 1920s. The acquisition may have been a sentimental memorial to her Russian émigré friend Andrey Avinoff, who had died in 1949, and his sister Elizabeth Shoumatoff, whose son Nicholas was taking a leading role in the activities and management of the Westmoreland Sanctuary. The pieces were bought from A La Vieille Russie, the New York store where Nicholas Shoumatoff's wife worked.

Antoine Le Nain (1588–1648), *Le Bénédicité* (*The Blessing*). Acquired by Helen Clay Frick in 1971 for the Frick Art Museum. Oil on copper, mounted on wood panel, 5 ⅝ x 7 in. © the Collection of the Frick Art & Historical Center, Pittsburgh, Pennsylvania. Photo credit: Richard A. Stoner.

Helen was pleased by the growth of the Frick Art Museum, but she was agitated by an abstract sculpture in the lobby of the University of Pittsburgh's Frick Fine Arts building. Helen asked the director to remove it, and wrote to Chancellor Wesley Posvar, "[I] was horrified to see an excruciatingly ugly modern work in the lobby. The lobby is a very important part of the building & you once promised me you would never have a modern work near the Renaissance part of the building & the lobby leads straight into the [Lochoff] Cloister." When asked if she would loan Pitt her father's collection of miniatures for an exhibition, she flatly refused.

She did, however, loan her Italian primitives to the Frick Collection for an exhibition curated by Edgar Munhall. Much as he admired Helen as a collector, as a lender she proved difficult. Mounting the show was "an ordeal, not a lot of fun." Once the checklist was printed and the paintings hung—with alarms on each one and masses of electrical cords running through the basement—Helen came over from the library every day and "fretted about the alarms." Two weeks after the exhibition opened, "Miss Frick suddenly announced, 'I think I will take them back now.'"

For the most part, however, Helen was comfortable at and content with the Frick Collection and its director, Harry Grier. But in June 1972, Grier was struck and killed by a truck when he was walking across Seventieth Street to enter the building. Helen was disconsolate. With many other Frick family members, she later attended Grier's funeral in Oxford, Pennsylvania.

The new director, Everett Fahy, pleased Helen. He was thirty-two, a former curator of European paintings at the Metropolitan Museum, young, handsome, charming, and knowledgeable. He got along very well with Helen, even though shortly after his appointment

Right: Jean-Honoré Fragonard (1732–1806), Study for *The Pursuit* panel in the Fragonard Room at the Frick Collection. Acquired by Helen Clay Frick in 1922 and given to the Frick Art Museum in 1973. Oil on canvas, 11 x 14 in. © the Collection of the Frick Art & Historical Center, Pittsburgh, Pennsylvania. Photo credit: Richard A. Stoner.

Below: Nicholas Lancret (1690–1743), *Young Lovers in a Landscape*. Acquired by Helen Clay Frick in 1973 for the Frick Art Museum. Oil on canvas, 18 ⅜ x 24 ⅝ in. © the Collection of the Frick Art & Historical Center, Pittsburgh, Pennsylvania.

Artist unknown, Period of Czar Alexei Michailovich (1660–1680), *bratina* (loving cup). Parcel-gilt silver made in Moscow, 5 ¼ in. Helen acquired eleven pieces of Czarist silver as a tribute to her émigré friend Andrey Avinoff and his sister, Elizabeth Shoumatoff, and her family. © the Collection of the Frick Art & Historical Center, Pittsburgh, Pennsylvania. Photo credit: Harold Corsini.

she muttered to him, "You are so young; you won't last long." Fahy in fact lasted fourteen years. The Frick Collection purchased an adjacent building, the home of George Widener, in 1972, and Helen responded positively to the subsequent creation of a small garden. The original driveway gate, moved by Childs and Dixie to their Long Island estate, would be reinstalled at the front of the new garden, evoking the original entrance. But an accompanying plan calling for a two-story wing had not met with her approval. She must have complained to John Walker, for he wrote Fahy, "It is sad and ironical that even the Frick and the Freer, the perfect galleries as to size, intend to grow larger. Enormousness is a disease endemic among museums. . . . Museum directors are incorrigible. Once they begin spending other people's money they will never leave well enough alone." Several years later, in 1977, both the garden, designed by the prominent British landscape architect Russell Page, and the wing were built—beautiful complements to the graceful architecture and serenity of the Frick Collection.

Meanwhile, the Nixon administration committed the final series of illegal acts that eventually toppled the presidency. On June 17, 1972, five burglars employed by CREEP were caught replacing a bug in the Democratic National Headquarters at the Watergate Hotel in Washington, D.C. Initially the story attracted little attention. Nixon quickly ordered a cover-up and hush money for the burglars, and in November, fifty-nine-year-old Richard M. Nixon won a second term by a landslide. As Stephen Ambrose remarked, "Thus began the political story of the century." On January 11, 1973, the Senate Democratic caucus voted to establish a special committee to investigate the Watergate break-in and other illegal activities by the Nixon staff in the 1972 election. By February, talk of Nixon's impeachment was growing, but Helen and Fife Symington were among the many Republicans who stood by the president. His only offense, they firmly believed, was surrounding himself with bad advisors. Symington continued to press the deputy presidential assistant, John Bennett, who was assistant to chief of staff Alexander Haig, for action on his hoped for ambassadorship. On July 23, Nixon's staff secretary, Jerry Jones, suggested Haig "should probably make a stroking call to Fife before he gets out of control."

Twenty-one resolutions for Nixon's impeachment were introduced in Congress and the press on October 23. Nixon's lawyers and Republicans concerned about the forthcoming 1974 midterm elections demanded his resignation. The new special prosecutor, Leon Jaworski, wanted to use Fife's testimony to convict the men involved in the sale of ambassadorships: Nixon, Stans, Kalmbach, Gleason, and Haldeman. Symington had left an incriminating paper trail evidencing quid pro quo in his dogged pursuit. The office of the special prosecutor alerted Symington's new lawyer, Thomas D. Washburne, who had replaced J. Nicholas Shriver on his death: "We wish to receive copies of certain correspondence between Mr. Symington and his attorneys, which refer to his contributions and efforts on his behalf for an ambassadorial position."

In February 1974, the *Baltimore Sun* broke the story of sixty-three-year-old Fife Symington's involvement in the sale of ambassadorships. "Mr. Symington's hopes for a European ambassadorship—or probably any other government position—went up in smoke yesterday with the disclosure [by Kalmbach that Fife] secretly contributed $100,000 to Nixon fund-raisers in apparent exchange for such an assignment." As the article explained, Fife Symington had been called to testify before the grand jury about the scheme and initially gave false testimony. When threatened with an indictment for perjury, he amended his statements. Kalmbach, Haldeman, and Gleason all pled guilty and joined the other officials from the Nixon presidency, including top White House advisors and four cabinet members, who were convicted and imprisoned for their crimes. But as the *New York Times* noted a few weeks later, Symington was "given a walk"—granted immunity from being prosecuted for bribery and perjury by Jaworski—"because his testimony was deemed essential to the bringing of charges against Mr. Kalmbach."

On April 12, Helen took up Nixon's defense, writing three letters to the *Pittsburgh Post-Gazette*. She warned that "the American people would regret it if Congress and the Senate wrongly accused Nixon" and urged that "the Senate Judiciary Committee . . . conducting the Watergate investigation be abolished." She blamed the scandal on the Communists: "The honor of our country is at stake if we allow our great president to be impeached by congressmen who cannot offer any proof of his wrongdoing. . . . The Judiciary Committee has fallen into a trap that has been laid by the Communists. President Nixon's name will go down in history as our greatest president."

The House Judiciary Committee approved the first of three articles of impeachment on July 27, and at 9:00 a.m. Friday, August 9, Richard M. Nixon became the first president of the United States to resign his office. According to Liza Fosburgh, daughter-in-law of Helen's friend Eleanor Whitney Fosburgh, Helen was "heart-sick about it. It was a deep blow to her; she admired him so much." True to what Bill Rea described as her "terrific loyalty," Helen continued to believe that Nixon had been maligned and persecuted by the Democrats, reasserting her position that "he got very bad advice" and that "his staff did things wrong. They handled things wrong." President Gerald Ford granted Nixon a full pardon in September, thus sparing him, his family, and the country years of litigation and trials. By resigning, Nixon could keep his $60,000 pension, a $96,000 allotment for office staff, free office space, and a $20,000 widow's pension for Pat.

Helen was miserable that fall, heartbroken about Nixon and suffering from a recurring cancerous growth on her eyelid. She remained upset with Fife Symington as well, but for the sake of her niece, Martha, chose to overlook his shortcomings. Nevertheless, she declined to join the family for Christmas in Baltimore. As she explained to Arabella, "Your mother. . . . was very sweet and cordial but I'm afraid I will be too tired to move again after my Pittsburgh [birthday] celebration."

Just before Christmas, still recuperating from the removal of a blood clot in his lung, Nixon telephoned Helen. She followed up with a letter on December 26, writing: "Your call added a great deal to my Christmas happiness. Your voice sounded so normal & as you said in two months you will be well again. At the present time, there does not seem to be war in any part of the world & this must make you exceedingly happy for it was you who brought Peace to the Earth & some day people will realize this & bless you for it!" She signed her letter, "With warm friendship," and ever after continued her tradition, begun after his 1952 "Checkers speech," of sending him a present at Christmas and a lily at Easter.

Helen returned to Westmoreland Farm and broke her hip in February 1975. Furious with herself, the eighty-seven-year-old wrote the Frick Art Reference Library staff that it was "something I have tried to avoid and stupidly had to have it happen in my own house." Taken from Bedford to the hospital in Mt. Kisco for surgery, Helen and the family feared that an operation at such advanced age might cause a stroke, heart attack, or pneumonia. After a frightened Helen tried to escape by climbing over the guardrails of her bed, one of her grandnieces spent the next night sleeping on the floor beside her bed. Arabella made special arrangements for Helen to visit her new cocker spaniel puppy, Laddie, in the psychiatric department where pets were permitted. Other family members decided she should have a downstairs bathroom at Westmoreland Farm and installed one in the dogs' quarters. When Helen returned, according to her friend Alice Thompson, "She had a fit, had the bathroom taken out, and had the dogs' room restored back to the way it was." Helen then purchased a recreation vehicle outfitted with a kitchen, a bed, and a bathroom, so she could maintain her Pittsburgh residency requirements and enjoy the eight-hour drive back and forth to Pittsburgh in comfort.

To Helen's delight, Nixon had telephoned her in the hospital. When he told her of the $2.5 million contract he had received for his memoirs, Helen wrote him, "We are all looking forward to your writing the history of your life. When it is published it will be the most popular autobiography of this age!" Nixon kept her letter and underlined the sentence reading, "It was a great pleasure to hear your voice and I hope you are feeling stronger everyday." Helen was supporting him both emotionally and financially through the President Nixon Justice Fund, established to defray his continuing legal bills. "I pray that you are feeling better," Nixon wrote her on March 21, 1975. "Pat and I will always treasure the friendship and support you have extended to us over the years." Helen replied, "The world is certainly in a mess and in my opinion, you with your brilliant mind could certainly help to straighten it out."

But times were changing, and the standards Helen set for herself and tried to impose on others were being challenged by the younger generations. In January 1975, the social activist and artist May Stevens, an ardent feminist, arrived at the Frick Art Reference Library wearing blue jeans. Ever since the library's opening in 1924, a sign in the lobby stated, "Ladies wearing very short skirts, shorts, slacks or spiked heels will not be admitted. Gentlemen must wear jackets or coats in [the] reading room." When the guard asked Stevens to change into the skirt kept for such emergencies, Stevens filed a lawsuit with the Human Rights Commission. She claimed that the Frick Art Reference Library was "acting illegally when it discriminates against my wearing clothes I find warm, practical and convenient. . . . Why am I prevented access to knowledge unless I conform to [Miss Frick's] taste in women's wear? . . . I do not see why my dress should be supervised and made to conform to the standards of someone whose income and way of life are indeed very different from mine." In addition Stevens thought the spare skirt "humiliating and unsanitary" and charged that she was "being treated differently than men who are *allowed* to wear pants."

The head librarian, Mildred Steinbach, responded to her argument. "We are a private library. . . . [and] after all, restaurants and clubs have a right to turn away women wearing pants, and we do too." She continued: "Spike heels are not permitted to protect the floors and to prevent accidents. . . . [and] the basis for these requests is [Miss Frick's] desire to create an atmosphere of dignity and decorum in accordance with the standards of good taste for the study of art. . . . This kind of apparel seems appropriate to the kind of research carried on here and we hope that our readers will help create a sense of repose where creative scholarship can thrive rather than an atmosphere of strident self-assertion." The suit failed, largely because the court had not classified matters of dress. Moreover, the library was a private endeavor and accepted no public funding. The dress code remained in place

Studio of Andrea della Robia (ca. 1435–1525), *Adoration of the Christ Child.* Acquired by Helen Clay Frick in 1976 for the Frick Art Museum. Terra-cotta relief, glazed, 25 x 17 ½ in. © the Collection of the Frick Art & Historical Center, Pittsburgh, Pennsylvania. Photo credit: Richard A. Stoner.

throughout Helen's lifetime and was not abandoned until 1989. As the *New York Post* stated, "the institution [remained] in the ranks of some of the snootiest restaurants in New York."

Although Helen's health was declining in 1976, she continued to acquire work for the Frick Art Museum. Her newest purchase was an Andrea della Robbia terra-cotta plaque previously in the Metropolitan Museum of Art and once owned by J. P. Morgan, *Adoration of the Christ Child.* Helen called it "my 'latest child'" and mused with Steinbach about her first, the Frick Art Reference Library. "To think that FARL has grown into an institution known the world over and filling a place that no other library can fill makes me so happy and so proud of those who have brought this perfection to a little creation that was never thought to be important when it was conceived."

Helen returned to the Mt. Kisco hospital in April 1976, this time for an operation on her foot, noting afterward, "I am thankful that it was a success." That summer Helen, now eighty-eight years old, faced yet another operation, this one on her right eyelid, now permanently closed. That surgery left the eyelid fixed open, a real blessing to Helen because she loved to read the newspapers and write letters. Her vision improved so much that when she visited the Frick Art Museum with Arabella—in a wheelchair with her hat on—she complained that the new della Robbia plaque recently hung over the mantel in the Italian Gallery was crooked. The carpenters thought she was just being fussy, but upon measuring they found it off by one-sixteenth of an inch.

Helen measured her time working at the Frick Art Reference Library, albeit at a slower pace and less often since her hip operation. She continued to visit her grandnieces and grandnephews and their families. And she traveled back and forth to Clayton in her recreation vehicle, casting her vote in the 1976 elections that fall, seeing family and friends, and enjoying the Frick Art Museum. In 1977 she purchased what would be her last work of art, Jean-Marc Nattier's portrait of Marie Leszczynska, wife of Louis XV. Fittingly, Nattier was the first Old Master her father had collected, the artist whose *Elizabeth, Countess of Warwick*, set Frick on his lifelong passion of reuniting long-separated portraits of family members.

Jean-Marc Nattier (1685–1766), *Elizabeth, Countess of Warwick*. Acquired by Henry Clay Frick in 1899. Oil on canvas, 32 ⅛ x 25 ¾ in. © the Frick Collection, New York.

Whether in New York or Pittsburgh, rarely a day passed when Helen did not share the company of someone who loved her. But those who visited noticed a change. Sometimes she imagined her mother was with her at Westmoreland Farm. Sometimes she would pack her bags and call for the chauffeur to take her to Pittsburgh; but after a drive around Bedford she forgot about Pittsburgh and happily returned to her garden paradise. In September 1978, when she celebrated her ninetieth birthday at the Westmoreland Sanctuary's little wildlife museum, the family noticed her hearing had deteriorated. Her vision troubled her again too, enough to prevent her from reading, seeing someone across the room, or fully enjoying her lovely pictures.

Helen's attorney, Holmes Wolfe, who had succeeded William F. Knox on his death, began to fine-tune her estate planning. The Westmoreland-Fayette Historical Society in West Overton, incorporated by Helen in 1949, was given deed and title to the Henry Clay Frick Birthplace. Additionally, to avoid paying taxes both in New York and Pennsylvania, and to consolidate the Frick family archives at Clayton and in the basement of the Frick Building, her papers and personal belongings were removed from the Frick Art Reference Library and sent to Pittsburgh. Later, Helen's office manager, Walter Cooley, asked Helen's trial lawyer, David B. Buerger, to send him Helen's files: "As part of my duties to Miss Frick, I have been endeavoring to keep her files complete and located in one place. A continuing consolidation process has, therefore, been underway for some time."

Remaining attentive to her political agenda, in February 1980 Helen asked Richard Nixon for advice on the Republican primaries. "There is such a good chance that we might have another fool like the one we have in the White House now [Jimmy Carter] and that would be most unfortunate for this country. . . . I am very much out of touch with the affairs of the world," Helen acknowledged, "and because of my eyes I am unable to read so I feel quite lost when there is a discussion regarding politics." Nixon gave her his "confidential appraisal" of Republican candidates and thanked her again, as he always did, "for [her] loyal support and particularly [her] generous contribution to the Senate and House campaigns I recommended in 1966." Both hoped for a landslide Republican victory in November and the restoration of the White House to Republicans through the election of Ronald Reagan.

On May 22, 1980, in advance celebration of the Frick Art Museum's tenth anniversary that fall, Helen gathered the Frick family at Clayton for the dedication of two sugar maples she had planted at the museum in memory of her parents. During the ceremony, her friend Austin Pardue, former bishop of the Episcopal Diocese of Pittsburgh, thanked God for Henry Clay Frick's great philanthropy, for "his genius in upholding the value in which he so firmly believed" and for his "sensitive teaching and training of his daughter, Helen, and her willingness to share his many treasures with millions of people." He also thanked God for Adelaide's "faithful acceptance of your will in the loss of her departed children." When blessing the trees he prayed, "May it please thee to grant favorable weather, temperate rain, and fruitful seasons," and then, with the family gathered around the family graves just up the hill in the Homewood Cemetery, the bishop blessed the souls of the departed Fricks.

Jean-Marc Nattier (1685–1766), *Marie Leczinska*. Acquired by Helen Clay Frick in 1977 for the Frick Art Museum. © the Collection of the Frick Art & Historical Center, Pittsburgh, Pennsylvania. Photo credit: Richard A. Stoner.

Over the Memorial Day weekend, Helen refused to leave Clayton for the farm. After much talking and reasoning with her, the nurses, by 4:30 p.m., were able to persuade her to go. But before departing, Helen slipped back into childhood and talked to pictures of her sister Martha and her parents as if they were alive, and as her nurse Barbara Hunter recalled, "held them personally, saying good-bye to them and explaining where she was going." She asked for her beloved canaries, Mr. Mignon and his family, embalmed by Childs in the early 1900s and preserved in a small glass case, and "she talked to them too and thanked them for the enjoyment they brought into her life."

Helen spent the summer of 1981 at the farm, where she entertained Richard Nixon. But she agreed that Clayton was a warmer, more efficient house than the ramshackle Bedford farmhouse, and Clayton had stairs that would accommodate a chair slide. So Helen deeded Westmoreland Farm to her namesake grandniece, Helen Clay Chace, and in June 1981 returned to Clayton, this time for good.

Back in her Father's House

In an old house there is always listening, and more is heard than is spoken.
And what is spoken remains in the room, waiting for the future to hear it.
And whatever happens began in the past, and presses hard on the future.
The agony in the curtained bedroom, whether of birth or of dying,
Gathers into itself all the voices of the past, and projects them into the future. . . .
There is nothing at all to be done about it.

—T. S. Eliot, "The Family Reunion"

Nurses assumed Helen Frick's care, and Holmes Wolfe completed additional details of her estate planning. One of the largest considerations was to sell the Frick Building and remove it from her estate. Even though Childs had created trusts for her fifteen grandnieces and grandnephews, and in the 1960s Helen too had formed a small trust for each of them, Helen's niece Martha Symington was concerned about the financial future of her children and the other Frick descendants in their generation. She asked Helen to place the $14 million proceeds from the Frick Building sale in a generation-skipping trust for the family, and Helen obliged. In February 2007, Henry Clay Frick II, the last of Helen's nieces and nephews, died. Accordingly, the trust was distributed to the next generation, Helen's fourteen grandnieces and grandnephews, just as Martha Symington had hoped.

In addition, Helen decided to give her *Pietà* to the Frick Collection so there would be no confusion over its status on her death. She was certain, however, that the trustees would honor their agreement never to exhibit the Rockefeller artworks, still at Princeton University, in her father's house.

When her beloved spaniel Laddie died at the veterinary hospital during the summer, no one wanted to tell Helen the bad news. The day after the dog's death, Clay Frick summoned his courage and told her by telephone. According to one of Helen's nurses, Barbara Hunter, she didn't cry. "Yes," she said, "I understand. No pain. Thank you, Clay." Stoic though she appeared, Helen was devastated. She insisted on having Laddie's body brought to her, and even though he had been dead more than twenty-four hours, she stroked his fur and talked

Opposite: Helen returned to her childhood bedroom, unchanged since 1901, when this photograph was taken. Above the mantel is a portrait of Martha (left), Helen (center), and Childs (right). A posthumous photograph of Henry Clay Frick Jr. is on the left corner of the mantel. Jean-François Raffaëlli's *Woman in a Dressing Gown* is on the right.
Private collection.

to him. Then she had a small grave dug for him in the dog graveyard next to the playhouse, and with Helen "all dressed up," the funeral service began. Helen recited the prayers, but she couldn't see Laddie or the flowers. After his body was lowered into the ground she asked Barbara to describe every detail, and then flatly began to deny his death.

A new black cocker spaniel named Welcome brought Helen much enjoyment that year, as did the autographed copy of Nixon's latest book, *Leaders,* sent by Nixon for Christmas 1982. Walter Cooley, thanking him on her behalf, wrote "As you may remember, Miss Frick's sight has not been good enough for her to read for herself. . . . [but] her nurses have been reading to her. . . . I just wanted you to know that she has received and is enjoying your thoughtful gift and under other circumstances she would convey her most cordial greetings." Nixon replied ten days later. "Of the literally thousands of people all over the world we have met in our travels, Miss Frick rates at the top of the list as far as Mrs. Nixon & I are concerned. For grace, intelligence & courage, there are few who are in her league."

Helen's nurses in the Clayton library in spring 1984. In the front row, left to right, are: Donna Williams and Sister Miriam of the Sisters of Charity in Pittsburgh. Standing, from left to right are: Sarah Gallagher, Barbara Hunter, Helen Kutch, and Ruth Mansfield. Courtesy Hills Studio.

In her decline, even Helen's sense of humor never waned. According to her grandniece Arabella Symington Dane, in these last two years of her great-aunt's life she "still did funny things." One day when Barbara Hunter brought in the breakfast tray, Helen said, "You look tired," and beckoned the nurse to take her place in the bed. Helen, giggling, then proceeded to serve Barbara breakfast.

For Barbara and the night nurse, Ruth Mansfield, taking care of Helen was "a very challenging home case," and not just because of her personality. Helen was "always awake and kept three shifts moving. Hyper-vigilant, she was afraid of sleep, afraid of dying." To calm her, the nurses wheeled Helen from one room to another during the day, letting her sit in each room, surrounded by childhood memories and falling silent "as if she were in some deep communion, in deep and private thoughts, reliving her experiences with her parents." Many days Barbara also wheeled Helen down to the Frick Art Museum.

Despite her weakening condition, Helen never turned away a visitor. One Easter, when Helen organized a piano recital at Clayton by Byron Janis, whose career she had patronized, Barbara kept the secret that Helen's hearing "had become so bad you had to speak right into her ear." When Janis played "many of her favorite pieces . . . after each she applauded and smiled. I don't think to this day that anyone realized she hadn't heard a note of the music. . . . She pretended to listen attentively, and she watched and applauded at the right moments." Afterward, when Barbara helped Helen get back into bed, "she asked, as she had on other occasions, 'Well, Barbara, did I carry it off?' "

In these dark, sleepless hours in the stillness of a house where time had stopped, Helen turned to ruminations about Martha's death. She explained to Barbara and Ruth that painkillers, X-rays, and antibiotics were largely unknown in the early 1890s, and remembered how her father told Martha "to just bite his fingers when the pain was bad," and how this left a scar on his hand. Then she enumerated all the things her father had done for her, Helen, and claimed that she was number one in his life. Yet at the same time she complained of being "unworthy of him, and of her mother, and of God because she had not lived up to Martha." Pointing to the large picture over the mantel in her bedroom of herself with Martha and Childs, Helen identified herself as "that homely little girl in the middle."

Her immutable and finally ungovernable sadness for what was and for what might have been unleashed a stream of guilt and self-recrimination for having failed her father, and for not being able to fill the void left by her deceased sister. Fortunately, the Reverend Philip Tierney, a man Helen liked and trusted, entered her life and earnestly tried to bring her peace. "Why," she pleaded to Tierney and Barbara, "won't God let me die so that I can be with my father and mother?" And then came chilling words: "My Father in heaven will not accept me because I have failed my Father on earth."

When Tierney left Helen's room, having tried to assure her that God's love was not based on debt and payment or her obligations to her father, she was able to sleep, sometimes for an hour and a half. Struck by her imploding despair, her haunting emotional, psychological, and spiritual rupture, Tierney later confessed he saw Helen Frick as a "prisoner of her father and of the Frick family, a museum-piece too fragile to be touched, and unable to leave." To him "Miss Frick was the ultimate scapegoat, locked away in Clayton, a cold, dark, lifeless, and oppressive mausoleum, a person who had lived—and was about to die—to redeem her father."

In 1984, Clay Frick and the Frick Collection trustees, knowing that Helen could not live much longer, and assuming that she was going to leave a handsome endowment to the Frick Art Reference Library, had embarked on a plan of expansion and revitalization. Although Helen was still the director and legally it belonged to her, not the Frick Collection, Clay and the trustees had officially merged the two entities. That summer, Clay flew in from New York and joined Helen's Pittsburgh office manager, Walter Cooley, and her lawyer, Holmes Wolfe, for a meeting in Helen's bedroom. Clay insisted Helen resign from the library "for voting purposes [and] because having her as director was inconvenient. They needed an active participant, someone who could be on top of things." Maintaining her dignity and composure, while Barbara explained what the men demanded, Helen offered alternative after alternative. She could vote by absentee ballot. They could hold meetings at Clayton. She could fly to New York. But the men were insistent. Helen finally capitulated, but not until, her nurse Barbara remembered, "putting each of them through the ringer before she did. There was never a tear, no expression that a major calamity had happened, that they had stripped her." The effect on Helen was as if "her child had been stolen, and her power had been completely taken away. And then," according to Barbara, "a big change came over her. She withdrew, rarely spoke, and began to lose her will to live."

Helen Clay Chace, then a trustee of the Frick Collection and of the library, often visited her great-aunt and remembered the aftermath of the meeting: "She turned to the wall and wanted to die." Helen Sanger, who had succeeded Steinbach as head librarian, claimed that after the torturous meeting "Miss Frick was sorry she had signed the papers and felt she got talked into it." But Helen had a secret, some cold comfort she could take from being pressured to abandon her child. The fallout from her will would settle old scores with the trustees, and this one as well. With no endowment bequeathed, financial havoc would follow for the Frick Collection.

Helen soon refused to eat. She chose the clothes for her burial and the format of her funeral service, including the message she wanted Tierney to deliver in his eulogy and the selection of her favorite hymns. Tierney had become "her dearest friend," and somehow he was able to move Helen beyond fear and guilt, beyond her feelings of unworthiness, into a space where she could accept death, "thrilled," as Barbara said, "and delighted to know she was worthy of God's love, that she hadn't had to earn it."

Though Helen was ready to die, her nephew Clay Frick, a doctor, believed he had to stop her from starving herself. Against Helen's expressed wishes, Clay ordered intravenous feeding. Helen ripped the needle out of her arm. When Martha Symington came to Clayton about two weeks after the feeding had started and heard "the unmerciful screams from Miss Frick, screams that took a lot of effort," she put a stop to the ordeal. "This will not happen again," Martha promised her aunt. "We will not hurt you any more." She also asked the family to pay their last respects, and then to visit no more. "The visits," she said, "just keep her here."

Helen continued to refuse nourishment and lingered, without pain, during the autumn of 1984. She had recurring visions of her sister Martha and of Adelaide. Then, on November 9, around 12:30 p.m., the telephone rang. Martha Symington had called to see how her aunt was doing, and in that moment, Helen Frick slipped away.

At about 4:30 that afternoon, Clay Frick told the Frick Art Reference Library staff that his aunt had died. Helen Sanger assembled everyone in the main reading room, and in a small ceremony she and Edgar Munhall placed an arrangement of white flowers beside a framed photograph of Helen. The library remained open, and at the Frick Collection the American flag was lowered to half-mast for a week. The faculty of the Henry Clay Frick Fine Arts Department at the University of Pittsburgh purchased a twelve-volume set of *Storia dell'Arte Italiana* in her memory.

Helen's funeral took place on Monday, November 12, in the enclosed porch at Clayton. Family members, numbering about thirty, were seated there, facing the burl wood coffin; guests filled the adjoining parlor. Tierney prayed that the mantle Henry Clay Frick had passed to his daughter Helen—the pain, the suffering, the wrongs she defended against—would now be borne by Jesus Christ, and not by any other member of the Frick family. Snow swirled as the mourners walked to Helen's grave in Homewood Cemetery and watched her coffin being lowered into the steel vault.

Former president Richard Nixon wrote Clay Frick on November 29, "What I particularly admired about her was her fierce loyalty to the memory of her father." But the *Pittsburgh Press* saw this loyalty in another light, describing Helen Frick as "a shadowy queen ruling an empire of family art and fortune . . . [who] cast only a faint outline across the public landscape. . . . Indomitable, generous, intensely private, and to some, eccentric, she labored through the decades as the fierce protector of her father's name."

Helen Frick's will, executed on December 8, 1981, caused much consternation. Although her personal possessions not reserved for exhibition in Clayton—various books, paintings, jewelry, furniture, china, glass, silver, and linen—were given to family members, her fortune was bestowed elsewhere. Having created the $14 million trust from the sale of the Frick Building, her will stated that no further monetary bequests to family members were forthcoming, "not only in view of earlier gifts by me to them, but also because of my concern, which I know they share, that . . . the Helen Clay Frick Foundation be adequately funded to further objectives to which we have long been devoted."

More than $250,000 was given to staff at the Frick Art Reference Library, the Westmoreland Sanctuary, the Henry Clay Frick Birthplace, and the Frick Art Museum at Clayton. In addition, Helen established $500,000 in pensions for two personal employees. She donated the two Francesco Guardi paintings of Venice in the main reading room at FARL to the Frick Collection, along with Andrea di Bartolo's *Madonna and Child* and five English portrait prints she had inherited from her father. Her collection of Italian primitives was given to the Frick Art Museum in Pittsburgh, as well as Fragonard's study for *The Pursuit,* de Lyon's *Gabrielle de Rochechouart,* and her three Houdon sculptures: *Bust of Claudine Houdon, Bust of Madame Houdon,* and the *Vestal Virgin.* Her valuable research on Jean-Antoine Houdon and the manuscript whose publication had been halted during the Rockefeller controversy was given to the Bibliothèque de la Ville de Versailles in France. She left the Eagle Rock piano to the Frick Art Museum, where it had resided in the trustees' room since the opening. The piano, like all her gifts to the museum, was never to be disposed of or sold. Helen also left $30,000 for the maintenance and upkeep of the Frick family graves and directed that fresh flowers from the Clayton greenhouse be placed on them regularly. Bequests totaling $80,000 went to the churches she frequented, and a $300,000 trust for the maintenance of Westmoreland Farm passed almost immediately to the Westmoreland Sanctuary when her grandniece sold the property.

Jean-Antoine Houdon (1741–1828), *Vestal Virgin.* Plaster, 25 ½ in. Acquired by Helen Clay Frick in 1973 for the Frick Art Museum. © the Collection of the Frick Art & Historical Center, Pittsburgh, Pennsylvania. Photo credit: Richard A. Stoner.

To ensure Clayton remain an all-Frick house museum, Helen instructed that the house and the surrounding property and buildings, with all the tangibles not otherwise bequeathed, become the property of the Helen Clay Frick Foundation "for the purposes of public exhibition and preservation, as a historic house and estate, of a home occupied in the late Nineteenth Century and early Twentieth Century by an industrialist, philanthropist and connoisseur of the Fine Arts and his family." Her will retained the 1950s stipulations that no gifts or objects could be accepted for exhibition unless given by blood relatives of Henry Clay Frick (and then only if in keeping with the house) and that the architectural style could not be altered and the internal structural arrangement could not be changed or additions made.

Helen's will was a blow to the expectations of the Frick Collection. There was no endowment for the Frick Art Reference Library. On March 31, 1947, at the inception of the Rockefeller crisis, when Helen established the Helen Clay Frick Foundation, she put all her trust funds into it, including FARL Trust 1, created in 1933 when she signed the agreement with the Frick Collection, and FARL Trust 2, created on December 7, 1934, just prior to the opening of the new library. Upon her death, the income from Trust 1 in excess of the $113,300 required by the 1933 library agreement reverted to the foundation, as did the more than $33 million in assets. From this account, only enough principal to produce the agreed to $133,300 in annual income could be placed into a new trust for the library. Regarding Trust 2, Helen had retained her power of appointment, and at her death its assets of $310,000 were transferred to her foundation; only income on this amount was to be paid to the Frick Collection. By the terms of Helen Frick's will, the library stood to receive only an approximate $150,000 annually—less than one-fifth of its budget.

In abandoning the library, she had placed its financial burden squarely on the shoulders of the Frick Collection trustees. According to Holmes Wolfe, who drafted Helen's final

Piero della Francesca (1410/20–1492), *The Crucifixion*. Tempera on panel (irregular), 14 ¼ x 16 ¼ in. © the Frick Collection, New York, bequest of John D. Rockefeller Jr., 1961.

will, she had changed the document many times over the years, but provisions concerning the library had always remained the same. "Toward the very end of her life she felt she had done all she had to do for FARL and that the principal of her concern was the future of Clayton as a house-museum. . . . She felt after the trusts for the benefit of [FARL], she did not owe more to it. When the last version of her will was drafted, she had mentally cut her [financial] connection to the library."

When the library staff and the Frick Collection trustees learned the terms of the will, Helen Sanger said they were "astonished, mystified," and even "puzzled." The library required an endowment of $34 million to continue operating, "not one cent of which," as the *Pittsburgh Post-Gazette* pointed out, "was yet secured [at Helen Frick's death]." Noting that the assets Helen had set aside for the library in Trust 1 and Trust 2 had for the most part passed to her foundation, "a shudder went throughout the international art world."

A shudder also went through the Frick Collection. Bitterness over Helen Frick's will was extreme. The Frick Collection trustees were so furious with Helen they delivered her a posthumous insult. Although she had given her *Pietà* on the understanding that the Rockefeller works would never be exhibited in the Frick Collection, immediately after Helen's death her nephew Clay called for a standing vote to provide for the return of those pieces from Princeton, including the badly damaged "rag," *The Crucifixion*. Some family trustees abstained because, according to Helen Clay Chace, "they felt this was a betrayal of our great-aunt." Yet Helen Clay herself voted for the return and exhibition of the Rockefeller pieces: "I was mad at her for not funding the library," she recalled. The trustees in fact were so mad at Helen Frick that they made no statement about her death in the Frick Collection trustee minutes.

Meanwhile, a bewildered Clay Frick tried to assure everyone that library operations would continue in the same manner as before. He was, after all, president of the Frick Collection, the Frick Art Reference Library, and now the Helen Clay Frick Foundation. The library, he reasoned, could still be funded with annual grants from the foundation. But in a backhanded way, Helen had at last succeeded in taming the Frick Collection trustees, who henceforth had to come begging to her foundation.

Within two years of her death, by 1986, the library's financial need was so acute that Martha Symington, by then trustee emerita, suggested the collection "divorce" the library—sell it to the Helen Clay Frick Foundation or to another entity "in view of the fact that the Frick Collection faces a huge annual deficit now and in the future, and [because] the Collection has become (and will become even more so) dependent on hand-outs from the Helen Clay Frick Foundation over which it has no control except the good will of its present president [her brother Clay Frick]." She continued:

> I am aware of the time and effort that went into combining the portfolios and pension funds of the two institutions but in my opinion this has proven to be an experiment that failed. What was done can and *must* be undone. I assume that the Library will continue to be dependent on the H.C.F.F. which is completely correct. The F.A.R.L. is a Helen Clay Frick thing—as is the project at "Clayton". . . . The Frick Collection is not. It is Grandfather's monument and should stand on its own feet, totally independent of anything his daughter subsequently created.

Trustee Alfred H. Howell replied to this suggestion, "We do have a legal obligation to take responsibility for the Library which cannot be set aside."

When Charles Ryskamp, a Princeton University professor of eighteenth-century English and the former director of the Morgan Library, became director of the Frick Collection the following year, operating costs for both the collection and the library had increased, placing, as the *New York Times* reported, "[an] added burden on the income from the [collection's] original endowment." Ryskamp complained, "No one understood it. . . . Miss Frick loved the Frick Library. Throughout most of her life it was the project that meant the most to her. The general feeling is one of having been orphaned."

By 1989, five years after Helen's death, the library's financial situation was dire. According to the *New York Times,* $15 million was needed "to avoid a curtailment in services." The Frick Collection trustees had wearied of making funding requests to the Helen Clay Frick Foundation and now lobbied for an endowment. Clay Frick, still head of the Frick Collection, the Frick Art Reference Library, the Helen Clay Frick Foundation, and now also the Clayton Corporation, a subdivision of the foundation to renovate Clayton into a public house museum, decided to simply transfer $30 million—almost one-third of the foundation's assets—to the Frick Collection for the library. Some of the foundation trustees were not so inclined. By their reckoning, since Helen had not provided an endowment for the library, she had indicated that no assets should be transferred to either the library or the Frick Collection. Her foundation had one priority—the restoration and maintenance of her home and art museum at Clayton.

Immediately after Helen's death, restoration of Clayton had commenced. The architect in charge, Thierry Despont, said, "We are trying to recapture the feeling, even the smell and the sound of the house." Two hundred craftsmen had been hired for the renovation, while the detailed archives provided the names of the original suppliers of anything that needed to be reproduced. In an effort to restore Clayton to its original splendor and to research the lives of Henry Clay Frick and his family as dictated by Helen's will, papers from the Frick Building basement had been brought to the Carriage House and incorporated with those from Clayton and the Frick Art Reference Library.

After much wrangling about the fate of the Frick Art Reference Library versus the future of Clayton, in 1989, the Helen Clay Frick Foundation trustees reached a compromise. They decided to curtail the foundation's grant program for other nonprofits and instead awarded the library a $15 million one-time-only challenge grant. To satisfy the grant, the Frick Collection trustees had to match that amount; should the library fail, the money was to be returned to the foundation. Although the challenge grant was met, it proved insufficient to sustain the library. Ryskamp remained concerned. "The Frick has never solicited money," he said, and "even if the [$34 million] goal is reached, the library will still need $500,000 a year in operating funds. . . . The Collection can't ruin itself for the library." Whereas "we were active in acquiring art in the 1960s," when Helen Frick was alive and funding the library, "we are not acquiring art now."

By March 1993, the endowment for the library stood at over $25 million, but to meet its estimated annual operating costs of $2.5 million, another $9 million still needed to be raised. The trustees never were able to make up the shortfall. In 2005, the library lost about $1 million, and although the reasons were not disclosed, the Frick Collection's assets had fallen from approximately $400 million in the 1980s to approximately $225 million in 2005. It, too, loses about $1 million per year. Helen Clay Chace, then president of the board, acknowledged in the 2005 annual report, the situation had made "our financial picture the most challenging in the institution's history." By 2007, the Frick Collection seemed to be on more stable financial footing. Board president Margot Bogert recognized this in the *Frick Collection Member's Magazine* of winter 2007. Although the financial statement did not include a cash flow analysis, Bogert claimed that the Frick Collection enjoyed a financial year that was "one of the strongest in the Frick's history." She confessed, however, to the very situation Helen Frick had anticipated. The collection must "raise a substantial portion of [the] annual budget from . . . other income beyond our endowment [and] now confronts steeply increased needs for fundraising."

At Clayton, almost $6 million was spent by the time the house, described by the *Pittsburgh Press* as "the sole surviving mansion in what was once a neighborhood of millionaires," opened to the public on September 22, 1990. David Sallinger of the *Daily News* acknowledged, "Clayton is considered one of the best preserved and documented examples of late Victorian life anywhere." In 1996, the foundation endowed the house museum, now known as the Frick Art & Historical Center, with $55 million, boosting its endowment to $75.6 million. In a reorganization effort, the non–Frick family trustees on the foundation board resigned to join the center's, and the foundation's charter was amended to expand the number of trustees so Helen's grandnieces and grandnephews could sit on its board. The foundation's grant program was revived, and from its remaining assets of $20 million, Clay Frick, his wife, and Helen's grandnieces and grandnephews were given the right to request funds for their favorite charities. With Clay Frick still head of the Frick boards, and with four of Helen Frick's grandnieces and grandnephews serving as trustees of the Frick Collection and the Helen Clay Frick Foundation, funding of the library and the Frick Collection has continued.

Helen Clay Frick was back in the news in 2000. Her grandnieces and grandnephews, wanting control over the family archives, voted to move the historic papers stored in Clayton's carriage house to the Frick Art Reference Library in New York, even though a professional archivist had been hired in the late 1990s to properly catalogue and maintain the papers on the historic site in Pittsburgh. Of the 1,500 linear feet of archival material, not more than an estimated 10 percent concerned the library or the Frick Collection; 90 percent dealt with the social, business, and philanthropic history of the Frick, Overholt, and Childs families, all legal residents of Pennsylvania. The center's lawyer, who was also legal counsel for the foundation, together with the Frick family trustees on the center's board—also serving in a conflicted capacity as trustees of the Frick Collection and of the foundation—had warned the nonfamily trustees of the center against filing an objection. The center often depended on the foundation for extra funding, and, the foundation argued, the archival material could be digitized.

In a family fight played out in the press and the Allegheny County Orphan's Court, Arabella Symington Dane and her cousin Edward Weidline Jr., formerly a trustee of the foundation and of the center, filed an objection to the removal of the archives, with the support of Arabella's sister, Martha ("Martie") Frick Symington Sanger (this author). They cited article 1 of Helen Frick's will:

> I give . . . to the Trustees of the Helen Clay Frick Foundation . . . all the paintings, statuary, works of art, books, furnishings, and equipment and other tangible personal property which at the time of my death shall be contained in or usually kept by me in said [Clayton] buildings. . . . [and they] shall be held, maintained and administered in perpetuity by said Trustees for the purpose of public exhibition and preservation, as a historic house and estate. . . . [and] maintained and administered for the sole use of the public by way of free exhibition within the Commonwealth of Pennsylvania.

Helen in her nineties. Author's collection.

Since the Frick Art & Historical Center did not want the papers, the University of Pittsburgh and the Historical Society of Western Pennsylvania offered to house them. But the foundation trustees, anxious to get the archives under Frick Collection control in New York, rejected their proposals. Working with the Frick Collection's counsel from Vanderbilt Webb's former firm, Patterson, Belknap, and Webb, they argued that because article 1 did not specifically mention the archives, the papers legally fell under article 7, the residuary clause giving the foundation trustees the right to dispose of "all . . . property . . . of whatsoever nature . . . not otherwise disposed of by the prior provisions."

Meanwhile, unbeknownst to Arabella and Edward, the foundation trustees and the University of Pittsburgh announced a "settlement agreement" to the press. They would split the papers between the Frick Collection and the university. Since the university had no legal standing and the so-called settlement agreement was hatched in secret, the court immediately ordered the foundation trustees and Arabella, Edward, and Martie into mediation. The negotiations failed and the case went to trial, but only as to the merits of the secret settlement agreement. The agreement stood. Helen Frick's intentions for the archives were not permitted into evidence, and the judge ruled that neither Arabella nor Edward had legal standing, even though at that approximate moment a Philadelphia court had recognized the legal standing of Barnes Foundation trustees in their battle to move that collection from Bryn Mawr to Philadelphia. The archives were, therefore, ordered split between the Frick Collection and the University of Pittsburgh. Helen's friend Liza Fosburgh, reacted: "She would roll over in her grave. She is really rolling over in her grave."

The Frick family archives removed from Clayton will play yet another role in years to come. Although the Frick Art Reference Library will run out of storage space by 2010 (even with digital conversions of data), the Frick Collection plans an architectural expansion, as funding becomes available, to house material on the decorative arts and to include a Center for the History of Collecting at the Frick Art Reference Library. The family archives will serve as the new center's nucleus.

The death of Helen Frick marked the end of the industrialist father–daughter heiress generation. True, multibillionaire Doris Duke would survive Helen by nine years, but the 1960s had seen the passing of Electra Havemeyer Webb and Ailsa Mellon Bruce; the 1970s the passing of Marjorie Merriweather Post, Ima Hogg, Peggy Guggenheim, and Barbara Hutton. Like Helen, these father's daughters had used their fortunes to serve art and humanity. Webb's passion for American folk art led her to found the Shelburne Museum, a twenty-acre property in Vermont, studded with thirty colonial houses that had been moved there and used as exhibition space for her vast collections of pottery, quilts, wrought iron, carriages, and paintings. Ailsa Mellon Bruce gave her collection of ninety Impressionist paintings to the National Gallery together with an endowment for future purchases, and also financed the acquisition of paintings for the Carnegie Art Museum and the Virginia Museum of Fine Arts in Richmond. Marjorie Merriweather Post endowed her home in Washington, D.C., Hillwood, with her extraordinary collections of eighty-four Russian icons and of Faberge, the finest examples known outside of Russia. Ima Hogg restored the birthplace and first home of her father, Governor Hogg, and donated parks in his name. She also followed her own course by founding the Houston Child Guidance Center, the first of its kind in America, establishing the Hogg Foundation for Mental Health and Hygiene, and endowing her home, Bayou Bend, a showcase of period rooms with furniture and decorative objects of upper-class Americans spanning the colonial period to the antebellum era. Outlandish Peggy Guggenheim left her house in Venice, together with her collection of modern art, to the Guggenheim Museum, and last of all, Barbara Hutton, tortured by her wealth, accomplished her goal, to dissipate her fortune, "This root of all evil, to get even with [her father]." On her deathbed, holed up in a bare room in the Beverly Wilshire Hotel in Hollywood, emaciated from years of alcohol and drug abuse, she asked of her fortune: "It's nearly all gone, isn't it?" "Just about," her lawyer replied. Hutton died with $3,500 in her bank account.

Unlike Helen Frick, however, these father-daughter heiresses (with the exception of Hutton) continue to have their achievements honored, celebrated, and upheld, leaving Helen a lone shadowy figure, largely unrecognized for her many endeavors, including the critically important role she played in the development of the Frick Collection; the creation of the Frick Art Reference Library; her many pioneering, philanthropic endeavors such as the Iron Rail; the founding of the University of Pittsburgh's Fine Arts Department and its building; the gifting of Frick Park and the Westmoreland Sanctuary; the restoration of Henry Clay Frick's birthplace; and her success in acquiring art for four different collections. The tributes to Helen at the Frick Collection are minimal: the dedication to her of the small Frick catalogue published in 1968, a slight reference to her contribution to the collection's development in the introductory video, and notations of her gifts in the provenance sections of Frick Collection publications. The direction of the collection, too, has moved away from Helen's undeniable influence. As she feared, many of her father's decorative objects and paintings are in the vault, and gifted or loaned objects are showcased in their stead. At a financial crossroads and no longer able to afford great paintings, the collection is instead purchasing less costly sculpture and decorative objects for display in the galleries and at a future date for the second-floor rooms once fancied by John D. Rockefeller Jr. for his porcelain collection. A curator of decorative objects is to be hired, and now, objects of scholarly interest are being purchased, some of them controversial because they lack the high standard of artistic beauty demanded by Helen and her father.

At Clayton in Pittsburgh, Helen Frick is also uncelebrated. Although she lived there for ninety-six years and founded the historic site, there is no founder's day celebration, no memorial plaque, no garden dedicated to her. Although a new visitors' center is being planned for the site, "to unify the entities and to place Henry Clay Frick and Helen Frick in historical context," the focus will remain primarily on Henry Clay Frick. And recently, although Helen stipulated that the house-museum illustrate "the kind of life that was lived within its walls," evidence of Martha and little Henry Clay Frick Jr.'s deaths, tragedies that shaped the Frick family and most particularly influenced Frick's art collection and the direction of Helen's life, have been eliminated. Instead of using these misfortunes to educate the public about Victorian mourning customs and the effect a child's death has on a family, or even to console those grieving today for the loss of a son, daughter, brother, or sister, the opposite has occurred. The vast Dagnan-Bouveret painting of family mourning, *Consolatrix Afflictorum,* once in the Clayton dining room, has been placed in storage. Although the bust of Martha has recently returned to its place in the reception room, the check with Martha's likeness no longer rests on Frick's desk, and the four photographs of infant Henry Clay Frick Jr.'s body lying in his bassinette, kept by Adelaide Frick in her bedroom from his death during the 1892 Homestead steel strike through her death in 1931 to 2004, have been removed. Visitors enjoy instead the Fricks' fantasy life—the collection of antique cars and carriages, the house with its fine paintings and decorative objects, the playhouse, greenhouse, and dog graveyard. They savor the exceptional lunch and tea in the café, the first Friday concerts on the lawn, and the tastefully presented exhibitions in the Frick Art Museum with their accompanying educational programs for adults and children. But in the last five years, attendance in the house has steadily declined by an average of 1,500 visitors per year, perhaps because it has become a stage set.

FRICK

EPILOGUE

Today, in the Frick family plot at Homewood Cemetery where Helen and her father are buried, there stands a large granite cenotaph that reads "Frick." At its base is a single line of graves. First comes Helen, then the mother and father who never recovered from their children's deaths, then the children themselves, Henry Clay Frick Jr. and little Martha. The grave of Helen's nephew, Henry Clay Frick II, is next, followed by those of Childs and Dixie, and finally Martha Symington.

The graves, for all their seeming peace and serenity, stand as markers of buried dreams, loves gone wrong, lives broken and unfulfilled, and hopes lost. Yet Helen Frick has not vanished. Her legacy may have left a wake of mixed and real successes: controversy, disagreement, perhaps even failure within a divided family, but also a mark on the world that cannot be erased. At Clayton, at the Frick Collection, at the Frick Art Reference Library, even at the Henry Clay Frick Birthplace and the Henry Clay Frick Fine Arts Building—in all the places she loved most—tangible evidences of her taste, her intelligence, her strong opinions, her love for family and friends, and, above all, her quest to please her father and carry out his wishes still stand. They are manifested in architecture, in art history books and catalogues, in images on canvas, in fresco, porcelain, and bronze, and in deep forest where songbirds still sing.

Opposite: The Frick family graves, Homewood Cemetery, Pittsburgh, Pennsylvania.

APPENDIX: HELEN CLAY FRICK, ACQUISITIONS AND GIFTS

I. Acquired for the Frick Collection by the Art Acquisition Committee, Helen Clay Frick, Chairman

A. Paintings

1924 Fra Filippo Lippi, *The Annunciation*
1926 Jean-Baptiste-Siméon Chardin, *Lady with a Bird-Organ*
1926 Gentile Bellini, *The Doge*
1927 Jean-Auguste-Dominique Ingres, *Comtesse d'Haussonville*
1927 French School, probably Burgundian, *Madonna and Child*
1927 Duccio di Buoninsegna, *Temptation of Christ on the Mountain*
1930 Paolo and Giovanni Veneziano, *The Coronation of the Virgin*
1935 Lazzaro Bastiani, *Adoration of the Magi*
1936 Piero della Francesca, *Saint Simon the Apostle (?)*
1937 François Boucher, *Madame Boucher*
1937 Jacques-Louis David, *The Comtesse Daru*
1938 Jacopo Tintoretto, *Portrait of a Venetian Procurator*
1938 Paul Cézanne, *Chestnut Trees at Jas de Bouffan* (deaccessioned 1949)
1939 Andrea del Castagno, *The Resurrection* (acquired as Francesco Botticinni)
1940 Paul Cézanne, *Antoine Dominique Sauveur Aubert, the Artist's Uncle, as a Monk* (deaccessioned 1949)
1940 Paul Gauguin, *Tahitian Landscape* (deaccessioned 1949)
1942 Claude-Oscar Monet, *Vétheuil in Winter*
1943 John Constable, *The White Horse*
1943 Francisco de Goya y Lucientes, *Don Pedro, Duque de Osuna*
1943 Jean-Baptiste Greuze, *The Wool Winder*
1943 Rembrandt Harmensz. Van Rijn, *Nicolaes Ruts*
1943 Sir Joshua Reynolds, *General John Burgoyne*
1945 Jean-Baptiste-Siméon Chardin, *Still Life with Plums*
1946 Thomas Gainsborough, *Grace Dalrymple Elliott*
1946 Thomas Gainsborough, *Richard Paul Jodrell*
1948 Georges de la Tour, *The Education of the Virgin*
1949 Jacob van Ruisdael, *Landscape with a Footbridge*
1950 Piero della Francesca, Workshop of, *An Augustinian Monk*
1950 Piero della Francesca, Workshop of, *An Augustinian Nun*
1950 Cimabue, Cenni di Pepi, *The Flagellation of Christ*
1952 Césarine-Henriette-Flore Davin-Mirvault (acquired as Jacques-Louis David), *Antonio Bartolomeo Bruni*
1954 Jan van Eyck and workshop, *Virgin and Child with Saints and Donor*
1960 Claude Lorraine, *The Sermon on the Mount*

B. Sculptures

1935 Jean-Antoine Houdon, *Armand-Thomas Hue, Marquis de Miromesnil*
1939 Jean-Antoine Houdon, *Diana, The Huntress*
1943 Jean Barbet de Lyon, *Angel*
1945 Antoine Coysevox, *Robert de Cotte*

C. Decorative Arts

1955 Tuscan or Umbrian, *Small Credenza*

D. Drawings

1936 Antonio Pisanello, *Studies of Men Hanging*
1936 Swabian, *Virgin and Child*
1936 Albrecht Altdorfer, *Mercenary Foot Soldier*
1936 Niklaus Manuel Deutsch, *A Lady on Horseback and a Foot Soldier*
1936 Tiziano Vecellio (Titian), *Landscape with a Satyr*
1936 Sir Peter Paul Rubens, Studies of Venus (?) (recto); *Studies for a Last Judgment* (verso)
1936 Francisco de Goya y Lucientes, *The Anglers*
1943 William Blake, *Pilgrim's Progress*
1959 Jean-Auguste-Dominique Ingres, *Study for the Portrait of the Comtesse d'Haussonville*

E. Prints

1940 Albrecht Dürer, *Melencolia* I
1958 Sir Anthony Van Dyck and Pieter Neeffs, *Portrait of Snyders (Franciscus Snyders)*

II. Gifts to the Frick Collection (See also VIII)

A. Paintings

1927 Barna da Siena, *Christ Bearing the Cross* (gift of Helen C. Frick)

1943 John C. Johansen, *Henry Clay Frick* (two versions, one Helen C. Frick gift to the Frick Collection; one for her office in FARL, now at the Frick Art & Historical Center)

1977 Anton Mauve, *Early Morning Plowing* (by direct descent from Helen C. Frick through Frances Frick Burden)

1979 Sir Joshua Reynolds, *Lady Cecil Rice* (by direct descent from Helen C. Frick through Martha Frick Symington)

1984 Francesco Guardi, *View of Venice*

1984 Francesco Guardi, *Regatta in Venice*

B. Pottery and Porcelains

1934 Thirty-nine pieces of French pottery and porcelain, including Saint-Porchaire, Vincennes, Sèvres, and Samson, some purchased by Henry Clay Frick, some gifts to Adelaide from Joseph Duveen's private collection

1956 Pair of Yongzheng Palace Jars, Chinese

C. Sculptures

From Adelaide Frick's Collection, or commissioned by Helen C. Frick

1934 Étienne-Maurice Falconet, *Friendship*

1934 After François-Jacques-Joseph Saly, *Bust of a Young Girl*

1935 French, Eighteenth Century, *Bust of a Young Girl*

1970 Antico (Pier Jacopo Alari Bonacolsi), *Hercules*, from the Eagle Rock–J. P. Morgan Collection

D. Decorative Arts

1935 Flemish (Brussels?), *Tapestry Showing Deer Hunt with Archer*

1935 Flemish (Brussels?), *Tapestry Showing Bear Hunt*

1953 Dukes of Devonshire, Gobelins Manufactory, *Firescreen*

1979 French, Last Quarter of the Eighteenth Century, *Gilt-Bronze Mantel Clock with Attributes of Ceres, Venus, and Bacchus* (by direct descent from Helen C. Frick through Martha Frick Symington)

E. English Reproductive Portrait Prints

1978 William Dickinson, *Jane, Duchess of Gordon*, after Sir Joshua Reynolds (by direct descent through Frances Frick Burden)

1978 Valentine Green, *Lady Louisa Manners*, after Sir Joshua Reynolds (by direct descent through Frances Frick Burden)

1978 James Walker, *Miss Frances Woodley, Later Mrs. Bankes*, after George Romney (by direct descent through Frances Frick Burden)

1978 John Raphael Smith, *Lady Louisa Stormont*, after George Romney (by direct descent through Frances Frick Burden)

1978 John Raphael Smith, *Lady Hamilton as 'Nature,'* after George Romney (by direct descent through Frances Frick Burden)

1978 Charles Knight and Francesco Bartolozzi, *Elizabeth Farren, Later Countess of Derby*, after Sir Thomas Lawrence (by direct descent through Frances Frick Burden)

1984 James Watson, *Miss Greenway*, after Sir Joshua Reynolds

1984 John Dean, *Lady Elizabeth Herbert and Her Son Charles*, after Sir Joshua Reynolds

1984 John Raphael Smith, *Mrs. Stables and Her Daughters Harriet and Maria*, after George Romney

1984 John Raphael Smith, *Lady Catherine Pelham Clinton*, after Sir Joshua Reynolds

1984 John Jones, Caroline, *Duchess of Marlborough*, after George Romney

III. Gifts to the Carnegie Museum of Art

A. Painting

1927 Jean-Julien Lemordant, *La Danse*

B. Porcelain

1971 Chienlung Chinese vases (2), 1662–1722, from the Eagle Rock-Morgan Collection, "Given in memory of Mrs. Thomas Childs Wurtz by an admiring friend."

IV. Gift to the Fogg Art Museum, Harvard University

1953 Jacob van Ruisdael, *Waterfall with a Half-Timbered House and Castle*, from the Eagle Rock Collection

V. Gifts to the Princeton University Art Museum

1935 Jean-Baptiste-Siméon Chardin, *Attributes of the Architect*

1935 Jean-Baptiste-Siméon Chardin, *Attributes of the Painter*

VI. Gift to an Individual

1945 To William S. Moorhead:
Claude Monet, *Rocks and Sea at Belle-Île*

VII. Gifts to Family from the Eagle Rock Collection

c. 1950 To Adelaide Frick Blanchard:
Narcisse Diaz de La Peña, (2) untitled
J. B. Robie, *Flower-piece Roses*

George Moreland, *Interior of Stable*
Sir Henry Raeburn, *Alexander Allan*

c. 1950 To Frances Frick Burden:
Anton Mauve, *Early Morning Plowing*
Théodore Rousseau, untitled
Jacob van Ruisdael, *Waterfall*
Constant Troyon, *Landscape (2)*

c. 1950 To Martha Frick Symington:
American School, Pennsylvania, *Martha Howard Childs (Mrs. Asa P. Childs)*
George Bellows, *Docks in Winter*
Edmund Tarbell, *View at Portsmouth, N.H.*
George Romney, *Mrs. Thomas Raikes (Charlotte Finch) and Child*

c. 1950 To Henry Clay Frick II:
John Constable, *Agitated Sea*
Francis Cotes, *Mrs. Boynton*
Francis Cotes, *Sir Griffith Boynton*
Jacob Maris, *Towing Path*
B. E. Murillo, *Self-Portrait*
Joseph R. Woodwell, *Landscape*

VIII. Acquistions for Helen's Private Collection, 1914–1938, Later Given to the Frick Art Museum, Unless Otherwise Noted

A. Paintings

1922 Follower of Konrad Witz, *Pietà* (given to Frick Collection 1981)
1922 School of Giotto di Bondone, *Madonna and Child with Saints: Scenes from the Life of Christ and the Life of the Virgin* (in 1926, Helen C. Frick reimbursed her mother for half the cost)
1922 Jean-Honoré Fragonard, study for *The Pursuit* panel
1924 Apollonio di Giovanni, *Scenes from the Odyssey*
1924 Matteo di Giovanni, *Madonna and Child with Saint Jerome, Saint Sebastian, and Angel*
1925 Sir Gerard Kelly, *Henry Clay Frick in the West Gallery*
1925 Giovanni di Paolo, *Nativity*
1925 Sassetta, *Virgin of Humility Crowned by Two Angels* (owned by Adelaide Howard Childs Frick; in 1931, Helen C. Frick purchased it from her mother)
1925 Sassetta, *Annunciation*
1925 Andrea di Bartolo, *Madonna and Child* (given to Frick Collection 1984)
c. 1925 Jean Julien Lemordant, *St. Malo*
1926 Bernardo Daddi, *Madonna and Child with Saint Francis and a Bishop; Saints Peter and Paul; Crucifixion; Annunciation*
1926 Walter Gay, *The Fragonard Room*
1926 Master of San Sepolcro (once attributed to Duccio), *Angel with Crown Thorns and Spear*
1927 Francesco di Vannuccio, *St. Catherine of Alexandria*
1928 Walter Gay, *The Living Hall*
1928 Walter Gay, *The Boucher Room*
1930 Arcangelo di Cola da Camerino, *Madonna and Child Enthroned; Crucifixion*
1931 Corneille de Lyon, studio of, *Gabrielle de Rochechouart, Dame de Lansac*
1938 Rainaldo di Rainuccio da Spoleto, formerly attributed to the Lucchese or Umbrian School, *Madonna and Child Enthroned with Four Scenes of the Passion; St. Francis; St. Anthony*

B. Sculptures

1914 Jean-Antoine Houdon, *Bust of Claudine Houdon*
1922 Malvina Hoffman, *Bust of Henry Clay Frick* (given to the Frick Collection in 1935)
1923 Alceo Dossena, *Annunciation* group (purchased as Simone Martini, kept at One East Seventieth Street until given to the University of Pittsburgh, 1933)
1936 Jean-Antoine Houdon, *Bust of Madame Houdon*

IX. Purchased for Henry Clay Frick Fine Arts Department

1925 *St. John the Baptist*, Umbrian fresco fragment
1925 *The Resurrected Christ*, Umbrian fresco fragment

X. Nicholas Lochoff Frescoes

A. Purchased for the Frick Art Reference Library

1928 Nicholas Lochoff, *Madonna and Child with Saints Francis and John*, after Pietro Lorenzetti, Lower Church, San Francesco, Assisi

B. Purchased for the University of Pittsburgh Fine Arts Department, now in the Cathedral of Learning

1928 Nicholas Lochoff, *Resurrection*, after Piero della Francesca, Museo Civico, Borgo San Sepolcro

C. Purchased for the Henry Clay Frick Fine Arts Building

1959 *Christ Appears to Two Apostles on the Way to Emmaus*, after Duccio di Buoninsegna, Maesta, Siena
1959 *Christ Appears to Mary Magdalen (Noli Me Tangere)*, after Duccio, Maesta, Siena
1959 *St. Francis Preaching to the Birds*, after Giotto di Bondone, Upper Church, San Francesco, Assisi
1959 *An Angel:* Detail of *Madonna and Child Enthroned*, after Giotto, Uffizi, Florence
1959 *Dream of St. Martin*, after Simone Martini, Lower Church, San Francesco, Assisi

1959 *Saint Clara,* after Simone Martini (in original condition), Lower Church, San Francesco, Assisi

1959 *Saint Clara,* after Simone Martini (in aged condition), Lower Church, San Francesco, Assisi

1959 *Annunciation,* after Simone Martini, Uffizi, Florence

1959 *Temptation,* after Masolino di Pancale, Santa Maria del Carmine, Florence

1959 *Expulsion from Paradise* after Masaccio, Santa Maria del Carmine, Florence

1959 *Male Donor:* Detail from *The Trinity,* after Masaccio, Santa Maria Novella, Florence

1959 *Crucifix with St. Dominic,* after Fra Angelico, Cloister of San Marco, Florence

1959 *Dominicans Receive Christ as Pilgrim,* after Fra Angelico, Cloister of San Marco, Florence

1959 *St. Peter Martyr, Enjoining Silence,* after Fra Angelico, Cloister of San Marco, Florence

1959 *Esther,* after Andrea del Castagno, then at Castagno Museum of Sant' Apollonia, Florence

1959 *The Duke of Urbino,* Federigo da Montefeltro, after Piero della Francesca, Uffizi, Florence

1959 *The Duchess of Urbino,* Battista Sforza, after Piero della Francesca, Uffizi, Florence

1959 *The Birth of the Virgin,* after Domenico Ghirlandaio, Santa Maria Novella, Florence

1959 *The Birth of Venus,* after Botticelli, Uffizi, Florence

1959 *The Madonna of the Pomegranate,* after Botticelli, Uffizi, Florence

1959 *Madonna and Saints,* after Giovanni Bellini, Sacristy, Santa Maria del Frari, Venice

1959 *The Arrival of the Ambassadors,* after Vittore Carpaccio, Academia, Venice

XI. Works Purchased for the University of Pittsburgh Collection, now at the Frick Art Museum at the Frick Art & Historical Center

A. Paintings

1965 Hubert Robert, *Grotto Baths of Apollo*

1965 Hubert Robert, *Memorial Garden of Lenoir's Museum of French Monuments*

1965 Jean-Louis Demarne, *The Seine at Saint Cloud*

1965 Lippo Memmi, *St. Agnes and St. Anthony* (panels)

1965 Luca Giordano, *The Calling of Sts. Peter and Andrew*

1965 Lazzaro Bastiani, *Madonna and Child with St. Dorothy and St. John the Baptist* (credited that year for Hubert Robert, *Adoration of the Magi*)

1965 Hubert Robert, *Adoration of the Magi*

1965 Biagio di Goro Ghezzi, *Madonna and Child with St. Catherine*

1965 School of Tintoretto, *Susannah and the Elders*

1965 Jean Bellegambe, *Virgin and Child with Rosary* (Diptych from Flines Convent)

1965 Italian Sienese, *Madonna and Child with St. Catherine and St. John*

1966 Francesco Melzi, *Madonna and Child in a Jasmine Bower*

1966 Carle Van Loo, *The Arts in Supplication*

1966 Jean-Honoré Fragonard, *Young Boy in White Collar*

1966 Jean-Baptiste Pater, *Le Repos dans le Parc*

B. Tapestries

1965 French, School of Loire, *Two Musicians*

1965 French, School of Loire, *Lady and Attendants*

C. Sculptures

1963 Antoine-Louis Barye, bronze, *Mountain Lion Mauling a Deer*

1963 French, n.d., bronze, *Lieut. Henri Farré*

XII. Gifts to the Frick Art Museum at the Frick Art & Historical Center (see also VIII and XI)

A. Paintings

1969 Francesco Ubertini (Il Bacchiacca), *Madonna and Child with Saint Elizabeth and Saint John*

1969 Peter Paul Rubens, *Charlotte-Marguerite de Montmorency, Princess of Condé*

1969 Bambino Vispo Master, *Madonna and Child with Scroll*

1969 1839 edition of lithographs, *Picturesque Architecture in Paris, Ghent, Antwerp, and Rouen*

1970 Thomas Gainsborough, *Richard Brinsley Sheridan,* from the Eagle Rock Collection

1970 Francesco Guardi, *View of the Grand Canal,* from the Eagle Rock Collection

1970 William Hogarth, *The Hon. John Hamilton,* from the Eagle Rock Collection

1970 William Beechey, attributed to, *Princess Sophia,* from the Eagle Rock Collection

1970 Jacob Maris, *Man Ploughing,* from the Eagle Rock Collection

1970 Narcisse-Virgile Diaz de la Peña, *Landscape,* from the Eagle Rock Collection

1970 Theodore Rousseau, *Woodland Scene,* from the Eagle Rock Collection

1970 Hans Vereycke, *Master of the Female Half-Figure, Madonna and Child with Angel; St. Catherine; St. Barbara* (triptych)

1970 Attributed to Michel Garnier, formerly attributed to Louis Leopold Boilly, *La Femme Qui Joué de la Guitare*

1971 Antoine Le Nain, *Le Bénédicité*

1971 Jean-François de Troy, *Portrait of a Gentleman*

1972 François Boucher, *Pastorale: Peasant Boy Fishing*

1972 Alexis Grimou, formerly attributed to Jean-Honoré Fragonard, *Portrait of a Woman Called Fragonard's Cook, or Portrait Study of a Head*

1972 Nicholas B. Lépicié, *Mother Feeding Her Child*

1972 Edward Haytley, formerly attributed to Arthur Devis, *The Gardnor Family*

1973 Nicholas Lancret, *Young Lovers in a Landscape*

1973 Jan Steen, *The Music Lesson*

1977 Jean-Marc Nattier, *Marie Leczinska*

1984 Arthur Devis, *Sir Joshua Vanneck and His Family of Roehampton House, Putney,* from the Eagle Rock Collection

1984 Francisco de Goya y Lucientes, *Portrait of Julio Ascencio,* from the Eagle Rock Collection

B. Works on Paper

1970 William-Whiston Barney, *Duchess of Devonshire,* after Thomas Gainsborough

1970 Thomas Shotter Boys, twenty-nine color lithographs, *Picturesque Architecture in Paris, Ghent, Antwerp, and Rouen*

1970 Valentine Green, *Countess Harrington,* after Sir Joshua Reynolds

1970 Attributed to Peter Paul Rubens, *Head of an Old Man*

1970 Charles Turner, *Lord Newton,* after Sir Henry Raeburn

1970 Attributed to Antoine Watteau, *Young Woman*

C. Decorative Arts: Carpets and Runners

1970 Four antique runners for tables and piano

1970 Savonnerie carpet, 1715–1723

1970 Persian, nineteenth-century Bijar carpet from Eagle Rock

1971 Antique runner

1973 Antique runner

D. Furniture

1. American

1970 Eighteenth-century Chippendale-style side chair

1970 Nineteenth-century Chippendale-style side chair

2. English

1970 Twelve eighteenth- and nineteenth-century pieces mostly from Eagle Rock

3. French

1970 Henry II-style 1547–1589, pair of armchairs, late nineteenth century

1970 French Renaissance walnut cabinet c. 1580, purchased by Henry Clay Frick in 1916

1970 Louis XV *Commode Bombé* by Roger Vandercruse from the Eagle Rock Collection

1970 Louis XVI sofa and five armchairs from the Eagle Rock Music Room

1970 Louis XVI-style armchair from Eagle Rock Music Room

1970 Louis XVI pair of armchairs, possible Boucher tapestry of series depicting the *Arts and Sciences,* possibly by Georges Jacob

1970 Louis XVI pair of side chairs by Georges Jacob

1970 Louis XVI, *Console Desserte* by Charles-Claude Saunier

1970 Louis XVI, *Console Desserte* from the Eagle Rock Breakfast Room

1970 Louis XVI *Bergère* from Eagle Rock

1970 Louis XVI-style tulipwood table, nineteenth century

1970 Louis XVI style, three armchairs

1970 Louis XVI-style piano stool, nineteenth century from Eagle Rock

1972 Two French eighteenth-century and two nineteenth-century vitrines

1972 Louis XV-Louis XVI, *Table à Ecrire* by Roger Vandercruse

1973 Louis XVI *Serviteur Fidèle* by Martin Carlin

1973 Louis XVI *Secretaire à Abattant* from Clayton

1973 Louis XVI *Bureau Plat,* tulipwood, Sèvres porcelain, attributed to Martin Carlin

1973 Louis XVI *Commode,* mahogany, oak, satinwood, by Jean Henri Reisener

1973 Nineteenth-century table with Sèvres porcelain plaque

4. Spanish

1970 Refectory table, sixteenth century

1974 Pair of oak benches, eighteenth century

5. Italian

1967 Stool, seventeenth century

1967 Table, walnut, eighteenth century

1970 Sgabello chair, sixteenth century

1970 Bishop's chair, sixteenth century

1970 Travel chest, sixteenth century

1970 *Prie-Dieu,* seventeenth century

1970 Pair of armchairs in the Italian Renaissance style

1970 Sixteenth-century style Savonarola stool, nineteenth century

1970 Seventeenth-century style refectory table from Eagle Rock, early nineteenth century

1973 Pedestal, n.d., for *Bust of Madame Houdon*

1973 Three wall seats, nineteenth century in the seventeenth style, oak

E. Musical Instruments

1970 Regal parlor organ, French, eighteenth century, by Jean-Pierre Latz, cabinet maker to Louis XV

1971 Louis XVI style Harpsicord, American, 1963, by William Dowd

F. Porcelain

1. German

1970 German, Pair of Meissen Rose du Barry-like lavender double gourd vases, c. 1730–1740, Eagle Rock Collection, possibly J. P. Morgan Collection

2. Chinese, from the Eagle Rock–J. P. Morgan Collection

1970 Ming Dynasty, Celadon bottle-shaped vase with long neck, Chongzhen period, 1628–1644

1970 Ming Dynasty, Cloisonné, enamel on copper, bottle-shaped vase

1970 Kangxi period, 1622–1722, nine examples, including 12 inch- to 1-inch high vases, jars, temple vases, and temple jars

1970 Yongzheng period, 1723–1735, ovid-shaped jar

1970 Qianlong period, 1736–1795, eight examples from 6 ½ inches to 31 ¾ inches high, including punch bowls and vases

1985 Kangxi period, 1622–1722, three 10-inch-high vases

3. French

1970 French (?), eighteenth century, urn-shaped vase of Celadon, n.d.

1985 French, c. 1754, Pair Sèvres cache-pots

1985 French, 1757–1766, Pair of Sèvres Aromatic

1985 Paris (?) Standish, porcelain and bronze

G. Sculptures

1967 Pierre Blondeau, after Françios Boucher, *La Petite Fille au Tablier,* c. 1753–1757

1967 Pierre Blondeau, after Françios Boucher, *La Jeune Suppliant,* c. 1753–1757

1970 Claude-Michel Clodion, Urn

1970 Twenty-nine Italian Renaissance bronzes from the Eagle Rock–J. P. Morgan Collection

1970 Two German sixteenth-century bronzes from the Eagle Rock–J. P. Morgan Collection

1970 One Italian, Rome or English, London, second half of the nineteenth century from the Eagle Rock–J. P. Morgan Collection, *Hunter with Hound*

1970 One Flemish seventeenth-century bronze from the Eagle Rock–J. P. Morgan Collection, *Charging Bull*

1970 John MacCallen Swan, bronze, English c. 1900, *Panther,* purchased by Helen C. Frick c. 1898 for Clayton

1970 Art Nouveau style c. 1910, stamped "V.W.," bronze, *Dish as a Pond with Female Figure*

1973 Four Italian Renaissance bronzes from the Eagle Rock–J. P. Morgan Collection

1973 Jean-Antoine Houdon, *Vestal Virgin*

1976 Andrea della Robbia, *Madonna and Child*

1991 Italian Renaissance gilt bronze statue from the Eagle Rock–J. P. Morgan Collection, *Venus with Apple*

1991 Italian, nineteenth century, bronze candlesticks from the Eagle Rock–J. P. Morgan Collection

H. Silver

1. English

1970 English, 1774, silver-plated Punch Bowl by Boulton and Watts

1970 English, Sheffield, Wine Cooler

1971 English, Pair of c. 1706 Muffineer by F. Garkhorne

1971 English, 1723, Tankard with Cover by Thomas Tearle

1971 English, 1780, Teapot by Hester Bateman

1972 English, Coffee Pot, Teapot, Sugar Bowl, Creamer, n.d., monogrammed "FAM"

1973 English, Old Sheffield Kettle on Stand

1973 English, Tea Strainer, n.d.

1973 English, Sugar Tongs by Tiffany & Company, 1912

2. Irish

1971 Irish, c. 1735, Mug by John Hamilton

1971 Irish, c. 1710, Two-handled Cup by David King

3. Russian

1973 Russian, twelve Czarist seventeenth- and eighteenth-century pieces including Bratina, Tea Pot, Stopas (Beakers), Stakans (Small Beakers), Creamer, and Tray

I. Tapestries

1969 Flemish, early sixteenth century, *Rest on the Flight to Egypt*

1969 Flemish, early sixteenth century, *Court of Love*

1970 Flemish, early sixteenth century, *Carnations and Peonies or Roses*

1971 Tapestry Screen, Brussels, late eighteenth century, from Eagle Rock dining room

NOTES

ABBREVIATIONS USED IN THE NOTES

ASCUP	Archives Service Center, University of Pittsburgh
DCD	David C. Duniway Collection, Salem, Ore.
FARL	Frick Art Reference Library, New York, N.Y.
FC	Frick Collection, New York, N.Y.
FC/FARL Archives	Frick Collection-Frick Art Reference Library Institutional Archives, New York, N.Y.
GCA	Girls Clubs of America, Inc., Schlesinger Library, Radcliffe Institute for Advanced Study, Cambridge, Mass.
HCFFA	Helen Clay Frick Foundation Archives at FARL/FC
HCFFUP	Helen Clay Frick Foundation Archives at the University of Pittsburgh
HUA	Harvard University Archives, Cambridge, Mass.
KA	Knoedler Art Gallery Archives, New York, N.Y.
LC	Library of Congress, Washington, D.C.
NARA CA	National Archives and Records Administration, Pacific Region, Laguna-Niguel, Calif.
NARA MD	National Archives and Records Administration, College Park, Md.
NGA	National Gallery of Art Archives, Washington, D.C.
OPM	Office of Paul Mellon, Washington, D.C.
RAC	Rockefeller Archive Center, Sleepy Hollow, N.Y.
RFA	Rockefeller Family Archives, Sleepy Hollow, N.Y.
SFA	Shelburne Farms Archives, Shelburne, Vt.
UP	University of Pittsburgh, Pittsburgh, Pa.
WOMA	West Overton Museums Archives, Scottdale, Pa.
YU	Yale University, New Haven, Conn.

PART ONE: SISTER (1888–1891)

3 "Hell with the lid": quoted in Toker, *Pittsburgh: An Urban Portrait*, 10, 11.

4 "One time, when insulted": Charles F. Booher, quoted in "Henry Clay Frick's Boyhood Days Recalled," *New York Sun*, December 28, 1919, Henry Clay Frick Scrapbook, 1849–1919, HCFFA.

4 "Oh how proud I was": Helen C. Frick, "Grandfather," memoir, c. 1920, HCFFA.

5 Frick "desire[d] to get on"; "There is nothing to hinder me": Helen C. Frick, Timeline Diary 1849–1890, HCFFA.

5 Frick's reliance on his mother and grandmother: Karl Overholt Diary, HCFFA, and Harvey, *Henry Clay Frick*, 31.

6 "one of the talented": Florence Speer, "To the Alumnae Association of the Former Pittsburgh School of Design," 1899. The author is grateful to Betty Shields of the Sewickley Valley Historical Society for bringing this article to her attention.

6 "leaving him alone": Abraham Overholt Tinstman, January 25, 1875, Helen C. Frick, Timeline Diary 1849–1890, HCFFA.

9ff. All material on Martha's suffering, death, and its immediate aftermath is from Annie Blumenschine Stephany, "Memoir," HCFFA, unless otherwise noted.

17 "When I was very little"; "used to take out [Martha's] beautiful little curl": Helen C. Frick, "Grandfather," memoir, c. 1920, HCFFA.

PART TWO: DAUGHTER (1892–1903)

21 "the only remarkable thing": Sauder, "Meadow Mart Hall of Distinction," 5.

22 "Many of the gentlemen here": George McGrew to Childs Frick, undated, HCFFA.

22 "Poor Childs—go away": Myra B. Crandall to Clyde Augustus Duniway, December 20, 1892, DCD.

22 "I have one more request": Adelaide Howard Childs Frick to Clyde Augustus Duniway, undated, DCD.

22 "I know I am a very": Adelaide Howard Childs Frick to Clyde Augustus Duniway, May 20, 1894(?), DCD.

22 "I hope to have": Henry Clay Frick to Childs Frick, October 3, 1893, HCFFA.

22 "It is about as I expected": Henry Clay Frick to Clyde Augustus Duniway, October 30, 1893, DCD.

22 "How hard it will be to tell [your father]": Martha Howard Childs to Childs Frick, November 1, 1893, HCFFA.

22 "I got the unpleasant news": Henry Clay Frick to Childs Frick, November 2, 1893, HCFFA.

22 "He is exceedingly diffident": Henry Clay Frick to Clyde Augustus Duniway, January 9, 1894, DCD.

22 "once became well acquainted": Henry Clay Frick to Clyde Augustus Duniway, January 3, 1894, DCD.

22–23 "I regret to say that": Henry Clay Frick to Clyde Augustus Duniway, February 3, 1894, DCD.

23 "Using red ink": Henry Clay Frick to Childs Frick, December 1895, HCFFA.

23 "You should always date your"; "[I] was much pleased to hear": Henry Clay Frick to Childs Frick, January 1894, HCFFA.

23 "Sorry to hear of your illness": Henry Clay Frick to Childs Frick, undated, HCFFA.

23 "Helen now occupies your place": George McGrew to Childs Frick, undated, HCFFA.

23 "Lady Helen": Andrew Carnegie to Henry Clay Frick, November 26, 1894, HCFFA.

24 "Whenever a gentleman": Helen C. Frick, "Mr. Mignon and Family," essay, undated, HCFFA.

24ff. All material related to Helen C. Frick's recollections of life at Clayton: Helen C. Frick, "Clayton Memoir c. 1950," HCFFA, unless otherwise noted.

27 "What this extra space meant"; "earnest young men": Judge Joseph Buffington, draft of public address, "Last Thirty Years," undated, ASCUP.

28 "If all the children had such a pretty bedroom": Helen C. Frick, "Description of My Bed-room," essay, March 1898, HCFFA.

28 "This afternoon Melle and I": Helen C. Frick to Adelaide Howard Childs Frick, December 15, 1903, HCFFA.

28 "arranged doll furniture"; "poor children": Helen C. Frick, Diary, 1904–1905, entries for January 9 and December 24, 1904, HCFFA.

28 "We will have to give him a trial": Henry Clay Frick to Clyde Augustus Duniway, February 3, 1896, DCD.

28 "Very glad to be able to say": Henry Clay Frick to Clyde Augustus Duniway, November 30, 1896, DCD.

28 "They are real": Childs Frick to Clyde Augustus Duniway, 1896, DCD.

28 "On every Decoration Day": Helen C. Frick, "Clayton Memoir, c. 1950," HCFFA.

28 "the squirrel, allegator": Childs Frick to Clyde Augustus Duniway, 1896, DCD.

28 "a great 12 B shotgun": Childs Frick to Clyde Augustus Duniway, January 2, 1898, DCD.

28 "Today I shot": Childs Frick to Clyde Augustus Duniway, undated, DCD.

28 "[Helen] has good practical business capabilities"; "The head altogether is far too hot": Cecil Twyford, "The Character of Miss Helen Frick," August 24, 1896, London, HCFFA.

29 "I regret having had a scene"; "Mr. Frick, you ought to consider": Miss R. A. Châtelain to Henry Clay Frick, May 7, 1897, HCFFA.

29 "Helen, since our return": Henry Clay Frick to Roland F. Knoedler, September 22, 1896, HCFFA.

30ff. Description of Marika Ogiz and her position regarding "a young student": the author is exceedingly grateful to Marcel Gerber of Eclépens, Switzerland, for bringing this undated, unidentified article to her attention.

30 "If it wasn't for that little Swiss woman": Helen C. Frick, "Grandfather," memoir, c. 1920, HCFFA.

30 "The Daisy Story": Helen C. Frick, essay, May 19, 1897, HCFFA.

30 "Her time is completely taken up": Henry Clay Frick to Clyde Augustus Duniway, November 30, 1896, HCFFA.

31 "Cultivate your mind"; "I know you are anxious to": Henry Clay Frick to Helen C. Frick, July 7, 1903, HCFFA.

31 "We had a good morning with our studies": Marika Ogiz to Adelaide Howard Childs Frick, November 24, 1899, author's collection.

31 "pictures by Jules Breton"; "[The] walls of the house": Helen C. Frick, "Grandfather," memoir, c. 1920, HCFFA.

31 "When my Father and I": Helen C. Frick, "Clayton Memoir, c. 1950" HCFFA.

31 "Mr. Woodwell was over yesterday": Henry Clay Frick to Roland F. Knoedler, January 26, 1897, HCFFA.

31 "[My father] encouraged me": Helen C. Frick, "Grandfather," memoir, c. 1920, HCFFA.

32 "Helen would not consent": Henry Clay Frick to Roland F. Knoedler, January 26, 1897, HCFFA.

32 "it does not please me": Henry Clay Frick to Roland F. Knoedler, March 1, 1897, HCFFA.

32 "that I proposed to exchange"; "She promptly said"; "So you see": Henry Clay Frick to Roland F. Knoedler, December 8, 1897, HCFFA.

32 "As for the Rembrant": Helen C. Frick to Roland F. Knoedler, November 5, 1899, HCFFA.

32 "Papsie was so ambitious for me"; "he would relent": Helen C. Frick, "Grandfather," memoir, c. 1920, HCFFA.

32 Conversation on Gillespie house: Henry Clay Frick to Andrew Carnegie, March 19, 1898, HCFFA.

32 "Helen's no slouch": Helen C. Frick, "Grandfather," memoir, c. 1920, HCFFA.

32 "He used to make me feel": ibid.

32–33 "When foreigners came"; "But I wonder what": Helen C. Frick, "Clayton Memoir," HCFFA.

33 "It is forty feet": Childs Frick to Clyde Augustus Duniway, June 10, 1897, DCD.

34 "Wish we had Helen": Andrew Carnegie to Henry Clay Frick, April 23, 1897 (?), HCFFA.

34 "[He] loved to tease": Helen C. Frick, "Grandfather," memoir, c. 1920, HCFFA.

34 "often poked fun"; "was always pleased": Helen C. Frick, *My Father*, 28.

34 "One of his favorite methods": Helen C. Frick, "Grandfather," memoir, c. 1920, HCFFA.

35 "because it resembled a daughter": Gimpel, *Diary of an Art Dealer*, 232.

35 "unwell and overstrained": Henry Clay Frick to Andrew Carnegie, January 1, 1895, Andrew Carnegie Papers, vol. 30, 5707–5111, LC.

35 "tired state"; "your face appears to me": Andrew Carnegie to Henry Clay Frick, December 18, 1894, HCFFA.

35 "too old—too infirm": Warren, *Triumphant Capitalism*, 450.

35–36 "Her death was felt": Sauder, "Meadow Mart Hall," 5.

36 "The greatest sorrow"; Frick's rituals: Helen C. Frick, "Grandfather," memoir, c. 1920, HCFFA.

36 "Four Little Sunbeams": Helen C. Frick, essay, January 24, 1900, HCFFA.

36–37 "Sympathy": Helen C. Frick, essay, November 21, undated, HCFFA.

37 "Helen and her mama compromised": Henry Clay Frick to Roland F. Knoedler, April 25, 1896, HCFFA.

37 "would make a splendid": Twyford, "The Character of Miss Helen Frick," August 24, 1896, London, HCFFA.

38 "For years I have been convinced": quoted in Wall, *Andrew Carnegie*, 755.

38 "bitter personal struggle"; "The suit is the most important"; "The entire world will": "Frick At Last Appeals to the Courts for Aid," *Pittsburgh Dispatch*, February 14, 1900, author's collection.

38 "perfectly satisfied to let": unidentified news article, March 21, 1900, "Break with Carnegie Newspaper Clippings Album," author's collection.

38 "an opportunity to gloat": March 22, 1900, ibid.

38 "encompass[ing] the mines and": March 23, 1900, ibid.

38 "Utmost cordiality now exists": March 22, 1900, ibid.

39 Description of the Frick Building, *Frank Leslie's Weekly*, March 19, 1903.

40 Psalm 55: verses 5–6 and 23, King James Version.

40 "always smiled"; "My father often got": Helen C. Frick, "Grandfather," memoir, c. 1920, HCFFA.

40 "[An apartment] may be very attractive": Helen C. Frick, "An Apartment at Sherry's," essay, December 10, 1903, HCFFA.

42 "I hope you are not": Helen C. Frick to Adelaide Howard Childs Frick, December 11, 1900, HCFFA.

42 "Don't you be trying to do": Helen C. Frick to Adelaide Howard Childs Frick, November 9, 1903, HCFFA.

42 "I was so sorry tonight": Helen C. Frick to Adelaide Howard Childs Frick, November 11, 1903, HCFFA.

42 "Darling little Mamma": Helen C. Frick to Adelaide Howard Childs Frick, December 4, 1904, HCFFA.

43 "Jane": Helen C. Frick, essay, 1903, HCFFA.

44"I was Papsie's": Helen C. Frick, "Grandfather," memoir, c. 1920, HCFFA.

45 "your loving little girl": Helen C. Frick to Adelaide Howard Childs Frick, December 11, 1900, HCFFA.

45 "your loving little kid": Helen C. Frick to Adelaide Howard Childs Frick, November 11, 1903, HCFFA.

45 "You are so sweet to write": Helen C. Frick to Adelaide Howard Childs Frick, January 25, 1900, HCFFA.

45 "keep stacks of that stuff": Helen C. Frick to Adelaide Howard Childs Frick, December 13, 1903, HCFFA.

45 "If he violates her sexually": Murdock, *Hero's Daughter*, 63.

PART THREE: YOUNG WOMAN (1904–1912)

50ff. Helen's comments on her behavior, her travels, her grandmother, and on New York: Helen C. Frick, Diary, 1904–1905, HCFFA, unless otherwise noted.

50 "the gem of my collection": Henry Clay Frick to Andrew Carnegie, August 2, 1898, Andrew Carnegie Papers, vol. 54, ms. division, letter no. 1042, LC

54 "That is all I shall ever want": quoted in Harvey, *Henry Clay Frick: The Man*, 270.

55 "afforded such excellent hanging space": Helen C. Frick, "Grandfather," memoir, c. 1920, HCFFA.

55 Statistics on the marriages of American heiresses: Fowler, *In a Gilded Cage*, xiii.

55 "no other place could compare with it in my opinion": Helen C. Frick, "Clayton Memoir, c. 1950," HCFFA.

55 Helen's comments on Spence School: Helen C. Frick to Mary Duff, October 8, 1905, HCFFA.

55–56 "a docile student": McCarten, "Profiles," pt. 1, 23.

56 "I hope and expect to go home"; "Two days": Helen C. Frick to Mary Duff, October 8, 1905, HCFFA.

56 "enabled me to stay home": Childs Frick, Composite Diary, 1883–1965 (notation by Helen C. Frick), author's collection.

56 "the cutest little trick": Helen C. Frick to Howard Childs, September 17, 1906, HCFFA.

56 Biographical information on Clara Bebbe Spence: Edmondson, *Profiles in Leadership*, 2–3.

56 "fit men and women for": New York School of Philanthropy, 1905 Handbook, box 1, Columbia University Library.

56 "heroic imagination": Meier, *History of the New York School of Social Work*, 31.

57 "Frick's ambition [was] to have [Helen] attend": McCarten, "Profiles," pt. 1, 24.

57 "Not infrequently the strong willed"; "Papa, mine": ibid, 23, 24.

58 "It has been quite like old times": Martha Howard Childs, Diary, 1908–1909, entry for December 9, 1908, HCFFA.

58 Helen's debutante party: unidentified news article, "Mrs. Henry Clay Frick Introduces Her Young Daughter at 'Clayton,'" and other unidentified news articles about the debut, HCFFA.

58 "Helen as a young lady": Martha Howard Childs, Diary, 1908–1909, entry for December 9, 1908, HCFFA.

58 "real and grave evils"; "square deal": quoted in *World Book Encyclopedia*, 1972, s.v. "Theodore Roosevelt," 428, 430.

58 "We bought him, but": author's interview with Henry Clay Frick II, September 8, 1994.

59 "The children of Pittsburg[h] who have not": *New York Times*, June 15, 1909.

All material about Helen C. Frick's 1909 trip abroad and return home: Helen C. Frick, Diary, 1908–1909, HCFFA, unless otherwise noted.

61 "holiday mood": Knox, *Story of the Frick Art Reference Library*, 5.

61 "the one who developed": Sir Joseph Duveen, article handed to *New Yorker* Magazine Representative (Mr. McElway), January 15, 1936, Duveen Archives, box 452, reel 307, folder 5.

68 "the much discussed *Christina of Denmark [Duchess of Milan]*": Helen C. Frick, Diary, 1908–1909, entry for May 14, 1909, HCFFA.

70 "Do All That You Can": Helen C. Frick, essay, March 18, 1898, HCFFA.

71 "ten promising, needy": Khalife, "True Blue Girls," *Heyday Magazine*, May–June 1993, 35.

72 "I was a very tired young girl": Hazel Sargent Clement to Helen C. Frick, 1939, GCA, Letters 1939, vol. 1., Schlesinger Library, Radcliffe Institute for Advanced Study, HUA.

72 "I'll never forget the time": Mabel Lawrence to Helen C. Frick, 1939, ibid.

73 "I recall being just spellbound": Martha Cord to Helen C. Frick, 1939, ibid.

73 "You Miss Frick": Ida Arthur to Helen C. Frick, 1939, ibid., vol. 2.

73 "You could do such different things": Anna Morrison Ruiter to Helen C. Frick, 1939, ibid, vol. 1.

73 "If we had little problems": Melo Corrow to Helen C. Frick, 1939, ibid, vol. 2.

73 "It was his custom to give"; "while we were at dinner": Ellen R. Boyd to William J. Naughton, January 13, 1922, HCFFA.

73 "Mr. Frick did": *Newsletter for True Blue Folks*, July 9, 1928, HCFFA.

74 "How sweet of you": Henry Clay Frick to Helen C. Frick, December 19, 1910, HCFFA.

74–75 "beamed for days": Helen C. Frick, "Grandfather," memoir, c. 1920, HCFFA.

75 "It gives me the keenest pleasure": Henry Clay Frick to Roland F. Knoedler, May 13, 1910, HCFFA.

75 "When we have trouble we go": quoted in Cameron, *Radicals of the Worst Sort*, 131.

76 "A hundred years from now"; "And they will point": Helen C. Frick, "Grandfather," memoir, c. 1920, HCFFA.

76 "hot to go to Egypt": author's interview with Helen Clay Chace, June 1992.

77 "unrivaled outside of Cairo": Gardiner M. Lane to Henry Clay Frick, November 2, 1911, HCFFA.

77 "help you to see Egypt": Gardiner M. Lane to Henry Clay Frick, November 2, 1911, HCFFA.

77 "raised in five minutes": George A. Reisner, unpublished memoir, "Adventures of an Archaeologist," 51. The author is indebted to Peter Der Manuelian for sharing this memoir.

77ff. All material concerning Helen C. Frick's 1912 trip abroad and to Egypt: Helen C. Frick, Egypt Diaries 1 and 2, HCFFA, unless otherwise noted.

77 "promised [Adelaide]": Reisner, "Adventures of an Archaeologist," 52.

77–78 "You'd swear that Egypt becomes a province": quoted in Blottière, *Vintage Egypt*, 171.

81–82 "no trace of [it] had shown"; "tomb carefully cleared": notation on February 13, 1912, box C13, Giza Photographs, G2184, Museum of Fine Arts, Boston.

82 Henry Clay Frick's conversation with Reisner: Reisner, Expedition Diary, 1912, entry for February 21. The author is exceedingly grateful to Peter Der Manuelian for sharing this diary.

82 "packing cases were soaked": box C13, Giza Photographs, G2184, Museum of Fine Arts, Boston.

83 Helen and the *Titanic*: author's interview with Alice Thompson, April 28, 2004. The author is exceedingly grateful to Alice Thompson for sharing this story.

85 "fought like Hell": author's interview with Henry Clay Frick II, September 8, 1994.

85 "utterly failed to treat many": Garland, *Boston's Gold Coast*, 181.

85 "so ultra-democratic as to be plebian": "Society Objects to Trades People," *Pittsburgh Post*, August 17, 1912.

85 "known as one who rarely": ibid.

86 "had their hands full": "H. C. Frick's Party Draws Thousands," *New York Times*, August 17, 1912, author's collection.

86 "a veritable fairyland": "Society Objects to Trades People," *Pittsburgh Post*, August 17, 1912.

86 "a gathering of society notables": "Society Throngs to Frick's Brilliant Fete," *Pittsburgh Gazette Times*, undated, HCFFA.

86 "an event which caused": *New York Times*, August 17, 1912.

86 "We have nothing to say": *Pittsburgh Gazette Times*, undated, HCFFA.

86 "Helen's my girl"; "after perhaps giving me"; "never mind": Helen C. Frick, "Grandfather," memoir, c. 1920, HCFFA.

86 "Indeed Papsie would have done anything": ibid.

PART FOUR: FATHER (1913–1919)

89 "carry out some of her ideas": "Miss Frick's Club Opens," *New York Times*, May 26, 1919, author's collection.

89ff. Details of Childs and Dixie's wedding: The author is exceedingly grateful to Polly Simpson Gorman for sharing her Frances Dixon Frick material.

89 "slight indisposition": unidentified news article, Polly Simpson Gorman Collection.

90 "demure"; "dark beauty": unidentified news article, October 14, 1913, ibid.

90 "The many guests": "Huge Frick Gift to Son," *New York Times*, October 16, 1913.

90 "decide what had better": Henry Clay Frick to Childs Frick, June 5, 1909, HCFFA.

91 "I shall not limit"; "I know you will not over-do": Henry Clay Frick to Elsie de Wolfe, April 24, 1915, HCFFA.

91 Frick was pleased with the purchases: Henry Clay Frick to Elsie de Wolfe, May 27, 1914, HCFFA.

92 "Well it is too bad": Henry Clay Frick to S. L. Schoonmaker, August 13, 1914, HCFFA.

92 "When you get to the end": True Blue Almanac 1925, True Blue Club Calendar, entry for 1917, HCFFA.

93 "Weddings make me sad"; "Often in connection with the future": Helen C. Frick, "Grandfather," memoir, c. 1920, HCFFA.

93–94 Bridge's comments about the system of lighting: Bridge, *Millionaires and Grubb Street*, 86–87, and "Agreement by James Howard Bridge with Helen C. Frick," April 21, 1931, Exhibit C, FC/FARL Archives.

94 "After dinner we visited the Gallery": quoted in William Rieder, *Charmed Couple*, 188.

94 "Often late at night": Harvey, *Henry Clay Frick*, 335.

94 "sufficient to make us comfortable": Henry Clay Frick to W. D. Sloane, October 1, 1914, Henry Clay Frick Letter Press Book, no. 34, HCFFA.

94 "the owner's direction": Helen C. Frick, "Henry Clay Frick and His Collection," in The Frick Collection, *Art in the Frick Collection*, vol. 1, *Paintings*.

94–95 Frick's themes in collecting: See also Sanger, *Henry Clay Frick: An Intimate Portrait* (Abbeville Press, 1998).

97 "Arrange at once to pay": quoted in *Newsletter*, Frick Art & Historical Center, Autumn 1998.

97 "Mr. Frick has earned": "Mr. Frick's Fine Gift," *Rambler*, January 1, 1916, HCFFA.

97 "Next to Santa Claus": quoted in *Newsletter*, Frick Art & Historical Center, Autumn 1998.

97 "People in general looked": quoted in ibid.

97 "visited the Fragonards": Helen C. Frick, Alice Braddel Daily Diary, entry for February 22, 1915 (notation), HCFFA.

97 "very impatient": Sir Joseph Duveen to Embellishment London, January 26, 1915, Duveen Archives, box 453, reel 308, folder 1–5.

98 "The house is in": Helen C. Frick, Alice Braddel Daily Diary, entry for October 18, 1915 (notation), HCFFA.

98 "saw the [Iron Rail] porch": Helen C. Frick, Alice Braddel Daily Diary, entry for June 7, 1915 (notation), HCFFA.

98 "How I should like": Helen C. Frick, Alice Braddel Daily Diary, entry for June 11, 1915 (notation), HCFFA.

98 "How fascinating it would be": Adelaide Howard Childs Frick to Sir Joseph Duveen, September 14, 1916, Duveen Archives, box 452, reel 307, folder 2.

100 "I have decided to do nothing": Henry Clay Frick to Thomas Hastings, January 12, 1917, HCFFA.

100 "While I differ": quoted in Harvey, *Henry Clay Frick: The Man*, 318.

101 "an easy out": quoted in Jeff Meyers, "'Plattsburgh Idea' Helped Prepare U.S. for WWI," *Press Republican*, September 26, 1999.

101 "tendered through the Mayor": Helen C. Frick, Alice Braddel Daily Diary, entry for April 30, 1917 (notation), HCFFA.

101 "Papsie, Mamma, & I": May 9, 1917, ibid.

102 "distinguished looking man": quoted in Backlund, "World War I: Jane I. Rignel St. John '13 and Dr. Fordyce B. St. John, P&S '09," 29–30.

102 "he adored her": author's interview with Liza Fosburgh, summer 2003. The author is exceedingly grateful to Liza Fosburgh for sharing her understanding of Helen Frick.

102 "considered one of the most beautiful": "The Autumn Wedding Bells Are Ringing," *New York Times*, September 28, 1913.

102 "ever running herself as family favorite": author's interview with Helen Clay Chace, June 1992.

103 "I have what I want": author's interview with Julia B. Egan, July 21, 1993.

103 "promised to marry": author's interview with Liza Fosburgh, summer 2003.

103 "Papsie wrote me a sweet letter": Helen C. Frick, Diary, 1919, entries for April 9 and April 11, HCFFA.

103 "Army officers who knew": McCarten, "Profiles," pt. 1, 25.

103 "poor old man": author's interview with Henry Clay Frick II, April 25, 1995.

104 "held first place": Harvey, *Henry Clay Frick*, 372.

104–5 "down to the dirtiest little specimens": Schneider and Schneider, *Into the Breach*, 50.

105 "ten of our soldiers": Helen C. Frick, Alice Braddel Daily Diary, entry for November 29, 1917 (notation), HCFFA.

105 "Papsie told us"; "He decorated me": Helen C. Frick, "Grandfather," memoir, c. 1920, HCFFA.

105 "My dearest Helen": Henry Clay Frick to Helen C. Frick, November 30, 1917, HCFFA.

105 Helen's descriptions of transatlantic crossing: Helen C. Frick, War Diary, 1917–1918, entry for December 8, 1917, HCFFA.

106 Helen's description of Paris: Helen C. Frick to Adelaide Howard Childs Frick, December 12, 1917, HCFFA.

106 "Three of us are going with"; "And all must be finished": Helen C. Frick to Adelaide Howard Childs Frick, December 16, 1917, HCFFA.

106 Gift of Christmas pins: Helen C. Frick, "Grandfather," memoir, c. 1920, HCFFA.

106 "Thank you again": Helen C. Frick to Henry Clay Frick, December 25, 1917, HCFFA.

106 "under real orders": Helen C. Frick to her parents, January 14, 1918, HCFFA.

106–7 Helen's stories and description of her work: Helen C. Frick to her parents, December 29, 1917, HCFFA.

107 "No French people are allowed": "Helen Frick Tells Red Cross Work," *New York Times*, August 26, 1918, HCFFA.

107 "One poor, old man": ibid.

107 "studying geography": Helen C. Frick to her parents, January 4, 1918, HCFFA.

107 "Except for the stories": Helen C. Frick to her parents, January 8, 1918, HCFFA.

107–8 "the townspeople wanted"; "The people are little more than": Helen C. Frick to her parents, January 10, 1918, HCFFA.

108 "quantities of old people"; "most touching scene": Helen C. Frick, War Diary, 1917–1918, entry for January 16, 1918, HCFFA.

108 "one large dish": Helen C. Frick, "Glimpses Along the Road," newsletter, January 24, 1918, HCFFA.

108 "turned completely over": Helen C. Frick, War Diary, 1917–1918, entry for January 31, 1918, HCFFA.

108 "[W]ith small valises full of": Helen C. Frick, "Glimpses Along the Road," February 3, 1918, HCFFA.

108 "It was time for our Unit"; "we began distributing": Helen C. Frick, "Glimpses Along the Road," February 3, 1918, HCFFA.

108 "Found a stone wall": Helen C. Frick, War Diary, 1917–1918, entry for February 6, 1918, HCFFA.

108–9 "Tomorrow we take": Helen C. Frick to Adelaide Howard Childs Frick, February 12, 1918, HCFFA.

109 The convoy arriving at Evian: Helen C. Frick, "Glimpses Along the Road," February 15, 1918, HCFFA.

109 "four of us to take their histories"; "our lists showed"; "This is a sample": Helen C. Frick to unknown, possibly members of the Goodwill Section, February 15, 1918, HCFFA.

109 "busily engaged in the study": Childs Frick to Rev. William Holland, January 20, 1918, Directors' Correspondence 1910–1924, Carnegie Museum of Natural History.

109 "I am so happy": Helen C. Frick to her parents, February 20, 1918, HCFFA.

109 "We thought we were busy before": quoted in Schneider and Schneider, *Into the Breach*, 60.

110 "Last night . . . bombs"; "seems so never ending": Helen C. Frick to her parents, day after Easter, 1918, HCFFA.

110 "organize and finance"; "large enough": Helen C. Frick to Henry Clay Frick, March 6, 1918, HCFFA.

110 "I do want to start it": Helen C. Frick to her parents, March 17, 1918, HCFFA.

111 "hadn't been well for ten days": Gertrude Hill to her mother, April 2, 1918, HCFFA.

111–12 "Do you know that she has had"; "While Helen was here": Louise Freeman to Henry Clay Frick, April 4, 1918, HCFFA.

112 "You can be sure": Helen C. Frick to her parents, April 15, 1918, HCFFA.

112 "Papsie & Mamma [were] down at"; "My first glance": Helen C. Frick, Alice Braddel Daily Diary, entry for June 5, 1918 (notation), HCFFA.

112 "When you got a letter": Helen C. Frick, "Grandfather," memoir, c. 1920, HCFFA.

114 "glorified rummage shop": Sir Joseph Duveen to Helen C. Frick, January 13, 1919, Duveen Archives, box 452, reel 307, folder 4.

114 "in the cause of humanity": Helen C. Frick, "Summons," Red Cross Clipping Scrapbook, HCFFA.

114 "to our great melting pot": ibid.

114 George W. Bellows paintings: The author is exceedingly grateful to Sarah Hall, curator of exhibitions and registrar at the Frick Art & Historical Center, for bringing these paintings to her attention, as well as the thank you note Helen C. Frick to George W. Bellows, March 27, 1919, George W. Bellows papers (box 2, folder 12) Archives and Special Collections, Amherst College Library.

114 "a dollar trinket": unidentified newspaper clipping, December 9, 1918, Scrapbook, on the Red Cross Shop, HCFFA.

114 "more keen to see Mrs. Frick": *Town Topics: The Journal of Society*, December 12, 1918, vol. 80, no. 24, Red Cross Clipping Scrapbook, HCFFA.

116 "Society" women: *New York Tribune*, December 8, 1918, Red Cross Clipping Scrapbook, HCFFA.

116 Henry Clay Frick's tour of the shop: *New York Sunday Herald*, December 8, 1918, Red Cross Clipping Scrapbook, HCFFA.

117 "a true appreciation": *Evening Mail*, undated, Red Cross Clipping Scrapbook, HCFFA.

117 "I have not lost my leg": ibid.

117 Red Cross Shop raises $50,000: ibid.

117 "he asked me if I": Helen C. Frick, Alice Braddel Daily Diary, entry for March 25, 1919 (notation), HCFFA.

117 "I sat on his lap"; "[We] went early: Helen C. Frick, Diary, 1919, entry for April 9, HCFFA.

118 "My string of pearls"; "the dearest little note"; "clasped them": Helen C. Frick, Alice Braddel Daily Diary, entry for May 23, 1919 (notation), and "Grandfather," memoir, c.1920, HCFFA.

118 "delighted over his purchase": Helen C. Frick, Alice Braddel Daily Diary, entry for June 26, 1919 (notation), HCFFA.

118 "The effect of the pictures": Helen C. Frick to Roland F. Knoedler, undated, KA.

118 "I can only hope that the public": quoted in Harvey, *Henry Clay Frick: The Man*, 336.

118 "went down [the] drive": Harvey, *Henry Clay Frick: The Man*, 363.

118 "threw it three times": Helen C. Frick, Alice Braddel Daily Diary, entry for July 13, 1919 (notation), HCFFA.

121 Helen's return to One East Seventieth Street, Frick's lobster luncheon, his illness, his fatal decline, and his death: Helen C. Frick, Diary, 1919, entries from November–December, HCFFA, unless otherwise noted.

121 Henry Clay Frick's conversations with Helen on death: Helen C. Frick, "Grandfather," memoir, c. 1920, HCFFA.

126 Henry Clay Frick's conversation with Bridge: Bridge, *Millionaires and Grubb Street*, 68–69.

127 "enable her to make effective": article 2, Will of Henry C. Frick, June 24, 1915, author's collection.

127 "indicate[s] his appreciation of"; "Much of the interest of": "Coke King Makes Bequests to Local Region Hospitals," *Weekly Courier*, Connellsville, Pa., December 9, 1919, Carnegie Library, Connellsville.

128 "the largest single testamentary": unidentified news article, RFA, RG 2, series H, box 63, folder 473, RAC.

128 "It so surpasses any other": Hilaire S. Dean to Helen C. Frick, December 8, 1919, HCFFA.

128 Suspicions that Helen had killed her father: author's interview with Helen Clay Chace, June 1992.

128 "All amounts which I thus give"; "It would, nevertheless, be agreeable": article 7, Will of Henry C. Frick, June 24, 1915.

128 "dangerous in the sense that she": William L. O'Neill, *Everyone Was Brave*, 238.

PART FIVE: THE FAMILY CLAIM (1920–1931)

131 "considers her creative ability": Woodman, *Addiction to Perfection*, 168.

132 "I would like to personally settle the bills": Helen C. Frick to Karl Overholt, February 6, 1920, HCFFA.

132ff. All material about Helen C. Frick's 1920 trip abroad: Helen C. Frick, Album Diaries, 1920: Three Weeks in England; France; Belgium-France, HCFFA, unless otherwise noted.

132 "much unnecessary time": Knox, *Story of the Frick Art Reference Library*, 7.

133 Helen's conversation with Witt and its effect: quoted in ibid., 8, 12–14.

134 "Monsieur Maçon": ibid., 10.

135 Hines's letter about Helen's vision for an art history library: Walker D. Hines to Lewis Cass Ledyard, August 27, 1920, HCFFA.

136 "Miss Frick's initial problem": Howell, "The Frick Art Reference Library," National Portrait Gallery Archives, Smithsonian Institution.

136 "one of the greatest": quoted in Knox, *Story of the Frick Art Reference Library*, 11.

136 "the Frick mausoleum": quoted in Hadley, *Letters of Bernard Berenson*, 619.

136 "I was shocked": Bryson Burroughs to Edward W. Forbes, December 11, 1920, Fogg Art Museum, HUA.

136–37 "I like the spirit"; "I told her": Edward W. Forbes to Bryson Burroughs, December 13, 1920, Fogg Art Museum, HUA.

137 Letter noting later change in gallery lighting: Adelaide Howard Childs Frick to Sir Joseph Duveen, April 17, 1929, Duveen Archives, box 452, reel 307, folder 6.

137 "A great weight": Helen C. Frick to Edward W. Forbes, December 14, 1920, Fogg Art Museum, HUA.

137 "The change was so startling": Helen C. Frick to John D. Rockefeller Jr., April 8, 1921, RFA, RG 2, series H, box 63, folder 432, RAC.

137 "best not to touch them": Helen C. Frick to John D. Rockefeller Jr., May 4, 1921, RFA, RG 2, series H, box 63, folder 473, RAC.

137 "Many of them [were] taken": Everett Fahy, foreword to Knox, *Story of the Frick Art Reference Library*, xii.

138 Childs's attempts to restructure Frick Collection board: Lewis Cass Ledyard to John D. Rockefeller Jr., August 3, 1921, RFA, RG 2, series H, box 63, folder 473, RAC.

138 "made any plans for the disposal"; "I hope very much": quoted in Knox, *Story of the Frick Art Reference Library*, 65.

138 "a distinct pleasure"; "deeply interested": ibid.

139 "Your cable of greetings": Sir Robert Witt to Helen C. Frick, November 9, 1921, FC/FARL Archives.

139 "very well pleased": Helen C. Frick to George P. Butler, August 21, 1921, HCFFA.

139 Comments on the farm: Helen C. Frick, Westmoreland Farm Diary, 1922–1926, HCFFA.

139 "a great help": quoted in Knox, *Story of the Frick Art Reference Library*, 25.

141 "began to slowly rise"; "by morning": Ruth Savord to Helen C. Frick, June 16, 1922, FC/FARL Archives.

141 "First of all": Helen C. Frick to Ruth Savord, June 16, 1922, FC/FARL Archives.

142 "My future lies": "Prowler Is Arrested at Mrs. Frick's Home," *New York Times*, May 7, 1922. The author is indebted to Patrick Trimble for bringing this article to her attention.

143 "Do you consider it": Helen C. Frick to Edward W. Forbes, February 26, 1922, Fogg Art Museum, HUA.

143 "I do want you to feel": Helen C. Frick to Malvina Hoffman, undated, Malvina Hoffman Papers, box 3, Getty Research Institute.

143 "that unless the Library": Knox, *Story of the Frick Art Reference Library*, 26.

143 "a copy . . . by a craftsman": Sir Joseph Duveen to Helen C. Frick, March 22, 1922, Millard Meiss Papers, reel 270, Archives of American Art, Smithsonian Institution.

143–44 "show[ed] the [pair] to everyone": Gimpel, *Diary of an Art Dealer*, 230.

145 "the pearl of the collection"; "Tell your brother-in-law": ibid., 218, 220.

145 "like the old speckled floors": R. H. Shreve to Helen C. Frick, September 26, October 30, 1923, FC/FARL Archives.

145 Sleeper's plans for American rooms: Harry D. Sleeper to Helen C. Frick, December 18, 1923, HCFFA.

145 "I think the expense": Helen C. Frick to Karl Overholt, October 9, 1923, HCFFA.

145–46 "early America had no art": quoted in David Bubier, "Collector Profile: Katharine Prentis Murphy," February 16, 1993, New Hampshire Historical Society.

146 "It was quite an undertaking": Ellen R. Boyd to Jesse Trindle, November 20, 1923, HCFFA.

146–47 "I shall be thinking": Sir Robert Witt to Helen C. Frick, May 13, 1924, FC/FARL Archives.

147 "This may sound like a large number": Helen C. Frick to True Blue Girls, June 1925, HCFFA.

147 "If your place of business": True Blue *Newsletter*, June 18, 1924, HCFFA.

148 "I will *not* have Schling": Helen C. Frick to Carrère and Hastings, undated, FC/FARL Archives.

148 "The part I object to": Helen C. Frick to Edward W. Forbes, January 20, 1924, Fogg Art Museum, HUA.

148 "It would be intolerable"; "Only this morning": Helen C. Frick to Edward W. Forbes, March 12, 1924, Fogg Art Museum, HUA.

148–49 "[Valentiner] replied": Edward W. Forbes to Helen C. Frick, March 29, 1924, Fogg Art Museum, HUA.

149 "If I may add a word of counsel": Sir Robert Witt to Helen C. Frick, May 13, 1924, FC/FARL Archives.

149 "I am fully aware": Paul Sachs to Helen C. Frick, November (?) 1924, Fogg Art Museum, HUA.

149 "so kind"; "My principle": Helen C. Frick to Paul Sachs, November 15, 1924, Fogg Art Museum, HUA.

149 "*This is it!!*": Paul Sachs to Edward W. Forbes, November 15, 1924, Fogg Art Museum, HUA.

149 "I venture to disagree": Paul Sachs to Helen C. Frick, November 22, 1924, Fogg Art Museum, HUA.

149 "a cultivated gentleman": Paul Sachs to Helen C. Frick, November 27, 1926, Fogg Art Museum, HUA.

149 "You may not agree": Paul Sachs to Edward W. Forbes, notation on Helen C. Frick to Paul Sachs, November 30, 1926HUA.

150 "hop[ed] he & Sachs": Helen C. Frick to Edward W. Forbes, March 12, 1924, Fogg Art Museum, HUA.

150 "It is a most heart-rending": Helen C. Frick to Henry Fuller, October 2, 1924, FC/FARL Archives.

152 "Miss Fr. will *not* consider": Helen C. Frick, notation to her secretary, on Thomas Hastings to Helen C. Frick, November 5, 1924, FC/FARL Archives.

152 "Alas. . . . It was expected": Thomas Hastings to Helen C. Frick, February 27, 1925, FC/FARL Archives.

153 "your work was not": Helen C. Frick's secretary to Hermann & Grace Co., May 2, 1925, FC/FARL Archives.

153 "It looks so very shabby": Helen C. Frick's secretary to Hermann & Grace Co., March 11, 1925, FC/FARL Archives.

153 "It is just under a year": Helen C. Frick to Thomas Hastings, undated, FC/FARL Archives.

153 "The opinion expressed": Helen C. Frick to Gerard Kelly, June 9, 1925, HCFFA.

153–54 "last great center in the country": Bowman, *Unofficial Notes*, 6.

154 "about which all the activities": University of Pittsburgh Bulletin, Report of the Chancellor to the Trustees, January 1, 1921 to June 30, 1921, Chancellor's Files, RG 2/10, 1921–1945, ASCUP.

154 "Without making any": Helen C. Frick to John Gabbert Bowman, May 22, 1925, HCFFB Files, Department of Fine Arts and Architecture, UP.

154 "In making this gift": Helen C. Frick to John Gabbert Bowman, May 22, 1925, Fogg Art Museum, HUA.

154 "No Italian photographer would work by contract": quoted in Knox, *Story of the Frick Art Reference Library*, 30–31.

156 "I think you have reversed"; "Where is this one": Helen C. Frick, comments in Polly Wells-Helen C. Frick Diary, 1925, HCFFA.

156 "splendid teaching material": John Gabbert Bowman to Helen C. Frick, December 3, 1925, HCFFB Files, History of the Department of Fine Arts and Architecture, Chairman's Office, UP.

156 "It was quite an unusual": True Blue *Newsletter*, September 28, 1925, HCFFA.

156 "They gave us": ibid., January 6, 1926, HCFFA.

156–57 "a fine 'Crucifixion'": Helen C. Frick to John D. Rockefeller Jr., Marchc12, 1926, RFA, RG 2, series H, box 63, folder 473, RAC.

157 "I was very much impressed": Thomas Hastings to Helen C. Frick, July 29, 1926, FC/FARL Archives.

157 "Indeed"; "I recall being": Thomas Hastings to Adelaide Howard Childs Frick, August 9, 1926, FC/FARL Archives.

157 "Your letter addressed to my mother"; "as a trustee": Helen C. Frick to Thomas Hastings, August 9, 1926, FC/FARL Archives.

157 "You will probably laugh": Thomas Hastings to Adelaide Howard Childs Frick, August 3, 1926, FC/FARL Archives.

157 "Your last letter to me": Thomas Hastings to Helen C. Frick, August 12, 1926, FC/FARL Archives.

157 "Not until they have attended": Helen C. Frick to her secretary, undated memorandum, FC/FARL Archives.

157 "Art"; "reveals the story": quoted in Agnes Lynch Starrett, "Through One Hundred and Fifty Years," 1937, HCFFUP.

158 "With your vision": Frederick Mortimer Clapp to John Gabbert Bowman, October 4, 1926, HCFFB Files, History of the Department of Fine Arts and Architecture, Chairman's Office, UP.

158 "I shaved for a week": Frederick Mortimer Clapp to Harrison Griswold Dwight, August 28, 1927, Frederick Mortimer Clapp Papers, YU.

158 "a little Bernardo Daddi"; "The left panel": Helen C. Frick to Edward W. Forbes, July 24, 1926, Fogg Art Museum, HUA.

158 "intend[ed] moving heaven": Helen C. Frick to Paul Sachs, August 4, 1925, Fogg Art Museum, HUA.

158 "one of the jewels": Royal Cortissoz to Helen C. Frick, January 26, 1926, HCFFA.

158 "has felt that a cracked wall": Metcalf, *Ogden Codman*, 176.

158 "on her back": Helen C. Frick secretary to Ellen R. Boyd, May 18, 1927, HCFFA.

160 "should [she] purchase the French Primitive": Minutes of the FC Board of Trustees, May 4, 1927, HCFFA.

160 "a great secret. . . . [but] I naturally": Sir Joseph Duveen to Adelaide Howard Childs Frick, July 6, 1927, Duveen Archives, box 452, reel 307, folder 6.

160 "My daughter and I deeply interested in Benson Duccio": Adelaide Howard Childs Frick to Sir Joseph Duveen, 1927, ibid.

160 *New York Times* assessment of Duccio: "Frick Gallery Gets Two Art Treasures," *New York Times*, November 19, 1924, HCFFA.

160 "The Trustees decided to purchase": Helen C. Frick to Paul Sachs, November 16, 1927, Fogg Art Museum, HUA.

160 "from time to time [to] borrow": Special Meeting of the FC Board of Trustees, November 15, 1927, FC/FARL Archives.

160 "The glow of the beautiful color": Edward W. Forbes to Helen C. Frick, December 9, 1927, Fogg Art Museum, HUA.

163 "In spite of the fact": Helen C. Frick to Paul Sachs, December 19, 1927, Fogg Art Museum, HUA.

163 "Every now and again": Paul Sachs to Helen C. Frick, December 2, 1927, Fogg Art Museum, HUA.

163 "Again it is with deep regret": Helen C. Frick to Paul Sachs, December 5, 1927, Fogg Art Museum, HUA.

163 "*Here it is again!*": Paul Sachs to Edward W. Forbes, notation on Helen C. Frick to Paul Sachs, December 5, 1927, Fogg Art Museum, HUA.

163 "It all looks so stylish": Daphne Hoffman, October 7, 1927, Frick Art Reference Library Scrapbook 1920–29, FARL Archives.

163 "Is it not a strange coincidence": Helen C. Frick to Ethelwyn Manning, December 31, 1927, FC/FARL

163 "a bad sister and a bad daughter"; "I am unworthy": author's interview with Helen Clay Chace, June 1992.

163–64 "some of the pictures": Helen C. Frick to Paul Sachs, April 2, 1928, Fogg Art Museum, HUA.

164 "stimulate interest in": unidentified news article, Historical House Scrapbook, WOMA.

165 "two statues . . . of such important": Frank Mason Perkins to Helen C. Frick, April 22, 1924, FC/FARL Archives.

165 "this great work": Frank Mason Perkins to Helen C. Frick, December 18, 1925, FC/FARL Archives.

165 "I suppose you have heard": Helen C. Frick to Edward W. Forbes, September 13, 1928, Fogg Art Museum, HUA.

165 "One glance around": quoted in *Twelve Masterpieces of Italian Painting*, 2.

166 "barbarous restoration": Nicholas Lochoff to Helen C. Frick, c. 1923, FC/FARL Archives.

166 "to see the 'Piero'": Helen C. Frick to Ethelwyn Manning, September 30, 1928, FC/FARL Archives.

166 "You are fortunate": Ernest C. Moore to Frederick Mortimer Clapp, 1928, Frederick Mortimer Clapp Papers, YU.

166 "wrapped 1400 packages": Ellen R. Boyd to Miss Brown, December 6, 1928, HCFFA.

168 "a willing but none too competent amateur": McCarten, "Profiles," pt. 2, 25.

168 "any other matter in connection with our family": Helen C. Frick to G. H. Dorr, December 7, 1928, HCFFA.

168 "I would like to know": Helen C. Frick to Roland F. Knoedler, November 15, 1928, KA.

168 "We took [the] courtesy": Helen C. Frick to Charles R. Henschel, November 14, 1928, with Roland F. Knoedler notation, KA.

168 "[I] will support": Helen C. Frick to Ellen R. Boyd, January 28, 1929, HCFFA.

168 "The tenements did look poor"; "with the spirit and the loyalty": Ellen R. Boyd to Helen C. Frick, March 3, 1929, HCFFA.

169 "I cannot half express": Helen C. Frick to Karl Overholt, February 12, 1929, Westmoreland-Fayette Historical Society, box 3, HCFFA, ASCUP.

169 "Orders were given": Helen C. Frick to Edward W. Forbes, April 18, 1929, Fogg Art Museum, HUA.

169–70 Helen's description of trustees meeting; changes to her will: Helen C. Frick to Karl Overholt, April 19, 1929, HCFFA.

170 "a supreme small Diptych": Helen C. Frick to William S. Moorhead, October 29, 1845, HCFFA.

170 "It is one of the world's great masterpieces": Adelaide Howard Childs Frick to Louis Cass Ledyard, undated, FC/FARL Archives.

170 "a picture of that period": Frank J. Mather Jr. to Helen C. Frick, November 23, 1927, HCFFA.

170 "high figure"; "their lack of appreciation and knowledge": Helen C. Frick to William S. Moorhead, October 29, 1945, HCFFA.

172 "before the other Trustees": Helen C. Frick to unnamed attorney, Preparation of the Facts, May 3, 1947, HCFFA.

172 "not to have any 'business'": Paul Sachs to Helen C. Frick, December 10, 1929, Fogg Art Museum, HUA.

172 "I am sick at heart": Helen C. Frick to Paul Sachs, December 10, 1929, Fogg Art Museum, HUA.

172 "say nothing whatever": Paul Sachs to Helen C. Frick, December 12, 1929, Fogg Art Museum, HUA.

172 "Be a listener": Paul Sachs to Helen C. Frick, December 24, 1929, Fogg Art Museum, HUA.

172 "Maybe 1930 holds better luck": Helen C. Frick to Paul Sachs, January 6, 1930, Fogg Art Museum, HUA.

172 "I feel that you are": Helen C. Frick to Paul Sachs, February 12, 1930, Fogg Art Museum, HUA.

173 Helen's view of contemporary art as "trash": The author is grateful to Arabella S. Dane and Nicholas Shoumatoff for these insights.

173 "an attempt to give": Assistant Professor John Rothenstein, Department of Fine Arts Announcement, February 7, 1929, Chancellors Files, RG 2/10, 1921–1945, ASCUP.

175 "[There] are some wonderful": Walker D. Hines to Helen C. Frick, April 25, 1930, Fogg Art Museum, HUA.

175 "Those are the four pieces": John D. Rockefeller Jr. to Louis Cass Ledyard, December 26, 1930, RFA, RG 2, series H, box 63, folder 472, RAC.

175 "I do not think that this": Louis Cass Ledyard to John D. Rockefeller Jr., December 22, ibid.

175 "It is amazing how many": Ellen R. Boyd to Helen C. Frick, February 7, 1930, HCFFA.

175 "many beauties in the mosses": True Blue *Newsletter*, July 14, 1930, HCFFA.

176 "a copy, no matter how fine": Helen C. Frick to Edward W. Forbes, March 18, 1931, Fogg Art Museum, HUA.

176 "Mother": Childs Frick, Composite Diary, 1883–1965, entry for October 4, 1931, author's collection.

176 "All is over": Helen C. Frick, Westmoreland Farm Diary, 1927–1931, entry for October 4, 1931, HCFFA.

176 "Sacred": Helen C. Frick notation on envelope of Adelaide Howard Childs Frick to Helen C. Frick, September 10, 1931, HCFFA.

177 "one of America's"; "He knows more": Paul Sachs to Childs Frick, October 15, 1931, Frederick Mortimer Clapp Papers, YU.

177 "one of the leading scholars in the world": John Gabbert Bowman to Childs Frick, October 10, 1931, Chancellors Files, RG 2/10, 1921–1945, ASCUP.

177 "pending appraisal": Special Meeting of the FC Board of Trustees, November 5, 1931, HCFFA.

177 "The trustees meetings": Helen C. Frick to Edward W. Forbes, April 17, 1932, Fogg Art Museum, HUA.

177 "to think of either a fable or": Helen C. Frick's secretary to Ethelwyn Manning, August 1, 1930, HCFFA.

PART SIX: ON HER OWN (1932–1939)

179 "The first load": Ellen R. Boyd to Helen C. Frick January 11, 1932, HCFFA.

179 "[We] remembered eighty-three": Ellen R. Boyd to Helen C. Frick, January 25, 1932, HCFFA.

179 "tunnel": quoted in Frederick Mortimer Clapp memorandum, June 15, 1932, Frederick Mortimer Clapp Notebook 4, FC/FARL Archives.

180 "The Library should continue its development": quoted in Fazio, "Helen Clay Frick, Architectural Patron and Art Collector," 38.

181 "Miss Frick said"; "She said that in these times": Frederick Mortimer Clapp memorandum, November 25, 1932, Frederick Mortimer Clapp Notebook 4, FC/FARL Archives.

181 "healing hand and voice": Sir Robert Witt to Malvina Hoffman, October 5, 1932, Malvina Hoffman Papers, box 11, folder 5, Getty Research Institute.

181 "This wretched": Sir Robert Witt to Malvina Hoffman, October 6, 1932, ibid.

181 "thanks to you she will": Sir Robert Witt to Malvina Hoffman, October 14, 1932, ibid.

181 "state of mind and body"; "But isn't it sad": Sir Robert Witt to Malvina Hoffman, December 12, 1932, ibid.

181–82 "As for my 'reputation'"; "I cannot see why": Helen C. Frick to Malvina Hoffman, undated, ibid.

182 "This requires no answer!": Helen C. Frick, notation on Mary Witt to Helen C. Frick, March 28, 1933, FC/FARL Archives.

182 "Miss Frick is now retrenching": Ethelwyn Manning to Sir Robert Witt, March 11, 1933, FC/FARL Archives.

182 "You must . . . realize"; "old wounds hidden": Malvina Hoffman to Sir Robert Witt, October 10, 1932, Malvina Hoffman Papers, box 11, folder 5, Getty Research Institute.

182 "like a sick woman": Sir Robert Witt to Malvina Hoffman, January 24, 1933, ibid.

182 Conditions in Lawrence: Ellen R. Boyd to Helen C. Frick, April 17, 1932, HCFFA.

182 Conditions in Lowell: Ellen R. Boyd to Helen C. Frick, May 27, 1932, HCFFA.

182 "the first such plan": "Heir to Frick Fortune Succumbs," *Pittsburgh Tribune Review*, November 10, 1984, HCFFA.

183 "were worth their weight": Ellen R. Boyd to Helen C. Frick, February 2, 1933, HCFFA.

183 "to keep their self-respect": Ellen R. Boyd to Helen C. Frick, February 20, 1933, HCFFA.

183 "So many of our families": Ellen R. Boyd to Helen C. Frick, March 29, 1933, HCFFA.

183 "It was only because of": Frederick Mortimer Clapp, Helen C. Frick memorandum, April 19, 1933, HCFFA.

183 "I realized from the outset": John D. Rockefeller Jr. to Mrs. Walker D. Hines, March 15, 1934, RFA, RG 2, series H, box 63, folder 472, RAC.

183 "instantly there was a 'huddle'"; "I withdrew from the meeting": Helen C. Frick memorandum to unnamed attorney, "The Frick Collection," February 4, 1949, HCFFA.

183 "have always admitted": Minutes of the FC Board of Trustees, April 13, 1933, HCFFA.

183 "She is not for an artificial skylight": Frederick Mortimer Clapp memorandum, March 13, 1935, FC/FARL Archives.

184 "Miss Frick expressed herself": John D. Rockefeller Jr. to Walker D. Hines, April 28, 1933, RFA, RG 2, series H, box 63, folder 472, RAC.

184 "If we now yield": ibid.

184 "the income of which": Minutes of the FC Board of Trustees, April 13, 1933, HCFFA.

184 "until they had seen [the] 'light'": Helen C. Frick to unnamed attorney, "The Frick Collection," February 4, 1949, HCFFA.

184 "While The Frick Collection": Minutes of the FC Board of Trustees, April 13, 1933, HCFFA.

184 "A little bird tells me": Helen C. Frick to Andrew W. Mellon, May 12, 1933, Andrew W. Mellon Papers, OPM.

185 "in the acquisition of important"; "Instead of owning": Helen C. Frick memorandum, April 19, 1933, HCFFA.

185 Helen's comments on FC interior: Helen C. Frick to Frederick Mortimer Clapp, May 10, 1933, FC/FARL Archives.

185 "she is very anxious": Minutes of the FC Board of Trustees, April 13, 1933, HCFFA.

185 "as it was always a very personal one": Helen C. Frick to Frederick Mortimer Clapp, January 29, 1933, Clapp Papers, YU.

186 "Last night the pictures were"; "Tremendous pounding"; "What an adventure": Frederick Mortimer Clapp to Helen C. Frick, June 29, 1933, FC/FARL Archives.

186 "[It] has lifted from my mind": Frederick Mortimer Clapp to Helen C. Frick, June 4, 1933, HCFFA.

186 "the fine ornamental iron stair": Frederick Mortimer Clapp to John Gabbert Bowman, October 27, 1933, Frederick Mortimer Clapp Papers, YU.

187 "You must know at heart": Helen C. Frick to Frederick Mortimer Clapp, June 19, 1933, Frederick Mortimer Clapp Papers, YU.

187 "When the door is closed": L. W. Eisinger to Helen C. Frick, July 30, 1934, FC/FARL Archives.

187 "*No.* I prefer": Helen C. Frick to L. W. Eisinger, July 30, 1934, FC/FARL Archives.

188 Taking Virginia Musselman to task: Helen C. Frick to Virginia Musselman, June 22, 1934, HCFFA.

188 "She is so very tired": Eleanor B. Howland to Ellen R. Boyd, November 23, 1934, HCFFA.

188 "just the color she wanted": *Time*, December 23, 1935, Frick Collection Scrapbook, 1931–1945, FC.

188 "The Library appears to be": Helen C. Frick to Edward W. Forbes, November 7, 1934, HCFFA.

188 "the furniture throughout": Frederick Mortimer Clapp Memorandum, November 19, 1934, FC/FARL Archives.

188 Childs's complaints: Frederick Mortimer Clapp memorandum, October 27, 1934, FC/FARL Archives.

188 "a knotty problem"; "To advance the knowledge": Frederick Mortimer Clapp to Harrison Griswold Dwight, October 19, 1934, Frederick Mortimer Clapp Papers, YU.

189 "not what might be expected"; "she could stand such": Frederick Mortimer Clapp memorandum, October 4, 1934, FC/FARL Archives.

190 "Miss Frick could rush": author's interview with Helen Sanger, July 22, 1993.

190 "bothered by [the] dreadful lawsuit": Edward W. Forbes to Helen C. Frick, February 1, 1935, Fogg Art Museum, HUA.

190 "full of inaccuracies": *New York American*, January 16, 1935, FARL Scrapbook, 1930–1939, FARL.

190 "not a recognized specialist in art"; "he was not employed"; "slander[ing] him by calling him": *Pittsburgh Press*, undated news article, HCFFA.

190 "gotten in the neighborhood": H. A. Rosenberg to Helen C. Frick, January 17, 1935, FC/FARL Archives.

190 "Trial!": Helen C. Frick, Westmoreland Farm Diary, 1932–1935, entry for January 15, 1935, HCFFA.

190 "left my fate in"; "curt note"; "[She] dismissed me": *New York Herald Tribune*, January 18, 1935, FARL Scrapbook, 1930–1939, FARL.

190 "I once had a request": quoted in "Rich Man's Man," *Time*, January 28, 1935, author's collection.

191 "A psychosis of unconscious arrogance"; "the arrogance malady"; "I guess moral delinquency": "Art Suit Plaintiff Attacked on Book," *New York Times*, January 17, 1935, author's collection.

191 "the White Plains Supreme Court": *New York American*, January 17, 1935, FC.

191 the "'conscious arrogance' of Miss Helen Frick": "Wealthy Woman 'Needs Psychiatrist' Asserts Plaintiff," *New York American*, January 18, 1935, FC.

191 "Well I suppose I have"; "lifted"; "corrections": "Gifts to Wealthy Decried in Art Suit," *New York Times*, January 18, 1935, author's collection.

191 "Although she confessed": *New York Herald Tribune*, February 6, 1935, FC.

191 "never liked": *New York Times*, February 7, 1935, FC.

191 "in a timid, frightened voice"; "in a determined whisper": *New York World Telegram*, FARL Scrapbook, 1930–1939, January 16, 1935, FARL.

192 "very ungraciously"; "[So] you're going to do": ibid.

192 "a willing but none too competent amateur": McCarten, "Profiles," pt. 2, 25.

192 "a guide not a curator"; "in 1914 her father moved": *New York World Telegram*, January 16, 1935, FARL Scrapbook, 1930–1939, FARL.

192 "Despite the fact he was a Princeton graduate": *New York Herald Tribune*, February 6, 1935, FC.

192–93 "the satisfaction of a rich woman's hate": *New York Herald Tribune*, February 7, 1935, FC.

193 "still regrets the portal": Frederick Mortimer Clapp memorandum, March 12, 1935, FC/FARL Archives.

193 "the excellent suggestion": Frederick Mortimer Clapp memorandum, December 11, 1934, FC/FARL Archives.

193 "as a trustee"; "father was not there": Helen C. Frick to unnamed attorney, "The Frick Collection," February 4, 1949, HCFFA.

193 Helen's comments on FC decor: Frederick Mortimer Clapp memorandum, May 23, 1935, FC/FARL Archives.

193 "the lattices . . . should be of bronze": Frederick Mortimer Clapp memorandum on Childs Frick, October 3, 1934, FC/FARL Archives.

193 "amateurish and ineffectual"; "thought the matter of wall fabrics": Frederick Mortimer Clapp memorandum, May 27, 1935, FC/FARL Archives.

193 "was entirely unnecessary": Frederick Mortimer Clapp memorandum, May 28, 1935, FC.

194 "Being a Jew": *New York Post*, September 21, 1935, FARL Scrapbook, 1930–1939, FARL.

194 "She said they had been selected": Frederick Mortimer Clapp memorandum, August 29, 1935, FC/FARL Archives.

194 "without even taking off her hat": *Time*, December 23, 1935, Frick Collection Scrapbook 1931–1945, FC.

194 "I told her the committee"; "new reflectors that Mr. Frick liked": Frederick Mortimer Clapp memorandum, October 15, 1935, FC/FARL Archives.

194 "The building seems to have reached": Helen C. Frick to John D. Rockefeller Jr., November 21, 1935, RFA, RG 2, series H, box 63, folder 472, RAC.

194 "Thank you for your": John D. Rockefeller Jr. to Helen C. Frick, November 26, 1935, ibid.

195 "a marble bust by Malvina Hoffman"; description of the Frick Collection opening; "two mysterious primitives": *New York Herald Tribune*, December 12, 1935, ibid.

196 "The opening was indeed": Helen C. Frick to Maude Clapp, undated, Frederick Mortimer Clapp Papers, YU.

196 "One forgets all about": *New York World Telegram*, December 12, 1935, Frick Collection Scrapbook, 1931–1943, FC.

196 "the very beautiful and impressive arrangement": Sir Joseph Duveen to Frederick Mortimer Clapp, December 12, 1935, Duveen Archives, box 452, reel, 307, folder 5.

196 "I count it my great good fortune": Frederick Mortimer Clapp to John D. Rockefeller Jr., January 13, 1936, RFA, RG 2, series H, box 64, folder 485, RAC.

196 "little enough in view of": John D. Rockefeller Jr. to Frederick Mortimer Clapp, January 14, 1936, ibid.

196 Martie Smith Perry's experience at the Frick Collection: The author is grateful to Martie Smith Perry for sharing her experience of Helen C. Frick.

196 "the domination of the Frick"; "ill"; "not active much longer": John D. Rockefeller Jr. to Maitland F. Griggs, July 8, 1935, RFA, RG 2, series H, box 63, folder 472, RAC.

196–97 Rockefeller advises against meeting minutes: John D. Rockefeller Jr. to George Baker, January 27, 1936, ibid., box 65, folder 491.

197 "It has become necessary"; "Then you can say": Frederick Mortimer Clapp to John Henry Hammond, January 27, 1936, Frederick Mortimer Clapp Papers, YU, with Hammond's reply.

197 "There is no woman whose business achievement": quoted in Ware, *Holding Their Own*, 75.

197–98 The argument between Helen and Clapp: Helen C. Frick, "Conversation Between Miss Frick and Mr. Clapp," January 27, 1936, HCFFA, and Frederick Mortimer Clapp memorandum, February 1, 1936, Frederick Mortimer Clapp Papers, YU.

198 Morgan "heartily endorses": George Baker to John D. Rockefeller Jr., January 30, 1936, RFA, RG 2, series H, box 65, folder 491, RAC.

198–99 "possible election of officers": John D. Rockefeller Jr., notation on George Baker letter, January 30, 1936, ibid.

199 "a permanent record of": John D. Rockefeller Jr. to Andrew W. Mellon, April 24, 1936, ibid.

199 "the members of the Board . . . are entitled": Thomas M. Debevoise to John D. Rockefeller Jr., May 19, 1936, ibid.

199 "This letter of course"; "it indicates the basis": John D. Rockefeller Jr. to Andrew W. Mellon, April 24, 1936, ibid.

199 "It is both natural and proper"; "it was the Founder's wish"; "Miss Frick is in complete charge"; "dominance": John D. Rockefeller Jr. to Childs Frick, February 3, 1936, ibid, box 64, folder 485.

199 "The situation as it exists": John D. Rockefeller Jr. to Frederick Mortimer Clapp, February 16, 1936, Frederick Mortimer Clapp Papers, YU.

199 "No Trustee . . . shall": Resolutions and Preambles Adopted by the Executive Committee, February 18, 1936, RFA, RG 2, box 64, folder 485, RAC.

199 "[Childs] got it"; "As for the sister"; "All went merry": Harrison Griswold Dwight to Frederick Mortimer Clapp, March 3, 1936, Frederick Mortimer Clapp Papers, YU.

199 "F. announced": Harrison Griswold Dwight to Frederick Mortimer Clapp, March 15, 1936, Frederick Mortimer Clapp Papers, YU.

200 "I am very much impressed": Helen C. Frick to Frederick Mortimer Clapp, March 4, 1936, FC/FARL Archives.

200 "another such opportunity": Helen C. Frick to Maitland F. Griggs, February 14, 1936, FC/FARL Archives.

200 "The condition of the pictures in the Collection": Helen C. Frick to Edward W. Forbes, March 6, 1936, Fogg Art Museum, HUA.

200 "the usurpation of authority": John D. Rockefeller Jr. to Frederick Mortimer Clapp, April 14, 1936, Frederick Mortimer Clapp Papers, YU.

200 "You should be the director"; "The way in which pictures"; "Besides I am sick": Frederick Mortimer Clapp to Harrison Griswold Dwight, April 17, 1936, ibid.

201 "I have come to the inescapable"; Helen's further comments in rejoinder: Helen C. Frick to Childs Frick, May 13, 1936, RFA, RG 2, series H, box 65, folder 491, RAC.

201 "It will be the source": Helen C. Frick to Childs Frick, May 14, 1936, Frederick Mortimer Clapp Papers, YU.

201 "fearing I have not the reserves": Frederick Mortimer Clapp to George Baker, May 22, 1936, ibid.

201 "I want you to know this": Frederick Mortimer Clapp to Helen C. Frick, June 5, 1936, ibid.

202 "Miss Frick told me"; "Though [it] rises above me": Frederick Mortimer Clapp to Mr. Porter, June 13, 1936, ibid.

202 "One wonders just how much": Harrison Griswold Dwight to John D. Rockefeller Jr., June 19, 1936, RFA, RG 2, series H, box 64, folder 485, RAC.

202 "[It] does not impress me"; "The drapery": Helen C. Frick to Frederick Mortimer Clapp, July 31, 1936, HCFFA.

202"I am deeply interested": Helen C. Frick to Paul Sachs, April 14, 1936, Fogg Art Museum, HUA.

202 "Miss Frick would like to": Eleanor B. Howland to Ellen R. Boyd, May 11, 1936, HCFFA.

202 "On the whole": Ellen R. Boyd to Helen C. Frick, June 22, 1936, HCFFA.

203 "Owing to the close"; "In light of": Horace Havemeyer to John D. Rockefeller Jr., August 25, 1936, RFA, RG 2, series H, box 64, folder 487, RAC.

203 Letter of protest: John D. Rockefeller Jr. to Helen C. Frick, August 26, 1936, ibid.

203 "Miss Frick was just terribly upset": Eleanor B. Howland to Ellen R. Boyd, November 17, 1936, HCFFA.

204 "I think you will be proud": Helen C. Frick to Edward W. Forbes, October 13, 1937, Fogg Art Museum, HUA.

204 "The Fine Arts Department is no longer"; "illustrating art"; "A complete sound motion picture apparatus": "The Department of Fine Arts Courses 1936–1937," ASCUP.

204 "smooth running machine"; "perhaps your greatest": John D. Rockefeller Jr. to Frederick Mortimer Clapp, October 27, 1936, Frederick Mortimer Clapp Papers, YU.

204–5 "I have been slyly cultivating"; "I wrote a soothing"; "I . . . wrote the Duchess"; "A reply arrived": Harrison Griswold Dwight to Frederick Mortimer Clapp and Maud Clapp, November 20, 1936, Frederick Mortimer Clapp Papers, YU.

205–6 Helen's opinion of the Fra Carnevale: Helen C. Frick to Harrison Griswold Dwight, December 14, 1936, FC/FARL Archives.

206 "How will [the trustees]": Harrison Griswold Dwight to Frederick Mortimer Clapp, December 1, 1936, Frederick Mortimer Clapp Papers, YU.

206 "a second-tier somebody"; "little more than a name": "An Artist who Kept His Day Job as a Priest," *New York Times*, January 28, 2005, author's collection.

206 Philippe de Montebello's comments: foreword to Christiansen, *From Filippo Lippi to Piero della Francesca*, 12–33.

206 Helen's walk through the Frick galleries: Harrison Griswold Dwight to Frederick Mortimer Clapp, December 1, 1936, Frederick Mortimer Clapp Papers, YU.

206 "expressed a desire"; "a sketch of a possible program": Vanderbilt Webb to Helen C. Frick, April 5, 1937, RFA, RG 2, series H, box 64, folder 480, RAC.

206–7 Frederick Mortimer Clapp's sketch, "Toward a Policy of Acquisitions," April 5, 1937, ibid.

207 "that it may be wise to consider": Minutes of the FC Board of Trustees, May 19, 1937, HCFFA.

207 "We are not made for large mobs": Frederick Mortimer Clapp to Harrison Griswold Dwight, November 11, 1937, Frederick Mortimer Clapp Papers, YU.

207 "[the] fold in [the] drapery"; "go back to [the] original": Edward W. Forbes to Helen C. Frick, November 4, 1937, HCFFA.

208 "I am getting things": Helen C. Frick to Edward W. Forbes, February 8, 1938, HCFFA.

208 Russian Room tapestry: The author is grateful to Antonia and Nicholas Shoumatoff for bringing this story to her attention and to Antonia for making her aware of their great-uncle, Andrey Avinoff's, watercolors of the Nationality Rooms.

208 Miss Frick regrets it is impossible": Eleanor B. Howland to F. X. A. Eble, February 19, 1938, HCFFA.

208 "our American job holders": Helen C. Frick to Ellen R. Boyd, March 26, 1938, HCFFA.

208 "We worked hard": Ellen R. Boyd to Helen C. Frick, April 1, 1938, HCFFA.

211 Boyd on Germans at the Iron Rail: Ellen R. Boyd to Helen C. Frick, May 18, 1938, HCFFA.

211 "She thought it a pity"; "These things must be quietly discussed"; "Sooner or later": Harrison Griswold Dwight to Frederick Mortimer Clapp, May 12, 1938, Frederick Mortimer Clapp Papers, YU.

211 "Francofile [*sic*] feminist": Harrison Griswold Dwight to Frederick Mortimer Clapp, June 17, 1938, ibid.

212 "Of course what is required"; Dwight's complaints about Childs: Harrison Griswold Dwight to Frederick Mortimer Clapp, June 23, 1938, ibid.

212 "I don't suppose it ever"; "We simply have to make": Harrison Griswold Dwight to Frederick Mortimer Clapp, 1938, ibid.

212 "I hope there is someone": Frederick Osborn to John D. Rockefeller Jr., October 10, 1938, RFA, RG 2, series H, box 64, folder 480, RAC.

212 "everyone's purse strings": Helen C. Frick to Edward W. Forbes, June 18, 1935, Fogg Art Museum, HUA.

214 "One little girl": Ellen R. Boyd to Helen C. Frick, August 15, 1938, HCFFA.

214 "declared she would come": Helen C. Frick to Edward W. Forbes, February 21, 1939, HCFFA.

214 "It doesn't seem to me": Harrison Griswold Dwight to Frederick Mortimer Clapp, January 9, 1939, Frederick Mortimer Clapp Papers, YU.

214–15 Clapp's plan for acquisitions: Frederick Mortimer Clapp to Acquisition Committee on Policy, February 14, 1939, RFA, RG 2, series H, box 64, folder 480, RAC.

216 "The condition is perfect": Helen C. Frick to Edward W. Forbes, March 25, 1939, Fogg Art Museum, HUA.

216 Clapp's frustration: Frederick Mortimer Clapp to Harrison Griswold Dwight, May 5, 1939, Frederick Mortimer Clapp Papers, YU.

216 Clapp's desire to see John D. Rockefeller as president: Frederick Mortimer Clapp to Harrison Griswold Dwight, July 24, 1939, Frederick Mortimer Clapp Papers, YU.

216 "profound regret": Helen C. Frick to Herbert Hoover, April 24, 1939, Herbert Hoover Papers, Herbert Hoover Presidential Library.

217 "I'm always at the fireside": Helen C. Frick to Gertrude Davis, undated, 1939, Iron Rail Thirtieth Anniversary Book of Letters, vol. 1, GCA, Schlesinger Library, Radcliffe College, HUA.

217 "beautifully made": Eleanor B. Howland to Ellen R. Boyd, December 13, 1939, HCFFA.

217 "The expenditure of money": Ellen R. Boyd, 1939 Report to Officers and Board Members of the Iron Rail, HCFFA.

217 Quotations from McCarten, "Profiles," pts. 1 and 2.

PART SEVEN: WAR (1940–1950)

219 "I am very much upset": Helen C. Frick to Ellen R. Boyd, January 5, 1940, HCFFA.

219 "clear to Miss Frick": John D. Rockefeller Jr. to Frederick Osborn, March 12, 1940, RFA, RG 2, series H, box 64, folder 480, RAC.

219 "The question as to whether": John D. Rockefeller Jr., undated memorandum, ibid.

219 Osborn's report on decision to purchase Gauguin and Cézanne: Frederick Osborn to John D. Rockefeller Jr., April 23, 1940, ibid.

219–21 "would like to see armored plate"; "at a considerable distance from": Frederick Mortimer Clapp memorandum, May 17, 1940, Frederick Mortimer Clapp Papers, YU.

221 "The world is in such an upset condition": Helen C. Frick to John Gabbert Bowman, June 12, 1940, Chancellors File, RG 2/10, 1921–1945, ASCUP.

221 "This looks like the first ray": Helen C. Frick to Edward W. Forbes, June 28, 1940, HCFFA.

221 "because . . . it seems a pity": Helen C. Frick to Edward W. Forbes, June 18, 1940, HCFFA.

221 "I do not doubt that you are as absorbed"; "It is hard to believe": Edward W. Forbes to Helen C. Frick, June 27, 1940, Fogg Art Museum, HUA.

221 "merry and kind": Sheila Inglis, "Birdseye View of Christmas at Thissell House," December 25, 1940, HCFFA.

222 "her little boy, Bobby": author's interview with Shelia Inglis Milliken, June 4, 1993. The author is deeply grateful to Mrs. Milliken for sharing her recollections of Helen C. Frick.

222 Parents' letters to Helen: T. Alan Stuchbery, September 30, 1940; Phyllis Sayers, August 31, 1941; Elsie Horn, November 8, 1940, HCFFA.

223 "Never in any letter": Phyllis Sayers to Helen C. Frick, July 13, 1941.

223 "the terrific results make": Helen C. Frick, Westmoreland Farm Diary, 1937–1941, entry for November 5, 1940, HCFFA.

223 "We have never kept a record": Ellen R. Boyd to Helen C. Frick, September 11, 1940, HCFFA.

223 "considerable doubt exists": R. G. Rankin & Co., "Iron Rail Vacation Home Report on the Investigation of the Accounting System," December 2, 1940, HCFFA.

223 "after Mrs. Boyd's wedding announcement": Helen C. Frick interview with Miss Elizabeth Limmond, reported to William J. Naughton, August 25, 1941, HCFFA.

223 "forbidden person": Eleanor B. Howland to William J. Naughton, July 5, 1941, HCFFA.

223 "Isn't this an *amazing* letter": Helen C. Frick to William J. Naughton, February 24, 1941, HCFFA.

223–24 "so as to eradicate the memories"; not "to be bothered by [Boyd]": Eleanor B. Howland to William J. Naughton, March 31, 1941, HCFFA.

224 "The Collection is more of a grave": Frederick Mortimer Clapp to Harrison Griswold Dwight, August 20, 1940, Frederick Mortimer Clapp Papers, YU.

224 "Heaven give me strength": Frederick Mortimer Clapp to Harrison Griswold Dwight, December 16, 1940, ibid.

224 Description of Christmas: Sheila Inglis, "Birdseye View of Christmas at Thissell House," December 25, 1940, HCFFA.

224 "There is so much to be done": Helen C. Frick to John Gabbert Bowman, January 8, 1941, Chancellors Files, RG 2/10, 1921–1945, ASCUP.

224 "busy after work knitting sweaters": Helen Sanger, "Recollections of Miss Frick by the Senior Staff of the Frick Art Reference Library," 1984, 3, FARL.

225 "Completion of the [new] vault": Henry O. Milliken to Helen C. Frick, June 25, 1941, HCFFA.

225 "after all represent": Henry O. Milliken to Helen C. Frick, July 22, 1941, HCFFA.

225 "Most of our people are working": Iron Rail Report, July 1941, HCFFA.

225 "The most marked change": Iron Rail Report, August 1941, HCFFA.

226 Preparation of the cottage: Helen C. Frick to William J. Naughton, undated, HCFFA.

226 "satisfied in leaving all but the *Pietà*"; "in the safest place": Helen C. Frick to Paul Sachs, December 19, 1941, Fogg Art Museum, HUA.

227 "I have been giving thought": Helen C. Frick to John Gabbert Bowman, May 23, 1942, Chancellors File, RG 2/10, 1921–1945, ASCUP.

227 "a good deal of the chicken wire"; "put [the meat] up": Helen C. Frick to Ruth W. Larsen, September 23, 1942, HCFFA.

227 "trying so hard to save": Eleanor B. Howland to Ruth W. Larsen, January 30, 1942, HCFFA.

227 "Has it occurred to you"; "A profession": Helen C. Frick to True Blue Girls ages 18 to 30, October 9, 1942, HCFFA.

229 "wander about"; "became very close friends" author's interview with Shelia Inglis Milliken, June 4, 1993.

229 "Just as a matter of record": Helen C. Frick to Childs Frick, February 10, 1943, RFA, RG 2, series H, box 63, folder 474, RAC.

229 "in an appropriate place in the Collection": John D. Rockefeller Jr. to Childs Frick, March 1943, ibid.

229 "have drawings made at my expense": Helen C. Frick to unnamed attorney, "The Frick Collection," February 4, 1949, HCFFA.

229 "Of course the hanging of the picture": Frederick Mortimer Clapp to John D. Rockefeller Jr., February 26, 1943, Frederick Mortimer Clapp Papers, YU.

229 "accepted the gift": John D. Rockefeller Jr. to Childs Frick, March 1943, RFA, RG 2, series H, box 63, folder 474, RAC.

229 "would not have anyone dictate": Helen C. Frick to unnamed attorney, "The Frick Collection," February 4, 1949, HCFFA.

229–30 "I reminded him that I had been accustomed": ibid.

230 "Some museum not obsessed": Frederick Mortimer Clapp to Harrison Griswold Dwight, June 25, 1943, Frederick Mortimer Clapp Papers, YU.

231 "to tell you how deeply grateful we are": Sumner McK. Crosby to Helen C. Frick, July 2, 1943, HCFFA.

231 "more than a hundred expert scholars": Knox, *Story of the Frick Art Reference Library*, 83.

232 "a test of whether or not": "Europe's Looted Art, Can It Be Recovered?": *New York Times*, September 19, 1943, FARL Scrapbook, 1940–1949, FARL.

232 "Would it be possible": Helen C. Frick to Owen J. Roberts, November 30, 1943, HCFFA.

232 "It may well be": Owen J. Roberts to Helen C. Frick, December 2, 1943, HCFFA.

232 "Since it is impossible to live or work": Ruth W. Larsen to Helen C. Frick, November 24, 1943, HCFFA, with notation by Helen C. Frick.

232–33 Helen's decision to change the Iron Rail: Helen C. Frick to True Blue Girls, December 15, 1943, HCFFA.

233 "The Lowell and Lawrence girls": Ruth W. Larsen to Helen C. Frick, January 27, 1944, HCFFA.

233 "To some of us the need of Iron Rail's free vacations": Boston True Blue Club to Helen C. Frick, March 1944, HCFFA.

233 "a few [in the other clubs were]": Ruth W. Larsen to Helen C. Frick, January 27, 1944, HCFFA.

233 "French Babies"; "Our purpose would be"; "old enough to ensure": Helen C. Frick to Mrs. Edward J. Holmes, February 24, 1944, HCFFA.

233 "very crowded and not very pleasing": Helen C. Frick to Frederick Mortimer Clapp, January 6, 1944, HCFFA.

233 "Although this was the last time we'll see you": Molly Stuchbery to Helen C. Frick, July 14, 1944, HCFFA.

233 "Three of us stood in the stern of the ship"; "so each had something nice": interview with Sheila Inglis Milliken, June 4, 1993.

233–34 "not to mention business of any kind to her": Eleanor B. Howland to Ruth W. Larsen, September 6, 1944, HCFFA.

234 "sick at heart!": Helen C. Frick to Edward W. Forbes, September 21, 1944, Fogg Art Museum, HUA.

234 "as long as your committee finds it necessary": Helen C. Frick to William B. Dinsmoor, October 26, 1944, HCFFA.

234 "[The] damage to historical monuments in France": Rensselaer W. Lee to Frank Aydelotte, November 28, 1944, Rensselaer W. Lee Papers, Historical Studies-Social Science Library, Institute for Advanced Studies, Princeton, N.J.

234 "I was surprised and shocked": Frank J. Mather Jr. to Helen C. Frick, April 25, 1945, HCFFA.

234 "The flags have been omitted at my direction": Helen C. Frick to Frank J. Mather Jr., April 28, 1945, HCFFA.

234 "You are so desperately muddled"; "monstrously sophistical"; "[I] hate to think": Frank J. Mather Jr. to Helen C. Frick, May 5, 1945, HCFFA.

234 "This morning heard that unconditional surrender": Helen C. Frick, Ready Reference Diary, 1945, entry for May 7, HCFFA.

235 "Under your generalship": Helen C. Frick to Ethelwyn Manning, FARL Scrapbook, 1940–1949, FARL.

235 "never get to go anywhere.": Ruth W. Larsen to Helen C. Frick, January 31, 1945, HCFFA.

235 "turned my mind"; "where we could": John D. Rockefeller Jr. to Horace Havemeyer, March 1, 1945, RFA, RG 2, series H, box 63, folder 474, RAC.

235 "I . . . hit the skies!": Helen C. Frick to William S. Moorhead, memorandum of meeting with Frederick Osborn, undated, 1946, HCFFA.

235 "I am very much concerned": Helen C. Frick to William S. Moorhead, March 22, 1945, HCFFA.

236 "The Frick Collection just *breathes* my father's and mother's taste": Helen C. Frick, answers to William S. Moorhead questions, 1948, HCFFA.

236 "study the Will and [the] Charter"; "Childs will not fight": Helen C. Frick to William S. Moorhead, March 22, 1945, HCFFA.

236 "shall encourage"; "to be expended from time to time": article 4, sections 2 and 4, Will of Henry C. Frick, June 24, 1915, author's collection.

236 "Mr. Moorhead's conclusions": Vanderbilt Webb to John Henry Hammond, June 12, 1945, SFA.

236 Hammond's list of Helen's gifts to the collection: quoted in William S. Moorhead, memorandum, "Gifts from Miss Frick as Related to the Frick Collection and the Power of the Trustees of the Collection to Accept Gifts," April 4, 1947.

236 "a man's will should be interpreted": William Watson Smith to William S. Moorhead (?), July 6, 1945, HCFFA.

236 "This list is what I thought"; "felt it belonged in [the] Collection": "Gifts From Miss Frick with Comments and Notations by Miss Frick," 1947 (?), HCFFA.

236–37 "by agreement"; "an agreed exchange": memo for William S. Moorhead, "Gifts From Miss Frick," April 4, 1947, HCFFA.

237 Smith's response to Hammond's list: William Watson Smith to William S. Moorhead, July 9, 1945, SFA; also in the HCFFA.

237 "to prepare a list of artists": Helen C. Frick to Edward W. Forbes, October 19, 1945, Fogg Art Museum, HUA.

237 Clapp's analysis of FC: Frederick Mortimer Clapp, "Special Report on the Frick Collection," October 9, 1945, HCFFA.

237 "Mr. Clapp's uncomplimentary remarks"; "I want to frankly say": Helen C. Frick to Edward W. Forbes, October 19, 1945, Fogg Art Museum, HUA.

237 "the distinction of the collection"; "will have to decide": Edward W. Forbes to Helen C. Frick, October 24, 1945, Fogg Art Museum, HUA.

238 "TRIPE"; "Should this paper be shown": Helen C. Frick to William S. Moorhead, October 15, 1945, HCFFA.

238 "If paintings by all"; "it would be wise": William S. Moorhead to Helen C. Frick, October 9, 1945, HCFFA.

238 "hints that we should invest in Impressionists": Helen C. Frick memorandum, October 23, 1945, Malvina Hoffman Papers, Getty Research Institute.

238 Helen's report of the trustees meeting and decision to go to court: Helen C. Frick to William S. Morehead, October 23, 1945, and enclosure; October 29, 1945, HCFFA.

238 "J. D. R.'s 'henchman'": Helen C. Frick to William S. Moorhead, January 19, 1946, HCFFA.

238–41 "I would not wish"; "sorry that Childs is not with us"; "It may be easier"; "to remove Childs' name": Helen C. Frick to William S. Moorhead, October 29, 1945, HCFFA.

241 "some of the trustees are a bit scared"; "I would not do so": Helen C. Frick to William S. Moorhead, January 10, 1946, HCFFA.

241 "Every mail contains requests": Ruth W. Larsen to Eleanor B. Howland, April 12, 1946, HCFFA.

241 "Of course they have just moved": Eleanor B. Howland to Ruth W. Larsen, April 1, 1946, HCFFA.

241 "for Mrs. Symington": Eleanor B. Howland to Ruth W. Larsen, March 11, 1946, HCFFA.

241 "I have undertaken a big job": Helen C. Frick to Edward W. Forbes, July 14, 1946, Fogg Art Museum, HUA.

241 "[Miss Frick] is certainly enjoying": Ruth W. Larsen to Eleanor B. Howland, July 27, 1946, HCFFA.

241 "because we are all swamped": Ethelwyn Manning to Helen C. Frick, August 21, 1946, HCFFA.

241 "otherwise six months time": John D. Rockefeller Jr. to Vanderbilt Webb, June 1, 1946, SFA.

241 "no personal interest"; "the undesirability": Helen C. Frick to unnamed attorney, Helen C. Frick notes of FC board meeting October 11, 1946, HCFFA.

243 "Put my name in": Helen C. Frick to unnamed attorney, notations on FC Board of Trustees meeting, October 11, 1946, HCFFA.

243 "rather heatedly inquired": Helen C. Frick to William S. Moorhead, October 25, HCFFA.

243 "What will happen after"; "I can pull out quietly"; "Rockefeller was *furious*": Helen C. Frick to unnamed attorney, notations on FC Board of Trustees meeting, October 11, 1946, HCFFA.

243 "I can see the prospect": Helen C. Frick to William S. Moorhead, October 19, 1946, HCFFA.

243 "Don't forget the Executive Committee": Helen C. Frick to William S. Moorhead, October 19, 1946, HCFFA.

243 "such a right": Helen C. Frick to Vanderbilt Webb, December 9, 1946, HCFFA.

243 "officially advised"; "any trustee could make": William S. Moorhead to John Henry Hammond, February 15, 1947, HCFFA.

243 "very much dissatisfied"; "[Sachs] regretted": Helen C. Frick to William S. Moorhead, "Miss Frick . . . is making all sorts of preparations": Eleanor B. Howland to Ruth W. Larsen, April 9, 1947, HCFFA.

244 "I am familiar with some of the paintings": Helen C. Frick to Frederick Osborn, February 28, 1947, SFA.

244 Helen's comments on Frederick Mortimer Clapp's selections: Helen C. Frick to Frederick Osborn, March 22, 1947, SFA; also HCFFA.

244 "Your opinion I should naturally value highly": Frederick Mortimer Clapp to Paul Sachs, February 13, 1947, Frederick Mortimer Clapp Papers, YU.

244 "tangible basis for a consideration": Thomas M. Debevoise to Vanderbilt Webb, May 28, 1954, RFA, RG 2, Series H, box 64, folder 477, RAC.

244 "something to shoot at": John D. Rockefeller Jr. to Vanderbilt Webb, July 17, 1947, ibid.

244 "add to the interest": quoted in Thomas M. Debevoise to Vanderbilt Webb, April 23, 1947, SFA.

244 "to take the narrow view": Thomas M. Debevoise to Vanderbilt Webb, May 28, 1954, SFA.

244 "The success of the Collection": John Henry Hammond to Vanderbilt Webb, April 24, 1947, SFA.

244 "My understanding is": Helen C. Frick to Frederick Osborn, April 29, 1947, SFA.

244 "still a great work of art": Helen C. Frick, "Re Mr. Rockefeller's Offer," April 23, 1947, HCFFA.

244–45 "Before Duveen sold it to your father": Helen C. Frick to John D. Rockefeller Jr., undated, HCFFA.

245 "would feel like recommending": John D. Rockefeller Jr. to Frederick Mortimer Clapp, February 25, 1947, RFA, RG 2, series H, box 64, folder 477, RAC.

245 "deeply impressed"; "I feel sure that there does not exist": Frederick Mortimer Clapp to John D. Rockefeller Jr., March 19, 1947, ibid.

245 "The male members": John D. Rockefeller Jr. to Harrison Griswold Dwight, May 27, 1947, Harrison Griswold Dwight Papers, box VI, folder 16, Amherst College.

245 "she [was] going to resign"; "No": Helen C. Frick, record of telephone conversation with William S. Moorhead, May 6, 1947, HCFFA.

245 "Were the trustees to do so": Helen C. Frick to FC trustees, May 7, 1947, HCFFA.

245 "the application to the court is going forward": John D. Rockefeller Jr. to Harrison Griswold Dwight, June 5, 1947, Harrison Griswold Dwight Papers, box VI, folder 16, Amherst College.

245 Helen's jubilant response to the court filing: Helen C. Frick to Edward W. Forbes, May 29, 1947, Fogg Art Museum, HUA.

246 Helen's preparation for testimony about Henry Clay Frick's intentions: unnamed attorney, Evidence to Be Introduced at the Trial, undated, HCFFA.

246 "opinion as to the artistic quality": Helen C. Frick to Richard Offner, May 14, 1947, HCFFA.

246 Helen withdraws Houdon manuscript: Helen C. Frick to Edgar Munhall, September 17, 1976, HCFFA.

246 "While [the court] decision is most gratifying": John D. Rockefeller Jr. to Frederick Mortimer Clapp, July 22, 1945, Frederick Mortimer Clapp Papers, YU.

246–47 "You will agree, I am sure": John D. Rockefeller Jr. to Helen C. Frick, July 17, 1947, RFA, RG 2, series H, box 64, folder 477, RAC.

247 "Whether your letter of July 17th": Helen C. Frick to John D. Rockefeller Jr., July 24, 1947, ibid.

247 "'Obsession' is a polite": Thomas M. Debevoise to John D. Rockefeller Jr., July 30, 1947, ibid.

247 "Her letter was the last thing needed": Vanderbilt Webb to John D. Rockefeller Jr., August 17, 1947, SFA.

247 "many years ago now": Sir Robert Witt to Helen C. Frick, July 3, 1948, FARL Scrapbook, 1940–1949, FARL; also FC/FARL Archives.

247 "Rockefeller Gift of Art Is Refused": *New York Times*, January 30, 1948, HCFFA.

247 "Miss Frick seems to be taking this trial": Eleanor B. Howland to Ethelwyn Manning, February 11, 1948, HCFFA.

247–48 "Acquisition of pictures has become": Frederick Mortimer Clapp to John D. Rockefeller Jr., March 15, 1948, RFA, RG 2, series H, folder 474, RAC; also Frederick Mortimer Clapp Papers, YU.

248 "friendly action"; quoted in "Decision Reserved in Frick Gift Case," *New York Times*, May 1, 1948, David E. Finley Papers, RG 28, box 33, NGA.

248 "the art collection [was] too broad in nature": "Big Names in Friendly Suit over Frick Art Collection," *Sun Telegraph*, April 30, 1948, HCFFA.

248 "slight, graying"; "conservative brown suit and a small hat": "Frick Daughter Testifies in Art Collection Suit," *New York World Telegram*, April 30, 1948, HCFFA.

248 "his monument"; "my collection"; "our collection"; "my paintings": "Decision Reserved in Frick Gift Case," *New York Times*, May 1, 1948, HCFFA.

248 "that acceptance of outside gifts": "Big Names in Friendly Suit Over Frick Art Collection," *Sun Telegraph*, April 30, 1948, HCFFA.

248 "relieved to have this ordeal"; "Bedford as fast as possible": Helen C. Frick, Ready Reference Diary, 1948, entry for April 30, HCFFA.

248 "Miss Frick seemed pleased with the outcome": Eleanor B. Howland to Ruth W. Larsen, May 4, 1948, HCFFA.

248 "affords no ground for imputing to the testator": quoted in "Court Opens Way to Frick Art Gifts," *New York Times*, July 13, 1948, David E. Finley Papers, NGA.

248 "this morning's paper carried": Frederick Mortimer Clapp to John D. Rockefeller Jr., July 13, 1948, RFA, RG 2, series H, box 64, folder 477, RAC.

248 "In a rage for the next two days": Helen C. Frick, Ready Reference Diary, 1948, entry for July 13, HCFFA.

248 "So depressing. There is nothing": ibid., entry for July 15.

249 Helen rejects the Giorgione: Helen C. Frick to Charles R. Henschel, January 11, 1949, HCFFA.

249 Helen rejects Piero panels and Titian: Helen C. Frick to Edward W. Hutton, February 4, 1949, HCFFA.

249 "rank injustice": Helen C. Frick, Dante Day by Day Diary, 1949, entry for January 24, HCFFA.

249 "She is fighting mad about it": Eleanor B. Howland to Dagmar Holmes, February 1, 1949, HCFFA.

249–50 Helen's letter to "Your Honors": February 8, 1949, HCFFA.

250 "Terrific blow in afternoon"; "I will fight on!": Helen C. Frick, Dante Day by Day Diary, 1949, entry for May 26, HCFFA.

250 "similarity . . . to the matter uppermost"; "As a bird lover": Helen C. Frick to William S. Moorhead, memorandum, June 4, 1949, HCFFA.

250 "the utter unhappiness I have felt"; "For the past thirty years": Helen C. Frick to John T. Loughran, June 22, 1949, HCFFA.

250 "Not another soul knows about this": Helen C. Frick to William S. Moorhead, June 25, 1949, HCFFA.

250 "Now that Hammond is dead": Helen C. Frick to Childs Frick, July 1, 1949, HCFFA.

251 "discordant notes" Helen C. Frick, Art Acquisition Committee Report, January 13, 1949, FC/FARL Archives.

251 "The decision was a matter of opinion": Grier, interoffice memo, telephone conversation with Franklin M. Biebel, May 26, 1949, Minneapolis Institute of Arts.

251 "a haven for Communist sympathizers": quoted in Ross C. Anderson, "Politics and Aesthetics in the State Department Exhibition 1946–1948," in Littleton and Sykes, *Advancing American Art*, 23.

251 "Marshall Halts World Tour of Red-Linked U.S. Art": quoted in Littleton and Sykes, *Advancing American Art*, 54.

251 "controlled and manned overwhelmingly"; "an intimate of Picasso"; "the role of the artist"; "We are dealing with": George A. Dondero, "Communists Maneuver to Control Art in the United States," *Congressional Record*, March 25, 1949, 3234, 3235.

252 "Mr. Biebel stated confidentially": Harry D. M. Grier, interoffice memorandum, telephone conversation with Franklin M. Biebel, May 26, 1949, Minneapolis Institute of Art.

252 "When we were speaking of my Chinese porcelains"; "could easily be arranged": John D. Rockefeller Jr. to Frederick Mortimer Clapp, October 31, 1949, RFA, RG 2, series H, box 63, folder 474, RAC.

252 "generosity and for the tribute": Childs Frick to John D. Rockefeller Jr., November 3, 1949, RFA, RG 2, series H, box 64, folder 477, RAC.

252 "cannot accept or decline to accept": Thomas Debevoise to John D. Rockefeller Jr., November 10, 1949, ibid.

252 "most difficult"; tried to "tame": Helen C. Frick, Dante Day by Day Diary, 1949, entry for October 13, HCFFA.

252 "dead tired": ibid., entry for October 14.

252 "listened to [Norman] Spicer": ibid., entry for October 31.

252 a "nasty spill"; "quite sick": Helen C. Frick, Dante Day by Day Diary, 1949, entry for November 17, HCFFA.

252 "bare and institutional"; "homelike feeling": Minutes of the FC Board of Trustees, October 13, 1949, HCFFA.

252–53 "The Great Centennial Celebration": Helen C. Frick, Westmoreland Farm Diary, 1949–1951, entry for December 18, 1949, HCFFA.

253 "Your beautiful tributes to my father"; "You are making the world of art understand": Helen C. Frick to Sir Osbert Sitwell, July 5, July 10, 1947, HCFFA.

253 "That which sets [the Frick Collection] apart": Osbert Sitwell, introduction to The Frick Collection, *Paintings*, vol. 1 of the Frick Collection illustrated catalogue, 1949.

254 "There never was any question regarding": Helen C. Frick, "Henry Clay Frick and His Collection," ibid.

254 "I can think of no finer memorial": quoted in Knox, *Story of the Frick Art Reference Library*, first draft, FC/FARL Archives.

254 "additions to The Collection could then be housed": Frederick Osborn to FC trustees, January 10, 1950, HCFFA.

254 "injury . . . to the wholeness"; "the dissent of a minority of one"; "Miss Frick is pretty upset": Frederick Osborn to John D. Rockefeller Jr., January 16, 1950, RFA, RG 2, series H, box 63, folder 474, RAC.

254 "I wish to state that I am not yet through fighting": Helen C. Frick to Frederick Osborn, January 12, 1950, HCFFA.

254 "Trustees meeting—awful": Helen C. Frick, Zodiac Diary, 1949–1951, entry for January 12, 1950, HCFFA.

254 "a museum housing the art collection of others": Helen C. Frick to Vanderbilt Webb, April 12, 1950, SFA.

254 "to see if there is some furniture in the house": Helen C. Frick secretary to Platt Ketcham, February 16, 1950, HCFFA.

255 "We shall have to be extremely careful": Vanderbilt Webb to Frederick Osborn, February 23, 1950, SFA.

255 Helen's radio address and leopard story: Helen C. Frick, undated memorandum, March 1950, HCFFA.

255 David Finley's diplomatic reply: David Finley to Helen C. Frick, March 8, 1950, HCFFA.

255 "I feel that your son-in-law's chances"; "I am going to find other means": Helen C. Frick to Theodore Rousseau, March 15, 1950, HCFFA.

256 "Miss Frick regrets she does not feel": Helen C. Frick's secretary to Germain Seligman, April 14, 1950, HCFFA.

256 "a number of the Trustees feel that the present facilities": Frederick Osborn to John D. Rockefeller Jr., May 12, 1950, RFA, RG 2, Office of the Messrs. Rockefeller, John D. Rockefeller Jr., Personal Series, box 44, RAC.

256 "carry the thing along"; "get a more wholly favorable result": ibid., undated.

256 "There is to say the least grave doubt": Charles Harding to Helen C. Frick, May 17, 1950, HCFFA.

256 "piecemeal or step-by-step basis"; "I am sure that every responsible trustee": Helen C. Frick to Vanderbilt Webb, June 1, 1950, HCFFA.

256 "In my attempt to help the Frick Collection": John D. Rockefeller Jr. to Vanderbilt Webb, June 30, 1950, RFA, RG2, series H, box 64, folder 477, RAC.

256 "planning certain additions"; "That they should go to the Metropolitan": John D. Rockefeller Jr. to Vanderbilt Webb, July 26, 1950, RFA, RG 2, Office of the Messrs. Rockefeller, John D. Rockefeller Jr., Personal Series, box 44, RAC.

256 "Time should be taken by the forelock": Helen C. Frick to Vanderbilt Webb, December 14, 1950, SFA.

256 "pretty drastic treatment in New York": Eleanor B. Howland to Ruth W. Larsen, October 17, 1950, HCFFA.

256 "requiring such a program [had] not yet": Vanderbilt Webb, memorandum of December 19, 1950, FC Executive Committee Meeting, SFA.

256 "American, and Americans of American extraction": Helen C. Frick's secretary to G. La Montagne, December 5, 1950, HCFFA.

256 "on top of the world": Eleanor B. Howland to Ruth W. Larsen, November 8, 1950, HCFFA.

256 "a superb example of this master's work": Charles R. Henschel to Frederick Mortimer Clapp, November 30, 1950, HCFFA.

256 "This is really most unusual and very beautiful": Helen C. Frick to Charles B. Harding, November 3, 1950, HCFFA.

256 Helen rejects paintings by Bartolo di Fredi and Manet: ibid.

257 "I cannot now truthfully say": Frederick Mortimer Clapp to John D. Rockefeller Jr., January 1, 1951, SFA.

257 "While I feel with Dr. Clapp": John D. Rockefeller Jr. to Vanderbilt Webb, January 15, 1951, SFA.

257–59 "It seems to me that the final conclusion": Vanderbilt Webb to John D. Rockefeller Jr., January 23, 1951, SFA.

259 "All you aspire to is done": Maud Clapp to Helen C. Frick, undated draft, Frederick Mortimer Clapp Papers, YU.

259 "Trustees meeting—Very Weary!": Helen C. Frick, Westmoreland Farm Diary, 1949–1951, entry for January 11, 1951, HCFFA.

PART EIGHT: THE MANTLE (1951–1964)

261 "It is the policy": Helen C. Frick, Proposed Resolution on Art Acquisition, May 21, 1951, HCFFA.

261 Helen rejects Titian painting: Helen C. Frick to Madeleine Loiseau, March 27, 1951, HCFFA.

261 Helen rejects Francesco di Giorgio painting: Helen C. Frick to B. S. Boggis, April 4, 1951, HCFFA.

261 Helen rejects Sassetta painting: FC Board Minutes, October 16, 1951, HCFFA.

262 "We have taken quite a strong stand": Ruth W. Larsen to Helen C. Frick, April 3, 1951, HCFFA.

262 "My personal opinion of the U.N.": Helen C. Frick to assistant director of Iron Rail, April 4, 1951, HCFFA.

262 "We have found that [it] is by Eleanor Roosevelt": Helen C. Frick to Ruth W. Larsen, April 4, 1951, HCFFA.

262 "perpetuate [Clayton] and [its] contents as a landmark of the Victorian era": quoted in Helen Clay Frick Foundation, *Clayton: The Furnishings Plan*, 309.

262 "[I am] deeply impressed with the importance": David E. Finley to Helen C. Frick, May 21, 1952, HCFFA.

263 "a scrapbook in my possession at Bedford": quoted in Helen Clay Frick Foundation, *Clayton: The Furnishings Plan*, 1.

263 "As far as possible, the paintings": ibid., 2.

263 "to choose from among my thousand memories": Helen C. Frick, "Clayton Memoir, c. 1950s," HCFFA.

263 "I wish to make it clear": quoted in Helen Clay Frick Foundation, *Clayton: The Furnishing Plan*, 309.

264 Nixon's "Checkers Speech"; "You're my boy": quoted in "Richard M. Nixon," *World Book Encyclopedia*, 1972, s.v. "Nixon, Richard."

264 "When you made [your] television appearance": R. W. Bramwell to Richard M. Nixon, June 11, 1953, Richard M. Nixon Pre-Presidential Papers, series 320, box 601, "Pittsburgh & West Virginia Railway Company," NARA CA.

264 "Resolved: That it is the policy of the Frick Collection": quoted in Charles Ryskamp, introduction to The Frick Collection, *Art in the Frick Collection: Paintings, Sculpture, Decorative Arts*, 31.

264 "It concerns me more personally"; "What induced him": Helen C. Frick to William Knox, January 26, 1953, HCFFA.

265 "I may only say that I can thoroughly": Childs Frick to John D. Rockefeller Jr., December 4, 1954, RFA, RG 2, series H, box 64, folder 477, RAC.

265 Transporting the Westmoreland railroad car to Clayton: Walter F. Cooley Jr. to Charles Harding, September 1 and September 21, 1953, HCFFA.

266 Helen's recounting of events while in Scotland and London: Helen C. Frick, Scotland 1953 Album, author's collection, unless otherwise noted.

266 "having a great deal of trouble": Helen C. Frick's secretary to Ruth W. Larsen, September 2, 1953, HCFFA.

266 "overcome by [the] bad news": Helen C. Frick telegram to Fred L. Rath, October 12, 1953, HCFFA.

267 "mentioned that she owned a large piece": Gooch, *History of the Girls Clubs of America*, 14.

267 "the thought had never occurred to me"; "I know this is not easy": Helen C. Frick to Ruth W. Larsen, April 10, 1954, HCFFA.

267 Snapshots "taken many years ago": Eleanor B. Howland to Walter F. Cooley Jr., September 8, 1955, HCFFA.

267 "shocked [and] distressed"; "appearance in the Pittsburgh papers": Helen C. Frick to Fred L. Rath, June 9, 1954, Abstract of Major Correspondence on Clayton, National Trust Archives, Special Collections, Hornbake Library, University of Maryland.

267 Charles J. Graham's comments to the press: *Pittsburgh Post-Gazette*, June 5, 1954, HCFFA.

267 Helen's corrections: *Pittsburgh Sun Telegraph*, June 5, 1954, HCFFA.

267 "Your discussion of me in any way"; "In view of your disclosure": Helen C. Frick to Charles J. Graham, June 7, 1954, HCFFA.

267–68 "With all the building activity": Helen Duprey Bullock to Walter F. Cooley Jr., June 9, 1954, HCFFA.

269 "may not be *all* Van Eyck": Helen C. Frick to FC trustees, June 10, 1953, HCFFA.

269 "most important ever acquired": *New York Herald Tribune*, August 20, 1954, FARL Scrapbook, 1950–1959, FARL.

269 "perhaps the most important single painting": *New York Herald Tribune*, October 24, 1954, FC curatorial files, FC.

269 "The other day I was stunned"; "In view of the fact"; "I merely bring this": Helen C. Frick to Childs Frick, May 21, 1954, HCFFA.

269 "It is my desire that the library" Helen's request that FARL records not be copied: Helen C. Frick to FC trustees, 1955, HCFFA.

271–72 Westmoreland Farm bequests: Helen C. Frick, "Inventory of Furnishings at Westmoreland Farm," January 28, 1956, HCFFA.

272 "They are . . . getting to look rather crumbly": Rudolfe M. Riefstrahl to John Coolidge, November 1, 1956, Fogg Art Museum, HUA.

272 "I fear that I have some distressing news": John Coolidge to Helen C. Frick, July 2, 1957, Fogg Art Museum, HUA.

272 "I am both shocked and grieved"; "Because my faith": Helen C. Frick to John Coolidge, July 11, 1957, Fogg Art Museum, HUA.

272 "Her letter is an outrageous and typical": Paul Sachs to John Coolidge, July 11, 1957, Fogg Art Museum, HUA.

272 Agnes Mongan "thinks that Miss Frick": Rudolfe M. Riefstrahl to John Coolidge, July 12, 1957, Fogg Art Museum, HUA.

272 "I am deeply distressed": John Coolidge to Helen C. Frick, July 15, 1957, Fogg Art Museum, HUA.

273 Importance of a university art museum: Walter Reed Hovey to Edward Howard Litchfield, February 28, 1956, Chancellors Files, RG 2/1 1956–1965, ASCUP.

273 "Miss Frick apparently has a very strong dislike": A. C. Van Dusen to Edward Howard Litchfield, November 12, 1957, ibid.

273 "what was happening": Walker, *Self-Portrait with Donors*, 18.

273 "neither beautiful nor educational": quoted in "Helen Clay Frick Dies at 96," *Pittsburgh Post-Gazette*, November 10, 1984, HCFFA.

273 "try[ing] to avoid any estimates of cost at this time": A. C. Van Dusen to Edward Litchfield, November 12, 1957, Litchfield Papers, RG2/10, ASCUP.

273 "wherein wild bird and animal life": Certificate of Incorporation of Westmoreland Sanctuary, Inc., March 16, 1957, Bedford Village Archives, New York.

273 "substantial additional acreage": quoted in "New Wildlife Sanctuary Opens Today Near Bedford," *New York Times*, January 1, 1958.

274 "It looks as though"; "last summer"; "for [his] kind letter": Helen C. Frick to Bernard Berenson, March 17, 1958, Villa I Tatti Archives, HU Center for Italian Renaissance Studies.

274 "I wonder what is to become of the pictures"; "museums would rather spend their money": Edward W. Forbes to Bernard Berenson, September 15, 1948, Villa I Tatti Archives, HU Center for Italian Renaissance Studies.

274 "if the Lochoff collection"; "He was very encouraging": quoted in news article, undated, Fine Arts Library Records, Fine Arts Library, UP.

275 "Should I erect a building": quoted in unidentified news article, undated, Fine Arts Library Records, Fine Arts Library, UP.

275 "bus-loads after bus-loads of Germans": Martha Frick Symington [Sanger], Italy Album, 1958, author's collection.

275 "As you know Miss Frick has definite likes": Walter Reed Hovey to Edward Howard Litchfield, November 12, 1958, Chancellors Files, RG 2/1 1956–1965, ASCUP.

275 "Our problem is to keep": Edward Howard Litchfield to Charles H. Peake, December 11, 1958, Chancellors Files, RG 2/1 1956–1965, ASCUP.

275–76 "gradually" abandoned; "should be given to the Henry Clay Frick Fine Arts"; "an appropriate building would have to be erected"; "seemed . . . the only suitable": quoted in unidentified news article, undated, Fine Arts Library Records, Fine Arts Library, UP.

276 "contribute significantly to the intellectual": Charles H. Peake to Edward Howard Litchfield, March 31, 1959, Chancellors Files, RG 2/1 1956–1965, ASCUP.

276 "1.2 million is *all* we can get"; "While photographs are a proper means": Charles H. Peake to Edward Howard Litchfield, March 31, 1959, ibid.

277 "In the old days"; "bear the entire cost": Helen C. Frick to Edward Howard Litchfield, October 6, 1959, Chancellors Files, RG 2/1 1956–1965, ASCUP.

277 "displaying the history of the arts": "Plans Bared for Pitt Fine Arts Building," *Pittsburgh Post-Gazette*, November 5, 1959, author's collection.

277 "very much impressed": Helen C. Frick, Report to Art Acquisition Committee, January 14, 1960, HCFFA.

277 Helen hospitalized: Helen C. Frick, "Clochers et Pâturages" Calendar, 1960, entries for January 20 and 21, HCFFA.

277 "may try to dump their acquisitions": Bernard Berenson to Helen C. Frick, July 12, 1958, HCFFA.

277 "Should the Trustees vote to purchase": Helen C. Frick, Report to Art Acquisition Committee, January 14, 1960, HCFFA.

278 Nixon "would go down in history": quoted in unidentified news article, undated, WOMA.

278 "to comment directly on reports": unidentified news article, December 26, 1959, WOMA.

278 "The court is really lovely": quoted in Fazio, "Helen Clay Frick, Architectural Patron and Art Collector," 119.

278 "Each year I would present the budget": quoted in Alberts, *Pitt: The Story of the University of Pittsburgh*, 331.

278 "If [Hovey] was forced to step down": ibid, 352.

278 "a force that gave a privileged elite the authority": *New York Times*, January 1, 1989, Fine Arts Library, UP.

279 "about the only newspaper person"; "*no statement on the cost of the building*": Charles H. Peake to Edward Howard Litchfield, June 23, 1960, Chancellors Files, RG 2/1 1956–1965, ASCUP.

279 "Although we Republicans have not yet recovered": Helen C. Frick to Richard M. Nixon, March 2, 1961, box 275, NARA CA.

279 Condition of the Verrocchio bust: John Pope Hennessy, "Draft," FC curatorial files, FC.

280 "both bright and pretty": Simpson, *Partnership*, 240.

280 "skillful and artistic work": John D. Rockefeller Jr. to Frederick Mortimer Clapp, May 10, 1954, Frederick Mortimer Clapp Papers, YU.

280 William Suhr's condition report for *Crucifixion*: William Suhr to John D. Rockefeller Jr., March 8–October 29, 1951, William Suhr Papers, Getty Research Institute, Getty Research Library.

280 "that rag": author's interview with Helen Clay Chace, fall 1993.

280 "teasing and tormenting": ibid.

280 "had to declare out loud, one at a time": ibid.

280 Helen's departure from the trustees' room: author's interview with Henry Clay Frick II, September 27, 1993. The author is exceedingly grateful to Henry Clay Frick II for describing this event.

280 Helen's reaction at lunch: The author is deeply grateful to Ingrid and Bill Rea for describing this scene during an interview of June 2002.

280–81 Helen's resignation in the press; "he could make no statement": *New York Herald Tribune*, January 18, 1961.

281 Higginson's letter to Helen: Thomas H. Higginson to Helen C. Frick, January 13, 1961, HCFFA.

281 "Miss Frick stated that in view of the fact": Annual Meeting of the FC Board of Trustees, January 12, 1961, HCFFA.

281 "If Miss Helen C. Frick has resigned": *New York Herald Tribune*, January 1961, HCFFA.

281 "far below [the] average of [the] Collection"; "I applaud your courageous": Richard Offner to Helen C. Frick, January 5, January 20, 1961, HCFFA.

281 "Neither bust would seem"; "They might on the other hand": Charles Seymour Jr. to Helen C. Frick, January 9, 1961, HCFFA.

281 "on the magnificent way"; "It takes only one or two": Kenneth Clark to Helen C. Frick, January 4, January 18, 1961, HCFFA.

282 "The desire to preserve the Frick Collection intact": Helen C. Frick to FC trustees, January 20, 1961, HCFFA.

282 "I hope sufficient interest will be awakened": Helen C. Frick to Harvey Childs, March 21, 1961. The author is exceedingly grateful to Harvey Childs for sharing this letter.

282 "I would like to feel free to go ahead": Helen C. Frick to Edward Howard Litchfield, October 16, 1961, Chancellors Files, RG 2/1 1956–1965, ASCUP.

283 "does not fear gnats": Friends of Frick Fine Arts, *History of the Henry Clay Frick Fine Arts Department*, inside cover.

283 "Miss Frick indicated that it was not necessary"; "Do we insist": E. B. Cale to Edward Howard Litchfield, August 14, 1962, Chancellors Files, RG 2/1 1956–1965, ASCUP, with notation by Litchfield.

283 "This handsome memorial to your father's interest": Edward Howard Litchfield to Helen C. Frick, September 11, 1962, Chancellor's Files, RG 2/1 1956–1965, ASCUP.

283 Helen receives credit at the opening: Remarks by the Honorable Joseph M. Barr, Monday September 17, 1962, Buildings, ASCUP; Remarks by Edward H. Litchfield, 1962, Chancellors Files, RG 2/1 1956–1965, ASCUP.

283 "I am so delighted that everything went so well": Helen C. Frick to Charles H. Peake, September 27, 1962, Chancellors Files, RG 2/1 1956–1965, ASCUP.

283 "Proceed": Helen C. Frick to Edward Howard Litchfield, January 22, 1963, Chancellors Files, RG 2/1 1956–1965, ASCUP.

283 "It is beautiful!": Helen C. Frick, California Calendar, 1963 (altered by Helen C. Frick to be a 1964 calendar), entry for April 7, 1964, HCFFA.

283–84 "[Miss Frick] is making no commitment at this time": William F. Knox to Charles H. Peake, November 19, 1962, Chancellors Files, RG 2/1 1956–1965, ASCUP.

284 "I . . . want [Hovey] to have a great deal to say": Helen C. Frick to Frank W. Wadsworth, March 7, 1963, Office of the Dean, Division of the Humanities, RG 90/4/3, ASCUP.

284 "I do not look with favor upon German scholars"; "This is a very personal request": Helen C. Frick to Frank W. Wadsworth, April 10, 1963, Office of the Dean, Division of the Humanities, RG 90/4/3, ASCUP.

284 "Let me first try to answer the question"; "academic"; "The other persons"; "made a very favorable impression": Frank W. Wadsworth to Helen C. Frick, May 2, 1963, Chancellors Files, RG 2/1 1956–1965, ASCUP.

284 "I think her attitude"; "I do not think that Miss Frick"; "can afford to allow her": Frank W. Wadsworth to Charles H. Peake, June 5, 1963, Dean's Files, Division of the Humanities, ASCUP.

284 "is an American, about as American"; "He is a first-class person": Frank W. Wadsworth to Helen C. Frick, June 5, 1963, Chancellors Files, RG 2/1 1956–1965, ASCUP.

284–85 "Loerke is a very masculine, aggressive person": quoted in Alberts, *Pitt: The Story of the University of Pittsburgh*, 354.

285 "marked those sections having to do with her prejudice": Frank W. Wadsworth to Edward Howard Litchfield, May 31, 1963, Chancellors Files, RG 2/1 1956–1965, ASCUP.

285 "My belief is that donors are donors to the whole University": William C. Loerke to Frank W. Wadsworth, undated, Chancellors Files, RG 2/1 1956–1965, ASCUP.

285 Loerke's statement to the press: Edward Howard Litchfield to Messrs. Cale, Jalbert, Peake, Wadsworth, June 10, 1963, ibid.

285 "I would have thought that in consideration"; "Please remember that, as the sole donor": Helen C. Frick to Frank W. Wadsworth, June 21, 1963, Office of the Dean, Division of the Humanities, RG 90/4/3, ASCUP.

285 "most anxious to respect [her] wishes": quoted in Alberts, *Pitt: The Story of the University of Pittsburgh*, 355

285 "I am glad that although"; "I do not wish to be"; "Dr. Birkmeyer is an exception": Helen C. Frick to Edward Howard Litchfield, July 6, 1963, Dean's Files, Division of the Humanities, ASCUP.

285 "a gamble worth taking": quoted in Alberts, *Pitt: The Story of the University of Pittsburgh*, 355.

285 "1963 was the crucial year"; "mounting deficits and alarming"; "was close to being out": ibid., 306.

286 "other fresh farm products"; "one of the most pleasant afternoons"; "In view of what you told me about your opinion": Richard M. Nixon to Helen C. Frick, September 16, 1963, series 320, Richard Nixon Library and Birthplace Collections.

286 "I have started to read it"; "a mutually convenient date": Helen C. Frick to Richard M. Nixon, October 1, 1963, ibid.

286 "in every way"; "This time *you must win*": Helen C. Frick to Richard M. Nixon, January 29, 1964, series 320, Richard Nixon Library and Birthplace Collections.

286 "work out dates by phone": Richard M. Nixon, notation, ibid.

286 "a year hence"; "asking Miss Frick for a temporary exhibit": Charles H. Peake to Edward Howard Litchfield, October 15, 1963, Chancellors Files, RG 2/1 1956–1965, ASCUP, with notation by Litchfield.

286 "run[ning the collection] very sternly": Paul Cummings, interview with Harry Grier, April 21, 1970.

287 "nobody did anything but read the circulating mail folders": "Comments Made by Harry Grier," Peggy Kahn Collection.

287 "to look around and see"; Helen's relationship with Grier: author's interview with Peggy Kahn, October 31, 2003.

287 Loerke's letter to Lewis: William C. Loerke to Virginia E. Lewis, February 7, 1964, HCFFA.

287 Helen's response to Loerke's letter: Helen C. Frick to William C. Loerke, February 15, 1964, HCFFA.

287–88 Loerke's apology to Helen: William C. Loerke to Helen C. Frick, February 28, 1964, HCFFA.

287–88 "that a man capable of such boorishness": Helen C. Frick to Richard K. Mellon, February 27, 1964, Buildings, ASCUP.

288 Litchfield's statements on the Loerke controversy: Edward Howard Litchfield to Richard K. Mellon, April 6, 1964, Buildings, ASCUP.

288 "The pressure is getting intense": William H. Rea to Edward Howard Litchfield, March 27, 1964, Buildings, ASCUP.

288 "it would be absolutely impossible"; "truly magnificent structure": William H. Rea to Helen C. Frick, April 22, 1964, HCFFA.

288 "I am deeply sorry"; Helen's ultimatum: Helen C. Frick to William H. Rea, April 24, 1964, HCFFA.

288 Helen attacks Loerke's character and demanded his removal: Helen C. Frick to William H. Rea, April 24, 1964, HCFFA.

289 Helen solicits John Walker for support: Helen C. Frick to John Walker, August 18, 1964, HCFFA.

289 "distressed beyond description"; "it is both wise and fair"; "give him a chance to show": John Walker to Helen C. Frick, August 25, 1964, HCFFA.

289 "You suggest that I 'forgive him'": Helen C. Frick to John Walker, September 5, 1964, HCFFA.

289 "of uncontrollable temper": Helen C. Frick to Ernest T. Dewald, August 25, 1964, HCFFA.

289 "a campaign to overwhelm Miss Frick"; "Strategically, there is much to be said": Frank W. Wadsworth to Edward Howard Litchfield, "Possible Lines of Action in the Fine Arts Impasse," September 18, 1964, Dean's Files, Division of the Humanities, ASCUP.

289 "I will not have that man": quoted in Alberts, *Pitt: The Story of the University of Pittsburgh*, 357.

289 "You will be wise if you make"; "The lack of courtesy and consideration": Helen C. Frick to Charles H. Peake, October 5, 1964, HCFFA.

289 "It seems very strange": Helen C. Frick to Arabella S. Dane, undated, Arabella S. Dane Collection.

290 "darling little Skipper": Helen C. Frick, California Calendar, 1963, entry for November 4, HCFFA.

290 "the basis for textbooks for high schools": "Frick's Daughter Accuses Stevens of Portraying Her as 'Book Burner'": *Philadelphia Evening Bulletin*, September 27, 1966, author's collection.

290 Quotes from Stevens's book: Exhibit A to Complaint, Court of Common Pleas of Cumberland County, Pa., January 19, 1965, HCFFA.

290 "Your book was given to me": Helen C. Frick to Sylvester K. Stevens, Virginia Calendar, 1964, enclosure, HCFFA.

290 "As you have endorsed": Helen C. Frick to William Scranton, December 30, 1964, HCFFA.

290 "I have tried to make it clear": Sylvester K. Stevens to Helen C. Frick, January 7, 1965, HCFFA.

290–91 "I got a copy of the book and checked the references": William Scranton to Helen C. Frick, January 8, 1965, HCFFA.

291 "In my opinion, no basis exists"; "'tending to blacken the memory'"; "never been instituted": William F. Knox to Helen C. Frick, January 6, 1965, HCFFA.

291 "If you wish to avoid litigation": David B. Buerger to Sylvester K. Stevens, January 8, 1965, HCFFA.

291 "I might add that I have discussed this situation": Sylvester K. Stevens to David B. Buerger, January 21, 1965, HCFFA.

291 "has devoted her life to the promotion of projects": Exhibit A to Complaint—Complaint in Pennsylvania Suit, January 19, 1965, HCFFA.

291 "delete what was offensive"; "publish an errata": David B. Buerger to Helen C. Frick, June 25, 1965, HCFFA.

PART NINE: LAST STAND (1965–1980)

293 "I want to erase from the record": Frederick Mortimer Clapp to Helen C. Frick, March 23, 1960, Frederick Mortimer Clapp Papers, YU.

293 "It is a lot of water over the dam": Helen C. Frick to Frederick Mortimer Clapp, March 24, 1960, ibid.

293 "not of the caliber": Frederick Mortimer Clapp to Helen C. Frick, October 12, 1965, ibid.

293 "I want to tell you something exciting": quoted in Fazio, "Helen Clay Frick, Architectural Patron and Art Collector," 133.

295 "This as you well know": Edward Howard Litchfield to William H. Rea, April 2, 1965, Chancellors Files, RG 2/1 1956–1965, ASCUP.

295 "One important apprehension keeps coming up": Aaron Sheon to William C. Loerke, February 22, 1964, Buildings, ASCUP.

296 "I fear that if I were to please [Miss Frick]"; "It is, in my opinion, little short of tragic": Joseph C. Sloane to Edward Howard Litchfield, March 27, 1965, Chancellors Files, RG 2/1 1956–1965, ASCUP.

296 "Hovey and Lewis are going ahead": Frank W. Wadsworth to Charles H. Peake, March 26, 1965, Fine Arts Library Archives, Fine Arts Library, UP.

296 "I don't know how much longer I can": Charles H. Peake to Edward Howard Litchfield, March 22, 1965, Buildings, ASCUP.

296–97 Terms of agreement: "Memorandum of Understanding," June 16, 1965, Buildings, ASCUP.

297 Wadsworth argued against the agreement: Frank W. Wadsworth to Charles H. Peake, 1965, Buildings, ASCUP.

297 "He was sleeping": Helen C. Frick, Bird Watchers Date Book, 1965, entry for May 3, HCFFA.

297 "Childs wouldn't receive me": author's interview with Julia B. Egan, July 21, 1993.

297 "nothing could alter in any way the jurisdiction": Charles H. Peake to "Monty" [Edison Mongomery?], September 6, 1981, Buildings, ASCUP.

298 "no publicity will be given": David B. Buerger to Charles H. Peake, May 13, 1965, Buildings, ASCUP.

298 "Morally offended"; "I reject categorically": Charles H. Peake to David B. Buerger, 1965, Buildings, ASCUP.

298 "The great day": Helen C. Frick, Bird Watchers Date Book, 1965, entry for May 28, HCFFA.

298 "It seems to me you are making progress": John Walker to Charles H. Peake, July 6, 1965, Buildings, ASCUP.

298 Faculty and staff criticized Memorandum of Understanding: Alberts, *Pitt: The Story of the University of Pittsburgh*, 357.

298 "overzealous bookkeeping"; forced his retirement: "When an Immovable Object Meets and Irresistible Force," *Pittsburgh Post-Gazette*, November 24, 1984, HCFFA.

298–99 "The newspapers, especially in Pittsburgh and New York": James B. Stevenson to Helen C. Frick, March 9, 1965, HCFFA.

299 "The urgent purpose of history is not": quoted in Brent D. Glass, "The Public Is Entitled to Know," *Pennsylvania Heritage*, 18, no. 1: 8.

299 "not unusual": Roger B. May, "Stop the Presses!" *Wall Street Journal*, November 30, 1966, WOMA.

299 "The courts are bulging with suits": Alistair Cooke, "Mrs. Kennedy Suffers Grief She Sought to Avoid," *Manchester Guardian*, December 20, 1966, Stevens-Outman Family Papers, MG 149, box 6, folder D, Pennsylvania State Archives.

299 "concerned about the increase"; "There's not enough": quoted in *Wall Street Journal*, November 30, 1966, WOMA.

299 "an interested attendant at court sessions"; "could hear better": unidentified, undated news article, WOMA.

299 "so far admitted that three of his comments": David B. Buerger to editor, *Pittsburgh Post-Gazette*, July 26, 1965, regarding its article, "History in Court," HCFFA.

299 "People will get a strong feeling": David B. Buerger to Helen C. Frick, July 29, 1965, HCFFA.

299 "produce detailed original source materials"; "sweeping constitutional and practical implications": "Frick's Daughter Sues Historian Over Appraisal," *New York Times*, July 25, 1965, WOMA.

299 "[I] am just as capable as an Historian": George F. Douglas to Sylvester K. Stevens, June 23, 1965, Stevens-Outman Family Papers, MG 149, box 4, folder D, Pennsylvania State Archives.

299–300 "denigrated into the questioning of historical facts": Sylvester K. Stevens to Richard McCormick, December 1, 1965, Julien Boyd Papers, box 33, folder 5, Princeton University Libraries.

300 Helen's inspection and outrage: Helen C. Frick to Edward W. Weidline Sr., August 31, 1965, Buildings, ASCUP.

300 "not [to] give a negative report": Stanton C. Crawford to Robert Dunkelman, undated, Buildings, ASCUP.

300 "promise that [she] would never": author's interview with Helen Clay Chace, June 17, 1993.

301 "Certain misunderstandings have been built up": quoted in Alberts, *Pitt: The Story of the University of Pittsburgh*, 359.

301 "how very serious and how very difficult the situation": Charles H. Peake to John Walker, February 7, 1966, Buildings, ASCUP.

301 "The Department of Fine Arts is reaching a crisis" Peake's proposed remedy: Charles H. Peake to David Howard Kurtzman and Gwilym A. Price, March 7, 1966, Buildings, ASCUP.

301 "Unfortunately, there have been too many"; "Ever since the Fine Arts Department": Helen C. Frick to David Howard Kurtzman, March 24, 1966, Buildings, ASCUP.

301 "I was both outraged and embarrassed"; "menacing presence": Frank W. Wadsworth to Charles H. Peake, March 29, 1966, Buildings, ASCUP.

301–2 "Miss Lewis and the guards"; "Guards have even": William C. Loerke to David Howard Kurtzman, June 24, 1966, Buildings, ASCUP.

302 "progressively worsening situation": quoted in Alberts, *Pitt: The Story of the University of Pittsburgh*, 359.

302 "I, as well as the rest of the faculty, was appalled": Leonard Slatkes, May 11, 1966, resignation letter, Buildings, ASCUP.

302 "The Fine Arts Department has now become known": Frank W. Wadsworth to David Howard Kurtzman, May 20, 1966, Buildings, ASCUP.

302 "more controls than Pitt ever dreamed": Ralph Brem, "Kennedys Influence Harvard," *Pittsburgh Press*, 1966 (?), ASCUP. The author is grateful to Donald Miller for identifying Brem as the writer of this article.

302 "The University [of Pittsburgh] will have no jurisdiction": Helen C. Frick to John Walker, March 16, 1966, Frick Fine Arts Center, NGA.

302 "You can count on my help": John Walker to Helen C. Frick, May 23, 1966, ibid.

302 Buerger notified Helen that the university had changed its mind; his analysis and recommendations: David B. Buerger to Helen C. Frick, October 28, 1966, John Walker Papers, Frick Fine Arts Center, NGA.

303 "I think the enclosed statement": Helen C. Frick to John Walker, November 2, 1966, John Walker Papers, NGA.

303 "ridiculous and tragic position": Virginia Gambrell to Oliver Jensen, August 19, 1966, Stevens-Outman Family Papers, MG 149, box 4, folder D, Pennsylvania State Archives.

303 "presents a serious danger"; "assault . . . if successful"; "the first case we know of": "The American Historical Association and the Organization of American Historians Announce the Formation of the Joint Committee for the Defense of the Rights of Historians under the First Amendment," undated, Buildings, ASCUP.

303 "unlimited funds": George F. Douglas to Sylvester K. Stevens, February 7, 1966, Julien Boyd Papers, box 33, folder 5, Princeton University Libraries.

303 "victory . . . would encourage others": "The American Historical Association and the Organization of American Historians Announce the Formation of the Joint Committee for the Defense of the Rights of Historians Under the First Amendment," undated, Buildings, ASCUP.

304 "Miss Frick is not conducting a crusade": David B. Buerger to editor, *Pitt News*, September 17, 1966, HCFFA.

304 "Wonderful Republican victory": Helen C. Frick, Medieval Treasury Calendar, 1966, entry for November 8, HCFFA.

304 "G.O.P. Candidates Aided by Heiress": *New York Times*, June 8, 1966, Richard Nixon Library and Birthplace Collections.

304 "Nixon is Mum on Angle Role": *New York Daily News*, June 9, 1966, ibid.

306 "excommunicated": author's interviews with William H. Rea, June 17, 2002, and April 7, 2004.

306 "It really was a phenomenal thing": *Pitt News*, undated, William H. Rea Papers, ASCUP.

306 "rare, perhaps unique, act of a university": Alberts, *Pitt: The Story of the University of Pittsburgh*, 360.

306 "quest for academic freedom: "Pitt Gives Up Frick Millions in Art Fight" *Pittsburgh Press*, February 8, 1967, FARL Scrapbook, 1960–1969, FARL.

306 "We were given to understand"; "It was either this or lose": quoted in "University of Pittsburgh Cuts Frick Ties," *New York Times*, February 9, 1967, HCFFA.

306 "that you tell Helen Frick": Leonard Stein to the chancellor, February 9, 1967, Buildings, ASCUP.

306 "A Brave and Wise Stand": *Pitt News*, February 10, 1967.

306 "Whatever the facts"; "our art resources"; "this will be regretted": "The Frick Museum/School," *Pittsburgh Press*, February 10, 1967, John Walker Papers, RG 28, box 34, Frick Fine Arts Center, NGA.

306 "sorry that there has been"; "a working department"; "historical museum of art": "Miss Helen Frick Called Good Loser," *Pittsburgh Press*, February 8, 1967, John Walker Papers, RG 28, box 34, Frick Fine Arts Center, NGA.

306 "not give any more"; "Miss Frick will not permit": *Pittsburgh Press*, February 11, 1967, Department of Fine Arts and Architecture, UP.

306 "Miss Frick thought you might": Julia B. Egan to Richard M. Nixon, February 10, 1967, Richard Nixon Library and Birthplace Collections.

306 "I can't tell you how distressed I am": John Walker to Helen C. Frick, February 14, 1967, John Walker Papers, RG 28, box 34, Frick Fine Arts Center, NGA.

307 "It seems to me incredible": Frederick Mortimer Clapp to Helen C. Frick, February 16, 1967, Frederick Mortimer Clapp Papers, YU.

307 "nice letter"; "I know how it must sadden": Helen C. Frick to Frederick Mortimer Clapp, February 21, 1967, ibid.

307 "from the home of her father and mother": Theodore Bowman to David Howard Kurtzman, April 5, 1967, Buildings, ASCUP.

307 "a 'fast buck' operator"; "press the issue"; "First Amendment protection": Joseph T. Kingston to Sylvester K. Stevens, January 13, 1967, Stevens-Outman Family Papers, MG 149, box 4, folder D, Pennsylvania State Archives.

307 "himself an arbiter": Sylvester K. Stevens to George F. Douglas and Sylvia Rambo, January 25, 1967, ibid.

307–8 "milder"; "proud"; "If everyone read a book"; "By analogy, Miss Frick": quoted in "Defender of a Memory: Helen Clay Frick," *New York Times*, May 26, 1967, HCFFA.

308 "really something of a masterpiece": Sylvester K. Stevens to Oliver Jensen, May 26, 1967, Stevens-Outman Family Papers, MG 149, box 4, folder D, Pennsylvania State Archives.

308 "Miss Frick is bound to appeal": Sylvester K. Stevens to Julien Boyd, July 26, 1965, Julien Boyd Papers, box 32, folder 11, Princeton University Libraries.

308 "I am hopeful that we will win": Helen C. Frick to David F. Maxwell, June 14, 1967, HCFFA.

308 "As it stands, just about any crackpot": Sylvester K. Stevens to Julien Boyd, July 26, 1965, Julien Boyd Papers, box 32, folder 11, Princeton University Libraries.

308 Helen withdrew her suit "with prejudice": *New York Times*, August 10, 1967, Julien Boyd Papers, box 33, folder 5, Princeton University Libraries.

308 "You know we can't control Miss Frick": quoted in *Pittsburgh Post*, August 11, 1967, WOMA.

308 "I am delighted to announce"; "While some inaccuracies": Helen C. Frick, press release, August 8, 1967, Richard Nixon Library and Birthplace Collections.

308 "delighted"; "this has been a very unpleasant": Richard M. Nixon to Helen C. Frick, August 15, 1967, ibid.

308 "positively vicious and obviously face-saving"; "very minor points": quoted in *New York Times*, August 10, 1967, Julien Boyd Papers, box 33, folder 5, Princeton University Libraries.

308 "give rise to misinterpretation": Sylvester K. Stevens to Members of the Joint Committee, August 18, 1967, Julien Boyd Papers, box 33, folder 5, Princeton University Libraries.

308 "deception"; "undisclosed": press release, "Frick Book Legal Tiff Reactivated," *Pittsburgh Post*, August 11, 1967, WOMA.

308 "to file an opinion on the 103 exceptions": quoted in "Frick Book Court Fight Reactivated," *Pittsburgh Press*, August 11, 1967, WOMA.

308–9 "in the minds of many": Sylvester K. Stevens to George F. Douglas, August 22, 1967, Stevens-Outman Family Papers, MG 149, box 5, folder D, Pennsylvania State Archives.

309 "I realize that my success"; "But it will encourage": Helen C. Frick, press release draft, August 16, 1967, HCFFA.

309 "finally [been] able to clear her father's name": Howard B. King statement to members of the Westmoreland-Fayette Historical Society, November (?), 1968, HCFFA.

309 "I must go abroad": Helen C. Frick, Virginia Calendar, entry for August 15, 1967, HCFFA.

309 Quotes from "Filial Piety": Oliver Jensen, "Filial Piety and the First Amendment," *American Heritage* 18, no. 6 (October 1967): 3, WOMA.

309 "Your organization has chosen to glorify": David B. Buerger to Gordon Gray, November 14, 1967, HCFFA.

309 "The Trust may be better off": Sylvester K. Stevens to Gordon Gray, January 23, 1968, Stevens-Outman Family Papers, MG 149, box 5, folder D, Pennsylvania State Archives.

309 "She could be absolutely ruthless": author's interview with William H. Rea, June 17, 2004.

309 Quotes from King's letter: Howard B. King, statement to members of the Westmoreland-Fayette Historical Society, November (?), 1968, WOMA, also HCFFA.

309 "I compliment you": Sylvester K. Stevens to Howard B. King, December 9, 1968, HCFFA.

310 "It is hard to understand": David B. Buerger to editor, *Pittsburgh Post-Gazette*, September 27, 1968, HCFFA.

310 "I think something should be done": Helen C. Frick to James G. Fulton, January 10, 1968, Fulton Papers, HCFFUP.

310 "Miss Frick has reproduced two photographs": Julia B. Egan to Rose Mary Woods, January 11, 1968, Richard Nixon Library and Birthplace Collections.

310 "I hope that yesterday's results in New Hampshire": Helen C. Frick to Richard M. Nixon, March 13, 1968, ibid.

310 "great rejoicing": Helen C. Frick to Richard M. Nixon, May 29, 1968, ibid.

311 "the Early Italian Rooms in the National Gallery of Art": Walker, *Self-Portrait with Donors*, xv.

311 "when few Pittsburghers were either collecting": Fazio, "Helen Clay Frick, Architectural Patron and Art Collector," 153.

311 "An exciting evening": Helen C. Frick, France Engagement Calendar, 1968, entry for October 28, HCFFA.

311 "preserving the records": dedication to Helen C. Frick, The Frick Collection, *Paintings*, vol. 1 of the Frick Collection illustrated catalogue, 1949.

311 "Crowds. Didn't see Pres. or Mrs. Nixon": Helen C. Frick, Khamsa of Nizami Calendar, 1969, entry for January 21, HCFFA.

311–12 "with the care given to the cutting of a precious diamond": "60-Room Frick House Will Be Dismantled," *Beverly Times*, December 17, 1968, Beverly Historical Society.

312 Episode with David Rockefeller: author's interview with Liza Fosburgh, summer 2003.

312 "I didn't ask if you wanted it": author's interview with Arabella S. Dane, spring 2005.

312 "desired a European post": Roger M. Witten, Information Pertinent to Questioning of Fife J. Symington [*sic*], October 19, 1973, Watergate Special Prosecution Force, Sale of Ambassadorships, NARA MD.

312 "I have had a life long ambition to be ambassador": J. Fife Symington Jr. to Maurice W. Stans, November 29, 1968, Watergate Special Prosecution Force, Sale of Ambassadorships, NARA MD.

314 "a small reception on December 19": Paul Cummings, interview with Harry Grier, April 21, 1970.

314 "was not merely to honor a great American": David B. Buerger to Wesley W. Posvar, March 4, 1970. Buildings, ASCUP.

314 "One of the discussed targets of dissident protest": Donald E. Gordon to Wesley W. Posvar, May 11, 1970, Buildings, ASCUP.

316 "greatest interest": Helen C. Frick, "Account of Her Life History, 1981," Helen C. Frick Biographical Files, FARL.

316 "Opening of FAM. Many out of town guests": Helen C. Frick, France Calendar, 1970, entry for October 10, HCFFA.

316 "It was an exciting evening": Helen C. Frick to FARL Staff, October 11, 1970, FC/FARL Archives.

316 "the same delightfully warm and intimate atmosphere": Hovey, *Treasures of the Frick Art Museum*, 11.

316 "She remembered every detail"; Helen "walked to a draped grand piano": Donald Miller, "When an Immovable Object Meets an Irresistible Force," *Pittsburgh Post-Gazette*, November 24, 1984.

316–17 "encouraged that you 'at the top'": J. Fife Symington Jr. to Peter M. Flannigan, July 7, 1970, Watergate Special Prosecution Force, Sale of Ambassadorships, NARA MD.

317–18 "Spain, Portugal, Italy"; "I want 50 [thousand dollars] this year": Herbert W. Kalmbach worksheet, September 19, 1970, Watergate Special Prosecution Force, Townhouse Project, NARA MD.

318 "It certainly was the most expensive lunch": J. Fife Symington Jr. to Herbert W. Kalmbach, September 28, 1970, Watergate Special Prosecution Force, Sale of Ambassadorships, NARA MD.

318 "Regarding the 'commitment to move Fyfe [*sic*] Symington'": Peter M. Flannigan to H. R. Haldeman, June 17, 1971, Watergate Special Prosecution Force, Sale of Ambassadorships, NARA MD.

318 "I am not accustomed to ask favors": Helen C. Frick to Richard M. Nixon, June 16, 1971, Arabella S. Dane Collection.

318 "Knowing what a splendid job he is doing": Richard M. Nixon to Helen C. Frick, June 23, 1971, Watergate Special Prosecution Force, Sale of Ambassadorships, NARA MD.

319 "be encouraged to resign": Gordon Strachan to H. R. Haldeman, August 10, 1971, ibid.

319 contribution "should be returned": Herbert W. Kalmbach, Political Action Memorandum, September 24, 1971, ibid.

319 Kalmbach relayed the bad news: Gordon Strachan to H. R. Haldeman, memorandum of phone conversation with Herbert W. Kalmbach, October 11, 1971, ibid.

319 "I feel sure that Peter [Flanigan] will work things out": J. Fife Symington Jr. to H. R. Haldeman, November 13, 1971, ibid.

319 "a terrific ambassador"; "incompetent"; "to discuss the matter": Gordon Strachan to H. R. Haldeman, October 11, 1971, Watergate Special Prosecution Force, Sale of Ambassadorships, NARA MD.

319 "Before we leave for the trip to China": Rose Mary Woods to Helen C. Frick, February 16, 1972, HCFFA.

319 "Concerning Fife Symington, Flanigan remains vehemently opposed": Gordon Strachan to H. R. Haldeman, April 5, 1972, Watergate Special Prosecution Force, Sale of Ambassadorships, NARA MD, with notation by Gordon Strachan, April 11, 1972.

320 "[I] was horrified to see": Helen C. Frick to Wesley Posvar, October 19, 1972, Buildings, ASCUP.

334 "an ordeal"; "fretted about the alarms"; "Miss Frick suddenly announced": author's interview with Edgar Munhall, August 2, 1993.

322 "You are so young, you won't last": interview with Everett Fahy, 2005.

322 "It is sad and ironical that even the Frick and the Freer": John Walker to Everett Fahy, May 8, 1974, John Walker Papers, NGA.

322 "Thus began the political story of the century": Ambrose, *Nixon: The Triumph of a Politician*, 558.

322 "should probably make a stroking call": Jerry Jones to Dan Todd, July 23, 1973, Watergate Special Prosecution Force, Sale of Ambassadorships, NARA MD.

322 "We wish to receive copies": Thomas F. McBride to Thomas D. Washburne, November 13, 1973, ibid.

322–23 "Mr. Symington's hopes": "Gentleman Farmer Sought Greener Pastures Elsewhere," *Baltimore Sun*, February 26, 1974, ibid.

323 "given a walk"; "because his testimony was deemed essential": "Nixon Denies Prosecutor Data on Ambassadorships," *New York Times*, March 17, 1974, ibid.

323 Helen took up Nixon's defense: Letters to the editor, *Pittsburgh Post-Gazette*, November 10, 1984, in reference to the obituary, "Helen Clay Frick Dies at 96," author's collection.

323 "heart-sick about it": author's interview with Liza Fosburgh, summer 2003.

323 "terrific loyalty": author's interview with William H. Rea, May 7, 2004.

323 "he got very bad advice"; "his staff did things wrong": author's interview with Liza Fosburgh, summer 2003.

323 "Your mother. . . . was very sweet and cordial": Helen C. Frick to Arabella S. Dane, 1974, Arabella S. Dane Collection.

323 "Your call added a great deal": Helen C. Frick to Richard M. Nixon, December 26, 1974, Richard Nixon Library and Birthplace Collections.

323 "something I have tried to avoid": Helen C. Frick to FARL Staff, February 12, 1975, FC/FARL Archives.

324 "She had a fit, had the bathroom taken out": author's interview with Alice Thompson, April 27, 2004.

324 "We are all looking forward": Helen C. Frick to Richard M. Nixon, February 6, 1975, Richard Nixon Library and Birthplace Collections.

324 "I pray that you are feeling better": Richard M. Nixon to Helen C. Frick, March 21, 1975, ibid.

324 "The world is certainly in a mess": Helen C. Frick to Richard M. Nixon, April 4, 1975, ibid.

324 "acting illegally when it discriminates": quoted in "Woman Artist Challenges Frick Library on Pants," *New York Times*, January 14, 1975, HCFFA.

324 "humiliating and unsanitary"; "being treated differently than men": quoted in "Human Rights Suit Filed by Elin Lake Ewald," *May Stevens vs. FARL*, Case no. 6809, The City of New York Commission on Human Rights, February 4, 1975, HCFFA.

324 "We are a private library"; "Spike heels are not permitted": Steinbach, "Answers to the Questions," unpublished notations, April 8, 1975, HCFFA.

325 "the institution [remained] in the ranks": "Frick's Dress Code Finally Phased Out," *New York Post*, March 26, 1989, HCFFA.

325 "my 'latest child'"; "To think that FARL has grown": Helen C. Frick to Mildred Steinbach, April 24, 1976, FC/FARL Archives.

325 "I am thankful it was": Helen C. Frick to Alice Thompson, June 26, 1976. The author is grateful to Alice Thompson for bringing this letter to her attention.

326 The off-center terra-cotta plaque: author's interview with Arabella S. Dane, April 5, 2005. The author is grateful to Arabella Dane for sharing this story.

326 "As part of my duties": Walter F. Cooley to David B. Buerger, January 30, 1984, HCFFA.

326–27 "There is such a good chance that we might have another fool": Helen C. Frick to Richard M. Nixon, January 22, 1980, HCFFA.

327 "confidential appraisal"; "for [her] loyal support": Richard M. Nixon to Helen C. Frick, February 8, 1980, HCFFA.

327 The tree planting: "Dedication Ceremony of Two Sugar Maple Trees in Memory of Mr. and Mrs. Henry Clay Frick, May 22, 1980," author's collection.

327 "held them personally, saying good-bye"; "she talked to them too": author's interview with Barbara Hunter, October 14, 1993.

PART TEN: BACK IN HER FATHER'S HOUSE (1981–1984)

329ff. Helen Frick in her last years at Clayton: author's interviews with Barbara Hunter, October 14 and October 24, 1993; Ruth Mansfield, October 17, 1991; and Ed and Alice Boyle, September 25, 1993, unless otherwise noted.

330 "As you may remember, Miss Frick's sight": Walter F. Cooley Jr. to Richard M. Nixon, December 17, 1982, Richard Nixon Library and Birthplace.

330 "Of the literally thousands of people": Richard M. Nixon to Walter F. Cooley Jr., December 27, 1982, ibid.

330 The breakfast tray incident: the author is grateful to Arabella S. Dane for sharing this story.

331 "prisoner of her father"; "Miss Frick was the ultimate scapegoat": author's interview with Rev. Philip Tierney, August 31, 1991.

331 "She turned her back to the wall": author's interview with Helen Clay Chace, 1993.

331 "Miss Frick was sorry she had signed the papers": author's interview with Helen Sanger, July 20, 1993.

332 Helen's funeral service: "The Office of Burial for Helen C. Frick," undated, author's collection.

332 Helen's coffin and grave: The author is grateful to David Wilkens for bringing this information to her attention.

332 "What I particularly admired about her": Richard M. Nixon to Henry Clay Frick II, November 29, 1984, Richard Nixon Library and Birthplace Collections.

332 "a shadowy queen": "Helen Clay Frick Dies at Point Breeze Estate," *Pittsburgh Press*, November 10, 1984, author's collection.

332 "not only in view of earlier gifts by me": Will of Helen C. Frick, December 8, 1981, author's collection.

333 "for the purposes of public exhibition and preservation": ibid.

334 "Toward the very end of her life she felt": author's interview with Holmes Wolfe, August 30, 1992.

334 "astonished, mystified"; "puzzled": author's interview with Helen Sanger, July 20, 1993.

334 "not one cent of which"; "was yet secured"; "a shudder went throughout": "NYC's Frick Art Library Needs Funds," *Pittsburgh Post-Gazette*, March 22, 1993, HCFFA.

334 "they felt this was a betrayal"; "I was mad at her": author's interview with Helen Clay Chace, July 1993.

335 Martha Symington suggests divorce: Martha Frick Symington to FC Board, 1986, author's collection.

335 "We do have a legal obligation": Alfred H. Howell to Martha Frick Symington, October 10, 1986, author's collection.

335 "[an] added burden on the income": "Frick Awaits New Director," *New York Times*, January 9, 1987.

335 "No one understood it": quoted in Klinkenborg, "The Frick Art Reference Library: Art-Historical Legacy on East 71st Street," 88.

335 "to avoid a curtailment in services": "Frick Reference Library Is Obliged to Seek Funds," *New York Times*, December 30, 1990, HCFFA.

335 "We are trying to recapture": quoted in "A Triumph of Restoration," *Architectural Digest*, December 1990, 2, author's collection.

336 "The Frick has never solicited money"; "we were active": quoted in "Frick Reference Library Is Obliged to Seek Funds," *New York Times*, December 30, 1990, HCFFA.

336 "our financial picture the most challenging": quoted in "Making a Less Fusty Frick (And Hoping Nobody Notices)," *New York Times*, July 31, 2005.

336 "one of the strongest in the Frick's history"; "raise a substantial portion": Margot Bogert, *The Frick Collection Member's Magazine* (Winter 2007): 21.

336 "the sole surviving mansion": "A Piece of Pittsburgh Past," *Pittsburgh Press*, September 23, 1990, author's collection.

336 "Clayton is considered one of the best preserved and documented": David Sallinger, *Daily News*, undated, author's collection.

337 Quotes from article 1 and article 7 of Helen's will: Will of Helen C. Frick, December 8, 1981, author's collection.

337 "She would roll over in her grave": interview with Liza Fosburgh, summer 2003.

338 "This root of all evil": Rensselaer, *Million Dollar Baby*, 14.

338 "It's nearly all gone": *Poor Little Rich Girl*.

339 "to unify the entities": William Bodine, e-mail to the author, April 23, 2007.

339 "the kind of life that was lived within its walls": Helen C. Frick, "Clayton Memoir, c. 1950s," HCFFA.

BIBLIOGRAPHY

PRIMARY SOURCES BY HELEN C. FRICK

All sources listed below are located at the Helen Clay Frick Foundation Archives at the Frick Collection/Frick Art Reference Library and in the Institutional Archives for the Frick Art Reference Library and the Frick Collection, New York, N.Y., unless otherwise noted.

Album Diaries, 1920: Three Weeks in England; France; Belgium-France

Alice Braddel Daily Diary, 1914–1919

"An Apartment at Sherry's," essay, December 10, 1903

California Calendar, 1963

"Clayton Memoir c. 1950"

"Clochers et Pâturages" Calendar, 1960

Dante Day by Day Diary, 1949

"Description of My Bed-room," essay, March 1898

Diary, 1904–1905

Diary, 1908–1909

Egypt Diaries 1 and 2

"Four Little Sunbeams," essay, January 24, 1900

France Calendar, 1970

"Glimpses Along the Road"

"Grandfather," memoir of Henry Clay Frick, c. 1920

Henry Clay Frick Scrapbook, 1849–1919

"Jane," essay, 1903

Khamsa of Nizami Calendar, 1969

Medieval Treasury Calendar, 1966

"Mr. Mignon and Family," essay, undated

Polly Wells-Helen Clay Frick Diary, 1925

Ready Reference Diary, 1945

Ready Reference Diary, 1948

Red Cross Clipping Scrapbook

Scotland Album, 1953

Scrapbook on the Red Cross Shop

Sunny Side School Diary, 1901–1904

"Sympathy," essay, November 21, no year

"The Daisy Story," essay, May 19, 1897

Timeline Diary, 1849–1890

Untitled essays, listed by date

Virginia Calendar (annual calendar, multiple years)

War Diary, 1917–1918

Westmoreland Farm Diary, 1922–1926

Westmoreland Farm Diary, 1937–1941

Will of Helen Clay Frick, December 8, 1981, author's collection

Zodiac Diary, 1949–1951

ARCHIVAL COLLECTIONS AND RESOURCES

American Museum of Natural History, New York, N.Y.

Amherst College, Amherst, Mass.

Andrew Carnegie Papers, Library of Congress, Washington, D.C.

Arabella S. Dane Collection, Center Harbor, N.H.

Archives of American Art, Smithsonian Institution, Washington, D.C.

Archives of American Gardens, Smithsonian Institution, Washington, D.C.

Archives Service Center, University of Pittsburgh

Author's collection, Stevenson, Md.

Bedford Village Archives, Bedford, N.Y.

Beverly Historical Society, Beverly, Mass.

Carnegie Library, Connellsville, Pa.

Carnegie Museum of Natural History, Pittsburgh, Pa.

Columbia University Library, New York, N.Y.

David C. Duniway Collection, Salem, Ore.

Duveen Archives, Thomas J. Watson Library, Metropolitan Museum of Art, New York, N.Y.

Dwight D. Eisenhower Presidential Library, Gettysburg, Pa.

Frederick Mortimer Clapp Papers, 1885–1965, unprocessed, Yale Collection of American Literature, Beinecke Rare Book and Manuscript Library, Yale University

Frick Art & Historical Center, Pittsburgh, Pa.

Frick Art Reference Library, New York, N.Y.

Frick Art Reference Library and the Frick Collection Institutional Archives, New York, N.Y.

Frick Collection, Central and Curatorial Files, New York, N.Y.

Frick Collection, Helen Clay Frick Foundation Archives at the Frick Art Reference Library, New York, N.Y.

Girls Clubs of America, Inc., Schlesinger Library, Radcliffe Institute for Advanced Study, Cambridge, Mass.

Harrison Griswold Dwight Papers, Amherst College, Amherst, Mass.

Harvard University Archives, Cambridge, Mass.

Helen Clay Frick Foundation Archives at FARL/FC

Helen Clay Frick Foundation Archives at the University of Pittsburgh

Knoedler Art Gallery Archives, New York, N.Y.

Malvina Hoffman Papers, Research Library, The Getty Research Institute, Los Angeles, Calif.

Minneapolis Institute of Arts, Minneapolis, Minn.

Museum of Fine Arts, Boston, Mass.

National Archives and Records Administration, College Park, Md.

National Archives and Records Administration, Pacific Region, Laguna-Niguel, Calif.

National Gallery of Art Archives, Washington, D.C.

National Portrait Gallery Library, Smithsonian Institution, Washington, D.C.

National Trust Archives, Special Collections, Hornbake Library, University of Maryland, College Park, Md.

Office of Paul Mellon, Washington, D.C.

Peggy Kahn Collection, North Bennington, Vt.

Pennsylvania State Archives, Harrisburg, Pa.

Philadelphia Museum of Art, Philadelphia, Pa.

Polly Simpson Gorman Collection, Ruxton, Md.

Princeton University Libraries, Princeton, N.J.

Red Cross, Hazel Braugh Records Center and Archives, Washington, D.C.

Rensselaer W. Lee Papers, Historical Studies-Social Science Library, Institute for Advanced Studies, Princeton, N.J.

Richard Nixon Library and Birthplace Collections, Yorba Linda, Calif.

Rockefeller Archive Center, Sleepy Hollow, N.Y.

Rockefeller Family Archives, Sleepy Hollow, N.Y.

Shelburne Farms Archives, Shelburne, Vt.

University of Pittsburgh, Pittsburgh, Pa.

Villa I Tatti Archives, Harvard University Center for Italian Renaissance Studies, Settingnano, Italy

West Overton Museums Archives, Scottdale, Pa.

Wright State University Archives, Dayton, Ohio

Yale University, New Haven, Conn.

ART HISTORY

Ausfeld, Margaret Lynne, and Virginia M. Mecklenburg. *Advancing American Art: Politics and Aesthetics in the State Department Exhibition, 1946–48.* Montgomery, Ala.: Montgomery Museum of Fine Arts, 1984.

Blottière, Alain. *Vintage Egypt: Cruising the Nile in the Golden Age of Travel.* Paris: Flammarion, 2003.

Bridge, James Howard. *Portraits and Personalities: Imaginary Conversations in the Frick Galleries.* New York: Brentano's, n.d.

Christiansen, Keith, et al., eds. *From Filippo Lippi to Piero della Francesca: Fra Carnevale and the Making of a Renaissance Master.* New Haven: Yale University Press, 2005.

Fazio, Vincent Carl. "Helen Clay Frick: Architectural Patron and Art Collector." Master's thesis, Department of the History of Art and Architecture, University of Pittsburgh, 1998.

Frick Collection, The. *Art in the Frick Collection: Paintings, Sculpture, Decorative Arts.* New York: Harry N. Abrams in association with the Frick Collection, 1996.

———. *Chinese Blue-and-White Porcelain in the Frick Collection.* New York: The Frick Collection, 1992.

———. *Documents Relating to the Frick Collection.* New York: The Merrymount Press, 1940.

———. *Drawings, Prints, and Later Acquisitions.* Vol. 9 of the Frick Collection illustrated catalogue. New York: The Frick Collection, 2003.

———. *Furniture and Gilt Bronzes: French.* Vol. 6 of the Frick Collection illustrated catalogue. New York: The Frick Collection, 1992.

———. *Furniture: Italian and French.* Vol. 5 of the Frick Collection illustrated catalogue. New York: The Frick Collection, 1992.

———. *A Guide to Works of Art on Exhibition.* 7th ed. New York: The Frick Collection, 1996.

———. *A Guide to Works of Art on Exhibition.* 13th ed. New York: The Frick Collection, 2003.

———. *Handbook of Paintings.* New York: The Frick Collection, 1978.

———. *Handbook of Paintings.* New York: The Frick Collection, 1985.

———. *Paintings.* Vol. 1 of the Frick Collection illustrated catalogue. Pittsburgh, Pa.: The Frick Art Reference Library, 1949.

———. *Paintings: American, British, Dutch, Flemish and German.* Vol. 1 of the Frick Collection illustrated catalogue. New York: The Frick Collection, 1968.

———. *Paintings: French, Italian and Spanish.* Vol. 2 of the Frick Collection illustrated catalogue. New York: The Frick Collection, 1968.

———. *Porcelains: Oriental and French.* Vol. 7 of the Frick Collection illustrated catalogue. New York: The Frick Collection, 1974.

———. *Potteries and Porcelains.* Vol. 8 of the Frick Collection illustrated catalogue. New York: The Frick Art Reference Library, 1955.

———. *Sculpture: German, Netherlandish, French and British.* Vol. 4 of the Frick Collection illustrated catalogue. New York: The Frick Collection, 1970.

———. *Sculpture: Italian.* Vol. 3 of the Frick Collection illustrated catalogue. New York: The Frick Collection, 1970.

Friends of Frick Fine Arts. *History of the Henry Clay Frick Fine Arts Department, the University Art Gallery, the Frick Fine Arts Library at the University of Pittsburgh, Pa.: 1927–1987.* Pittsburgh, Pa.: The Henry Clay Frick Fine Arts Department, 1987.

Helen Clay Frick Foundation, *Clayton: The Furnishings Plan.* Pittsburgh: The Helen Clay Frick Foundation, 1988.

Hovey, Walter Read. *Treasures of the Frick Art Museum.* Pittsburgh, Pa.: The Helen Clay Frick Foundation, 1975.

Howell, Hannah Johnson. "The Frick Art Reference Library," *College Art Journal* (Winter 1951–1952): 123–26.

Klinkenborg, Verlyn. "The Frick Art Reference Library: An Art-Historical Legacy on East 71st Street." *Architectural Digest,* October 25, 1991, 80–88.

Knox, Katharine McCook, with assistance of the Frick Art Reference Library Staff. *The Story of the Frick Art Reference Library: The Early Years.* New York: The Frick Art Reference Library, 1979.

Littleton, Taylor D., and Maltby Sykes. *Advancing American Art: Painting, Politics, and Cultural Confrontation at Mid-Century.* Tuscaloosa: University of Alabama Press, 1989.

Metcalf, Pauline C., ed. *Ogden Codman and the Decoration of Houses.* Boston: David R. Godine, in association with the Boston Athenaeum, 1988.

Twelve Masterpieces of Italian Painting from the Fourteenth and Fifteenth Centuries. Pittsburgh, Pa.: Henry Clay Frick Fine Arts Department. University of Pittsburgh, 1959.

AUTOBIOGRAPHY, BIOGRAPHY, MEMOIR

Ambrose, Stephen E. *Nixon.* Vol. 2, *The Triumph of a Politician, 1962–1972.* New York: Simon and Schuster, 1989.

———. *Nixon.* Vol. 3, *Ruin and Recovery, 1973–1990.* New York: Simon & Schuster, 1991.

Bowman, John G. *Unofficial Notes.* Pittsburgh, Pa.: privately printed, 1963.

Bridge, James Howard. *Millionaires and Grubb Street: Comrades and Contacts in the Last Half Century.* 1931. Reprint, Freeport, New York: Books for Libraries Press, 1968.

Bubier, David. "Collector Profile: Katharine Prentis Murphy." For continuing education class, Harvard University, 1993.

"Essay: Filial Piety and the First Amendment." *American Heritage* 17, no. 6 (October 1967): 2–4.

Frick, Helen Clay, as told by Mary O'Hara. *My Father, Henry Clay Frick.* N.p., 1958.

Gimpel, René. *Diary of an Art Dealer.* Trans. John Rosenberg. New York: Farrar Straus and Giroux, 1992.

Hadley, Rollin Van N., ed. *The Letters of Bernard Berenson and Isabella Stewart Gardner, 1887–1924.* Boston: Northeastern University Press, 1987.

Harvey, George. *Henry Clay Frick: The Man.* New York: Charles Scribner's Sons, 1928.

Heymann, C. David. *Poor Little Rich Girl: The Life and Legend of Barbara Hutton.* New York: Random House, 1983.

Hodges, Julia Shelley. *George Hodges.* New York: Century Co., 1926.

McCarten, John. "Profiles: Daughter of Her Father." Parts 1 and 2. *New Yorker,* July 15, 1939, 21–25; July 22, 1939, 23–26.

Poor Little Rich Girl: The Barbara Hutton Story. VHS. A Lester Persky Production in association with ITS Productions, 1993.

Rieder, William. *A Charmed Couple: The Art and Life of Walter and Matilda Gay.* New York: Harry N. Abrams, 2000.

Sanger, Margaret. *Margaret Sanger: An Autobiography.* New York: Dover Publications, 1971.

Sanger, Martha Frick Symington. *Henry Clay Frick: An Intimate Portrait.* New York: Abbeville Press, 1998.

———. *The Henry Clay Frick Houses: Architecture, Interiors, Landscapes in the Golden Era.* New York: The Monacelli Press, 2001.

Sauder, Glenn M. "The Meadow Mart Hall of Distinction: Henry Clay Frick." *Meadow Mart* 9, no. 2 (February 1977): 1–7.

Shoumatoff, Elizabeth. *FDR's Unfinished Portrait: A Memoir by Elizabeth Shoumatoff.* Pittsburgh, Pa.: University of Pittsburgh Press, 1990.

Simpson, Colin. *The Partnership: The Secret Association of Bernard Berenson and Joseph Duveen.* N. p.: Bodley Head, 1987.

Sterne, Margaret. *The Passionate Eye: The Life of William R. Valentiner.* Detroit: Wayne State University Press, 1980.

St. John, Fordyce. "Yesterday." *Proceedings of the Charaka Club.* Vol. 11, 1947.

Van Rensselaer, Philip. *Million Dollar Baby: An Intimate Portrait of Barbara Hutton.* New York: G. P. Putnam's Sons, 1979.

Walker, John. *Self-Portrait with Donors: Confessions of an Art Collector.* Boston: Little, Brown, 1969.

Wall, Joseph Frazier. *Andrew Carnegie.* 1970. Reprint, Pittsburgh, Pa.: University of Pittsburgh Press, 1989.

Ware, Susan. *Partner and I: Molly Dewson, Feminism, and New Deal Politics.* New Haven: Yale University Press, 1987.

DEATH, DYING, MOURNING, AND THE AFTERLIFE

Altschul, Sol, ed. *Childhood Bereavement and Its Aftermath.* Madison, Conn.: International University Press, 1988.

Baty, James Marvin, and Veronica B. Tisza. "The Impact of Illness on the Child and His Family." *Child Study* 34 (January 1956): 15–19.

Bowlby, John. "Grief and Mourning in Infancy and Early Childhood." *Psychoanalytic Study of the Child* 15 (1965): 9–52.

Cain, Albert C., and Barbara S. Cain. "On Replacing a Child." *Journal of the American Academy of Child Psychiatry* 3 (1964): 443–56.

Cain, Albert C., Irene Fast, and Mary E. Erickson. "Children's Disturbed Reactions to the Death of a Sibling." *American Journal of Orthopsychiatry* 34 (July 1964): 741–52.

Cobb, Beatrix. "Psychological Impact of Long Illness and Death of a Child in the Family Circle." *Journal of Pediatrics* 49, no. 6 (October–December 1956): 746–51.

"Death in Childhood." *Canadian Medical Association Journal* 98 (May 1968): 967–69.

Deutsch, Helen. "Absence of Grief." *The Psychoanalytic Quarterly* 6 (1937): 13–22.

Fanos, Joanna H., and Bruce G. Nickerson. "Long-Term Effects of Sibling Death During Adolescence." *Journal of Adolescent Research* 6, no. 1 (January 1991): 70–82.

Rando, Therese A. *Treatment of Complicated Mourning.* Champaign, Ill.: Research Press, 1993.

Raphael, Beverly. *The Anatomy of Bereavement.* New York: Basic Books, 1983.

HISTORY

Alberts, Robert C. *Pitt: The Story of the University of Pittsburgh, 1787–1987.* Pittsburgh, Pa.: University of Pittsburgh Press, 1987.

Brown, Raymond Shiland. *The New York Hospital in France: Base Hospital No. 9 A.E.F.: A History of the Work of the New York Hospital Unit During Two Years of Active Service.* New York, 1920.

Dengler, Eartha, Katherine Khalife, and Ken Skulski. *Lawrence, Massachusetts.* 1995. Reprint, Charleston, S.C.: Arcadia Publishing, 2001.

Edmondson, Mary Dillon. *Profiles in Leadership: A History of the Spence School, 1892–1992.* West Kennebunk, Maine: Phoenix Publishing, 1991.

Fowler, Marion. *In a Gilded Cage: American Heiresses who Married British Aristocrats.* New York: St. Martin's Press, 1993.

Garland, Joseph E. *Boston's Gold Coast: The North Shore, 1890–1929.* Boston: Little Brown, 1981.

Maxwell, Marianne. "Pittsburgh's Frick Park: A Unique Addition to the City's Park System." *Western Pennsylvania Historical Magazine* 68, no. 3 (July 1985).

Meier, Elizabeth G. *A History of the New York School of Social Work.* New York: Columbia University Press, 1954.

Toker, Franklin. *Pittsburgh: An Urban Portrait.* Pittsburgh, Pa.: University of Pittsburgh Press, 1986.

PSYCHIATRY, PSYCHOLOGY, AND SPIRITUALITY

Gelinas, Denise J. "The Persisting Negative Effects of Incest." *Psychiatry* 46 (November 1983): 312–32.

Leonard, Linda. *The Wounded Woman: Healing the Father-Daughter Relationship.* Boston: Shambhala, 1983.

Miller, Alice. *The Drama of the Gifted Child: The Search for the True Self.* Trans. Ruth Ward. New York: Meridian, 1986. Originally published as *Prisoners of Childhood.*

———. *For Your Own Good: Hidden Cruelty in Child-Rearing and the Roots of Violence.* Trans. Hildegard Hannum and Hunter Hannum. New York: Farrar, Straus & Giroux, 1983.

———. *Thou Shalt Not Be Aware: Society's Betrayal of the Child.* Trans. Hildegard Hannum and Hunter Hannum. New York: Farrar, Straus & Giroux, 1984.

Murdock, Maureen. *The Hero's Daughter: Through Myth, Story, and Jungian Psychology, an Exploration of the Shadow Side of Father Love.* New York: Ballantine Books, 1994.

Perera, Sylvia Brinton. *The Scapegoat Complex: Toward a Mythology of Shadow and Guilt.* Toronto: Inner City Books, 1986.

Woodman, Marion. *Addiction to Perfection: The Still Unravished Bride (A Psychological Study).* Toronto: Inner City Books, 1982.

WOMEN'S HISTORY

Backlund, Addie Nelson. "World War I: Jane I. Rignel St. John '13 and Dr. Fordyce B. St. John, P&S '09." *Academic Nurse: The Journal of the Columbia University School of Nursing and its Alumni* 15, no. 2 (Fall 1998): 28–31.

Cameron, Ardis. *Radicals of the Worst Sort: Laboring Women in Lawrence, Massachusetts, 1860–1912.* Urbana: University of Illinois Press, 1993.

Edmondson, Mary Dillon. *Profiles in Leadership: A History of the Spence School, 1892–1992.* West Kennebunk, Maine: Phoenix Publishing, 1991.

Fowler, Marian. *In a Gilded Cage: From Heiress to Duchess.* New York: St. Martin's Press, 1993.

Friedan, Betty. *The Feminine Mystique.* New York: W.W. Norton, 1997.

Gooch, Jane Bradford. *A History of the Girls Clubs of America, 1945–1977.* New York: Girls Clubs of America, 1978.

O'Neill, William L. *Everyone Was Brave: The Rise and Fall of Feminism in America.* Chicago: Quadrangle Books, 1969.

The Red Cross Courier: Official Journal of the Red Cross. Washington, D.C.: The American Red Cross, 1923.

Rosenberg, Rosalind. *Divided Lives: American Women in the Twentieth Century.* New York: Hill and Wang, 1992.

Schneider, Dorothy, and Carl J. Schneider. *American Women in the Progressive Era, 1900–1920: Change, Challenge, and the Struggle for Women's Rights.* New York: Doubleday, 1993.

———. *Into the Breach: American Women Overseas in World War I.* San Jose: toExcel Press, 1991.

Stein, Leon. *The Triangle Fire.* Ithaca, N.Y.: ILR Press, 1962.

Ware, Susan. *Holding Their Own: American Women in the 1930s.* Boston: Twayne Publishers, 1982.

ACKNOWLEDGMENTS

In spite of three and a half years of litigation with the Frick Art Reference Library, the Frick Collection, and the Helen Clay Frick Foundation, including over one year in the Orphan's Court of Allegheny County, to secure high-quality prints from the Helen Clay Frick Foundation Archives at the Frick Art Reference Library and permission for their reproduction, *Helen Clay Frick: Bittersweet Heiress* has been published. To that end I owe a sincere debt of thanks to my publisher, Cynthia Miller, for her enthusiastic interest in the project and for her support and understanding during these difficult years. The skillful assistance of my attorneys must also be acknowledged. Franklin Molin spent six months proving copyright of these images to the Frick Collection's satisfaction. H. Woodruff Turner, my lead attorney, supervised all aspects of the litigation while he and his able assistant, Kristen del Sole, doggedly championed my rights in the Orphan's Court. And my designer, Alex Castro, stood by year after year, offering hope and encouragement when all seemed lost, patiently waiting (as he did with my two other books, also subjects of litigation with the Frick entities) for the moment he could get his hands on the final work. In this, the third Frick book he has composed and designed for me, Alex again included me in the process and once more I reveled in the high level of elegance and beauty he has attained. And to Everett Fahy, former director of the Frick Collection and curator of European painting in the Metropolitan Museum of Art, I owe a special debt of gratitude. He knew my great-aunt Helen professionally and by giving this work a critical read and writing an endorsement of her biography on the jacket, he has honored Helen Clay Frick in a most meaningful tribute to her memory.

Freelance editor Susan Leon helped me develop the initial draft for this book and another person, who wishes anonymity, gave valuable editorial comments critical to its scholarship. Deborah Meade, senior editor at the University of Pittsburgh Press, brought the manuscript to greater height with her unique ability to focus and condense the story, proving once again that less is more. At all times she was gracious to me and sensitive to the needs of this biography. In having Deborah as my editor, no author could have been luckier than I.

Grant Gerlich, director of the Henry Clay Frick Birthplace, was generous with his time, as was archivist Mary Ann Mogus. William Bodine, director of the Frick Art & Historical Center, was always encouraging and interested in this project. He, too, was generous with his time and resources. Also at the Frick Art & Historical Center, Amanda Gillen and Sarah Hall worked tirelessly to provide transparencies and photographs for use in this book and accurate documentation of the gifts Helen Frick made to the University of Pittsburgh and to the Frick Art Museum. Charles Altman was as always interested, supportive, and informative.

In the course of my research, I conducted many interviews with members of the Frick, Dixon, Childs, and Rea families and with individuals who knew Helen Frick. I would like to thank them all for granting these interviews and for being honest in their comments. Within the Frick, Childs, and Rea families I thank Arabella S. Dane, Liz Childs, Mernie Berger, Lowrie Ebbert, Sally Childs, Peggy Rea, William Rea, Ed and Wicker Weidline, Mabon Childs, and Harvey Childs. Within the Dixon family I thank Grace Turner Hazard, Harry Turner, Milly Wharton, Polly Gorman, Frances Colston, and Pat Dixon. Of those who knew Helen Frick I thank Nicholas Shoumatoff, Alex Shoumatoff, Antonia Shoumatoff, Alice Thompson, Lucy Moorhead, Rev. John Harper, Peggy Kahn, Bailey Buchanan, M.D., Henrietta Suhr, Liza Fosburgh, Ann Rath, Sue Ann Grier, Jane St. John Roe, Anne dePayster Todd Osborn, and particularly Sheila Milliken.

At the University of Pittsburgh Press, I am grateful to all staff members, including Lowell Britson, David Baumann, Maria Sticco, and Ann Walston. At the University of Pittsburgh, I extend my gratitude to former chairman of the Henry Clay Frick Department of Fine Art and Architecture, David Wilkens; as well as Kirk Savage, chairman; Linda Hicks; and Derek D. Churchill. Ray Anne Lockhard, director of the Henry Clay Frick Fine Arts Library, provided invaluable help and insights, as did Marcia Rosteck. Mike Dabrishus, director, Archive Service Center, Marianne Kasica, Matthew Yount, and Sarah Cranston worked tirelessly on my behalf and suggested material critical to this work.

The following individuals provided invaluable information from their collections: Susan K. Anderson, Philadelphia Museum of Art; Ronald M. Bulatoff and Carol Leadenham, the Hoover Institution Archives at Stanford University; Jessica Collins, National Gallery, London; Madlyn Deming and Michele Haberland, the Spence School; Julie Edwards, Shelburne Farms Archives; Polly Darnell, Shelburne Museum Archives; Michelle Gachette, Andrea B. Goldstein and Abigail G. Smith, the Harvard University Archives; Jennifer A. Gaudio and Betty Parisi, Lynn Museum; Lisa B. Gezelter, National Archives and Records, Pacific Region; David R. Grinnell, Kerin Shellenbarger, and Sharon Watson-Mauro, Senator John Heinz Pittsburgh Regional History Center; Stephen P. Hall, Beverly Historical Society; Spencer Howard, the Herbert Hoover Presidential Library; Pat Jaysane, Immigrant City Archives, Lawrence; Meghan Lee, the Richard Nixon Library and Birthplace; Pat Lynagh, Smithsonian Institution Archives; Dana McGinnis, Wright State University; Senator Barbara A. Mikulski; Philip Montgomery, Rice University; Marty Newsom, Girls Clubs of America; Sarah Nichols, chief curator and curator of decorative arts, Carnegie Museum of Art; at the North Woods Club, members Sherman Gray, Elizabeth Gray Lilleston, Richard Douglas Lilliston, Edward Whitcraft, and Terry Brune; Christina Rae, Town of Bedford Archives; Kristan Regina, the Hillwood Museum Library; David Paynter, the National Archives; Megan Rich, Princeton University Special Collections; Rugby Realty; Tracey Schuster, Getty Research Institute; Ellen M. Shea, Arthur and Elizabeth Schelsinger Library, Radcliff Institute; Clare M. Sheridan, the American Textile History Museum; Betty Shields, Sewickley Valley Historical Society; Jennifer A. Smith, Columbia School of Nursing; Jonathan Stayer, the Commonwealth of Pennsylvania State Archives; Emily Stearns, director, J. Tracey deJong, curator, and Rosemary Loring Campbell, trustee, Wenham Museum; George Stevenson, the North Carolina State Archives; Sally Sims Stokes and Kevin Hammett, National Trust for Historic Preservation; Fiorella Gioffredi Superbi, Villa I Tatti; Alfred Tannler,

Pittsburgh History and Landmarks Foundation; Tessa Veazey and Wendy Hurlock, Archives of American Art, Smithsonian Institution; Jean Waldman, RN, American Red Cross Historical Resources; and Susan Wolfe, Calvary Episcopal Church. Additionally I extend my thanks to Paul Hudon for giving me a tour of Lowell, Massachusetts; to Kate Thomas, clinical sexologist, for her insights on the father-daughter syndrome; to Marjorie Lang for giving me valuable material about the *Titanic;* and to those individuals who provided material and insights on Childs Frick: Susan Bell, John Flinn, Chris Norris, and Barbara Mathe, Richard Tedford, American Museum of Natural History; Suzanne B. McLaren, David R. Watters, and John Wible, Bernadette G. Callery, Carnegie Museum of Natural History; and Douglas M. Morton, University of California, Riverside.

Many other institutions provided valuable art historical assistance: Hope Alswang, Shelburne Museum; Christina Brody, Isabella Stewart Gardner Museum; Maygene F. Daniels, National Gallery of Art Archives, Washington, D.C.; Matthew J. W. Drutt, chief curator, and Vance Muse, the Menil Collection; John Hagood, the National Gallery of Art Library in Washington, D.C.; Erica Holmquist-Wall, the Minneapolis Institute of Arts; Cheryl Hutchens, the Tate Gallery; Sona Johnston, curator, the Baltimore Museum of Art; Peter Der Manuelian, Museum of Fine Arts, Boston; Ellen Buie Niewyk, the Hamon Art Library at Southern Methodist University; Kerry Schauber, the Fogg Art Museum; David B. Warren, former director, Bayou Bend, and docents Judy Baldwin and Linda Lamb; and Ed Watkins and Richard A. Stoner, photographers.

In spite of my difficulties with the Frick Art Reference Library and the Frick Collection, individuals in both organizations deserve mention. Their courteous, efficient, and professional behavior was much appreciated when researching this book, and when working on my two previous books, *Henry Clay Frick: An Intimate Portrait* (1998) and *The Henry Clay Frick Houses* (2001). At the Frick Art Reference Library, I thank Lydia Dufour, art historical research librarian, and Susan Chore, institutional archivist. At the Frick Collection, my thanks go to Susan Grace Galassi, curator, and to Joanna Sheers, her assistant.

My publicist, David Mashek, and readers Donald Miller, Susan Ware, Isabel Roberts, Ellen Reeder, PhD, Barbara Trimble, John Davis, PhD, Lucy Moorhead, and Josephine Trueschler gave me their valuable time and insights. To Patrick Trimble I remain indebted for conducting Internet research that saved me many tedious hours on the computer. A special thanks to Jack Wilkens, Alison Wardrop, Mark Weigman, Melissa Cantekin, Kurt Rosenthal, and, of course, Robert Talbert, all of whom kept me sane through the hard years of writing and litigation. And to my children, who knew their great-great-aunt Helen Clay Frick, and to my grandchildren, who can know her now, you will never know how deeply I have appreciated your interest, encouragement, and support.

INDEX

THIS BOOK WAS DESIGNED AND COMPOSED BY

ALEX CASTRO

IN ADOBE KEPLER AND EDWARDIAN SCRIPT FONTS

AND WAS PRINTED BY

AMILCARE PIZZI, S.P.A., MILAN